Old Somerset on The Eastern Shore of Maryland

A Study in Foundations and Founders

Hearken to me...look unto the rock whence
ye are hewn... —Isaiah 51:1.

Whatever happens in any part of the globe has now
a significance for every other part.—Lord Bryce.

Clayton Torrence

HERITAGE BOOKS
2006

HERITAGE BOOKS
AN IMPRINT OF HERITAGE BOOKS, INC.

Books, CDs, and more—Worldwide

For our listing of thousands of titles see our website
at
www.HeritageBooks.com

A Facsimile Reprint
Published 2006 by
HERITAGE BOOKS, INC.
Publishing Division
65 East Main Street
Westminster, Maryland 21157-5026

Copyright © 1935 Whittet & Shepperson
Richmond, Va.

— Publisher's Notice —
In reprints such as this, it is often not possible to remove blemishes from the original. We feel the contents of this book warrant its reissue despite these blemishes and hope you will agree and read it with pleasure.

International Standard Book Number: 978-1-58549-237-X

To
CASSIUS M. DASHIELL
and
HENRY FILLMORE LANKFORD
GENTLEMEN OF OLD SOMERSET ON THE EASTERN SHORE OF MARYLAND

*Friendship is not made of age and time and place;
but of love and kindness and sympathetic
understanding.*

PREFACE

WHY the foundations and founders of "Old Somerset" on the "Eastern Shore" of Maryland have not previously become the subject of a thorough study, and compilation of results from such study, I cannot imagine. Here and there someone interested in family history, or a particular historical fact or sequence of facts, in relation to a particular Somerset County subject, has looked up the matter and written thereon. But such researches and writings seem to have been few and far between; certainly any published studies of such subjects are most rare. I know of several excellent papers which have been written on certain aspects of Somerset's history; but which remain unpublished. However, none of these studies deal with the subject of origins—foundations and founders—unless the study is one in genealogy, which of course markedly limits its interest. With the exception of the late Doctor Bowen's *Days of Makemie,* of which the origin of Presbyterianism in Somerset County is the subject of study, I have discovered no publication relating to Somerset's "origins"; or for that matter to later aspects of the county's history.

This present study has been confined to the subject of the foundations and founders of Somerset; and its purpose is that of an introduction to any succeeding studies, by whomsoever made, in later aspects of the county's history. The wealth of original material in the local and provincial archives, on which this study is based, has proved incomparable in quantity and quality. My inquiries of, and discussions with, persons in regard to the actual origins of Somerset have been extensive, and yet very few of them have known, and fewer of them seem to realize, the greatness of these origins and the significance of the early events in the county's history.

Incomparably rich in natural resources—only lightly touched by the aborigines—the Lower Eastern Shore of his province of Maryland was Cecil, Lord Baltimore's rightly careful interest. The territorial area was unquestionably in danger of encroachment by other parties. Naturally, Lord Baltimore desired permanent settlements made here in order the better to protect his rights. At last his opportunity arrived in most dramatic fashion. Virginia's law against the Quakers in 1660 sent certain Northampton-Accomack Quakers in quest of new homes. They crossed the Maryland-Virginia line to the Lower Eastern Shore of Maryland. This was "Land of Sanctuary" for them. Lord Baltimore seized upon the opportunity thus presented him and organized a territorial unit near the boundary line between his province and Virginia; and gave every encouragement to the Virginians who would come there and settle. The Quakers—seeking refuge—were first to arrive and make homes. These Quakers who settled largely along the Annemessex River within a short time proved themselves the most stalwart defenders of his Lordship's rights in this quarter when most powerful interests sought to rob him of many square miles of his territory. The Quakers—refugees for conscience sake—came first; but they were followed very soon by other men, who for other reasons sought homes in this area. Together these people laid the foundations of Somerset. This part of Maryland was the objective and the scene of a conflict which gravely endangered a large and valuable area of Lord Baltimore's territory when Colonel Edmund Scarburgh, "Surveyor-General and Treasurer of his Majesty for Virginia," sought by every means within his power to re-locate the first marker of the Maryland-Virginia boundary line, transferring it thirty miles to the north of its actual location. But, in this attempt, Colonel Scarburgh was not successful, though he waged relentless warfare in behalf of his unscrupulous contention.

From this early conflict over the Maryland-Virginia boundary line on the "Eastern Shore," and its immediate results, came the stabilizing of affairs in this lower "Eastern Shore" area. The territorial unit was more strongly organized and progress ensued; immigrants increased in numbers; settlement expanded over the area; and finally the county of Somerset was created. The political and economic foundations were laid of strongest materials.

No less significant are the religious foundations of "Old Somerset." Quakers and other non-conformists made up a goodly part of the population in the beginning; but there was also a large element—and strong—of Church of England men. These loyal Churchmen were of a markedly liberal type of mind. Finally there came to the settlement a strong element of Presbyterian faith and order. Quakers, Churchmen, Presbyterians, (and doubtless other religious elements now undiscoverable), lived together in peace, and labored abundantly for the strengthening and upbuilding of the community. In 1672 Somerset County became the scene of a most remarkable experiment in religious unity. The Grand Jury in March of that year rendered an "opinion" that there should be regular religious services in the county, and designated the preacher and four preaching stations at which such services should be conducted successively on four Sundays of the month. Quakers, Churchmen, Presbyterians joined in this plan of worship and instruction. Robert Maddock was the preacher designate, and it has been impossible to discover his religious affiliation—the source of his "ordination and authorization" has so far remained a secret of history.

The life of the Reverend John Huett, a clergyman of the Church of England, who came to Somerset County about 1680 or '81 as a missionary, is the very foundation of the organization of his Church in Somerset; while it was to this county that the Reverend Francis Makemie, of the Presbytery of Laggan in the North of Ireland, came in 1683 and laid here the foundation of his faith and order from which organized Presbyterianism in America was derived.

Imperishably imbedded in the foundation of "Old Somerset," like a strengthening element holding its several parts together in unbreakable unity, is the spirit of William Stevens, of "Rehoboth"—Churchman of liberal mind, jurist, assemblyman and provincial councillor. Stevens was a man of ability in the affairs of his county and the province at large; a veritable genius in promoting development in a new land. Stevens' business acumen brought him a fortune in his day, but the handling and accumulation of that substance left his honor untarnished.

Somerset—"as it was in the beginning"—has proved a charming study. Though a so-called "foreigner"—having connection neither by birth nor tradition with this county—yet with mind and heart to which the eternal values discoverable in Somerset's foundations and founders are by no means "foreign"—I have attempted to gather, classify, and to relate the facts I have found. If I have been able to evoke the significance from their remarkable reality I shall be glad; while my only regret would be to find that I had in any instance failed to bring forth from one of these facts the meaning of its abiding value. And so I pass this story of "Old Somerset" not only into the hands, but, I hope, the minds and hearts as well, of the present generation of Somerset's sons and daughters—a challenge from Immortals to the living.

Throughout the course of preparation of this study I have received most kindly encouragement and assistance in various ways from a number of persons. Henry Fillmore Lankford, Esq., and Cassius M. Dashiell, Esq., both of Princess Anne, Maryland, have been interested in my undertaking from its very beginning. Mr. Lankford placed his splendid collection of publications on Maryland history at my command. Without Mr. Dashiell's urgent request and kindly interest, manifested in various ways, this study would never have assumed form for publication. The late Doctor Henry R. McIlwaine, State Librarian of Virginia, was invariably kind in meeting my request for the loan of books which could not otherwise have been obtained by me. The authorities of the Maryland Historical Society have granted me every privilege in the use of material in their library; while Miss Florence J. Kennedy, of the Society's staff, has been unremitting in kindly courtesy and guidance to me as I worked among the Society's manuscript treasures. Miss Louise Magruder, of Annapolis, William B. Marye, Esq., of Baltimore, Benjamin J. Dashiell, Esq., of Towson, and Mrs. R. R. Norris, of Crisfield, have generously contributed items of value and interest. James R. Stewart, Esq., Benjamin L. Barnes, Esq., and Miss Ruth Ward, of the office staff of the Clerk of Court for Somerset County, and Miss Florence Dryden, of the Somerset Register of Wills office, Doctor Paul Jones, Register of Wills for Worcester County and his assistant, Miss Frances Truett, and Miss Bessie Bowen, Clerk of Court for Worcester County, have shown me every courtesy possible as I made researches in the original record sources in their keeping. Doctor Earl G. Swem, Librarian of William and Mary College, Williamsburg, Virginia, Daniel G. Henry, Esq., of Easton, W. C. Thurston, Esq., C. J. Truitt, Esq., and Mrs. W. H. Tilghman, all of Salisbury, Maryland, have greatly encouraged me in the publication of this study; while the writings of Matthew Page Andrews, Esq., on Maryland history, and a bit of correspondence with him, have been an inspiration to this work. Doctor J. Hall Pleasants, of Baltimore, Mrs. Henry H. Sasscer, the Reverend J. Paul Trout, and Professor C. N. Baughan, of Princess Anne, and W. Coulbourn Brown, Esq., of Philadelphia, at my request most kindly read the manuscript of this book in whole or in part, ably assisting me by their suggestions and criticism. I am deeply indebted to Miss Nell Jones and Miss Dorothy Denwood Jones, of Princess Anne; to the former for her excellent typing of the manuscript of this book, and to the latter for her gracious assistance in comparing the typewritten copy with the "original manuscript." To my wife, Elizabeth Green Neblett Torrence, I am indebted for the encouragement of her power of acute criticism of the written word and her incomparable proof-reading ability; and, as always, for her inexhaustible patience with my scribbling moods. To my friend of many years, R. McLean Whittet, Esqr., of Whittet & Shepperson, the printers of this book, I am indebted more deeply than I can ever say, for his interest in my undertaking to publish the results of my investigation of "Old Somerset's" origins. His generosity afforded me the opportunity of "going to press" with this work; while his genius has shaped the chaste form in which this book appears . To him and to every member of his establishment who has had his, or her, hand upon the work of printing this book, I am deeply grateful. Then there are two others—beloved friends—who may not read this "written words" of thanks, but who, I believe, still know and understand the "word that is in the heart." Stratton Nottingham and Roy Rolfe Gilson—now in the presence of Him from Whom all History derives—you who so greatly assisted and encouraged me in this undertaking—know and understand.

—CLAYTON TORRENCE.

CONTENTS

Part I

I—BREAK OF DAY 3
Somerset, 1666—References to Area 1608, 1620 and 1656—The Eastern Shore of Maryland and Isle of Kent Settlement—The Lower Eastern Shore, where Maryland joined Virginia—Lord Baltimore fears encroachment on his territory—Settlements directed "for the better publication and remembrance of the bounds between Maryland and Virginia"—Virginia and the Quakers—November 6, 1661: Maryland's response to the petition of certain "inhabitants of Northampton, otherwise called Accomack, in Virginia"—Territorial unit of "the Eastern Shore"—Settlements Established—Wicomico Indians Object—State of Plantation, May, 1662—Progress: Civil and Military Organization—Commissions of 1662 and 1663.

II—A STORM AT SUNRISE 23
Annemessex and the Quakers—Manokin: Seat of Authority—Scarburgh, "Surveyor General and Treasurer of his Majesty for Virginia," claims lands of Manokin-Annemessex settlers—Elzey, of the Commission for the Eastern Shore, refuses demand for subjection—To his Lordship's Council for Maryland: Elzey's appeal on behalf of the settlement—Maryland authorities appeal to the Governor of Virginia—Virginia Assembly's "Act Concerning the Bounds of This Colony on the Eastern Shore"—Scarburgh invades Manokin-Annemessex—Annemessex, the Defiant, and Manokin, the Amenable—Accomack Court's response to Manokin settlers' appeal—Governor Calvert "in person" to Governor Berkeley, of Virginia, and the Commission to Chancellor Philip Calvert to conclude the affair—The agreement of June, 1668.

III—AS CLOUDS ROLLED AWAY 55
Manokin-Annemessex secured in their allegiance to the Maryland government—Commissions for "the Eastern Shore" in February, 1663/4, and May, 1664—The Commission of August 25, 1665—Significance of this Commission—Increase in population and expansion of settlements—First court, of which record remains—"A Person to Keepe ye Records"—Governor Calvert sends the court a clerk.

IV—THEN A PERFECT DAY IN SUMMER 65
    Somerset County created by proclamation, August 22, 1666—The proclamation, commission of the peace, clerk of court and sheriff "Captain of All the Forces"—First court for Somerset, September 4, 1666—First marriages, constables, surveyors of highways, and grand jury—Highway for the county and boundaries of the hundreds—Affairs from March, 1667, to October, 1668—The first free Negroes—Somerset County's first election of representatives to the General Assembly.

V—THE HOUSEHOLD OF FAITH 81
    (1) *Followers of the Inner Light:* The Quakers who settled Annemessex—Meeting places and the "Meeting House"—A lone beacon of the Inner Light on Wicomico—George Fox, founder of the Society of Friends, visits Somerset—The Quakers of Monie—Meeting place and the "Meeting House" and burial ground—The Bogerternorton meeting and its membership—Meeting place, the "Meeting House" and burial ground. 83

    (2) *Voice of the People:* Earliest remaining record of a Baptism in Somerset, 1669—The grand jury of Somerset Court, March, 1671/2, renders "opinion" that regular religious services should be held in the county—Four places designated—Religious affiliations of grand jurymen rendering the "opinion," and of members of the court to whom it was rendered—Locations of preaching places in Pocomoke, Annemessex, Manokin and Wicomico Hundreds—Robert Maddock, preacher—Benjamin Salisbury, Morgan Jones, Robert Richardson and David Richardson. 113

    (3) *Of Ancient and Apostolic Lineage:* The Church of England in Somerset—Early Churchmen—Liberal type of churchmanship—Earliest remaining records of Burial, Baptism and Marriage, according to the rites and ceremonies of the Church of England—Captain Thomas Walker's bequest in May, 1680—John Huett, first resident clergyman of the Church of England in Somerset—Organization of the church in Somerset under the Assembly's Act of 1692 establishing the Church of England in the Province of Maryland—Parishes of Somerset, Coventry, Stepney and Snow Hill created—Time and places designated by the court for first election of vestries—Members of the first vestries—Parish Churches erected—Trotter, rector of Stepney and Somerset, Brechin, rector of Coventry. 129

    Notes: *Pocomoke Church, 1692; Parish Churches and Chapels of Ease* 167

    (4) *Children of the Covenant:* Planting of the Presbyterian Church in Somerset—Earliest identified Presbyterians—William Stevens' appeal to the Presbytery of Laggan in 1680—First min-

isters of Presbyterian faith and order—Francis Makemie, father of organized Presbyterianism in America—William Traile, of Rehoboth—Samuel Davis, of Snow Hill—Thomas Wilson, of Manokin—Erection of Presbyterian Church buildings in Somerset: Rehoboth, Snow Hill, Manokin and "at the road going up along the Sea Side." 209

Notes: Wicomico Presbyterian Congregation; Meeting House of 1697 "at the road going up along the sea side"; Buckingham Presbyterian Congregation; "Meeting House near Mrs. Edgar's," 1706; Pitts Creek Presbyterian Congregation; Some Other Early Presbyterian Places of Worship 251

VI—ORIGINS 273

Human, Professional, Mercantile and Industrial.
The Northampton-Accomack background of Somerset's first settlers—Social and economic status in Virginia—Names of the first settlers of Somerset—European origins of settlers—Status of families in Somerset—The first doctors, teachers, attorneys, traders, merchants, tradesmen.

VII—FOUNDERS 295

Stephen Horsey—Ambrose Dixon—Randall Revell—John Elzey—William Thorne—John Odber—Thomas Price—George Johnson—Henry Boston—William Coulbourne—William Bosman—William Stevens—James Jones—John White—John Winder—Edmund Beauchamp.

VIII—SOMERSET IN THE PROTESTANT REVOLUTION AND IN THE ROYAL PROVINCE 335

With notes on David Brown, Robert King, Francis Jenckins, George Layfield, William Whittington, William Brereton.

Part II

APPENDIXES

I—Governor Calvert's Commission for Settlement of the Eastern Shore Below Choptank River, November 6, 1661 386

II—Randall Revell's Report on Conditions at Manokin-Annemessex, May, 1662 387

III—Colonel Edmund Scarburgh's Report of His Proceedings at Mankin-Annemessex, October, 1663 388

IV—Somerset County Officials Before 1700 393

V—Somerset County Marriages 396

VI—First Court House Sites and First Towns in Somerset 402

VII—A Proposed County on the Seaboard Side 423

VIII—Worcester County (1742) and Wicomico County (1867) 428

IX—The King Homes in Somerset County: (1) "Kingsland"; (2) Beverly"; (3) "Kingston Hall" 430

X—Early Settlers 434
    (a) First Settlers' (1662-1666) Families: Genealogical Notes.
    (b) Names of Settlers in Somerset County, 1666-1700.
    (c) Names of Quaker, Church of England and Presbyterian Families.
    (d) Patentees of Land in the Old Somerset Area, 1662-1666.

Part III

References and Index 481

OLD SOMERSET
ON
THE EASTERN SHORE OF MARYLAND

PART I

I

BREAK OF DAY

⁕

Somerset, 1666—References to Area 1608, 1620 and 1656—The Eastern Shore of Maryland and Isle of Kent Settlement—The Lower Eastern Shore, where Maryland joined Virginia—Lord Baltimore fears encroachment on his territory—Settlements directed "for the better publication and remembrance of the bounds between Maryland and Virginia"—Virginia and the Quakers—November 6, 1661: Maryland's response to the petition of certain "inhabitants of Northampton, otherwise called Accomack, in Virginia"—Territorial unit of the "Eastern Shore"—Settlements Established—Wicomico Indians Object—State of Plantation, May, 1662—Progress: Civil and Military Organization—Commissions of 1662 and 1663.

SOMERSET, eighth of Mother Maryland's family of "county children," is no longer young. In truth, she is ancient, for the passing years since her birth have carried her well past the mark of two and a half centuries—her natal day having been the 22nd of August in the year of our Lord, 1666. But her life has been one so filled with nobility of purpose and great interests that ancientness rests upon her like a mantle of glory. Beauty, as in youth, adorns her countenance; grace lingers in every contour of her fair form; her heart is filled by strong mother-love, nurturing the ever-increasing generations of her line; and her ample bosom is in very truth home to hearts who claim her blood. "Her children rise up and call her blessed."

Cecil, Lord Baltimore, Lord Proprietary of the province of Maryland, by proclamation dated 22nd August, 1666, issued through the Honorable Charles Calvert, governor of the province, announced the erection of Somerset County on the Eastern Shore of Maryland; named "in hon^r to our dear Sister, Lady Mary Somersett,"[1] and created "for the ease & benefit of the people of this o^r pvince & the speedy and more exact Adm^{con} of Justice." To him who has an eye for natural beauty the Lord Proprietor's delineation in his proclamation of Somerset's proportions veritably miniatures her wondrousness—"bounded south with a line from Watkin's Point (being the north point of th^t bay into wch the River Wighco form^{ly} called Wighcocomoco afterwards Pocomoke & Wighcocomoco againe, doth fall exclusively) to the Ocean on the east; Nanticoke River on the North & the Sound of Chesipeake Bay on the West." Great virgin forest, flowing stream, billowy wave and graceful isle are here enshrined, abounding natural beauty and resource for subsistence.

Thus created and named, the purpose of her being announced, her physical proportions delineated, his Lordship then proceeds to name the "sponsors" for this new addition to Mother Maryland's household—eight gentlemen—justices of the peace, "Com^{rs} Jointly & severally to keepe the peace": Stephen Horsey, William Stevens, William Thorne, James Jones, John Winder, Henry Boston, George Johnson and John White. So does the ancient register of such matters—the Archives of Maryland—record Somerset County's advent into the life of the province. The record of birth, of naming and of sponsoring are clear facts of history.[2] But back of these plain "household facts" lies a series of important events—"reasons and reasons" from which this "county being" grew—shaping her into life. Every birth involves a lineage; every birth's setting is against a background of "origin." Somerset's is not otherwise.

Very early—in fact near the beginning of permanent settlement on North America's eastern seaboard—we catch a glimpse, in mere outline though it be, of the bayside contours of the territory which in after years became Somerset County. For this rather imperfect picturing of the ancient land we are indebted to Captain John Smith's *Map of Virginia* published in 1612, embodying the discoveries made during his exploration of the Chesapeake Bay region in the summer of the year 1608. This *"Map"* interestingly indicates the bayside section of "Old Somerset" from the Pocomoke River (which Smith designates as the "Wighco") to the Nanticoke (which he indicates by the name of "Kus"). From the text of the pamphlet which accompanies the *"Map"* it is evident that Captain Smith and members of his party made investigations on the land itself, gathering bits of information relative to the country, its Indian population and their villages. Thus may we with certainty say that "once upon a time," and very near the beginning of English colonization in America, the section which later became Somerset County received a visit, fleeting though it was, from the redoubtable Captain John Smith and his companions, during the memorable summer of the year 1608.[3]

In various sections of this territory, later embraced by the boundaries of Somerset County, we find locations of the towns and villages of the several Indian tribes whose names have become familiar through local lore. On the banks of the winding streams these "Native Americans" had their homes. Of Indians within this territory there were apparently five branches of one tribe: Pocomoke, Annemessex, Manoakin, Nassawattox and Aquintico; while to the northward—on the river bearing their name—were the Nanticokes.[4] In addition to these groups there was yet another, whose presence is disclosed by remaining records in the name of "Manny" or "Monie," with a village in the vicinity of the creek which bears the name of "Great Monie."[5]

From remaining records it appears that as early as the year 1620 white men were coming into the Manokin River to trade with the Indians (evidently the "Manokins"), whose town was located in an upper fork of that river (on the south side thereof), a section which we find in later records designated as the "Indian Neck" and today may be identified under the name of "Stewart's Neck." This bit of information comes to us in a deposition of John Westlock, of Somerset County, who in the year 1670, then in the 90th year of his age, was called upon to testify as to the location of the "Trading Branch" (now King's Creek). Westlock in the course of his testimony refers to having traded with the Indians at "the point" of the "Trading Branch" some "fifty years agoe." From depositions made by German Gillett and Henry Hooper, in 1670, it also appears that traders were coming from Rappahannock (in Virginia) to trade with the Indians in the Manokin River in the year 1656.[6]

These references, though scanty, give us a glimpse at least of this section of "Old Somerset" as a trading-place between the resident Indians and white men coming from a distance. The first reference, (that of John Westlock), to trading with these Indians at "the point" in 1620, carries us back to a period fourteen years prior to the founding and settlement of the province of Maryland in March, 1634; while the reference to the trading here in 1656, brings us down to a period within five or six years of the first permanent settlement by white men within the limits of "Old Somerset." No doubt, through the intervening years, white traders were frequently passing through this section conducting commerce with the Indian residents.

Lord Baltimore's province of Maryland was a fair land, great in extent, endowed with a mighty purpose, and rich in natural resources. By natural conformation Maryland fell into two sections, one east, one west, of the Chesapeake Bay. When in March, 1634, the first shiploads of colonists arrived from England, settlement was made in that section west of the Bay; and for every Marylander there is charm unreckonable in the tradition of "St. Mary's." Though this settlement at St. Mary's in 1634 was technically and veritably the first settlement of the province of Maryland, there had been for some years a trading post on the Isle of Kent in the upper Chesapeake Bay, around which gathered a not inconsiderable group of settlers. From the year 1627 this upper section of territory lying along the Bay had been the objective of development for purposes of trade by Captain William Claiborne, a Virginia official of high rank, who, with the cooperation of certain English merchants, had been successful in establishing interests there. In 1627, 1628 and 1629 Claiborne conducted his business in this vicinity under license from the Virginia local authorities. Finally, in 1631, under license from the Crown, he made a permanent settlement and trading-post on the southern end of the island, to which was given the name Isle of Kent. When the charter for the province to be called Maryland was granted to Lord Baltimore, June 30, 1632, this Isle of Kent, with its established trading-post and settlement, fell within the territorial limits defined by the charter. Claiborne and his associates had bitterly opposed the granting of this charter, and matters had even gone so far in attempting to include the Isle of Kent settlement in the Virginia colony, that it was represented in the Virginia Assembly of February, 1631/2. It is not surprising, therefore, to find that this settlement and its *de facto* ruler did not constitute an angelic choir chanting hymns of peace at the actual birth of the province of Maryland; but, on the contrary, marshalled an impish little army sowing a thorny way of travel for the sponsors and guardians of the infant government at St. Mary's. After a time, however, questions of governmental authority over the island settlement were solved through the enforced recognition of the Lord Proprietor's charter rights, and Kent came fully under the goverance of Lord Baltimore and his deputies resident in Maryland.[7] In the year 1642, this settlement having extended itself from the island well onto the mainland of the "Eastern Shore," the section was erected into a county under the name of Kent.[8] This Isle of Kent settlement, made before the province of Maryland actually came into being, and thereafter extensively increasing, represents the first settlement of English colonists *east* of the Chesapeake Bay within the limits of the section known historically and geographically as the

"Eastern Shore." This settlement was, however, far to the north of the scene which invites our attention, and actually did not extend in its various ramifications so very far to the southward.⁹ In reality there was no connection whatsoever between this Kent settlement and the later settlement in the extreme southern part of Maryland's portion of this peninsula—the settlement far to the south which assumed the role of "Genesis" in the drama which through the years developed into that remarkable and wonderful climax—"Old Somerset."

Southward, then, we turn our eyes. On this peninsula, formed by the Atlantic Ocean and the Chesapeake Bay, and below the Choptank River, on the Eastern Shore of the province of Maryland, lay a fertile territory consisting of thousands upon thousands of acres of wonderful forests and rich level fields touched and deeply penetrated by great, deep, winding streams—streams winding westward to the "Sound of Chesapeake Bay"; a territory so far peopled only by "true native Americans." This naturally rich part of Lord Baltimore's province extended southward on this peninsula to the northern limit of the ancient colony of Virginia's territory east of the Chesapeake Bay, where there lay "like a bone of contention" between the authorities of Virginia and Maryland, the specified—though unsurveyed and unmarked—southern boundary line of Lord Baltimore's territorial possessions in this section of his province. To secure the recognition of this boundary line as defined in his charter and to save the southernmost part of his possessions east of the Chesapeake Bay from encroachments by Virginia officials and settlers "pressing up shore" from the south, his Lordship became increasingly interested in opening up the lands thereabouts to settlers and obtaining immigrants who would come into this area, take up lands there under patent from him, and establish homes. Under conditions actually obtaining, Lord Baltimore could sufficiently and effectively fortify his charter rights in this territory only by organizing settlements on his lands near the boundary line.

As the years passed, this necessity bore with increasing force upon Lord Baltimore's mind, and with marked insistence he emphasized this matter of necessity in communication to his officials resident in the province. In his official letter of April 26, 1651, to his provincial governor, the Honorable William Stone, and the members of the General Assembly, he urged upon them the necessity for encouraging the establishment of permanent settlements "on or near the Bounds of our Province on that tract of land which is commonly called the Eastern Shore lying between the Bay of Chesapeake and the Sea." In this communication, Lord Baltimore specifically stated his reason for the urgency of establishing such settlements to be "for the better publication and remembrance of the bounds between Virginia and Maryland and Prevention of Controversies which may otherwise hereafter happen between the Inhabitants of Virginia and those of our Province." With this end in view, his Lordship, by this same communication, requires that his officials "encourage some English as soon as you can to take up such land as shall be due them in our said province" as near as possible to this boundary line between Maryland and Virginia.[10] In instructions to his governor and council under date of October 23, 1656, Lord Baltimore again emphatically approaches the question of securing this boundary line of his province "on that part of the country known there by the name of the Eastern Shore."[11] Thus was his Lordship insistent on the protection of his territorial rights in the southernmost part of his province east of Chesapeake Bay.

Seldom did there arise a more vexing question in the relations of Maryland and Virginia in colonial times than this one of the boundary line between them on the "Eastern Shore." Nor did a question arise between this ancient colony and province with more far-reaching consequences in litigation, for the final settlement thereof did not come until more than two and a half centuries had passed; well within the memory of living men. Though the geographical limits of the province of Maryland were stated in Lord Baltimore's charter and the boundary line between Maryland and Virginia specifically described, yet the line had not been actually surveyed, run out and marked at this early day, and there was a shadowiness about it which tended to the confusion of rights, encouraging unscrupulous persons to take advantage of both governments, while other residents thereabouts were "really unable to tell whether they were citizens of Maryland or Virginia."[12] There was uneasiness on both sides of this "boundary line." Lord Baltimore's misgivings relative to the proper insurance of his territorial rights in the area were matched by the frequent perplexity of the authorities in the then adjoining county of Northampton in Virginia as to what was proper procedure in regard to certain developing settlements in this area. Certain residents of the "Eastern Shore" of Virginia sought to make settlements in this area under the authority of the Virginia government; while Lord Baltimore most sincerely believed that he was being unjustly dealt with by certain officials of the Virginia colony. This feeling of Lord Baltimore's was wholly justified by the fact remaining of record that grants for land made by the Virginia authorities about this time were, a few years later, determined by actual survey to lie within his territorial possessions as granted and guaranteed by his charter.[13]

The beginning of the controversy over the boundary line between Maryland and Virginia on the "Eastern Shore" came at a time when his Lordship's proprietary rights were in grave peril. With the dethronement of Charles I, and his subsequent execution; with first Parliament and later the Lord Protector in the saddle of affairs in England, old enemies of his Lordship and the Maryland adventure— enemies because of his staunch religious affiliation, and enemies from jealousy of his chartered rights and his successful prosecution of those rights—sought by every means to wrest from his hand the provincial government and territory with its accruing revenues. The times were indeed fraught with grave peril for the interests of Cecil, Lord Baltimore; but his "caution and carefulness"—exercised with great astuteness—and the fairness displayed toward him by the powers of government in England, brought him safely through in possession of all his rights until, finally, in March, 1657/8, we find him again secure in the government of his province. Not one particle did Lord Baltimore yield in the rights granted him by charter. Not once did he admit the contentions of his prejudiced assailants. Calmly, guardedly, wisely did he battle with his foes and offset them at every turn.

We have noted the insistence with which Lord Baltimore, in 1651 and 1656, directed and required his authorities in the province to make every effort to organize settlements in that section where his territorial rights were in danger, near the boundary line, between Maryland and Virginia, on the "Eastern Shore." Even in the hour of his greatest peril he worked vigorously to fortify and secure his rights. This conduct of affairs by Lord Baltimore is deeply involved in that which is of interest to us in this study; for, had he relaxed his vigor in maintaining his territorial rights, we may rest assured that the southernmost part of Maryland's "Eastern Shore"—the section which in due season became Somerset County—would have passed to another government. This is the inevitable conclusion reached from study of the facts clearly set forth by investigators and historians of the matters pertaining to this boundary line controversy—the only just and fair interpretation of the situation.[14]

"Up to . . . March 1657/8," writes an authority, "no settlement upon the Eastern Shore within the limits of Maryland, below the Choptank River, had been made under grants of land from Lord Baltimore so far as we have been able to ascertain."[15] However, it was not a long period of waiting that Lord Baltimore had to endure before his urgently expressed desire for permanent settlements in this area, and as near as possible to the boundary line between his province and the colony of Virginia, should meet with fulfilment, and that fulfilment after most dramatic fashion.

The General Assembly of the colony of Virginia, meeting in March, 1660 (1659/60), early in its session framed a drastic law against Quakers, whom it describes as "an unreasonable and turbulent sort of people who daily gather together unlawful assemblies of people, teaching lies, miracles, false visions, prophecies, and doctrines tending to disturb the peace, disorganize society and destroy all law and government and religion." This Act forbade any more of this "faith and practice" to enter Virginia, exacting the removal of such adherents thereto as were then resident in the colony. Penalties of heaviest nature were enjoined for violation of the provisions of this Act. In the enforcement of this law that irreconcilable royalist and Churchman, Sir William Berkeley—recently restored to the governorship of Virginia on the restoration of Charles II to the throne of England—spared no pains. Whatever defence may be found for this "law against Quakers" in the political and military exigencies of that day and time (and there is unquestionably a defence to be found therein), its provisions and their execution met with strong resistance from those at whose practices it was aimed. "Pacific resistance" it may be termed, yet most effective in the long run; resistance through endurance of prosecution (not to say persecution); resistance by evasion; and most powerful of all, resistance by exodus. Then, too, there was resistance by defiance. Again and again these followers of the "Inner Light" defied the law and the authorities by persistently practicing their faith. The remaining records of Virginia of that day are imperishable testimony to the Quakers' faithfulness in witnessing to "Conviction."[16]

This law against Quakers was enacted by the Virginia Assembly at a session convened March, 1659/60. Many of the Quakers—a large majority no doubt—remained in Virginia offering resistance by defiance of law and authority; yet many of them sought a place of refuge where they would be free from the harassing humiliation of the execution of the law's provisions. For those who desired a more serene and sympathetic atmosphere there was near at hand an "open door of escape"—the province of Maryland—where a more liberal policy in matters of religion was both tradition and law.

With the situation as it was developing in Virginia under the enforcement of the law against Quakers, it is not surprising to find the authorities of the government in Maryland petitioned by "divers persons well affected to this province, now or late inhabitants of Northampton, otherwise called Accomack, in Virginia, who are desirous to transplant themselves and their families into this province." Nor are we surprised by the cheerful readiness with which the Maryland authorities responded to the desire of these petitioners. "Favor and gain" were double edged. The petitioners from Northampton County (otherwise called Accomack) in Virginia wished to migrate from the Virginia colony, and Lord Baltimore wished to have settlers for the lands in the immediate vicinity of his southern boundary line on the "Eastern Shore" so that he could effectively organize this area.

No copy of this petition of the Northampton-Accomack Virginians praying right to settle in Maryland has been so far discovered. The names of the petitioners are not now known. Nor is the date of this petition known. But, on November 6, 1661, Governor Philip Calvert issued a proclamation (countersigned by "C. Baltimore"; i. e. Cecil, Lord Baltimore) directing that the petitioners "now or late inhabitants of Northampton otherwise called Accomack, in Virginia," who were desirous of moving into the province of Maryland, should be granted lands "upon the Eastern Shore of the province in any part below the Choptank River" for the purpose of "the more speedy and effectual prosecution of his Lordship's command to me to see that Parte of this Province next adjoining to the county aforesaid [i. e. Northampton, otherwise called Accomack] peopled."[17]

The Virginia Assembly's Act against Quakers was passed in March, 1659/60. The date of the petition of the Northampton-Accomack people desiring settlement in Maryland is not known; neither do we know the names of the petitioners. The proclamation of the governor of Maryland granting this petition and directing the area in which the settlement was to be made bears date November 6, 1661. Under the terms of this proclamation, and in the specific area named by the authorities for settlement by the petitioners, we find a group of Northampton-Accomack Quakers and their dependents and sympathizers settled in the early part of the year 1662. Unquestionably, we have at the foundation of the settlement, whose foundation and development we are studying, a stone rejected by the builders of Virginia—cast out—to be laid as the very corner stone of Somerset's structure! There were unquestionably other elements in the foundation of Somerset—we shall find them as we explore; but, of the Northampton-Accomack (Virginia) Quaker element—we believe that it was the first to come. The Virginia Assembly's Act against Quakers in March, 1659/60, really "blazed the trail" over which was brought the very "corner stone" of the lower "Eastern Shore" structure.

Under the terms of Governor Calvert's proclamation of November, 1661, we find the first settlement made within the area which later became Somerset County. The first settlers were all from Northampton-Accomack in Virginia; and the settlements made, some very near, some at greater distance from, the boundary line. This territorial unit was officially designated the "Eastern Shore"—extending from the Choptank River south to the boundary line of the province; with "ocean's wave-beat shore" as eastern limit, and the "wondrous emerald inland sea" (as Chesapeake Bay has been called) its western extent. From the southern part of this unit (the territory south of Nanticoke River) Somerset County was erected in August, 1666.

In passing (we shall later take up the details of the matter) it may be stated that the first settlements within the area which finally became Somerset were made by Quakers, and their sympathizers, about the south bank of the Great Annemessex River (near its mouth), and by an element, predominantly Church of England in religious affiliation (though numbering a few Quakers), along the Manokin River and its creek tributaries. These first settlements were very early called by the names of "Annemessex" and "Manoakin."

The proclamation of the Maryland authorities, November 6, 1661, not only granted the request of the Northampton-Accomack petitioners, designating the area for their settlement; but established a commission of three members for the purpose of effecting this "Eastern Shore" settlement near the Maryland-Virginia boundary line. Lord Baltimore, by his deputies, was striking while the iron was hot. Here, indeed, was good material ready for the shaping. By the proclamation a commission was named, consisting of Edmund Scarburgh, Randall Revell and John Elzey—"any two of them being within the province"—which was authorized to grant lands to the petitioners; fifty acres for every person "transplanted"; and to administer the "oath of fidelity" to the immigrants so obtaining land. The commission was directed to keep careful record of its land transactions, this record to be returned into the provincial secretary's office. All persons to whom land was thus granted were to be accountable to the secretary for any fees attached thereto.

Scarburgh, Revell and Elzey, the commissioners named, were prominent Northampton County, Virginia, residents. Edmund Scarburgh—of whom, later, we shall hear a great deal—was indeed the most powerful citizen of his county and, in fact, among the most powerful men and officials in the Virginia government. Of unquestioned ability and distinction; possessing brain, wealth and the advantage of high office in his county and colony; Scarburgh was no doubt named in this commission by the Maryland authorities in hope of obtaining his favor in behalf of the venture. It was no doubt with Scarburgh's intention to remain a citizen of Virginia in full view that the proclamation in naming the land commission for the "Eastern Shore" required that only two of the commissioners should be resident in the province. Scarburgh did retain his Virginia citizenship and high political office, and it was not long before he was retired from membership in the Maryland commission. Scarburgh indeed played quite a different role from that of "good genius" to the "Eastern Shore" venture, becoming in fact an implacable foe to the whole undertaking. Revell and Elzey, however, came into Maryland to reside, both of them becoming officers in Lord Baltimore's "Eastern Shore" settlement, and both of them seating extensive plantations immediately on Manokin River—Revell to the south of the river on a tract called "The Double Purchase" (which today bears the name of "Revell's Neck") and Elzey to the north of the river at "Almodington." Revell and Elzey were the first officials of the "Eastern Shore" settlements of "Manoakin" and "Annemessex," and "Manoakin" was the first seat of the "local government." Revell—living to a goodly old age—saw the settlements grow into a county well established; while Elzey passed on beyond all earthly settlements while "Manoakin" and "Annemessex" were still in infancy.

Positive evidence of the exact date of the "Eastern Shore" settlements of "Annemessex" and "Manoakin" is lacking; though the term used in the proclamation of November 6, 1661, relative to the Northampton-Accomack petitioners seeking settlement in Maryland—"now or *late* inhabitants of Northampton, otherwise called Accomack in Virginia," would seem to indicate that some of these petitioners had before that date "crossed the line" and seated themselves upon "Eastern Shore" Maryland lands. We shall not, however, labor over this question, for at best the issue would remain but a surmise. Whatever the exact date of these settlements, there remains evidence that by the spring of the year 1662 they were well planted and healthily growing, by the river sides of Annemessex and Manoakin.

The first direct reference to actual settlement made in the area, whose foundations we are unearthing, comes to us in the official records of the province of Maryland under date of April 9, 1662. This reference fully warrants the belief that the arrival of the settlers on the "Eastern Shore" of Maryland was attended by attempted opposition which, had it not been "nipped in the bud," would have resulted in conditions of discomfiture hardly less unpleasant (though of an entirely different nature) than those which caused the exodus from Virginia of a prominent element among these first settlers.

At a meeting of the Council of the province of Maryland, held at St. Mary's, April 2, 1662, John Elzey (one of the commission for the "Eastern Shore") made a sworn deposition:

"that beeings at Wiccocomaco on the Eastern Shore certain of the greate men of that towne came . . . and sayd that Mr. John Nuttall had told them that . . . this deponent and others that came hither to take upp land did belong to the County of Accomack and that wee weare not heere to inhabit, for that land did belong to the Province of Maryland, and if wee weare suffred to seate there amongst them wee would serve them as we have don our neighbor Indians at Accomack, and further this deponent sayeth that hee heard there was a letter went to that effect, and som of Mr. Revels servants told this deponent that there was a letter directed to this Deponent to that effect by Mr. Wright he referring to this deponent whoe might be the author, and further sayeth not."

Thus we see that it was believed that "seeds of disaster" to the new settlement were being sown, whose growth in the Indian mind would surely prejudice the Red Man against his newly arrived neighbors. The "Wiccocomico" referred to in Mr. Elzey's deposition is of course the seat of the Indians of the Wicomico tribe and "the greate men" of that tribe were evidently the ones whose minds were the object of "inflammation" by the gossip of one John Nuttall. Upon "the oath of John Elzey" the Council proceeded to order that Nuttall "doe give security to appear at the next Provinciall Courts to cleere himself of the things he is accused by John Elzey and Francis Wright" and that "Wright's deposition concerning the same" be taken and returned into the secretary's office.[18]

One would really like to know what amount of truth was at the bottom of this report of "the greate men" of the Wicomicos from which we infer that John Nuttall was attempting to sow the seed of strife between the Indians and the white settlers in this area. Unquestionably there was a party in Accomack, headed by Edmund Scarburgh (one of the commission for the settlement of the "Eastern Shore" of Maryland), known for its bitter hatred toward and openly avowed policy of extermination of the Indians.[19] Nuttall, if indeed he were "guilty as charged in the indictment" of disseminating this seed of strife, was not untruthful in his statement of Accomack affairs. On the other hand, Nuttall was a trader in furs and animal skins under license of the Maryland authorities, and the Indians were his profitable source for obtaining the articles of his commerce. Was his "talk," though its "kernel be truth," the trick of a trader, jealous of encroachments on his ground of gain? Francis Wright, whose name is also brought into this matter as an accuser of Nuttall, was also a trader in skins and furs. The conclusion of this complaint against Nuttall has not been discovered; though it seems probable that he was cleared of the charge, as he continued to hold license as a trader. It should be further noted that, however true was the report of the treatment of the Indians in Virginia by the Accomackians, there is no evidence to show that the settlers from Accomack who came to the "Eastern Shore" of Maryland ever attempted persecution of, or adopted a policy of antagonism towards, the Indians of this locality.

Whatever may have been the strength or the weakness of the opposition offered by the Indians to the first settlers in this area of the "Eastern Shore," accomplishment soon crowned the efforts made by Randall Revell and John Elzey, the resident commissioners of Lord Baltimore, in making the settlement. On May 2, 1662, Revell, appearing at a Council held for the province at St. Mary's, the seat of government, sketched, in encouraging detail, for that august body the state of affairs in the infant plantation.

"There weare now at this present (May 1662)" reported Mr. Revell, "seated there fifty tithable persons viz. at Manokin and Annamessicks a place distant some fower miles from Manokin." He reports an agreement made with the Emperor of the Nanticoke Indians (evidently the Indian "overlord" of this territory) in regard to compensation for every plantation settled; for the return of runaway servants; for prohibiting murders, either of the settlers by the Indians or *vice versa;* for preventing stealing from either one by the other; regulations agreed upon regarding trade by the Indians with the Dutch; and of the requirement of "passes" from the governor or a magistrate duly authorized to issue them, before an Englishman could go through the quarters of the Indians. Revell also requested that "course might be taken for the supply of the plantation or continuance to himself and others Graunted for Graunting of warrants and survey of lands in that part of the province dated 6th of November last past."[20]

On receiving this report, which was evidently deemed most satisfactory, the Council of the province ordered that a fit person be authorized to conclude terms of peace with the Nanticoke Indians on the basis of the agreement outlined by Revell and that the agreement be "entred uppon Rec^d [record]." The commission of November 6, 1661, for granting warrants for land in this specified area was renewed to Scarburgh, Revell and Elzey, "till his Lo^p [lordship] or his Heirs, or his or their Lieut. or chief Governor of this Province for the tyme being shall recall the same." The Council further ordered that copies of the proclamations of December 7, 1661, and January 31, 1661/2—one prohibiting trade with the Indians and the other for the better observing of the Act of Navigation and the increase of shipping[21]—be given to Randall Revell, and that a commission be granted to him and John Elzey empowering them to carry the provisions of these proclamations into effect.

The progress and condition of the settlement at Manokin-Annemessex on the "Eastern Shore," as reported by Mr. Revell in May, 1662, seemed to warrant the civil and military organization of this area by the provincial authorities, the Council at this time entering the order "that a Commission be Graunted to William Thorne to command the Company of foote to be leaveyed and raised at Manokin in usuall forme, and that he choose his Lieutenant and Ensigne... that Commission be granted to Randall Revell, John Elzey and William Thorne to heere and determine any causes to the vallue of 2000 l. of tobacco or under and that they make choyce of some man who may serve in the nature of a Sheriffe or Martiall to bring such people before them as shall be delinquent or in debt till a County be erected and further order taken therein."[22]

In accordance with orders of Council there were issued under date of May 2, 1662, commission to William Thorne to be captain at "Manoakin" and "Anamessick"; to Scarburgh, Revell and Elzey a renewal of the former commission to grant land warrants in this area; to Randall Revell, John Elzey and William Thorne "Com[on] (commission) to keepe the peace"; and a commission was granted for the protection of the rights of trade by the seizure of vessels operating in the waterways of the area without due license and authority. At the same time licenses to trade were granted to Francis Wright and a person named Clausen; while on the following day, May 3rd, licenses were given Revell, Wright and Elzey to export stipulated amounts of corn.[23]

These orders and commissions of the Council of Maryland clearly disclose the objective of the provincial authorities to develop as soon as possible this settlement at Manoakin-Annemessex into an organized political unit—a county; and in the meantime to insure its every interest by the due authorization of commissioners, both civil and military, for the proper conduct of affairs.

In this first "commission to keepe the peace" granted for the "Eastern Shore" May 25, 1662, to Randall Revell, John Elzey and William Thorne, we find "priority" given to Revell. This was in reality a confirmation by the authorities of Revell's actual position in the settlement; for, from all appearances, he was the chief resident official, and it is evident that it was in such capacity that he made the first report to the provincial authorities on the "state of the plantation." With the issuing of this first commission of the peace, and the commission to the captain of the company of foot to be leveyed and raised, there is introduced into the affairs of the settlement a new human factor in the person of William Thorne, whose life from now on we shall find closely interwoven in the affairs of the "Eastern Shore" and later in the early events of Somerset County, both as military commander and magistrate.

The archives of the province afford no data relative to the life and development in the Manokin-Annemessex settlement during the ten months period between Revell's report to the Council in May, 1662, with the action by the Council on that report, and the following February, 1662/3, at which time we are able to again pick up the thread of events. On February 4, 1662/3, we find the Governor of Maryland again issuing a commission for the "Eastern Shore" (between Choptank River and the Maryland-Virginia boundary line), this time naming John Elzey, Randall Revell and Stephen Horsey as commissioners to grant land warrants and to "keep the peace." In this commission, John Elzey is given priority as being the first named, while Randall Revell takes "second place," and Stephen Horsey is nar ed third and replaces William Thorne of the commission of May 2, 1662, but now omitted. However, when the matter of confirming the governor's appointment of "Commissioners for that part of the Eastern Shore newly settled and adjoining Virginia" came up to the Council on February 20th, it was "ordered that Mr. John Elzey and Stephen Horsey be continued. That Randall Revell bee out. And that William Thorne and Captain John Odber be joined to Mr. John Elzey and Stephen Horsey in the said commission."[24] Thus the commission for the "Eastern Shore" issued in February, 1662/3, carried the names of John Elzey, Stephen Horsey, William Thorne and John Odber.

February, 1662/3 marks the retirement from official connection with Manokin-Annemessex of Edmund Scarburgh and Randall Revell, a retirement which was inevitable because of their attitude towards Lord Baltimore's insistent maintenance of his territorial rights on the "Eastern Shore'" his determination to hold to the boundary line between his province and the colony of Virginia as specifically designated in his charter. Edmund Scarburgh's appointment by Lord Baltimore as one of the commissioners for settling this area was indeed an anomalous one, for which his Lordship could not possibly have had any other reason than that he wished to curry favor with the powerful Virginian. What part Scarburgh played in active pursuit of his commission from Lord Baltimore we do not know, and most certainly we can only believe that he toyed with the matter simply to enable him to gain a firmer hold on territory which later developments clearly prove he exercised every particle of his power in attempting to wrest from Lord Baltimore's possession. In all probability Scarburgh did not actively participate in this commission, and with his frank and violent nature did not long successfully conceal his motive and desire from the Maryland authorities; and his Lordship, seeing the utter futility of his flattering appointment, ordered an avowed enemy dropped from the commission. Randall Revell did, however, actively participate in effecting the settlement at Manokin under the terms of his commission and, as we have seen, held "priority" in office there. No doubt, Revell was more in sympathy with Scarburgh's schemes than with Lord Baltimore's defense of his territorial rights, and so finally was excluded from official connection with the "Eastern Shore" settlement.

Revell and Scarburgh were intimate in their association and a constant and invariable tradition gives them as brothers-in-law, relating that Revell's wife was a sister of Scarburgh. However, whatever cause may have finally cast weight into the scales against them, Scarburgh and Revell were certainly retired from official connection with the "Eastern Shore" settlement at Manokin-Annemessex by omission from the commission of February, 1662/3.

This commission of February, 1662/3, introduces two new men to the official life of the "Eastern Shore" settlement—Horsey and Odber. Stephen Horsey had for some years prior to his coming to Maryland been in conflict with the authorities in Northampton County, Virginia. He cannot be identified as a Quaker, though he seems to have been constantly in rebellion against the "established order," refusing to pay parish tithes in Virginia. He was one of the first Northampton-Accomack men to flee to the "Eastern Shore" of Maryland and his home on the Annemessex River was in the very midst of the Quaker element. We shall meet him time and again as our story unfolds.

In Captain John Odber we find a man who before entering the service of the "Eastern Shore" had figured conspicuously as a military officer in Calvert County across the Bay, and, after but a year's service in the settlement of Manokin-Annemessex, apparently "moved on"—only to be murdered a few years later by a Wicomico Indian.

By this Commission of the Peace and for granting land warrants issued for the "Eastern Shore" in February, 1662/3, we have noticed the priority given to John Elzey. He now becomes the resident head of the settlement. Elzey's career as "chief magistrate" in this settlement was marked from first to last by the display of fine ability in meeting the difficult situations which now began to confront the authorities; an ability which truly entitles him to the distinction of "a founder among founders" of this historic territorial unit from which was evolved the county of Somerset.

In April, 1663, and again in August, 1663, the government's commission of the peace and for granting warrants for land on the "Eastern Shore" below Choptank River was renewed to John Elzey, Stephen Horsey, William Thorne and John Odber,[25] with priority given to Elzey.

So the "Commission for the Eastern Shore" stood with Elzey as "chief magistrate" and Thorne as military commander of the area when in October, 1663, a time which veritably tried the souls of officials and settlers, came upon the infant settlement, and across it swept a storm of opposition, whose fury was aimed at wresting the area from Lord Baltimore's territorial possession.

II

A STORM AT SUNRISE

Annemessex and the Quakers—Manokin: Seat of Authority—Scarburgh, "Surveyor General and Treasurer of his Majesty for Virginia," claims lands of Manokin-Annemessex settlers—Elzey, of the Commission for the "Eastern Shore," refuses demand for subjection—To his Lordship's Council for Maryland: Elzey's appeal on behalf of the settlement—Maryland authorities appeal to the Governor of Virginia—Virginia Assembly's "Act Concerning the Bounds of This Colony on the Eastern Shore" — Scarburgh invades Manokin-Annemessex — Annemessex the Defiant, and Manokin the Amenable—Accomack Court's response to Manokin settlers' appeal—Governor Calvert "in person" to Governor Berkeley, of Virginia, and the Commission to Chancellor Philip Calvert to conclude the affair—The agreement of June, 1668.

UNUSUALLY rich in dramatic episodes, Maryland colonial history presents none more dramatic than that of the Manokin-Annemessex settlement on the "Eastern Shore" in the storm of opposition which swept upon it during the earliest days of its life.

Lord Baltimore's determined effort to establish permanent settlements in his territory near the boundary line between his province and Virginia on the "Eastern Shore" met with success in the year 1661. About this time certain Northampton-Accomack Virginians petitioned for the right to settle in the province of Maryland, thereby affording his Lordship opportunity of obtaining settlers for this area. With marked readiness the prayer of these petitioners was granted and they were directed to lands adjacent to the boundary line. The officials of the local territorial unit set up for these would-be settlers by proclamation in November, 1661, reported well established plantations in May, 1662: "now at this present seated there fifty tithable persons viz. at Manokin and Anamessicks a place distant some fower miles from Manokin." Day by day these plantations grew as men came forward to take advantage of the opportunities thus afforded.

The settlement of this "Eastern Shore" area was made in two distinct sections: Manokin and Annemessex; and made, we are inclined to believe, by men of differing motives. There is unquestionable evidence in the human composition of the Annemessex section that the settlers were men who sought refuge in Maryland from the drastic execution of Virginia's laws against Quakers and other nonconformists; while in the Manokin section we find men who, though of a liberal type in matters religious, yet conformed to the Church of England, having no other apparent reason for leaving the colony of Virginia than the economic one of greater opportunity afforded them by newly opened lands. The settlers at Annemessex were men who had come into conflict with the Virginia authorities because of their Quaker and other non-conformist sympathies and affiliations. The Manokin men (probably with a few exceptions) had met with no such difficulties in Virginia. This is not meant for invidious comparison; but simply as statement of fact which is disclosed by careful consideration of evidence. To each element its motive for leaving the Virginia colony was an urgent one; and each element seems to have found in the "new home" in Maryland the liberty which was sought. To both there came with removal to Maryland the opportunity "to live and let live."

We are not able to determine the exact date of the settlements of Manokin-Annemessex, though we are certain that the Annemessex men came first, to be followed very shortly by the Manokin men. The Annemessex settlement was made on the south side of the Great Annemessex River (not far from its mouth), along the river side immediately to the northwest of Coulbourne's Creek, extending several miles up the river to the present Gale's Creek (which appears in old land records as Red Cap Creek). In this section we find Stephen Horsey, Ambrose Dixon, Thomas Price, George Johnson and Henry Boston settled. Dixon, Price, Johnson and Boston were Quakers, and Horsey, though we cannot identify him as a member of that sect, was a rabid non-conformist who, in years gone by, had taken an active part in popular agitations against the government in Virginia. These men had come into conflict with the local authorities in Northampton County, Virginia, because of their non-conformity. Horsey and Dixon, with their families, had certainly departed from Northampton by January, 1661/2. Having refused to pay "minister's tithes and dues," they were summoned for this delinquency, and were reported at that date as having fled the jurisdiction of that court. It seems, beyond reasonable doubt, that they had gone to Annemessex on the Eastern Shore of Maryland, and thus we believe that the settlement at Annemessex was forming in the latter part of the year 1661.[1] To this section other refugees from the drastic Virginia laws against Quakers soon came to make their abode.

By March, 1661/2, the second section of the settlement within the newly created area of the "Eastern Shore" was certainly being made.[2]

This section, designated as Manokin, was made principally in the neck of land between Manokin River (north) and Back Creek (south), with a plantation or so to the north side of the river and the south side of the creek. Though a trifle later (only a few months at most) in formation than Annemessex, Manokin took priority from the fact that it was the seat of the commissioners for the "Eastern Shore." Randall Revell, first presiding resident official of the settlement, took out (with a certain Mrs. Anne Toft) a warrant for a large tract of land in the neck between Manokin River and Back Creek, extending several miles up both the river and the creek. This tract, called "Double Purchase," soon became known as "Revell's Neck" (a name which it bears to this day) and on this tract Revell made his home. Within this section, south of Manokin River and extending to the south side of Back Creek, the Manokin settlers established themselves. On the north side of Manokin River, just west of Goose Creek (and opposite to Revell's plantation), John Elzey, the other resident member of the commission for the "Eastern Shore," located by warrant, a large tract of land which he called "Almodington," and there established his home. Warrants and patents for the Revell and Elzey tracts were not issued until sometime later; but all evidence points to the fact that these men made homes on their respective lands from the first.[3] William Thorne (soon following the Revells and Elzeys), also an official in the new settlement, settled on the north side of Manokin River at "Thornton," about a mile above Elzey's "Almodington." The Revell, Elzey and Thorne families were staunch Church of England people. The only Quaker element discoverable, at this very early time, in the Manokin section of the settlement, was the Covington family on Great Monie Creek on the very outskirts of the section.

Differing in human composition, Manokin and Annemessex were each a part of "the whole adventure," knit together politically and industrially into the unit officially designated the "Eastern Shore"; while both sections in the first blush of infancy were occupied with matters of economic adjustment in the new environment of their living. Having been "begotten and born," the question of sustenance was foremost during early hours of the settlement's conscious life.

Thus we find the "plantation" with its fifty tithable persons (and probably as many more not reckoned as tithable), when Randall

Revell, senior commissioner, made report to his Lordship's council in May, 1662.

Unfortunately no local records remain for this earliest period of the "Eastern Shore's" life; but, it is clear from remaining general records, that the settlement was constantly receiving additions from Northampton County in Virginia. Through the remainder of the year 1662 and on to the fall of 1663, these new acquisitions were fitting themselves into the life of this frontier settlement.

The settlement of Manokin-Annemessex made progress from its very beginning, but progress shadowed by a cloud of opposition, from time to time muttering thunder of disapproval.

The location of the boundary line on the "Eastern Shore" between Maryland and Virginia had always been a vexing question. Clearly indicated, if not clearly marked, in Lord Baltimore's charter for his province, it proved a tender spot with a certain class in Virginia officialdom. His Lordship's constant insistence on the location of this boundary line was his warning that he intended to secure his territorial right in this section, while the settlement at Manokin-Annemessex was a clear declaration of his method of policy in maintaining those rights.

In Northampton County (later Accomack), in Virginia, adjoining this boundary line, there was always a party opposing Lord Baltimore's possession of this area—a party whose opposition increased and strengthened with passing years. In Northampton resided a most powerful factor in the Virginia government, the Honorable Colonel Edmund Scarburgh, his Majesty's treasurer and surveyor-general for Virginia, who with all his strength was at the bottom of Virginia's supposed contention over this boundary line. He it was who brought about the unhappy strife, which, but for the Maryland authorities' sturdy resistance, backed by the loyalty of the settlers at Manokin-Annemessex, would have swept this area from Lord Baltimore's possession, and annexed it to the colony of Virginia.

Granted that the Virginia authorities did at first protest against the issuing of the Maryland charter to Lord Baltimore, and that chagrin may have been felt over the grant; yet it was not in the nature of Virginia to lay hands on territory which had been declared not hers, by charter rights granted another. It was not so, however, with certain individuals in that colony. Edmund Scarburgh never let the matter rest in his mind from the time he was old enough to think thereon, and when opportunity presented itself he strenuously lined up a party of aggressive opposition. The fact that Lord Baltimore had been successful in obtaining settlement of the area of his province nearest this boundary line—and this by means of drawing settlers from Northampton (otherwise called Accomack) in Virginia, roused Scarburgh's ire to "the nth degree," making him strike with all his power to break Lord Baltimore's hold upon his lower "Eastern Shore" possessions. To say that this attempt to take an area of the Maryland province into the colony of Virginia was a scheme of the Virginia government would be untrue; for the scheme was not Virginia's, but Scarburgh's, whose forceful though fruitless action—be it said to the everlasting praise of Virginia of that day—was repudiated by the chief authority of that colony.

Edmund Scarburgh at this time (1662-1663) had a precious pet scheme of his own. His uncontrolled and ungovernable love of power, his almost maniacal genius for being a law unto himself and bending men to his own will, had just brought about the disruption of the territory of the county of Northampton in Virginia and the creation of the new county of Accomack out of its northern portion, which was immediately south of the Maryland boundary line. In this new county of Accomack Scarburgh was supreme authority. Now was the time to hurl his thunderbolt at Lord Baltimore, to strike with the lightning of his self-imagined power and sweep by the torrent of his force the newly settled area of the "Eastern Shore" of Maryland—Manokin-Annemessex—into the county of Accomack in the colony of Virginia. This genius of storm marshalled every element at his command to accomplish this purpose.

As "Surveyor-General and Treasurer of his Majesty for Virginia" (for Virginia was a crown colony), Edmund Scarburgh brought every particle of his authority to bear by demanding of the Manokin-Annemessex settlers "obedience and acknowledgment to his Majesty's dues in payment of rights for land and government." He was claiming that the area of their settlement was "the King's" (remember, Virginia was a crown colony) and not Lord Baltimore's chartered province of Maryland! To support his contention, Scarburgh attempted to re-locate the land-mark of the first bounder of Lord Baltimore's charter-described southern boundary line on the "Eastern

Shore." Without scruple Scarburgh made oath, and made others swear, that "Watkin's Point" (the first marker of this line) should be located at the mouth of the Wicomico River instead of the mouth of the Pocomoke River—thirty miles to the north of its actual position. All the while the evidence for the correct location of this marker was in existence on Captain John Smith's *Map of Virginia*, based upon discoveries made by him in 1608 and published in 1612. Scarburgh's testimony plainly and vastly "varied with fact," his ungovernable greed for power making him "unscrupulously jealous of Virginia's rights and his own."[4]

By degrees Scarburgh marshalled the elements for making his storm against the Manokin-Annemessex settlement. The settlement was well established by May, 1662, and the year passed on to its close; with a new year—1663—coming to birth. Then—muttering of the brewing storm is heard.

In January, or early February, 1663 (old style 1662/3), *"Colonel Scarburgh writ to Mr. Revell concerning their claim to this place."* Thus quaintly, though succinctly, does John Elzey, an official of the Manokin-Annemessex settlement, give the first intimation of Scarburgh's opening of proceedings to extend Virginia's authority over the Manokin-Annemessex settlement and a portion of Lord Baltimore's territorial possessions on the "Eastern Shore."[5] The "Mr. Revell," to whom Scarburgh addressed his statement of "claim," was of course Randall Revell, who at the time was presiding officer of the "Eastern Shore" settlement. Within a month of the receipt of this "claim" from Colonel Scarburgh, Mr. Revell was relieved of his office by the Council of Maryland. No answer to the inevitable question as to why Revell was thus relieved of office has been found; though imagination will not be forbidden its picture that something led the honorable Council of Maryland to believe that he was being drawn into sympathy with Scarburgh's scheme, and that it would be safer to Lord Baltimore's interests in the settlement to have him relieved of his official capacity. "This place" to which claim was made was, of course, the Manokin-Annemessex settlement. Scarburgh was claiming these lands as Virginia's territory; inferentially (if not specifically) denying Lord Baltimore's chartered territorial rights. What reply the commissioners of the "Eastern Shore" made to Scarburgh at this time, we are not informed; but if they did make reply it is certain that the gentleman's zeal in pursuit of his purpose was no whit abated thereby.

When Randall Revell was dropped from the commission for the "Eastern Shore" on February 20, 1662/3, John Elzey was named "first" in the new commission then issued, given priority among the commissioners, and hence chief command in the "Eastern Shore" settlement of Manokin-Annemessex. In this position, Elzey became the target for Scarburgh's continued attack on the plantation.

However, before Elzey had time to receive this commission (dated February 20th) giving him priority and chief magistracy in the settlement, he was called to Accomack County in Virginia on business. While there, on February 23rd, he was arrested by Colonel Scarburgh "at his Majesty's suit" with accompanying "demand for obedience and rights for land." Scarburgh's written demand and Elzey's reply have both come down to us.[6]

[COLONEL SCARBURGH TO MR. ELZEY]

"Mr. John Elzey. This day as I am his majesty's treasurer and substitute I do demand of you obedience and acknowledgment to his majesty's dues in payment of rights for land and government, which though hitherto upon some reasonable pretense you have declined I have upon better information, and doe by these presents demand your immediate obedience to his sacred majesty in payment of right for land and gov'mt to which your answer and submission is required by me, his majesty's officer, this 23d of February 1662 (1662/3).

E[DMUND] S[CARBURGH]."

"Upon some delays and scruples by Mr. John Elzey I demand right of land in and upon the place he lyveth, and submission to his majestie's government, being in a place called Manokin, formerly in Smith's Map Wicomico River.

E[DMUND] S[CARBURGH]."

[MR. ELZEY'S ANSWER]

"Mr. Scarburgh. Honered Sir: Having perused your demand of obedience and acknowledgment to his majestie's dues in payment of rights for government I can give no other response than this that I shall decline as long as I live all authority that shall not be derived from him, his heirs, or lawful successors, and am, and shall always be ready, to yield obedience to them that is or shall be the gov'mt by an authority granted from him, or any of his lawful successors, and will willingly pay all such rights and dues as shall be lawfully demanded of me, whether of right of land or otherwise; and so shall subscribe this 23rd of February 1662 (1662/3).

J[OHN] E[LZEY]."

At the time Scarburgh made this demand, February 23rd, Elzey was probably not aware that he had replaced Revell as presiding officer of the "Eastern Shore" settlement of Manokin-Annemessex, for the commission giving him this priority was not issued at St. Mary's (seat of government of the province) until February 20th, and certainly had not had time (as travel went in those days) to reach Elzey at Manokin before his departure for Accomack, where we find him on February 23rd.

Scarburgh's demand was a directly personal one on Elzey, who was seated on land in the Manokin section; and was (as appears by the wording of Scarburgh's note) a repetition of a former demand, whose date is missing. Scarburgh's designation of the location of Elzey's home as "being in a place called Manokin formerly in Smith's Map Wicomico River" is interesting, as it is by virtue of thus locating this land that Scarburgh makes his demand. Scarburgh is here directly misreading Smith's Map, on which the "River Wighco" (which the Colonel is here confusing with the Wicomico), is most clearly shown to be the present Pocomoke River. It was at the mouth of the River Wighco (now Pocomoke and at times referred to as the Wighgocomoco), on the north side thereof, that "Watkin's Point," first marker named for the Maryland-Virginia boundary line, was located on Smith's Map. To bring Elzey's land onto the Virginia side of this boundary line Scarburgh was replacing "Watkin's Point" some thirty miles to the north of its actual location, at the mouth of the present Wicomico River, which estuary does not even appear on Smith's Map. John Elzey's lands were located on the north side of Manokin River many miles north of the *actual* location of "Watkin's Point." The Colonel never permitted actuality to take precedence of the "Scarburghian" senses of omniscience and omnipotence. The "wall of fact" has, however, a certain way of unhorsing the rider who attempts to leap its heights and Scarburgh was most certainly riding to a fall.

Mr. Elzey's reply to Colonel Scarburgh's demand shows the honorable Colonel's scheming disposition well met by ready wit. Elzey's reply is a masterpiece in steering a safe course through stormy waters. Taking up Scarburgh's challenge in his demand for "obedience and acknowledgment to his Majesty's dues in payments of rights for land and government," Elzey clearly lays his safe course in astute and wittiest fashion. Elzey will ever refuse all authority not derived from the King, and will ever "be ready to yield obedience to them that is or shall be the gov[ernme]nt by an authority granted from him." It is perfectly clear that Elzey considered Lord Baltimore's government lawfully derived from the King, and that his allegiance to his Lordship's government was allegiance to the King. Elzey, a subject of Lord Baltimore's government and seated upon lands within the charter-defined territory of his Lordship's province, by his allegiance to Lord Baltimore and refusal of obedience to the demand of his Majesty's treasurer for the Virginia colony, proved his "obedience to his Majesty." Scarburgh, himself possessed of no mean wit, appreciated Elzey's finely made point, and attempted to cover his confusion with the statement that Elzey's "answer was like to that of the Oracle of Delphos." For the time being Elzey gained his point and kept his liberty, also keeping clean his loyalty to Lord Baltimore and the King.

Mr. Elzey, very wisely, did not overestimate the value of his present escape from Scarburgh's clutches. Back of this personal demand lay Scarburgh's scheme that in gaining one advantage he would gain all. Elzey's submission would have proved a powerful weapon in Scarburgh's hand to turn upon every settler on the Manokin-Annemessex lands; but he did not submit and the seemingly conciliatory tone of his reply was clearly for the purpose of gaining time to act with that wisdom which the seriousness of the situation demanded of an adherent to, and officer of, Lord Baltimore's government.

On his return to Manokin, John Elzey sent the following communication to his Lordship's Council through the secretary of the province. The letter, bearing date March, 1662/3, was placed before the Council at its meeting early in April, 1663.

"At a Council held at St. John's 8th April 1663 was read a letter from Mr. John Elzey to Mr. Sewall, Secretary.[7]

Honorable Sirs: By the last opportunity of conveyance which was by John Anderson we gave your honors account of what Col. Scarburgh writ Mr. Revell as concerning their claim to this place and have ever since expected some instructions from the hon'ble lieut: gen'l how we should answer him if he should come up. But as yet none has come Since the time of writing my business drew me down to Accomack where Colonel Scarburgh arrested me at his majesty's suit and made his demands of obedience and rights for land the copie whereof I have enclosed, and the copie of my answer to it, without which I could not have done my business nor have returned home before I had been to Jamestown, where I do believe it would have been exacted more particularly. Colonel Scarburgh telling me that my answer was like to that of the oracle of Delphos. When he had my response he told me if he could he would be with us before Jamestown court, if not, presently after, and make the same demand of every particular person, and on denial would, according to his order, set the broad arrow on the house of him that should refuse to give a satisfactory answer, and promises great protection on submission.

Now I beseech your honors that you will, with what speed you can, urge his lieut: to consider our condition, how we lie between Sylla and Charibdis, not knowing how to get out of this labarynth. I could not understand but that he doth intend to come up with a competent company to force us, who are not in a capacity to defend ourselves against the pagans, who do grow more insolent, and tell us we are lyars, and that our great men care not for us, because they come not to us.

I would gladly have waited on your honors, but cannot at present by reason of an extreme cold that hath seized on me. But because I would not have this miscarry I have sent my friend, by whom I shall expect your answer, to the satisfaction of all the inhabitants, who do much desire to serve his lordship faithfully and live quietly under his protection and government to enjoy what little goods they have in peace, and not have it macerated and torn from them because they are ignorant. Thus hoping you will think of us and provide for our safety that cannot help ourselves. I shall omit at present what further discourse I have heard unt'l it shall please God that I shall see you and rest. Your honors' ever faithfull and ready servant.

Manokin this _____ th
March 1662/3. JOHN ELZEY."

The gravity of the situation of the settlement at this juncture and the peril so stoutly confronting Lord Baltimore's territorial rights in this area could not be more vividly pictured than is done by Elzey's letter to the Council. The persistence with which Scarburgh made his demands, first on Randall Revell, then doubly on Elzey, and his threat to come up to the settlement and demand submission of all the settlers, confiscating their lands where refusal of submission was made, were indeed alarming. Why the Council and the Lieutenant-General (the governor) of the province paid no attention to the former communication of the state of affairs by the commissioners for the "Eastern Shore," sent by one John Anderson, and withheld the urgently requested advice, we are at a loss to understand. The communications from Scarburgh to Revell and from the commissioners to the Council (through John Anderson) reporting

Scarburgh's demand and requesting advice in regard to action, must have passed in January or early February, 1662/3. Now, in late March, Elzey makes this further appeal, and it is April 8th before this goes before the Council. The silence of the provincial authorities looks indeed like the veriest folly of procrastination. Elzey's escape from Colonel Scarburgh by his wise reply to that gentleman's demand made upon him while in Accomack in late February seems alone to have prevented his being carried before the authorities of the colony of Virginia at Jamestown, "where I do believe," says he, "it would have been exacted more particularly." Such words from Elzey reveal the power which Scarburgh exercised over the chief authorities in the Virginia government in attempting to carry out his unholy scheme for robbing Lord Baltimore of his territorial rights by the use of such unscrupulous methods as falsifying testimony as to boundary markers and intimidating settlers by threats of the use of force and confiscation of property. The whole situation is charged with grave peril. Elzey had indeed escaped, but only for the time being. The fact was impressed upon his mind that Scarburgh meant to relentlessly pursue his design by drastic measures.

In face of all this peril from without, there were foes within. There was menace in the form of an Indian enemy ("the pagans," as Elzey refers to them), contemplating attack on the settlement, contemptuous of the unprotected condition of the settlers and of the policy of neglect which marked the attitude of the provincial authorities towards the affairs of the settlement. In the light of this Indian menace, would it be surprising if the weight of offered protection, thrown into the scales of the situation by Scarburgh, overbalanced the settlers' loyalty to Lord Baltimore's government? Such seems to be the tenor of Elzey's plea that immediate attention be given by his Lordship's Council to these urgent matters. Elzey's letter to the Council is a penetrating analysis of the grave situation and a courageous challenge to the provincial authorities to make clear their intentions at once. But, as is so often the case, "the vision of the man in the field" seems to have been discounted by a bureaucratic board sitting within doors, about a polished table, far away from the field of action. We find no record of action by the Council in providing protection for the defenceless settlers of the "Eastern Shore" against the Indian enemy; though an order (as we shall presently see) was entered to send a letter of protest to the Governor of Virginia against the harassing and unscrupulous conduct of Colonel Scarburgh. It must be admitted, though not without blush of shame for the conduct of the honorable Council, that the question of territorial rights seems by far to outweigh with them the settlers' rights to protection for their lives.[8]

Be the facts as they may relative to the Council's action on Mr. Elzey's appeal that protection against the Indian enemy be given the settlers, it is certain that the governor and councillors went at once to serious consideration of the menace presented to Lord Baltimore's territorial rights by Colonel Scarburgh's persistently threatening demands. Immediately upon the reading of Mr. Elzey's letter relative to conditions at the "Eastern Shore" settlement, the Council directed the following order entered, April 8, 1663:

> "That a letter bee sent to Sir William Berkeley, governor of Virginia, from the governor and council, signifying unto him Col. Scarburgh's demand of obedience and acknowledgement to his majestie in pay'mt of rights of land from the people inhabiting at Manoakin and Annamessex, as well as submission to his majesties government of Virginia. And that on their part they would appoynt a time, when we on our part, shall attend on them to determine that place which shall be accounted Watkins point according to his lordship's patent for Maryland."[9]

Now fully aroused to the Scarburghian menace to his Lordship's territorial rights in the area adjoining the Maryland-Virginia boundary line on the "Eastern Shore," the Maryland authorities make direct appeal to the Governor of Virginia for the only sure and just means of quelling the strife raised by that colony's official Treasurer, Edmund Scarburgh. Going at once to the crux of the alleged claim, the actual location of Watkin's Point, first marker given in Lord Baltimore's charter as the beginning of this boundary line, the Maryland authorities appeal to the Virginia governor for a commission composed of representatives of both the Maryland and Virginia governments to determine the actual location of this first marker. Scarburgh's whole attitude in this matter was fully known to the Maryland authorities, while his attempt to justify by false evidence his claim that Watkin's Point was situated thirty miles to the north of is actual position is a matter of record.[10] With unreckonable persistence Scarburgh reiterated his claim and demand, while with unrelenting zeal the Maryland authorities offered resistance to the unscrupulous scheme.

We have neither the date nor the text of the communication sent by the Maryland authorities to Sir William Berkeley, Governor of Virginia, in accordance with the order of Council of Maryland, April 8, 1663, as quoted above. At what date Governor Berkeley received this communication has not been discovered; nor have we any record of his reply.

For a period of months the records afford no further word of transactions by either Maryland or Virginia authorities in regard to this matter. Springtime of the year 1663 passed; summer came and was near an end when, with terrific fury, the cloud of opposition to the Manokin-Annemessex settlement hurled a crashing bolt which struck the field of action with mighty force of warning. The Virginia Assembly convened September 10, 1663, had passed that staggering Act of assumacy: *"An Act Concerning the Bounds of this Colony on the Eastern Shore."*[11]

Considering "His majesty's interests on the Eastern Shore of Virginia, to gether with some other concernments of Lord Baltimore," this Act directs "that publication be made as soone as possible by Collonel Edmund Scarburg, his majesties' surveyor generall of Virginia commanding in his majesties name all his inhabitants of the Eastern Shore of Virginia from Wattkins point southward to render obedience to his majesties government of Virginia and make payment of his majesties rents and all publique dues to his majesties colony of Virginia." The act then proceeds: "And whereas it hath binn controvesed by some ignorant or ill disposed persons, where Wattkins point, the Lord Baltimores southermost bounds on the Easterne shore, is scituate, this grand assembly, by the care and speciall enquiry of five able selected surveyors and two burgesses, and the due examination thereof conclude the same place of Wattkins point to be the northside of Wicomocoe river, on the Eastern shore, and neere unto and on the south side of the streight limbe [Limbo] opposite to Potuxent river, which place according to captain John Smith and discoverers with him, in the yeare 1608 was so named, being the lord Baltimores bounds on the Eastern shore within which bounds his majesties subjects that are now seated are hereby comanded to yeild due obedience at their perill, and in case the said lord Baltimore his lieutenants or deputies shall not be fully convinced of his or their actuall or pretended intrusions, this grand assembly of Virginia in due obedience, makeing this perticular parte of Virginia their present care on his majesties behalfe doe ingage and command collonel Edward [Edmund] Scarburgh, Mr. John Cultlett [Catlett] and Mr. Richard Lawrence, or any two of them (whereof his majesties surveyor general to be one) that upon convenient notice and assignment of time and place, at Manokin or any other parte of his majesties country of Virginia on the Eastern shore, they or any two of them shall give a meeting to the lord Baltimores lieutenants or deputies, or his or their substitutes as aforesaid, the account whereof to be retorned to his majesties governor and councell of Virginia, and in the meantime, all inhabitants on the Eastern shore as aforesaid are required in his majesties name to conforme due obedience to this act of assembly. *Be it also enacted* that the surveyor generall of Virginia aforesaid is hereby commanded and authorized to improve his best abilities in all other of his majesties concerns of land relating to Virginia espetially to the northward of forty degrees of latitude, being the utmost bounds of the said lord Baltimores grant, and to give an account of his proceedings therein to the right honorable governor and council of Virginia."

The content of this Act of the Virginia Assembly of September, 1663, *"Concerning the bounds of this Colony on the Eastern Shore,"* should be carefully noted. First, it directs Colonel Edmund Scarburgh, his Majesty's surveyor-general in Virginia, to command in his Majesty's name all the inhabitants on the Eastern Shore *"from Watkin's Point southward"* to render obedience to the government of Virginia and make payment of all quit rents and dues to that colony. This done, the Act proceeds definitely to locate Watkin's Point at the mouth of Wicomico River—*thirty miles north of its actual position*—embodying as support of this statement as to location the unscrupulously misread evidence of Smith's *Map,* daringly asserting that the location of this Point as decreed by this Act is made upon the examination and inquiry of "five able surveyors and two burgesses." It is indeed a deprivation to posterity not to have been given the names of these "five able surveyors and two burgesses" who so shrewdly foisted false evidence on the Virginia Assembly, entrapping that otherwise able body into such a display of ignorant assumacy as this assertion as to the location of Watkin's Point. By this act the whole area of Lord Baltimore's territory south of the Wicomico River, including the Manokin-Annemessex settlements, and more than half of the province of Maryland's recently created territorial and magisterial unit of the "Eastern Shore," is swept into Accomack County in the colony of Virginia and into the rapacious grasp of Edmund Scarburgh—the "all powerful" of Accomack. Thus decreeing, the Act then suavely and with magnanimous gesture proceeds to name a commission to meet with Lord Baltimore's provincial authorities, and should they object to this decreed location of Watkin's Point, to hear the objections and return an account of the proceedings to the authorities of the Virginia government. A more audacious reply could not have been made to the Maryland authorities' protest (under direction of the Council order of April 8, 1663) to the Governor of Virginia concerning Colonel Edmund Scarburgh's demands and claims to Lord Baltimore's territory within his territorial unit officially designated the "Eastern Shore." This "Act" is writ large in characters, evidencing the powerful influence of Colonel Edmund Scarburgh, at whose instigation we unhesitatingly say that it was "framed and passed."

Though this Act of the Virginia Assembly of September, 1663, *"Concerning the bounds of this Colony on the Eastern Shore,"* specifically directs that the Maryland authorities be given opportunity to question or protest its decree before commissioners from Virginia named for that purpose, such opportunity was not afforded. Colonel Edmund Scarburgh, who was entrusted by the Act with the exercise of authority in demanding submission of the inhabitants *south of the decreed location of Watkin's Point,* did not, however, fail to proceed at once to "improve his best abilities" in this matter. Without informing his own government of his intention, and without due warning to the Maryland authorities of his intended proceedings, but by the sanction of his own authority and power, Scarburgh invaded the Maryland settlement, and the storm, so long a-brewing, broke in all its fury upon the plantation of Manokin-Annemessex.

The ink with which was inscribed the Virginia Assembly's *"Act Concerning the bounds of this Colony on the Eastern Shore"* was hardly dry before Colonel Scarburgh began detailed preparations to subdue the Manokin-Annemessex settlement. Early October saw the full maturing of his plan of attack, and with a well marshalled force he invaded Lord Baltimore's territory, viciously assailing the settlers on their patented lands. "Accompanied wth Coll Stringer four of ye Commission & about fourty horsemen whom I tooke wth me for pomp of Safety and to repell y^t Contempt wch I was informed some Quakers and a foole in office had threatened to obtrude: wee came to Anamessecks on Sunday night ye 11th of October . . ." So the Honorable Colonel Scarburgh opens his "account of proceedings in his Maties affaires at Anamessecks and Manoakin on ye Eastern Shoare of Virginia" (note the gentleman's designation of location!)—which he was pleased to make to the "Honble Govn^{or} & Councill of Virginia."[12]

This army of invasion under Scarburgh's general command—raised under his direction and by his authority—was composed of Accomack County Virginia men. Colonel Stringer was an officer of the militia in that county; the "four of ye Commission" to whom he refers were doubtless four members of the Commission of the Peace (magistrates of the court) in Accomack; and the "fourty horsemen" members of the troop of horse of the Accomack militia. Monday morning, the 12th of October, found Colonel Scarburgh early engaged in demanding submission of Annemessex settlers. These Annemessex settlers were, with one exception, Quakers who had fled Virginian prosecution for their religious faith and had taken refuge in Lord Baltimore's province of Maryland. The one exception was the notable Stephen Horsey, whom we cannot definitely place as ever having become a Quaker; but whom we do know was as valiantly and rabidly "non-conformist" in his religious attitude as a man could well be. First in order, Scarburgh proceeded to the house of Stephen Horsey—"the foole in office," as Scarburgh brands him—a member of the commission for the "Eastern Shore"—an officer of Lord Baltimore's settlement. Horsey's submission was stoutly demanded, and as stoutly refused. He was placed under arrest and the "broad arrow" (sign of confiscation) placed upon his door. From Stephen Horsey's home, Scarburgh and his cohorts proceeded to Ambrose Dixon's house, where, finding George Johnson and Thomas Price together with Dixon, he "published ye Act of Assembly wth a becoming Reverence wch ye Quakers scoft & dispised." Again did the Colonel demand submission and obedience and again was his demand rejected, while Dixon, Johnson and Price were arrested and "I sett ye broad arrow on ye doore." Then followed an encounter with Henry Boston, and the Act of Assembly was again read. Boston "desired Consideration a day or two" with promise that "then he would attend," but who, Scarburgh relates, "hid himself & so scaped arrest." Later in the day, after Scarburgh had gone to Manokin, Horsey and Boston again "appeared according to promise," when Horsey (according to the Colonel's account) "pretended hee would visit us next morning" and after resigning his commission as an officer of Lord Baltimore would "then subscribe his Conformity. But hee never saw us more & wee are informed carried away Boston wth him & advised others to Rebellion & to this Day wth the Quakers bid defiance to ye Govm^t of his Maties County of Virginia boasting their insolence & forgeries."

Horsey, Dixon, Johnson, Price and Boston—rebel non-conformist and Quakers—once suffering for their faith at the hands of the Virginia authorities, wishing now only to be let alone in the home of their newly found freedom, were as adamant to the Colonel's demands. The "pomp and circumstance" of Scarburghian authority mattered not to these men, now at liberty from the "iron heel" of the Colonel's dominating power. Their flight to freedom had been made from the jurisdiction of Scarburgh's home court and they would resist his clutches to the utmost.[18] Now they had him on their own ground, as it were, and Horsey, Dixon, Johnson, Price and Boston are the only men whom abundant remaining records show, ever successfully defied him and derided his authority, leaving him only the power of his vitriolic imagination with which to attempt to everlastingly shadow their characters by his descriptions of them which appear in the report of his proceedings at "Anamessecks." Read with imagination, Colonel Scarburgh's report of his proceedings at Annemessex on the notable 12th of October, 1663, though by him intended quite otherwise, is in reality a vivid picture of the ultimate discomfiture of that would-be "All Powerful" at the hands of a small but select company—"some Quakers and a foole in office."

From Annemessex, the defiant and unyielding Scarburgh made his way, still accompanied by his body-guard of officers and horsemen, to Manokin, seat of local authority in the "Eastern Shore" settlement. Here he entered (accepting his report at face value) a different atmosphere of attitude toward his mission, and was received with open arms. Here his summons and demand were readily obeyed by all but the presiding officer of the settlement and the military commander of the area: "Mr. Elzey & Capt William Thorne who being officers for ye Lord Baltimore desired respite of time untill they could returne their commissions wch they engaged their words and Reputations to performe as soon as possible." At a "Court of Survey" which Colonel Scarburgh held at Manokin; in which court he relates that he "had the assistance of ye Commission^{rs} therein," . . . "all the people made entries of their Lands & acknowledgments of Conveyances of Land, they all desiring ye Honble Govno^r of Virginia protection as his Maties subjects, which we did assure them of, so far as was in o^r

power." At Manokin we find that Scarburgh's strength was largely able to exercise itself because of the weakness of the Maryland provincial authorities, in not responding sympathetically and understandingly to the appeals of the local commissioners and the settlers for protection in their supposed imminent danger from Indian invasion. Scarburgh writes in his report: "They [i. e. the Manokin settlers] also complained of a late invasion from ye Indians and great danger of being cut off, and said they sent to Maryland to ye Lord Lieut: [i. e. the governor] for aid who after about fourteen daies delay had a letter of advise to stand on their owne guard, for they had more than enough to do in Maryland, so that these people said they were owned for profit and deserted in distress. That if a report of Coll: Scarburgh's coming wth troopes of horse had not prevented together with a sloope of his full of armed men seeking Ranawais had not hapned their [there] in y^t juncture of time to ye terror of ye Indians they had undoubtedly bin cut off therefore desired course to be taken therein wch accordingly was done. They further desired y^t in regard of ye remoteness of officers and ye intermixed neighborhood of Quakers together wth ye frequent access of boats full of Quakers and the Confusion they did & might produce That officers might be their [there] appointed." Thus Scarburgh in his report of his proceedings at Manokin, reveals the anxiety of the settlers in this section in regard to the Indian menace, and their "conformist" fear of the influence of the Quakers. Here indeed, if Scarburgh's statement may be considered as evidence, we find the essential difference in the Manokin and Annemessex sections of the "Eastern Shore" settlement. Into this discussion with the Manokin settlers over the matter of their submission to the Virginia authority as represented by Colonel Scarburgh there was injected, by the Manokin men themselves, the question of the correct location of the boundary line between Lord Baltimore's province and the colony of Virginia. Whereupon Scarburgh appealed to the Act of the Virginia Assembly, under whose supposed authority he was conducting his present proceedings, as settling this question by its decreed locations of Watkin's Point—first marker of the boundary line—at the mouth of Wicomico River, thus bringing within the territory of the Virginia colony and the jurisdiction of that colony's authority the Manokin area where these settlers resided and held lands. What mattered it to them what claim "ye Lord Leif^t of Maryland" laid to Manokin and places to the south? Had not the Act of the Virginia Assembly declared "ye certaine bounds of ye Lord Baltimore's pattent"? And thus Scarburgh promoted his scheming intentions among the Manokin element. So far, so good, and with every assurance of "protection of their persons & estates from any pretenders under ye s^d Lord (Baltimore) . . . they departed well satisfied."

Having completed his proceedings under his assumed interpretation of the authority granted him by the Act of the Virginia Assembly of September, 1663, "Concerning the bounds of this Colony on the Eastern Shore," Colonel Scarburgh returned to his home in Accomack, leaving Annemessex in a state of "rebellion and defiance," and apparently having gained the submission of Manokin to his demands. The essential difference between Annemessex and Manokin is developed through the Colonel's report of his proceedings there in October, 1663; a difference found in the contrast noted of the receptions respectively accorded him in each of these places as he made his invasion to conduct his proceedings.

Colonel Scarburgh had barely chance to settle himself comfortably again in Accomack before the court of that county was appealed to by the Manokin settlers who had "lately conformed their obedience by subscription to ye Act of [Virginia] Assembly . . . for means of protection" in a peril which they felt to be rising.[14] These Manokin men charged the still rebellious and defiant Quakers, their adherents, and other factious people of the settlements, with disseminating threatening reports of action which the Governor of Maryland proposed towards the parties who had submitted to Scarburgh's demands, and that these Quakers and other factious people had made threats against the Governor of Virginia, and declared that Scarburgh should be hanged for his "proceedings." No doubt there was much plain speaking on the part of those in the settlement who objected to Scarburgh's invasion, while those who succumbed to his demands, thereby practically forswearing allegiance to Lord Baltimore's government, feared for the consequences of their action, and so sought protection from the Accomack County, Virginia, court. In reply to the appeal of the Manokin settlers, the Accomack Court on November 10, 1663, ordered "that until his Maties Govno^r [of Virginia] can be fully informed of this affaire & provide a fitter expedient, that Capt Wm. Thorne, an officer under Coll: Scarburgh, Mr. Randall

Revell, Mr. Wm. Bosman and Mr. Jno Rhodes, all or any of them be qualified wth sufficient Authority to call together & Command all his Maties good subjects at Manoakin & all other parts of this County [i. e. Accomack] so farr as Pocomock River to come together and arme themselves only for defence against any person or persons y^t shall invade them to ye disturbance of ye people and their estates..."
The Accomack Court is careful to record its belief that the rumors of intended drastic punishment for the defectors which were being spread by "ye Quakers and factious fooles" did not proceed from the Maryland authorities but rather from the desires of those who were disseminating the rumors. But, note that the Accomack Court claims jurisdiction over the Manokin settlement and south to the Pocomoke River, describing these points as being within "this county" [i. e. Accomack] thus inferentially claiming the area as part of Virginia. However wild may have been the reports emanating from "ye Quakers and factious fooles," the picture presented discloses seething rebellion in a certain element of the population in the settlement. Though the Court of Accomack, responding to the fear-stricken Manokin men, appointed a commission to act in the section from "Manoakin & all other parts of this County so farr as Pocomok River," there is no evidence that this commission was ever called upon to act.

Thus remaining records relate the effects wrought upon the "Eastern Shore" of Maryland settlement by the sweeping storm of Scarburgh's invasion of Manokin and Annemessex, in October, 1663.

Colonel Scarburgh's action in attempting to reduce by armed force the Annemessex and Manokin settlers to submission to the Virginia government and thus fortify his false claim that the area in which they were settled was within the colony of Virginia, brought the long vexing question of the Maryland-Virginia boundary line to an acute issue. The chief authorities in the Maryland government were now fully aroused to the grave peril shadowing the rights of the Lord Proprietor and the interests of the settlers in this section of the province.

The result of Scarburgh's invasion was that the Governor of Maryland went in person to the Governor of Virginia, to make protest against the employment of such measures, whereupon Virginia's governor emphatically disclaimed any responsibility for the forcible methods used by Scarburgh. The real issue was that of the location of the boundary line between Maryland and Virginia, and this must be settled, though several years were to elapse before any conclusion of the matter could be had.

For evidence of what transpired between the Maryland and Virginia authorities in settling, for the time being, this disputed boundary line, we are dependent on a commission issued in June, 1664, by Charles Calvert, Governor of Maryland, by which he appoints Philip Calvert, Chancellor of the province, to go to the Governor and Council of Virginia and lay before them the just grievances of the province of Maryland and seek redress therefor. This proclamation fully reviews the facts in the case from the time of Scarburgh's invasion of Annemessex and Manokin, in October, 1663, until the date of its issuance, June 3, 1664; so we turn to this document for enlightenment.[15]

By way of introducing, as it were, the main objective of his commission, Governor Calvert recites:

"Whereas, divers persons, ill willers to the good correspondence of long time held between the Gov'm'nt of Virginia and that of this province, have of late endeavored to raise differences between the said governments, touching the ancient and known bounds between them on the Eastern Shore; and whereas the Honorable Sir Wm. Berkley, gov. of Virginia, did appoint Col. Edmond Scarborough, Mr. John Catlett and Mr. Richard Lawrence, or any two of them, whereof the said Scarborough to be one, to give a meeting to the deputies or substitutes of this government, by the governor thereof to be appointed (in case any dispute should arise where Watkins point was, that being the bound of this province), to determine what should be reasonably proposed by the said Deputies. In pursuance whereof, the said Col. Scarborough, without the said Catlett or Lawrence, or convenient notice given to me, did, about the tenth day of October last [1663] in a hostile manner, enter many miles into this province, to the terror of the people of Manrakin [Manoakin] and Annamessick, beating, abusing and imprisoning the people there, by him long before seated by virtue of a commission from the government, and contrary to his certain knowledge of the bounds of the said province. And whereupon, remonstrance of this undue proceeding to the Honorable Sir Wm. Berkley, by myself in person, he did not only disclaim any order from him to the said Scarborough alone, or before notice given and debate had, touching the point in question, to proceed by force as he did . . ."

This statement clearly shows that Scarburgh in invading the "Eastern Shore" settlements in October, 1663, had taken the law into his own hands, stretching the authority granted him to meet his own desire and inclination in the matter. Calvert states that Berkeley, Governor of Virginia, had appointed Scarburgh, Catlett and Lawrence (or any two of them, Scarburgh being one), to meet with "deputies or substitutes" to be appointed by the Maryland authority, should there be any dispute as to the location of Watkin's Point (the acknowledged first marker in the boundary line between Maryland and Virginia on the "Eastern Shore"), and that this commission on the part of Virginia was "to determine what should be reasonably proposed by the said Deputies." No copy of, or other reference (than in this proclamation), has been found to Governor Berkley's commission to Scarburgh, Catlett and Lawrence. Such a commission may indeed have been issued by Berkeley and now lost through the destruction of the executive department records of Virginia for that period. However, we have the Virginia Assembly's Act of September, 1663 *"Concerning the bounds of this Colony* [i. e. Virginia] *on the Eastern Shore."* The provisions of this Act most clearly bear out Governor Calvert's statements, proving that Scarburgh acted unlawfully in invading the Annemessex-Manokin settlement without first holding a meeting of the Virginia commissioners with deputies from the Maryland government, giving the latter opportunity to protest the Act's decreed (and as we have seen incorrectly decreed) location of Watkin's Point, and referring such proceedings to the Virginia governor and council for debate and determination.*

Another statement of Governor Calvert's must not be overlooked. Calvert specifically charges Scarburgh with invading and attacking the people of Annemessex-Manokin settlement "by him [i. e. Scarburgh] long before seated by virtue of a commission from the government [i. e. Maryland] and contrary to his [i. e. Scarburgh's] certain knowledge of the bounds of this province." We recall that Scarburgh was the first named in the commission of November, 1661, for establishing the settlement of this area of the "Eastern Shore" of Maryland, and for granting warrants for land to the settlers there under "oath of fidelity" to the Lord Proprietor of that province. Scarburgh was again named in the commission of May 2, 1662, but was omitted from the commission of February, 1662/3, obviously

---

*See this Act given in full, ante page 37.

because "as his Majesty's Treasurer for Virginia" he had been pressing claim to this area as belonging to the colony of Virginia.* We have hesitated heretofore to say that Scarburgh *actually* served under his commission from the Maryland authorities in assisting to establish the settlements of Manokin-Annemessex in this area of the "Eastern Shore" of the Maryland province; and that too, with settlers who had come out from Northampton-Accomack in Virginia. Governor Calvert makes the direct charge that Scarburgh did so serve and that he actually knew the boundaries of the province in that quarter; a boundary that he now was alleging to be thirty miles north of its actual location.

Can we wonder that the Governor of Maryland went *in person* to the Governor of Virginia with his charge against Edmund Scarburgh of unlawful proceedings; proceedings unlawful not only from the standpoint of the province of Maryland but unlawful also under the specific terms of the Virginia Assembly's Act of September, 1663, "*Concerning the bounds of this Colony* [Virginia] *on the Eastern Shore*"? In view of the evidence are we surprised that Governor Berkeley, of Virginia, "did . . . disclaime any order from him to the said Scarburgh, or before notice or debate had, touching the point in question, to proceed by force as he did . . . "? While to this we cannot forbear adding the Honorable Colonel Edmund Scarburgh's own confession of stretching, to suit his own inclination and desire, the authority given him as his Majesty's Surveyor-General of Virginia. In making his report to the Governor and Council of Virginia in regard to his proceedings in what he terms his "rout" of the Manokin-Annemessex settlement in October, 1663, Colonel Scarburgh wrote with charming naivete: "I writt to ye Lord Left: of Maryland [i. e. the governor] & sent ye copy of ye Act [i. e. Act of the Virginia Assembly of September, 1663] to wch I aded my readiness to attend wth Mr. Catlett & Mr. Lawrence if his Hon^r did desire it, but have received no answer But a capitulatory letter wch I have sent herewith p^{r}suming ye Lord Leift: hath personated his afaires wth ye Honble Govno^r at Jamestown *though I suppose according to ye Act of Assembly their ought to have beene a meeting on ye Easterne Shoare.*"[16]

---

*See ante pages 19 and 21.

Thus does the strife and confusion raised in the Manokin-Annemessex settlements of Lord Baltimore's province in the area of the unit territorially and magisterially designated the "Eastern Shore," appear Scarburghian in its true temper and disposition. This is here most clearly revealed.

Let us now return to Governor Calvert's commission of June 3, 1664 (taking up the document at the point we left off), for the conclusion of the matter:

"And whereupon remonstrance of this undue proceeding [Scarburgh's invasion of Manokin-Anamessex in October 1663] to the Honorable Sir Wm. Berkeley [Governor of Virginia] by myself in person, he did not only disclaime any order from him to the said Scarburgh alone, or before notice given and debate had, touching the point in question, to proceed by force as he did, but was pleased further by his order of the 28th of March last [1664] to order the said Scarborough, with one or both of the surveyors, Catlett or Lawrence aforesaid, Capt. Joseph Bridger, Capt. Robt. Elkson [Elkison?] and Mr. Bulmer Mitford, to give a meeting to such commissioners, as should by me be appointed, at Manoakin 10th May last, and in case of my refusal of that so just a proposal, to proceed according as in that commission they were ordered. Now know ye, that forasmuch as neither the said Catlett, nor Richard Lawrence, appeared at Manoakin at the time appointed, without one of which nothing could be legally by the rest done that did appear; and to show how we are not to be tired out of our desires of fair correspondence with the hon'ble gov. and council of Virginia, I have constituted, ordained, appointed and impowered Phillip Calvert deputy lieutenant and chancellor of this province, to repair to the Hon. Sir Wm. Berkeley, gov. of Virginia, and the council there, and after delivery of a duplicate of these presents, and to treat and determine the said difference concerning Watkins point; also to demand justice against the said Edmond Scarborough for entering into this province, in a hostile manner, in October last, and by blows and imprisonment outraging the inhabitants of Manoakin and Annamessex, without commission, as also for attempting to mark a tree upon a point of land above thirty miles to the Northward of Watkins Point, in Maryland, without commission or order, and for publishing a proclamation at Manoakin, on Monday, 16th May [1664] contrary to the order dated 28th of March [1664] aforesaid, I have appointed commissioner the said Philip Calvert, and Jerome White, surveyor general, to meet at Manoakin aforesaid, who did accordingly come at the time and place appointed, which unless I had refused to do, they, the said commissioners, had no order to publish any command or proclamation whatsoever had they been present (according to the tenor of the same order) as they were not ... "

This section of Governor Charles Calvert's commission is revelation indeed of proceedings in this matter subsequent to his personal visit to Governor Berkeley of Virginia to remonstrate with him against Scarburgh's invasion of Manokin-Annemessex. Governor Berkeley's "disclaimer" of responsibility for Scarburgh's action we have before analyzed, finding that Scarburgh had absolutely acted in this matter on his own initiative, and contrary to the provisions of the Act of the Virginia Assembly of September, 1663, under whose authority he professed to be acting; though himself confessing that before any such proceeding as he had engaged in *"I suppose according to ye Act of Assembly their ought to have beene a meeting on ye Easterne Shoare."*

Evidently the Virginia authorities did not take any action against Colonel Scarburgh personally for his proved unlawful proceedings, though the Governor of Maryland made personal remonstrance against him, the Governor of Virginia fully concurring in his view of the unlawfulness of Scarburgh's act. It might well have been that the Virginia governor and council could not proceed further against Scarburgh than to disclaim responsibility for his forceful invasion of the Maryland settlement and to issue a further order directing him, with other specifically named commissioners, to meet with commissioners from the Maryland government to determine the point in question as to the boundary mark. Scarburgh was "his Majesty's surveyor-general and treasurer for Virginia"; his commission of office was derived from the crown, not from the Virginia governor and council. However this might have been, Scarburgh wielded tremendous influence; he had scarcely his match in power and influence in the Virginia government; and indeed had a substantial following to whom his will and word were law.

In order, however, to try and placate the Maryland authorities, who, justly outraged by Scarburgh's proved and admittedly unlawful action, were seeking redress against him personally, the Governor of Virginia (Sir William Berkeley) issued an order March 28, 1664, to Scarburgh, with Catlett or Lawrence (the surveyors), and Bridger, Elkson [Elkison?] and Mitford, as a commission on the part of Virginia, to meet with a commission to be named by the Governor of Maryland to settle this contest over the location of Watkins Point. This meeting was directed to be held at Manokin, May 10, 1664. Governor Calvert of Maryland, appointed Philip Calvert, chancellor of the province, and Jerome White, surveyor-general of the province, as commissioners to act on the part of Maryland in this directed conference. At the time appointed, neither Catlett nor Lawrence appeared, and under the terms of the order of the Governor of Virginia "without one of which [whom] nothing could be legally by the rest done that did appear." Philip Calvert and Jerome White, on the part of Maryland, were present; and certainly Edmund Scarburgh was present (and probably Bridger, Elkson and Mitford) on Virginia's part; but the absence of both Catlett and Lawrence halted all *legal* procedure in the matter. But again the omnipresent, omniscient and omnipotent Scarburgh threw down the gauntlet to authority, challenging law and order, *"attempting to mark a tree upon a point of land above thirty miles to the northward of Watkins point, in Maryland, without commission or order, and (published) a proclamation at Manoakin, on Monday, 16th May [1664] contrary to order [of the governor of Virginia] dated 28th of March aforesaid [1664]."* Comment is unnecessary on the lengths to which Scarburgh allowed his overweening and audacious sense of personal power to carry him; and if the record were not clearly before us, the actuality of this staggering sense of personal authority in an individual would be unbelievable. No wonder, in the light of this last affront, the Governor of Maryland appoints and empowers (as he does by this commission of June 3, 1664) a commissioner to go to the Governor and Council of Virginia "to treat and determine the said difference concerning Watkin's Point" (the boundary marker); "to demand justice against the said Edmund Scarborough for entering into this province in a hostile manner, in October last" (conducting his invasion of Manokin-Annemessex); for "attempting to mark a tree above thirty miles to the Northward of Watkin's Point in Maryland and for publishing a proclamation at Manoakin" in May, 1664. That the Governor of Maryland, in issuing his proclamation appointing a commissioner to treat with the Governor and Council of Virginia concerning the matters involved, should employ such a term as—*"to show how we are not to be tired out of our desires of fair correspondence with the hon'ble gov. and council of Virginia,"*—bespeaks not only the formal gracefulness of the language of his day and generation; but, also, that incomparable "grace of patient endurance of wrong" of which Charles Calvert, Governor of Maryland, seems remarkably possessed when we consider what had transpired.

In the light of all that had happened since the Virginia Assembly's daring act of assumacy of September, 1663, *"An Act concerning the bounds of this colony [Virginia] on the Eastern Shore"*—the Act decreeing a false location of Watkin's Point, and with whose authority granted him Edmund Scarburgh proceeded to run completely away—in the light of these events, we are not surprised to find the Governor of Maryland concluding his commission of June 3, 1664, with this trenchant instruction to his commissioner:

"And further, to represent to Honorable Sir William Berkeley (governor of Virginia) the under [undue] proceedings of the assembly of Virginia, who undertake to take cognizance of things relating to this province and the people thereof. Whereas his majesty of happy memory by the charter hath by express words exempted both the province and people thereof from the government of Virginia, and made both it and them dependent only of the crowne of England; and to desire of him, the said Sir Wm. Berkeley, to take care for the future that the assembly, meddling with things relating to us, and beyond their power, be no cause of future difference between us; which we in our assembly on our part, shall industriously avoid. Whereof I desire that the said Philip Calvert may be credited and believed, promising to ratify and confirm whatsoever shall be done by him, according to this my commission, as if it were done by myself. Given at St. Maries, under my hand, and the lesser seal of this province of Maryland, this 3ᵈ day of June, 1664."

And so Philip Calvert, chancellor of the province of Maryland, commissioned by the governor of the province, was sent in person to Sir William Berkeley, the governor, and the council of the colony of Virginia, with the matters so forcefully presented in this proclamation.

By the fact of the tragic destruction (as part of the ill fortunes of war) of the executive records of the colony of Virginia, we are unable to trace in full the proceedings of the Governor and Council of Virginia on the matters of the grievance thus presented to them by the Maryland authorities. However, it so happens that a devoted Virginia historical student, the late Conway Robinson, many years ago, before the destruction of these precious and priceless records, made certain notes therefrom which have been preserved to us. In Mr. Robinson's notes appears the following:

"1664. June 2 (*sic.* 20th?). Power from the Governor of Maryland to Philip Calvert to repair to Virginia and treat with the governor (of Virginia) concerning Watkins Point and to demand justice against Edmund Scarburgh for entering the province of Maryland in a hostile manner. Agreement between Calvert and Sir William Berkeley that persons living near the land shall live peacably together until the difference be settled between the two colonies. Concerning Colonel Scarburgh."[17]

Thus, with tantalizing brevity, we learn the bare fact that Philip Calvert, commissioner of the government of Maryland, did present his commission and the grievance of Maryland to the Governor of Virginia, and that the Governor of Virginia and Calvert entered into an agreement for the peace of the settlers in this area until the question of the boundary should be settled. How enlightening would be the possession of that old record—now gone—which led the student to enter in his notes the simple comment: *"Concerning Colonel Scarburgh."* What indeed may not that record have told us about the Virginia authorities' view of Scarburgh's relation to this whole matter?

Philip Calvert, commissioner on the part of Maryland, and Sir William Berkeley, Governor of Virginia, may have indeed willed peace for the Maryland settlers living near this disputed boundary line between the province and colony; and indeed may have desired a just and peaceable conclusion of this harassing question; but what of Edmund Scarburgh? Neither the will nor the desire of any single individual or any governmental authority could make him keep peace if he could possibly accomplish strife. With supreme contempt for fact, and assurance in his ability to establish his prejudiced opinions— to supplant fact with his own highly bred fictions—to actually prove his contention in defiance of all evidence in regard to the location of Watkin's Point, on July 19, 1664, Edmund Scarburgh made oath in open court in Accomack County, Virginia, to a statement as to the location of Watkin's Point which, though indeed it may have been his own opinion, is proved to have been absolutely incorrect. This sworn statement is signed not only by Edmund Scarburgh but by his son, Charles Scarburgh; his brother-in-law, John Wise (who married Scarburgh's sister); Edward Revell (son of Randall Revell of Manokin); Will[iam] Jones, George Parker, Anto [Anthony] Hodgkins and John Renny. At the same time Captain William Jones, a justice of the Court of Northampton County, Virginia, made a sworn statement to an incorrect location of Watkin's Point. The purpose of both of these sworn statements was to fix the location of this boundary marker at the mouth of Wicomico River,[18] which was some thirty miles north of its actual location at the mouth of Pocomoke River.

From June, 1664, when Philip Calvert, commissioner on the part of Maryland, and Governor Berkeley, of the colony of Virginia, had their conference (as by terms of the Governor of Maryland's commission of June 3, 1664), to June, 1668, we have no record of transactions relative to the settlement of the vital question in all this controversy: the correct location of Watkin's Point. One might assume with reasonable certainty that such a question could be settled in much less time than four years, particularly with the *evidence* at hand all the time. But in a matter of such vexing proportions and involvements with the constant presence of so persistent an evil genius as Colonel Edmund Scarburgh to keep the pot of strife boiling, no "reasonable certainty" of anything may be assumed.

In June, 1668, we do, however, find the conclusion of this matter so far as we are concerned with it here; and four years were consumed in "the concluding" of the actual location of Watkin's Point. In the meantime Lord Baltimore's territorial and magisterial unit of the "Eastern Shore below Choptank River" had been divided and two counties established therefrom: Dorchester County (from Choptank River south to Nanticoke River) and Somerset County (from Nanticoke River south to Watkin's Point). Lord Baltimore's provincial authorities had the evidence on their side all the time,—the Virginia authorities admitting it—and so the Maryland authorities created the counties of Dorchester and Somerset from this old unit of the "Eastern Shore," including in Somerset (whose "foundations" are our consideration), the area of the Manokin-Annemessex settlement over which the bitter "Scarburghian" warfare was waged and over which the storm of Scarburghian invasion swept.[19]

Finally Philip Calvert, chancellor of the province of Maryland, and Edmund Scarburgh, surveyor-general of his Majesty's colony of Virginia, were appointed by their respective governments as commissioners to settle the whole vexed question, being instructed to *"meet upon the place called Watkins Point and thence run a divisional line (between Maryland and Virginia) to the ocean sea &c."* As instructed, these commissioners met at the place designated and *"after a full and perfect view taken of the point of land made by the North side of Pocomoke bay and the south side of Annamessex Bay have and do conclude the same to be Watkins Point."* Let us carefully note that this is just where the Maryland authorities had always contended Watkin's Point was located and just the location given it on Smith's Map, to which appeal was continuously being made, both by the true contenders, the authorities of Maryland, and the false pretender, Edmund Scarburgh. Having thus settled the true location of Watkin's Point, the commissioners then proceeded to run the Maryland-Virginia boundary line to the Atlantic Ocean.

On June 25, 1668, articles of agreement were signed by Philip Calvert and Edmund Scarburgh making provisions for guaranteeing the titles of lands held by settlers in this area, and on the same day they confirmed their findings in regard to Watkin's Point and made official statement of the line run by them from thence to the Atlantic Ocean.[20]

In this agreement of June 25, 1668, between Calvert and Scarburgh we find the conclusion of the settlement of the question of the Maryland-Virginia boundary line, in so far as the period of our study is concerned.[21] Thus do we see the Honorable Colonel Edmund Scarburgh, mighty contender for a fiction, and manipulator of evidences to satisfy his greed for power, unhorsed by the stubborn wall of fact into which the storm of his own brewing relentlessly swept him, as he attempted to ride rough-shod over Lord Baltimore's territorial rights. But, as he rode even to his fall, this stubborn Knight of a Wild Delusion, did not lose his sense of Scarburghian shrewdness, for as he fell he grasped and by his powerful grasp held on to "some twenty three square miles of territory that, by terms of the charter, belonged to Maryland"—dragging it safely into his county of Accomack in Virginia![22]

III

AS CLOUDS ROLLED AWAY

*

Manokin-Annemessex secured in their allegiance to the Maryland government—Commissions for the "Eastern Shore" in February, 1663/4, and May, 1664—The Commission of August 25, 1665—Significance of this Commission—Increase in population and expansion of settlements—First court, of which record remains—"A Person to Keepe ye Records"—Governor Calvert sends the court a clerk.

WHILE strife and contention, marshalled in fine fashion by Colonel Edmund Scarburgh, swept over the infant settlement, and the Maryland and Virginia authorities were desperately seeking to break the wilfully aggressive spirit of "the evil genius" of the Manokin-Annemessex settlements, life mightily surged in the plantation. The Annemessex element, defiantly rebelling against Scarburgh's pretentions, yielded not an iota to his demands or to his harsh attempts at their enforcement. It was but briefly, too, that the Manokin element wavered in allegiance to Lord Baltimore. Scarburgh and his minions raged; but all the while Lord Baltimore's resident provincial authorities guerdoned with the assurance of right, stood like giant forest oaks against the storm of opposition.

The seeming defection of John Elzey and William Thorne—Manokin men, local officials of the "Eastern Shore" settlement of Manokin-Annemessex, was short-lived. In October, 1663, they desired, before making their submission to Colonel Scarburgh's demand, "respite of time until they could return their commissions" to Lord Baltimore— "which they engaged their words and reputations to performe as soon as possible." Elzey and Thorne were again soon restored to places in the "commission", if indeed they were ever looked upon by the provincial authorities as "legally absent" therefrom. From all evidence that remains it would seem that not a settler at Manokin-Annemessex left his lands while the authorities at St. Mary's held resolutely to a policy of development for the area in question. We do not know what methods of procedure were employed by the local commission for the "Eastern Shore" during the first months of the period of "storm and stress"; but there can be no doubt about the attitude of the Governor and Council of Maryland. Colonel Edmund

Scarburgh, the Virginia Assembly's Act, and the Court of Accomack County in Virginia, might reiteratingly din the ears of the settlers of Manokin-Annemessex with the cry that the area inhabited by them was part of the territory of the Virginia colony; but, to the governor and other officials of the Maryland province, this area was the territorial unit of the "Eastern Shore" of the province of Maryland—Lord Baltimore's chartered right—and all procedure was according thereto.

When time again arrived for renewal of the commission for the "Eastern Shore," John Elzey, Stepney Horsey, William Thorne and John Odbur were renamed in February, 1663/4. Here we find Elzey and Thorne—the seeming "defectors" of October, 1663, renewing their oath of office as commissioners and magistrates in this area to the Lord Proprietor of the province of Maryland. On March 26, 1664, an addition to the military establishment of the settlement was made by commissioning William Coulbourne as "Lieutenant under Captain William Thorne of the Foot Company at present and to be raised by him between Choptank River and a line drawne east into the Mayne Ocean from Watkins Point." This commission to Coulbourne not only supplies a side-light revealing Thorne as still actively engaged as military commander of the area; but interestingly introduces a reference to the celebrated first land marker of the Maryland-Virginia boundary line, Watkin's Point, at the mouth of Pocomoke River; showing how doggedly the Maryland authorities swung to the Lord Proprietor's territorial rights.

In May, 1664, another commission from the governor naming commissioners for granting land warrants and administering justice in the "Eastern Shore" settlement below Choptank River was directed to Stephen Horsey, William Thorne and William Bosman.[1]

In the commissions just granted we notice the appearance of new men in the field of local affairs: William Coulbourne and William Bosman; and the absence of the familiar names of John Elzey and John Odbur; while the invincible Annemessex man, Stephen Horsey, is given priority in the commission of the peace—"chief magistracy"—thus succeeding to the official leadership of the "Eastern Shore" settlement below Choptank River. John Elzey, that most worthy official who from the very beginning of the settlement had so faithfully and courageously served its best interests, has now passed, not only from office, but from the world; his retirement not the act of man, but of God. John Odbur's removing—an earthly one—was to regions "up shore" whence he, too, soon was "gathered to his fathers," through the bloody avenue of Indian massacre. William Coulbourne, at this time first appearing in records as within this jurisdiction, was another Annemessex man who had recently gone to live there; but of the "same stuff" which is an invariable mark of the Annemessex tradition. Coulbourne was another defiant spirit who stood against the intolerance of the Virginia law against Quakers; though we cannot prove that he himself was ever of that "faith." We find him in the clutches of the court of Northampton because of his sympathies with these brethren; and his removal to Annemessex (where he settled near to Stephen Horsey) was no doubt due to his desire for less cramped spiritual quarter as well as ampler acreage of an earthly one. Coulbourne became one of the most distinguished residents of this area, though his numerous services were mostly rendered after the erection of Somerset County in August, 1666. William Bosman, the other "new man" in the commission of the peace named in May, 1664, had come into the settlement sometime in the year 1663 and was a "Manokin man." His home on the north side of Manokin River was just east of John Elzey's place of residence; Goose Creek being the dividing line between Bosman's "More and Case It" tract and Elzey's "Almodington." Bosman, we recall, was one of the commission named by the Court of Accomack County, Virginia (in extending its jurisdiction to Manokin), in November, 1663, appointed to "call together & command" the settlers there "to come together and arm themselves for defence" against any invasions; the fear of which seemed at that time to have alarmed these people to the point of outcry to the Accomack authorities for protection. Now Bosman passes into the service of Lord Baltimore through this commission of May, 1664, doubtless serving out his commission before death overtook him sometime prior to December, 1665.

The next commission for the "Eastern Shore" was issued August 25, 1665, at which time Stephen Horsey (with priority) and William Thorne were continued in office, while added with them to the magistracy were George Johnson, William Stevens, John White, John Winder, James Jones and Henry Boston; and on February 23, 1665/6, Horsey, Thorne, Johnson, Stevens, White, Winder, Jones and Boston were again named as "Comm^{rs} on the Eastern Shore," these commissioners continuing in office until the erection of Somerset County six months later. In September, 1665, a new commission was issued to "Capt William Thorne to Command all the Forces (as Capt) on the Eastern Shore of this province from Wiccocomico that joynes upon Manny to that part of Pocomoke on the said Eastern Shore that is or shall be inhabited, wthin this s^d province of Maryland, them to muster, exercise, &c."[2]

The augmentation of the commission for the "Eastern Shore" in August, 1665, is interesting from several points of view. The number of commissioners named is marked evidence of the solid progress which the settlement was making. Population had increased and with it the demands in legal affairs. The new settlers were evidently taking up lands in parts of the area beyond the limits of the original settlements at Annemessex and Manokin. The commission was increased from three to eight members, with a more general distribution of the magistrates throughout the area to meet the needs of the now widely distributed population. Horsey, Johnson and Boston were Annemessex men; Thorne was to the north of Manokin River; Stevens and White were on Pocomoke River, well inland from its mouth; Winder and Jones were on the Wicomico River well in the northern part of the settled area. In this commission we find Annemessex given a majority in the magistracy, with Horsey (first place), Johnson and Boston, leaving Thorne alone to represent the Manokin element of the population. The center of affairs in the plantation has shifted. Another interesting fact about this commission is the marked display in attitude of religious liberality in the appointments. Johnson, Boston and Jones were Quakers; while Horsey, whom though we cannot at any time positively identify as a Quaker, seems to have been a thorough-going radical in matters religious. Thorne, Stevens and Winder were of the Church of England, while White was also probably at this time affiliated with that body, though later found with the Presbyterian element along the Pocomoke. This is William Stevens' introduction to the official life of the "Eastern Shore" and from this time forward we shall find him steadily gaining supremacy in the affairs of the settlement. Stevens was unquestionably a Church of England man; but of markedly liberal type. It was he who some years later was largely responsible for the introduction of Presbyterian ministers into Somerset, while there is evidence of his profound interest in the visit of George Fox, the apostle of Quakerism, to the settlement. This commission, named in August, 1665, was a body of vigorous, able men, well representative of the spirit of the settlement and well qualified to direct the rapidly developing interests of the area.

Between the spring of the year 1664 (when the sweeping storm of opposition had subsided) and the summer of 1666, when all requirements for the erection of a legally constituted county were apparently met, the development of this section was pronounced. Through an ever-increasing population of sturdy and steady settlers bound into the economic and industrial interests of the community, a healthy spirited progress took place and we find the lower "Eastern Shore" passing through this era of 1664-1666 into larger being—to full political status as a "County." In the summer of 1666, we find the county of Somerset emerging from the territorial chrysalis of the "Eastern Shore," strongly winged for flight through the years.

Unfortunately there remain no records of proceedings of the courts of the commissioners of the peace for the "Eastern Shore" from the time of their first authorization in May, 1662, to December 11, 1665. Just what records were kept by the local magistrates during this period we do not know, for these records have long since disappeared. The records of these commissioners as a body for granting land warrants, however, have survived in the general land records of the province and are to be found today in the warrants, surveys and patents of the present Land Office of the State of Maryland.

The earliest record remaining from the old courts for the "Eastern Shore" bears date December 11, 1665 (something over three years after this court was established), and comes to us from "a Courte helld att Thomas Poole Monday ye 11th December in Manoakin on ye Easterne Shore in ye province of Maryland," when the following order was entered:

"This day ye Inhabitants moved ye Court y^t a parson [person] might be nominated to keepe ye records and upon deliberat Consideration of [as?] to y^l necessity of ye thinge required The Court doth hereupon think fitt & ord^r y^t George Johnson keepe ye records & y^t they remayne att ye said Johnson's howse in Annamessex."[3]

The justices present at this first court for which we have records preserved to us were: Stephen Horsey (who evidently was "presiding justice"), William Thorne, William Stephens (Stevens), George Johnson, John Winder, James Jones and Henry Boston. The court is designated as a court "on ye Eastern Shore in ye province of Maryland." Courts held in January, 1665/6, and April and May, 1666, are designated as courts "houlden for y^t part of ye province of Maryland lying and being betweene Choptank River & Watkins Pointe." The business transacted in the courts thus held consisted of trials for cases of debt and trespass, assault and battery, bastardy, defamation of character, and the recording of conveyances of land and deeds of gift, or sale, of cattle. These courts had also jurisdiction over orphans' estates, the appointment of guardians, adjudging ages of indentured servants, registration of cattle marks, the settling of controversies between indentured servants and their masters as to conditions and length of terms of service, and the publication of banns of matrimony. The magistrates of this local court were also empowered to perform marriages. The records of proceedings of the "Eastern Shore" courts which remain to us cover the period from December 11, 1665, to the erection of Somerset County in August, 1666.

The careful keeping of records was a matter of great importance to the authorities of the province and the local community as well as to the individuals inhabiting the developing settlement of the "Eastern Shore." In December, 1665, as we have seen, the inhabitants themselves requested the court to appoint a fit person to "keepe ye records" and in accordance with the request this duty was assigned to George Johnson, of Annemessex. Such records as we have for the courts held in the months between December, 1665, and July, 1666, were made by him, or under his direction. In the summer of 1666 the matter of keeping records again came up for consideration by the authorities and it is evident that the governor of the province at this time recommended Edmund Beauchamp for the office of clerk of the "Eastern Shore." At a court held July 3, 1666, the following interesting letter from the commissioners of the "Eastern Shore" to Governor Charles Calvert found its way into the records:

"Right Honnorable

Wee re^{cd} yor honn^{rs} Letter by Mr. Edmund Beauchamp & had answered itt sooner onely wanted a fitt oppertunity to meete together, wee have entertayned him as o^r clerke & take it as a singular favour yor hon^r giveinge us y^t Libertie to add to yor hon^{rs} presentation o^r approbation of y^t officer (wch all though of small profitt) yett itt is evident That ye well or ill keeping of Records is of great Consequence itt being a Considerable means to p^{r}serve ye right & proprietyes of ye Inhabitants & wee hope ye party recommended will Carefully dischardge ye same. honored S^r wee humbly pray y^t yor hon^r will add that favour to ye oth^r alsoe to Cause acts of ye last Session of grand assembly to be sent over to us That wee may knowe ye better to keepe o^{r}selves in due (?) observance of ye Lawes established wch is all y^t p^{r}sent wee have to trouble yor honour with But to tend^r ye humble Duties & faithfull service to yor hon^{ors} we Crave leave to subscribe o^{r}selves

   Your Honn^{rs} Most Humble servants
   in all duty to be Commanded

Manonoakin 3^d July 1666	STEVEN HORSI
To ye right hon^{ble} Charles Calvert	CAPT. WILLIAM THORNE
Lieu^t Generall & Governour of y^e	WILLIAM STEVENS
Province of Maryland These p^{r}sent	GEORGE JOHNSON
Att St. Maryes.^{4}	JOHN WINDER
	HENRY BOSTON."

Thus are we brought to the conclusion of legal affairs of the area officially designated as the "Eastern Shore" of the province of Maryland, for within a month's time this "unit" gives place to the counties of Somerset and Dorchester; the former erected from that part of its territorial area south of Nanticoke River, and extending southward to the Maryland-Virginia boundary line; the latter erected from the territory north of Nanticoke River and extending northward to Choptank River. Thus, also, is introduced to the "Eastern Shore" of the province of Maryland a personage whose name stands in the history of the community for all that is worthy in citizenship, a man found ever faithful in discharge of public and private obligations—"Mr. Edmund Beauchamp," last of the great worthies who came into the settlement of "the Eastern Shore below Choptank River" before the erection of Somerset County, into whose service his name is wrought in imperishable characters.

IV

THEN A PERFECT DAY IN SUMMER

1

Somerset County created by proclamation, August 22, 1666—The proclamation, commission of the peace, clerk of court and sheriff "Captain of All the Forces"—First court for Somerset, September 4, 1666—First marriages, constables, surveyors of highways, and grand jury—Highway for the county and boundaries of the hundreds—Affairs from March, 1667, to October, 1668—The first free Negroes—Somerset County's first election of representatives to the General Assembly.

THE season's day of mature leaf for nature's trees brought also maturity to the avowed purpose of Lord Baltimore, in planting settlements on the "Eastern Shore" near the Maryland-Virginia boundary line, to organize and erect that area into a "county." The vexed and vexing question of this "boundary line" was still unsettled in the minds of Lord Baltimore's opponents to his chartered territorial rights in this section; but to Lord Baltimore and his provincial authorities there was no such question, for they viewed the whole matter as so much false pretension of disgruntled trouble makers. The area in question now met all requirements for erection into a county, so ignoring the would-be trouble makers, and standing on his chartered rights, Cæcilius, Lord Baltimore, by proclamation, August 22, 1666, issued through his resident provincial representative, "Charles Calvert, Esq. our Lieutennant Generall, Chiefe Governo^r and Chiefe Justice of our sayd Province of Maryland," erected, established, and defined the limits of Somerset County, giving to the county complete civil and military organization.

[A Proclamation Establishing Somerset County]

"Caeilius Absolute lord & Prop^{ry} of the pvinces of Maryland & Avalon Lord Baron of Baltimore &c to Stephen Horsey, Wm. Stevens, Wm. Thorne, James Jones, John Winder, Henry Boston, George Johnson, & John White, gent. Greet^g. know yee that wee for the case and benefitt of the people of this o^r pvince & for the Speedy & more exact Adm^{con} of Justice hav erected & doe by theis pnts erect all th^t tract of land wthin this our province of Maryland bounded on the South with a line drawne from Watkins point (being the North point of th^t bay into wch the River Wighco form^{rly} called Wighcocomoco afterwards Pocomoke & now Wighcocomoco againe doth fall exclusively) to the Ocean on the East. Nanticoke river on the North & the Sound of Chesipiake bay on the West into a County by the name of Sommersett County in hono^r to our

Deare Sister the Lady Mary Somersett & for the great trust & confidence we have in your fidelityes Circumpeccons Providdnces and Wisdomes have Constituted Ordeyned & appyinted & doe by theis pnts constitute Ordeyne & appoint you Stephen Horsey, W^m. Stevens, W^m. Thorne, James Jones, John Winder, Henry Boston, George Johnson, & John White gent. Com^{rs} Jointly & sev^{r}ally to keepe the Peace in Sommersett County afores^d & to keepe & cause to be kept all laws & Ord^{rs} made for the good & conservacon of the peace & for the quiett rule & gov^{r}m^t of the people in all & ev^{r}y the Articles of the same & to chastice & punish all psons offending ag^t the forme of any lawes & Ord^{rs} of this our pvince or any of th^m in Som^{r}sett Co^{nty} afores^d as according to the forme of those lawes & Ord^{rs} shall be fitt to be done Wee have alsoe Constituted & Ordeyned you & every four or more of you of wch you the s^d Ste: Horsey W^m. Stevens & Wm Thorne (vnless some one of our Councill be pnt) are alwaies to be one Com^{rs} to enquire by the Oath of good & lawfull men of your County afores^d of all maner of fellonies Whitchcrafts inchantm^{ts} Sorceryes Magick Arts Trespasses forestallings ingrossing & extorcons w^{t}soev^r & of all & singler other Misdeeds & offences of wch Justices of the Peace in England may or ought lawfully to enquire by whomesoeve^r or whensoev^r done or ppertrated or wch hereafter shall happen to be done or ppetrated in the County afores^d ag^t the laws & ord^{rs} of this o^r pvince Provided you pced not in any of the cases afores^d to take life or member but th^t in ev^{r}y such case you send the prisoners wth their Indictn^{ts} & the whole matter dpending before you to o^r Justices of o^r Prv^{all} Court next to be holden of this our province whensoev^r or wheresoever to be holden there to be tryed, And further wee doe hereby authorize you to yssue Writts, processe arrests & attachm^{ts} to hold Plea of heare & determine and after Jugm^t execucon to award in all causes Civill whether in accons reall or personall where the thing in accon doth not exceed the value of three thousand pound weight of tobacco according to the lawes Orders & reasonable Customes made & vsed in this o^r pvince of Maryland In wch causes Civill to be tryed we doe Constitute Ordeine & appoint you the s^d Ste. Horsey Wm Stevens & Wm Thorne or either of you to be Judges afores^d vnlesse some one of our Councill be then in Co^{rt} And therefore we Command you th^t you dilligently intend the keeping of the peace lawes & ord^{rs} & all & singler other the premisses & att certayne daies & places wch you or any such foure or more of you as afores^d shall in th^t behalfe appoint ye make inquire upon the pmsses & pforme & fulfill the same in forme afores^d doing therein th^t which to Justice appurteyneth according to the lawes Ord^{rs} & reasonable Customs of this our pvince Saving to us the Am^{r}ciam^{ts} & other things thereof to us belonging And we command the Sheriffe of you s^d County for the tyme being by v^{r}tue of theis pnts th^t at c^{r}taine daies & places wch you or any such foure or more of you as afores^d shall make knowne to him to give his attendance on yo^w & if need require to cause to come before you or any such foure or more of you afores^d such & as many good & lawfull men of your County by whome the truth in the premisses may be the better knowne & enquired of. And lastly we have appointed Edmond Beuchchampe Clarke & Keeper of the Records of pceedings in this yor County Court & therefore you shall cause to be brought before you at the said Daies & places the writts pcepts processes Indictmn^{ts} to yor Court & Jurisdiction belonging to the same may be inspected & by a due course dete^{r}mined as afores^d Given vnd^r the Great Seale of this our pvince of Maryland the two & twentieth day of Augt in the five & thirtyeth yeare of our Dominion over the s^d Province & in the yeare of our Lord One thousand Six Hundred Sixty Sixe. Witness our Deare Sonn Charles Calvert Esq. our Lievtennant Generall Chiefe Governo^r and Chiefe Justice of our sayd Province of Maryland."[1]

With the above proclamation erecting and establishing Somerset County—naming commissioners of the peace and clerk of court—there were also issued commissions for a sheriff and military commander. Stephen Horsey was commissioned, as of August 22, 1666, "to be Sheriffe of the said County for one whole year from the date hereof to be Computed and after untill the Governo^r shall depute another Sheriffe for the said county"; while, under the same date, "Commission then issued and Granted to Capt Willm Thorne to be Capt (under Charles Calvert, Esqr Capt Generall) of all the forces on the Easterne Shore of this province from Wiccocomoco that Joynes uppon Manii to the north point of Pocomoke on the Eastern Shore."[2]

The documents above recited: the proclamation establishing Somerset County, the commissions to Stephen Horsey as sheriff, and to William Thorne as commander of the military forces, were immediately dispatched to the authorities therein named and in the first book of the records of Somerset County we find these documents given in full: "Entred ye 27th August 1666"; together with "the Oath of a Sheriffe"; while an additional commission—dated July 20th, 1666—to Stephen Horsey to be one of "ye Deputy Surveyors of this province under Jerome White, Surveyor General," is also made a matter of record. To Stephen Horsey—we can but note what prominence he had attained in the affairs of the settlement: first named in the commission of the peace, first named for the three judges designated for the court; commissioned as high sheriff of the county and a deputy surveyor for this area—to Stephen Horsey was directed authority "to swear ye rest of ye Commissioners mentioned in this Commission afore they act as Justices for ye County." Such was the endorsement of his excellency, Charles Calvert, the governor of the province, on the proclamation embodying the first commission of the peace for Somerset County.[3]

Of prime importance to the provincial authorities would be a list of the tithables of the newly erected county, for such would be the basis of taxation "per poll." In this matter the authorities were not negligent and "Entred ye 27th August 1666" we find this order:

"Theis are to will & require you y^t ye by ye tenth day of October next you Cause a List to be taken of all ye tithables within yor County & in ye said List ye name & Surname of each tithable person & the house of his abode be distinctly sett down & A Copy thereof fayre written & sent Immediately up to ye Governo^r & Councell And another Copy of ye said List sett up att yor Court house att yor next County Court to remayne there for ye whole yeare to ye end y^t iff any errors be therein they may be corrected & ye same certified to ye Governor & Councell before ye next provinciall Court being to be helld on ye 16th day of October next ensueing herein fayle not as you will answer ye Contrary and for soe doing this shall be yor warrant Given under my hand & seal this 22th day of August A^o 1666.

CHARLES CALVERT.

To Stephen Horsey, gent.
high Sheriffe of Somersett County."[4]

It is most unfortunate that no copy of this list of tithables of 1666 has been found, for it would give to us a census of male taxable inhabitants of "Old Somerset" at the time of the county's establishment.

On September 6, 1666, William Stevens, John Winder and Henry Boston took the oath in "open court" as commissioners of the peace for Somerset County; and James Jones and George Johnson "desired time to consider the oath wch was graunted untill ye next Court wch is ordered to be ye last tweseday in the Month. Mr. Steven Horse sworne high Sheriffe in open Court for the County of Sommersett Mr. Steven Horse & Capt Will: Thorne were Sworne Com^{rs} att St. Maries by ye right hon^{ble} Charles Calvert."[5] Thus were items recorded from time to time in the first records of proceedings of Somerset County court.

On September 4, 1666, was held the first apparently fully organized court to sit for Somerset County and on that day were present on the bench: William Stevens, William Thorne, John Winder and Henry Boston; with Stevens "presiding." At this court, "Bonds [Banns] of Matrimony" were published for John Okee and Mary Vincent, both of Manonoakin, and of Thomas Tull, of Anamessicke, and Mary Mitchell [Minshall] of Morumsco.[6] There had been prior marriages in the "Eastern Shore" settlement (we have records of three as having taken place in 1663 and 1664), but the Okee-Vincent and Tull-Mitchell (Minshall) are the first banns recorded as "published" after Somerset County was erected. John Okee and Mary Vincent—Thomas Tull and Mary Minshall (as the bride's name is given in the record of marriage) were married in October, 1666; the former couple by John Winder, the latter by George Johnson, both of whom were "his Lordship's justices of the peace for Somerset."[7]

At this court held for Somerset, September, 4, 1666, was also entered a proclamation of Governor Charles Calvert, dated July 20, 1666, addressed to the "Commissioners of the Eastern Shore," directing them to give notice to all persons within their jurisdiction that the said commissioners are authorized to issue grants for lands on the seaboard side of "the shore" to all who wish to seat themselves there; the lands to be granted under a yearly rent of one shilling for each fifty acres.[8] Thus early do we find the provincial authorities encouraging settlement in the extreme eastern portion of this area towards the Atlantic Ocean. Of this venture we shall hear more.

Later, in September, 1666, record was made in the minutes of the court of the fact that oath as commissioners of the peace for Somerset County by "Mr. George Johnson & Mr. James Jones was taken att St. Maries by le lieut: Generall ye 11th of September 1666 being subscribed & annexed to ye oath in these words (vizt) The above s^d oath was taken by George Johnson & James Jones before me this 11th of September 1666, Charles Calvert."[9] By Johnson and Jones thus taking "oath of office," the commission of the peace for Somerset was complete but for the proper "qualification" of John White. White does not appear to have taken "oath of office" and there is no record of his having sat as member of courts held between September, 1666, and October, 1668. However, he appears to have qualified under another commission in 1671.

With great precision the authorities proceeded with the organization of affairs in the new county. At a court held on September 25, 1666, "were sworne Constables in open Court for ye County of Somersett in ye pvince of Maryland, John Hillyard, constable for Pocomoke & Morumsco, Robert Hart, constable for Anemessick, James Caine, constable for Manonoakin, Nicholas Rice, constable for ye Mannyes & Wiccocomoco"; while at court on November 27, 1666, the Com^{rs} for ye Countie of Sommersett Doe order & appointe Jinkin Prise

[Price], Ambrose Dixon, Roger Wollford [Woolford], John Waller & James Dashiell to be surveyors for ye highways & to proceed to ye making A highway according to Act of Assembly" and "This day Mr. Steven Horse high Sheriffe psented A Jury of Inquest who were Sworne viz: Mr. James Davis, foreman, Jeffery Minshall, Alexander Draper, Edward Southern, Daniell Hast, William Furnis, William Boyes, Robert Cattling, Robert Hignett, William Jones, James Price, John King, & they took oath." It was further ordered that "The jury of Enquest meet at ye house of Tho: Poole ye 26th December next and that those constables wch were absent from ye Court this day be summoned before ye Jury, the parties absent were Nicholas Rice and John Hillyard." On November 27, 1666, "Nehemiah Covington was sworne this day constable" and on January 29, 1666/7, "were added to ye Jury of Enquest & sworne in Courte: John Manlove, Owen Mackra & Daniell Curtis" and on the same day we find that "Edmund Beauchamp Clerke to ye Court was Sworne."[10] In passing it will not be amiss to call attention to the fact that the "Jury of Inquest" sworne November 27, 1666, and whose number was enlarged January 29, 1666/7, was the first grand jury summoned and sworn for Somerset County.

It will be noticed that a meeting of this "Jury of Enquest" was directed to be held at the house of Thomas Poole. It will be recalled that the court of the "Eastern Shore" held in December, 1665, is described as "A Court held *att Thomas Poole . . . in Manoakin.*" Thomas Poole's home at this time was on a tract called "Poole's Hope," on the south side of Back Creek, near the headwaters of the creek, and it was doubtless there that the first courts for Somerset County were held.[11]

The court for Somerset County held January 17, 1666/7, was one of great importance, for it was then that steps were first taken for obtaining ground for the erection of a court house; the commissioners of the peace compelled under penalty (in accordance with Act of Assembly) to remain at sessions of court; provision made for a proper review of proceedings of sessions of court by the commissioners and their due and proper entry upon record; "the highway" for the county was directed to be laid out; and the boundaries of the several districts—designated "hundreds"—definitely described. The following extract is from the records of this court:

"Orders agreed upon by ye Com^rs of Sommersett Countie this 17th of January 1666/7.¹²

Present:

 Mr. William Stevens   Mr. George Johnson
 Capt William Thorne   Mr. James Jones
 Mr. John Winder   Mr. Henry Boston
    Mr. Steven Horse, high Sherriffe.

Imprimas: That A Tract of Land in ye most Conveniente place for the whole Countie be taken up for ye Counties use & a house builded thereupon.

2^ly That ye Com^rs according to Act of Assembly ye Court being setting not any one of Com^rs to depart without leave of ye Court upon penalty of tenne pounds of tobacco for every hour being absent.

3^ly That at every Court after ye Causes are all dispatch upon adjournment of ye Court ye orders of y^t p^rsent Court to be reviewed by ye Commission^rs then to be entered according to their direction.

The highway for ye Countie of Sommersett¹³ from ye Landing place upon Capt. Goyeders Land in Pocomoke river to Morumsco Dambs neare ye house of Robert Hignett & from thence downe to ye head of Thomas Price's Creeke to ye head of William Coleborne's Creeke And from ye head of Will Colbornes Creeke to Wattkins point from ye Dambs y^t lyeth by Robert Hignetts to ye Lower Dambs y^t lyeth at ye head of Anamessicke river from thence to ye Lower Dambs y^t lyeth at ye head of ye back Creeke of Manonoakin river And from thence to ye head of Manonakin river & from thence to the head of Wiccocomoco Creeke.

The bounds of Pocomoke hundred.¹⁴

Pocomoke river & ye eastermost side of Morumsco Creeke to Morsumco Dambs.

The bounds of Anamessick hundred.

Anamessicke beginning at Watkins pointe running to the mouth of Morumsco Creeke up ye westermost side of ye said Creeke to Morumsco Dambs & from Watkin's pointe to the north point of Anamessicke river & from thence running up ye middest of y^t neck of Land Called desert.

The bounds of Manonoakin hundred.

Manonoakin beginning at ye north pointe of Anamessicke river running up ye middest of ye said neck called desert on ye north side And from ye north point of Anamessicke to ye north pointe of Manonakin running up ye middest of y^t neck of Land Lyeing betweene ye north side of Manonakin & ye south side of Little Manny.

The bounds of greate & Little Manny hundred.

Manny beginning at ye north pointe of Manonoakin running up ye middest of ye said neck of Land Lyeing between ye north side of Manonakin river & ye

South of Little Manny on ye north side of ye said neck And from ye north pointe of Manonoakin river to ye South point of Wiccocomoco river and soe running up the middest of the said neck on the south side thereof.

The bounds of Wiccocomoco hundred.

Wiccocomoco begining at ye south pointe of Wiccocomoco river & running up ye northermost side of ye said neck that lyeth betweene ye north side of greate Manny & ye south side of Wiccocomoco river in ye middest thereof And beginning at ye South pointe of Wiccocomoco and running to ye north pointe of Wiccocomoco so running up the middest of y^t neck Lyeing betweene the north side of Wiccocomoco on ye south side of Nanticoke.

These five "hundreds," Pocomoke, Annemessex, Manokin, Great and Little Monie and Wicomico, were the five districts into which Somerset County was originally divided in January, 1666/7. Later there were four additional "hundreds" created: Nanticoke (to the north of Wicomico) Hundred; Bogerternorton (to the east and north of Pocomoke) Hundred, and extending along the seaside; Mattapany Hundred, in the extreme southeastern section of the county; and still later, Baltimore (to the north of Bogerternorton) Hundred, extending to the seaside.[15]

Again to resume our narrative. At a court held for Somerset County March 26, 1667 (with Stevens, Winder, Boston and Johnson present), the commissioners presented for the consideration of the provincial authorities the names of Stephen Horsey, William Thorne and William Coulbourne, one of whom to be appointed and commissioned sheriff of the county for the ensuing year. Stephen Horsey (who already occupied the office) was the successful nominee and was commissioned high sheriff on April 23, 1667, continuing in office until June, 1668, when he was succeeded by George Johnson. It is evident that the question of a sufficient road constructing force was considered by this court of March 26th, as the record shows: "It is ordered that every man shall make out & cleare his owne Land (excepting where bridges are judged needfull) for A highway by the direction of the Surveyors." On July 30, 1667, John Panter was named surveyor of the highways for Great and Little Manny Hundred in place of John Waller, deceased, and on April 10, 1668, "Will: Furnice constable for Manoakin hundred in place of James Caine, deceased, & take his oath in y^t behalfe before ye next justice of ye peace." On June 30, 1668, George Johnson was sworn high sheriff of Somerset County; Alexander Draper, constable for Annemessex Hundred; and David Spence, constable for Wiccocomoco Hundred. On October 1, 1668, George Johnson, the high sheriff, announced his appointments of George Hossfoord (Horsford), of Somerset, Cirurgeon (Chirurgeon; surgeon) to be his "under sheriff" and the said Hossfoord qualified to that office by taking oath as "deputie sheriff."[16]

Let us now retrace our steps somewhat—but only in order to glance at an important and most interesting item in connection with Somerset County's earliest history—and reenter the court held for Somerset on July 2, 1667. At this session of court we discover Randall Revell suing one *"John Johnson, Negro,"* in an action of debt.[17] This mention of "John Johnson, Negro," is the first reference so far discovered to Negroes within the boundaries of the original Somerset County (from Nanticoke River south to the Maryland-Virginia boundary line and from the Atlantic Ocean on the east to Chesapeake Bay on the west). Furthermore, it seems probable that the Johnson family to which this "John Johnson, Negro," belonged, were the first Negroes resident within the area designated officially in November, 1661, as the "Eastern Shore" (from Choptank River south to Watkin's Point at the mouth of Pocomoke River, and the Maryland-Virginia boundary line). Then, too, of yet greater interest, is the fact that these Johnsons (of whom there are records of several generations) were "free negroes" and came to the "Eastern Shore" of Maryland—now Somerset County—in late 1661 or early 1662, from Northampton County in Virginia, where they had resided for many years as "free negroes." This family had its origin in Anthony Johnson and Mary, his wife, "free negroes," who were residing as early as 1622 in old Accomack, later Northampton County, on the "Eastern Shore" of the colony of Virginia, and stated to have been the first free Negroes in Virginia. In 1652, these Johnsons suffered great property loss by reason of a devastating fire and were thereafter exempted from payment of taxes.

These Johnsons not only were owners of landed property, but also apparently held other Negroes as slaves. Anthony and Mary Johnson were the parents of at least two sons, John Johnson and Richard Johnson, who were grown men by the year 1654, when they appear in land transactions in the records of Northampton County, Virginia. When settlement was made on the "Eastern Shore" of the province of Maryland under proclamation of Lord Baltimore, dated November 6, 1661, we find as two of the "headrights" of Randall Revell and Ann Toft to their patent for "Double Purchase," dated November 10, 1662, the names of Anthony and Mary Johnson. Thus we find these Johnsons coming into the Manokin section of the "Eastern Shore" Maryland settlement, transported thither by Randall Revell and Anne Toft. Anthony Johnson and Mary, his wife (identified by records to be quoted presently as "negroes") certainly came among the first settlers of the area which later became Somerset County and lived for a while in the Manokin section. On August 10, 1666, Stephen Horsey, of Annemessex, in the province of Maryland, Gentleman, leased to "Anthony Johnson, of Manonoakin, in the province aforesaid, planter," a tract of 300 acres of land called "Tonies Vineyard," on the south side of Wiccocomoco Creek and lying by the creek side adjoining William Bosman's land; the said tract having been granted said Horsey by patent February 24, 1665/6. This lease was for the term of 200 years to the said Johnson and his wife at the yearly rent of "one pepper corne" and the payment of his Lordship's rents and other dues. The lease was entered on the Somerset records September 10, 1666, with William Thorne and William Stevens as witnesses thereto. The exact date of Anthony Johnson's death is not known, but it took place prior to June, 1670, for on the tenth day of that month Stephen Horsey, of Somerset County, made a 99-year lease of the land called "Tonies Vineyard," on south side of Wiccocomoco Creek, to Mary Johnson, relict of Anthony Johnson, late of Somerset County, deceased, and after her death to John Johnson and Richard Johnson (sons of the said Anthony and Mary Johnson) and their, or either of their, heirs. The yearly rent again was stated as one ear of Indian Corn. On September 3, 1672, Mary Johnson, of Somerset County, *Negro* (relict of Anthony Johnson, late of the said county, *Negro,* deceased), made deed of gift for cattle, to her grandchildren, viz: Anthony Johnson, son of John Johnson, *Negro,* and Francis and Richard Johnson, sons of Richard Johnson. On the same date, Mary Johnson, Negro, of Somerset County (widow and relict of Anthony Johnson, late of Somerset, Negro, deceased), gave a power of attorney to her son, John Johnson, Negro, of Somerset County. This power of attorney was witnessed by Edmund Beauchamp and "John Cazara, Negro." No attempt has been made to trace these Johnsons further and the items here given are merely for the purpose of identifying the first generations of this notable "first negro family" in Somerset. This is indeed a notable family, having been the first free Negroes in the colony of Virginia (according to Jennings Wise, *Ye Kingdome of Accawmacke, or the Eastern Shore of Virginia in the Seventeenth Century*) and resident in Accomack County as early as 1622 (the first Negroes imported into the colony of Virginia having been carried there in 1619). These Johnsons came into the Manokin section of the "Eastern Shore" of Maryland settlement late in 1661 or early in 1662, and were the first Negroes to come, or be brought, there. They were the first Negroes in Somerset County, and as "free negroes," the first free Negroes of *this* "Eastern Shore" of Maryland settlement and of Somerset County, and certainly if not the first, then among the first, free African Negroes to appear in the province of Maryland.[18]

We come now to that interesting feature in early Somerset history—the first representation of the county in the General Assembly of the province.

The erection and organization of Somerset County brought as a matter of course to the new political unit the right of representation in the General Assembly, and we find the authorities of the province, on February 16, 1668 (1668/9), issuing a writ to George Johnson, sheriff of Somerset, directing him to conduct an election of burgesses (or delegates) to represent the county in an Assembly to be held at St. Mary's, seat of government of the province, April 13, 1669, and to make due return of the representatives so elected. In the record of the General Assembly, convened April 13, 1669, we find duly returned as burgess (or delegate) for

"*Som'sett County: Mr. William Stevens.*"[19]

Thus was Somerset County's first representative in the provincial Assembly seated; but behind this dignified act lies a remarkable bit of procedure which the records of the province disclose with perfect frankness. Stevens was indeed returned by Sheriff Johnson as duly elected by the vote of Somerset's citizens and took his seat in the Assembly which was in session from April 13 to May 26, 1669; but, in the course of the session, it was developed that two representatives had been elected for Somerset under the writ of February, 1668/9;

two burgesses (or delegates) being the number to which the county was entitled. By the election, William Stevens and Stephen Horsey were both entitled to seats in the Assembly, though for some reason (which is not stated) the people of Somerset meeting after the election in an "Ale House" told Sheriff Johnson that "they would have but one burgess." Thereupon, Johnson, assuming authority to act as judge in the matter of choice between Stevens and Horsey, made return of Stevens as "duly elected," while informing Horsey "that he need not come to the Assembly for he would not return him." On May 4th, the matter of Stephen Horsey's due election to a seat in the Lower House as a representative from Somerset County, and his absence from the Assembly, were brought before that august body for consideration, together with a charge of Sheriff Johnson's failure "to make due return of the said Member." It appears, however, that Horsey had sent a letter to a member of the House informing him that he "was sick & could not attend" and the gentleman recipient "produced a letter from him (Horsey) sent to the House for that purpose." But this did not satisfy the Lower House, to which Horsey had been "duly elected," though not "duly returned." The gentlemen composing that body manifested considerable indignation over such procedure, devoting grave consideration to the matter. In the course of discussion provoked by such behavior, evidence was produced from the chancellor of the province and the clerk of the House showing that Sheriff Johnson, when he had come to St. Mary's on April 10th to make return on the writ, had informed the chancellor of the due election of both Stevens and Horsey and also of the refusal of the people of Somerset County to send two burgesses to the Assembly; and of his, the sheriff's, action in regard to Horsey. The chancellor, it appears, was outspoken in his censure of Sheriff Johnson's conduct, frankly telling him "that he was not to be his own Judge of Election but ought to return & thereupon returned Mr. Horsey." With this evidence before it, the House was most emphatic in its rebuke of the sheriff. Hearing these facts plainly stated "the Question thereupon was put whither his evidence shall aquit said Member from Fine or no? It passed in the affirmative. The Question again put whither the said Sheriff be not finable for his Proceedings on the Election & Return. Yea or no? It passed in the affirmative. Yea.

Ordered that these votes be sent to the Upper House to whom this House leaves the matter as to fining the Sheriff."[20]

Unfortunately there is no record of the action taken by the Upper House of Assembly in this matter.

Thus we find record of Somerset County's first representation in the General Assembly of the province of Maryland; and thus are we enlightened as to "politics" as played in Somerset County "in the beginning." Why Sheriff Johnson should have given way to the high-handed method employed by the electorate in Somerset in setting aside one of its duly elected representatives, we do not know; nor have we been able to discover why the sheriff assumed to act as judge in choosing between the men so elected; nor has there been discovered any reason as stated by the electorate of Somerset for refusing to send two representatives to the Assembly. We have only the facts as recited above. At any rate, the chancellor of the province and the Lower House of Assembly did not hesitate to censure the whole proceeding—explicitly censuring Sheriff Johnson, and implicitly the electorate of Somerset. Needless to say, we do not find again any record of such assumption of authority. We cannot, however, leave this matter without commenting on the cleverness of the Somerset men in attaining their end. The writ demanded the election of two burgesses (or delegates). The two were duly elected; then the people refused to send but one. This proceeding, which gained at least the support of the sheriff, was virtual nullification of the legal demand and met with merited reproof. Then fate—if we may call it such—took a hand in affairs ordaining the "intention" of the Somerset men that "they would have but one burgess"—for Stephen Horsey's illness prevented his attendance in the Assembly, and Somerset was represented alone by William Stevens!

We have compassed the political foundations of Somerset on the "Eastern Shore" of the province of Maryland—seven years in their laying; but solidly laid by the genius of the craft of early community builders. Deluge of opposition indeed impeded progress in this work and attempted to sweep away the very foundation as it was being laid. But the strong purpose and right in which this foundation was laid, held—and the storm beat in vain. At last came the clear day of completion of the venture and through the long ages the work of the builders has stood—a house built upon a rock!

V

THE HOUSEHOLD OF FAITH

1. *Followers of the Inner Light.*
2. *Voice of the People.*
3. *Of Ancient and Apostolic Lineage.*
4. *Children of the Covenant.*

1. FOLLOWERS OF THE INNER LIGHT

1

The Quakers who settled Annemessex:—Meeting places and the "Meeting House"—A Lone Beacon of the "Inner Light" on Wicomico—George Fox, founder of the Society of Friends, visits Somerset—The Quakers of Monie:—Meeting place and the "Meeting House" and burial ground—The Bogerternorton Meeting and its membership:—Meeting place, the "Meeting House" and burial ground.

THERE is no more fascinating story of religious foundations in any community of colonial times in America than that disclosed by research among institutional origins of "Old Somerset."

Lord Baltimore's objective in promoting settlements in the extreme southeastern section of his "Eastern Shore" territory was for the specific purpose of reenforcing his territorial rights in that area, in order to develop them in the interest of the proprietary revenue. It is also evident that the first settlers in this region were not unmindful of the economic advantage which would be theirs in possessing the new, rich and fertile lands now opened for settlement by the Lord Proprietor of Maryland. These elements are self-evident in the opening up of this area. But in fully evaluating such factors and then laying them aside there is disclosed a stone in the foundation of this adventure whose significance is far richer than the acquirement of silver and gold. The imagination, inspired by this discovery, finds new light flooding the ancient truth that "man does not live by bread alone."

Among the founders of the settlement on the lower "Eastern Shore" (which developed into the county of Somerset), we find a group of men who, with their families, were seeking homes within a political area which primarily afforded them the right of the free exercise of conscience in matters of religion. This liberty was afforded them both by tradition and statue in the province of Maryland, whose governing authority was offering lands for settlement. Somerset County's true origin is in nature identical with the origin of the province of Maryland—in this exemplifying the old adage: "like mother, like daughter." Underlying both of these historic territorial and political structures is the principle of religious liberty; though the spirit which created the "Mother" and the spirit creating the "Daughter" represent the polarities in the realm of religious philosophy. Maryland's creation issued from the desire of a great soul primarily to secure a colony where English Roman Catholics might be free to worship God according to the dictates of conscience. The settlement which developed into Somerset County had its genesis in a group of religious radicals—Quakers, and other religious non-conformists—whose "form of faith" represented in its expression the extreme of Protestantism. True humanness and the strength of the over-ruling providence of the Divine are brought out vividly and clearly through this historic illustration of true oneness of purpose, with vast contrast in the expression of that purpose, as found in the creation of "Mother" Maryland and "Daughter" Somerset. It is a picture of real life in the living which will never lose charm for those who love to view life as it actually is.

Insistently and persistently Lord Baltimore urged upon his provincial authorities the necessity of protecting territorial rights on the lower "Eastern Shore" of Maryland, near the Maryland-Virginia boundary line, by making permanent settlements in that area. In dramatic fashion, this desire of his Lordship found consummation through the drastic law against Quakers which was promulgated by the Virginia authorities in March, 1659/60. In November, 1661, the Governor of Maryland issued his proclamation (countersigned by the Lord Proprietor) opening to settlement the lands on the "Eastern Shore" near the boundary line for certain Northampton-Accomack Virginians who had petitioned the Maryland authorities for premission to settle in the province. Almost immediately after the date of issue of this proclamation, we find certain notable Northampton-Accomack Virginia Quakers, and other religious non-conformists, in residence along the south bank of the Great Annemessex River. In this settlement designated as "Annemessex" we find such men as Stephen Horsey, Ambrose Dixon, Thomas Price, Henry Boston, George Johnson, William Coulbourne, Robert Hart and Alexander Draper, all of whom had been in conflict with the authorities in Northampton County, Virginia, because of their Quaker and other non-conformist attitudes, and for refusing to pay ministers' and other church dues. "Annemessex" was the foundation settlement in the area which later became Somerset County. In Northampton County, Virginia (which in that day immediately joined the Maryland boundary line on the south of the peninsula forming the "Eastern Shore"[1]), there was a very strong element of religious and political liberalism, which laid hold with tenacity upon the tenets of Quakerism. The "faith of the Inner Light" found a particularly rich plot in this quarter for the germination of seed sown by the apostles of that faith, while the resultant luxuriant growth afforded a rich harvest for the legal scythe put into the hand of Northampton County officialdom by the Virginia Assembly's Act against Quakers. The records of Northampton County, Virginia, Court yield abundant evidence of the industry of the authorities in wielding the keen blade of this law.[2]

These Northampton-Accomack, Virginia, "religious rebels" were not long in transferring allegiance to the proprietary government of Maryland when Lord Baltimore through his resident governor issued the proclamation of November, 1661, opening for settlement the area of the province near the Maryland-Virginia boundary line. It may be that "Annamessex men" had even crossed the boundary into Maryland before the proclamation was issued. It is certain that Horsey, Dixon, Price, Boston, Johnson, Coulbourne, Hart and Draper stood upon no ceremony, either in leaving Virginia or in entering Maryland. They were all under ban by the Virginia authorities because of their defiant religious non-conformity.

This Annemessex settlement on the "Eastern Shore" of Maryland was composed of men from Northampton County, in Virginia, who were non-conformists to the Established Church of England; the majority of them definitely affiliated with the Quakers. In Northampton County, Virginia, Court, January 28, 1661 (1661/2), Stephen Horsey, Ambrose Dixon, Robert Hart and Alexander Draper, of Hungars Parish, who had been "delinquent in payment of ye dues belonging to ye Minister of ye sd Parish and other pish [parish] dues belonging to ye Church had accon entrd ag't [against] them by the Church wardens of ye sd parrish of Hungers and by ye Sherr [sheriff] returned non est inventus." Attachment was ordered against their estates if any should be found in Northampton County. At the same court, William Coulbourne, Jeffrey Minshall, John Marcum and others, of Hungars Parish, were also reported because of delinquency "in paymt of ye dues to ye Minister and other parish dues belonging to ye Church," and were ordered to "make p^r sent payment of what shall appear by ye Church wardens to bee due to be paid by them from ye years 1654 ye Church wardens pducing their severall Respective accot^s als exec^n [also execution]."³ Stephen Horsey, Ambrose Dixon, Robert Hart and Alexander Draper were certainly out of Northampton County by January, 1661/2; and doubtless were then at Annemessex in Maryland. We cannot say when George Johnson, Henry Boston and Thomas Price arrived at Annemessex. Johnson was still residing in Northampton County, Virginia, in March, 1662/3.⁴ Johnson, Boston and Price were certainly at Annemessex in October, 1663.⁵ William Coulbourne was at Annemessex by January, 1663/4; evidently not having arrived there by October, 1663.⁶ Jeffrey Minshall and John Marcum also came to this settlement in Maryland at a later date.⁷ Another prominent rebel against the Virginia law against Quakers, who finally found his way to Annemessex, was Ambrose London; the date of whose arrival we do not know, but who was still in Northampton County, Virginia, in February, 1663/4, when he was before the court for his Quakerism.⁸

We cannot "religiously denominate" Stephen Horsey. Never once is he specifically referred to as a Quaker; but is described by Edmund Scarburgh as "of all sects yet professing none," who "left ye lower parts [i. e. Northampton] to head rebellion at Annamessex." William Coulbourne cannot be identified as a Quaker though he was most friendly to the followers of the "Inner Light." Boston, Hart, Draper, and Marcum, though evidently "sympathetic," do not appear in the records under specific designation as Quakers. Of Ambrose Dixon, George Johnson and Thomas Price we have, however, the "sure and certain sign."

Thus it is that we find in Annemessex on the "Eastern Shore" of Maryland the first organized religious group in the area which later became Somerset County. Here this stone in the ancient foundation of the settlement is laid in religious liberty; a stone bearing through eternity the decipherable names of Ambrose Dixon, George Johnson and Thomas Price; with markings, no doubt signifying the names of others, which the passage of time has made undecipherable.

Ambrose Dixon, himself a Quaker, was certainly the very heart of this group of Quakers and other non-conformists who sought sanctuary in this quarter. "A receiver of many Quakers, his home ye place of their Resort, and a conveyor of o˞ ingaged perons out of the county [i. e. Northampton-Accomack in Virginia]," so wrote Colonel Scarburgh, of Ambrose Dixon. George Johnson is termed "ye proteus of heresy," and Thomas Price "a creeping Quaker." Ambrose Dixon's house on the land called "Dixon's Choice," on Annemessex River, was the first place of "meeting" for the Quakers and their sympathisers who fled from Virginia and settled on this lower "Eastern Shore" of the province of Maryland. On this tract of land, not far distant from Dixon's house, the first regular Meeting House of the Annemessex Quakers was erected at a later day and continued to stand for some years; while in the hallowed ground about this Meeting House the blessed dead of the faith were buried.[9]

Unfortunately no records of the Annemessex Meeting have been discovered, and it is only from other sources that we have been able to gather fragmentary references to its membership. We know that Ambrose Dixon, George Johnson and Thomas Price were members of this meeting. Doubtless there were many others though we do not now possess their names. Annemessex Meeting certainly continued for more than half a century, the latest evidence of its existence being found in the will of Richard Waters, who lived at "Water's River," a plantation on the north side of Annemessex River, and who died in the year 1720. We find that the "Men's Meeting" of the Society of Friends, held on the Western Shore of Maryland in 1679, received reports from several local meetings of the monthly type, among them one from the Annemessex Meeting. In 1684, the Friends' Yearly Meeting of Maryland, composed of particular meetings, numbered Annemessex Meeting among them. Again, "At a Yearly Meeting [of the Society of Friends] at Tredhaven Creek [Talbot County] 5th 8mo 1697, inquiry was made into the estate and welfare of Weekly Meetings belonging to the Yearly Meeting," among which is named the "Weekly Meeting" at Annemessex.[10]

Few names of members of this Annemessex Meeting have come down to us; but these few are of great interest. Ambrose Dixon remained faithful to the end—until the "Inner Light," ever brightening as the years gathered about his pathway through this mortal life, lighted his way into "the land beyond." In the year 1687 the mortal part of this "Old Somerset" immortal was laid in the earth at the "Meeting House at Annamessex." In the same year the body of Dixon's daughter, Mrs. Elizabeth Dukes, was interred in the same hallowed ground.[11] We are not less certain that George Johnson, that "Proteus of heresy," "abided" unto the end in the faith which he so valiantly espoused. Johnson (who died in 1681) indited his will *"In the Name of the Light which enlighteneth every Man that cometh into the World that was my Condemer but now my savior, So be itt."* After providing for his family, he directed certain property "to be given unto such Poor friends" as shall be chosen by the trustees of his estate, or such as may be chosen (under certain conditions) by *"ye meeting."* It is interesting to note that one of the witnesses to Johnson's will (dated November 23, 1680; probated December 23, 1681) was one "Th^s Price," who at the probate thereof appeared as an evidence in proving the document, when he *"did declare (but not upon oath)"* to the signature of the deceased testator. Certainly in Price we find another Quaker, and though we have no means for proving his "identity," we suspect that in him we have Thomas Price, the "creeping Quaker," and one of the original Annemessex men. Thomas Price—"the original"—was certainly living as late as September, 1685. As belonging to this Annemessex Meeting we can also identify Thomas Evernden (who married Katherine, widow of George Johnson), and John Goddin (who married Katherine, daughter of George and Katherine [Butcher] Johnson). Goddin and Evernden first appear in Somerset County, in the Annemessex neighborhood, in the 1670's and the 1680's, respectively. John Goddin removed sometime after 1685 to a plantation called "Rochester," near the head of Pocomoke River (south side), becoming a member of the Bogerternorton Meeting of Friends. He died intestate in 1712. Thomas Evernden, soon after the beginning of the eighteenth century, removed to Dorchester County, where he died in 1710; leaving a will which fully attests his abiding loyalty to the Society of Friends.[12] It was Thomas Evernden who brought Thomas Chalkley, the celebrated Quaker preacher, to Somerset County on his first visit in 1698; Evernden crossing the Bay in his own sloop to meet him. While Evernden's guest, Chalkley records holding a meeting "where many people came" and that he, with "about ten friends," attended the funeral of one Robert Cathing (a neighbor of Evernden's), "and there were a great many people, among whom we had a good opportunity, and many weighty truths were opened to them in the love of

God; and some of them were tender and wept; and the most if not all, I think I may say, were solid and weighty."[13] Chalkley at this time visited George Truitt and his brother near the head of Pocomoke, and at Levin Denwood's on Great Monie. About 1699, or 1702/5, Thomas Story—"who was the Paul among the Friends of America"—in making a tour of the "Eastern Shore" of Maryland, spent two days with Thomas Evernden at Annemessex after having visited George Truitt and holding a meeting at Walter Lane's (whose home was on the south side of Pocomoke River); going from Evernden's to Richard Waters' home, which was on the north side of the Annemessex River.[14]

Thus we have been able to gather items from remaining records relative to the Annemessex Meeting of the Society of Friends. As these records have afforded items relative to some of the members of this meeting; so, too, they disclose several references to the places of meeting of the Annemessex Quakers. In the beginning this group of Quakers evidently held meetings in the home of Ambrose Dixon. Colonel Scarburgh in 1663 refered to Dixon as "A receiver of many Quakers, *his house ye place of their Resort."* Certainly Dixon, as the very heart of Annemessex Quakerism, gave his house as a place of assembly for worship before the erection of a Meeting House. Doubtless the homes of other members of this group were used from time to time for this purpose; but to Dixon's home certainly goes the honour of the "chief sanctuary." At what date the Annemessex Quakers erected a public Meeting House we do not know; but undoubtedly sometime before the spring of 1687, for we have the record that "Ambrose Dixon, Senr died and was buried at the meeting house in Anemessex the 12th day of Aprill Annoq Do^m one Thousand Six hundred eighty & seaven." When finally the Friends' Meeting House of Annemessex was built, where indeed should it have been erected but on the land of Ambrose Dixon? Of this fact we have evidence. In November, 1739, a question arose about certain boundary markers of "Dixon's Choice," the original land grant and home place of old Ambrose Dixon. In an attempt to restore the ancient land marks depositions were taken, in one of which reference is made to a location where "a Gum stood in a valley or branch and Leaned over the road *near to a place where the Quaker Meeting house stood."*[15] Just as we have no evidence of the date of the erection of this Meeting

House in Annemessex, so we have no evidence of the date of its abandonment. We are doubtless correct in assuming that its destruction or abandonment took place somewhat before the year 1700, and that this group of Quakers again resorted to the use of private homes for the purpose of meetings. In June, 1704, the court of Somerset County granted the petition of Somerset Quakers, that certain private houses be appointed "meeting houses for the people Called Quakers to worship god in pursuant to an act of Parliam^t and the good Lawes of this province." One of these was "the house of Richard Waters in Annemessex." Doubtless Richard Waters' home remained the regular place of meeting through the remainder of his life. Richard Waters, who "abided faithful unto the end," died in the summer of the year 1720 and by his will directed that "the Monthly Meeting ... at West River" (which was in Anne Arundel County on the Western Shore of the province) should have supervision of the marriages of his children. Madam Elizabeth Waters, widow of Richard Waters, we shall later meet in our study of the Monie Meeting.

Every one of the persons named above in connection with the life of the Annemessex Meeting of Quakers, save Thomas Price, were people of very substantial means; several of them possessing wealth compared with others of their day and time. Moreover, the worldly possessions of these Quakers consisted not only in houses and lands and currency; but also included Negro slaves. Then, too, all of those whom we can positively identify as Quakers, save Thomas Price, were appointed or elected to political office. Ambrose Dixon was elected a delegate from Somerset County to the Lower House of the Maryland Assembly in January, 1670/1, though there is no evidence that he qualified to that office. George Johnson and Henry Boston served for years as members of the court of Somerset; and Johnson was at one time sheriff of the county. Thomas Evernden and John Goddin were elected to the Lower House of the Assembly in 1692, but Maryland having become a Royal Province, "conscience" precluded their taking the required oath of office. Richard Waters belonged, both by birth and marriage, to one of the most distinguished "office holding" connections on both the "Eastern Shore" of Maryland and Virginia. We cannot, in a single instance, positively label as Quakers the distinguished Stephen Horsey, William Coulbourne and Ambrose London; but of their deep sympathy with Quakerism there can be no doubt, and of their rebellious spirit of non-conformity there is no question. Horsey, Coulbourne and London were all men of first rank in the office-holding class of "Old Somerset." Thomas Price remains, among the group, the only man of simple means and "walking the common ways of life."[16] Horsey, Dixon and Price are referred to as having been originally tradesmen, "a cooper," "a caulker" and "a leather dresser," respectively. Horsey and Dixon became well-to-do planters. Price we should best designate as a farmer; and probably he also continued his "trade." George Johnson, a wealthy planter, was extensively engaged in trading with both Old and New England. Coulbourne, Boston, London, Evernden and Goddin were most substantial planters; though Coulbourne seems to have devoted his time largely to military and political pursuits. Richard Waters was a very wealthy planter. So much for the "worldly station" of these *known* Annemessex Quakers and their sympathsizers. No doubt this Meeting numbered likewise many poor, unfamed, and more simple folk, whose names are not written upon perishable parchment; but surely imperishably in "the Lamb's book of life."

What of the continuance of Quakerism and other non-conformity in the families of these valiant defenders of liberty of conscience in matters of religion? It is a strange story we have to relate—Dixons, Bostons, Horseys, Coulbournes, of the *second generation,* are all found within the fold of the Church of England as established in the province of Maryland. A Dixon, a Horsey and a Coulbourne found themselves elected to membership in the first parish vestries chosen in 1692 for Coventry and Somerset Parishes in Somerset County. These names, together with that of Boston, appear frequently upon remaining fragmentary parochial records as of persons baptized, married and buried in the faith of the Church of England. Of the religious affiliation of Thomas Price's descendants we know not; nor of Ambrose London's. George Johnson's line died out with the demise of his Goddin grandchildren, unmarried. How long Thomas Evernden's line held to Quakerism we have not searched to discover. Richard Waters' descendants all came within the fold of the Church of England.

This is the story of the Annemessex Meeting of Quakers as we have been able to gather it from remaining records. Truly this was the first "Meeting" of the Society of Friends on the "Eastern Shore" of Maryland below Choptank River, dating back to the year 1662 (not improbably late 1661), with Ambrose Dixon as founder and very heart of the adventure. This stone is in the very first layer of the foundation of "Old Somerset."

The date at which the Annemessex Meeting of Quakers ceased to exist has not so far been discovered. Towards the middle of the 18th Century we have evidence, however, that its Meeting House made with hands, had disappeared. We can but wonder if by that time the erstwhile worshippers of that House had not been all gathered to the Temple not made with hands, eternal in the heavens.

* * * *

Before proceeding with our story of the Quaker Meetings in this area, let us turn for a moment to two interesting characters of this faith who appear in vital connection with the affairs of "Old Somerset"—James Jones, who came to reside there; and George Fox, the founder and great apostle of Quakerism, who paid a most notable visit to the county.

Like a lone beacon of the "Inner Light" on the outpost of the settlement, James Jones—identified Quaker—occupied his plantation on the west side of Wicomico River. Jones' plantation was situated on a tract of land called "Jones Hole," about opposite to where the present Wicomico Creek enters the larger stream, and about a mile above the present town of Whitehaven, in Wicomico County (at the time of James Jones' life—and for nearly two centuries after—Somerset County). James Jones was evidently a native of Monmouthshire in Wales; going thence, at a date now unknown, to Northampton County, Virginia. In May, 1660, he evidenced his disrespect for earthly magistrates in Northampton County by "moveing into ye court in an irrevent manner wth his hatt on his head." For such unseemly behavior he was placed under bond; then committed to the sheriff's custody until he should pay "that part of y^e [parish?] Leavie for himself & family wch should have been paid last year." In July, 1660, Jones was "released from his Imprisonment, the Court think fitt to release him Mr. Revell being security for his good behavior & paying his fees & c^{rt} charges." Jones appears again in the records of

Northampton County, Virginia, in January 1660/1, as living at the house of George Johnson—most probably the same George Johnson who later came to reside at Annemessex. At what date James Jones came into the settlement of the "Eastern Shore" (later Somerset County) in the province of Maryland, we do not know, but his grant for 250 acres of land, called "Jones Hole," on the west side of Wicomico River bears date February, 1663/4. Here he made settlement, and by August, 1665, had attained such degree of prominence as to find himself named in the commission of the peace; an office which he retained until his death in 1677. He appears as a lone beacon of the "Inner Light" on this true outpost of the settlement. In 1672, George Fox, the great founder of this faith, on his visit to Somerset, visited James Jones, at whose house (he writes in his journal) "we had a large and very glorious meeting."[17]

* * * *

So we come to that memorable event in "Old Somerset's" historic life—the visit of George Fox, founder and apostle of the Society of Friends. It is no slight honor thus bestowed upon Somerset in her early days, that George Fox should leave his foot-prints in the sand of her time, that he should give his voice to echo agelessly through the course of her life. No doubt familiar, at least from hear-say, with the earnest interest in his gospel of the "Inner Light" manifested by a large element of Somerset's population, Fox's anticipation of a visit to these parts could hardly have been greater than the desire of many Somerset people to receive him. After his arrival from Jamaica (where he had spent sometime en route from England to America), Fox stayed for awhile in Calvert County, Maryland, on the western side of the Chesapeake Bay. From Calvert he went to Talbot County on the upper "Eastern Shore," and thence to New England. Returning from the north by way of the province, he sailed for Virginia and Carolina. In November, 1672, Fox returned to the Patuxent River section in Calvert County, Maryland.

Leaving "the Cliffs," in Calvert, on 12th 12mo. 1672 [February 12, 1672], Fox and his party set sail across the Bay for Somerset. Passing through Tangier Sound and sailing after nightfall into a creek of Manokin River,[18] the boat ran aground, forcing the party to remain until morning and returning tide. The bitter cold of the weather encountered in this experience neither chilled the fervor of the great missionary nor was it in the slightest indicative of the atmosphere of the reception which awaited him in the hearts and homes of Somerset people. Morning and in-flowing tide again set the boat afloat, thus enabling the party to make land and a good fire whereby to restore greatly benumbed hands and to warm thoroughly chilled bodies. Idleness played no part in the itinerary of this witness to the "Inner Light"—a spiritual imperative driving him ever "about his Father's business." As soon as could be, he was again in the boat, "pushing forward." And thus, as he goes on his mission, we shall let George Fox tell for us the story of his triumphal visit to "Old Somerset":[12]

". . . returning to our boat we passed on about ten miles further to a Friend's house[20] where next day we had a very precious meeting at which some of the chief of the place were. I went after it to a Friend's house about four miles off at the head of Anamessy River[21] where on the day following the judge of the county and the justice with him came to me and were very loving and much satisfied with Friend's order.[22] The next day we had a large meeting in the justice's barn, for his house could not hold the company. There were several of the great folks of that country and among the rest an opposer; but all was preserved quiet and well; a precious meeting it was and the people were much affected with the truth; blessed be the Lord! We went next day to see Captain Colburn,[23] who was also a justice, and there we had some service; then returning again we had a very glorious meeting at the same justice's, where we met before; to which came many people of account in the world, magistrates, officers and others. It was large and the power of the Lord was much felt, so that the people were generally well satisfied, and taken with the truth, and there being several merchants and masters of ships from New England, the truth was spread abroad, blessed be the Lord.

A day or two after we traveled about sixteen miles through the woods and bogs heading Anamessy River and Amoroca River part of which last we went over in a canoe and came to Manaoke,[24] to a friendly woman's house; where on the 24th we had a large meeting in a barn. The Lord's Living presence was with us and among the people; blessed be his holy name forever more! Friends had never had a meeting in those parts before.[25] After this we passed over the River Wicocomoco through many bad and watery swamps and marshy ways, and came to James Jone's,[26] a Friend, and justice of the peace where we had a large and very glorious meeting; praised be the Lord God! Then passing over the water in a boat, we took horse and travelled about twenty-four miles through woods and troublesome swamps and came to another justice's house where we had a very large meeting, much people and many of considerable account being present; and the living presence of the Lord was amongst us, praised forever be his holy name! This was on the 3rd of the 1st month [March 3] 1672/3 and on the 5th we had another living heavenly meeting at which divers of the justices, with their wives and many of the people, were; amongst whom we had very good service for the Lord; blessed be his holy name! At this meeting was a woman that lived at Anamessy, who had been many years in trouble of mind and sometimes would sit moping near two months together, and hardly speak or mind anything. When I heard of her, I was moved of the Lord to go to her and tell her 'that salvation was come to her house.' After I had spoken the word of life to her, and entreated the Lord for her, she mended, went up and down with us to meetings, and is since well, blessed be the Lord!"[27]

Being now clear of these parts we left Anamessy on the 7th [of March 1672/3] and passing by water about fifty miles came to a friendly woman's house at Hunger River.[28] We had very rough weather in our passage to this place and were in great danger for the boat had nearly been turned over; but through the good providence of God we got safe thither; praised be his name!"[29]

For nearly a month one of the world's great "human sons of God" lived and labored in Somerset on the "Eastern Shore" of Maryland; this George Fox, founder of that great "Order of the Spirit,"—the Society of Friends. In the mighty power of the Spirit, this man preached in the newly opened and settled lands by the waters of Annemessex, Manokin and Wicomico. He sought the great; he sought the humble. Greatness and humbleness were both alike to him. Imagination can but be enlivened by the poetic cast of the record of the meeting held by Fox on 24th 12 mo 1672—[February 24, 1672/3]: "... came to Manaoke [Manokin], to a friendly woman's house; where ... we had a large meeting in a barn. The Lord's living presence was with us and among the people; blessed be his holy name forevermore!" As one reads this brief entry he can but think a long, long way into the past; far, far beyond the ancientness of Somerset, to Bethlehem in Judea—a Judean peasant woman friendly to God's bidding—and a stable—and a stall—and "the Lord's living presence." Light of Light shining from the manger of a stable in Bethlehem of Judea down the ages across land and sea to Somerset in Maryland! No wonder with his living mind and heart, his silver tongue, George Fox drew to him and deeply touched "all sorts and conditions of men." What an ideal environment for his witness bearing Fox must have found in Somerset: "God who made the world did not dwell in temples made with hands" so the Apostle of the gospel of the "Inner Light" quoted the immortal words of the first Christian Martyr. Somerset's wondrous waters and forests incomparable—"A temple not made with hands!"

And the voice of the mighty prophet sounded through this wilderness. Today no memorial in man or "Meeting House" of this great order of faith remains in Somerset. But who will deny that something of the spirit of Fox and his Friends does abide in the spiritual fabric of the county—an element in Somerset's eternal life?

* * * *

We have traced the origin, and fragmentarily, the development of the Annemessex Meeting of Friends following its Light even to what seems the vanishing point. Annemessex Meeting, though truly first, was not the only Quaker Meeting in Somerset. Not many years elapse before we find evidence of the Monie and Bogerternorton Meetings; the former located about the headwaters of Great Monie Creek; the latter near the headwaters of Pocomoke River. We have not discovered the exact dates at which the Monie and Bogerternorton Meetings originated; but certainly they were not in existence at the time of George Fox's visit to Somerset in February-March, 1671/2. The organization of the Monie Meeting was no doubt the result of Fox's visit to Somerset. The Bogerternorton Meeting seems, however, to have been a much later foundation.

* * * *

Let us first consider the Monie Meeting. In the year 1670 there came to live in Monie Hundred, Somerset County, one Levin Denwood (then about twenty-two years of age) and his wife, Priscilla, from Accomack County in the colony of Virginia. He seated a large tract of land called "Hackland" on the south side of Great Monie Creek and at the headwaters thereof. Levin Denwood's sister, Mary, had married (in Northampton-Accomack, in March, 1661/2), Roger Woolford and had come with him into Somerset County as early as the year 1666. Susanna Denwood (another sister of Levin Denwood) married Thomas Browne, of Accomack; and she and her husband became leading members of the Society of Friends in Accomack. Several years later, after Levin Denwood had settled in Somerset County, Maryland, his younger sister, Rebecca Denwood, married, in 1679, Nehemiah Covington, Junior, who lived on the north side of Great Monie Creek (about a mile below the Denwood plantation) at "Covington's Vineyard." Roger Woolford and his immediate household (living on a plantation on the north side of Manokin River) were staunch Church of England folk; but Levin Denwood and his sister, Rebecca, and Rebecca's husband, Nehemiah Covington, Junior, were staunch Quakers. This Levin Denwood and his sisters, Mrs. Susannah Brown, Mrs. Mary Woolford and Mrs. Rebecca Covington were children of an elder Levin Denwood, of Northampton and Accomack Counties in Virginia, a man of means and high social position (at one time a magistrate of Northampton Court), who was certainly most friendly to the Quakers. He most probably became a member of their "Society," and is reported to have erected (about 1657) the first Quaker Meeting House on the "Eastern Shore" of Virginia—a simple log structure on Nassawaddox Creek. This elder Levin Denwood, we are told, was "a receiver of Quakers" who were imported into Northampton County, Virginia, by the celebrated Henry Vaux, who, under pretense of transporting them to Patuxent in Calvert County, Maryland, would land them at Nassawaddox Creek in Virginia.[30]

The young Levin Denwood seems to have spent some of his time with his brother-in-law, Roger Woolford, in Somerset, before finally going there to reside permanently, appearing as having been transported to Maryland by Woolford in 1665, when he was about seventeen years old. However, young Denwood evidently married in Accomack County, Virginia, and there is record of a son having been born there to him and his wife in November, 1670. In this same month he obtained land rights in Somerset County for having transported his wife Priscilla into the province of Maryland. Thus we may safely say that it was in late 1670 or early 1671 that Levin Denwood and Priscilla, his wife, with their infant son, Levin, established their home in Somerset on Great Monie Creek, where a son was born to them in February, 1671/2.

Young Levin Denwood and Priscilla, his wife, were no doubt well established in the faith of Quakerism before making permanent residence in Somerset in 1670 or 1671. His estate on Great Monie was an extensive one and in the course of years he became a man of very substantial means. Nehemiah Covington (Denwood's brother-in-law) was also a man of extensive possessions. That Denwood and Covington were the very heart of this Quaker Meeting in Monie there can be no doubt; and though it would be interesting to know the names of others who were numbered among this worthy group, no records seem to remain by which to identify them. Arthur Denwood and Madam Betty Gale, children of Levin Denwood, were prominent in later years in the affairs of the Monie Meeting, though Madam Gale's husband, Colonel George Gale (who died in 1712), a distinguished official of Somerset, was so stiff a "Churchman" that he directed in his will that their four children (all sons) should be brought up in the faith of the Church of England. This was done, and in this Church they and their descendants most faithfully continued. Also, it may be said in passing, that in the marriage of Sarah Covington (daughter of Nehemiah and Rebecca [Denwood] Covington), a traditionally beautiful Quaker maiden, to the young nabob, Edward Lloyd, of Wye, in Talbot County (afterwards major-general of militia and governor of the province), centers one of the charming romances of provincial Maryland. From the Covington roof-tree went forth also a daughter, Priscilla, born and bred a "Quaker lady," to become wife and mother of Kings of "Kingsland" in Somerset— uncompromising ruling elders of the Presbyterian Church. "Denwood of Hackland" and "Covington of Covington's Vineyard" were names to conjure with in their day and generation; and their Friends' Meeting in Monie was one in which the "Spirit of truth" moved amidst all the refinement and culture of Maryland provincial society.

Unlike the Annemessex Quakers, we wish to record here, the Monie Quaker gentlemen seemed never to have troubled themselves with political life. Denwood and Covington did not seem to seek office, nor were they apparently drafted into official life; though Nehemiah Covington was charged with the great responsibility of General Indian Interpreter for the government of Maryland on the "Eastern Shore."

Levin Denwood, still a very young man, had established his home in Somerset on Great Monie but a brief year or so when George Fox came into Somerset, preaching with mighty power his gospel of the "Inner Light." At this same time, Nehemiah Covington—also but a very young man—was living at "Covington's Vineyard" with his father, the elder Nehemiah Covington. We can but wonder if Fox's visit set young Denwood and young Covington to thinking about organizing a Meeting in the Monie section. The stalwart Quaker, James Jones, lived just a mile or two away (as the crow flies) across Wicomico River; and we wonder if Denwood and Covington may not have been at the "large and very glorious meeting" which George Fox conducted at Jones' house in late February(?), 1672. And may not James Jones in his stalwart faith have given encouragement to the formation of this Meeting in the area just across the river from his plantation? We can prove nothing of this, but such thoughts inadvertently arise as we think on these things.

Whatever the source of encouragement back of the formation of the Monie Meeting of Friends, that "Meeting" was most surely formed. The first recorded reference we have discovered to this Monie Meeting bears date of the year 1679. It appears that the Men's Meeting for Maryland, held in 1679 (convened on the Western Shore of the province) received reports from several "meetings" of the monthly type, one of which was from "Munny," a readily recognizable variation in spelling "Monie." In 1684, "Munny" Meeting was one of the "particular meetings" composing the Friends' Yearly Meeting of Maryland.[31] This Monie Meeting evidently continued active, resolving itself into a Weekly Meeting, for at the Yearly Meeting of the Society of Friends held at Tredhaven Creek in Talbot County, 5th 8mo 1697, inquiry was made "into the estate and welfare of Weekly Meetings belonging to Yearly Meeting," among them the meeting at "Monnye."[32] In 1688, Levin Denwood was one of the signers of an address of thanks from Friends' Quarterly Meeting at Herring Creek, 7th 9mo that year, to Lord Baltimore, who by proclamation had dispensed Quakers from taking oaths in testamentary cases.[33] In 1698, Thomas Chalkley, the great Quaker missionary visiting in Somerset County, records in his "Journal" that he went to Levin Denwood's. Thomas Story, another great Quaker missionary traveling with friends on the "Eastern Shore," recorded a visit to Levin Denwood's in Somerset about 1699 or 1702/5.[34] Again, we find another Quaker traveler and observer, William Edmundson, in Somerset certainly sometime after 1712, recording a visit to "the Widow Gale's at Monay," from here journeying to Annemessex and thence into Virginia.[35] In this lady whom Edmundson visited we recognize Madam Betty Gale, daughter of Levin Denwood, and widow of Colonel George Gale, who died in 1712.

At this point we would like to introduce one whom we have discovered to have been a faithful Quaker and whom, from the proximity of his place of residence to the Monie Meeting, we believe to have been a member thereof—"Richard Stevens of Wiccocomoco," as he is designated in the records in July, 1666. Stevens (who was born about 1641) came from England and was soon thereafter at the residence of John Winder. Though we do not know just the date of his arrival, we do know that he was in the settlement somewhat before the area was erected into Somerset County in August, 1666. In 1668, Richard Stevens purchased lands of Daniel Haste, which he later (in 1680) sold. Then he took up certain lands by patent: "Stevens Conquest" and "Goddard's Folly"; and purchased a tract called "Fairfields." These lands were immediately in the fork of the present Wicomico River and Wicomico Creek, bordering on both the river and the creek and extending some distance on both. However, we should bear in mind that at the date of Stevens' patent and purchase of these lands the *creek* was then frequently referred to as Wicomico *River* and the *river* was designated *Rockawalkin River*. Stevens' lands were on the north side of the *then* Wicomico River (now Creek) and on the east side of the *then* Rockawalkin River (now Wicomico River). Stevens certainly made his home on these lands after 1680, and there he was residing at the time of his death in the fall of 1713. Stevens' home was not more than a mile or two (in direct line northwest) from Levin Denwood's home, though Wicomico River (now Creek) lay between them. Richard Stevens, it appears, was twice married, *first* to Frances (whose surname is unknown); and *secondly* (in the latter part of October, 1676) to Abigail Kibble, widow of John Kibble, and daughter of the celebrated Stephen Horsey, of Annemessex. That Richard Stevens was a loyal Quaker is attested by his will which contains this emphatic clause: "Item and in case any difference or dispute should arise betwixt any of my three sons herein mentioned about there (their) lands then my will is and I do empower my Overseers whom I shall hereafter mention or any two of friends of meeting of the People called Quakers in this County for to settle and moderate matters in that nature betwixt y^m And whatsoever they shall see meete to order betwixt them shall be as final as if I ware (were) in being myself." Stevens then names as "overseers," to assist his wife, Abigail (named as sole executrix), his "well beloved friends," Richard Waters, Benjamin Cottman, William Kibble, George Truitt and John Truitt. Richard Waters was he whom we have before met as so prominent a member of the Annemessex Meeting of Friends, and George Truitt and John Truitt we shall later meet as members of the Bogerternorton Meeting. Benjamin Cottman (whose religious affiliations we do not know) was a neighbor of Stevens, while William Kibble was Stevens' stepson. Kibble (though we have no evidence to that effect) may also have been a Quaker. We place Richard Stevens as a member of the Monie Meeting because of his evidenced Quakerism and the close proximity of his home to that Meeting. Thus passeth Richard Stevens.[86]

Let us now turn to a consideration of the "meeting place" and "Meeting House" of the Monie Friends Meeting. We make this distinction between "meeting place" and "Meeting House" because during the early years of the life of the Monie Meeting their assemblies for worship were no doubt held in the homes of members (as were the earliest Annemessex Meetings held at the home of Ambrose Dixon), and because we find no reference to the erection of a "Meeting House" in Monie until 1711. We have no positive evidence of the "meeting place" in Monie until 1704, but it is not unlikely that the Quakers in this vicinity met from the first at Levin Denwood's, whose "home place" can today be "located" on the south side of the head of the Great Monie Creek (on the farm now [1934] owned by Grover Ross), about four miles northwest of the town of Princess Anne and about a quarter of a mile south of the so-called Waterloo Bridge (over the head of Monie Creek) at the present Somerset County Alms House (once the beautiful Waggaman mansion). That the first, and principal, "meeting place" of the Monie Quakers was at Levin Denwood's home seems beyond question, though no doubt "meetings" were also held from time to time in the Covington home, on the north side of Great Monie Creek (not far distant below Denwood's), and probably in homes of other members of the Meeting whose names are now lost to us. But in June, 1704, we have positive evidence of a petition that *"the house of Levin Denwood att Mony"* be appointed a "meeting house for the people Called Quakers to worship god in pursuant to an act of Parliament and the good Lawes of this province": and that the petition, granted by Somerset Court, was entered upon record.[37] At this same time, the "house of Richard Waters in Annemessex and the house of George Trewetts upon Pocomoke" were named as "meeting houses" for Quakers in those respective parts. From June, 1704, until the erection of a public Meeting House in Monie in 1711, we know that Levin Denwood's home was the officially licensed place for the Monie Meeting. In the fall of the year 1711, we find record of the erection of a "meeting house":

"At a Court held for Somerset County 29th 9ber [November] 1711 . . . On Motion Made to ye Court By Mr. Samuel Worthington on behalf of Mr. Livin Denwood, Mr Auther (Arthur) Denwood & other of the people Called Quaquers that a house Built by them on Husk Ridge Lying between Wiccomoco & Munny is allowed by this Court to be a Publick Mee(t)ing house for ye People called Quaquers. Entred pr Order Alexn Hall, Clck."[38]

Samuel Worthington, who made this motion before the Somerset Court, was a prominent attorney of the county. "Livin Denwood" we recognize as our old friend, Levin Denwood—dare we say "founder of the Monie Meeting"? Arthur Denwood was the son of Levin, and the first of the Denwood children born after his parents moved to Somerset. We could wish that "& other of the People called Quaquers" had been named; but the record is silent beyond this formal indication that the Denwoods, though apparently leaders in the movement, were not the only ones so interested. This "Publick Meeting house" erected in 1711 evidently remained the Meeting House for Monie until the final termination of this "Meeting." This Meeting House, so erected and "licensed" by the court and "recorded," was situated on an acre of ground back in the woods about midway between Great Monie Creek and Wicomico Creek (the present creek) and about a mile north of Levin Denwood's home. On June 9, 1712, Daniel Jones, of Somerset County, made (for 20 shillings currency) conveyance of this property to Levin Denwood *"containing one acre with all and singular the Houses and appurtenances thereunto be-*

longing ... To have and to hold the said one Acre of Land to him ye s^d Levin Denwood his Heirs and Assigns forever to be a meeting place and Burying place for ye People called Quakers forever ..."
On the same date Daniel Jones made acknowledgment of this conveyance before George Gale and Charles Ballard, two magistrates of Somerset Court; and it was recorded June 17, 1712.[39]

Nearly fourteen years after the above recited conveyance of the Monie Meeting House, we find the trust therein and thereby reposed in Levin Denwood, passed on to other hands and hearts as he passed into the life beyond. In the will of Levin Denwood (dated April 21, 1725, and probated May 9, 1726), we find this significant clause:

"unto my Daughter Betty Gale & Elizabeth Waters Fifteen pounds to be by them disposed off among Friends commonly called Quakers. I also give to the (said) Betty & Eliz & their Heirs & Assigns forever one Acre of Land Lying between Weccocomico & Manny whereon there now is a Quaker Meeting House wth the s^d Meeting House to be kept for that purpose."[40]

Thus Levin Denwood passes the trust so confidently reposed in him to two women. Here we have for the first time in Somerset County's history, the trusteeship of sacred (we dare not say "church") property given into the hands of women! But such practice was in keeping with the tenets of the Society of Friends, and indeed Levin Denwood could not have committed the trust to abler persons. This daughter of his, Madam Betty Gale, was a factor to be reckoned with in Somerset; a woman of splendid executive ability, concerned in large affairs in the administration of a great estate; a veritable regent in the social realm; and the mother of four gifted sons whose ability was not traceable only to their paternal ancestor. Madam Elizabeth Waters (the other "trustee" of the Monie Meeting House) was a close second—if not an equal—to Madam Betty Gale. Born a Littleton—daughter of Southly Littleton, of Accomack, in Virginia—able child of an able race; and widow of Richard Waters, of "Waters River" in Somerset, in Maryland; who was a moving spirit in the later life of the Annemessex Meeting of Friends; and whose home for some years was the officially designated place of their "meeting." And so the Monie Meeting of Friends came into the hands and hearts of Madam Betty Gale and Madam Elizabeth Waters. What a charming bit of history would be the record of their administration of this trust if we but possessed it. We have no record, but imagination will not be denied its dues as we think on this circumstance.

We have no further recorded facts of the Monie Meeting save one. In November, 1746, a question was raised as to the boundaries of a tract of land adjoining the original tract from which was taken the acre on which the Meeting House stood. In depositions then taken, we find reference to "An Antient Quaker meeting house" and to "a low swamp where the Quaker meeting house did stand."

Thus vanishes the glory that was Monie!

*   *   *   *

We journey now to the southeastern section of "Old Somerset," about the headwaters of Pocomoke River, several miles east of the town of Snow Hill, where we find the third of the Somerset Quaker Meetings in existence before the end of the seventeenth century. The date of the formation of Bogerternorton Meeting is not now known, and the first reference to it (so far discovered) is in 1697. From consideration of all circumstances discoverable in regard to this Meeting we have reached the conclusion that its origin was most probably due to the influence of John Goddin and Katherine, his wife, who removed (sometime between 1685 and 1690) to this section from Annemessex.* John Goddin settled at Annemessex sometime during the 1670's and later married Katherine, daughter of George Johnson, a leading spirit of the Annemessex Meeting. In October, 1687, John Goddin obtained a patent for 2,900 acres of land, called "Rochester," on the south side of Pocomoke River, near the head-

---

*There remains of record an intimation that a very early settler in Bogerternorton Hundred was at least possessed of Quaker tendencies. Jenkin Price, one of the very earliest settlers in this region (having come from Accomack County, Virginia, about 1665 appears in a court record of 1667 as "affirming" in a certain matter. Evidently Price had scruples against taking the usual oaths. This, however, is all that we have discovered about Jenkin Price's religious inclinations. He continued to live in this section of the county certainly as late as 1670. There is no evidence of his connection with the Bogerternorton Meeting. It should also be stated that there is no evidence of any relationship between Jenkin Price and Thomas Price, who was one of the original Quaker settlers at Annemessex.[41]

waters thereof. John Goddin and Katherine, his wife, settled, and made their home on this "Rochester" tract somewhat prior to the year 1690. In 1689, George Truitt, who came from Accomack County, Virginia, purchased from Madam Elizabeth Stevens a 600-acre tract of land which he called "Mulberry," being part of a larger tract called "Mulberry Grove." Truitt's "Mulberry" tract is described as adjoining John Goddin's "Rochester" plantation. In 1710, John Goddin sold off a part of his "Rochester" tract to Affradozi Johnson, who, like Truitt, had come from Accomack County, Virginia; and on this land Johnson made his home. "Rochester" and "Mulberry" were situated just south of the headwaters of Pocomoke River and about six to eight miles northeast of Snow Hill Town. The Goddin and Truitt families seem to have formed the nucleus of the Bogerternorton Meeting. Into this Meeting were gathered the Powell family, and later still the family of Affradozi Johnson. Of Goddin's Quaker connection and affiliation there is absolutely no doubt. After his election as a delegate from Somerset County to the Lower House of the Maryland Provincial Assembly in 1692 he was excluded from taking his seat, owing to the fact that he would not take the required oath of office because he was a Quaker.[42] There is no less certainty that Walter Powell and his son, William Powell, were Quakers. Walter Powell arrived in Somerset County from Accomack, in Virginia, about the year 1669 or 1670, purchasing lands called "Greenfield," "Middle" and "Exchange," on the north side of Pocomoke River near its headwaters. Walter Powell lived at "Greenfield," bequeathing this plantation, at his death in 1696/7, to his son, William Powell. William Powell likewise made his home at "Greenfield" and, dying in 1715, devised the plantation to his son, John Powell. Walter Powell directed by his will, dated March 27, 1695, probated February 4, 1696/7, that his body *"be buried in the Quaker burying ground."* William Powell's will, dated April 15, 1715, probated June 22, 1715, requests *"to be buried according to the direction of the Quakers."*[43]

In July, 1689, we find George Truitt (also spelled Truit and Trewett) purchasing from Madam Elizabeth Stevens (widow of Colonel William Stevens) a six-hundred-acre part of the "Mulberry Grove" tract on the south side of Pocomoke River and adjoining John Goddin's and Samuel Davis' lands. George Truitt came to this section about this time, or somewhat earlier, from Accomack County, in

Virginia, and now purchasing this tract of land proceeded to settle and make his home here.[44] Truitt's home seems to have been the center of the "Bogerternorton Meeting"; and he was indeed, as we shall see, the great benefactor of this Meeting.

There remain several interesting items on record relative to this Meeting. The Yearly Meeting of the Society of Friends, held at Tredhaven Creek in Talbot County, 5th 8mo 1697, made inquiry "into estate and welfare of Weekly Meetings belonging to Yearly Meeting," among them the meeting at "Pocotynorton" (one of many variations in spelling the name "Bogerternorton").[45]

Thomas Chalkley, the celebrated Quaker missionary journeying through Somerset County in 1698, enters in his "Journal" that having visited Thomas Evernden's at Annemessex:

"we went to George Truit's at whose house we had a meeting. This Friend and I went to an Indian town not far from his house, because I had a desire to see these people, having never seen any of them before. When we came to the town they were kind to us, spoke well of Friends and said they would not cheat them, as others did. From George Truit's in Maryland we went down to Virginia and in Accomack and Northampton Counties had large meetings . . . (in returning from Virginia) went by the sea side the nearest way to Philadelphia and afterwards I had a meeting at George Truit's brother's and on the first day (Sunday) another near the Court house . . . "[46]

Thomas Story, another Quaker missionary, on his visit to Somerset County about 1699 or 1702/5 records, in his *"Journal,"* making two visits to George Truitt's and holding meetings there.[47]

In June, 1704, *"the house of George Trewetts upon Pocomoke"* was (together with the houses of Richard Waters in Annemessex and Levin Denwood in Monie), upon petition, approved and recorded by the court of Somerset County as a *"meeting house for the people Called Quakers to worship god in pursuant to an act of Parliament and the good Lawes of the province."*[48]

Then at last we come to George Truitt's munificent gift to the "Bogerternorton Meeting." Having thrown himself wholeheartedly into the work of this Quaker Meeting, and living to a good old age, George Truitt, by his will dated August 15, 1720 (probated November 21, 1721), devised to *"the Quakers one acre of land for a burying ground and a meeting house where the burying ground now is; and* *personalty and dwelling house for a meeting place until the meeting house shall be built."*⁴⁹ Of the erection of this intended Meeting House we have no record; but we do not doubt that it was finally constructed at the location directed for it in Truitt's will. Though the records do not afford us the information we should like to have in regard to this building, yet through the years the spot hallowed by the burying of the Quaker dead has remained in the tradition of the community. In 1867, reference is made to this burying ground in Neill's *Terra Mariæ*. Referring to George Truitt's residence as having been not very far from the town of Snow Hill (in Worcester County, which was up until 1742 a part of Somerset), Doctor Neill writes: "There still exists [1867] an old Quaker graveyard about five miles above that place [Snow Hill] on the road that leads to Berlin." Doctor Littleton P. Bowen, in his *Days of Makemie*, wrote in 1885, "A hill between Snow Hill and Berlin is called the 'old Quaker Burying Ground' ... " The hallowed spot is still pointed out in this year of our Lord 1933.⁵⁰

We leave the Bogerternorton Meeting at this point; not having attempted to trace its history further. Though it probably had a longer life than the Annemessex and Monie Meetings, we do not believe that as a "Meeting" its continuance was beyond the middle of the eighteenth century, if that long.⁵¹

* * * *

Before concluding our study of the Quaker element in the "foundations" of "Old Somerset," we cannot forbear commenting upon a report of the Sheriff of Somerset County in 1697, in which he states that of Quakers and their meeting houses in Somerset: *"none as I know of particularly."* The Governor and Council of Maryland on August 10, 1697, ordered the Sheriffs of the several counties in the province to return a list of Roman Catholic priests and lay brothers resident in their respective counties and of their churches, chapels and places of worship, and also make a like return about Quakers and other Dissenters from the Church of England. The Sheriff of Somerset, in making his return on this order of the Governor and Council, writes of his county: "Here are neither Popish Priests, Lay Brothers nor any of their Chapels. As to the Quakers and other Dissenters, *to the first, none as I know of particularly.*"

We have produced evidence of Quaker Meetings in Somerset County at this specific period—three of them, Annemessex, Monie and Bogerternorton. How then may we reconcile this statement of the Sheriff of Somerset County with the facts which we have related? We would quote an item from the late Reverend Ethan Allen, D.D., which seems to us to reconcile these conflicting statements. Doctor Allen first quotes the inquiry made by Tredhaven Yearly Meeting on 5th 8mo 1697, into estate and welfare of Weekly Meetings at Monnye [Monie], Annemessex and Pocatynorton [Bogerternorton], among others, and then adds: "Apparent discrepancies between returns of the Sheriffs and this list of weekly meetings may possibly be explained by the fact that some of these meetings were held in private houses, which some of the Sheriffs may not have considered as embraced in the order of Council, while others included them in their returns." We think this explanation offered by Doctor Allen not only a possible, even a probable one, but, in so far as it bears upon the conflict between the Somerset County Sheriff's statement and the actual facts, the correct solution of the problem presented. The Monie Meeting House was not erected until about 1711, and the house for the Bogerternorton Meeting had not been built prior to August, 1720 (the date of George Truitt's will). The Monie and Bogerternorton Meetings were certainly being held prior to 1711 and 1720, respectively, in private houses. There was certainly a Meeting House in Annemessex prior to 1687 when we have record that Ambrose Dixon and his daughter, Mrs. Elizabeth Dukes, were buried there. (See *ante* page 91). Had the Annemessex Meeting House disappeared by 1697 or 8, when the sheriff of Somerset made his return; and were the Annemessex Quakers again holding their Meetings in the homes of members? This seems most probably the case. Certainly by 1704 (see ante pages 91, 104 and 108) Annemessex, Monie and Bogerternorton were holding Meetings in the homes of Richard Waters, Levin Denwood and George Truitt, respectively. For these reasons we believe that the Sheriff of Somerset did not consider that Quaker Meetings held in private homes were embraced by the order commanding him to make return on the houses of worship of Roman Catholics, Quakers and other Dissenters from the Church of England.[52]

* * * *

So we bring "to an end as a tale that is told" the story of Quakerism in "Old Somerset." "Three score years and ten," possibly into its fourth score of years, the life of Friends' Meetings in Somerset lasted. The passing of the old order, and numberless defections from the faith among the new, added but labour and sorrow to the valiant remnant which "soon passed away and was gone."

2. VOICE OF THE PEOPLE

1

Earliest remaining record of a Baptism in Somerset, 1669—The grand jury of Somerset Court, March, 1671/2, renders "opinion" that regular religious services should be held in the county—Four places designated—Religious affiliations of grand jurymen rendering the "opinion," and of members of the court to whom it was rendered—Locations of preaching places in Pocomoke, Annemessex, Manokin and Wicomico Hundreds—Robert Maddock, preacher—Benjamin Salisbury, Morgan Jones, Robert Richardson and David Richardson.

DURING the first ten years of the life of the Manokin-Annemessex settlement on "the Eastern Shore of the Proince of Maryland below Choptank River"—established in 1662 and created in county form as Somerset in 1666—there is no evidence whatsoever of any provision for regular religious ministrations among the settlers, other than the Quaker Meeting at Annemessex.

From the very beginning, we find Quakers and Church of England men and their families; and doubtless, if we could but identify them, an element in the population strongly influenced by contact with Congregationalism from New England, for there seems to have been constant passing back and forth between the Eastern Shore of Virginia (from which the first settlers of Manokin-Annemessex in Maryland came) and the colonies in New England.

By 1670 there was an abundance of Quakers and Church of England men and a sprinkling of Presbyterians and we know not how many touched by Congregationalism; but prior to this date we have not discovered the name of a single *resident* ordained minister of the Gospel in this area. In fact, a very close study of remaining local and provincial records reveals the name of only one "minister of the Word and Sacraments" as recordedly connected in any way with Old Somerset prior to November, 1671, when Robert Maddock (or Maddox, as his name is most often spelled) first appears on the records.

This one instance is interesting indeed. There was a man named Edmund Lum (his patronymic spelled variously Lum, Lunn and Lunne) who appeared in the Manokin section of "the Eastern Shore below Choptank River" settlement as early as January, 1664/5. From the ancient register of "births, marriages and deaths," which no modern simplified numerical system of classification can rob of its honored title of "Liber I K L" of Somerset Court, we ascertain the fact that

"Elizabeth Lum ye daughter of Edward Lum was borne att Manokin ye seaventent day of January Anno domini one Thousand six hundred sixty foure (1664/5)."

Then from the same source we draw the record that

Elizabeth Lum ye daughter of Edward Lum *was baptized by Mr. George Moonerow ye* eight and twentieth day of November Anno Domini one Thousand six hundred sixty nine."

Here certainly we have "a minister of the Sacraments" in this "Mr. George Moonerow." But did he come on a brief pilgrimage to Somerset County (as it was in 1669); or was this child, Elizabeth Lum, on a journey away from home with her parents when the baptism took place? It has been suggested that maybe a grave emergency had arisen and "believing parents" had lay baptism administered to their child; though this we hardly think possible—not to say probable—for a "believing parent" would have baptized the child himself. But *"Mr. George Moonerow,"* who administered Holy Baptism to the four-year-old Elizabeth Lum (born in Manokin and the child of Manokin parents) is as much a "human mystery" as his act is a "Divine Mystery." We know not who he was, whence he came, nor what "order of ministry" was his. We do not even venture to assert from the basis of the scant record that he was ever on Somerset soil. We simply give the record as it stands, of his having baptized a Somerset County child in the year 1669, and of the entry of the record of that act in the Somerset County official register. We may indeed have imaginings about this matter, but we have no evidence beyond the record.[1]

We have this single reference to "Mr. George Moonerow's" connection with the religious life of this area in 1669. Then, too, there is a tradition (nothing more) that Parson Teackle, rector of Hungars and St. George's Parishes, in Northampton and Accomack Counties in Virginia, "kept in touch" with the English Churchmen who came from his parishes into this Maryland settlement; and of this "Teackle tradition" we shall hear more later on.[2] But there is absolutely no evidence that there was a resident minister of the Church of England in this area prior to the year 1680;[3] while the Presbyterians certainly cannot claim the resident presence of an ordained minister in Somerset until the arrival of Makemie and Traill late in 1682 or early in 1683.[4]

The period of 1664/5 marked notable increase by immigration in the population of this "Eastern Shore" of Maryland settlement. From this time there was steady growth in numbers and consequent expansion of population through the territorial area. Such increase and expansion unquestionably had grave bearings on the religious and moral needs of the community, as well as upon its economic, civil and military life.

As we scan the remaining records, we can, in imagination, see the full inflowing tide of immigration extending the limits of the settlement. No longer are the confines of settlement marked by "Manokin" and "Annemessex"; but "Pocomoke," "the Monies," "Wicomico," "Nanticoke," come before us frequently—with the section referred to "as the sea side"—as the infant Somerset begins to exercise itself. As we follow the names of the rapidly immigrating settlers we can easily trace strains of English, Scotch, Welsh and Irish blood mingling in the veins of this new life. We find increasing contacts with the "outside world," and discover enlarging numbers of planters, merchants, traders and tradesmen; even a sprinkling of men of the professions—"chirurgeons," "attorneys," "surveyors," a "teacher" or two (after a fashion). "All sorts and conditions of men" are here gathered together in settlements; and yet—"no minister of the Word and Sacraments."[5] Only were the Quakers adequately provided for in the matter of religious ministration. Certainly the "other than Quakers"—of whom there was an abundance—had "spiritual needs." We turn page by page the ancient records—a decade of this new life passes—and yet no "shepherd for the fold."

Then, as we turn the fast fading pages of the ancient court ledger, there comes to us from the early spring of the year 1672 (late 1671/2), the most singular and impressive record of "the opinion" of the Grand Jury of Somerset County that the "Word of God" should be regularly "taught" by sermon, appointing four places (homes of planters) as preaching stations, and expressing a "desire" as to the man who should so minister "the Word." We shall let this imperishable record speak for itself:

"At a Court held for Somersett County the 12th day of March in the XXXXth years of the Dominion of the R^t hon^{ble} Cælius ^{etc} Annoq Domini 1671 before his Lopp^s Justices thereunto assigned & Authorized

	Mr William Stevens	Mr John Winder	
Present	Mr Henry Smith	Mr George Johnson	Comm^{rs}
	Mr James Jones	Capt Wm Colebourne	

The rules of the Co^{rt} being read & the Co^{rt} Setting the Sheriffe presents his grand Jury of Enquest who are sworne vizt

	David Brown, fforeman	Alexander Draper	
	Robert Hart	Peter Dowtey	
	Marcum Thomas	Robert Houlstone	
	Tho: Covington	Thos Davis, Carpente^r	
	James Dashiell	Thomas Roe	
Grand Jurymen	Beniamin Cottman	Cornelius Johnson	grand Jurymen
	Levin Denwood	John Bossman	
	Richard Ackworth	John Williams	
	John Dorman, coop(er)	Richard Tull	
	Wm Woodgate	Philip Askew	
	Richard Davis		

The grand Jury having rec^d their Chardge goe from the board. The grand Jury returne & being agreed in their presentments which they give in writing and is read vizt^6 . . . [and following the presentments is this item]

It is the opinion of us Grand Jurors That sermon Shoulld be taught in ffoure severall places in the County (vizt) one the first Sunday at the house of Mr William Stevens at Pocomoke one the second Sunday at the house of Daniell Curtis in Anamessicks one the third Sunday at the house of Christopher Nutter in Manoakin And one the fourth Sunday at the house of Thomas Roe at Wiccocomoco. And it our desire that Mr Matix shoulld here preach.

David Brown fforeman."[7]

* * * *

In this action of the Grand Jury of Somerset Court, March, 1671/2, we have declaration of "opinion" of the necessity for the regular preaching of the Word of God throughout the county, by a legally constituted authority charged with inquiring into matters pertaining to the moral welfare of a community. Such an "opinion" rendered by such an authority we have indeed; but there is more than this. Through this declaration of opinion—and the provisions for making it effective—we have the voiced consciousness of the spiritual needs of the community—the voice of the people, crying out, as it were, a deep sense of need through the mouth of the duly constituted "wardens of welfare." This "opinion" may indeed have been formulated behind the closed door of the jury room; but the stuff of which it was made had been borne in on the winds of public sentiment from field and forest and river-way, great house and humble cabin, of the county. This is indeed the finest expression that has come down to us in the annals of Somerset history of the people's loyalty to the true and deep spiritual need of their community; and we doubt that this record can be duplicated in American colonial history—of colony or province—for it is not the voice of an "established form of religion" but the voice of a people left free as to choice in such matters.[8]

In view of the deep, abiding significance of this action of the Somerset Grand Jury; an analysis will not be amiss in regard to religious affiliation and location of residence of the court who received this "opinion" and the grand jurymen who rendered it.

Of the "Court," his honor, William Stevens (presiding magistrate), Henry Smith and John Winder, were Church of England men.[9] James Jones and George Johnson were Quakers, and William Coulbourne (though probably a "liberal Churchman"), was certainly deeply in sympathy with the tenets of Quakerism. Of the grand jurymen, David Brown, the foreman, was a Scotch Presbyterian; Levin Denwood was a Quaker, while Robert Hart and Alexander Draper were—if not actually Quakers—markedly in sympathy with that expression of faith. James Dashiell, Benjamin Cottman, John Bossman, Richard Ackworth, Thomas Tull and Philip Askew were Church of England men. Of the remaining ten grand jurors, we cannot even hazard a guess as to their religious affiliations or predilections.

Now for the "territorial distribution" of the members of this court and grand jury. Stevens lived at "Rehoboth" on Pocomoke River; Henry Smith in the upper fork of Manokin River (just south of the river); James Jones lived on the west side of Wicomico River (just opposite the mouth of the present Wicomico Creek, his plantation being immediately along the river); John Winder lived on the north side of Cutmaptico Creek (north of the then Wicomico River [now Creek] and east of the *present* Wicomico River, at the present time [1934] in Wicomico County); George Johnson lived near the headwaters (and on the south side) of the Great Annemessex River; while William Coulbourne lived south of Coulbourne's Creek, near the mouth of the Great Annemessex. So much for the residences of the members of the Court.

The grand jurymen were equally well "distributed territorially." David Brown, John Bossman, Richard Ackworth and John Dorman lived on the north side of Manokin River, on lands from Goose Creek to the headwaters of the river. Robert Hart and Alexander Draper lived to the south side of Annemessex River and immediately west of Hart's (now Jones') Creek; Richard Tull, near Marumsco Creek (or on Annemessex River?); Robert Houlstone, on the south side of Pocomoke River at the point where the Maryland-Virginia boundary line strikes a due east course; Benjamin Cottman lived on the north side of what is now Wicomico Creek; Thomas Roe (or Row), on the east side of Wicomico River, immediately north of Dashiell's Creek; James Dashiell lived on Wetipquin Creek, a tributary of Nanticoke River (and now in Wicomico County); Levin Denwood, on the south side of Great Monie Creek (near the headwaters); Thomas Covington, to the north of Great Monie; Cornelius Johnson, on lands near Monie Bay; Philip Askew, in the neighborhood of Passadike Creek (a branch of the *then* Wicomico River, now Creek); and Richard Davis, on the south side of Back Creek. While we cannot state definitely the location of the residences of Peter Dowtey (also spelled Douty) and Marcum Thomas, it is probable that Dowtey was living at that time near Little Monie Creek and Thomas doubtless lived in the neighborhood of the headwaters of Pocomoke River (on the north side). We have not been able to locate the "home places" of William Woodgate, John Williams and Thomas Davis, carpenter, at the time of this notable grand jury service. As there was diversity of religious "denominationalism" and utter absence of territorial "sectionalism" in the composition of this grand jury; so we find that its membership was drawn from all classes in the population, from men of wealth and highest social position down to the simplest farmer and tradesman.

Having analyzed the court and grand jury "religiously" and "territorially," let us now locate the homes of the four worthies named by the grand jury as places at which *"Sermon Should be taught"* successively on four Sundays in the month.

Let us say, first, that the homes of the men thus chosen and named as "preaching stations" for this evangelistic adventure, were (as we shall see from descriptions of the places which follow) centrally located in relation to the areas of population which this preaching was intended to reach. Moreover, these four homes were located on principal waterways into which led various creek tributaries, so that boats (a common means of travel in this section during the early days) could be used by people coming from greater distances and who did not travel by road, or who found the former method of travel more convenient and expeditious.

The first of the "preaching stations" named was *"the house of William Stevens at Pocomoke."* Of course this was the home of his honor, William Stevens, the presiding magistrate of the court at the session of March, 1671/2. That the house is described as being *"at Pocomoke"* is designation of it as in Pocomoke Hundred. William Stevens' home was "Rehoboth," on Pocomoke River, a name apparently given by him to his home plantation with full recognition of the Biblical significance of the word—"roominess" or "room for all." Stevens, though a Church of England man (as can be proved), was a pronounced "religious liberal," in the sense that he was generously and genuinely sympathetic (as we shall later see) towards any sincere expression of the Christian faith.[10] "Rehoboth," the home of William Stevens and the place designated by the grand jury as the first of these "preaching stations," was located on the west side of Pocomoke River (immediately on the river), in the southern part of Somerset County, just about a mile northeast of the later (1686) town of Rehoboth; at this present time the village and post office of Rehoboth, Maryland.[11]

The second of these "preaching stations" was designated as *"the house of Daniell Curtis in Annamessicks [i. e. Annemessex Hundred]."* Daniel Curtis' home was located on the north side of Annemessex River, about a half mile east of Swanny Creek, also called in olden times Tull's Creek, and at this present time "Hall's Creek" (?). The tract of land on which Daniel Curtis lived in March, 1671/2, was in his day made up from portions of tracts known (from their patent names) as "Armstrong's Purchase" and "Armstrong's Lott" and "commonly knowne by the name of Scipers [Skipper's?] plantation." This "home site" of Daniel Curtis in March, 1671/2 is at this present time (1934) included in the farm of Mr. Cameron, east of the village of Upper Fairmount.

We come now to the third mentioned of these "preaching stations," which was designated as *"at the house of Christopher Nutter in Manoakin."* At the date of the grand jury's rendering its "opinion," in March, 1671/2, Christopher Nutter was living on a tract called "Nutter's Purchase," on the west and north sides of Manoakin River very near its headwaters. This location is, in this year of Lord 1934, discoverable in a tract of land to the west and north of Manokin River as it winds through the town of Princess Anne. The easternmost section of this original "Nutter's Purchase" tract is within the present northern limits of Princess Anne, and on this portion of the land is the Manokin Presbyterian Church with its surrounding "God's Acre," and St. Andrew's Cemetery. Somewhere in this immediate vicinity—we cannot be more definite—stood *"the house of Christopher Nutter in Manoakin."* It is interesting to note that this immediate vicinity seems in all probability to have been the scene of religious services for an almost unbroken period of two hundred and sixty-two years (1671/2-1934). Certainly very near was *"the house of Christopher Nutter in Manoakin"*—somewhere on the tract of 300 acres of "Nutter's Purchase," on a small parcel of which now stands Manokin Presbyterian Church. "Mr Matix," who was chosen by the grand jury of March, 1671/2, to preach at Nutter's house on the third Sunday of each month, preached certainly until March, 1674/5; maybe somewhat later. By 1685 the Reverend Thomas Wilson, first pastor of the Manokin Presbyterian congregation, was settled in Somerset, living on a farm about two miles south of the present town of Princess Anne. In 1697, we have the record that the Presbyterians had a meeting house at Manokin. How much earlier than 1697 this house of worship had been erected we have not discovered. Can we doubt that with a pastor settled in their midst in 1686 this congregation (which was a comparatively large one) was long in erecting a church building of some kind or fashion? Then age by age, since Thomas Wilson first came to Manokin, a Presbyterian congregation has worshipped on this ground. We have not an "unbroken title" with which to support this lengthy claim of religious services on this spot; but circumstances seem to justify the belief that here, from the year 1671/2 to the present day—with the exception of the ten-year period, 1674/5-1686 (from the disappearance of "Mr. Matix" until the arrival of Mr. Wilson) this has been a spot hallowed by religious services.[13]

And now for the location of the fourth, and last, of these grand jury selected places for monthly preaching—*"the house of Thomas Roe at Wiccomoco [i. e. in Wicomico Hundred]."* We have been able to trace Roe's home place in March, 1671/2, to a tract of 500 acres on the east side of Wicomico River extending from the mouth of Dashiell's Creek (on the south) north on the river. Thomas Roe bought this place from James Dashiell in November, 1670, and continued in possession of the river side part thereof—the part of the tract on which his plantation houses stood—until June, 1675, when he conveyed the place to Thomas Walker. In this present year (1934), we can locate this fourth preaching station as on the east side of Wicomico River just north of Dashiell's Creek, and about a mile south of where the present Wicomico Creek enters the river. Thomas Roe's plantation of 1671/2 is at this time (1934) included in lands belonging to the estate of the late Daniel W. White.[14]

Thus today, more than two and a half centuries since the memorable action of Somerset County's Grand Jury of March, 1671/2, in rendering an opinion *"that sermon Shoulld be taught in ffour severall places in the County"*—specifically designating them—we can with certainty locate the four sacred sites—veritable "Stations of the Cross"; for is not the preaching of the Word—the Gospel of the blessed God in very truth—to "preach Christ Crucified"?

It would be interesting to know something of the services held at the specified places on four successive Sundays in the month as recommended by the Grand Jury of Somerset in March, 1671/2. No further record, though, seems to remain of this remarkable evangelistic adventure. This absence of record does not prevent, however, the belief that Sunday after Sunday, at Stevens' house at Pocomoke, Curtis' in Annemessex, Nutter's in Manokin, and Roe's at Wicomico—at each in succession as directed—the Gospel was fully preached by "Mr. Matix," and that the planters and other settlers with their families in these respective regions gave of their best in encouragement of this religious work.

Remaining records reveal, as we have seen, considerable information relative to the officials of "Old Somerset" who were the means by which this general spiritual need assumed concrete form, thereby becoming the channel through which the adventure was launched. There is no lack of data relative to the locations of the homes of the four planters designated as preaching stations in this work. Yet research in the ancient documentary sources has failed to disclose more than a few facts in regard to "Mr. Matix," who, it was the expressed desire of the grand jury, should conduct this undertaking.

The conclusion of the jury's recommendation in regard to these preaching services in "Old Somerset" reads very simply: *"And it is desire that Mr. Matix should here preach."*[15]

This is our introduction to the prophet who was charged with making straight paths for the Prince of Peace through the wilderness of rugged frontier souls. "Mr. Matix"—who was he?—what of him? In the first place, whoever he may have been, he must indeed have been a man of stalwart Christian faith and character; a man commanding profound respect from his fellow human beings in order to have been desired to undertake such a mission. We have not been able to discover when this man actually first came into the settlement and there remains no recorded transaction showing that he owned any property in Somerset. There is no conveyance of land either to or by him in the remaining records of the county, and no indication that he possessed any personal property. We have discovered no evidence of wife or children, or of any other bond of human connection for him in Somerset. This man's name appears in the records only in connection with his work and office in ministering in the things of the Gospel. Various references to him in this capacity show, however, that his baptismal name was *Robert* and that his surname was variously spelled *Matix, Madock, Maddock, Maddocks, Madox* and *Maddox:* seventeen times as *Maddock* and eighteen times as *Maddox;* once each as *Matix, Madock* and *Maddocks;* and four times as *Madox*. From this variety in the spelling of the man's surname we are almost tempted to wonder what in actuality the name was; though the preponderance in references certainly gives it to Maddox, with Maddock a close second. We have no reference in records, and no tradition (worthy the name), as to this man's "orders of ministry." He is designated as "clerke" or "clarke" and once as "minister." He has been claimed as "Presbyterian"; he has been claimed as "Church of England" (probably in deacon's orders); and it has been suggested that he might have been a "Congregationalist." No evidence whatsoever has been found in this matter of his "orders." He certainly was not a Quaker, for he officiated in the capacity of minister at marriages. In fact, the only times he is referred to in the remaining Somerset County records (with the exception of the one time that he was chosen as "county evangelist") is as officiating at marriages—forty-two marriages in all. This man's other acts and deeds in Christ's name and for Christ's sake, though unrecorded in the perishable materials of earth, doubtless found record in imperishable terms in the spiritual fabric of the lives which he touched through his ministry; and certainly in the "Lamb's Book of Life."

The first recorded appearance of this man on the records of Somerset was in November, 1671, when he officiated as "Robert Maddox, Clarke" at the marriage of Richard Partridge and Margaret Lee. His last appearance in the records was March, 1674/5, when he officiated as "Robert Maddox" at the marriage of William Loudridge and Katherine Jones.

Like Melchizedek of old, this man simply appears—and disappears; and we should like to believe that, as Melchizedek's, so was his blessing—the blessing of peace.

In passing it may be of interest to note that Robert Maddox (to give the name the form most frequently used in the records) was ministering in Somerset at the time of the visit of George Fox, the great Quaker, to the county in the late winter of 1672/3. No doubt Maddox's simple ministry truly prepared the hearts of the people for the preaching of "the one who was greater than he"; and we trust that the very great man's preaching proved an easing of the rugged way for the constant shepherd of the fold who must labor on in days that followed.

The official register of births, deaths and marriages in "Old Somerset": "Liber I K L" of Somerset Court,[16] which discloses facts of such vital interest in regard to Robert Maddox (or Maddock) gives us also fleeting glimpses of several other ministers hurriedly crossing this scene of affairs. In January, 1673/4, the name of "Benjamin Salisbury, Clarke" appears as officiating at the marriage of William Howard and Mary Hobday. This is the only appearance which we have found recorded in the Somerset records of Mr. Salisbury. In 1678, there appears one "Morgan Jones, Minister," officiating at the marriage of Alexander Thomas and Cecill Shaw. Strangely, the record of the marriage of this couple is twice entered in old "Liber I K L"—in both entries only the year of the marriage is given (without month or day). Only this once have we found the name of "Morgan Jones, Minister," in the remaining records of "Old Somerset." Salisbury, it will be noted, makes his appearance during the time that Robert Maddox was resident in Somerset, while Morgan Jones' appearance was not until at least three years after the disappearance of Maddox's name from the records. Then in the year 1679, on November 9th, we pick up our first reference to another minister, "Mr. David Richardson," as officiating at the marriage of James Sangster and Mary Benston. Between this date, November 9, 1679, and September, 1689, David Richardson appears as officiating at marriages eighteen times and is designated variously as "minister," "minister of the gospell," and "clarke." Then we have another of this surname appearing in the records as officiating at two marriages: "Mr. Robert Richardson, Minister." One of these marriages, that of George Benson and Anne Roberts, took place in May, 1682; while the other, the marriage of William Henderson to Sarah Bishop was celebrated in August, 1684. After this "Mr. Robert Richardson, Minister," disappears from the records.[17]

Here we have the names of four men appearing on the Somerset County records between 1673/4 and 1689—Salisbury, Jones, David Richardson and Robert Richardson—and described as "ministers," "ministers of the gospell" and "clarkes"; and yet there is no indication as to the nature of their "orders of ministry"—through or by what succession, church or sect they were ordained. So far we have not been able to discover what became of Salisbury, Jones and Robert Richardson after the disappearance of their names from the Somerset County records, nor have we discovered from whence they came to "Old Somerset."

Of "Mr. David Richardson, Minister," we have, however, more detailed information as to his life in Somerset, finding that he remained here until death overtook him in the year 1696. On March 10, 1681/2, as "David Richardson, Minister," this man purchased of Captain Henry Smith (for 7,000 pounds of tobacco) a tract of 500 acres of land called "Wiltshire"; and on September 18, 1682, as "David Richardson, Clarke," he purchased from Colonel William

Stevens (for 10,000 pounds of tobacco) 500 acres of land called "Weymouth." Both of these tracts are described as being on the seaboard side at a place called Boquetenorton (Bogerternorton) in Somerset County, and as on Boquetenorten Bay. Richardson continued to hold these lands throughout his lifetime, disposing of them by will to his two sons. While the parties who were married by Richardson lived in various sections of Somerset County, it is evident that the minister himself lived on a plantation on Bogerternorton Bay on the "seaboard side," in the southeastern section of Somerset (now Worcester) County. Of Richardson's exercise of his ministry, beyond the various marriages which he celebrated (the last appearing in the old register under date of September, 1689), we have no record, though we doubt not that he traveled about the county holding services and preaching. Toward the end of his life he tragically gained unsavory prominence. At a court held for Somerset County, March 15, 1692/3, David Richardson was presented by the grand jury "for being drunk at his own house at Bogotee Norton upon the Seaventh of March 1692/3." On June 14, 1693, Robert Pirrie gave bond for £15 sterling for "Mr. David Richardson, Minister's" appearance at next court to answer to charges against him.

On September 13, 1693, the court heard the case (on the foregoing presentment of the grand jury) of "David Richardson of this County, Cl'k, for that the said David of the seventh day of March afores[d] at the house of him the said David in Bogotonorton Hundred in the County afores[d] then and there with drinking became drunk to ye evil example of others..." Judgment of the court against Richardson was prayed by the clerk of presentments, one Peter Dent. The conclusion of the matter, fully set forth in the court's order, was to the effect that "No evidence appearing against the said Richardson the Court orders the action to be dismist & Orders that Robert Pirrie pay all fees." In view of this action of the court, one of two things is evident: either "an enemy had done this"—sown seed of scandal against the man; or else when the charge against him in the indictment came up to the court for trial, an intervening spirit of charity restrained "evidence." This indictment, and the dismissal of the action by the court because of "No evidence appearing," is the only time that there is any intimation of any delinquency on the part of Richardson.[18] In this connection we should like to add that, during the whole course of our study of the old court records, this is the only instance (prior to the year 1700) that we have discovered of any charge resting against a minister of the Gospel in "Old Somerset."

With the few facts which we have been able to present in regard to Robert Maddox (or Maddock), Benjamin Salisbury, Morgan Jones and the Richardsons, we bring to a conclusion the study of that period in the early religious life of Somerset County before there was any apparent attempt at organizing regular congregations among the people, other than the Quaker Meetings. The appearances of Benjamin Salisbury and Morgan Jones were indeed fleeting ones. Robert Maddox and David Richardson (whose "orders of ministry" are not known), together with John Huett (of the Church of England), who arrived about 1680, with Makemie, Traill, Wilson and Davis (of the Presbyterian Church), who came between 1682-1685, carried forward the religious life in "Old Somerset" to the day of regularly organized congregations of the Church of England and the Presbyterian Church.

3. OF ANCIENT AND APOSTOLIC LINEAGE

❡

The Church of England in Somerset—Early Churchmen—Liberal type of Churchmanship—Earliest remaining records of Burial, Baptism and Marriage, according to the rites and ceremonies of the Church of England—Captain Thomas Walker's bequest in May, 1680—John Huett, first resident clergyman of the Church of England in Somerset—Organization of the church in Somerset under the Assembly's Act of 1692 establishing the Church of England in the province of Maryland—Parishes of Somerset, Coventry, Stepney and Snow Hill created—Time and places designated by the court for first election of vestries—Members of the first vestries—Parish Churches erected—Trotter, rector of Stepney and Somerset, and Brechin, rector of Coventry.

IT IS incontrovertible that adherents to the Church of England—"Churchmen" tried and true—came into the Manokin section of this Eastern Shore of Maryland settlement at the very beginning. When, late in the Fall of 1661 or early Spring of 1662, the Manokin section of this settlement was made, "Churchmen" were first on the ground. Randall Revell and John Elzey, the two resident members of the commission named for establishing settlements in this area, were, with their families, adherents of the Church of England. So, no doubt, were the majority at least of the first planters at Manokin, and the white indentured servants brought in by them. "In the beginning" we find Randall Revell, John Elzey, Nicholas Fountain (or Fontaine), William Furniss, Thomas Poole, George Mitchell, who were "Churchmen." Doubtless we may number among "Churchmen" Anthony and Mary Johnson and their family,—the "free negroes," first of their race and kind to appear in this area. The parties just named were all settled in Manokin by May, 1662. The year 1663 brought William Thorne and William Bosman to Manokin—officials and "Churchmen"; while between 1663 and 1666 came Roger Woolford, Charles Ballard, James Barnabe (or Barnaby), Philip Barré (or Berry), John Nelson, John Panter, George Downes, George Betts, Gideon Tillman and Richard Ackworth—"Churchmen." About the Monies, the Ingrams, Wallers, Cornelius Johnson and William Jones settled; and on the Wicomico River (or very near by) David Spence, James Dashiell, John Winder, Thomas Shiall and Daniel Haste. On the Pocomoke were William Stevens and Donnock Dennis. Others who came into the sections mentioned may have been "Churchmen"—those whom we have mentioned were unquestionably such. Somewhat later the Breretons, Askews and Cottmans, settling to the north and south of Wicomico (now the Creek), came with their "Churchmanship."

"In the beginning" the Quaker hue of Annemessex was untouched by any "shadow of conformity"; but such a shadow did at last cast itself upon this section in the persons of John Rhodes, Charles Hall, John Roach, Cornelius Ward, Thomas Tull, Richard Tull and Edmund Beauchamp.

There is a singular matter of record in regard to religious life and practice in the Beauchamp household which, in passing, we cannot forbear relating. Sarah, wife of Edmund Beauchamp (the first clerk of Somerset County), was a daughter of Ambrose Dixon, the uncompromising rebel Quaker, or Quaker rebel—"as you like it." Edmund Beauchamp and Sarah Dixon were married in Annemessex, June 11, 1668, by the relentless non-conformist and genius of religious dissent, Stephen Horsey, who was a magistrate in the settlement. This estimable lady, Mrs. Edmund Beauchamp, was born and bred in the heaviest atmosphere of rebellion against conformity to anything in the religious life savoring of a sacramental nature. And yet it was thought worthy of record in the register of births, marriages and burials (Liber I K L of Somerset Court) that Mrs. Sarah Beauchamp (wife of Edmund Beauchamp) and her three oldest children, Thomas, Alice and Edmund Beauchamp, Junior, were *baptized*. Mrs. Beauchamp and her infant son, Thomas (then about four months old) were baptized in April, 1671; Alice Beauchamp (before the first month of her life was concluded) was baptized in May, 1674,* and Edmund Beauchamp, Junior (at about the age of seven months), was baptized in July, 1677.[1] Mrs. Beauchamp's baptism was indeed "adult baptism," for the lady was born certainly as early as 1652/4 and was at least in the 16th or 18th year of age at the time of her baptism. This is the least in years that we feel that we may assign to her as wife and mother, though neither marriage nor motherhood in this early day stood upon the "ceremony of age." The three Beauchamp children were mere infants at the respective times of their baptisms. There is no intimation in the record of the name of the minister who officiated at the baptisms of the four Beauchamps. The

---

*Benjamin Salisbury, Clerke, was in Somerset County in January, 1673/4. He may have been there as late as May, 1674, and hence "the baptizer" of Alice Beauchamp.

first three of these baptisms may, of course, have been at the hand of Robert Maddox (or Maddock)—the Somerset County "evangelist"—whose religious affiliations we do not know; though hardly the last—for Maddox's name disappears from the records of Somerset two years and five months before Edmund Beauchamp, Junior, was baptized in July, 1677. Duly considering the matter, we are inclined to think that Mrs. Beauchamp and her three children, recorded as baptized in 1671, 1674 and 1677, probably received baptism at the hands of a minister of the Church of England. There was, it is true, no minister of the Church of England resident in Somerset County at the respective dates of these baptisms; but it is possible that some minister of this Church who was passing through the county may have administered baptism to these members of the Beauchamp household. There is, however, a much more tenable theory in regard to these Beauchamp baptisms. Immediately south of the Maryland-Virginia boundary line—and thus immediately south of Old Somerset County—was Accomack County in Virginia, where the Reverend Thomas Teackle was rector of St. Georges' Parish from 1662 to 1694. Though there is no "record evidence" to that effect, there is a tradition that the Reverend Mr. Teackle ministered to members of the Church of England in Somerset before the days in which there was any resident minister of this Church in the county. Mr. Teackle had been in Northampton (later Accomack) in Virginia since 1652. Nearly every man, woman and child who came as "first settlers" into the area which became Somerset County, was known to Mr. Teackle; for all of the "first settlers" (with four or five notable exceptions) came from "Northampton (otherwise called Accomack) in Virginia." There was unquestionably a strong Church of England element in the first settlement of Somerset; an element strengthened by each succeeding wave of immigration. The Somerset County settlements were reasonably accessible to Accomack owing to the wonderful waterway course of travel of the Bay and rivers; and the distance was not great. A glance at the map of the Eastern Shore of Maryland and Virginia shows this. The tradition that from time to time worthy Parson Teackle visited "Churchmen" in Somerset is not at all unreasonable. It is well within probability that Mrs. Beauchamp and her three children received the sacrament of Holy Baptism according to the rite of the Church of England and at the hand of the Reverend

Mr. Teackle. Doubtless we are on treacherous ground in thus appearing to try to force baptism according to the form of the Church of England on the heads of long dead and thus defenceless Beauchamps. This may be special pleading. We can almost hear old Ambrose Dixon and Stephen Horsey bitingly rebuke us: "Much ado about nothing"! However, the Beauchamp baptisms stand, and we believe they stand as a witness to baptism according to the ministration of that sacrament of the Gospel as set forth by the Church of England.[3]

Before passing on to consider the detail of facts in regard to the growth and development of the Church of England in Somerset, it may be well to remind ourselves that there is every indication that the "Churchmanship" (technically speaking) of Church of England people in Somerset in the earliest days (and before the "establishment" by law of this Church in the province in 1692) was of a liberal, tolerant type—in keeping with the spirit of early Maryland as a proprietary province. It was a type of "Churchmanship" best described as absolutely loyal in principle, yet marked by the absence of any sense of bigotry. The flower of this spirit, whose long buried fragrance is inescapable as one unearths the foundations of this truly great settlement, is found in the religious character of the incomparable William Stevens of "Rehoboth" on Pocomoke River. Stevens was the friend and trusted official of the Roman Catholic proprietor of the province; a trusted magistrate, military commander and a representative (both in the Lower House of Assembly and the Council) of the ultra Protestant county of Somerset. He was a sympathetic supporter of the county's early non-sectarian, evangelical adventure (committed for exercise to the hands of the godly Robert Maddox). He was an admirer of the preaching of the great George Fox, Apostle of Quakerism; and it was he who appealed to the Presbytery of Laggan in the north of Ireland to send "a godly minister" of their great covenanting faith to Somerset in Maryland. This was the spirit of the "Churchman," William Stevens, of "Rehoboth" in "Old Somerset"—a spirit which has made lesser spirits doubt the sincerity of his "Churchmanship." Yet, as attesting the genuineness of his "Churchmanship," we find Stevens' name signed to a document in defence of the Roman Catholic proprietor, whose policy of administration was being attacked by Protestant sectarian interests—a document which concludes with the words: "We therefore, the subscribers, *pro-*

fessing the gospell of Jesus Christ, according to the Litturgy of the Church of England* and Protestants against the Doctrine and Practice of the Church of Rome . . . " To this document is attached (among others) the unmistakable signature: *"Will: Stevens"*—"Old Somerset's" immortal "Stevens of Rehoboth," whose name and blood passed with his passing from Somerset. At the time he signed this document William Stevens was a member of Lord Baltimore's Council for the province of Maryland. Let us note at this juncture that three other "Churchmen" of Somerset also signed this same document: James Dashiell, Roger Woolford and Henry Smith, who were the county's representatives at that date in the Lower House of Assembly.[4]

From the beginning then, we find Church of England men and their families located and seated in the Manokin section of the settlement of "the Eastern Shore below Choptank River," and not long afterward "Churchmen" appeared in Annemessex. Following record evidence we have named these "Churchmen." Doubtless there were as many more of this faith whom the old records fail to identify. While Church of England men and their families were not an inconsiderable number in the settlements—yet no evidence appears of the residence in the area of any minister of this "ancient and apostolic lineage."

These are indeed facts: the *presence* of "Churchmen and the *absence* of ministers of this faith. The imagination at play upon these primary facts will not, however, be forbidden to picture a group of loyal ones here and there gathered together on the "Lord's Day," with a "reader of prayers" chosen from among themselves, for wherever "Churchmen" may be found in any age or time there will be found that most precious child of the "Word of God"—the *Book of Common Prayer*. Who, with any real knowledge of "Churchmen," will dare say that men and women of this faith did not gather with their little ones, and other dependents, and say the sacred offices to lay-tongues permitted, and chant the ancient Psalms? Will the imagination be denied picturing the visits of Parson Teackle, of Accomack—that veritable institution of the faith on Virginia's Eastern Shore not so many miles away? Did he, "Shepherd of Souls," let souls which once had been his care depart, and at that into not so great a distance, with never a look or gesture towards them afterwards? Did these departing ones—who really had not gone so very far away—never look back or make gesture towards that "Shepherd of Souls" whose "fold" for years had been their spiritual home? Manokin—Annemessex—Pocomoke—Wicomico were only some fifty-odd miles from Accomack and there is ample evidence of much passing back and forth. Trading boats and sail-vessels were constantly passing to and fro between these points. Again the silence of records prevents our speaking authoritatively upon matters "most surely believed among us"; but tradition holds in the realm of spiritual certainties "beyond the written word." We profess our belief in the "unrecorded," resting that belief upon a sure and certain knowledge of the spirit of "Churchmen," both lay folk and ministers. There are facts of life which are part and parcel of "things spiritual," which may be most truly believed, though no evidence of a tangible and material nature remain wherewith to "prove" them.[6]

For the period of earliest settlement at Manokin-Annemessex—1662-1666—we have found no recorded evidences of just what transpired in "outward and visible form" in a Church of England way in that area.[7] We do have the names of settlers during this early period, who are clearly identified as "Churchmen." We have, too, certain inescapable elements in the tradition of "Churchmanship" which insistently appeal to the imagination and will not be forbidden as we think about these things. Few and far between as recorded facts may be, yet, here and there, when records once begin, items of great significance are found. Such indeed is the first discovered item of record in regard to "Churchmanship" as given in the first volume of ancient Somerset Court records. Like the breaking of day after long, silent night comes a simple bit of testimony of loyalty to the Church of England from an early settler in Manokin, for whom the light of "Eternal Day" would soon be breaking.

In his will dated January 26, 1665/6, probated May 28, 1667, "James Barnabe, Living in Manoakin in ye Province of Maryland, being weak of body, but of perfect memory," after committing his "soul to God that gave it mee," and his "body unto ye Dust from whence it was taken, in full assurance of a resurrection to come through ye Merits and Death of my blessed Savior Jesus Christ," continues his last will and testament in these words: "My will and desire is to be buried with a soleme and desente buriall according to the anchente

Custom that is used in [the] Trew Prodistant Church in England." From the register kept in Somerset Court, we have this further record of this man: "James Barnabe, Senio^r died and was buried at Manoakin the Seventeenth day of February A° Dom one thousand six hundred sixty and six (1666/7)." Can we doubt what words were read over the lifeless body and above the new-made grave of James Barnabe at Manokin? Whether read by presbyter, deacon or layman is of slight moment.[8]

A decade is to pass from the time of this memorable direction in the will of James Barnabe before another item breathing the spirit of devoted "Churchmanship" is disclosed by the records of Somerset.

In the fork of the present day Wicomico and Passerdyke Creeks there came to settle, probably about the year 1675, one William Brereton, from Northumberland County, Virginia. The Brereton family was one of distinguished connection with church and local administrative affairs, as well as social life, in Northumberland County, and this tradition followed William Brereton in his life in Somerset in Maryland. The tract of land on which he settled in Somerset County (bordering on both Wicomico [at that day called the river] and Passerdyke Creeks) was one of 500 acres out of a larger grant called "Smith's Adventure," patented in April, 1667, by one Colonel Samuel Smith, of Little Wiccocomoco in Northumberland County, Virginia, and deeded by him in June, 1672, to "my son in law William Brereton, of Wiccocomoco afsd and Sarah, his now wife ... and the heirs of the said Sarah forever." William Brereton had evidently married Sarah, a daughter of Colonel Smith, and on coming to Somerset in Maryland to live, simply exchanged one "Wiccocomoco locality" for another. When Brereton and his wife came, with their elder children, to reside in Somerset, their family was but half complete. After their arrival the records give entries of the births of several more children. It is the record entered in regard to the first child born to this couple after their settlement in Wicomico Hundred, Somerset County, that concerns us here.

"Hannah Brereton ye daughter of William Brereton was born at Wiccocomoco the ninth day of February of Sarah his wife Annoq Do^m one thousand six hundred Seaventy six and baptized the third day of June following by Mr. John Fransele at Wiccocomoco in ye County of Northumberland in Virginia."[9]

Such is the evidence of Brereton loyalty to the Church of England which we find among the fragments of the foundations of Somerset. A four-months-old girl baby was carried miles across the waters of river and bay from Wicomico in Somerset, on the "Eastern Shore" of the province of Maryland, to Wicomico in Northumberland in the colony of Virginia—carried home—back among her kindred to the sacred font, to be symbolically gathered from the arms of the woman who gave her birth, into the arms of her spiritual "Mother Church," and "made a member of Christ, the child of God, and an inheritor of the Kingdom of Heaven." A mere fragment such as this record of little Hannah Brereton's birth and baptism opens vistas to the imagination of a "Churchman."

Again, in the year 1678, we find record evidence of the loyalty of Church of England people in Somerset. In the old register of Somerset Court this entry appears:

"Cap[t] William Coulbourne and Anne Revell was marryed by M[r] Parkes Minister of ye Gospell in Accomack The 15th day of June an[o] Domini One thousand Six hundred Seaventy eight."[10]

The man and woman thus united in marriage belonged to two of the "great families" of "Old Somerset." Anne Revell, the bride, was a daughter of Randall Revell, first resident chief executive officer of the Manokin-Annemessex settlements, owner of extensive plantations, dweller on the south side of Manokin River not far from its mouth. The young groom—for he was only in the twentieth year of his age—William Coulbourne, was the eldest son of that Annemessex worthy, Colonel William Coulbourne, who, in the eyes of the Virginia law, was tainted by his Quaker sympathies. Seeking larger liberty in Maryland he became a wealthy planter and one of Somerset's leading officials. The Revells, as a household, were "Churchmen." We are not able to prove that the Coulbournes went further toward Quakerism than in "loving sympathy"; but certain it is that William Coulbourne—the bridgeroom—was a "Churchman" (later to become a vestryman) as were indeed all of the second generation of the house to which he belonged. "Churchmen" were being united in this marriage and their undoubted sense of "the fitness of things" made them desire the blessing of the Church upon their union. So we find the Reverend Henry Parkes, "minister of ye Gospell in Accomack"—rector of Accomack Parish in Accomack County, Virginia—summoned to Mr. Revell's, on the Manokin, in Somerset, in the province of Maryland, to unite in the bonds of Holy Matrimony young William Coulbourne and the fair Anne Revell.

By the year 1680 Somerset was truly alive with Church of England men and their families. It must indeed have been a question as to how Church of England men should be provided with the regular ministrations of their Church. As yet no minister of the Church was resident in the county. The sacraments of the Gospel and the ordinances of the Church could be had only from the hands of some passing presbyter. There was no "Sacred Font"; no "Table of the Lord" in their midst. However liberal and tolerant may have been the spirit of "Churchmanship," yet these people were "Churchmen," and the spirit must have cried out, above the peace of tolerance, for the ingrained and sacredly accustomed "family ways." Even the glory of liberality in matters religious could not abate the spirit of loyalty.

For many years there had resided in Somerset a rather notable merchant and mariner; a man whose business acumen brought him wealth for his day and whose sturdy character gained recognition for him in the official life of the county. This man was Captain Thomas Walker. Appearing in Somerset County as early as 1666, he was several times sheriff of the county, naval officer and magistrate. Captain Walker was extensively engaged in coast-wise and English trade, and after his marriage, in 1674, to Jane Coppinball, he acquired by purchase from Thomas Roe (in June, 1675) a plantation on the east side of Wicomico River (in the fork of the river and Dashiell's Creek). This plantation, while the home of Thomas Roe, had been one of the "preaching stations" of Robert Maddox, as designated by the Somerset Grand Jury of March, 1672/3. On this plantation Captain Walker made his home, here died, and here was buried in the month of February, 1680/1.

Captain Thomas Walker was a staunch Church of England man, manifesting his deep interest in the Church by making a bequest in his will towards the encouragement of a resident minister. Captain Walker's will, dated May 1, 1680, probated March 10, 1680/1, contains this item:

"I give to the first Protestant Minister that shall hereafter come from England to live in this County towards his transportation one thousand pounds of good tobacco."

Then, from the account of Captain Walker's estate, rendered by Edward Day (who married Jane Walker, executrix of Captain Walker's will), admitted to record October 8, 1685, we have this interesting and enlightening item:

"paid John Huett as p^r receit being a legacy left to him by the deceased in his will 1000 lbs. tob°."

Captain Walker does not even mention in his will the name of John Huett; much less leave to him a specific legacy. John Huett, to whom the 1,000 pounds of tobacco was paid from Walker's estate as a legacy, is proved to have been a clergyman of the Church of England. The fact that Walker devised this amount of tobacco towards the expenses of transportation of "the first Protestant Minister that shall hereafter come from England to live in this County," coupled with Huett's receipt for the legacy of like amount, plus the fact that Huett was a minister, explains the item quoted above from the estate account.[11]

Though the estate account rendered by the executor of Captain Walker was not recorded until 1685, we have evidence (presently to be quoted) that the Reverend John Huett had arrived in Somerset County prior to the month of January, 1680/1, while Captain Walker did not die until February, 1680/1. The official record of Walker's death and burial reads as follows:

"Capt Thomas Walker died & was buryed at his Plantation in Wiccocomoco ye sixth day of February Annoq Dom one Thousand six hundred & Eighty [1680/1]."

There is no record evidence of the fact, but can we doubt that the Reverend John Huett committed to earth the body of Captain Thomas Walker, of Wicomico, with the service of his beloved Church?

Thus are we introduced to the first resident clergyman of the Church of England in the county: John Huett, "Father-Founder" of the organized Church of England in Somerset, identified as a son of the Reverend John Huett (1614-1658), of St. Gregory's by St. Paul's, London, who was a royalist divine and forfeited his life for his loyalty to the Stuart cause.[12]

Eighteen years passed from the first settlement made at Manokin-Annemessex, on "the Eastern Shore below Choptank River," and fourteen years from the time that Somerset County was created from territory taken out of that area, before the Church of England had a resident representative of her "orders and ministry" in that section. Now that such a representative of the Church appears, we find in him a man fully measuring in character to the responsibility thus coming into his hands.

The exact date at which the Reverend John Huett arrived in Somerset County from England has not been discovered. He evidently had not arrived in May, 1680, when Captain Thomas Walker made his will providing a bequest towards the transportation of "the first Protestant Minister that shall hereafter come from England to live in this County"; while there is evidence that he had arrived in the county before, and at least by, January, 1680/1. From one source we have an intimation that Mr. Huett may have been in Maryland as early as the year 1677 or 8; though this record does not indicate the part of the province in which he then resided. Certainly he did not come to reside in Somerset until somewhat later than May 1, 1680. The first appearance of his name in the records of the county is on January 29, 1680/1, when he officiated at the marriage of Alexander Price and Rebecca Thomas.[13]

The spirit which guided Mr. Huett to Somerset County for the exercise of his ministry indeed guided him to a field of labor rich in opportunity. Somerset was an important center of life in the province of Maryland, and its vast territory was wholly lacking in any organized religious work other than the Quaker meetings. Church of England men and their families numbered a large percentage of the population by 1680. "Churchmen" were scattered from Nanticoke on the north to the Maryland-Virginia boundary line on the south and from the Ocean to the Bay—east and west. Each of the eight "Hundreds" had its full quota of "Churchmen." One who knows the great extent of Somerset's original territory can, in imagination, picture the "field ripe unto harvest" which confronted this man. As for tenure of office and material support, they were entirely questions of the man's ability to securely fix himself into the life of the people and of his dependence on any financial resources which he may himself have possessed. The ministry in this place was purely missionary in nature. The minister's work was veritably "from door to door." Diligent research in the ancient records has failed to discover reference to even the rudest semblance of a house of worship at that time. Whatever services of worship were held must have been held in homes of the planters, in store houses, barns or, in seasonable weather, in open air.[14] It was with the raw materials of human desire and will only that this man went to work in the building of the Church in Somerset; dependent wholly upon the power of the Spirit of the living God in himself and the people, for strength sufficient for his undertaking. Once for all it may be said that there is no evidence afforded by remaining records that John Huett had been misguided in his undertaking. The results accruing from his ministry constitute evidence of the man's genius for pastoral work and organization. Huett's work as first minister of the Church of England resident in Somerset (and for the first fifteen years of that ministry, which totalled only eighteen years, the only resident minister of that Church) gives to the Church of England, and her daughter, the Protestant Episcopal Church, in this county a "Father-Founder," from whose true and courageous spirit ministers and laity may timelessly draw inspiration.

John Huett had certainly entered upon his work in Somerset by the beginning of the year 1681. He is designated in the records as "Minister of the Gospell of Jesus Christ," "Minister of the Gospel," "Minister" and "Clerke." As a regularly ordained presbyter of the Church of England, his work was not only pastoral and prophetic—to counsel and to teach the people under his care—but also faithfully to minister the sacraments of the Gospel. There remain no records of his celebrations of the Holy Communion—such records were very rarely kept in those days. In the absence of early congregation and later parish records, we have been able to discover from another source only two records of his having administered Holy Baptism.

On the north side of Great Monie Creek (about two miles above its mouth) was the town of the Monie Indians, among whom no doubt Mr. Huett extended his labor of ministry. The first of the two baptisms referred to above was that of "John Puckham, an Indian, baptized by Mr. John Huet minister ye 25th day of January one Thousand Six hundred eighty two (1682/3)." John Puckham was doubtless a member of this Monie tribe, as we have evidence from remaining records that people by the name of Puckham were living at a later date in the neighborhood of this Monie Indian town site. John Puckham's baptism into the Christian faith by a minister of the Church of England was no doubt in preparation for his marriage according to the Christian rite; for we find the "sd. John Puckham & Jone Johnson, negro, married by said Mr Huett ye 25th February Annoq Do^m one Thousand six hundred Eighty Two (1682/3)." We cannot, in passing, but wonder if "Jone Johnson, negro," was a member of that Johnson family of free Negroes, first of their race and kind in Somerset. This Johnson family lived on the south side of Wicomico (the present creek), not more than five or six miles northeast of the Monie Indian town. It is little less than certain that the Johnson free Negroes were all Church of England people by virtue of baptism.

The second of the records of baptisms by Mr. Huett is as interesting as the first:

"Thomas Brereton ye fourth son of William Brereton & Sarah his wife was born at Wiccocomoco on the Easterne Shore March ye Seaventh A° D° 1682/3 being Wendsday about 12 of ye Clock at noone & was Christened at Wiccocomoco aforesaid by Mr. Huett ye 25th day of March in ye same year."[15]

The Thomas Brereton baptized by Mr. Huett was a younger brother of that Hannah Brereton whom we have before learned was carried in 1676 by her parents, faithful and loyal Church people, from Wicomico in Somerset County, Maryland (where there was at that time no minister of the Church of England), to Wicomico in Northumberland County, Virginia (the old home of the Breretons), there to be baptized by a minister of the Church.

The baptisms of John Puckham, the Indian, and of Thomas Brereton, are the only two which have found their way into remaining public records from among many others which Mr. Huett doubtless administered during the eighteen years of his ministry in Somerset. There remain records of twenty marriages at which Mr. Huett officiated between 1680/1 and 1695, affording evidence, from the locations of the residences of the brides, of the far-reaching extent of Huett's ministerial work. The "Hundreds" of Nanticoke, Wicomico, Monie, Manokin and Annemessex are all represented in these records of marriages. There is also a *tradition* of Mr. Huett's ministry in Bogerternorton and Pocomoke Hundreds, along Pocomoke River and towards the seaside. "Churchmen" in abundance lived in these two last named "Hundreds," but *records* are silent as to any ministry among them.

The absence of any Church records for this early period of Somerset's history makes it impossible for us to discover just what transpired—with the exception of events having more than local significance—in the area of Mr. Huett's ministry.[16] Of the first twelve years of this ministry—from 1680-1692—we know only that Mr. Huett must have labored diligently to minister to the members of the Church of England widely distributed through the large extent of Somerset County's territory, and to carry the comfort of the Gospel to those who were without.

It was in June, 1692, after the "Protestant Revolution" had deprived Lord Baltimore of all rights (but those of revenue) in his proprietorship of Maryland, that having received its first governor under royal commission the province also received an Established Church. The Church of England became the Established Church of the province by Act of the first Assembly held after the arrival of Governor Lionel Copley: "An Act for the Service of Almighty God and the Establishment of the Protestant Religion in this Province." Under this Act parishes were organized in the several counties of Maryland; vestries elected for the governance of parishes; rectors and ministers commissioned; and the support of the clergy and other parochial expenses provided for by a levy of forty pounds of tobacco on each tithable person regardless of religious affiliation.[17] This establishment by law of the Church of England in the province gave to the work of the Reverend Mr. Huett, as a clergyman of that Church, assured security in Somerset County.

With the organization of parishes and the election of vestries under the act of establishment in 1692, the Reverend John Huett became, by appointment, the first minister of Stepney Parish in Somerset County and, by election, a member of the first vestry of Somerset Parish. It also appears that he was the first minister of Somerset Parish. Though the clerical official head of a parish is designated as "rector," no remaining reference which we have found so designates Mr. Huett. He is invariably referred to as "minister," though the office which he exercised in Stepney Parish was certainly that of a rectorship.[18] We have, too, a statement to the effect that Mr. Huett in 1691, the year before the establishment of the Church by law, had extended his ministry to Dorchester County; though it does not appear that his service there was of long duration. It is probable that he went only occasionally to preach.[19] In both Stepney and Somerset Parishes, Mr. Huett seems to have continued his ministry until the year 1696.

First, last and always, a "minister of the Gospell of Jesus Christ"—a clergyman of the Church of England—missionary—the parish minister, yet we find the Reverend Mr. Huett broadening the field of his activities. In one instance we find the reverend gentleman ranging beyond the legal limits of his profession, entering—O unholy of unholies!—the realm of politics; encouraged in his pursuit of office —("read, mark, learn and unwardly digest" this fact, ye moderns)— by an electorate of which his own "church members" formed a goodly proportion. What brought about Huett's entrance into the political arena, what methods were employed towards furthering his election, whether a feeling of partisanship growing out of "loyal sectarianism" was utilized in gaining numerical advantage for his candidacy, we do not know. We only know that it is a fact that the Reverend John Huett, clergyman of the Church of England in Somerset County, was elected by the freeholders of his county on April 28, 1692 (together with Thomas Evernden and John Goddin, Quakers, and William Whittington, a "Churchman") to represent Somerset in the Lower House of Assembly of the province, called to convene at St. Mary's in the following month of May. Whatever else this election of Huett to the Assembly may mean, it seems certainly to indicate belief in the man's ability to occupy such an office, and evidence of the esteem in which he was held personally by a large number among the electorate. Furthermore, we must not forget that the election of a clergyman in active service to a seat in the Assembly was against the tradition, if not the law, of England and the province of Maryland. However, Mr. Huett was elected and consented to his election. Then came the "testing." When the Assembly convened Mr. Huett presented himself to take oath of office in order to qualify for his seat. The oath was administered and the delegate took his seat. The question was then raised as to the right of men in "holy orders" to occupy "the seats of the mighty." By no uncertain action the Assembly thereupon deprived and debarred from its membership the Reverend

Mr. Huett, of Somerset; but with the consequence that this reverend gentleman was immediately named—this, too, by action of that body —a chaplain to the Assembly. His fellow chaplain for the session was the Reverend John Clayland, of Talbot County, also a clergyman of the Church of England.[20] A chaplaincy to the first Assembly of Maryland as a Royal Province was no inconsiderable honor. Thus we find the abilities of the Reverend Mr. Huett recognized beyond local environs.

Later we again find Mr. Huett's ability recognized and enlisted for service by the authorities of the now Royal Province. That incomparable champion of both church and school, Francis Nicholson, while Governor of Maryland in 1694, proposed by message to the Assembly the passage of an Act "for a free school for the province."[21] The result of the plan thus advanced was the Petitioning Act of the Assembly of 1696 for the establishment of "a Free School or Schools, or place of study of Latin, Greek, writing and the like," and declaration of the necessary masters and one hundred scholars to "a school." The Archbishop of Canterbury was nominated as chancellor of this institution, which, in honor of the King, was called "King William's School." This school was to be built in Anne Arundel Town (Annapolis), with other schools to be erected "at such other places as by the General Assembly of this Province shall be thought convenient and fitting to be supported and maintained in all time coming." The Visitors and Trustees of this province-wide plan of schools were chosen from the most prominent citizens and officials of the province—among whose names we find "the Reverend Divine . . . Mr. John Hewett of Somerset County," together with Colonel Francis Jenckins, also of Somerset, a member of the first vestry of Coventry Parish (though later intimately associated with Presbyterianism in the county).[22] The honor thus bestowed upon Mr. Huett, minister of Stepney and Somerset Parishes, in Somerset County, was one of great dignity. Evidently he represented the Church on the "Eastern Shore" in this beginning of a great adventure in popular education which was the seed (though lying long dormant) which finally sprung to life in one of the best of colonial systems of education. The Reverend Perigrine Cony, of William and Mary Parish, St. Mary's County, represented the Church on the Western Shore as a member of this board. Thus did Mr. Huett, through the exercise of his abilities as man and clergyman, together with the distinguished layman, Colonel Francis Jenckins (an official of both county and province), connect up "Old Somerset" with "the beginnings" of the province of Maryland's adventure in popular academic education. This first plan (of 1696) did not carry out, it is true; but unquestionably it lies beneath the later "Academy Act" of 1723 (nearly a quarter of a century after Huett's death) which did prove effective, reaching province-wide proportions, and in which Somerset County was most creditably represented.[23]

But let us retrace our steps a bit. We find that Mr. Huett was, in September, 1694, the preacher at a "Fast Day Service" held at St. Mary's, the capital of the province, a service attended by the members of the General Assembly in a body. At this service he preached so acceptably that he was voted the thanks of that august body.[24]

The Reverend John Huett, from the time of his coming to Somerset County to reside, late in the year 1680, appears to have been the only clergyman of the Church of England resident in Somerset from that time until the year 1696 (only two years before his death), when the Reverend George Trotter appears as "incumbent" of both Stepney and Somerset Parishes.

We have reviewed at length the activities of Mr. Huett's notable life. Surely we may without question pronounce him a man of rare genius in the pursuit of the purpose to which he had dedicated himself. His name comes to us as that of a man who bore himself most honorably in the high calling of the ministry of the Gospel. Not once is there, in record or tradition, the slightest intimation of any unworthiness in regard to his manhood, or to his life in the "office and ministry of the Church." This is, of course, as it should be; but how rare a jewel it is to be found in colonial times in the crown of clerical office. His name comes down to us through two centuries with every mark of the character of a true Christian gentleman and minister, highly esteemed in his own day and worthy of honor in all time thereafter: Huett—Apostle of the Church of England to Somerset in Maryland.

In early Springtime of the year 1698, John Huett was led forth by the Good Shepherd from beside the still waters of Wicomico in "Old Somerset" to walk without fear through the valley of the shadow of death—"to dwell in the house of the Lord forever." "I have fought a good fight; I have finished my course, I have kept the faith. Henceforth there is laid up for me a crown..." Amen—John Huett—man and minister—"Father-Founder"—we have no doubt whatever.

We are particularly fortunate in having discovered some very interesting details relative to the Reverend John Huett's home plantation and the burial place of his body in Somerset County. Just where Mr. Huett lived when he first came to Somerset County we do not know; but of the plantation on which he finally made permanent settlement we have definite information. This plantation was a tract of land called, in the final grant therefor, "Contention," and was situated on the west side of Wicomico River, about a mile and a half slightly northeast of the town of Whitehaven, in the present Wicomico County (formed in 1867), and during Mr. Huett's lifetime in Somerset County and Stepney Parish. This plantation extended from Maningettoes (now known as Cherry Bridge) Creek northward (or slightly northeastward), along the west side of Wicomico River, to Rice's Creek (a small stream whose name has been lost from the tradition of the county), and was directly opposite the plantation of Captain Thomas Walker, which lay on the east side of Wicomico River. It was this Captain Walker who, dying in February, 1680/1, devised the thousand pounds of tobacco to the first Protestant minister who should come thereafter into Somerset County to reside, which legacy Mr. Huett received.

On this plantation, which bore the patent-name "Contention" (evidently from some circumstance in relation to establishing its boundaries), Mr. Huett made his home. The patent was not issued until some years after Huett's death; but a warrant of survey for the tract had been issued to him in 1695. It is, however, apparent that Huett had made settlement on this land and was living here several years prior to this date, and it was here, no doubt, that the freeholders of Wicomico and Nanticoke Hundreds met in December, 1692, when directed, by order of Somerset Court, to *"meet at Mr. John Huett's"* for the election of the first vestry of Stepney Parish. Though we cannot prove the matter, it is our belief that Mr. Huett settled on this property soon after his marriage to Rachel Battian, which certainly did not take place until after May, 1686, at which date the lady witnessed the will of John Evans, signing with her maiden name. By a recent careful examination of this tract of land, Mr. Benjamin J.

Dashiell, a surveyor and student of Somerset County history, was successful in locating the old house site (close by which was the graveyard) near the northeast boundary of the plantation (old Rice Creek) and only about a stone's throw back from the river. It was no doubt not long before Mr. Huett's death that he erected a new house (in succession to an older dwelling) on this plantation, for we find Joseph Venables (doubtless the contractor for this building) presenting and proving a bill in Somerset Court on March 19, 1699 (1700), against "Mr. John Huett," among the items appearing:

"To the building of Dwelling House att 10,000 lbs. tob^o
To the Shingling the Same House   4,000 lbs. tob^o"

Here it was that the Reverend Mr. Huett lived with his family, his wife, Rachel (nee Battian), and their two daughters, Ann (later the wife, *first,* of Matthew Nutter, and *secondly,* of Alexander Leckie) and Susanna, wife of Joseph Johnson. After Mr. Huett's death this home-place was the residence of his widow, Mrs. Rachel Huett, and her second husband, Colonel Nicholas Evans. Still later it became the property (if not for a time the residence) of Ann Huett and her second husband, Alexander Leckie. The Reverend John Huett died intestate in 1698, his estate being administered by his widow, Mrs. Rachel Huett. An inventory was presented and recorded in Somerset County, June 29, 1698. From personalty and lands of the Huett estate, it is certain that the reverend gentleman left not only to posterity and his community that richest of all legacies: "a good name," but that he left also to his immediate family an estate which proved his wisdom and faithfulness in handling things seen and temporal comparable to his faithfulness and wisdom in dealing with "things unseen and eternal."

As to the immediate cause of the Reverend John Huett's death we are not informed, but several rare items in relation to his funeral and place of burial have been discovered. That he died at his plantation seems certain, that his body was interred there is an established fact. The name of the minister officiating at Mr. Huett's funeral is not positively known to us; but we have evidence that a funeral service was held for the reverend gentleman at his home on this Wicomico River plantation and that a funeral sermon was preached during the course of that service. We strongly suspect that the Reverend

George Trotter, who was in 1698 "incumbent" of Stepney and Somerset Parishes, conducted the memorable service for Mr. Huett. Nearly fifty years after Mr. Huett's death the venerable Thomas Dashiell, then nearly eighty years old, testified "that the day the Reverend John Hewit was buried" he came "to the plantation and in the yard where the said Hewit did live and went within forty yards of the grave." A few months after Thomas Dashiell's testimony, we find John Evans, Senior (then about sixty-eight years old) referring to "the next day after Mr. Huett's death," and then to "the next day as this deponent was hearing the funeral Sermon."[25]

Thus, as related, we have been able to locate the home-place of the Reverend John Huett and the place of the burial of his earthly remains.

* * * *

Somerset County's first resident minister of the Church of England, the Reverend John Huett, arriving late in 1680, came at the time when events in the province were beginning to shape effectively the movement which finally resulted in the overthrow of Charles, Lord Baltimore's authority in the government of his province. Out of this movement arose the Protestant Revolution in Maryland, part and parcel of the Revolution in England which finally brought about the dethronement of the House of Stuart. Whatever truth there may have been in the charges brought against him by an element in his province, Lord Baltimore's loyal Roman Catholicism was most successfully used by his opponents as a lever to prize him out of his government. The House of Stuart had disappeared from the throne of England, and William and Mary had been seated thereon in a Protestant succession. Now the throne could be successfully reached by the enemies of the Roman Catholic Lord Proprietor; with the result that Maryland was taken from his governmental control, becoming the ward of the Crown as a Royal Province.[26]

The passing of Maryland from a Proprietary to a Royal Province brought many changes in affairs of state, but none more far reaching in its effects than *"An Act for the Service of Almighty God and the Establishment of the Protestant Religion in the Province,"* by which the Church of England became by law the Established Church in

Maryland. This Act was the second passed by the first Assembly convened by the first royal governor, Lionel Copley, May 10, 1692, having been specifically directed by the Crown's instructions to Governor Copley. It was the Sovereign's will and desire.[27]

The third section of the *"Act for the Service of Almighty God and the Establishment of the Protestant Religion in this Province"* concerns us here, for this section is the one directing the division of the counties into parishes and the election of vestries. The provision is made that the local courts in the province should, before September 1, 1692, give notice to "the most principall Freeholders" of their respective counties to meet with them in an advisory capacity to lay out a convenient number of parishes in each county. These local bodies were to define and record the boundaries of the parishes, certifying the same to the governor. After thus creating the parishes the courts were directed to order meetings of freeholders to be held in the most convenient places within the respective parishes to elect vestries. Each parish vestry was to be composed of six members. This Act also made provision for the full legal constitution of vestries, prescribing their duties in detail.[28]

Nothing is now known of the detail of organization of congregations of Church of England folk in Somerset from the arrival of the Reverend John Huett, late in 1680, to the time of the passage of the Act of May, 1692, establishing the Church of England in Maryland. There remains nothing in the way of Church records for this period; nor, as a matter of fact, of any such records until a date many years later. References gleaned from reading county records and provincial archives are very rare.[29] Though no records relating to such transactions remain, "Churchmen" familiar with canons and precedents governing and directing the work of ministers in the Church of England in colonial fields of labor will have "a sense" of what transpired. The eye of the "Churchman's" spirit will discern things that the passing of the years has made invisible to the physical eye. No "Churchman" doubts that under the vigorous leadership of the Reverend John Huett, during the twelve years of his ministry in virtually a missionary capacity, that Church people in Somerset were made fully ready for organization into parishes by the time the Act of 1692 was passed. No doubt the foundation of parochial organization, in so far as the ecclesiastical side of the matter was concerned (there was also a definitely political side to the matter), had been laid in groups of "Churchmen," banded together in congregational life in various parts of the county. Though we have only one record (to be quoted presently) of the erection of a church building prior to 1692, yet we doubt not that other simple structures of like nature had been erected before this date by "Churchmen" as visible witnesses in Somerset to the spirit of the corporate worship of God.

In 1692 the Church of England in Somerset, represented heretofore by sporadic congregations, passed (with such congregations in other parts of the province) into fulness of organization. As we follow the facts of the organization of the Church of England in Somerset under the Act of establishment, we must not forget that this work had also a political side, and was not committed solely to the hands of "Churchmen" (in the religious and ecclesiastical sense), but to the Court and Freeholders of the county. The courts, with advice of "the most principall Freeholders" laid out the parishes. The Freeholders were charged with the election of the vestries; and any Freeholder (regardless of his religious affiliation) had right of election to a seat on a vestry.[30] Among the twenty-eight appointees to assist Somerset Court in the matter of laying out its parishes, we find four whom we can definitely identify as Presbyterians; while there may have been other "dissenters" among the number whose definite sectarian affiliations we cannot identify. In so far as the members of the first vestries elected for Somerset County parishes are concerned, all of the gentlemen—with possibly the exception of Colonel Francis Jenckins, Mr. William Round and Mr. John Franklin—may be identified as "Churchman."[31]

There is an interesting item contained in the provincial archives of the period which we believe justifies the estimate which we have placed upon the Reverend Mr. Huett's character and work in the ministry. After the Act of establishment was passed, but before Somerset Court had proceeded with the organization of the Church in that county, there was, at a Council for the province held September 30, 1692,

"Produced and read a petition signed p Severall of the Inhabitants of Somersett County to the Number of one hundred and twelve Persons, praying the continuance among them their Ministers (vizt) *one of them of the Church of England* [italics ours], other three dissenters in some small matters but willing to qualify themselves so far as in conscience they can by taking the Oaths of allegiance and abhorrency—Referred for further consideration."[32]

We shall consider the three worthy "dissenters" later (in an account of Presbyterianism in Somerset), but in the one minister who was *"of the Church of England,"* we find the Reverend Mr. Huett (as well as the "dissenting" ministers) in "high favor" among the people of Somerset—the one hundred and twelve signatories to the petition being representative of the population at large. Though the "further consideration" to which the petition was referred has not been discovered it was no doubt favorable. At least we judge that it was, because Mr. Huett (as well as the three "dissenters") continued in the field of his labors for some years—even rising, as we have seen, to marked local and provincial dignity.

We now turn to consideration of the legal organization of the Church of England in Somerset County under the terms of the act of Assembly of June, 1692. Though the Act specifically directed the courts to divide their respective counties into parishes prior to September 30th, following; for some reason (not now apparent) the Somerset County officials did not get to the matter until late in the fall. In accordance with the provisions of the Act, the court of Somerset County, at its meeting November 8, 1692, entered the following order:

"Persons appointed p Court to appear to assist ye Justices in laying out & dividing ye County into Parishes as followeth viz—upon 22th of this Month [November]—

from Mattapony Thomas Purnell, Henry Hall, Wm. Stevenson & Richard Holland

from Pocomoke Mr. John Cornish, John Starrett, Alexander Maddox & Wm. Noble

from Annimessex Capt William Coulbourne, Mr. Wm. Planner, Mr. Thomas Dixon & Mr. Cha: Hall

from Manokin Mr. Arnold Elzey, Richard Chambers, Capt Rich: Whitty, Mr. Jno: Strawbridge

from Mony George Betts, John Laws, John Renshaw, John White

from Wiccocomoco Daniel Hast, Wm. Elgate, Wm. Alexander, Matthew Wallis Nanticoke—Robert Collier, James Weatherley, John Bounds, Capt. Wm. Piper

Sheriffe had in Court the Copy of ye persons & there Ordered to Sumon them unto app^r ut Supra."[33]

With this order of court entered, and the notice of appointments duly given, the Court of Somerset, at a "Special Session" held November 22, 1692, proceeded to establish and define the boundaries of four parishes for the county; and to order meetings of freeholders to be held for the election of vestries, designating the places at which these elections were to be held.

"At a meeting of their Maties Justices of the Peace at the Court house for the County of Somerset with the freeholders in each hundred for the lying out the County int° parishes this 22th day of Novem^r an° 1692.

Com^rs in Court were   Co^ll David Browne, Council, Mr. Francis Jenckins, Capt Jn° Winder, Mr. James Dashiels, Mr. Roger Woolford, Mr. Edmund Howard, Mr. George Layfield, & Capt John King

The abovsed Commissioners and the freeholders have the day and year abovse^d agreed & have divided the said County of Somerset into four parishes That is to Say—

Manokin & Mony hundred into one parish Called by the name of Somerset

Pocomoke and Annimessex into one parish Called Coventry

Wiccoccomocoe and Nanticoke into one parish Called Stepney

BogateeNorton & Mattapony hundred into one parish Called Snow Hill

The time Appointed for the freeholders to meet to Chuse Vestrymen att the places hereafter named is the 27th day of Devember next.

The freeholders of Manokin & Mony hundreds to meet at *Somerset Towne*.

The freeholders of Pocomoke & Annimessex to meet at *Pocomoke Church*.

The freeholders of Wiccocomocoe & Nanticoke to meet at *Mr. John Huett's*.

The freeholders of BogatteeNorton & Mattapony to meet at *Snow Hill*.

Ord^ered that the Clerk draw Coppies to each Constable as also four Coppies of the Laws Concerning the act of Religion and that the Constables of each hundred doe Summon the freeholders to meet at the time & places afores^d Thomas Ackworth Joy Hobbs George Wilson & Nicholas Cornehill to deliver the Coppies of ye s^d Act of Religion to the freeholders at the time & places afores^d

Ord^ered the Sheriffe Carry the Coppies & Orders to the Constables."[34]

In tracing further this matter of the organization of the Church in Somerset County, we gather several interesting items from the provincial archives, though no additional ones from the county records.

"At a meeting of the Council for the province on July 30, 1694, there was rendered to the Governor by members of the Council then present, a report of the State of the constitution of the Government of Maryland Viz^t as to Ecclesiasticall, Civill & Military Affaires . . ." in which the item appears:

"*Somerset County has ffour Parishes laid out, but never a Church Mr John Hewet, A Clergy Man . . .*"[35]

Then in February, 1696/7, we find a report made to a meeting of the Governor and Council of "An Acco^t of the Severall Parishes within the Province (according as they were by Act Laid out) together with the Bounds of the same the Names of the Vestrymen and Number of Tithables within Each Parish, Viz^t . . ."[36]

"Somerset County is divided into ffour Parishes Viz^t Somerset, Coventry, Stepney, Snow Hill. Somerset Parish Consists of Manokin and Many Hundreds Vestrymen for the s^d Parish as by Return Viz^t

    Mr John Huett   Mr Nath: Horsey
    Mr Richd Chambers   Mr Miles Gray   } Taxables 304
    Mr John Panter   Mr Peter Elzey

Coventry Parish Consists of Pocomoke and Annimessex hundreds. Vestrymen for the s^d Parish as by Return Viz^t.

    Mr Francis Jenckins   Mr Wm Planer, Senr } Taxables 414
    Mr George Layfield   Mr Thomas Dixon   Ann^o 96 (1696) 369
    Mr Thomas Nuball   Mr Wm Coleburn

Stepney Parish Consists of Wiccocomocoe and Nanticoke Hundreds. Vestrymen for the s^d Parish as by Return Viz^t.

        Mr John Huett, Clergym^n
Mr Jam: Weatherly   Mr Robert Collyer   } Taxables 381
Mr John Bounds   Mr Thomas Holbrooke   A^o 96 (1696) 362
Mr Philip Carter   Mr Philip Askue

Snow Hill Parish Consists of Bogettenorton & Mattapany Hundreds. Vestrymen for the s^d Parish as by Return Viz^t.

    Mr Matt: Scarborough   Mr Thomas Pointer
    Mr Wm Round   Mr Thomas Selby   } Taxables 353."
    Mr John Franklin   Mr Edward Hamond

The record as quoted above is given in the *Archives of Maryland. Proceedings of Council 1696/7—1698, page 22.* The compilation of statistics for this report, and its drafting, must have preceded by some time its presentation. This fact is attested by the changes noted and dated *"Ann° 96"* and *"A° 96,"* respectively, of the numbers of taxables for Coventry and Stepney Parishes. This seems to indicate that the number of taxables in these parishes had somewhat decreased between the compilation of the report and its presentation in February, 1696 (1696/7). This report as we have given it from the provincial archives is indeed interesting; but we are fortunate in having a copy thereof as it actually reached the Board of Trade in England in October, 1697, and was entered in that Board's record under the caption:

"An Account of the Parishes with their Bounds, Vestrymen, and Taxables of every Parish, as also of the Clergymen of the Church of England within this his Majesty's Province of Maryland viz...

Sommersett County is divided into Four Parishes, vizt. Sommersett, Coventry, Stepney, Snowhill

Sommerset Parish consists of Moriokin and Manny Hundreds.

The Reverend Mr John Hewett who hath been in the Country about 20 year..."

(Then follows a list of the Vestry of Somerset Parish, in which the six names of vestrymen are identical with those given in the account as quoted above from the published Archives of Maryland).
"Coventry parish consists of Pocomoke and Annamessex Hundreds.
The Reverend Mr James Breechin who came into the Countrey in the yeare 1696..."

(Then follows a list of vestrymen identical with the names quoted above for Coventry Parish; then a list of the minister and vestry of Stepney Parish, identical with the list quoted above except that Huett appears as "Mr. John Hewett, Clk"; then the list of vestrymen for Snow Hill Parish, identical with the list quoted above).

The number of taxables for the respective parishes is given in this paper as Somerset, 304; Coventry, 369; Stepney, 362; Snow Hill, 353. We here notice that the numbers of taxables follow the *"Ann° 96"* numbers as given for Coventry and Snow Hill Parishes in the former list. We have here the interesting additional information in regard to Mr. Huett's having been in the "countrey" about 20 years, and that he was evidently at that date (as he certainly was later) in charge of Somerset Parish (of which he was also a duly elected vestryman) as well as in charge of Stepney Parish. Somerset and Stepney were adjoining parishes.

This "Account" which came to the Board of Trade in October, 1697, included, of course, all of the parishes and vestries throughout the province. We have quoted only the section devoted to Somerset County. The "Account" is attested *"A true Copy Hen. Denton, Clk Council."* Denton was clerk of the Council for the province of Maryland.[37]

It should be noted that the number of taxables given in these reports for each parish were given as the basis for levying the tithes for ministers and other parish dues as provided by law. These taxables represent not only "Churchmen," but all taxable males of whatever religious denomination.

The documents above quoted give a complete statement of the political and ecclesiastical organization of the Established Church in Somerset County, according to the provisions of the Act of Assembly of June, 1692. In the names of several of "the most principall freeholders" who assisted the court in dividing the county into parishes, the justices who composed the court which effected this "Establishment" as it related to Somerset County, and of the vestrymen elected for the four parishes, we find interesting suggestions of historical importance.

The names of William Stevenson of Mattapony, John Strawbridge of Manokin, William Alexander and Matthew Wallis of Wicomico, are suggestive of Presbyterianism as represented in this body of "advisers" to the court in laying out the boundaries of the parishes in Somerset. Stevenson was a representative of the family of that name resident in the town of Snow Hill, which contributed so largely to the building of the Presbyterian Church in that neighborhood, while at a later date (1720) the house of James Stevenson was a "meeting place" for a congregation of that faith. William Alexander later became a ruling elder of the Manokin Presbyterian congregation, while Matthew Wallis and John Strawbridge were likewise members of Manokin; Strawbridge's relation (probably his son), James, was an elder in the Session of that church.[38] William Coulbourne and Thomas Dixon were sons of men who were the staunchest among the supporters of Quakerism in early Somerset.[39] It was on Arnold Elzey's land at "Almodington," on Manokin River, that the first church building for Somerset Parish was erected.[40] Captain William Piper, who appears to have been a "Churchman," married a daughter of Christopher Nutter, of Manokin (later of Nanticoke), whose home in Manokin was one of the four "preaching stations" designated for "Mr. Matix" by the Somerset Grand Jury of March, 1671/2. Captain William Piper's son, Christopher Piper, married a granddaughter of the Reverend John Huett. Another son of Captain Piper was that William Piper, who, dying in 1734, left an incomparable memorial to his "Churchmanship" and family piety by directing in his will that his four children "be well brought up in the fear of God & well instructed in the Religion of the Church of England and that they fail not to perform Prayers in Family discipline at least every Night & Morning."[41]

The names of "their Majesties Justices of the Peace," under whose direction, as "the county court," the original parishes in Somerset County were laid out, are also historically suggestive. Colonel David Brown, the presiding magistrate (and also one of their Majesties' Council for Maryland) was, so far as the records give evidence, the "original Scotch Presbyterian" in Somerset, having been in the county as early as 1670. He was a member of the "Committee of Twenty" of the "Associators Government" of 1689, the provincial power which finally overthrew Lord Baltimore's proprietary rule in the province. He was, we recall, "foreman" of the Somerset Grand Jury of March Court, 1671/2, which recommended the county-wide evangelistic adventure for "Mr. Matix."[42] Dashiell, Woolford, King, Winder and Layfield were "Churchmen"; and Francis Jenckins, though probably at one time a "Churchman," was "exceeding strong in his love of Presbyterianism."[43] It was on land once belonging to Captain John King that the first Chapel of Ease for Somerset County was erected in 1715/20, after the land had passed to his son, Captain John King, the second.

The four places directed by the court as the meeting places of freeholders for the election of vestries arouse interest. *"Somerset Town"* was on the south side of the lower Manokin River, the first town established in Somerset. This town was established by the Lord Proprietor as a "port of entry" on land deeded by Randall Revell and Katherine, his wife, in 1668.[44] *"Pocomoke Church"* is the first church to which reference is found in the records, and was at Rehoboth Town (also called Pocomoke Town).[45] *"Mr. John Huett's"* was the residence of the Reverend John Huett (who at the time was the only Church of England minister in Somerset) and was located on the west side of Wicomico River, about half a mile above the present town of White Haven (now in Wicomico County).[46] *"Somerset Town," "Pocomoke Church"* and *"Mr. John Huett's* are today only hallowed memories. *"Snow Hill"* was, of course, the ancient town of Snow Hill on the upper Pocomoke River, founded in 1686, and still in existence, "a thing of beauty and a joy forever"—the only one of the seventeenth century Somerset County towns still in existence. Snow Hill, since 1742, has been the seat of Worcester County, which was organized at that date from part of the original area of "Old Somerset."

Among the names of the first vestrymen of Somerset, Coventry, Stepney and Snow Hill Parishes, we find "historic links." Huett, the Clergyman, was a duly elected member of Somerset Parish's vestry, and appears as *first* in the list. It seems that the popular trust, confidence, respect and, we dare say, love and affection, in and for this man knew no limits. Nathaniel Horsey (of Somerset Parish) and William Coulbourne and Thomas Dixon (of Coventry) bring the three most notable of Somerset County Quaker-sympathizing families into the fold of the Church of England. Francis Jenckins (of Coventry Parish) has been claimed as "a most worthy Presbyterian." He may have "held out" in allegiance to the Church of England; but if amidst his surroundings he did, he is veritably the eighth wonder of the world. Jenckins' second wife was that celebrated Mary, daughter of Major Robert King I, himself strongly suspect of Presbyterianism—a "committeeman" of the "Associators' Government"—anti-Lord Baltimore and anti-Roman Catholic. This King became afterwards an able and trusted official in the Royal Province and was the founder of the colonial Somerset house of great wealth and prestige—"King of Kingsland," with its subsequent branches distinguished as "King of Beverley" and "King of Kingston Hall." The second Robert King of "Kingsland" (Francis Jenckins' brother-in-law) was for years a ruling elder of the Session of Manokin Presbyterian Congregation (as were his sons and grandsons). So indoctrinated with the faith of the Covenanting fathers was Madam Mary (King) Jenckins that when, "in the course of Divine Providence," her beloved Francis was removed, she took unto herself as *second choice* the Reverend John Henry, minister of the Presbyterian Congregation of Rehoboth; and at his decease made *third choice* in the silver-tongued and scholarly John Hampton, minister of the Snow Hill Congregation. Francis Jenckins and Mary, his wife (as someone has facetiously described her "a King who became a Queen") were the most trusted friends of the Reverend Francis Makemie—founder of organized Presbyterianism in America—and to whom he entrusted jointly the execution of his will and the guardianship of his children should his wife, Namoi Makemie, predecease him (which, however, she did not).[48] So surrounded how could Francis Jenckins withstand "the faith of the Covenant"?

In George Layfield, of the Coventry Vestry, we have the greatest of rebels against the canon law of the Church of England; at least that was the final end of this man. "In love" he set his will like adamant against the canon law of the ancient church and the "law of the land," and in Quaker fashion (though witnessed by both a Church of England and a Presbyterian divine) took unto himself as his second wife "his niece, Mistress Priscilla White." As a matter of fact, this charming young lady was the niece of Layfield's deceased first wife, who was none other than Madam Elizabeth Stevens, widow of William Stevens, of "Rehoboth." In consequence of his defiance Layfield and his second wife were both subjected to indictment by a Somerset Grand Jury and fined. Of this celebrated case we shall hear in full later on.[49] We shall also see how Presbyterianism in Somerset is indebted to Stevens, of "Rehoboth"—Church of England man—for its Father-Founder, Makemie.

In regard to the men whose names appear as members of the first vestries of Somerset, Coventry, Stepney and Snow Hill Parishes, but who have not been singled out by any particular historically significant fact or connection in their lives, a word must be said in passing. Richard Chambers, John Panter and Peter Elzey, of the Somerset Vestry; Thomas Nuball (or Newbold, as appears by the local records to have been the proper spelling of the name) and William Planer, Senior (Planner is the proper spelling of the name) of Coventry; Weatherly, Bounds, Carter, Collyer (Collier) and Askue (also Askew) of Stepney; Scarborough, Round, Francklin, Pointer and Selby, of Snow Hill Parish, were apparently all gentlemen of a quiet and serviceable way of living and founders of families of substantial worth in "Old Somerset." Matthew Scarborough and John Francklin were trusted officials; both of them members of the court, and Scarborough a representative of the county in the Lower House of Assembly. William Round (again a "suspect Presbyterian") belonged to a family of prominent merchants of the "Sea board side" and Snow Hill Town neighborhoods. Scarborough married the daughter of the first John Wise, of Accomack in Virginia, and a niece of the celebrated Colonel

Edmund Scarburgh; though Matthew, bearing the name of Scarborough, does not show in the records as "kin" to the *Scarburghs*.[50]

Miles Gray, of the Somerset Vestry (who was residing in Accomack in Virginia in 1670, aged thirty-three years, coming at a later date to Somerset), appears in the records of Somerset in 1671 as quite at odds with his wife, trying to abandon her. The court, upon investigation, saw no reason, however, why he should not live with and support her, and so ordered him to do.[51] Edward Hammond, of Snow Hill Parish, became a notorious and defiant evil liver and was, in 1706, "after warning & admonishment given by Mr. Robert Keith, Minister," presented to the Grand Jury by the Vestry of Snow Hill Parish.[52]

It may be added that no lists have been found of vestries of the four Somerset County parishes for the period prior to the year 1700, other than the lists of the first elected vestries as given above. No vestry records for the period remain, and a reading of the Somerset Court records prior to the year 1700 has failed to discover the names of any other vestrymen of these parishes.

Though exceedingly rich in detail relative to several aspects of Church of England affairs in "Old Somerset," the remaining records, both local and general, are singularly silent relative to the erection of church buildings in this area during the early days.[53] No reference has so far been discovered to any church building used for Church of England purposes in this area from the first settlement in 1662 up to the year 1692, when this Church was established by law in the province of Maryland. We know that loyal "Churchmen" were in this settlement from the time of its planting and we may think it exceedingly improbable that men and women loyal to this form of faith did not see to it that houses of worship of some nature—however simple they may have been—were erected for regular gatherings of the faithful. Yet no positive evidence of even the simplest of such structures appears prior to the year 1692.

The first recorded reference discovered to a building used for Church of England purposes is in November, 1692, when the court of Somerset County designated *"Pocomoke Church"* as the place, on December 27th following, for the freeholders of Pocomoke and Annemessex Hundreds to meet for the purpose of electing the first vestry for Coventry Parish. No reference has been found which gives any indication of the exact location, the date of erection, or of the nature of the structure of this *"Pocomoke Church."* In fact, this one reference to this *"Pocomoke Church"* is all that has been discovered regarding it.[54] From all circumstances, however, we are led to believe that this *"Pocomoke Church"* of 1692 stood somewhere within the grounds at present surrounding the remaining walls of the old Coventry Parish Church in the village of Rehoboth, on the west side of Pocomoke River in Somerset County. The town of Rehoboth (now but a village) was a thriving center of trade in Somerset County during the latter part of the seventeenth and early eighteenth centuries, and was alternately called *"Pocomoke Town."*[55] The records are as silent as to the time of disappearance or abandonment of this *"Pocomoke Church"* as they are to the date of its erection. We cannot even say with certainty that this *"Pocomoke Church"* was originally erected exclusively for purposes of worship according to the use of the Church of England. We only find it designated by the Somerset Court to be used as the place for the election of the first vestry of Coventry Parish after the Church of England had by law become the established church of the province. In this connection we must not fail to remember that the organization of the parochial life of the Church of England was not a matter left exclusively to "Churchmen" (technically speaking), but comprehended all "freeholders" within the respective parishes regardless of their religious affiliations. Pocomoke and Annemessex Hundreds, by whose combination Coventry Parish was created, were marked by diversity in their religious composition—Presbyterians and Quakers being found in abundance in this section; while Church of England adherents in this vicinity at the time seemed to hold a more or less liberal attitude towards "Dissenters."* Whatever may have been the exact nature of this *"Pocomoke Church,"* we find it referred to only once and that in November, 1692. Whatever may finally have become of this *"Pocomoke Church,"* it seems quite certain that it was not taken over and used as the "parish church" of Coventry. On July 30, 1694, in a report on the "State of the Constitution of the Government [of Maryland] vizt as to Ecclesiasticall, Civill & Military Affaires, delivered to his Ex[celle]^{ncy} [Francis Nicholson, governor of the province] by Members of the

---

*See post page 169, note, "Pocomoke Church, 1692."

Councill at the Board" we have the specific statement: *"Somerset County has four parishes laid out; but never a Church."* The report for Somerset County was evidently made by Colonel David Brown, of Somerset, member of the governor's council, who was present "at the Board" on that date.[56] The statement *"but never a Church"* refers, of course, to the fact that none of the parishes in Somerset County had by that date erected parish church buildings in accordance with provisions of the Act of 1692.

In considering the question of the erection of parish churches for Stepney, Somerset, Coventry and Snow Hill Parishes in Somerset County, we begin then with the fact that in July, 1694, though *"Somerset County has four parishes laid out"*; no parish church had been erected. Such a condition did not long continue, and the vestries of the parishes in Somerset County were soon engaged in fulfilling the provision of the Act of Assembly of June, 1692—establishing the Church of England in the province—which directed that vestries elected in accordance with that Act should build Parish Churches and Chapels of Ease in parishes which already did not have such buildings within their precincts.[57]

Unfortunately no records remain of the proceedings of the vestries of the four parishes in Somerset County relative to the building of the first Parish Churches. Fortunately for our purpose, however, other records contain certain items of circumstantial evidence pointing to the erection of the Coventry Parish Church prior to May, 1696, and Stepney, Somerset and Snow Hill Parish Churches as probably having reached completion during the years 1697 or 1698. There is evidence of a positive nature as to the existence of church buildings in Stepney Parish in 1701 and in Coventry, Somerset and Snow Hill Parishes in 1705.*

These "Parish Churches" were all erected on large waterways and in locations most convenient to their respective bodies of parishoners. The church of Stepney Parish was erected on the west side of Wicomico River, near the fork created by the confluence of Haste's Creek with that river, a location identified today as about 150 yards "north by west" of the present Parish Church—familiarly referred to as "Green

---

*See post page 174, *et seq.*, for Parish Churches and Chapels of Ease.

Hill Church." This site is a few miles down Wicomico River from the city of Salisbury, Maryland. Stepney Parish Church was at the date of its erection in Somerset County; but today—by sub-division of territory in 1867—is in Wicomico County. The first Parish Church of Somerset Parish was built on the north side of Manokin River, on the ancient Elzey estate of "Almodington," and immediately opposite from old Somerset Town, which was on the south side of this river. The site of this first Parish Church of Somerset Parish may today be identified as a spot of ground—now under water, but reachable at low tide of the river—about a half mile west of the mouth of Goose Creek and about six miles southwest of the town of Princess Anne. The site of this old first Parish Church of Somerset Parish is, by actual measurement (made by Benjamin J. Dashiell in 1933) 387 feet southwest of the brick mansion house on the "Almodington" estate. Coventry Parish Church was erected in the town of Rehoboth on Pocomoke River, and today the lines of its foundations may be found immediately back of the classic fragmentary walls of old "Rehoboth Church," which stand at the western end of the village. The Parish Church of Snow Hill (later All Hallow's) Parish was erected in the town of Snow Hill, near the head of tidewater on Pocomoke River, and on a town lot of ground just back from the riverside. At the time of its erection, the Snow Hill Parish Church was, of course, in Somerset County; but since 1742 has been within the limits of Worcester County, which was established at that date from part of the area of the original Somerset County. Today these original Parish Churches are but memories.

With the division of the county in 1692 into four parishes, Stepney, Somerset, Coventry and Snow Hill, the election of vestries, and the erection of Parish Churches, we find the Church of England fully organized in "Old Somerset"—the foundation, as it were, of this Household of Faith securely laid for the building of the Church through the coming ages.

During the early years of the period immediately succeeding the organization of the parishes in Somerset County, we find the Reverend John Huett, who for twelve years prior thereto had served practically as a missionary of the Church of England in Somerset County, acting in the capacity of minister of Stepney and Somerset Parishes. Mr. Huett's ministry in these parishes covered the period between 1692 and 1696, during which time (as for many years before) he appears to have been the only minister of the Church of England resident in Somerset County.[58] Coventry and Snow Hill Parishes do not appear to have had resident ministers prior to 1696, though a tradition prevails to the effect that Mr. Huett, as he was able, rendered to these parishes what service he could. In 1696, we find the Reverend George Trotter as incumbent of Stepney and Somerset Parishes, and the Reverend James Brechin as incumbent of Snow Hill Parish. Mr. Brechin does not seem to have remained long in Snow Hill Parish, but transferred his ministry to Coventry Parish before the end of the year; remaining in charge there from 1696 to 1698. The Reverend Mr. Trotter remained as incumbent of Stepney and Somerset Parishes from 1696 to the Fall of 1703, when he became rector of All Faith's Parish in St. Mary's County. The Reverend Mr. Brechin seems to have given up the incumbency of Coventry Parish in 1698; and Coventry does not appear to have had another minister until 1703, when the Reverend Robert Keith came to the parish, remaining until the year 1707.[59]

Thus we are able to trace the record of the Church of England in "Old Somerset" from the arrival in this territorial area of "Churchmen" with the first settlers in 1662.

Notes

1. *Pocomoke Church, 1692* — 2. *Parish Churches and Chapels of Ease*—The Parish Churches: (a) Coventry Parish Church; (b) Stepney Parish Church; (c) Somerset Parish Church; (d) Snow Hill (All Hallows) Parish Church—The Chapels of Ease: (1) Stepney Parish: (a) Goddard's Chapel; (b) Spring Hill Chapel; (c) Broad Creek Chapel—(2) Somerset Parish: (a) King's Mill Chapel; (b) The Chapel of Ease in Princess Anne Town—(3) Coventry Parish: (a) Annemessex Chapel; (b) Dividing Creek Chapel; (c) Proposed Chapel near Stevens' Ferry, 1774—(4) Snow Hill (or All Hallows) Parish: (a) Chapel near St. Martin's River; St. Martin's Church and Worcester Parish; (b) A Chapel in Worcester Parish (Prince George's Chapel, Sussex County, Delaware); (c) Chapels in All Hallows Parish, 1771 and 1774.

Pocomoke Church, 1692

In considering the all too brief reference to *"Pocomoke Church"* in 1692, we cannot help wondering if by any probability this structure was identical with a certain *"Rehoboth Church"* referred to in Somerset Court records in 1691. No church records from the vicinity of these churches—or this church (if the two references are to the same structure)—remain to us, and a search in the Somerset Court records has not been successful in producing any evidence whatsoever to assist in solving the problem. However, if *"Rehoboth Church"* of 1691 and *"Pocomoke Church"* of 1692 were one and the same, then "Old Somerset" possessed a house of worship which was used in common by a congregation of the Presbyterian Church and a congregation of the Church of England for the services of their respective religious bodies.

"Rehoboth Church"—so called in the records—is referred to in 1691 as the place in which the Reverend Francis Makemie, the Presbyterian divine, had in that year preached a funeral sermon. The reference is as follows:

"Memorandum: That upon the second of this present April A° 1691 there being a funeral Sermon preached at Rehoboth Church by Mr. Francis Makemy, minister" (Somerset Court, Judicials, Liber A. W. [1687-89 and 1690-91], page 90).

Thus we find *"Rehoboth Church"* in use by a Presbyterian minister.[1]

"Pocomoke Church" is referred to in November, 1692, as the place at which the freeholders of Pocomoke and Annemessex Hundreds were directed to meet, December 27th following, to elect a vestry for Coventry Parish, which parish was composed of the said Hundreds (Somerset Court, Judicials, Liber 1692-3, page 154).

"Rehoboth Church" of 1691 was certainly situated in the town of Rehoboth on the Pocomoke River. *"Pocomoke Church"* may certainly, from its very name, be located as in the vicinity of the Pocomoke River and as being in Pocomoke Hundred. There is remaining record evidence from the year 1708 which describes the town of Rehoboth as *"Pocomoke Town called Rehoboth,"*[2] while years before (in March, 1671/2) *"the house of William Stevens at Pocomoke"* is named as one of the preaching stations of the Reverend Robert Matix (or Maddocks), a minister whose denominational affiliation is now entirely unknown.[3] "The house of William Stevens at Pocomoke" was immediately on the Pocomoke River on his plantation which bore the name "Rehoboth." The town of Rehoboth was laid out in 1683 on a portion of this tract of land

---

[1] See post page 234 *et seq.*, for the Presbyterian Church at Rehoboth.
[2] Will of Reverend Francis Makemie (the Presbyterian minister) dated April 27, 1708, probated in Accomac County, Virginia, court, August 4, 1708, refers to a lot in *"Pocomoke Town called Rehoboth."* For excerpt from Makemie's will giving this item, see post.
[3] See ante page 121 for account of Matix's preaching stations in Somerset County.

which Stevens had sold; the town site being only about half a mile below Stevens' house site on the river.[4]

Of course, there is a tradition to the effect that the Presbyterian Congregation—organized about 1683-4—had its individual church building at Rehoboth Town at a very early date; a tradition which has secured itself in print from a writing by the Reverend Samuel McMaster (1744-1811), who was for many years pastor of the Rehoboth Presbyterian Church. Mr. McMaster wrote an account of early Presbyterianism in Somerset County, but unfortunately his manuscript (for his account was never put into print) has long since disappeared. Only a bare fragment of the McMaster manuscript remains, having been quoted by Irving Spence in his *Letters on the Early History of the Presbyterian Church in America* (published in Philadelphia in 1835). Mr. Spence in his book (page 97) quotes from McMaster's manuscript as follows: "The first congregation [of Presbyterians] which worshipped at Rehoboth . . . formed themselves into a religious society for the public worship of God. A house for public worship was built on the west side of the [Pocomoke] River at a place called Rehoboth."[5] Mr. Spence quoting Mr. McMaster's statement, but supplying no date, argues that the building referred to by McMaster preceded the so-called "new Meeting House" in Rehoboth Town, which is so referred to in the Reverend Francis Makemie's will in 1708. This so-called "new Meeting House" was erected between 1705 and 1706 as proved by records of that period.[6] Spence rests his argument for a prior building on the ground of Makemie's use of the term *"new* Meeting House." Spence argues that the term *"new"* is used by Makemie in contradistinction to an older building that had been erected and used by the Presbyterian congregation at Rehoboth. The Reverend L. P. Bowen, in his *Days of Makemie* (page 529) quoting the recorded reference to the Reverend Francis Makemie's (the Presbyterian divine) having preached a funeral sermon in *"Rehoboth Church"* in April, 1691, says that this reference proves "that the 'new church' of Makemie's will [1708] was the *second* there built." Thus the tradition in its classic form comes down through the local historians.[7]

The Church of England side also has its tradition as to a church building erected at Rehoboth Town at a very early date. This tradition in its classic form comes down to us in a historical sermon preached by the Reverend Samuel F. Hotchkin in August, 1892. Mr. Hotchkin refers to *"Pocomoke Church"* as being in existence in 1692 and at that time designated as the place of meeting of the freeholders for the election of a vestry for Coventry Parish. On the ground that this so-called *"Pocomoke Church"* was designated for this purpose Hotch-

---

[4]See post for note on Rehoboth Town. This town was located on that part of the Rehoboth tract which Stevens sold to James Weedon and Weedon's heir sold to Francis Jenkins. Jenkins was the owner of the land when the town was laid out.
[5]Spence comments on the passage from which we have made this excerpt: "Copied from the autograph of the Rev. Samuel McMaster, for many years pastor of the Church [Rehoboth]."
[6]See post page 234, *et seq.* for account of this "new Meeting House" erected on Makemie's lot in Rehoboth Town between 1705 and 1706.
[7]There is also a local tradition which places a Presbyterian church building, antedating the so-called "new Meeting House" (1705-1706 and 1708) on a site near the old mill dam at Rehoboth Town, which site is some yards northwest of the site of the "new Meeting House."

kin claims it as an edifice of the Church of England, and refers to it as the "first [church building] probably built of logs, built before 1692."[8] The Reverend Ethan Allen, in his *Who Were the Early Settlers of Maryland?* also claims this so-called *"Pocomoke Church"* as exclusively a Church of England edifice: "Somerset [County] four parishes, *one church* . . ."[9]

Thus we have the Presbyterian tradition of *"Rehoboth Church"* of 1691 as a house of worship erected by Presbyterians sometime prior to that date; and the Church of England tradition of *"Pocomoke Church"* of 1692 as a house of worship erected by a congregation of the Church of England, sometime prior to that date.

These traditions may contain and convey actual facts; we neither affirm nor deny them. But another view of the matter presents itself to this present writer, who cannot forbear setting it forth here for consideration.

May not the so-called *"Rehoboth Church"* of 1691 and the so-called *"Pocomoke Church"* of 1692 have been in reality identical, and in use by both Presbyterians and Church of England people for the services of their respective churches? No doubt this house of worship was erected, if not before, then probably about the time Rehoboth Town was laid out in 1683—*"Pocomoke Town called Rehoboth."* We know that in other parts of the province of Maryland there were houses of worship used in common (though not in unity) by colonists who differed in their religious denominational affiliations. There was the ancient "Chapel" (so called) in St. Mary's County which was used, near the beginning of the settlement of the province, by both Protestants and Roman Catholics for their respective services of worship. Then there is record of a house of worship in Cecil (now Kent) County which was so used by Protestants of differing religious persuasions.[10] May not this *"Rehoboth Church"-"Pocomoke Church"* in Somerset County have had its origin from the services held by Robert Matix at *"the house of William Stevens at Pocomoke"* in 1671/2 and later. Certainly this rather populous section along the Pocomoke River provided some place—some kind of a house—for regular purposes of public worship—Rehoboth Town was laid out in 1683. Rehoboth Town and Pocomoke Town were, we have seen, two names for the same town. This was a center for gatherings of people. *"Rehoboth Church"* of 1691; *"Pocomoke Church"* of 1692—may they not have been one and the same, and called alternately *"Rehoboth Church"* and *"Pocomoke Church,"* as the town itself was evidently alternately referred to as Rehoboth and Pocomoke Town? We simply ask the question. We cannot answer it. But, from all circumstances, the question has framed itself and will not lie quiet in the mind. Maybe some day there will be light of evidence dispelling the shadow of uncertainty.

---

[8]*"Sermon by the Rev. Samuel F. Hotchkin 1892 (with) Addenda by the Rev. Oliver H. Murphy, rector of Coventry Parish," page 8.*
[9]Quoted by Thomas, *Chronicles of Colonial Maryland*, page 172-3, footnote 2.
[10]For the "Chapel" in St. Mary's County used by both Protestants and Roman Catholics, see Thomas, *Chronicles of Colonial Maryland*, pages 38-39; and for reference to a "Meeting House" in Cecil County (now in Kent County by division of territory) and used by all Christians regardless of denomination, see Skirven, *Ancient Shrewsbury [Parish, Kent County] Scenes of Early Protestant Struggles*, page 3.

Assuming that *"Rehoboth Church"* of 1691, (used by the Presbyterians), and *"Pocomoke Church"* of 1692, (used by Church of England people), were one and the same building, we think from the very names by which it was referred to, that the structure must have stood on a lot of ground within the limits of the town of Rehoboth.[11] We cannot even hazard a guess about the date at which the building was erected nor as to the material of which it was constructed—whether of log, boards, or brick.

As we know nothing of the date of the erection of this *"Rehoboth Church"-"Pocomoke Church"* building, so we know nothing positively about the date of its disappearance or abandonment. It is quite certain, however, that this building had disappeared by July, 1694, when report was made to the governor of the province that

> "Somerset County has four Parishes laid out, *but never a Church* . . ."[12]

Certainly the Church of England congregation in Coventry Parish, which included Rehoboth Town, had at that date, July, 1694, no church building in use. That the Presbyterian congregation about Rehoboth Town did not have any church building in use in 1697 is clearly shown by the sheriff's report of that year in regard to places of worship (technically called "Meeting Houses") of the "Dissenters" in Somerset County. The "Dissenters" were certainly Presbyterians. The sheriff's report, 1697, specifically mentions "Meeting Houses" at Manokin, Snow Hill and "on the road going up along the Sea Side." There is no reference whatsoever in the report to any "Dissenters'" house of worship at, or near, Rehoboth Town. In March, 1702/3, the Presbyterian congregation of Rehoboth Town was using a private dwelling for purposes of assembly for worship.[13] This *"Rehoboth Church"-"Pocomoke Church"* of 1691 and 1692—used, as we believe, by both Presbyterians and Church of England congregations for purposes of worship, had disappeared as a place of worship by 1694. This *"Rehoboth Church"-"Pocomoke Church,"* being as we believe one and the same building, was (we think) the *first* church building used by the Presbyterian congregation at Rehoboth Town (and vicinity) and the *first* church building used by the congregation of Church of England people in the same vicinity. But *"Rehoboth Church"-"Pocomoke Church"* was not exclusively used by either congregation.

With the establishment of the Church of England as the "state church" in the province of Maryland in June, 1692, the *"Rehoboth Church"-"Pocomoke Church"* could not any longer be used by "Churchmen" and "Dissenters" in common, and so each of these congregations must erect their own houses of worship. The Church of England congregation erected the first church of

---

[11]It may be (though there is no evidence to that effect) that this building stood on the lot of ground in Rehoboth Town, later occupied by the first erected parish church of Coventry Parish, at the west end of the town.

[12]For this report, given in full, see ante pages 162-3.

[13]For this report of the sheriff of Somerset County in 1697, see post page 236; and for the use of the former dwelling house of Reverend William Traile as a place of worship by the Presbyterian congregation in 1702/3, see post pages 236-7.

Coventry Parish about 1695 or 1696, and the Presbyterian congregation of Rehoboth erected their "new Meeting House" between 1705 and 1706.[14]

(For full discussion as to date of erection of the first church building for Coventry Parish, see post page 174; and for account of erection of the "new Meeting House" for the Presbyterian congregation at Rehoboth Town, see *post* page 237.)

---

[14]While no evidence has been discovered to that effect, it is believed by some people (and we think it not improbable) that this old "Rehoboth Church, 1691-Pocomoke Church, 1692" occupied a site very near or immediately on the ground surrounding the first and second parish churches of Coventry Parish—the latter of which became known, and was designated as, the "Rehoboth Episcopal Church" whose fragmentary walls (reclaimed in 1928) stand at this present time at the west end of the village of Rehoboth, Somerset County, Maryland. See post page 174 for note on Coventry Parish Church.

Parish Churches and Chapels of Ease

1

The Parish Churches

As circumstantial evidence that churches for the parishes of Coventry, Stepney, Somerset and Snow Hill in Somerset County were either built prior to 1697 or were in a state of erection, we quote a letter about the erection of parish churches in the province of Maryland generally, written by Governor Francis Nicholson to the Board of Trade, dated Port Annapolis, *March 27, 1697,* in which he says: "When I came hither [Sept., 1694] I found very few of the Churches built according to the former Act of Assembly; *but I hope in God that they will be all finished this year* and then we shall want Clergymen, and a Commissary to inspect Church affairs, for whose maintenance an Act is passed and now sent to your Lordships." (*23 Arch. Md., p. 82*). Certainly this reference by Governor Nicholson shows that parish churches in the province which had not been completed at this date, March, 1697, were under construction or contemplation for immediate building. This item is, of course, circumstantial evidence only after a general fashion, though we quote it as not improbably including church building operations in Somerset County parishes which were certainly within the provincial wide prospects of Governor Nicholson.

(a) *Coventry Parish Church.* In the following items there seem circumstantial evidence specifically indicating the process of erection, or probable completion, of the parish church of Coventry Parish prior to May, 1696. May 2, 1696, a motion introduced in Lower House of Assembly that as vestry of Coventry Parish had considerable amount of tobacco on hand they desired to know of the House whether they should purchase a glebe or build a schoolhouse therewith. The House directed that vestry purchase a glebe. (*30 Arch. Md., p. 344*). May 25, 1696, ordered by Governor (and Council) that order, or resolve, of Lower House this past Assembly, that the tobacco in the hands of the vestry of Coventry Parish, Somerset County, be used for the purchase of a glebe, was not to go into effect, but that the sheriff of the county give notice to said vestry "that they presume not to dispose thereof for that use but that same be sold pursuant to a former ordinance of Assembly." (*20 Arch. Md., p. 448*). The "former ordinance of Assembly" here referred to was one of Oct. 18-19, 1695, which directed parish vestries, "where there is no minister *and where churches are already built,*" to expend what tobacco "they shall collect, or shall be remaining *after Churches Built,*" in erecting Chapels of Ease in their respective parishes, and should said vestries not dispose of tobacco collectible, or which remains in their hands this year (1695), that they invest the same in ready goods or bills of exchange, etc. (*19 Arch. Md., p. 256*). From the order of the Governor and Council, May 25, 1696, directing vestry of Coventry to comply with terms of this ordinance in the disposition of tobacco on hand it would seem, inferentially, that the parish at this date had no minister, and *that the parish church had been built by this date.*

Positive evidence of erection of Coventry Parish Church prior to Nov., 1705, is found in the protest of the vestry of Coventry and of Reverend Robert Keith (rector of Coventry) and Reverend Alexander Adams (rector of Stepney), presented to Somerset Court, Nov., 1705, and referred to the Governor and Council, and acted upon by that body in Feb., 1705/6. These protests were against the preaching of Reverend George M'Nish, a Presbyterian minister, in a certain "Meeting house lately erected *very nigh to the Church at Rehoboth.*" (See post page ____ for these protests and action taken thereon by Somerset Court and Governor and Council).

The *"Meeting house lately erected,"* which is referred to, was the Presbyterian Church which today is yet standing in the village of Rehoboth on Pocomoke River. *"The Church at Rehoboth"* was evidently the building which had been erected as the first parish church of Coventry Parish and which stood on the present church lot in Rehoboth Town, about one 150 yards southwest of the then so-called "Meeting house." This first parish church of Coventry Parish stood immediately behind the present remaining walls of a later (second) parish church, on which work was begun during the year 1784. In the year 1933 Mr. Cassius M. Dashiell, of Princess Anne, Maryland, directed certain excavations on this ancient church lot in Rehoboth Town, which were successful in disclosing to view the foundations of this first parish church of old Coventry. These foundations of the first parish church of Coventry measure 28 feet 2 inches in width and 59 feet in length. The north line of the foundation of this first parish church building is only 3 feet 9 inches to the south of the wall of the second church building (erected about 1785-6), the reclaimed walls of which are standing today on the church lot. In August, 1934, Cassius M. Dashiell had concrete pillars erected as markers on the four corners of the foundations (which still remain) of the first parish church of Coventry Parish.

It is evident that the land on which the Coventry Parish Church was built in Rehoboth Town was not conveyed to the parish until years after the erection of the first parish church building, for in June, 1735, we find Robert Jenckins Henry (in whom the title to the land was vested) conveying to Rev. James Robertson, John Dennis, Junior, Thomas Dixon, Thomas Hayward, Thomas Williams, William Lane and Isaac Williams, Gentlemen, Vestrymen in and for the parish of Coventry "for the use and benefitt of the said parish of Coventry a certain part or parcell of Land in Rehoboth Town in the Parish, County and Province aforesaid *on which the Parish Church now standeth* and next adjoining the same," containing two acres. (Somerset Court, Deed Liber O-18, page 233). In his will (dated July 21, 1764; probated November 14, 1766) Mr.

Henry confirmed his former conveyance of this land in the following words: "It is also my will and desire that the small parcell of Land whereon the Parish Church of Coventry now stands in Rehoboth Town by me heretofore Conveyed for that Pious Use may be by the people of the said Parish Quietly and Peaceably held used and enjoyed without the least claim or Interruption of any of my Descendants." (Somerset Registry of Wills, Liber E B 4, pages 119-121). This first parish church of Coventry, probably erected by 1696, and certainly standing on this lot of ground in the town of Rehoboth in 1705, 1735, and 1766 (as we have given references), was apparently in use up to the year 1785, when, as we learn from excerpts from old vestry records of Coventry which have come down to us, the church building, of which only the broken walls now remain standing, was erected. That the hallowed walls of this "House of God" have been preserved as a vivid reminder to the present generation of a great past is due to the thoughtful generosity of Cassius M. Dashiell, Esquire, of Princess Anne, Maryland. (For notes on later history of Coventry Parish, see Rev. Ethan Allen's manuscript history of the Eastern Shore parishes. See also *Sermon by the Reverend Samuel F. Hotchkin, 1892 (with) Addenda by the Reverend Oliver H. Murphy, rector of Coventry Parish*.)

The evidence that the building, of which the fragmentary walls now remain, was erected in 1785 and 6 is contained in a manuscript entitled *"Noticae of Coventry Parish, consisting mostly of extracts from old Parish Register now in possesion of William Williams, M.D. By John Crosdale, Rector. January 1st, 1848."* This manuscript is entered in a Vestry Book of Coventry Parish now (1934) in possession of the vestry of that parish.

The items in the *"Noticae"* relating to the erection of the church building in question are as follows:

> "Sept. 1st [1783] 'Ordered that Mr. Thos. Bruff & Mr. Geo. Waters draw a subscription paper in order for building a Church at Rehoboth' which paper was afterwards approved" (page 6).

> "August 12th [1784] It was proposed to the parishioners assembled at Rehoboth according to previous notice 'where the new Church should be built when it was agreed by a great majority that it should be built on the church lands at Rehoboth on such parts of the church lands as the Vestry should think proper'" (page 6).

> Oct. 18 [1784] Vestry agree that two of them draw a petition to the General Assembly of Maryland for a law to pass to call a sum of money out of different sheriffs hands heretofore collected for to build a chapel of ease over Pocomoke River[1] and apply same to the building of Rehoboth Church. This petition was presented and granted. Vide Laws of Maryland (page 7).

---

[1]This is a reference to a Chapel of Ease proposed to be built in 1774 near Stevens' Ferry on east side the Pocomoke River (present, 1934, site of Pocomoke City). This chapel was never erected. For account of its proposed erection, see post, page 201.

March 7th 1785. Agreement as to place new church should be built and the vestry gave the building thereof to the lowest bidder and it was struck off to Isaac Marshall at 700 pounds; i. e. the brick work and roof, door frames and window frames. The size of the church to be *"a brick house seventy feet long and forty-six feet wide from inside to inside"* (page 8).

May 1st, 1786. *"It is agreed by the Vestry that the Church at Rehoboth should be two stories high"* (page 9).

May 22nd, 1786. Isaac Marshall dying before finishing his part of the contract Vestry agreed with his widow, Mrs. Sarah Marshall, to let her off from the building of the Church at Rehoboth, on having all the work of every kind valued by the judgment of certain gentlemen, and to allow Mrs. Marshall for the same (page 9).

June 10, [1786]. Agreement with Elijah Broughton to make 31 window frames at 3/9^d and with Robert Lankford to make bricks at 3/6 per M (page 10).

August 6th [1786]. Ways and means for to finish the Church discussed. Sale of pews agreed as best method. On August 27th the sale of pews was made (page 10).

1792. A lottery was gotten up in the parish for benefit of the new church (page 12).

January 9, 1793. The Vestry agreed with Littleton Long to plant trees in the Church Yard (page 12).

The church at Rehoboth Town, to which the above items refer was the second parish church building of Coventry Parish. This building was completely paid for by July, 1803, as in a "Journal of Bishop Claggett's Visitation to the Eastern Shore," which bears the heading *"Easton* [Talbot County, Maryland] *23d July 1803";* the following entry occurs:[2]

"The 17th [i. e. July 17th, 1803] (Sunday) joined by Dr. Gardiner, went to Rehoboth Church, *it was consecrated by the Bishop,* a sermon by him and a confirmation of 36 persons."[3]

This old Rehoboth Church—second parish church building of Coventry Parish; erected between 1784 (in which year work was begun on its construction) and 1792 (when there is evidence that the building had certainly been com-

---

[2]Utley, *The Life and Times of Thomas John Claggett* . . . pages 117-118.
[3]Somerset County and its four parishes were included in the Diocese of Maryland until 1868 when the Diocese of Maryland was divided and the nine counties (one of which was Somerset) on the Eastern Shore were erected into the Diocese of Easton; the diocese taking its name from the then principal city on the Eastern Shore, and place of residence of the bishop—Easton, Talbot County.

pleted), consecrated in 1803,[4] continued in use for something more than a century. By 1900 it had fallen into a sad state of repair and a movement was set on foot to restore it, though this restoration was never accomplished. By degrees the wonderful old building crumbled. In 1928 Cassuis M. Dashiell, of Princess Anne, with his true and uncompromising love for the "origins" of his venerated "Old Somerset" reclaimed the sacred ruins of this House of God, having the fragmentary remaining walls strengthened and capped in concrete; replacing the floor with concrete and erecting a cross-crowned altar to memorialize the hallowed place. Immediately to the south of (and only a few feet away) lie the foundations of the first parish church of Coventry, laid in this soil about 1695 or 6; while these two emblems—the foundations of the "Old" and the fragmentary walls of the "New"—bear silent yet glorious witness to the succession of a faith that cannot fail.

* * * *

(b) *Stepney Parish Church.* In account of indebtedness due by the estate of Rev. John Huett to Joseph Venables appears an item which gives a bit of circumstantial evidence as to the time of the erection of the first parish church of Stepney. In Somerset Court, March 19, 1699 (1699/1700), Joseph Venables filed the following account:

"Mr. John Huett D^r (debtor)

P^r (price) lbs. tob?

To the building of Dwelling House att	10,000	Contra C^r (credit)	
		To Tob^o paid Wm Keene	7,000
To the Shingling the Same House	4,000	To Tob^o paid Mr Dan^{ll} Hast	1,000
To 1 Pew att	500	To Tob^o paid in Earthen Ware	400
To 1 Weading harrow	400		8,400
Sum Totall	14,900		
	8,400		
due to ball^s (balance)	6,500		

Errors Excepted pr me Joseph Venables.

---

[4]There is a statement to the effect that "Rehoboth Church" was consecrated by Bishop Claggett in 1795, made by the late Reverend Oliver H. Murphy in his Addenda to the 200th Anniversary ("*Sermon by the Reverend Samuel F. Hotchkin . . . August 21st, 1892,*" page 11). Mr. Hotchkin (page 8 of his sermon) says "the present church was consecrated by Bishop Claggett on Sunday, July 17th, A.D. 1803." The quotation given above from "Journal of Bishop Claggett's Visitation to the Eastern Shore" in 1803 certainly seems to indicate that Rehoboth Church was consecrated by Bishop Claggett in July, 1803. Bishop Claggett certainly visited the churches in Somerset County (Coventry Parish Church-"Rehoboth Church"—among them in 1795; there are records remaining which list confirmations made by him in Somerset County churches at that date. It may be that the knowledge of this fact has led to the assumption that "Rehoboth Church" was consecrated by him during his visitation in 1795. We are, however, inclined to accept the statement of consecration as of July 17, 1803. In all probability the church building was not entirely free of debt in 1795 and so could not be consecrated at that time. By 1803 all indebtedness for its construction having been cleared off, the Bishop proceeded to its consecration at that time.

The above account being proved in open Court by the oath of the said Joseph Venables It is thereupon ordered by the Court that the said Joseph Venables recover ag^t the said Nicholas Evans and Rachel, his wife, adm^{rs} of Mr. John Huett, decd. the ballance of the above acco^t Viz^t Six Thousand five hundred pounds of Tobacco Cost alias Exon (execution)." (Somerset Court, Judicials, Liber D. F. 1698-1701, page 324).

The item in the above account *"To 1 Pew att 500* (pounds tobacco)" evidently refers to the cost of *a pew* built by Mr. Venables *in the parish church* for the Reverend Mr. Huett during Huett's lifetime. Mr. Huett was the first minister of Stepney Parish and died during the Spring (probably in March) of 1698. His widow, Rachel Huett, petitioned the Maryland Assembly, March 28, 1698, relative to arrearages in her late husband's salary as minister of Stepney and Somerset Parishes. (*22 Arch. Md., page 113*). The work for which Mr. Venables filed his bill in Somerset Court, March 19, 1699/1700, was certainly done prior to Mr. Huett's death, which evidently took place during early March of the year 1698. Therefore the *"Pew"* whose construction was charged in the account was built before March, 1698, and if—as we believe it was— built in the Stepney Parish Church, then we here have circumstantial evidence that *the first church of Stepney Parish was erected prior to March, 1698.*

While the circumstantial evidence (as recited above) certainly warrants our believing that the first church of Stepney Parish was erected prior to March, 1698, there is evidence of a positive nature showing that this first church had been built prior to September, 1701.[1]

The location of the first parish church of Stepney was on a lot of ground near the mouth of Haste's Creek (south side), about 150 yards above where this creek enters the west side of Wicomico River, which lot of ground was included in *"The Draught of Greenehill Towne and Pourtt, Anno Domini 1707 . . . Wm. Whittington, Serv^r,"* and marked on the said plat "C" with reference: *"C. ye Church ground."* (The original of this draught is in the Maryland Historical Society, Baltimore, presented thereto by Cassius M. Dashiell, of Princess Anne). We find references to *"Stepney Church"* in August, 1723, when overseers were appointed for the roads from the church to both Hutchins' and Crockett's Ferries (Somerset Court Judicials, 1722-4, page 92). This site remained the location of the Stepney Parish Church until the erection in 1733 of the brick church which stands today on the west side of Wicomico River on what was originally Lot No. 16 in Green Hill Town. This later location is about fifty yards southeast of the site of the first parish church. April

---

[1] The vestry of Stepney Parish petitioned Somerset Court, 11th 9ber [Sept.] 1701 stating that in 1699 the court charged the vestry with maintaining the poor of the parish; this they have done, but find that no other parish has the same burden and that the poor in them are maintained "out of the county stock"; the Stepney vestry though maintaining the poor of its parish out of the 40 pounds tobacco per poll, yet have the same assessment laid upon the parish for maintaining the poor throughout the county; statement is made of certain poor persons assisted by the Stepney Parish in 1699 and 1700; *"and we are yet considerably indebted to the workmen for the finishing of our church,"* therefore must leave the poor to the court's maintenance for time to come and pray for allowance out of the county stock in order to pay debts for which they are engaged for keeping the poor. "Signed pr order pr me Robt. Bowditch, Clerk of ye Vestry." (Somerset Court, Judicials, Liber P, 1701-1702, page 39.)

19, 1731, Neal McClester (for 38 shillings currency) conveyed to the vestry of Stepney Parish, Somerset County, Lot No. 16 in Green Hill Town, "to the said Vestry and their successors forever to the only Propper use and behoof of the Parrish aforesaid forevermore." (Somerset Court, Deed Liber O 17, page 315). In the year 1733 the second parish church of Stepney was erected—a substantial building of brick—on the Lot No. 16 of Green Hill Town plan. The date of erection of this church—1733—is worked in large figures into the construction of the east end of the building. In 1887 this church was consecrated, with the name of St. Bartholomew's Church, by the Right Reverend William Forbes Adams, Bishop of Easton. After years of desuetude and decay, this "Old Green Hill Church," as it is affectionately called and known, was wonderfully restored through the generosity of friends, chief of whom was Cassius M. Dashiell, of Princess Annee, and stands today with high boxed pews, high pulpit and clerk's desk (on the south wall), Holy Table with communion rail in the east, and double entrance on the west, a precious and wonderfully beautiful memorial of the old parish of Stepney—still retaining its dignity as "the Parish Church."[2]

* * * *

(c) *Somerset Parish Church.* The first parish church building for Somerset Parish was situated on the north side of Manokin River on an acre of ground of the "Almodington" estate of the Elzey family, the exact location of the church building being about half a mile west of the mouth of Goose Creek. This first church site is now covered by the waters of Manokin River, which have by their continuous washings detached it from the mainland. The old foundations (of brick) of this first parish church of Somerset Parish may still be reached and touched at low tide. One can even wade out, at certain times, in the river to the site of these foundations. In the Summer of 1932 Mr. Benjamin J. Dashiell, of Towson, Maryland (who is a civil engineer and student of historical sites in Somerset County), with the assistance of Mr. Cassius M. Dashiell, of Princess Anne (Senior Warden of Somerset Parish and for years a student of the parish's history), definitely located this site of the first parish church of Somerset, and Mr. Benjamin Dashiell examined the remaining foundations, in so far as the water covering them would permit. The site of this first parish church is on the opposite side of the river from the western boundary (somewhat northwest therefrom) of the original location of old "Somerset Town" (see post page _____ for account of this town). We have discovered no positive evidence as to the date of the erection of this first church of Somerset Parish; but we believe that it was erected between July, 1694 (at which date we have evidence that none of the parish churches had been built in Somerset

---

[2] In 1771 there was some question raised as to "Green Hill Church" being the Parish Church of Stepney Parish. All doubts and questionings were silenced by an Act of Assembly, Oct.-Nov. 1771, which declared "Green-hill" to be the parish church. (*Laws of Maryland*, Acts of Assembly 1771, chapter 9).

County (see ante page 163), and March, 1697, when Governor Nicholson in a letter to the Board of Trade, referring to the erection of parish churches in the province of Maryland, wrote: "I hope in God that they will be all finished this year." (See Governor Nicholson's letter given ante page ___). The first positive recorded evidence of the existence of the first parish church of Somerset Parish is on February 6, 1705 (1705/6), when "Arnold Elzey of Somerset County in ye Province of Maryland, Gent & Major, his wife" conveyed by deed to "our Sovereign Lady Queen Anne of England, &c. for ye use of Somerset Parish in ye Province & county af^d . . . a part or parcel of Land Taken out of ye . . . tract or Dividend of Land called Almodington standing near ye Riverside where the Church of ye above sd parish now standeth . . . containing and laid out for one acre of land." (Somerset Court, Deed Liber O 9, page 53-54). This parish church across the Manokin River from, and opposite, "Somerset Town" was evidently still in use in November, 1708, when a road was directed "to be cleared to Monocan Town [old Somerset Town] from Mr. John King's Mill" because "it would be convenient for all persons to go to *ye Church in Town.*" (Somerset Court, Judicials Liber E F H, 1707-1711, page 152). The road thus directed to be cleared is what is now known as the old road down Revell's Neck in Somerset County, and extends in a westwardly direction from about the site of old King's Mill, at the head of King's Creek, to a farm known as "Clifton," which embraces the tract of ground originally laid out as "Somerset Town" (also called "Sommerton" and "Monocan Town"). Just how long this first Somerset Parish Church continued in use we do not know and have found no recorded evidence to guide us in determining. Sometime after November, 1708, however—and tradition says in 1710—a new parish church was built inland from the Manokin River about three miles northeast of the first church site and near the head of Little Monie Creek. This second Somerset Parish Church (built, as tradition says, about 1710) was a frame structure on brick foundation, erected on a tract of fifty acres of land granted under the patent name of "Somerset" in August, 1723, to Captain John Jones and Thomas Dashiell, the tract of land described as lying in a neck of land between the head of Little Monie Creek and Manokin River, on the head of a tract of land called Hab Nab.[3] By his will, dated March 17, 1755, and probated February 17, 1756, Thomas Dashiell, Senior, of Somerset County, gave and bequeathed *"all that tract of land called Somerset whereon Monny Church now stands To the use of the said Church and Parish forever."* (Dashiell's *Dashiell Family Records, Vol. II, pp. 257 and 260*). Thomas Dashiell (1666-1756), the donor of the land on which the second Somerset Parish Church was erected, was the son of James Dashiell (circa 1634-1697), the immigrant, of Wicomico Hundred, and Wetipquin in Nanticoke Hundred, Somerset County. (See Dashiell family note, post). Thomas Dashiell was a member of the vestry of Somerset Parish

---

[3]By the year 1824 the boundaries of the tract of land on which this church building was situated were uncertain and the vestry petitioned Somerset Court for a re-survey of the land in order to re-establish the boundaries. The report of the commission appointed by the court for this purpose together with a survey and plat of the land were returned to the court, September, 1825, and are recorded in Somerset Court Judicial Record, 1825-1827, page 11, et seq.

in 1723 (Somerset Court, Judicials 1722-4, page 52, suit of Thomas Cary against the vestry of Somerset Parish).

The earliest recorded reference we have found to this second church of Somerset Parish appears in August, 1723, when "Robert Laws was appointed overseer of roads in Manigh [Monie] Hundred, from Little Creek to the head of Little Manigh [Monie] and from Capt. Jones *to the New Church,* and from the head of Little Manigh [Monie] to William Jones on Goose Creek." (Somerset Court, Judicials 1722-24, page 91). In orders of Somerset Court, March, 1733, relative to overseers of roads *"the new Church"* is again referred to. (Somerset Court, Judicials 1733-4, page 138). On Sunday, May 14, 1738, Andrew Theodore Bourdillon (son of Reverend Benedict Bourdillon, rector of Somerset Parish, and Johanna, his wife) was "baptized in Manny [Monie] Church in Somerset Parish" (Fragment of old Somerset Parish register, MSS.). In November, 1742, we find reference to "Manny Church" in a court order appointing William Jones overseer of roads (Somerset Court, Judicials 1742-4, page 28). Thus we find this second church of Somerset Parish referred to as "the New Church" and later "Manny [Monie] Church." This second church building (which was of frame construction on a brick foundation) stood about a quarter of a mile north of the present main highway leading from the town of Princess Anne to Deals' Island, and about five miles west of Princess Anne. This second church building (which from time to time received additions and changes) was consecrated by the name of All Saints' Church, by the Right Reverend William Rollinson Whittingham, Bishop of Maryland, on November 10, 1845, and was totally demolished July 31, 1879, by a severe windstorm that visited the section. Through the devoted efforts of the late Reverend John Oliver Barton, D.D., saintly and beloved rector of the parish, with the loyal assistance of his parishioners, and friends of the parish, a new church building (of frame construction) was erected on the old foundation. This new building was consecrated by the Right Reverend Henry Champlin Lay, Bishop of Easton, May 5, 1881,[4] and stands today, "All Saints, Monie," a witness to the devotion of Somerset Parish Churchmen. All Saints' Church, Monie, remains the parish church of Somerset Parish, though by Act of the Maryland Assembly (over a century ago) the Chapel of Ease in Princess Anne Town (now St. Andrew's Church, Princess Anne) was designated, and legalized, as the place for the regular annual meetings of the congregation for the election of vestry and transaction of parish affairs.

* * * *

(d) *Snow Hill, later All Hallows Parish.* This parish was established as Snow Hill Parish (consisting of Bogerternorton and Mattapony Hundreds) in 1692 (see ante page 154) and in 1713 we find it referred to as *All Hallows*

---

[4]Somerset Parish, Somerset County, was until 1868 included in the Diocese of Maryland. In 1868 the Maryland counties on the Eastern Shore (nine in number) were erected into a diocese under the name of the Diocese of Easton, the diocese deriving its name from the then principal city of the Eastern Shore, and place of residence of the bishop—Easton, Talbot County.

Parish (John Rustell, Jun., Church Warden; Christopher Wilkinson [rector?], Jno. Purnell, Jno. Sturges, Tho. Purnell, William Cord [vestrymen?]. Petition of Vestry of *All Hallows Parish,* 9 ber 1713, to be allowed to make assessment to meet parochial charges. Somerset Court, Judicials, in Deed Liber O 12, page 7). The "Parish Church" of Snow Hill, or All Hallows Parish, has always been situated in the town of Snow Hill on Pocomoke River (Somerset County up to 1742 and since that date Worcester County). The date of the erection of the first parish church is not now known; but probably was built sometime within the period between the years 1697 and 1700.[5] The site of the first parish church (a frame structure) was on the western (or lower) part of Lot 9 in the town of Snow Hill,[6] indicated on a plat of the town dated 1793 (a reconstruction of the original town plan) by the letter *"F"* with the reference: *"F = The Old Church Lot"* (Worcester Court, Deed Liber P, page 293).

A church had certainly been erected in the town of Snow Hill prior to November, 1705, and a church (or Chapel of Ease) in the section called the "Sea Side," in the neighborhood of St. Martin's River, before that date. The evidence for the existence of these two churches prior to November, 1705, is as follows:

(a) Roger Thomas, of Somerset County, Maryland, will, dated June 26, 1703; probated October 29, 1703, devising his estate to Ince Stockly, John Stockly and William Hall, concludes his will: *"I desire that my body may be burried in the Church Yard at St. Martin's."*[7] (Somerset Registry of Wills, Liber E B 5, page 115; and Worcester Registry of Wills, Liber M H 3).

(b) Somerset Court, November 17, 1705, by order forbidding that any persons should drive or catch any horses upon the Great Bridge on Pocomoke River under penalty of fine directed that "this order be published *at the Churches* and meeting houses *At Snow Hill and Sea Side."* (Somerset Court, Judicials 1705, in Liber A. B. (O 9), page 12).

It will be noticed that distinction is made in the above court order between "Churches" and "Meeting Houses," the term "church" referred to buildings erected for worship by a parish of the Established Church in Maryland, while "meeting house" was the term technically used to designate a house of worship erected by "Dissenters." From the will of Roger Thomas, quoted above, we learn of the presence of a church in 1703 at "St. Martin's."[8] This was certainly in the section about St. Martin's River in the northeastern part of Somerset

---

[5]See ante, page 174, Governor Francis Nicholson's letter to the Board of Trade, about expected completion of parish churches in Maryland in 1697.
[6]"The Church and all the houses [in Snow Hill Town] built of wood ... The Parson of the Parish ... has the only brick house in town." (From *Observations in Several Voyages in Maryland and Virginia.* Published, London, 1746.)
[7]Was this *"Church Yard at St. Martin's"* in reality the yard, and burying ground, of a Chapel of Ease of Snow Hill Parish which had been erected in the vicinity of St. Martin's River? See post, page 202, for Chapel of Ease at St. Martin's.
[8]On March 28, 1703, Matthew Scarborough, of Somerset County, Maryland, conveyed to "Roger Thomas, of Somerset County in the Kingdom of England, Dealler" (for 7500 pounds of tobacco) a tract of 500 acres called "North Petherton" in Somerset County, Maryland, on the Seaboard side about 3 miles to the south of Cedar Neck, and extending to the easterne sea. (Somerset Court, Deed Liber O 8, page 49).

(now Worcester) County and in the section designated as the "Seaboard side" and commonly referred to as the "seaside." From the order of Somerset Court, November, 1705 (quoted above) we learn that at that date there were *"Churches . . . At Snow Hill and Sea Side."* The Church at Snow Hill in 1705 was certainly the parish church of Snow Hill (or All Hallows) Parish; while the *church* at "Seaside," 1705, certainly seems identical while the church in whose "Church Yard at St. Martin's" Roger Thomas, in 1703, directed that his body be buried.

The parish church of Snow Hill (or All Hallows) Parish was certainly erected quite early. It is referred to in a record in 1748 as "being very ancient, is much gone to decay so that . . . it is not worth repairing and is much too small for Reception of the Parishioners when assembled to serve God . . . the Number of Inhabitants in the aforesaid Parish, at the Time of erecting said Church did not amount to four hundred . . ."[9] We have evidence that no parish churches had been erected in Somerset County in June, 1694. In February, 1696/7, the number of taxables in Snow Hill Parish was returned as 353.[10] Exactly when this number of taxables reached 400 we have no way of ascertaining. However, in that the parish church of Snow Hill Parish was erected *before* the number of [taxable?] inhabitants reached this number, and had certainly been erected before the year 1705, it would not seem unreasonable to date its erection within the period between 1696 and 1700. This first parish church building of Snow Hill Parish stood on a lot of ground near the Pocomoke riverside in the town of Snow Hill and continued to stand in this location until the erection, between 1748 (when it was proposed) and 1756 (when it was completed) of the new brick church which was built on the public land in Snow Hill Town and which stands at this present time (1934) on the southeast corner of the intersection of Church and Market Streets. The location of this "new Church" is indicated on the 1793 plan of Snow Hill Town (a reconstruction of the original town plan) by the letter *"H"* with reference: "H = the new Church."[11]

Evidently the old (and first) parish church in Snow Hill Town near the riverside had, owing to its delapidated condition, been giving concern for some time to the vestry and wardens of the parish, who planned repairs thereto. These parish authorities applied to the Worcester County justices of the peace for an assessment and levy on the inhabitants of the parish in order to repair the church. However, on careful inspection "they found [the church] so far decayed and gone to ruin as to render repair impossible." Then in the Spring of 1748 the vestry, church wardens and sundry principal inhabitants petitioned the General Assembly of the province for the erection of a new church building of brick. Their petition stated "that the Parish Church for Preaching and Propagating the Protestant Religion as by Law Established, standing in Snow Hill Town within the Parish and County aforesaid [All Hallows Parish, Worcester County] being very ancient is much gone to decay and that it is too

---

[9] 46 Archives of Maryland, Proceedings and Acts of Assembly, 1748-1751, page 126.
[10] See ante, page 155, for these returns.
[11] The 1793 plan of Snow Hill Town is recorded in Worcester Court, Deed Liber P, page 293.

small for Reception of the Parishioners when assembled to serve God, That the number of Inhabitants in the aforesaid Parish, at the time of the erecting said Church did not amount to four hundred and that now [i. e. 1748] they are upwards of fourteen hundred and in order to have a new church erected near the same place, of a larger size, and with more conveniency for the service of Almighty God" they pray an Act of Assembly to levy a sufficient quantity of tobacco to erect and finish a brick church for the use of the said parish. In answer to this petition the Assembly at its session, May-June, 1748, passed an Act empowering the Worcester County Court to assess and collect a levy not exceeding 80,000 pounds of tobacco to be applied to building, finishing and completing the said parish church; and as the ground laid out for public use in the said town would be a more proper and convenient location for the new church than the site of the old one, the Act directed the placing of the new church on part of this public ground, and that the site of the old church should be applied to public use as the commissioners of the town think fit. The levy formerly raised for repairs to the old church, and which is yet in the sheriff's hands, is to be applied to the building expense of the new church.[12]

This "new church" building, erected and completed about 1756, remains until today in the town of Snow Hill under the name of "All Hallows Church"—the parish church of All Hallows (or Snow Hill) Parish; a building of rare dignity of design and quiet beauty—a joy to the worshipful mind and heart.[13]

* * * *

In the year 1744 All Hallows Parish (formerly Snow Hill Parish) in Worcester (formerly Somerset) County was divided and the northern part thereof erected into a new parish to be called Worcester Parish. It is in this Worcester Parish that St. Martin's Church was built on the site of a former Chapel of Ease of All Hallows Parish. For a note in this Chapel of Ease and St. Martin's Church, see post, page 202, *et seq.*

* * * *

---

[12]46 Archives of Maryland, Proceedings and Acts of Assembly, 1748-1751, pages 126-129, *"An Act empowering the justices of Worcester County to levy on the taxable inhabitants of All Hallows Parish in said county a sum not exceeding 80,000 pounds of tobacco for the uses therein mentioned."* An Act of Assembly 1756 (chapter 7) empowered the court of Worcester to levy an additional 45,000 pounds of tobacco for the completion of the parish church of All Hallows in Snow Hill Town, the first levy not proving sufficient for the purpose. (See Bacon's *Laws of Maryland,* Acts of Assembly, 1756, chapter 7.)
[13]The exterior of this beautiful "All Hallows Church" is about as it was originally. The interior has been completely modernized.
It was in All Hallows Church, Snow Hill Town, that the writer of this book, on his first visit to the Eastern Shore of Maryland (in October. 1927) first attended divine service in the area whose history has become one of the rarest treasures of his "golden bound chest of historic associations." Here his heart for the first time experienced the ancient glory that is Old Somerset's; and his spiritual eye beheld the light of a great past within the tabernacle of the present.

The Chapels of Ease

The Act of Assembly of June 2, 1692, which established the Church of England in the province of Maryland, defined the method of organization and provided for the support of this ecclesiastical establishment, directed not only the erection of parish churches but also Chapels of Ease within the respective parishes where the extent of territory demanded such for the convenience of the scattered population. Though the Chapels of Ease erected in the parishes in Somerset County were not built until after the year 1700, the information we have discovered in regard to them is given here for the benefit of any future student of parochial history in Somerset County.

* * * *

(1) STEPNEY PARISH.[1] During the course of the eighteenth century three Chapels of Ease were erected in Stepney Parish.

(a) *Goddard's Chapel.* The *first* of these chapels was erected on the south side of what is now known as Wicomico Creek (at that time called Wicomico River) about the year 1710.[2] The site of this old chapel, called "Goddard's Chapel," was definitely located through research in Somerset County records and a survey of land made in 1932-3. The research in the old records covered a number of years and was conducted by Cassius M. Dashiell, of Princess Anne, and Benjamin J. Dashiell, of Towson, Maryland, with later contribution of inadvertently discovered items by Clayton Torrence, of Princess Anne. The survey of the land, thus definitely locating the site of this old Chapel of Ease, was made in 1932 by Benjamin J. Dashiell, of Towson. The chapel site is today included in the farm lands of Miss Edna J. Davey, inherited by her under the will of the late Doctor Edward Tull, of Somerset County, situated about five miles north of the town of Princess Anne and some yards back from Wicomico Creek's south bank. In 1665 Thomas Walley (one of the first three "chirurgeons" who appeared in the early days of the settlement of Somerset) obtained a patent for 300 acres of land designated as "Walley's Chance," on the south side of Wicomico River (now Creek). (Land Office, Annapolis, Maryland). Thomas Walley removed from Somerset to Calvert County and, by his will, dated October 20, 1669, probated September 3, 1670, devised to his son, John Walley, and heirs 300 acres on Wickocomico River (Wicomico Creek) in Somerset County. (Baldwin, *Maryland Calendar of Wills, Vol. I,*

---

[1] We wish to acknowledge here the inestimable value to us of Cassius M. Dashiell's *Manuscript History of Stepney Parish,* written in 1885, which has been constantly at hand in this writing and a guide to sources for additional information.

[2] We arbitrarily place this date as being about the time of the erection of this chapel. There is no positive evidence so far disclosed which gives the exact date. The chapel was certainly built prior to July, 1711.

page 55). John Walley by deed, April, 1687, conveyed this tract of 300 acres, called "Walley's Chance" (on the south side of Wicomico Creek, Somerset County) to Michael Judd and the said Judd by deed, October 9, 1693, reconveyed the said land to Edward Day, of Somerset County, and on June 3, 1695, Edward Day reconveyed the same tract to George Goddard. These facts are recited in deeds, John Walley to Michael Judd and Michael Judd to Edward Day, recorded in Land Office, Annapolis, Maryland; see also a deed from Edward Day to George Goddard recorded in Somerset Court, Deed Liber O 7, page 300. In 1705 George Goddard conveyed parts of "Walley's Chance," "Cranburn" and "Windsor," adjoining tracts on south side Wicomico River (Creek) to Alexander Carlyle, and in August, 1709, Carlyle reconveyed these same lands back to the said George Goddard (Somerset Court, Deed Liber O 9, page 24, Goddard to Carlyle; and Deed Liber O 2, page 25, and Deed Liber O 5, page 548, two deeds of Carlyle to Goddard). It was evidently while George Goddard was in possession of the tract called "Walley's Chance" that the Chapel of Ease of Stepney Parish was built thereon. This chapel is invariably referred to both in tradition and later in record under the name of "Goddard's Chapel." In November, 1720, a resurvey was made in order to re-establish the boundaries of the tract called "Walley's Chance" and in the record of this resurvey appears the statement that the "first bounder of Walley's Chance was a pine stump they were now at a Small distance from ye Westermost end of *the new Chapell*." (Somerset Court, Liber A, *Views of Land by Commissioners,* pages 134-9, survey and plat of "Walley's Chance" for George and John Goddard).

That this, the first Chapel of Ease in Stepney Parish, was erected prior to July, 1711, we have evidence in a letter written July 2, 1711, by Reverend Alexander Adams, rector of Stepney Parish, to the Lord Bishop of London, in which Mr. Adams says that his own parish (Stepney) has a church and *chapel.* (Library of Congress, Washington, D. C., Manuscript Division, British Transcripts, S. P. G. MSS A 6 No. 107, letter of Alexander Adams to the Bishop of London. See also Perry, *Documents Relating to the Church in America,* Maryland-Delaware). The part of the tract called "Walley's Chance" on which this Chapel of Ease, called "Goddard's Chapel," had been erected came (by purchase) into the possession of the Reverend Alexander Adams. On September 18, 1722, George Goddard conveyed to Alexander Adams parts of the tracts called *"Walley's Chance,"* "Windsor" and "Cranburn" on the south side of Wicomico Creek, alias river (Somerset Court, Deed Liber O 14, page 239), and in November, 1722, the Reverend Mr. Adams conveyed a half acre of land on which this chapel stood "to be the right of the Church (or Chappel) forever." The following is a copy of Mr. Adams' deed:

"This Indenture made this twenty second day of Novr one thousand Seven hund^d & twenty two witnesseth that whereas George Goddard did alienate and make over unto Alex: Adams his heirs and assigns forever a p^{te} of Track of Ld Called Whalleys Chance as appears by the Records of Somst County therefore the s^d Alex: Adams by these presents does alienate Convey & Confirm for the use of a Church now built on the sd Whalley's Chance according to the following Bounders beginning at a marked post being the first Bound of the sd Whalley's Chance thence running East nine perches thence South Eight perches from thence running west to the adjacent branch or gully thence down the next adjacent gully to the first Bounde Containing half an acre of Land more or less to belong unto the afd Church for ever & do warrant the same from me & my heirs for ever given under my hand & Seal the day & year afsd Alex: Adams (Seal) Sealed Signed & Delivered in the presence of us Jn⁰ Scot Mer: Ellis Somst County Ss.

Memorandum that this day to wit the twenty Second day of Nov^{eber} Anno Dom One thous^d Seven hund^r & twenty two the Reverend Mr. Alex: Adams acknowledged the Land within mentioned to be right of the Church (or Chapspel) within mentioned In open Court. Test Alex: Hall Clk Cir Court Som^t."

The above deed is recorded in Somerset Court, Deed Liber O 12, page 441, and is entered in the individual index in the back of this volume of records under the letter "A" as "Mr. Adams' deed of Gift to the Church," and was first discovered by Clayton Torrence in 1933 while going through certain "judicial orders" in this volume page by page. This deed is not listed in the Somerset Court General Index to Deeds 1666-1672, either under the name of the grantor or the grantee.

By this deed of gift of November 22, 1722, from "Mr. Adams . . . to the Church," we are able to definitely place the site of this chapel on the extreme northwestern corner of the tract called "Walley's Chance," while we believe that the half acre of land surrounding the chapel site was used as a general burying ground, and certainly in years afterwards the bodies of the Reverend Mr. Adams' son and grandson were interred here.[3] The Reverend Alexander Adams himself lived immediately across Wicomoco Creek (north side) and in full view of this chapel site, and at his death in 1769 gave by will to his son, William Adams, the lands on the south side of Wicomico Creek in which—the chapel having at that time been abandoned—the half acre on which the chapel stood was finally included. In 1768 the vestry of Stepney Parish petitioned the General Assembly of Maryland to the effect "that their Chapel of Ease known by the name of Goddard's Chapel was not only old, unfit to attend Divine Service in, but was ill conveniently situated for the Parishoners and that their Chapel of Ease known by the name of Spring Hill chapel is in a ruinous condition and unfit to be repaired . . ." The Assembly considering this petition did by an Act (Chapter 9, Acts of Assembly of 1768) authorize the vestry to "purchase two acres of land on the South side of Wicomico River and above the branch whereon the mill of William Venables is built" and to rebuild "Goddard's Chapel" thereon. (For action in regard to the Spring Hill Chapel,

---

[3]William Adams (son of Rev. Alexander Adams), who died in 1796, and William Adams (born 1765; died 1792, son of John Adams, and grandson of Rev. Alexander Adams), are buried (under inscribed stones) in this old chapel ground, though their bodies were interred there some years after the abandonment of the chapel. There were no doubt many burials in this ground about the chapel during the years the chapel was in use; though no marked graves of the period remain.

see post page _____). The Assembly directed a levy of 100,000 pounds of tobacco to be raised for the rebuilding of "Goddard's Chapel" at the place directed, this levy to be collected in 1768 and 1769. In accordance with this Act the vestry of Stepney Parish purchased the two acres of land as directed and rebuilt "Goddard's Chapel" thereon, completing it between 1770 and 1773. The contractor for this work was William Adams, son of the Reverend Alexander Adams; his contract price being £600. The site purchased, the two acres "on the south side of Wicomico River and above the branch whereon the mill of William Venables is built," is now in the very heart of the city of Salisbury, Maryland.[4] "Goddard's Chapel," thus removed from its original site on the south side of Wicomico Creek, and rebuilt here, is the "origin" of St. Peter's Church, Salisbury, Maryland, which is the parish church of Salisbury Parish.[5] Salisbury Parish was erected from Spring Hill Parish in 1878; Spring Hill Parish having been carved out of Stepney Parish in 1827.

In connection with this note on the location of "Goddard's Chapel," we cannot forbear mentioning a splendid paper on the History of Stepney Parish written by Cassius M. Dashiell, Esquire, of Princess Anne, Maryland, in 1885. In this account Mr. Dashiell in "placing" "Goddard's Chapel" arrived, by deduction from certain records, at a location approximately only a quarter of a mile from the site which is now proved to have been the exact location of this chapel. This historical paper of Mr. Dashiell's we regret to say has never been published, but certainly merits preservation in printed form. We believe Mr. Cassius Dashiell to be veritably the originator of critical historical research into Somerset and Wicomico County parochial history, and we are indebted to his interest and learning in such matters for untold inspiration to the work undertaken in this present study. To Mr. Dashiell the writer of these pages owes a debt of gratitude truly unpayable.

* * * *

(b) *Spring Hill Chapel.* The *second* Chapel of Ease erected in Stepney Parish was the so-called "Spring Hill Chapel," taking its name from the patent name of the tract of land on which it was erected. The earliest reference so far found to this "Spring Hill Chapel" is in a reply made by the Reverend Alexander Adams, rector of Stepney Parish, to inquiries made by the Bishop of London. Mr. Adams' reply, dated 1724, refers to *"both chapels"* in his parish. One of these was "Goddard's Chapel" (heretofore referred to), the other was unquestionably the "Spring Hill Chapel." (A manuscript account of Stepney

---
[4]In a fragment of an old account book of Stepney Parish, 1769-1805, we find the following items: "1769, Nov. 7. To William Venables for 2 acres of Land." . . . "1769, June 24. To William Adams for Building Chapple at the head of Wicomaco £600" . . . "1771, Mar. 3. To Sam'l McClemmy for Compleating Joiners work floor & plastering of Head of Wicomaco Chapple £377:10:0." "1772. To William Horseys account for Erect'g a Rough Pulpit &c in Head of Wicomaco Chapple, £1:5:0." This old manuscript is in possession of Cassius M. Dashiell, of Princess Anne, registrar of the Diocese of Easton.
[5]The "chapel" erected in 1770-72 was destroyed by fire in 1860; a second church on this site was burned in 1886, after which the present building, "St. Peter's Church," was erected on the same site.

Parish written by C. M. Dashiell). In March, 1725/6, we pick up in the county records a reference that Somerset Court named John Hoffington to be overseer of the road from the bridge in Nanticoke Marshes that leads from Lame's Ferry to Rickett's Road above *"Spring Hill Chapel."* (Somerset Court, Judicials 1722-4, page 91). In March, 1733, Thomas Covington was appointed "overseer of the roads from the Cyprus Bridge to *the Chappell at Spring Hill."* (Somerset Court, Judicials 1733-4, page 138). The "Spring Hill" tract of land was the property of Colonel Francis Jenckins and passed at his death to his wife, Mary, who later married John Henry, and after his death married John Hampton. The chapel was certainly built on this site prior to March, 1725/6—how much earlier we do not know—while in November, 1738, Madam Mary Hampton conveyed to the "Vestry that now is of Stepney Parish" the "piece or parcell of Land whereon the Chapel now stands at Spring Hill in the said Parish and two acres of Land to the same next adjoining." The land is described as "beginning at a marked white oak on north side the head of Rowastico Branch near an Indian path and footbridge over the said branch and at an elbow or turning of the said branch on the north east side of an Indian field where it makes old field up to the branch side." (Somerset Court, Deed Liber O 20, page 18).[6]

By 1768 the chapel known as "Spring Hill" had fallen into "a ruinous condition and unfit to be repaired." The vestry petitioned the Assembly to be allowed to rebuild it. By Chapter 9, Acts of Assembly, 1768, the Assembly directed the vestry to "purchase two acres of land near unto the place where Spring Hill Chapel now stands and to erect a chapel thereon," and a levy was directed to be raised—to be collected in 1770 and 1771—to defray the expenses of erecting this new "Spring Hill Chapel."[7] This new chapel was erected in 1770-1773 with one John Hobbs contracting for the building thereof, as is evidenced by an old account book of Stepney Parish, 1769-1805.[8] Items in this old account book show that John Hobbs gave his bond in January 8, 1771, for building "Spring Hill Chapell" for £509 currency. On January 8, 1771, "To John Hobbs for Building Spring Hill Chapple £509, one half of which to be paid this year . . . £254:10s0" and "1772 To John Hobbs for building Spring Hill Chapple for £509: one half of which due this year; deducting £3 for bad work £251:10:0." Another account shows payments made John Hobbs for work on this chapel in 1773. That the *new* chapel was probably completed by January, 1773, is evidenced by this item: "1773 Cash Jany 16. To inhabitants for Springhill Old Chapple sold for £1:10:0."

---

[6]The deed of Madam Mary Hampton to the vestry of Stepney Parish states that Madam Hampton "being desirous at all times to shew her good inclinations to promote and encourage the Sincere professors of the Christian Religion as now Reformed in their duty of Publick Worship and more especially that the inhabitants of Stepney Parish may have confirmed to them a Convenient place for a Chapel of Ease in the said Parish," conveys the said ground "in consideration of a good and convenient pew in such Chapel of Ease, and five shillings." Madam Hampton was a Presbyterian, member of the Rehoboth Presbyterian Church, was widow of Rev. John Hampton, a Presbyterian minister. For reference to Madam Hampton and her family connection, see the index under Hampton.

[7]Acts of Assembly of Maryland, 1768, chapter 9.

[8]A fragmentary old account book of Stepney Parish, 1769-1805; manuscript in possession of Cassius M. Dashiell, of Princess Anne, registrar of the Diocese of Easton.

Spring Hill Church (formerly "Spring Hill Chapel" of Stepney Parish) is the parish church of Spring Hill Parish (erected from Stepney Parish in 1827) in Wicomico County.[2] This chapel (now church) erected 1770-1773 (and replacing the older chapel which stood from certainly as early as 1724 to 1773) is situated on the highway running north from Salisbury to Easton, Maryland, and is immediately opposite (in a southwesterly direction) from the Airplane Landing Field near the village of Hebron. This "chapel" (now church) is on the north side of Rowastico Creek, at the headwaters thereof; a location practically identical with the location of the older chapel (1724-1773) as described in the deed of Madam Mary Hampton to the vestry of Stepney Parish in November, 1738. Though the Act of Assembly of 1768, directing the erection of this *new* chapel, also directed the purchase of two acres of land "near unto the place where Spring Hill Chapel now stands" for the erection thereof, we are firmly convinced that this *new* chapel was erected on part of the land conveyed by Madam Hampton in 1738 and therefore not far distant—probably only a matter of yards—from the site of the old chapel.

(c) *Broad Creek Chapel*. The third Chapel of Ease in Stepney Parish was the chapel erected near the head of Broad Creek (a tributary of Nanticoke River), the building of which took place during the years 1770 and 1772, and which stands at the present time (1934) under the name of "Old Christ Church," about one and a half miles east of the town of Laurel, in Sussex County, Delaware, at Chipman's Mill Pond. In 1770, when the erection of this chapel was petitioned for, the lands in that area were counted as being in that part of Stepney Parish which lay in Worcester County, Maryland. The determination of the Maryland-Delaware boundary line had not been wholly accepted.[10] Stepney Parish was at that time partly in Somerset County (Wicomico County not being created until 1867) and partly in Worcester County.

The inhabitants of Stepney Parish residing at, or near, the head of Broad Creek, "being very remote from any place of public Worship" [i. e. any church, or chapel, of the Church of England], petitioned the General Assembly of Maryland in 1770 that an Act might be passed levying 80,000 pounds of tobacco on the inhabitants of Stepney Parish for the purpose of enabling the vestry to purchase land on the north side of Broad Creek, at or near Broad Creek Bridge,[11] and to erect thereon a Chapel of Ease. In accordance with this petition the Maryland Assembly passed the Act in 1770,[12] and in accordance therewith two acres of land were purchased on the north side of Broad Creek (some little distance above the bridge) and the chapel erected thereon. This building, of frame construction, has remarkable wainscoting, gallery, high pulpit on the north wall (with reading desk below); Holy Table with enclosing rails in the east end, and high backed, boxed, double pews—the natural heart-pine wood left unpainted. Today the severely plain barn-like exterior encloses an original

---

[9]Wicomico County (of the present time) was until 1867 a part of Somerset County.
[10]See post, for note on the Maryland-Delaware boundary line in this area.
[11]This bridge crossed Broad Creek at the site of the present Laurel, Delaware.
[12]Acts of Assembly of Maryland, 1770, chapter 8.

pure, natural interior of charm and beauty. Fragments of an old account book of Stepney Parish, 1769-1805,[18] prove that Robert Holston was the contractor for the building of this chapel at the sum of £510 currency, and that he was paid for his work in two equal payments of £255 currency, the first payment made January 25, 1771, the second payment in 1772, and on September 25, 1772, the item appears: *"Mr Robert Houstin*[14] *in account with the Vestry of Stepney Parish, D^r £510:0:0. 1772, Sepr 25 pr Contra By Building a Chappell at Broad Creek, C^r £510:0:0."*

This "Broad Creek Chapel," erected 1770-1772, now called "Old Christ Church," is in Sussex County, Delaware, Diocese of Delaware.

* * * *

(2) SOMERSET PARISH. Somerset Parish has had only two Chapels of Ease; the first of which was known as the "King's Mill Chapel," and its successor, the Chapel of Ease in Princess Anne Town.

(a) *King's Mill Chapel.* Somerset Parish's first erected Chapel of Ease stood at the old King's Mill near the headwaters of King's Creek, about two and a half miles south of Princess Anne Town (ante-dating the town by some years), and was known as "King's Mill Chapel." Unfortunately the destruction of the early vestry book of the parish has so far prevented discovery of the date at which this chapel was erected. The first reference to this chapel found in the county records is in the year 1723, when the boundaries of a tract of land called "Chance" were determined by a commission named for that purpose at the request of Captain John King, the boundary line of whose land was at that time in question between him and his brother, Upshur King. Evidence was taken by the commission in November, 1723, and January, 1723/4, and recorded in Somerset Court, March 17, 1723/4. The deposition of one Richard Chambers (aged about eighty years) proved the first bounder of "Chance" to have been "a white oak standing on a point of high land . . . a little to the east of an ancient Road now stopt by the mill dam that comes across Trading Branch or King's Branch opposite to a point on the south side of the sd Branch on which the road entered the same Branch about 500 yards along the Banck of the Branch above the now Mill Damm and *New Church* being the first deep sharp point that makes in on the north side of the afsd Branch above the said Mill . . ." (Somerset Court, Judicials 1722-4, page 154, *et seq*). This mention of the *"New Church"* near the mill dam on "Trading Branch or

---

[18]The fragmentary old account book of Stepney Parish—loose pages, and many leaves missing—carried entries from 1769-1805. On some leaves appear vestry records from 1803 on, and Confirmations, 1803 and 1807, and names of many parties, both white and colored, who subscribed obedience to the canon law of the Church. Evidently the old book, begun as an account book, was later used for vestry records and as a parish register. This old manuscript is now (1934) in possession of Cassius M. Dashiell, of Princess Anne, registrar of the Diocese of Easton.

[14]The name of the contractor in this single instance "Robert *Houstin.*" In every other instance (many times) the name is distinctly and unmistakably *"Holston."*

King's Branch" is a direct reference in January, 1723/4, to the so-called "King's Mill Chapel," the first erected Chapel of Ease in Somerset Parish. Being referred to in January, 1723/4, as the *"New* Church" would indicate that it had not been erected so many years before. In all probability this chapel was built sometime between 1715 and 1720. Though erected on this site prior to 1723, no conveyance of the land on which the chapel stood was made to the parish until many years later. On June 20, 1745, Whittington King, of Somerset County (for 500 pounds tobacco), conveyed to "the Principal Vestryman and the rest of his brethren, Vestrymen of Somerset Parish," two acres of land (taken out of tract called "Chance"), "whereon the Chappel of Somerset Parish now stands at a place called King's Mill," beginning at a marked [tree?] standing at the northeast corner of the said Chapel yard (Somerset Court, Deed Liber O 21, page 160). The "King's Mill Chapel" was abandoned early in 1767, when on February 3rd of that year permission was obtained from the Court of Somerset County for the rector of Somerset Parish to hold services in the Court House in Princess Anne Town (Vestry Book of Somerset Parish, 1766-1825). The services were held in the Court House from this time until the completion of the chapel which was erected in Princess Anne Town as the successor to the "King's Mill Chapel." On May 12, 1767, the rector and vestry of Somerset Parish sold and conveyed to William Miles, of Somerset County (for £25:15 shillings currency), the tract of two (2) acres of land "whereon the chapel now stands of Somerset Parish at a place known by the name of King's Mill which is now in possession of the said William Miles" (Somerset Court, Deed Liber O 25, page 93).

The site of the old "King's Mill Chapel" has several times changed hands since the conveyance thereof to William Miles in May, 1767. The site of this chapel, however, is at this present time (1934) located on the farm of Mr. Benjamin Barnes, on the north side of King's Creek, immediately east of the highway leading from Princess Anne to Pocomoke City, Maryland; and immediately by the creek side, where there are still evidences of the old mill dam near which this chapel—described as the "New Church"—is stated to have been situated in the year 1723. This site is about two and one-half miles south of the town of Princess Anne.

(b) *The Chapel of Ease in Princess Anne Town.* With the enforced abandonment of "King's Mill Chapel" in 1767 it was replaced by the erection of a Chapel of Ease for Somerset Parish, in Princess Anne Town.

It appears that in 1766[1] the rector, vestrymen and sundry inhabitants of Somerset Parish believing that their Chapel of Ease—"King's Mill Chapel"— had become unusuable and in a short time would be dangerous for holding Divine Service in; that it was too small for the congregation and not so well

---

[1]April 15, 1766, the vestry of Somerset Parish agreed to have a new chapel to be built in Princess Anne Town, and the registrar of the parish was to advertise the same in the parish in order to obtain the approbation of the parishioners. (Vestry Book of Somerset Parish, March, 1766-May, 1825.) No doubt, as the result of this action, the petition was drawn and sent to the Assembly.

situated as it might be, petitioned the General Assembly of Maryland that they might be allowed to sell this chapel and land belonging thereto and to purchase ground in Princess Anne Town and erect thereon a new chapel; and that £800, or the value thereof in tobacco, might be levied on the taxable inhabitants of the parish for that purpose. As an answer to this petition, the Assembly passed an Act in November, 1766, empowering the Somerset Court to levy 128,000 pounds of tobacco for the purchase of the necessary ground in Princess Anne Town and the erection thereon of the desired new chapel, and empowering the vestry to dispose of the "King's Mill Chapel" by sale.[2] On February 3, 1767, the vestry had liberty from Thomas Hayward, clerk of Somerset County, for the rector of the parish to hold services in the Court House at Princess Anne Town; and on the same date appointed Andrew Francis Cheney to purchase a lot in Princess Anne Town on which to build the chapel agreeable to the late Act of Assembly (Somerset Parish Vestry Book, 1766-1825). On February 17, 1767, Robert Geddes (for £28 currency) conveyed Lots 27 and 28 (adjoining) to Hamilton Bell, rector; Jesse King, William Waller, John Jones (of Goose Creek), Revell Horsey, Isaiah Tillman and Andrew Francis Cheney, vestrymen; William Fountain and John McGraw, church wardens of Somerset Parish. The Lots 27 and 28 are described as adjoining ones and Lot 27 bounded by New Market Street and Lowe Alley, and Lot 28 bounded by New Market Street and Upper Alley and divided from the ends of the lots whereon Samuel Ingram and Thomas McNeill live by New Market Street[3] (Somerset Court, Deed Liber O 25, page 68).

On March 31, 1767, at a meeting of the vestry of Somerset Parish a plan was set forth in detail for the erection of the chapel in Princess Anne Town. The chapel was 60 x 40 feet in size and to be built of brick; with an arch or "Simey Circle" (semi-circle) for the Communion Table, or chancel; the wall of the "Simey Circle" to be carried up as high as the other walls of the building, and so to be made that the north and south alleys (aisles) of the chapel shall lead into it; and was to have two arched windows with 32 panes of glass each. The chapel was to have four arched windows on each side, each window containing 48 panes of glass 8 x 10 inches; and a small window at the back of the pulpit containing 15 panes of glass, each 8 x 10 inches. There was to be a gallery (at the west end of the chapel) with a small window in the end thereof. Two large arch folding panel doors were to give entrance at the west end of the building; with a door on the north side (of this west end) with brick steps to lead into the gallery stairs. The floor of the chapel was to be laid in "toyl" (tile); the chapel to be ceiled overhead; the inside walls to be plastered and

---

[2]Bacon's *Laws of Maryland,* Acts of Assembly, 1766, chapter 8. See, also, preamble to deed, February, 1767, from Geddes to vestry of Somerset Parish for lots in Princess Anne Town on which to erect a chapel. (Somerset Court, Deed Liber O 25, page 68). The Act of 1768 directed a levy of 144,000 pounds of tobacco; 128,000 pounds of tobacco (together with what was realized from sale of King's Mill Chapel and land) to be applied to the purchase of lots in Princess Anne Town and building the chapel thereon; and remaining 16,000 pounds of tobacco to be applied to enlarging the parish church at Monie.

[3]"New Market Street" is the present Church Street in Princess Anne Town; "Upper Alley" is Washington Street, and "Low Alley" is Beckford Avenue.

whitewashed to the ceiling; the roof to be covered with green cypress shingles. Also a belfry was to be built to the said chapel. Levin Ballard was awarded the contract for this work at £800 currency.

Work on this chapel must have reached an advanced stage by August 1, 1769, for an that date the vestry ordered an advertisement set up of their intention to petition the next General Assembly of the province for a sum of money with which to build the pulpit, chancel and pews in the new chapel at Princess Anne Town. On March 6, 1770, the vestry met in order to receive the chapel (the actual building evidently having been completed by that date), "and finding the work not Done agreeable to articles refused to receive the Chapel."[4] Again in April and May, 1770, the vestry ordered an advertisement set up to the effect that they intended petitioning the Assembly for a levy of 30,000 pounds of tobacco with which to build the pulpit, chancel and pews in the new chapel. On May 22, 1770, specifications were drawn (and recorded) for the building of 53 pews, ...feet long, 3 feet 10 inches high; to be double pews and floored; for the chancel to be floored as the pews; with rails and banister to be set 5 feet on the chancel floor and 3 feet 10 inches high; the banisters, upper rails and door to be of walnut. This work was undertaken by John Fountain, Samuel McClemmy and Thomas Maddox, for which they were to be paid £100 currency; and the work was to be finished by July 1, 1771. In August, 1770, an advertisement was ordered set up that the vestry would meet at Princess Anne Town on Wednesday of August Court in order to agree with a person, or persons, inclinable to undertake "to build a pulpit in the new Chapel in Princess Anne Town of the same form of the pulpit in the old Chapel at King's Mill only the back of the pulpit to be Pallester[d]." In September, 1770, the General Assembly of Maryland passed an Act empowering a levy of 30,000 pounds of tobacco to be assessed in November for the purpose of finishing the pews, chancel and pulpit in the new chapel.[5] In February, 1771, the vestry agreed with Samuel McClemmy to build the pulpit and reading desk in the chapel for £16 currency; the back of the pulpit to be "Pallester[d]"; the work to be done with pine plank, and to be completed by June 1st next [1771]. On July 2, 1771, it was ordered that the workmen be paid when the pews and chancel are finished; and that Samuel McClemmy be paid when the pulpit and reading desk are finished. On July 9, 1771, the vestry received the pews, chancel, pulpit and reading desk and approved the work; and Thomas Hall was appointed to be sexton of the chapel for one year at 40 shillings. In April, 1773, advertisement was ordered that the vestry intends to have the windows in the chapel painted inside and out with white lead; the glass to be pinned and puttied where needed; the outside of the doors to be likewise painted. On May 4, 1773, the vestry agreed with Jesse Evans to paint all the sash and windows, outside and inside, with white lead; to "oyl" the doors, likewise the corneshes (cornices?) of the covering and barge boards;

---

[4]Though the vestry records make no further reference to this unsatisfactory work on the part of the contractor, nor is there any statement of particular errors, the defects were no doubt remedied and the building received by the vestry in due time.
[5]Acts of Assembly of Maryland, September, 1770, chapter 3.

to pin all sash lights where wanting with spriggs (tin or brass) and to putty all glass where wanting and to find light of glass that is wanting; to paint the pulpit and reading desk below and the pews of said colour, and to find [furnish] all the white lead and oil; and to have it finished by the last of August ensuing [August, 1773]. Evans to be paid £20:10 shillings in money that shall then circulate at the time of payment. In September, 1773, Jesse Evans was ordered to be paid £20:10 shillings for painting and mending the glassing in the chapel. September 7, 1773, the pew on the east side of the pulpit ordered to be the right of the rector of the parish and his successors forever;[6] and on September 18, 1773, the vestry proceeded to allot the pews in the New Chapel at Princess Anne Town.

The above items, all of which are quoted from the Somerset Parish Vestry Book of 1766-1825, give us the story of the origin, erection and completion of the Chapel of Ease for Somerset Parish built in Princess Anne Town: begun in 1769 and entirely finished in 1773. From these detailed items the imagination can visualize the wonderful chapel as it stood "in the beginning" and for many years afterwards.

Today the walls of the building, and the gallery, are all that remain of the original chapel. Change after change, in keeping with the spirit of new days, new times, has carried away the last vestige of the original interior—save the gallery; and that has suffered change. But surely the ancient walls hold the echo of the worship—petition and praise—of successive generations, from "the first." The light which casts such wonderful colors through the medium of exquisite bits of stained glass is the Eternal Light which once shed radiance through plainer windows. The marble altar, stainless in its purity, reflecting the tapers' light, is the successor of the one time Holy Table of "beauty unadorned." The graceful modern cross-capped spire now rising from the northeast corner of the church certainly symbolizes the aspiration of generations of worshippers through the ages—the parents and the children and the children's children. Yet today from the ancient Cup and Paten—which were here used—"in the beginning"—each succeeding generation has been nourished and fed with "the spiritual food of the Body and Blood of Christ": surely a vivid reminder that all the generations are "knit together . . . in one communion and fellowship, in the mystical body of . . . Christ our Lord."

Today, with its "heart of purity"—the marble white altar within; and without, its heavenward pointing spire—its Cross lifted high above the little town whose very center the "Chapel" occupies—old and yet new, of ancient times and yet of today—"St. Andrew's" (for so the "Chapel" has been consecrated

---

[6]It has been impossible, so far, to determine on which wall, north or south, the pulpit (with reading the desk below it) was erected, and therefore we cannot give the exact location of the rector's pew in this original building. All that we know of the pew's location is that it was immediately east of the pulpit and therefore on the chancel side of the pulpit. No draft of the floor plan of this chapel has been found. The pews were evidently (from reference to the north and south alleys as leading into the chancel) arranged in three blocks; one against the south wall, then an "alley" (aisle); a center block of pews, and then an alley (aisle), and the third block against the north wall.
[7]Somerset Parish still possesses the Cup, large and small Patens and Flagon—the Communion Silver, which bears a hall-mark signifying that it was made in 1719.

as a church) witnesses to the Eternal Father's eternal giving of "daily strength for daily needs." While the new name of the ancient shrine—"St. Andrew's"—bears witness that He whose Cross is here borne aloft—whose Table here is spread—ever

> ". . . calls us o'er the tumult
> Of our life's wild, restless sea,
> Day by day His sweet voice soundeth,
> Saying, 'Christian, follow Me'."[8]

*   *   *   *

(3) COVENTRY PARISH. This parish had two Chapels of Ease and a third chapel was proposed, though never erected. The first of these was "Annemessex Chapel" (prior to 1726); the second, the chapel at Dividing Creek (1751); the third was proposed (1774) for a site on the east side of Pocomoke River, at or near Stevens' Ferry (about the site of the present Pocomoke City in Worcester County).

(a) *Annemessex Chapel.* The date of the erection of "Annemessex Chapel" is not now known, though we find it in use in 1726. In November, 1726, Somerset Court gave permission to William and Solomon Coulbourn to turn the road which ran from the head of Coulbourn's Creek to the head of Jones' Creek; and in the court's order it is stated that the *"road from Annemessex Chapple to the bottom of Little Annemessex"* goes through the lands of the said Coulbourns. At November Court, 1739, John Scott, who owned a piece of land described as lying between *"Annemessex Chappel and a dam called Beaver Dam,"* petitioned for turning the road formerly called Duke's Road. At August Court, 1741, on motion of Captain Thomas Williams, a new road was ordered to be made from the main road near Joseph Porter's, the most direct route, *"to the Chapple at the head of Coulborn's Creek."* In 1748 a road was directed to be run from Captain Thomas Williams' gate to *"Annemessex Chapel."* (Somerset Court, Judicials 1724-27, page 180; 1738-40, page 197; 1740-42, page 144; and 1747-49, page 183). The references of 1726, 1739 and 1748 specifically call this chapel *"Annemessex Chapel."* The record of 1741 definitely locates the chapel at the head of Coulbourn's Creek.

---

[8]The Chapel in Princess Anne Town was consecrated as a church under the name of "St. Andrew's Church," on November 11, 1845, by the Right Reverend William Rollinson Whittingham, Bishop of Maryland.
  Around this church today, in graves marked and unmarked, rest the bodies of several generations of "churchmen" who have worshiped in this House of God. "God's Acre" is still sacredly kept here. Just beyond the northwest door of the church is the grave of John Oliver Barton, Priest, and for many years pastor of this congregation and rector of Somerset Parish. Just beyond the southwest door is the grave of Henry Crosdale, a faithful and honored Priest. To the south of the church is the grave of Oliver H. Murphy, Priest, at one time beloved rector of Coventry Parish and an indefatigable student of parochial history in Somerset County. Near the southwest corner of the church the body of the venerable William W. Johnston, a great benefactor of this church, lies buried. Throughout the churchyard one finds on gravestones the honored names of Waters, Woolford, Dashiell, Dennis, Duer, Barton, Bratton, Dixon, McMaster, Polk, Kerr, Waller, Long, Jones, Johnston, Covington, Brittingham, Whittington, Sudler, Dougherty, Wilson, Wise, Stone, Stewart, Cottman, Young, Smith, and many others; while there is ample evidence of many unmarked graves.

This first constructed *"Annemessex Chapel"* at the head of Coulbourn's Creek, which appears in records of 1726, 1739, 1741 and 1748 evidently fell into wretched condition and required replacing. By Chapter 16, Acts of Maryland Assembly, 1762, the justices of Somerset and Worcester Counties were empowered to levy 62,400 pounds of tobacco on the inhabitants of Coventry Parish (which lay partly in Somerset and partly in Worcester Counties[1]) for uses specified in the said Act; the said uses being: (1) the empowering of the vestry of Coventry Parish to purchase, in fee, two acres of land in Somerset County, in the said parish, *at some place between the head of Coulbourn's Creek and Annemessex Dams and thereon to build a Chapel of Ease for the said parish;* (2) the said vestry is empowered to enlarge the Chapel of Ease on Dividing Creek in Coventry Parish (Bacon's *Laws of Maryland,* Acts of Assembly, 1762, Chapter 16).

From this Act of Assembly, 1762, we assume the unusable condition of the "Annemessex Chapel" of 1726, 1739, 1741 and 1748 references. We have been unable to discover any record of conveyance to the vestry of Coventry Parish for the land at the head of Coulbourn's Creek on which it is specifically stated this chapel stood. Then on November 10, 1763, Stephen Horsey and Michael Holland (for £4 each) conveyed to the rector, vestry and wardens of Coventry Parish,[2] two acres of land, *"it being the ground whereon the New Chappell now stands";* the said two acres *"beginning at a marked oak cedar stake being the bounder of a tract called Pomfret near the westermost corner of the new Chappell"* (Somerset Court, Deed Liber O 24, page 196).

This deed of November, 1763, locates the *"new Chappell"* near a bounder mark of the tract of land called "Pomfret," which bounder was near the west corner of the said chapel. The court order of August, 1741 (quoted above) refers *"to the Chapple at the head of Coulbourn's Creek."* The *"new Chappell"* mentioned in 1763 evidently replaced the *"Chapple at the head of Coulbourn's Creek,"* of the court order of 1741. The site of the *"new Chappell,"* in 1763, and the site of the *"Chapple at the head of Coulbourn's Creek,"* in 1741, are practically identical; the land is the same, though there may have been a slight variation in the building sites—certainly, however, not more than a matter of "yards and feet." The tract called "Pomfret," (whose boundary marker is named as "near the westermost corner of the new Chappell"), lay immediately to the southwest of the head of Coulbourn's Creek and bordered on that creek. The Horsey lands, called "Coulbourne," lay to the northeast of Coulbourne's Creek and bordered on the creek. In the year 1763 Stephen Horsey owned this *southeast* corner of the "Coulbourne" tract and Michael Holland owned the *northeast* corner of the "Pomfret" tract, and their lands joined at

---

[1]Worcester County was until 1742 a part of Somerset County. Coventry Parish (in which Annemessex Chapel stood) was from 1692-1742 wholly in Somerset County, but when Worcester County was created, in 1742, that part of Coventry Parish lying east and south of the Pocomoke River fell within the boundaries of the newly created Worcester County.

[2]This deed was made by Stephen Horsey and Michael Holland to Nathaniel Whitaker (present incumbent [rector] of Coventry Parish), William Allen, James Gunby, John Dennis, Outerbridge Horsey, Littleton Dennis and Elijah Coulbourne (vestrymen of Coventry Parish) and William Melvin and Thomas Marshall (church wardens of Coventry Parish).

this point. The "Annemessex Chapel" (both the old and the new ones) stood on Horsey land immediately north, or northeast, of the head of Coulbourne's Creek, but the limits of the two acres conveyed evidently extended over onto the Holland land and hence the necessity for Stephen Horsey and Michael Holland making a joint conveyance in 1763 to the rector, vestry and wardens of Coventry Parish for this land on which the *"new Chappell"* stood.

Thus we find that the older (and first) *"Annemessex Chapel"* of 1726, 1739, 1741 and 1748 references, disappeared and had been replaced by a *"new Chappell,"* 1763, (also called "Annemessex Chapel" in tradition and record); this *"new Chappell"* occupying the same land, if not the identical building spot, of the older chapel.

Among the fragmentary items relative to Coventry Parish which have come down to us through the manuscript *"Noticæ of Coventry Parish . . . by John Crosdale, Rector . . . 1848,"*[4] we find several relating to the "Annemessex Chapel," which are as follows:

"August 2 [1779] . . . Ordered that Mr Duett make application to the neighborhood of Annemessex to meet at the chapel and prevent if possible its falling."

August 5, 1782, Thomas Williams and William Dixon appointed to have Annemessex Chapel repaired.

1786. During course of this year extensive repairs made on Annemessex Chapel.

The site of the "Annemessex Chapel"—both old and new—at the head of Coulbourn's Creek may be at this present time (1934) located about one mile west of the town of Marion in Somerset County.

In 1818 subscriptions were made to rebuild "Annemessex Chapel" (the one which appeared in 1763 as the "new Chapel") and work was commenced thereon. This was the *third* building of this chapel. In 1821 this *third* building was completed and the pews sold. At the time of the erection of this third chapel building the building site was changed from the Horsey lands at the head of Coulbourne's Creek. This chapel, erected 1818-1821, was placed on the county road leading from Marion to Crisfield, on land belonging to Benjamin Coulbourne. At this site the *third* building of "Annemessex Chapel" stood for thirty years, when in June, 1848, Isaac Marshall contracted to build the church in Annemessex. Again the site was changed. This time the building was erected on land about two miles east of the town of Marion—where the church then built remains standing (and in use) at this present day. In July, 1848, the chapel (erected 1818-1821) was taken down, the materials carried to the new location east of Marion, and mostly used in the construction of the new church. On July 27, 1848, the cornerstone of this church was laid, and on

---

[4]The items relative to Annemessex Chapel from this point on are from the manuscript entitled "Noticæ of Coventry Parish. Consisting mostly of extracts from old parish Register now in possession of William Williams, M.D., by John Crosdale, Rector, January 1st, 1848." These notes by Mr. Crosdale were made on the first pages of an old Vestry Book of Coventry Parish now (1934) in possession of the vestry of that parish. The "old parish register" to which Mr. Crosdale had access and from which he made his notes has disappeared.

December 21, 1848, the church was consecrated under the name of "St. Paul's Church" by the Right Reverend William Rollinson Whittingham, Bishop of Maryland.

(b) *Dividing Creek Chapel.* Coventry Parish lay partly in Somerset County and partly in Worcester County, after the division of Somerset and creation of Worcester County in 1742. Dividing Creek constituted the eastern boundary of Somerset and the western boundary of that part of Worcester County lying north and northeast of Pocomoke River. For some years church services had been conducted by the rector of Coventry Parish at the "Old Somerset" County Court House site, which was immediately east of Dividing Creek and which remained in Somerset County at the time of the division of the county and the creation of Worcester in 1742. In course of time the old Court House property came under private ownership and the church services there were abandoned. In 1751 inhabitants of "the upper part of Coventry Parish which lies in Worcester County" set forth in a petition to the General Assembly of Maryland, the deprivation which they and their families suffered from lack of religious services and ministrations owing to their great distance from any chapel or church. Giving this petition favorable consideration, the Assembly of May-June, 1751, passed an Act empowering and directing the vestry and wardens of Coventry Parish to purchase (in the name of the rector, vestrymen and wardens, and their successors) two acres of land in Worcester County and Coventry Parish, near the dwelling plantation of Angelo Atkinson, and out of a tract of land belonging to John Scott, and to erect thereon a Chapel of Ease. This Act also empowered the justices of Somerset and Worcester Counties to levy on the taxable inhabitants of Coventry Parish, in their respective jurisdictions, the sum of £150 currency, to be assessed in three equal portions in 1751, 1752 and 1753, these assessments to be collected by the sheriffs of Somerset and Worcester and paid over to the vestrymen and wardens of Coventry Parish, who were to receive and apply the same to the uses specified in the Act. (*46 Arch. Md.*, page 628-9; Bacon's *Laws of Maryland,* Acts of 1751, Chapter 23).

In accordance with this Act of Assembly of 1751 the rector, vestrymen and wardens of Coventry Parish purchased of John Scott two (2) acres of land on the northside of Pocomoke River in Worcester County and about two miles east of Dividing Creek. At this present time (1934) this chapel site may be located on the McMaster farm (on the north side of Pocomoke River, Worcester County), just west of Cottingham's Ferry.[5]

---

[5] From the *"Noticae of Coventry Parish . . . by John Crosdale, Rector, January 1st, 1848* (contained in an old vestry record of Coventry Parish), we have the following items:
(Page 22). Sept. 4, 1848, title to the ground around the church at Dividing Creek appearing to be somewhat uncertain from the difficulty of establishing it, a deed for one acre around the church was this day given by S. S. McMaster and wife, and Angelo Atkinson.
(Page 24). "In the records of the Land Office in Annapolis the following memorandum appears, 'Two acres of land to the Rector, Church Wardens and Vestry of Coventry Parish from John Scott, Dec. 9th, 1753. Smith's Folly by name of Dennis' Purchase, so returned by Mr. Gillis.'"
(Page 284). A deed, Dec. 9, 1753, John Scott to the Rector, Wardens and Vestry of Coventry Parish for 2 acres near Dividing Creek.
(Page 284). A deed, Sept. 4, 1848, Samuel S. McMaster and Anne E., his wife, and Angelo Atkinson, to the Vestry of Coventry Parish; land around the church at Dividing Creek.

From the Reverend John Crosdale's manuscript, *"Noticæ of Coventry Parish . . . 1848"* (entered in the old Vestry Book of Coventry Parish), we gain the following information:

> April 17, 1797, the people of the Dividing Creek district [of Coventry Parish] permitted to repair the old chapel or build a new chapel as they may think proper.
>
> August 5, 1797, subscriptions to be immediately set forward for purpose of repairing and furnishing the chapel at Dividing Creek.
>
> August, 1848, congregation of Dividing Creek Church determined to rebuild their church.
>
> December 20, 1848, cornerstone of a new church to be erected at Dividing Creek was laid by the Bishop of the Diocese [Bishop Whittingham, of Maryland].
>
> November 20, 1849, the old church on Dividing Creek taken down and a few days afterwards the materials disposed of at public sale.
>
> December 13, 1849, the church newly erected on Dividing Creek consecrated under name of St. Stephen's Church, by the Right Reverend William Rollinson Whittingham, Bishop of the Diocese of Maryland.

This St. Stephen's Church remained on the old site near Dividing Creek in Worcester County for some years, when finally it was taken down and removed to Upper Fairmount in Somerset County (and Coventry Parish) and there reerected, remaining in use at this present time (1934).

(c) *Proposed Chapel near Stevens' Ferry, 1774.* The General Assembly of Maryland in 1774 passed an Act empowering the justices of Somerset and Worcester Counties to levy on the taxable inhabitants of Coventry Parish (which lay in both counties) 32,000 pounds of tobacco, which was directed to be paid over to the rector and vestry of Coventry Parish, and for them to purchase therewith two acres of land on the east side of Pocomoke River, at or near Stevens' Ferry and to build thereon a Chapel of Ease for the Parish (Acts of the Assembly of Maryland, 1774, Chapter 19). The site proposed for the erection of this Chapel of Ease was in the immediate vicinity of the present (1934) Pocomoke City in Worcester County, on the commonly called south side of the Pocomoke River.[6] Stevens' Ferry, starting from the north (or Somerset County) side of Pocomoke River, had its southside landing at this point.[7]

This proposed purchase of land and building of this Chapel of Ease "at or near Stevens' Ferry" was not, however, effected. In all probability the advent of the Revolutionary War stopped all proceedings in the matter. In 1784 an

---

[6]The Act of Assembly says "east side of Pocomoke River." This description is geographically speaking more accurate as the river makes one of its innumerable turns at this point, thereby throwing the site designated to the east of the stream.
[7]For account of Stevens' Ferry, see post.

Act of Assembly directed that the funds raised for this purpose by levy, under the Act of 1774, be turned over to the vestry and church wardens of Coventry Parish (Acts of Assembly of Maryland, 1784, Chapter 40). In accordance with this Act the money was turned over to the vestry and applied to the building of Rehoboth Church.[8]

* * * *

(4) SNOW HILL (OR ALL HALLOWS) AND WORCESTER PARISHES. This parish occupied from its organization in 1692 that part of the original Somerset County comprised within Bogerternorton and Mattapony Hundreds, and extended from the Maryland-Delaware line on the north to the Maryland-Virginia line on the south. Its eastern boundary was the Atlantic Ocean; its western boundary the Pocomoke River and the eastern line of Coventry Parish. In 1742, when Worcester County was created out of the section of Somerset County lying south of the Pocomoke River and east of Dividing Creek, Snow Hill, or All Hallows Parish, as it was then called, fell entirely within the boundaries of Worcester County. There appear to have been several Chapels of Ease in the parish from time to time, one of them at least erected on territory which fell within Delaware when the boundary line between that colony and Maryland was finally determined.

(a) *The Chapel of Ease near St. Martin's River.* In his will, dated June 26, 1703, Roger Thomas, of Somerset County, directed: *"I desire that my body may be buried in the Church Yard at St. Martin's"* (Somerset Registry of Wills, Liber E B 5, page 115; Worcester Registry of Wills, Liber M H 3). This is the first reference so far discovered to a church in the vicinity of St. Martin's River; for it was that vicinity in the northeastern section of the present Worcester (at that date Somerset) County to which Roger Thomas refers in designating *"the Church Yard at St. Martin's"* as the place for the burial of his body. It was, no doubt, to this same so-called "Church" that an order of Somerset Court, November 17, 1705, directed to be published "at the *Churches* . . . at Snow Hill and *Seaside,"* referred. The "Church . . . at St. Martin's"— 1703; and the "Church . . . at . . . Seaside"—1705, were in all probability identical.[9] All of the extreme eastern section of the original Somerset County (since 1742, Worcester County) was referred to as the "Seaside" (or the "Seaboardside"). The section in the extreme northeastern corner of this "Seaside" area, and about the St. Martin's River and its creek tributaries, was referred

---
See ante, page 176, for item to this effect which appears in Crosdale's "Noticæ of Coventry Parish.
Though the proposed Chapel of Ease, 1774, was not erected, nor land purchased for it, and funds raised therefor by levy were used in building "Rehoboth Church"; many years later an Episcopal church was erected practically on the proposed site of 1774. A town called *Newtown* was erected at the old Stevens' Ferry landing on the south (or east) side of the Pocomoke River. In 1845 William I. Long gave a lot on which to build a church. This church was erected, opened for service in July, 1845, and consecrated, under the name of St. Mary the Virgin, on November 13, 1845. At the present (1934) this is St. Mary's Church, Pocomoke City, Maryland.
[9]See ante, page 183, for reference to Roger Thomas' will; and to the court order of 1705.

to in ancient (as well as modern times) as *"St. Martin's."* However, instead of this so-called "Church" being technically a "Church," the building so referred to was most probably a "Chapel of Ease" in Snow Hill (later All Halows) Parish, erected at an early date in this remote section of the parish for the benefit of the residents there.[10]

The next definite indication[11] of the presence of a house of worship in this immediate vicinity ("St. Martin's") we find in August, 1739, when Samuel Shewell conveyed to Henry Lawrence part of a tract of land lying on the head of St. Martin's River known [i. e. the land known] by the name of "Cropton," "beginning at the mouth of Burch Branch thence running up *the Chappell Branch* to the lines of Rackliffe's purchases of the said parcel of land [i. e. of 'Cropton']"[12] then up said line in the woods till it includes 100 acres within a parallel line to the first between Rackliffe's line and Burch Branch being the part and parcel of 'Cropton' where Abraham Briscoe now dwells" (Somerset Court, Deed Liber O 20, page 86). In March, 1742/3, Henry Lawrence and Mary, his wife, of Worcester County, conveyed to Solomon Cropper, of Worcester County, 100 acres, part of a tract called "Cropton," lying on the head of St. Martin's River, Worcester County, said 100 acres beginning at the mouth of Burch Branch, thence running up the *Chapple Branch* to the lines of Rackliffe's Purchase of the said land [i. e. of "Cropton"]. (Worcester Court, Deed Liber A, page 23). From these two deeds we see that Lawrence, in 1742/3, reconveyed the land on *the Chapple Branch,* which Samuel Shewell conveyed to said Lawrence in 1739.

Examination of the map of the present (1934) Worcester County shows that the Shingle Landing Prong of St. Martin's River (which in reality is the head of St. Martin's River) is formed by three small branches (or creeks), viz: Middle Branch: the most northerly of the three; Birch Branch: which is the center one; and South Branch: which is the most southerly branch. Middle Branch enters the Shingle Landing Prong of St. Martin's River on the north side thereof; while Birch Branch and South Branch (flowing easterly) enter Shingle Landing Prong (the head of St. Martin's River) on the south side, and come immediately together at their point of entry. From the descriptions of directions and courses in the Shewell and Lawrence deeds of 1739 and 1742/3 (above quoted)—"beginning at the mouth of *Burch* [Birch] *Branch* thence

---

[10]Technically speaking, a "Church" was the principal ecclesiastical building of a parish—"the Parish Church." In Snow Hill (or All Hallows) Parish the "church" was in the town of Snow Hill some twenty miles south of the area referred to as "St. Martins."

[11]Though the next definite indication of a *chapel* in this immediate vicinity is in August 1739, when *"the Chappell Branch"* reference is found, there are items of prior date which circumstantially indicate the presence of a chapel, or church, near this point. In January 1725-6 James Hogg, of Somerset Co., devised by will to his son James, land called "Showell's Addition" on east side of *"Church Branch"* and to son John residue of said tract on north side *"Church Branch."* (Worcester Registry of Wills, Liber MH3, page 277-8; also *Maryland Calendar of Wills,* VI, page 74). The tract called "Showell's Addition" is proved to have been on branches of St. Martin's River, in 1725-6 in Somerset Co., and after 1742 Worcester Co. In a deed February 1735-6, Saml. Shewell conveyed part of tract called "Cropton" to Presgrave Turvile, the land described as "situate and being between *Church Branch* and Middle Branch [of St. Martin's River] beginning at mouth of Middle Branch thence up *Church Branch."* (Somerset Court, Deed Liber O 19, page 13.)

[12]See deed of Samuel Shewell to Sarah Rackliffe for 100 acres out of tract called "Cropton," being between the Middle Branch and Burch Branch of St. Martin's River. (Somerset Court, Deed Liber O 19, page 274).

running up the *Chappell Branch,"* we can identify this so-called *"Chappell Branch"* of 1739 and 1742/3 as being the so-called *"South Branch"* at this present time (1934). Thus certainly there was a *chapel* hereabouts from which this *"Chappell Branch"* took its name. Furthermore, it is a fact that the present St. Martin's Church in Worcester County (about five miles north of the town of Berlin), which was erected in 1755 on the site of a former chapel (as we shall presently see), is situated just about 150 yards south of the South Branch of St. Martin's River, which we can identify as formerly called the *"Chappell Branch."*

Taking together all of the items above quoted we find a "Church" at St. Martin's in 1703 (the "church yard" thereof referred to in Roger Thomas' will) and this "Church" probably identical with the *"Church ... at ... Seaside"* in 1705 (as referred to in Somerset Court order of that year); the "Chapel" of 1739 and 1742/3 (as indicated by references in deeds to the *"Chappell Branch"* —identical with the present South Branch of St. Martin's River) and the erection, in 1755, of the parish church of Worcester Parish (which is referred to in 1772 as "St. Martin's Chapel" and later as "St. Martin's Church") on the site of a former chapel.

From 1692 (when the parishes were first organized) until 1742 the area about St. Martin's River (here under discussion) was in Somerset County and in Snow Hill Parish, which was later designated and called All Hallows Parish. In 1742 Worcester County was erected from Somerset County and All Hallows Parish fell entirely within the boundaries of Worcester County. In 1744 All Hallows Parish was divided and the northern part thereof erected into a separate parish called Worcester Parish.[13] The Act of Assembly erecting Worcester Parish directed, however, that the division of All Hallows and the erection of Worcester Parish should not be made until after the death, or removal, of the Reverend Patrick Glasgow, the then incumbent. The Reverend Mr. Glasgow did not die until March, 1753. However, in the meantime, the Assembly at its session, May-June, 1748, passed an Act which directed that when the division of All Hallows Parish and the erection of Worcester Parish should take place that the new parish of Worcester should, by a levy, be reimbursed in the matter of certain funds "which [funds] shall be applied ... towards erecting and building a Parish Church, or Church and Chapel in the new Parish of Worcester, in such Place as ... shall seem most proper and convenient."[14]

We have before seen that the "Chapel of Ease" for All Hallows Parish was located on the south side of the South Branch of St. Martin's River. In March,

---

[13] The southern boundary of this Worcester Parish was described as "beginning at the mouth of Newport Creek running out of the sea and with the said creek and a branch thereof to the main road at a place called Buckingham thence down the main road which leads to Snow Hill a quarter of a mile to a main road between Mrs. Mary Hampton and Brickus Townsend and thence with the Pocomoke River." North of this line was Worcester Parish: bounded south by the line designated above; north by the Maryland-Delaware line; east by the Atlantic Ocean and west by Pocomoke River. (Bacon's *Laws of Maryland*, Acts of Assembly, June 4, 1744, chapter 24.)

[14] 46 *Archives of Maryland; Proceedings and Acts of Assembly, 1748-1751*, pages 128-129; Assembly of May 10-June 11, 1748, "An Act empowering the Justices of Worcester County to levy on the taxable inhabitants of All Hallows Parish in said County a sum not exceeding 80,000 pounds of tobacco for the uses therein mentioned." The fourth section of this Act makes the above recited provision for the Worcester Parish Church.

1753, the Reverend Mr. Glasgow, rector of All Hallows Parish, died. As provided by the Act of Assembly of 1744 All Hallows Parish was immediately divided and Worcester Parish erected from its northern portion. An old Vestry Book of Worcester Parish gives the proceedings.

On September 4, 1753, the vestry of Worcester Parish made choice of the place where the chapel then stood to build a new church on. On August 6, 1756, the vestry bought two acres where "St. Martin's Chapel" stood from James Mumford on which to build the new church; paying £5 for the land and 12 shillings 6 pence for the plans for the church. July 10, 1756, there was an agreement with one James Johnson to build a church 44 feet square where the old chapel stood. September 25, 1759, the vestry met to receive the church building, but as it was not done according to the agreement made with James Johnson he was therefore to paint all over, to make the reading desk six inches longer, to make a seat for the clerk, and to furnish three staples and a bar for the front door. This work was evidently done and the church building appears to have been received by the vestry in October. On November 18, 1759, the pews were laid out beginning at the northwest corner and so around the church; they were double pews numbering 1 to 16; the west square in the middle of the floor numbering 17 to 24. The single pews occupied the east square and were numbered 25 to 31, with one in the southwest corner numbered 31. On January 1, 1761, these pews were allotted by number to parishioners. In March, 1761, the building of these 31 pews was contracted for with William Tunnel at 19 shillings per pew, and the work was to be finished in five months [i. e. August, 1761]. On July 14, 1761, there was an agreement with Tunnel to finish the chancel and end gallery in the church. On July 19, 1762, George Cochran bought the vestry's right in the old chapel (private pews excepted) at public sale for £14:1:0, and was to remove it. On July 1, 1763, the Reverend Edward Dingle (rector of Worcester Parish since 1758) died and was buried in front of the pulpit in the church. The pews were finished by a separate contract and the church was finally completed and received in 1763.[15]

The following abstract of the deed for the land on which the Worcester Parish Church was erected, will be of interest. August 6, 1756, James Mumford conveyed to the vestry of Worcester Parish two acres of land out of a tract called "Vermin Drane" [so spelled in the deed] in Worcester County, "beginning at a marked white oak on the south side of a mill pond to the westward of a mill dam thence south forty eight degrees east sixteen poles, thence south thirty five degrees west twenty poles thence north forty eight degrees sixteen poles thence with a right line to the aforesaid white oak." The "Vermin Drane" tract is described by the deed as located on the south side of the main branch of St. Martin's River, and as devised by Thomas Mumford in his will to his

---

[15] All of the above references to the selection of the site and the building of the Worcester Parish Church (known as St. Martin's Church) are from an old Vestry Book of Worcester Parish dating from 1753-1765. This vestry book was for a long time lost, but was recovered by the Reverend Ethan Allen, who made excerpts therefrom for use in his Manuscript History of the Eastern Shore Parishes. The "original" of this old Vestry Book (which is the property of Worcester Parish) has been placed for safe keeping with the Maryland Historical Society, Baltimore. The Society has also a photostatic copy of this Vestry Book for use by students.

son, James Mumford (the grantee), said Thomas Mumford having purchased the tract by deed, June 23, 1694, from George Layfield and Elizabeth, his wife, relict and executrix of Colonel William Stevens (Worcester Court, Deed Liber D, page 79).[16]

Today, under the name of St. Martin's Church, the wonderful old brick building, erected between 1755 and 1759, with the interior finally completed in 1763, sentinels with eternal vigilance the highway leading north from the town of Berlin in Worcester County. The old church stands about five miles north of that town and on a slight knoll immediately south (about 150 yards) of the South Branch of St. Martin's River—an architectural gem.

(b) *A Chapel in Worcester Parish (Prince George's Chapel in Sussex County, Delaware).* The government of the province of Maryland laid claim (under the charter granted in 1632 to Cecil, Lord Baltimore) to territory which extended some miles north of the Maryland-Delaware boundary line as it was finally determined—and as we have it today.[17] An extensive area in the southeastern part of Sussex County, Delaware, was, at the date of which we are writing, considered a part of Worcester Parish, Worcester County, Maryland.

In the year 1755 many inhabitants of the upper part of Worcester Parish petitioned the Maryland Assembly for the purchase of land and erection of a chapel thereon; setting forth the fact that they were entirely destitute of any place of public worship (by reason of their remoteness of residence), and stating that there was, or shortly would be, a sufficient amount of tobacco in the hands of the vestry to purchase the said two acres of land and build thereon a convenient Chapel of Ease.

In answer to this petition the Maryland Assembly on July 8, 1755, passed an Act empowering the vestry of Worcester Parish to purchase two acres of land on the east side of Pepper's Branch near where it crosses the main road and to erect a chapel thereon.

It appears that on June 9, 1755, the vestry had agreed to build a chapel at Blackfoot Town on the east side of Pepper's Creek. Then with the passage of the Assembly's empowering Act in July, the vestry on the 19th of that month purchased two acres of land, at Blackfoot Town, from Walter Evans. August 12, 1755, James Johnson agreed to build the chapel for 39,200 pounds of tobacco. December 2, 1755, Captain Derickson was directed to buy plank to finish the chapel. December 6, 1756, there was an agreement with Daniel Hull to lay the gallery floors in the chapel, 45 feet long and 7 feet wide, with wainscoat all around, and to build two pairs of stairs, a pew for strangers, and

---

[16]The deed of Layfield and wife to Thomas Mumford (June 23, 1694) calls the tract *"Vernum Deane."* This deed was made to Thomas Mumford and Sarah, his wife, and states that Mrs. Sarah Mumford was the daughter of Robert Richardson, and that the said land was conveyed to her under instructions of the will of the said Richardson. (Somerset Court, Deed Liber O 7, page 215.) The tract is also called *"Vernam Deane"* in a deed of Nov., 1772, from James Mumford to William Roan, Jr., conveying 13 acres thereof, beginning at second bounder of said tract and thence running courses of the original grant until it intersects the road that leads from Mitchell's storehouse to *"St. Martin's Chappell,"* etc. (Worcester Court, Deed Liber I, page 172.) The deed of August 6, 1756, James Mumford to the vestry of Worcester Parish for 2 acres of land makes no reference to chapel as standing thereon.

[17]See post for note on the Maryland-Delaware boundary line.

one table, for £20. April 14, 1757, the vestry assigned the pews in the new chapel, and on June 30, 1757, the chapel was finished and received by the vestry.[18]

This Chapel of Ease in Worcester Parish was given the name of "Prince George's Chapel," and was erected on the east side of Pepper's Creek (which issues into the south side of the Indian River) in Sussex County, Delaware, which at the date of the chapel's erection was deemed by the authorities to be in Worcester Parish, Worcester County, Maryland. The chapel—"Prince George's Chapel"—a frame building of simple, yet beautiful, proportions, and with much of the original of the interior (of heart pine in its natural state) intact, stands today just east of the village of Daggsboro in Sussex County, a priceless possession of the Diocese of Delaware.

This old chapel—"Prince George's"—erected between 1755 and 1759—was built on land obtained by the vestry of Worcester Parish from Walter Evans— a "lot" out of a tract called "Daniel's First Choice." William Evans, of Somerset County, conveyed this "Daniel's First Choice" tract containing 100 acres and a tract called "Evans' Inlarging" (also containing 100 acres) to his son, Walter Evans, of Somerset County, in January, 1740 [1740/1] (Somerset Court, Deed Liber O 20, page 205). The deed from Walter Evans to the vestry of Worcester Parish, for the "lot" on which the chapel was erected, has not been run down. However, the fact that Walter Evans did sell this building site to the vestry is evidenced both by parochial records (quoted by Ethan Allen in his Manuscript History of the Eastern Shore Parishes: Worcester Parish account) and by a deed from Walter Evans, of Worcester County, to John Dagworthy, of Worcester County, in October, 1763, when conveying 15 acres out of "Daniel's First Choice" tract, the survey is stated "to begin at the North West corner of the Lot of land sold by sd. Walter Evans *for the use of the Church*" and one line thereof as "a line up the road to the Church thence south around the Church Lott,"and it is stated to be "near Blackford" [Blackfoot Town?]. (Worcester Court, Deed Liber F, page 27). It will be noted that the Evanses who conveyed these lands designate themselves as "of Somerset County" (in 1740) and "of Worcester County" (in 1763), yet their homeplaces were at these respective dates in what is now Sussex County, Delaware.[19]

---

[18]The Act of Assembly of 1755 under which this Chapel of Ease in Worcester Parish was erected, see Bacon's, *Laws of Maryland,* Acts of Assembly, 1755, chapter 14. The old Vestry Book of Worcester Parish, 1753-1755, contained the items relative to purchase of the land and the building of this chapel. The items were gathered from this old Vestry Book by the Reverend Ethan Allen and incorporated in his account of Worcester Parish, given in his Manuscript History of the Eastern Shore Parishes. See ante page 205 for reference to "original" of this Vestry Book.

[19]Scharff, *History of Delaware,* page 1337, identifies Prince George's Chapel, near Daggsboro, Sussex County, with a chapel referred to by the Rev. Mr. Ross, of Lewes, Delaware (a missionary of the Society for the Propagation of the Gospel), in his *Journal* under date of August 6, 1717. Mr. Ross writes: *"There are two houses of worship in this vicinity, one 16 miles from Lewes and one in the upper part of the county not yet finished."* Scharff says the "unfinished" chapel was St. Matthew's in Cedar Creek Hundred, and that *"the former was probably Prince George's as it approximates that distance"* [i. e., 16 miles from Lewes]. Scharff comments that the exact date of the erection of Prince George's Chapel is unknown and that no record is extant of its organization, and "that it was built under charge of St. Martin's Parish, Snow Hill, Maryland." Scharff's error here is obvious. We have, (as given above) all of the details as to date and erection of Prince George's Chapel, 1755-1757, as a Chapel of Ease in Worcester Parish. It is therefore impossible to connect up Prince George's Chapel (as we know the facts) with the chapel 16 miles from Lewes in 1717 as referred to in Mr. Ross' *Journal.*

(c) *Chapels in All Hallows Parish, 1771 and 1774.*

(1) In 1771 certain persons petitioned the General Assembly of Maryland setting forth that the church at Snow Hill was the only place for public worship in the parish [All Hallows]; greatly distant from exterior parts thereof; that numbers of persons could not attend; and that they were desirious of having a chapel built which they could more easily reach. In answer to this petition the Assembly of 1771 passed an Act empowering a levy of 32,000 pounds of tobacco to build a Chapel of Ease at, or near, Johnson's Mill in All Hallows Parish, Worcester County. (Acts of Assembly of Maryland, 1771, Chapter 10; Ethan Allen, *Manuscript History of the Eastern Shore Parishes;* account of All Hallows Parish).

(2) In 1774 a levy of 45,000 pounds of tobacco was directed by Act of Assembly, which was to be paid by Worcester County authorities to John Rosse, John Parramore, Eliakim Johnson, et al. [rector and vestry of All Hallows Parish] for the purpose of erecting a Chapel of Ease in All Hallows Parish, on one acre of land to be purchased near Sandy Hill,[20], or on the land of Michael Tarr (Acts of Assembly of Maryland, 1774, Chapter 10; Ethan Allen, *Manuscript History of the Eastern Shore Parishes;* account of All Hallows Parish). The chapel which was erected at Sandy Hill was consecrated in 1844 under the name of the "Chapel of the Cross" (Ethan Allen, *Ibid*) and today is represented by the Church of the Holy Cross at Stockton in Worcester County.

---

[20] Sandy Hill is ten miles south of Snow Hill Town. (Note by Dr. Ethan Allen.)

4. CHILDREN OF THE COVENANT

*

Planting of the Presbyterian Church in Somerset—Earliest identified Presbyterians—William Stevens' appeal to the Presbytery of Laggan in 1680—First ministers of Presbyterian faith and order—Francis Makemie, father of organized Presbyterianism in America—William Traile, of Rehoboth—Samuel Davis, of Snow Hill—Thomas Wilson, of Manokin—Erection of Presbyterian church buildings in Somerset: Rehoboth, Snow Hill, Manokin and "at the road going up along the Sea Side."

THE glory of Somerset County's Presbyterianism does not rest on any claim to priority—the claim that in the soil of this county was laid the foundation in Maryland and in America of this great "household of faith." Very true, the founder of organized Presbyterianism in America—the Reverend Francis Makemie—made his first headquarters in the New World at Rehoboth in Somerset; maintaining throughout the remainder of his life close contact with the Rehoboth congregation of the Presbyterian Church. At the end of his life's journey Makemie gave to that congregation the land on which their "Meeting House" had been recently erected; no doubt having, before his death, contributed substantially toward the building of that hallowed fane. Indeed, Somerset's Rehoboth did through Makemie—its first minister—contribute the genius of organization to the Presbyterian Church in America.

Some years before Makemie came to Somerset the foundation of Presbyterianism had been laid in the province—in that section across the Chesapeake Bay from Somerset—in Southern Maryland. In 1668, two years prior to a positive identification of a single individual Presbyterian in the Somerset population, Calvert County received as a settler the sturdy Fifeshire Scotchman, Ninian Beall, who was veritably born of, and into, the "faith of the Covenant." In him we find the first Presbyterian thus far identified in Maryland.[1] Then, waiving all others who as "ministers" may have officiated in the congregation of Presbyterian faith and polity which unquestionably grew up around Ninian Beall in his Calvert County settlement, we know that one Matthew Hill, ordained according to Presbyterian order, was in Charles County between 1669 and 1679; at least fourteen years before men duly ordained and accredited in the ministry of the Presbyterian Church appeared in Somerset County.[2]

Somerset, it is true, may not lay claim to having the foundation of Presbyterianism in Maryland—and America, laid in her soil; but the later section of this household of faith erected here was constructed of incomparable materials masterfully organized.* It was from Somerset that the genius went forth carrying the spirit of organization into the wider field of colonial life as a whole, the genius by whose efforts Presbyterianism throughout America was finally brought into one massive body. It was the appeal of the liberal-minded Churchman, William Stevens, of Rehoboth in Somerset, to the Presbytery of Laggan in the north of Ireland, for a minister of Presbyterian faith and order, that resulted in Francis Makemie's coming to Maryland—and America; soon to be followed by men of such marked pastoral abilities as William Traile, Thomas Wilson and Samuel Davis. While Traile, Wilson and Davis strengthened the stakes of the adventure in Somerset soil, Makemie lengthened the cords of the faith to reach far distant sections.

Though there may have been Presbyterians in Somerset prior to the date at which we are able to positively identify a man of that order of the faith among the population of the county, we reach the year 1670 before we find reference in the remaining local records to David Brown, a Glasgow Scotchman, whose credentials are abso-

---

*We cannot forbear giving the following critical estimate of this passage by one who graciously read this chapter at our request. This critical statement is couched in such splendid terms; bears the stamp of such clear and sincere thought and the mark of scholarship that it should be read and meditated upon by all who are interested in the subject under discussion. The following critical note on our passage in question was written by the author's personal friend, the Reverend Paul Trout, pastor Manokin Presbyterian Church—a worthy successor in every way of the men of God who have through years ministered in this congregation. Mr. Trout writes: "While not contesting the position that Somerset has no claim to priority: certainly there are existing Presbyterian churches older than the Somerset churches; I do hesitate to assert that *the foundation of Presbyterianism* was laid elsewhere. Considering the term Presbyterianism as distinguishing a system of church government rather than of doctrine; where else was the foundation of this system laid? Not in Marlboro [Prince George County, Maryland] by Hill or Taylor; not on Long Island among the semi-Independent churches there. By Francis Makemie in the congregations that asked Presbytery for him, and where he must have organized sessions with a Presbytery in mind, was the foundation if anywhere."

lutely beyond question. Brown is a "self-evidencing" Presbyterian, his will eloquently testifying to his respect and reverence for his church by a legacy "for his better support" left to Thomas Wilson, Sen[r], whom we identify as minister of the Manokin Congregation. David Brown appears first in the records of Somerset as witnessing a document April 30, 1670.[8] From his first appearance David Brown entered prominently into the life of Somerset County; as a merchant he made a goodly fortune for his day and time; he served on juries and grand juries; for years he was one of his Lordship's Justices of the Peace; a representative of Somerset in the Lower House of Assembly, and a militia officer of high rank. With Major Robert King (another, and later, Somerset County Presbyterian) Brown represented Somerset on the "Committee of Twenty," which was the resident executive body towards the close of the Protestant Revolution in the province; and finally he appears as "the Hon[ble] Coll David Brown," member of the Council of the royal Governor of Maryland.[4] David Brown by 1672 had married Winifred, widow of Captain William Thorne, of Somerset, and succeeded thereby to the estate of "Thornton" on the north side of Manokin River, where he resided until his death in 1698. Brown's home at "Thornton" came within the precincts of Manokin Congregation of the Presbyterian Church when that congregation was organized about 1683/5. "Thornton," the site of David Brown's home, is situated on Manokin River about three miles southwest of the present town of Princess Anne.

David Brown we have as the earliest positively identified Presbyterian in "Old Somerset"; we know that he was in the county by the year 1670. It is with regret that we have been so far unable to identify other actual Presbyterians among the residents of Somerset at this date, or, as a matter of fact, for some years afterwards. We do not doubt that David Brown had company in the matter of his faith; but it has been impossible to discover their names. Something over a decade later we find among Somerset County settlers the names of a goodly number of families who, if the faith of the first settlers of these names may be assumed from the faith of their children and their children's children, we may certainly classify as Presbyterians. The Kings of Manokin Hundred; the Alexanders, McKnitts, Strawbridges, Wallises (or Wallaces), all of Manokin Hundred; the Erskines of Snow Hill Town; the Fassits, Rounds and Croppers of the

Seaboard Side section, and others scattered here and there throughout the county, were ardent Presbyterians.[5]

Whatever may have been the names of these now unknown early Presbyterians in Somerset[6] it is undoubtedly true that between the years 1670 and 1680 the Presbyterian element in the county must have increased considerably.[7] Some of these Presbyterian immigrants were no doubt directly from Scotland; but by far the large majority came from the north of Ireland, where times were troublous and perilous for the children of this faith.[8] With the accession of this strong Presbyterian element to the population of Somerset County, there arose the necessity for providing "a ministry of the Word and Sacraments" in keeping with its "faith and order."[9]

Among the residents of Somerset County, none was more deeply interested and concerned in its development and the welfare of its people than Colonel William Stevens, of "Rehoboth", on Pocomoke River. Arriving in this area just before its erection into a county, Stevens, from his first appearance, contributed his genius for community building to the settlement. He unstintedly invested his means in promoting, after most worthy fashion, the upbuilding of the land that he chose for his home. First and last he was called upon to occupy every position of trust and honor in the area, in the final organization of whose territory into a county he had such a prominent part. He was trusted by all classes in the population and was, as well, a staunch and trusted friend of the Lord Proprietor of the province, one of whose council and deputy governors he became. Besides his powerful official and social position, his marked business acumen, Stevens was possessed of a mind both deep and liberal in matters pertaining to religion. We cannot escape the significance of the name which he gave to his home—"Rehoboth"; veritably indicative of the spirit which possessed the man. An avowed adherent of the Church of England, William Stevens unhesitatingly manifested a tolerant and sympathetic attitude of mind towards the then several expressions of Christian belief and practice manifesting themselves in the population of Somerset and of the province of Maryland.[10]

So it is at last that we find the appeal of the Presbyterians in the population of Somerset for "a minister of the Word and Sacraments" according to their faith and order,[11] voiced for them by that powerful and incomparable Somerset man, William Stevens, of "Rehoboth"; and so it is that we come to this "minute" from the record book of the Presbytery of Laggan, in the north of Ireland.

"Decem: 29, 1680 Col. Stevens from Maryland beside Virginia his desire of a godly minister is represented to us. The Meeting will consider it seriously and do what they can in it. Mr. John Heart is to write to Mr. William Keyes about it and Mr. Robt. Rule to the M'[eetin]gs of Route and Tyrone, and Mr. William Trail to the Meetings of Down and Antrim."[12]

This appeal of Somerset Presbyterians, in the latter part of the year 1680, was a challenge of great moment to the missionary spirit of the ministry of the Presbyterian Church in the north of Ireland; and it is not difficult to imagine the depth of the interest which it elicited. Though no further reference is found to this appeal and its consideration in the remaining minutes of the Presbytery of Laggan,[13] we find the quality of the response thereto in the ministers of this faith who came to Somerset County during the years between 1682 and 1684. Makemie, Traile, Wilson and Davis composed the response to this appeal, and the organization of the Presbyterian churches in Somerset proved to be the foundation on which rests the structure of organized Presbyterianism in the United States of America.

The Presbytery of Laggan, as we have seen, received and noted, in December, 1680, the appeal of Somerset County Presbyterians sent through Colonel Stevens, that "a godly minister" be sent to them. Without haste and with the careful deliberation which such an appeal merits, the Presbytery made this desire widely known, with the result that within the period of the next eighteen months or two years we find young Makemie, a veritable giant of this faith and order, answering Somerset's Macedonian cry. He soon was followed by a trio of men as remarkable, according to their several abilities, as was he who led the way. Probably by Springtime of the year 1683, the Reverend Francis Makemie had arrived at Rehoboth in Somerset. Certainly by June, 1683, the Reverend William Traile had reached the same destination. By September, 1684, the Reverend Samuel Davis was in the county. In January, 1685/6, the Reverend Thomas Wilson had arrived in Somerset and was purchasing land for his home.[14]

These four men from the north of Ireland, Makemie, Traile, Davis and Wilson, with Makemie as the guiding genius of the group, organized the congregations of the Presbyterian Church in Somerset.

Makemie devoted himself largely to visiting the colonies along the Atlantic seaboard, encouraging and strengthening isolated congregations of Presbyterians; engaging in true missionary labor; and laying the foundation for the organization of a Presbytery which was later to follow. Traile, Davis and Wilson ministered with great earnestness to the congregations in Somerset. In Makemie, Traile, Davis and Wilson, the Presbyterians in Somerset were given men fully capable of the work which came to their hands. Makemie, who was a very young man, is said to have been ordained specifically that he might go to America in response to the appeal for "a godly minister" from "Col. Stevens from Maryland beside Virginia." He had been raised and trained in an area which knew the full meaning of what a man must undergo in the ministry of the Gospel. The Presbyterian Church in the North of Ireland was one under persecution.[15] Traile, Wilson, and no doubt Davis, older men in years than Makemie, were well seasoned in the work of the ministry, having served honorably in the pastorate. Restricted as they must have been in the exercise of their several ministries in the North of Ireland, these men were now to enter upon work where they could freely exercise their abilities in strengthening, building up and organizing congregations of their faith in a new land with its growing population. It is not difficult to imagine the inspiration under which they entered upon this new work.

There has come down to us a considerable amount of data in regard to these first Presbyterian divines who came to Somerset County from the North of Ireland; and their personal histories are most interesting.

Francis Makemie, the first of his "order and ministry" in Somerset—later to become the founder of organized Presbyterianism in America—was born, about 1658, of Scotch parentage, at Ramelton, Donegal, Ireland, and was enrolled as a student in the University of Glasgow, in the third class, February, 1675/6. In 1678/9 he appeared before the Presbytery of Laggan at St. Johnstown, Ireland, recommended to that body by his minister, Mr. Drummond. His "trials" before Presbytery were held in May and July, 1681, in which year he was licensed; and in 1682 was ordained so that he could go to America. On April 2, 1682, Makemie was preaching in the Reverend William Hampton's church in Burt, the last record we have of his appearance in Ireland. The exact date of Makemie's leaving Ireland we do not possess, but taking passage by way of Barbadoes, he reached Somerset County in the province of Maryland, probably in the Spring of the year 1683, in the rich strength of young manhood, being not more than twenty-five years old. We cannot doubt that in Somerset he made his headquarters at "Rehoboth," the home of Colonel William Stevens, and had the advantage of the counsel and advice of that wise personage in formulating plans for his work. Makemie, soon followed by William Traile, who remained in charge of the work about Rehoboth, took himself upon an expedition to the southward. The Fall of 1683 found him on the way to Norfolk, in Virginia. In May, 1684, he went to Carolina, and also in July, 1684, and July, 1685, visited "dissenting" congregations at Elizabeth River in Virginia; and in 1686 made a preaching tour southward. In all of these travels Makemie was engaging his best efforts in encouraging isolated congregations and probably exploring fields for the settlement of ministers.

From the very first appearance of Makemie we recognize the impelling missionary spirit of the man and a genius in him for organizing work. The opening vistas of American colonial service must indeed have appealed to his imagination. His early journeys southward in behalf of the work of strengthening Presbyterianism soon established him in the minds of people as a man of incomparable energy and devotion in such a field of labor. In his visitations of distant fields, Makemie realized the necessity for well-organized congregational life among the adherents of the Presbyterian faith; while, as he beheld the isolation of these individual congregations, there was borne in upon his mind the value of unifying them through larger organization. To Presbyterianism in the American colonies must be brought the wonderful system of the Church in Scotland and the North of Ireland.

After the first five years of his ministry in America, spent largely in visiting among the congregations of "Dissenters" to the southward of Maryland, Francis Makemie established his permanent residence in Accomack County in the colony of Virginia. This residence he established certainly in 1687 or 8, finally settling at Matchatank, which remained his home until his death in 1708. His name appears in the list of tithables for Accomack from 1688-1693 continuously; and we find him during this time ministering to congregations of Presbyterian faith in Onancock, Accomack County, Virginia, and at Rehoboth, in Somerset County, Maryland. In this "settled pastorate" Makemie was able to obtain more intimate relationships with individuals, an opportunity for "the closer walk with men" which is forbidden the traveling evangelist. Then, too, in this more settled state, the man turned to the normal human ideals of family life, and we find him uniting in marriage with Naomi Anderson, daughter of William Anderson (a wealthy merchant and planter of Accomack County) and his wife, Mary Wise, daughter of Colonel John Wise, distinguished alike in the official and social life of Accomack. The wife of Colonel John Wise—and the grandmother of Mrs. Naomi Makemie—was Hannah Scarburgh, sister of that distinguished Edmund Scarburgh who figured so conspicuously in the earliest history of Somerset County. So it is that we find Francis Makemie established in Accomack, ministering to a Presbyterian congregation there and at Rehoboth in Somerset County, Maryland; taking to wife a daughter of the most exclusive circle of Accomack's social life; building a home; and becoming the father of two girl children. The eldest of these, Elizabeth, died in childhood, while a younger daughter, Ann, lived to a good old age through three successive marriages, first to Thomas Blair, second to Colonel Robert King, of "Kingsland," in Somerset, and third to George Holden, of Accomack.

It was during the period of his settled ministry in Accomack and Somerset, 1687-1693, that Mr. Makemie evidently began the building of that comfortable estate by which the latter years of his life were materially blessed; an estate which became something of a fortune in those days by the addition of his wife's inheritance from her father's estate. This man of God, while truly "fervent in spirit, serving the Lord," was certainly "not slothful in business." There is as ample evidence of his ability to lay up treasure upon earth, fearless of the threatening corruption of moth and rust, as there is of his fervency and devotion in "laying up treasure in heaven where neither moth nor rust doth corrupt." Francis Makemie was undoubtedly possessed of the spirit of accumulating both earthly and heavenly treasure. His was no unprofitable service whichever way rendered.

Again we find the spirit of adventure in wider fields taking possession of the man; and, as though being literally driven forth from his earthly Eden, we see him re-engaging in missionary endeavors and further promoting the welfare of his church by finally effecting the organization of a Presbytery. In 1692 he is seen journeying to Philadelphia; in 1696 and 1698 making trips to Barbadoes; and in 1704/5 going to Europe. On his return from Europe, Makemie brought with him the Reverend George M'Nish and the Reverend John Hampton, who were later to play so prominent a part in the history of Somerset County Presbyterianism as pastors of Manokin, Rehoboth and Snow Hill congregations. Then came the eventful year of 1706, when the Presbyterian Church was organized in America through the formation of the Presbytery of Philadelphia. This was the crowning glory of Makemie's able work in the ministry of the Presbyterian Church in America; for we cannot for an instant doubt that it was his genius which effected the organization of the Presbytery of Philadelphia in 1706. From this Presbytery was developed, through succeeding years, the organized Presbyterian Church in the United States. The ministers constituting this first Presbytery in America were Francis Makemie, of Accomack in Virginia and Somerset in Maryland; John Hampton, George M'Nish and Samuel Davis, all three of Somerset; John Wilson, of New Castle in Delaware; and Jedediah Andrews, of Philadelphia in Pennsylvania. Though the first leaf of the record of minutes of this first meeting of the Presbytery of Philadelphia is missing, the date is approximated from the records of succeeding meetings; and it is also believed that Francis Makemie was "Moderator" of that body.

On adjournment of this first Presbytery, Francis Makemie, taking with him the Reverend John Hampton, started on a journey towards Boston; but, on reaching New York and preaching there in January, 1706/7, he was subjected to imprisonment for two months before being released on bail. He was charged by the Governor, Lord Cornbury, with being "a strolling preacher" and "spreading pernicious doctrines." Finally released on bail, Makemie returned to his home in Virginia, stopping in Philadelphia to attend the meeting of Presbytery, March 25, 1707. In June of that year he returned to New York for his celebrated trial before Lord Cornbury, which occurred March 11, 1707/8, and resulted in his acquittal. Again this "wayfarer for the Lord of Hosts" came back to his home, from whence, in the Summer of 1708, his spirit returned to God who gave it, and his body was committed to the earth of Accomack.[16]

This is the record of the Reverend Francis Makemie. Thus he lived his earthly portion of Life Eternal, "steadfast, immovable, always abounding in the work of the Lord, knowing that his labor was not in vain in the Lord."[17]

* * * *

Though there is dearth of detailed material from which to sketch the story of his life (and the days of his life of which we have record were spent largely within the circumscribed area of the local pastorate), the Reverend William Traile who followed Francis Makemie to Somerset County is a personage scarcely less interesting than his "leader." William Traile, born about the year 1640, and thus probably eighteen years Makemie's senior, was the son of the Reverend Robert Traile, a Scotch minister. With the very blood of the Kirk in his veins, and nurtured in strong loyalty on the traditions of the Covenanting faith, William Traile early dedicated his life to the ministry, giving thereto years of true and approved service. When first we come across him in records he is at work in the pastorate of Lifford in Donegal, in the Presbytery of Laggan, in the North of Ireland. At one time he was "Moderator" and at another "clerk" of Laggan Presbytery; and to him was committed by this Presbytery the responsibility of communicating with the meetings in Down and Antrim relative to Colonel William Stevens' request that "a godly minister" be sent to Somerset in Maryland. It is not difficult, even at this day's distance from the matter, to see the vision which opened up to William Traile as he entered into correspondence with congregations in regard to the request from "Maryland beside Virginia." As the rigors of persecution fell upon him with imprisonment and deprivation of the exercise of his ministry in Lifford as his lot, we are not surprised to find Traile adventuring himself on the mission to Maryland, and to discover his name of record in Somerset in June, 1683, as a fellow laborer with Makemie, his younger brother in the faith. Just how long before this date Traile came to Somerset we do not know; but from comparison of this date with the approximate date of Makemie's arrival in the same place, probably in the Springtime of 1683, we can but wonder if the two men really came to this new land together. Be that as it may, we know that William Traile was in Somerset County by June, 1683, and advantageously placed for his work in the neighborhood of "Rehoboth," on Pocomoke; and that during Makemie's absence between the autumn of the year 1683 and 1688, he ministered at this point and through the immediately surrounding country. In May, 1686, William Traile purchased from Mark Manlove a tract of one hundred thirty-three and one-half acres of land, called "Brother's Love," on the north side of Pocomoke River; and in February, 1688/9, from Josiah Seward a tract of twenty-five acres, to be called "Killeleah," adjoining the aforesaid tract of "Brother's Love." These lands were situated on Pocomoke River, something over a mile below Rehoboth Town, and there Traile made his home. Then, after six years of pastoral work along the Pocomoke River in Somerset, William Traile returned home in late February, or March, 1689/90, when word had come of the success of the English Revolution and the re-establishment of Presbytery. It is stated that on leaving Somerset County, William Traile went to Scotland, there becoming minister of the congregation of Borthwick, near Edinburgh.

We cannot conclude this brief note on William Traile's life without reference to his wife, Mrs. Eleanor Traile, who appears as his true companion and helpmeet during his ministry in Somerset. We are not informed as to the maiden name of this lady nor do we know whether she was married to Traile before his leaving Ireland or after his arrival in Maryland. She simply appears as his wife, and to her, on his return to the North of Ireland in 1689/90, he gave power of attorney to hold in trust all of his property in Somerset County, and to sell or lease the same as she considered to be for the best interest, and to receive rents or debts due. In April, 1691, Mrs. Eleanor Traile, acting under this power of attorney given her by her husband, sold to Archibald White, of Somerset County, Weaver, ninety and one-third acres of the tract called "Brother's Love," and the adjoining tract of "Killeleagh" containing twenty-five acres. These lands had been the Traile home in Somerset. After this Mrs. Eleanor Traile disappears from the Somerset records, no doubt having gone to her husband in Scotland, dying prior to the year 1701, when Mr. Traile married, a second time, Mrs. Jean (Murry) Moncrief. Of the date of William Traile's death we are not informed, but that it occurred prior to August, 1723, we know from the record of suit at that date filed in Somerset Court by Margaret, Lady Baltimore (executor of her deceased husband) against "James Traile, son and heir of William Traile, late of Somerset County in the province of Maryland, Cl[er]k, decd."

There was nothing of glamour about the life of the Reverend William Traile. A spirit of quiet perseverance possessed him and intrepidly he lived the life God gave him to live. Persecution and imprisonment for conscience sake seemed only to strengthen his intention to serve his divine Lord and Master through the ministry of the church militant. Deprived by law of the exercise of his office in the pastorate of Lifford in Donegal, he simply turned to the open field of missionary adventure in Somerset in the province of Maryland; and then, when peace was restored to the "Kirk," he turned again home. We can but feel that his "patient, brave endeavor" for Christ's sake was most effective. The counsels and the examples of such men may not leave shining marks upon the life of their times; but surely the marks of such men are deep and ineradicable.[18]

* * * *

The remaining records afford a group of authentic items relative to the Reverend Samuel Davis, who soon followed Makemie and Traile to Somerset County, which reveal a vivid character in bold relief against a dark background of unknown origins. We have been unable to discover anything relative to Davis' "origins." The place of his birth, his parentage, education, time of ordination, his place of residence and pastoral connections before his appearance in Somerset County are at present unknown. His name does not appear in the list of ministers of the Presbytery of Laggan in 1680, though it is believed that he came to Somerset from the North of Ireland. Though the fact has been obscured by the passage of years, Davis must have belonged to that great tradition. The first reference which we have found to him is that a patent for land in Somerset was granted him in September, 1684, while in the Somerset records is stated that "Mr Sam^{ll} Davis, Minister," officiated, February 26, 1684/5, at the marriage of John Broughton and Elizabeth Bradshaw.

While no doubt preaching as occasion offered or demanded, in various sections of Somerset, Samuel Davis is by all recorded evidence definitely associated with the section of the county adjacent to the town of Snow Hill on the upper Pocomoke River, and is specifically referred to as minister of the Snow Hill congregation. In 1686, the year following Davis' appearance in Somerset, the Town of Snow Hill took "form and order" by legislative enactment, becoming a center for trade and attracting English, Scotch and Scotch-Irish merchants by its opportunities and advantages for business. Snow Hill Town became the "trade metropolis" of colonial Somerset; and with its stable population, steady stream of visiting traders and the farming population of the surrounding country, was indeed a challenging location for Mr. Davis' ministry. In 1687 we find the reverend gentleman establishing his home on a plantation about a mile and a half northeast of Snow Hill Town; a place which may today be located at that distance and to the east of the highway leading from Snow Hill to Berlin. These lands were in Davis' day and time designated as "Grove."

Samuel Davis is looked upon as being the veritable founder of the Snow Hill congregation of the Presbyterian Church, a congregation which numbered as the years advanced, Erskines, Galbraiths, Rounds, Spences, Stevensons, Hopkinses, Croppers, Fassitts, Aydelotts, Martins, Wises, and others whose names are now unknown. Samuel Davis is recorded as the first minister of the Snow Hill congregation from 1686 to 1698, and as serving a second pastorate there from 1718 until his death in 1725. We cannot refrain from calling attention to this fact of Mr. Davis' two pastorates in the Snow Hill congregation; the first of twelve years, the second of about seven years. Davis is not considered by a historian of his own church the peer, intellectually or spiritually, of his great contemporaries in the work of the Presbyterian Church in Somerset—Makemie, Traile and Wilson. While this estimate is no doubt true, there must have been something in the man which appealed to people and held them.

Whatever may have been Mr. Davis' abilities as a minister, it is unquestionably true that he appears to have been developing business interests at Lewes, in Delaware, as early as the year 1692. To this place he went to reside about 1698, and for some years continued to live there, apparently discontinuing for a time the regular exercise of his ministry. Just what Mr. Davis' secular pursuits were we do not know, but his speculation in lands and engaging in trading seems apparent. We also find him designated as "doctor," indicating no doubt his adoption of the practice of medicine in addition to his other interests. Like the great Makemie, Davis appears to have possessed a keen business sense, which he employed most profitably; but, unlike Makemie, who exercised masterful control of that sense (making it subject to higher interests, though exercising it with profit), Davis appears to have allowed himself to be controlled, at least temporarily, by a sense of material values.

Though Mr. Davis gave up, for the time being, the regular exercise of its functions, he certainly did not renounce the ministry; and when the Presbytery of Philadelphia was organized in 1706 he was deemed by virtue of his ordination, and residence within that Presbytery's bounds, a member thereof, and subject thereto in matters of discipline. Appearing to the Presbytery as neglectful of his obligation and duty in the matter of attendance on its deliberations, in March, 1707/8, that body did not hesitate to reject the reasons offered by Davis for "his absence from this and preceeding meeting of Presbytery" and to send him a letter requiring him to be present at its next meeting. Needless to say, the reverend brother appeared at the meeting of Presbytery on May 18th following, and it is noted that "Mr. Davis satisfied Presbytery for his absence the former year." But marvel of marvels in Christian charity and forgiveness, Presbytery elected Davis "Moderator" of the body. Regardless of this fact, we are unable to perceive any variation in his indifference to his obligation and duty to attend meetings of Presbytery. Though never engaging in work as regular pastor of the congregation at Lewes, we find that Davis would "supply" "as much as the condition and posture of his affairs would admit," and in 1715 he joined with that congregation in a request to Presbytery to have a minister settled over them. In September, 1710, Davis and the Reverend John Hampton were appointed by Presbytery to preach the "admission sermon of Mr. John Henry at Rehoboth"; which they did, reporting the same to the meeting on September 20, 1711; and in June, 1719, by direction of Synod (which had then been organized), Samuel Davis, with the assistance of John Hampton and John Thompson, was directed to ordain John Clement and William Stewart at Rehoboth. Mr. Davis' name appears as one of the three ministers set apart by Synod at its organization to form the Presbytery of Snow Hill in 1716. The formation of this Presbytery was, however, prevented by the death of the Reverend John Henry, of Rehoboth, and the declining health of the Reverend John Hampton, of Snow Hill. The fact that Davis was set apart to the Snow Hill Presbytery would seem to be evidence that he had returned to dwell on his plantation near Snow Hill.

Through twenty years this ordained man of God had laid aside his ministry in spiritual things to seek material gain, proving eminently successful in his search for earthly treasure. We do not know the motives which really governed him in this matter, therefore we may only record the fact. Whether a man ordained is forced by circumstances to relinquish the due exercise of his office and ministry; or whether a spirit of worldliness, possessing him, drives him into the wilderness of material desires; the mere fact of the relinquishment of the due exercise of his sacred office is deeply distressing to him who will stop to consider. For twenty years Samuel Davis pursued the search for material riches; now the heart of the wanderer turns again home. The able and brilliant John Hampton, who had occupied the pastorate in the Snow Hill Congregation of the Presbyterian Church since 1707 is failing in health; a trip to his native land across the sea failed to restore him; so coming again to his charge in Somerset, he is forced to retire from his pastoral care in the Fall of 1718. To succeed John Hampton in the Snow Hill pastorate we find choice resting upon the Reverend Samuel Davis. Again we cannot refrain from comment. Though not considered intellectually and spiritually the peer of his earlier great companions in the ministry of the Gospel in Somerset, nor even of the younger and later Presbyterian divines (and we admit this estimate of a historian of Presbyterianism), yet here is Samuel Davis called again to the pastorate of the very congregation which he had forsaken to pursue material gain; and recalled in succession to the man and minister, John Hampton, who from every evidence appears to have been without a superior in "the things of the spirit." We leave this matter here, with the action of the Snow Hill Congregation in recalling Samuel Davis. For nearly seven years Davis continued in his second pastorate in Snow Hill, and then the end came to him—still on duty—in the early

Spring of 1725. An inventory of Mr. Davis' personal effects was returned to Somerset Court in April of that year. In the minutes of the Synod of Philadelphia, under date of September 15, 1725, we find the simple notation: "Mr. Samuel Davis died since last Synod."

One cannot be insensible to the inner conflict of motive which is suggested by the items which the records disclose about the Reverend Samuel Davis. A man of God and yet strongly obsessed by desire for material gain—serving in the ministry—forsaking the exercise of his sacred office for business after a worldly fashion—and then returning to the work of prophet and pastor. His was indeed a life of inner conflict, yet through all "God proved him and found him worthy for himself."[19]

* * * *

We come now to consider the last of the four divines of Presbyterian faith and order who came from the North of Ireland to Somerset County in Maryland following Colonel Stevens' appeal to the Presbytery of Laggan in 1680. Makemie and Traile came in 1683; Davis was established in the county by September, 1684; and we find Thomas Wilson purchasing lands for a home in Somerset in January, 1685/6. Makemie, Traile and Davis left their impress upon the spiritual life of the county; but their blood and names passed out of Somerset. Makemie left an only surviving child—a daughter, Ann, who though thrice married, to Blair—King—Holden, left no issue. The only child of William Traile's of whom we know, a son, James Traile, continued his residence in Scotland or the North of Ireland. Samuel Davis apparently had an only surviving child, a son, Doctor Samuel Davis, who resided in Accomack County, Virginia, and so the strain of this blood was lost to Somerset. Then there is Thomas Wilson, the impress of whose character on the spiritual life of Somerset is indeed ineradicable, but whose contribution did not stop here. The strain of his blood has coursed through succeeding generations of the family descending from him, continuing to enrich the religious, educational, political, legal and social life of Somerset County; sending forth strong scions into the state and even the national fields of spiritual and intellectual endeavor.

Thomas Wilson, whose name first appears upon the Somerset records in January, 1685/6—the first pastor of Manokin Congregation of the Presbyterian Church—was a man whose strength in the ministry of the Gospel, and faithfulness in the work of the pastorate, had been proved in the fires of adversity before his coming to the work in Somerset. As a member of the Presbytery of Laggan in the North of Ireland and minister of the congregation of Killybegs in Donegal, he had become familiar with the way that must be trodden by him whose salvation in his work on earth, as well as his final entrance "into the joy of his Lord," is dependent upon endurance unto the end. His parentage and the place of Thomas Wilson's nativity are not known. Of the character of the family from which he came, however, we cannot be in doubt, in that the approved worthiness and worthwhileness of the man cannot but be indicative of some worthy strain in his blood. Man of God that he was, he would indeed be satisfied with his status as a "child of Grace"; but, with us, seeing what a magnificent "child of Grace" he was, this status does not preclude the belief in an hereditary quality in the man upon which the Divine Spirit could and did so wonderfully exercise itself.

When the name of Thomas Wilson first appears upon the minutes of the Presbytery of Laggan in August, 1674, he is referred to as one suitable to the charge at Killybegs, and Mr. Henry, of Donegal, is instructed to recommend him to the people of that place. In January, 1676, Wilson is appointed to "supply" there, and in the August following credentials are received in his favor from Route Presbytery. So Thomas Wilson went to Killybegs in Donegal, on the north coast of Donegal Bay; declared a "suitable" man for the charge. This charge was among people whose lot in life was a hard one. The people of Killybegs Congregation were poor, very poor, their living veritably "by the sweat of the brow"; and, as it proved, they could not support a minister. But this Thomas Wilson was a "suitable" man for the place, and he dared this adventure for God, no doubt finding a challenge, as well as the comfort intended, in the words of his Master—"and the poor have the gospel preached unto them." Thomas Wilson probably had some means—though very slight—of his own; certainly his wife, Margaret, as we shall later see, had a small "marriage portion." Maybe by the income from such means they sustained themselves and their young children during the ministry at Killybegs. It may be that the possession of some material means constituted a part of the man's declared suitability for this charge; but "material means" was not all of the name thus given him. There was character in Thomas Wilson and in Margaret, his wife, who went with him to this charge. We pause to pay tribute to Margaret Wilson, for, after all, the "better-half" of a "man of God" in his work of the Gospel, is his wife; for by her, whose part is that of simply "standing by," is the sacrifice of the Cross made luminous. The "man of God" has his work—that is not sacrifice (however hard and difficult and oftentimes discouraging the way may be), but consummation of holy desire. The wife of the "man of God"—in any age, in any clime—if she be true—carries the Cross of sacrifice. "As it was in the beginning, is now, and ever shall be."

So Thomas Wilson—and Margaret, his wife—went to Killybegs, and sustained the ministry of the Gospel there. The difficulty from the material side we have made plain to us by notations from the records of the Presbytery of Laggan. In October, 1677, we find that "Killybegs promises to support Mr. Wilson better." In July, 1678, "Mr. Wilson is asked to attend Presbytery and give an account of his ministry, as the people cannot be induced to come to tell how they supported him." In November, 1678, "Killybegs has paid him only twelve pounds a year for last two years. No prospect for improvement." And yet in the list of the ministers of the Presbytery of Laggan in 1680 we find this record: *"Thomas Wilson . . . Killybegs."* From this date to July, 1681, when the minutes of the Presbytery of Laggan break off, there is "no word of his removal from Killybegs." The Reverend Professor Witherow, of Derry, communicating the above facts to the Reverend Doctor L. P. Bowen (author of "The Days of Makemie"), concludes his report on the results of his research in the Laggan Presbytery records for data in regard to Thomas Wilson, with these significant words: "When the minutes resume, in 1691, no word of Killybegs and Wilson. I suspect he was starved out..."

This man—this Thomas Wilson—was he who came to Somerset in Maryland following Makemie, Traile and Davis on their American mission, becoming "Minister of the Gospel at Manokin," and serving as first pastor of Manokin Congregation of Presbyterian faith and order in Somerset from 1685 until his death, about 1702.

The exact date of the Reverend Thomas Wilson's arrival in Somerset County we have not been able to ascertain, though probably we shall not be far wrong in placing his arrival in the Summer or Fall of the year 1685. With him came his sons, Ephraim and Thomas. Whether there were other children we do not know; these two sons were certainly his only surviving children at the time of his death. We do not know whether Margaret Wilson, his wife, survived the rigors of the Killybegs ministry or not, coming to Somerset to enjoy, for a season at least, the more comfortable adventure of her reverend spouse. However, we fear that she did not; and this fear is engendered by a passage in Mr. Wilson's deed of division of his property, near the close of his life, between his two sons. The property thus divided was purchased by him in Somerset County in January, 1685/6, with the "marriage portion" of his wife, Margaret, in accordance with their marriage contract and with a renewal of "my former Covenant and bargain with her and Confirmed with her upon her death bed a Little before her decease." Killybegs, which claimed Mrs. Margaret Wilson in life, no doubt holds in its soil her sacred dust.

On January 20, 1685/6, we find Jacob Waring conveying (for the sum of 10,000 pounds of tobacco) to "Thomas Wilson, of Somerset County, Clerk," a tract of 130 acres of land known as the "Turner's Purchase," in Somerset County, situated between the branches of the upper fork of Manokin River. This is the earliest reference to the Reverend Thomas Wilson that has been discovered in the Somerset County records. By this purchase Wilson obtained the land on which he built his home, continuing his residence there through the remainder of his life. Today the site of this "home-place" of Thomas Wilson in Somerset County may be located about a mile and a half south of the town of Princess Anne and included in the farm of Mr. Milton Hickman. In the course of events, after Mr. Wilson's death, through the sale of the land by his granddaughter, Mrs. Margaret Lindow, the home and plantation of this Presbyterian minister became the Glebe of Somerset Parish of the Church of England, and thus for some years the residence of the rectors of that parish.

Whatever may have been the date of Mr. Wilson's arrival in Somerset, his ministry was exclusively confined to the pastorate of the

Manokin Presbyterian Congregation, whose "Meeting House" was situated from the very first at the headwaters of Manokin River (north side and by the river side), about two miles north of Wilson's residence and on the site which today is occupied by the Manokin Presbyterian Church of the town of Princess Anne. Of this congregation Thomas Wilson was pastor from 1685 to 1701 or 2; and it consisted, in his day, of the sturdy families of King, Brown, Alexander, McNitt, Wallace, Strawbridge, Polk, and others, whose names the passage of time has obliterated. Major Robert King, of "Kingsland," and Colonel David Brown, of "Thornton"—both men of large wealth and great official position in the county and in the province—men who figured conspicuously in the Protestant Revolution in Maryland in 1688-90, were members of the Manokin Congregation in Mr. Wilson's day.

We have no detailed record of Thomas Wilson's ministry in Somerset, his pastorate in the Manokin Congregation. His was what would be called a very quiet pastorate, living day by day among his people, week by week on each recurring Lord's Day leading them in the worship of the sanctuary, interpreting to them the deep truths of the Word of God, and in season breaking the Bread of Life and blessing the Cup of Redemption to their souls' true nourishment. He came to this field of service beside the quiet waters of Manokin a man certainly in middle life; a well proved soldier of the Cross of Christ. His were eyes well opened to the vision of eternal realities, eyes whose true sight the dazzling prospects of worldly gain could not dim. After exercising reasonable carefulness about provision for his family in material things—wisely administering the trust committed to him in this behalf by contract with his deceased wife as to her "marriage portion"—the man appears to have cared nothing further about "earthly treasure." With the simple dignity of responsibility for those dependent upon him he discharged this material obligation and then laid aside "earthly things." No doubt the people of his congregation saw to it that he was well provided for in the matter of physical necessities; and we doubt not that Mr. Wilson advantageously farmed the lands that he purchased. Killybegs in Donegal and its destitution may indeed have proved his true worth, "strengthening and stiffening his soul," while it played at the game of attempting to starve his body; but certainly the "reasonable success" of Somerset only liberated his splendid spirit and mind for the work to which he had come. From every evidence remaining he appears to have been a man whom neither hardship nor reasonable comfort could deflect from his "high calling." If remembrance after a material fashion be any evidence of the esteem in which a man is held by his contemporaries, then we have an indication of what at least two able men thought of the Reverend Thomas Wilson. John Galbraith, a prominent Scotch merchant who had settled in Snow Hill Town, bequeathed in 1691 to Mr. Wilson, and to Mr. Makemie and Mr. Davis, each five thousand pounds of pork; while Colonel David Brown, of "Thornton," member of the Manokin Congregation, dying in 1697 made the first item of his will (after directing the payments of his debts) to read: "It is my will that Mr Thomas Wilson, Senr for his better support have Ten Thousand pounds of tobacco to be paid of my best debts."

As the end of his life approached, doubtless warned by some malady that the time of his departure from earth was drawing near, "Thomas Wilson, Senr, Clerke, and minister of gospell upon Manokin River in Somerset County . . ." made a division, by deed, September 4, 1700, between his eldest son, Ephraim Wilson and his younger son, Thomas Wilson, Junior, of the land where he lived with the improvements and stock thereon, which represented the investment of the "marriage portion" of Margaret, late wife of the said Thomas Wilson. It appears that when Mr. Wilson married his wife, Margaret (whose family name is not revealed), this "marriage portion" of the bride had by "contract of marriage" been placed as a trust in Mr. Wilson's keeping "to Lay out & improve . . . for the good & benefitt of the issue and Children Lawfully to be begotten and procreate between us as also I did truly & faithfully renew this my former Covenant and bargain with her and Confirmed with her upon her death bed a little before her decease . . ." The estate divided was not marked by extensiveness but by substantiality. It represented wisdom in investment, good judgment and prudence in management. By the conclusion of this deed of division, a further fact in regard to the Reverend Thomas Wilson's "adventure in living" is revealed. He had married a second time, a lady whose baptismal name was Jane—her family name does not appear—and this deed specifically secures to Ephraim and Thomas, the sons of the Reverend Thomas Wilson by his former wife, Margaret, this property "particularly against any title claime or right that Jane my present wife may pretend unto the Contra[ry] as her right but falsely and unjustly." Madam Jane Wilson had no doubt disclosed her grasping desire a trifle too soon for her own gain. Whatever Madam Jane's intentions on this property may have been, they were successfully frustrated by this deed.

It is the entry on the records of Somerset County Court of the above recited deed of division that certifies to us the fact that the Reverend Thomas Wilson passed from this life sometime towards the close of the year 1702. The deed, dated September 4, 1700, was witnessed by "John Gray, John Polke, Wm $\overset{his}{XX}$ Allesccn^r Senr [William Alexander, Senior?], John $\underset{marke}{\overset{his}{FB}}$ Brown, Wm $\underset{marke}{\overset{his}{B}}$ Wilson," and its recordation bears "Memorandum that this day (vizt) the 18th day of Jan^{ry} 1702/3 Came before me the subscribed Wm. Wilson and made oath upon the holy Evangelists that he see *the deceased Mr Thomas Wilson* Seale Sign & deliver the within menconed deed of Guift for the uses within mentioned (signed) J. West, Cha: Ballard."

So lived and died—to live eternally—Thomas Wilson, first pastor of Manokin Congregation of the Presbyterian Church in Somerset. We know that Somerset's tradition of "faith and works" is richer by far because of the years that Thomas Wilson ministered in the things of Christ within this area, *"for to me to live is Christ."* And we believe that the eye of his faith, piercing the mist which envelopes the way called "Death," beheld God—"and not as a stranger."[20]

* * * *

With the passing of Makemie, Traile, Wilson and Davis, the era of laying the foundations of Presbyterianism in Somerset County, and by Makemie those of organized Presbyterianism in America, is brought to a close. William Traile returned to his home across the sea in 1690; Thomas Wilson serving his only American pastorate at Manokin in Somerset, died there in 1701 or 2; Francis Makemie, whose residence for some years was in Accomack County, Virginia, died there in 1708; and Samuel Davis finished his earthly course during his second pastorate at Snow Hill in 1725. Thus passed the first ministers of the Presbyterian Church in Somerset—and the founders of organized Presbyterianism on this continent.[21]

There is an item of record, September, 1692, among the proceedings of the provincial council, which clearly indicates the esteem in which the Presbyterian divines—Makemie, Wilson and Davis, together with the Reverend John Huett, of the Church of England—were held by the people of Somerset County.[22] Maryland, after the Protestant Revolution became a royal province, and by law the Church of England became the "established church"; therefore, ministers not of the Church of England—"dissenters," as they were called—were allowed to "qualify" for their ministries by taking the "oaths of allegiance and abhorrency." The record of the Maryland Council, September 30, 1692, above referred to, relates that a petition, signed by a hundred and twelve Somerset County inhabitants, had been made to that body, "praying the continuances among them of their Ministers, (vizt) one of them of the Church of England, *other three dissenters only in some small matters but willing to qualify themselves so far as in conscience they can by taking the Oaths of allegiance and abhorrency."* The minister of the Church of England referred to was, of course, the Reverend John Huett, the only minister of that Church at the time resident in Somerset County. In the *"other three dissenters"* we recognize Francis Makemie, minister of the Presbyterian congregation of Rehoboth, Thomas Wilson, minister of Manokin, and Samuel Davis, minister of Snow Hill. We know that these three men were ministers of these respective congregations at that time, and as Presbyterians they were "dissenters." It is interesting to note the honor paid them and the value placed upon their services by the Somerset petition requesting the authorities to permit their "continuance" in their fields of labor. While we have not the names of the signers of this petition, there would seem to be a double-edged significance to the matter in that its prayer was alike in behalf of the "continuance" of a minister of the Church of England, and three ministers of the Presbyterian Church. It signifies that "dissenters" joined with "Churchmen" in requesting that the Reverend Mr. Huett, of the Church of England, be continued in his work in Somerset; and that "Churchmen" joined with "dissenters" in requesting that the Reverend Mr. Makemie, the Reverend Mr. Wilson and the Reverend

Mr. Davis—"dissenters"—ministers of the Presbyterian Church, be continued in their work in Somerset. This was the spirit of the laity both "Churchmen" and "dissenters" in "Old Somerset."

Of course, in the willingness of the "three dissenters"—the Presbyterian ministers, Makemie, Wilson and Davis—"to qualify themselves so far as in conscience they can by taking the Oaths of allegiance and abhorrency," we recognize that these men were in full accord with the *Protestant* succession to the throne of England established at the time of the accession of William III and his honorable spouse, Queen Mary. But, furthermore, we recognize that by their willingness "to qualify themselves so far as in conscience they can" they reserved to themselves, as true to their Presbyterianism, the right to reject any subscription to belief in the "Articles of Religion" of the Established Church, the Church of England, which would savor of disloyalty to the "faith and order" in which they gloried.

The record of the Council reciting the petition of the Somerset inhabitants in behalf of the continuance of their ministers concludes with the statement that it was "Referred to further consideration." Of this "further consideration" we have found no record; but that Makemie, Wilson and Davis continued in their work in Somerset there is abundance of evidence.

* * * *

From the record of the lives of the first Presbyterian ministers in Somerset, we turn to the story of the first houses of worship which were erected by Presbyterian congregations in the county.

To Rehoboth Town on Pocomoke River has always been attributed the first house of worship of the Presbyterian Church in Somerset. There is abundant tradition and strong circumstantial evidence to this effect; and with no record evidence or tradition to the contrary we credit the statement with the value of fact.*

Can we doubt that, when the Reverend Francis Makemie came to Somerset County in 1683, he established "headquarters" at Rehoboth,

---

*We make this statement after most careful consideration of the account giving to Snow Hill Town priority over Rehoboth as put forward in Nevin's *Encyclopædia of Presbyterian Church in the U. S. A.;* Philadelphia, 1884; page 1,216.

the home of Colonel Wm. Stevens on the Pocomoke River? Makemie's coming was in response to the request made by Stevens to the Presbytery of Laggan that a "godly minister" of their faith and order be sent to Somerset. The Stevens' home was probably for a time also the abiding place of the Reverend William Traile, who very soon followed Makemie to Somerset (if, as a matter of fact, he did not actually accompany him). Makemie and Traile were both established in Somerset for their work by June, 1683. It was just at this time that active consideration was being given to the laying out of a town on Pocomoke River, about a mile to the south of Colonel Stevens' home. This town, which was finally established under the name of Rehoboth, had its actual legal genesis in certain legislative enactments of the session of the Maryland Assembly held October-November, 1683.[23] In and around this Rehoboth Town a congregation of Presbyterian faith soon developed.

Up to the present time no recorded evidence of the date of the erection of the first house of worship used by the Presbyterian congregation at Rehoboth Town has been discovered. Of course, there is a "tradition" that a church building was erected in the year 1684 in Rehoboth Town, for the use of the Presbyterian congregation; but this date lacks any verification.[24] In April, 1691, we have positive evidence, however, that the Presbyterian congregation in this vicinity was using for purposes of worship a church building called "Rehoboth Church." This evidence is contained in the following record:

"Memorandum. That upon the second of this present April An° 1691 there being a funerall Sermon preached at Rehoboth Church by Mr. Francis Mackemy, minister . . ."[25]

April, 1691, is therefore the first recorded evidence we have of a church building—"Rehoboth Church"—in use by the Presbyterian congregation of Rehoboth. We cannot doubt that, with the influential ministry exercised by both Makemie and Traile in this section, and the increasing strength of their following since their arrival in 1683, this "Rehoboth Church" building had been in use by this congregation at least several years prior to the date of the first reference thereto in the records. We do not know when the building thus used, and thus described by name, was erected, and no records consulted have shed even the faintest light upon the question. As a matter of fact, we do not feel at all sure that this "Rehoboth Church" building was erected exclusively for Presbyterian usage. We are rather inclined to believe that this "Rehoboth Church" was identical with a certain "Pocomoke Church" referred to in records in 1692, and that the building was used for purposes of public worship both by Presbyterians and Church of England ministers and congregations.[26] But whatever may have been the date and circumstance of the erection of this building—"Rehoboth Church"—which was apparently the first regular house of public worship used by the Rehoboth Presbyterian Congregation, it seems certainly to have disappeared by the year 1697 or 1698, as evidenced by a certain report made by the sheriff of Somerset County.

On August 10, 1697, the Governor and Council of Maryland issued an order commanding the sheriffs of the counties of the province to make return of certain religious statistics. In the record of sheriffs' returns made in compliance with this order we find the following item:

"The Sheriff of Somerset County:
Here are neither Popish Priests, Lay Brothers, nor any of their Chapels.
As to Quakers and other Dissenters to the first, none as I know of particularly; and the other [i. e. Dissenters] hath a house at Snow Hill, one at the Road going up along the Sea Side, and one at Nearoakin [Manokin] about 30 feet long, plain country buildings all of them."[27]

It will be noticed that the congregations of Somerset "dissenters," who are easily identified as congregations of the Presbyterian faith, are credited, in this report of the sheriff in 1697, with only three "meeting houses," and that none of these is referred to as being at Rehoboth Town. Evidently the "Rehoboth Church" specifically referred to in the records in April, 1691, had gone the way of all things material.

We have no record as to the exact date of the abandonment, or destruction, of this "Rehoboth Church"; we only know that this congregation had evidently ceased to use it in 1697, when the sheriff made his report as above quoted. Between the date of the abandonment of this "Rehoboth Church" and the completion of their "new Meeting House" in 1705, it is not improbable that the Rehoboth Presbyterian Congregation held religious services in the nearby homes of members. We have evidence that in March, 1702/3, the house of Peirce Bray (formerly the home of the Reverend William Traile) near Rehoboth Town was being so used.²⁸

Many years are not to elapse, however, before we find the Rehoboth Presbyterians completing the erection of a "new Meeting House" on a lot in Rehoboth Town which was the property of the Reverend Francis Makemie, and which several years later he directed by his will that his executrix should convey to the congregation. The Reverend Mr. Makemie was certainly pastor of the Rehoboth Congregation at the time that this new edifice was erected, and it was his voice that was first heard from its pulpit. This so-called "new Meeting House," a substantially constructed building, was of brick, and was completed by the latter part of the year 1705 or early in the year 1706. The date of its completion is certified for us in ample fashion as the result of a truly dramatic episode.

On November 14, 1705, the Vestry of Coventry Parish, through its rector, the Reverend Robert Keith, who was joined in that behalf by the Reverend Alexander Adams, rector of Stepney Parish, petitioned the Court of Somerset County, stating that they had "good grounds to believe that Mr. Francis Mackemmy and others his assistance are intended to address your Worshipps on account of a Tolleration granted to ... [the?] Dissenters for Preaching and building meeting houses and doing whatever else is incumbent on them as such." The prayer of the petitioners was that "the whole as to the Premises be remitted to his Ex^{ncy} the Govern^r of this Province and the hon^{ble} Councel of State thereof By them to be considered and ordered and determined as they shall think fitt And that nothing be done in the premises until warrant and order be obtained from them as to the whole premises, or any part thereof And the same presented to your Worpp^s in open Court, or the Vestry of the said Parish [Coventry] and the remain[ing?] Vestrys therein concerned." The petition was "signed p Order John Heath Clr'e Vestry." Immediately following the record of the presentation of this petition we find the Reverend George McNish, whom we recognize as a Presbyterian minister, petitioning the court "that the usual oaths according to law tendered to And to be taken by dissenting Ministers and Preachers may be tendered to y^r Petitioner." The action of the Somerset Court relative to the petitions was then embodied in the following order:

"The Petions afores^d being read in Open Court the Wor^ll Justices having heard and deliberately Considered the Premesis on both sides, it having reference to his Ex^ncy for result in Ecclesiastick matters &ca he being here Representative in Chief of Church and State Allow the said Vestrys Petion to have its final result and determina*con* by his Ex^ncy and hon^ble Council of State as prayed for Nothwithstanding the said M^cnish in decent manner Did require (he being a Dissenter from the Church of England) that he might be dignified as by law in this County to preach, offering to take the Oaths and subscribe the Declara*con*. Nevertheless the Wor^ll Court hath Resolved as aforesaid."[29]

In keeping with the judgment of Somerset Court we find this matter before the Governor and Council of Maryland in executive session held February 21, 1705/6. At this time:

"Mr Keeth and Mr Adams Petition and Letter to his Excellency and Councill on Mr. M^cicnishes [McNish's] Application being read, Ordered thereon that there be no meeting houses Built within Less than half a mile of any Established Church already built; that they give an Account of all the meeting houses they have to the County Court who are to give his Ex^ncy an Account thereof, And that before they build anymore they Acquaint his Excellency therewith & where Scituated."

This record of the Council proceedings clearly shows that "Mr. M^cicnishes [McNish's] Application" concerned the erection of a "meeting house" near a church building of the Established Church, while the prohibitive order passed by the board certainly was aimed at preventing the use of the "meeting house" for whose registration as a place of worship Mr. McNish was applying.

This order of Council, February 21, 1705/6, brought the question to an acute stage, and about six weeks later, on April 5, 1706, we find "Mr. Robert Keith & Mr. Alexander Adams Ministers of the Church of England in Somerset County with Mr. Francis M^ccemie [Makemie] a dissenting Minister," in person before the Council sitting as the Upper House of Assembly. Mr. Makemie "complayns of their [i. e. his and his congregation's] Libertys being infringed by a certain Order of Councill prohibiting their building a Meeting House within less than a half a mile of any Established Church allready built." Hearing the arguments from both sides the Council refused to rescind the order against which Makemie was protesting, concluding its deliberations with the following decision:

"Upon which both parties being heard and it appearing to his Ex^cy & her Ma^tys hon^ble Councill that the House [i. e. the 'meeting house'] was allready erected on Mr. M^ccemies own proper Lands Advised that this matter be layd before my Lord Bishop of London for his decision And that in the mean tyme Mr. M^ccemie be at liberty to preach in his house according to the Tolleration."

From the proceedings of the Council in executive session a year later, in February, 1706/7, and April, 1707, we learn that this matter of registering, according to law, the "meeting house" in question was being further warmly debated on the grounds of the former objection. Again in February, 1706/7, a petition of Keith and Adams is heard against McNish's application for registration of "the meeting house lately erected very nigh to the Church at Rehoboth . . . for that it might be of Disturbance to the Church Established by Law there." The Council again passed an order that "no Meeting house be built within a mile [sic: half mile] of any Established Church allready built and that before any more be built his Ex^{cy} be Acquainted therewith and where Scituate." This time we find as a "Memd. Mr. Francis Makemie had a copy of the above order." In April, 1707, we find Mr. Keith and Mr. Adams with Mr. Makemie again appearing in person before the Council sitting in executive session. This time Makemie "on behalf of himself and others of his Comunion complains of their Liberty being infringed by a Certain order of Councill prohibitting their building a meeting house within half a Mile of any Established Church already built." As before, the Governor and Council hear the parties on both sides of the question, and ascertain that "the Meeting house of Rehoboth in Somersett County is allready Erected on Mr. M^ccemies owne proper Lands." So, away they send—not the Meeting House, for that seems as veritably unmovable as the Rock of Gibraltar—but the complaint against its location to "the Rt hon^{ble} & Rt Reverend the Lord Bishop of London for his Decision and Advice"; while—"in the meantime Mr. M^ccemie be at liberty to preach in his house according to the Tolleration."[30]

The proceedings before the Governor and Council, which we have quoted at length, are very illuminating. *First,* they positively fix the date of the erection of the "New Meeting House" in Rehoboth Town (built for the Presbyterian congregation there) as between November, 1705, and April, 1706. We are positively informed that the building of the "meeting house" had been completed by April, 1706; while there seems no reasonable doubt that the building was either finished, or in an advanced stage of construction, when the Council issued its prohibitive order in February, 1705/6. It seems certain also that this "meeting house" was in the building stage, well on the way, if not completed, by November, 1705, when the Coventry Parish Vestry made its petition to Somerset Court in anticipation of the intended application of Mr. Makemie and his assistants "on account of a Tolleration granted to . . . Dissenters for Preaching and building meeting houses and doing whatever else is incumbent on them as such." *Secondly,* these Council proceedings show the persistence with which Mr. Makemie carried out his purpose; for we recognize that it was his genius which conducted this affair safely through the turbulent waters of opposition. We see also the persistence of the opposition of Keith and Adams—representing the Established Church in Somerset County generally, as well as Coventry Parish in particular. We should not forget that these ministers of the Established Church, as well as the Vestry of Coventry Parish, were only doing their duty in protesting against the placing of a Presbyterian house of worship within half a mile of an already erected building of the Established Church.[31] Keith and Adams, as ministers of the Established Church, were only being faithful to their trust and charge. Abler and godlier men than Keith and Adams—and we know whereof we speak—cannot be found among the Maryland colonial clergy; and certainly none worthier or more faithful—"in labors more abundant"—than Alexander Adams, who for sixty-five years (1704-1769) was rector of Stepney Parish and who at intervals ministered to all four parishes of the Church of England in Somerset. The church of Coventry Parish, which had been built some years prior to 1705, stood only about 200 yards to the southwest of the site at which this "New Meeting House" was erected. By the action of Council in April, 1706, and 1707, the Reverend Francis Makemie and the Presbyterian congregation of Rehoboth made marked progress towards the objective of their appeal. Mr. Makemie's action in erecting this house of worship on his own land, to which he still held title (the title thereto only passing under Makemie's will), was most astute. The "Meeting House" was admitted by the Council to have been built *"on Mr. M^ccemies owne proper Lands,"* therefore the board granted him *"libertye to preach in his house."* Though granting this liberty to Mr. Makemie, the Council, in view of the nature of the objections raised to the location of the "meeting house," could not do otherwise than to refer the question of its registration to "the Lord Bishop of London for his Decision and Advice." The parishes of the Church of England within the provinces and colonies were within the jurisdiction of the Bishop of London. The provincial archives fail to disclose the "decision and advice" given by this ecclesiastical authority.

Victory in this matter was with the Reverend Francis Makemie and the Presbyterian congregation of Rehoboth.

For over a year this whole vexing question seems to have remained in abeyance. Yet throughout this period the "New Meeting House" in Rehoboth Town was in constant use. Then, in June, 1708, just a few weeks at most before Mr. Makemie's death, (his will was probated in August, his death probably having occurred in July, 1708), the question of the registration according to law of the "New Meeting House lately built at Rehoboth Town" came up for its final test in Somerset Court. The immortal closing petition and the final order of "registration" by the court are among the priceless records of Somerset County, and read as follows:

"Att a Court held by her Maty[s] Worshipfull Justices of the Peace att Dividing Creek the 9th of June Annoq Dom 1708
Com[rs] Present Cap[t] John West, Cap[t] Jno Franklyn, Cap[t] Charles Ballard, Mr. Joseph Venables, Mr. Joseph Gray

Maryland Ss To ye Worship[ll] Court of Somerset County the Petition of Moses Fenton, Pierce Bray, Humbly Sheweth that in Obedience to an Act of Parliament made the first year of King William and Queen Mary Establishing the Liberty of Protestant Disenters We in Humble Manner Certifye to this Court y[t] ye New Meeting house lately built at Rehoboth Town is one of the fixed places for ye Publick service or worship of God by Protestant Dissenters and your Worships are in humble manner prayed to direct your Clk to record the same and give Certificate thereof to any who will require it for wch we are ready to pay the fee specified in ye Last paragraph of s[d] Act of Parliament and y[r] petitioners as In duty bound shall allways Pray.

The petition being read in open Court the Court entered into Judgm[t] whether ye sd Church lately Built by ye Dissenters at Rehoboth Towne should be recorded ye Court here gives Judgm[t] and Ordered ye Clerke record ye same

Cap[t] John West and Mr. Joseph Gray enters their desent these reasons following: That the same thing Concerning ye Church Built at Rehoboth Town by Dissenting Protestants was layd before y[e] Gov[r] & Council and y[t] no finall result has been returned to this Court since concerning the premises."

This petition of Moses Fenton and Pierce Bray (unquestionably ruling elders in the session of Rehoboth Congregation), though meeting with specific objection from Captain John West and Mr. Joseph Gray, was not to remain ungranted, for the court at its session on the following day, June 10th, entered this order:

"This day (Viz^t) the 10th day of June An° Dom 1708 Ordered y^t ye New Meeting house built by Protestant dessenters at Rehoboth Town in Somerset County in ye Province of Maryland be & is hereby appointed to be a house & place for ye Publick Worship of Allmighty God in; the Minister thereunto appointed having Qualified himself as Law required. Entered pr Order. Alex^r Hall, Clk."[32]

The "'New Meeting House" of the congregation of the Presbyterian Church erected in Rehoboth Town, its construction certainly completed between November, 1705, and April, 1706, and finally registered according to law by Somerset Court in June, 1708, yet stands at this day in the little village of Rehoboth by Pocomoke River in Somerset County. Considerable architectural change to meet the needs of "newer days" has modified to a marked degree the original form of the honored fane; while the ancient walls gathering within them this "newness" enshrine the most hallowed memories of "the beginning."[33]

* * * *

Having accorded to the Rehoboth Congregation that position of priority among the congregations of the Presbyterian Church in "Old Somerset" which by origin and organization it unquestionably merits, and having traced the record of the erection of its ancient church buildings, we turn to the subject of the erection of the first church buildings of the remaining three seventeenth century Presbyterian congregations in Somerset.

Snow Hill Town, on the south side of Pocomoke River near its headwaters, was established by direction of the Maryland Assembly of 1686. The Reverend Samuel Davis, third in the succession of the Presbyterian ministry in Somerset, had arrived in the county prior to February, 1684/5, and in June, 1687, purchased a plantation about a mile and a half northeast of this newly established town. On this plantation called "Grove," he established his home. Mr. Davis, almost from its very beginning, was associated with Snow Hill Town and the immediate vicinity, becoming pastor of the Presbyterian congregation then forming in this section. He is recorded as minister of the Snow Hill Presbyterian Congregation from 1686 to 1698, and again from 1718 until his death in 1725. Though the exact date of the erection of the first "Meeting House" (as it was invariably referred to in the early records) of the Snow Hill Congregation has not been discovered, we can hardly doubt that with a resident pastor and a growing congregation centering in a developing town, a house of worship was built at a very early day. Mr. Davis is referred to in 1689/90 as dwelling in this section; and in August, 1691, as "Mr. Samuel Davis minister at Snow Hill."[34] It is not improbable that the Snow Hill Congregation built its first "Meeting House" sometime between 1687 and 1690. No recorded evidence has been found to this effect; and the statement is based purely upon the circumstances related above. It is certain, however, that this building had been erected prior to the Summer of 1697, for the report of the sheriff of Somerset, in reply to the Governor's request on August 10th of that year for certain statistics, stated that *"Dissenters . . . hath a house at Snow Hill;* one at the Road going up along the Sea Side, and one at Nearoakin [Manokin] about thirty feet long, plain country buildings all of them."[35] We have then this definite record of "a house at Snow Hill" of "the Dissenters"—"about 30 feet long"—a "plain country building," as standing in the Summer of 1697. This "Meeting House" is again specifically referred to in the records in November, 1705, February, 1719, and August, 1721.[36] We are also able to approximately locate this sacred edifice as having been on the north side of the present Green Street, some yards west of the present Bank Street, and probably on part of Lot 10 in the original plan of the town of Snow Hill.

The date at which this first "Meeting House" was abandoned is not known; but the remaining Session records of the congregation prove that a new house of worship was erected between 1745 and 1747. A deed of conveyance made in the year 1748 for lot Number 32 in Snow Hill Town refers to it as the lot *"on which the Protestant Presbyterian Dissenting Meeting House hath been lately built and now standeth."*[37] Again in May, 1795, subscriptions were taken for building a "Meeting House" on this Lot Number 32. This site is on the south side of Market Street in the town of Snow Hill, and today (1933) is included in the lot of ground occupied by the

Makemie Presbyterian Church, manse and burying ground in Snow Hill.[38]

* * * *

Today there stands within the limits of Princess Anne Town in Somerset County, some seventy-five yards north of the Manokin River—now but a very small stream at this point—the Manokin Presbyterian Church. The walls of this building are those of the "Meeting House" erected for this congregation in the year 1765 as the result of the Session's "finding [in December, 1764] that the 'Meeting House' was decayed in almost every part, and not worth repairing and that it is too small to contain the people that often attend." This ascertained condition of the "Meeting House" resulted in that governing board's determination to "build a new one of brick 50 x 40 in the clear 16 feet from the water table to the plate . . ." The years have brought marked changes in the original design of this building—modernizations which indeed have carried away all of the "original" save the walls.[39] We cannot say positively but, from consideration of all circumstances, we believe that this building of 1765—"a new one of brick"—was either the immediate successor to the *first* "Meeting House" of the Manokin Presbyterian Congregation, or certainly not further moved than in a degree, which, expressed in terms of human relationship, would be described as "grandchild" of the original. It is, of course, the "original" with which we are here concerned.

The Manokin Congregation of the Presbyterian Church was "in the beginning" a purely rural one. No shadow of town building cast itself upon the brightness of such felicity for nearly a half century from the time of its organization. This congregation was certainly in the formative stages in 1683, while Princess Anne Town did not take shape until 1733. The people who composed the Manokin Congregation lived in that area of Somerset County from south of the present King's Creek, north to the headwaters of the present Wicomico Creek (in that day called Wicomico River), and from some distance west on Manokin River to the section then known as "the Forest" on the east. As a matter of fact, the first Presbyterians whom we have been able to positively identify, David Brown, the Kings, the

Alexanders and Strawbridges, we find in this section which became the realm of the Manokin Congregation. By 1685/6 there was ample material here for the organization of a congregation, and we find the Reverend Thomas Wilson settling in this vicinity on a plantation which he purchased at that time. Mr. Wilson was pastor of this congregation from 1686 until his death in 1701-2.

As in the question of the dates of erection of the first "Meeting Houses" for the Presbyterian congregations of Rehoboth and Snow Hill, so with the date of erection of the first Manokin Meeting House; we must confess that no record evidence is at hand on which to base a positive statement. A congregation of sufficient proportions and interest to have a settled pastor in 1685/6 probably did not remain so many years without its house of worship. We may safely say that the first "Meeting House" of the Manokin Congregation was probably erected some time within the period between 1686 and 1690. Certainly in the Summer of the year 1697 the "Dissenters ... hath a house ... at Nearokin [Manokin] about 30 feet long [a] plain country building..."[40] This is of course a reference to the "Meeting House" of the Manokin Congregation of the Presbyterian Church. In August, 1701, a court order relating to the Pocosan Road clearly refers to this "Church" (as it calls it) at the head of Manokin. In June, 1706, when the Reverend John Hampton and the Reverend George McNish were, upon order of the Governor and Council (dated March 13, 1705/6) to the Somerset Court, admitted to qualify in order to preach in the county (being "Disenting preachers"); one of the places specified for their preaching was *"the meeting house att ye head of Manocan."*[41] At Somerset Court, June, 1708, the "Meeting House" of the Manokin Congregation was registered as follows:

"To ye Worshipfull the Judge & Justices of the Court of Somerset Humbly Sheweth That Whereas Divers persons in & aboute Monokin of ye Presbityrian Interest and persuasion have built a Meeting house for ye Publick Exercise of their religious Worship & heard [hard] by Manokin Bridge & being Willing to Satisfie the Law according to Act of Parliament in Petitioning ye County Court where a Meeting house is or shall be erected y^t it may be put on Publick record In complyance therefore with ye end & design of the Law in such Case y^r petitioner in Name of ye persons foresd do request y^t house foresd may be legally recorded as Law will and your Petitioner Shall pray &ca. June ye 10th 1708.   George McNish

The above written petition being read in Court was by ye Whole Court allowed & Ordered y^t sd Meeting house Built by Protestant Desenters by Manokin Bridge in Somerset County in Maryland Be & is hereby appointed to be a place for ye Worship of Almighty God in; ye Minister having Qualified himself as Law required Entered p^r Order Alex^r Hall Clk."[42]

It is this petition of Mr. McNish in June, 1708, which raises the question as to whether the "Meeting House" near Manokin Bridge, for whose registration he is petitioning, may not have been a newly erected building and a successor to the "Meeting House" which appears by the Somerset Sheriff's report (before referred to) as being in use in the Summer of 1697. There has appeared to this present time no record evidence by which this question may be definitely settled. The petition (of 1708) does not refer to the "Meeting House" as *new,* or *lately built,* and we are inclined to believe that Mr. McNish is petitioning for the registration of the "Meeting House" which had been erected sometime before this date and which was still standing, and in use, in June, 1708. We believe that Mr. McNish and the Manokin Congregation were simply complying with the law requiring the registering in the court of the law described "Dissenting Meeting Houses." We may be in error in this assumption; but we venture this as our belief, and await its successful disproving. It was this house of worship erected sometime prior to 1697 (probably between 1686 and 1690) and recorded as in use in that year, again appearing in the records (as quoted above) in June, 1706, and June, 1708, which was still standing in August, 1723, when Charles Ballard "out of the good and respect which he hath for the service of God" conveyed to the "Elders of the Presbyterian Congregation of Monokin," a quarter of an acre of ground for "the use support maintainance of a Meeting House for the Worship and service of Almighty God according to the Presbeterian prSuasion."[43]

The several items quoted above relative to the "Meeting House at the head of Manokin"—"hard by Manokin Bridge"[44]—together with the title to the land as that has been traced, absolutely certifies the location of this "Meeting House" site, and discloses the fact that the tract of land on which the Manokin Presbyterian Church of Princess Anne today stands has been the scene of religious services since the year 1672—a period of two hundred and sixty-one years. In August, 1667, Christopher Nutter received a patent for three hundred acres of land called "Nutter's Purchase" on the north side of the Manokin River in Somerset County, and between the lands of Owen Macrah and John Nelson. Here Nutter made his home, and while living there, in March, 1671/2, his house was named as one of the four preaching stations appointed by the Somerset Grand Jury for the Reverend Robert Maddox (see ante, page 122, for Maddox's "preaching stations"). In November, 1672, Christopher Nutter sold and conveyed this tract called "Nutter's Purchase" to Charles Ballard, of Somerset County. This Charles Ballard dying intestate about 1675, the "Nutter's Purchase" plantation passed to his son, Charles Ballard (Junior), who in August, 1723, conveyed the quarter of an acre of ground from that tract to the Elders of the Presbyterian Congregation of Manokin for a "Meeting House for the Worship and service of Almighty God according to the Presbeterian prSuasion." Charles Ballard's deed of August 19, 1723, recites the fact that the quarter acre of land thereby conveyed is out of a tract of three hundred acres called "Nutter's Purchase" on the north side, at the head of Manokin River, granted Christopher Nutter by patent August 15, 1667 (and at that date between the lands of Owen Magraw and John Nelson); that the land had become the property of the said Ballard's father by purchase, and so descended to him, the said Charles Ballard (Junior). Nearly a century later there evidently arose some question as to the title to the land on which the Manokin Presbyterian Church stood, and in 1812 "all that lot or parcel of Land on which the Presbyterian Church near the town of Princess Anne now stands" was conveyed by Elizabeth Jackson (for £200 currency) to Samuel Ker and George Handy, while, in July, 1827, Samuel Ker and Elizabeth Handy (widow of George Handy, Senior, deceased) reconveyed the same to William Jones, Senior, Samuel Ker, William Stewart, Henry P. C. Wilson, George Handy and Robert Patterson, thus perfecting the title of the lands to the church.[45]*

Today, its ivy-covered ancient walls holding memories of a great past, Manokin Presbyterian Church stands, surrounded by "God's Acre," beside the highway of this new day, at the northern entrance to Princess Anne Town. Only the walls of this church have come down to us from the past. The hands of time and change have re-

---

*See post for note on "Wicomico Presbyterian Congregation."

modeled the hallowed "Meeting House"—the house wherein God meets with man, as the children of men meet together to worship the Eternal Father. Yet is this place Bethel to the Children of the Covenant—children of the fathers of this faith in Somerset: "Surely the Lord is in this place; . . . this is none other but the house of God; and this is the gate of heaven."

* * * *

In addition to the "Meeting Houses" of the Snow Hill and Manokin Presbyterian Congregations referred to by the Somerset County Sheriff's report of 1697 as then standing, we learn, from this same source, of the existence of a third "Meeting House" of this faith described as being *"at the Road going up along the Sea Side,"* and in construction, like its sister edifices—"about 30 feet long plain country buildings, all of them."[46] There is no question about the locations of the Snow Hill and Manokin "Meeting Houses," but neither record nor tradition brings to us with any degree of exactness the location of this third mentioned Presbyterian house of worship. "The Road going up along the Sea Side" was indeed "a long, long road," whose course we cannot now trace in detail. This road, however, must have been one which extended north and south paralleling the sea and was east of Snow Hill Town. This road could not have been so many miles inland from the Atlantic Ocean. The portion of "Old Somerset," which since 1742 has been Worcester County, and lying to the east of Snow Hill Town and extending from the Maryland-Virginia boundary line on the south to the Maryland-Delaware line on the north, was familiarly referred to in the old records as "the sea side" and "sea-board side." Unquestionably, this *"Road going up along the Sea Side"* in the year 1697 is today followed generally by the highway which leads from the town of Snow Hill in a northeasterly direction through Berlin, thence north, crossing the headwaters of St. Martin's River (the South and Middle Branches) and through the village of Bishopville, thence crossing the Maryland-Delaware line.[47] Somewhere along this road the "Meeting House" of 1697, here under discussion, was located.* Since Snow Hill Town had its own "Meet-

---

*See post for note on "Meeting House on the road going up along the seaside," 1697.

ing House," we believe that the "Meeting House" described as "at the Road going up along the Sea Side" must have been some miles to the northeast of that town. To this sacred edifice we find but two references, the one in the Somerset County Sheriff's report of 1697, and the other in November, 1705, when the court, forbidding (under penalty) persons to drive or catch horses "upon the great Bridge on Pocomoke River [at Snow Hill]," directed its order "published at the Churches & *meeting houses* At Snow Hill and *Sea Side.*"[48] The date at which this "Meeting House" was built we do not know, nor do we know how long it continued in use, nor the names of the families who composed its congregation. We simply know that it had "being and life" and we believe that it was the source of the origin of the well-known old Buckingham Congregation of the Presbyterian Church,† which today centers in the town of Berlin, in Worcester County.‡

---

†See post for note on Buckingham Presbyterian Congregation and Meeting Houses.

‡See post for notes on "Meeting House near Mrs. Edgars," 1706; and the origin of the Pitts Creek Congregation.

Notes

1. Wicomico Presbyterian Congregation and Meeting Houses. 2. Meeting House, 1697, "at the road going up along the Sea Side," and in 1705 at "Sea Side." 3. Buckingham Presbyterian Congregation and Meeting Houses. 4. "Meeting House near Mrs. Edgar's, 1706; and the congregation, 1718 and 1744, on "south side of Pocomoke near the Ferry." 5. Pitts Creek Presbyterian Congregation and Meeting House. 6. Some other early Presbyterian places of worship.

WICOMICO CONGREGATION AND "MEETING HOUSES"

The well-known Wicomico Presbyterian Congregation (whose present church is the Wicomico Presbyterian Church, Salisbury, Wicomico County, Maryland) was the offspring of Manokin Presbyterian Congregation and was organized from that section of Manokin Congregation living in the area of the then Somerset County (now Wicomico County) to the north of the present Wicomico Creek and extending to the north of Wicomico River. The exact date of the organization of this Wicomico Presbyterian Congregation has not been discovered; but what was its first erected "Meeting House" appears in the records in June, 1706, when the Reverend John Hampton and the Reverend George McNish qualified before Somerset Court to preach in the county at the several "Meeting Houses," one of which is described as, *"ye meeting house on Mr. Joseph Venables' Land."* (Somerset Court, Deed Liber O 9 (AB), Judicials 1705-1706, page 110). References in Somerset County court records make the location of this "meeting house on Mr. Joseph Venables' Land" quite certain. February, 1717/18, boundaries of Joseph Venables' land, called "What You Please," were established and survey and plat thereof recorded. This tract situated north side Wicomico River, extending from Mitcheller's Branch (west) to Keene's Branch (east), with boundaries extending well back into the woods; contained 300 acres. (Somerset Court, Views of Commissioners of Land, Liber A (1719-1720), pages 24-25). Joseph Venables died intestate, and the tract, "What You Please," descended to his son, Benjamin Venables. April 3, 1738, Benjamin Venables, of Somerset County, conveyed (for £30 currency) to John Handy, of same county, 25 acres, part of "What You Please" originally patented by William Keene; being upper part of said tract lying north side Wicomico River beginning at oak by side of Mitcheller's Branch, (first bounder of the tract "What You Please"), thence up river side to mouth of Keene's Branch, thence into woods by line of marked trees till intersects Mitcheller's Branch, thence down that branch to first bounder; *"excepting half an acre where the meeting house now stands during the time the congregation of decenters shall keep a house there for the worship of God";* being all the land said Benjamin Venables holds of aforesaid tract lying eastermost side Mitcheller's Branch (Somerset Court, Deed Liber O 19, page 256). June 14, 1696, William Keene conveyed to Joseph Venables the tract called "What You Please" containing 300 acres (patented to said Keene on June 28, 1669) and being on north side Wicomico River, beginning at a tree near mouth of Mitcheller's Branch and extending up the riverside to mouth of Keene's Branch, etc., etc. (Somerset Court, Deed Liber O 7, page 427). At Somerset Court, August, 1727, Thomas Humphreys and Adam Heatch reported they had laid out road to the "Meeting House" in accordance with order of court, June 22, 1727, directing them to "Lay out a road from the Upper Ferry Road over Wickacomocoe River to the Presbyterian Meeting house standing on or near the said Riverside ye said Road to be Laid out ye most nearest way & Least of Prejudice to any person &c." (Somerset Court, Judicials, 1727-30, page 37). These records definitely locate this "Meeting House" of the Wicomico Presbyterian Congregation as on, or near, the riverside, on north side Wicomico River between Mitcheller's Branch (west) and Keene's Branch (east) not far west, or east, of the Upper Ferry landing on the north side of the river. The site is probably not more than a half mile west of the mouth of Rockawalkin Creek. In March, 1718/19, the Reverend William Stewart qualifying in Somerset Court to preach, named as one of his stations the "Meeting House" on north side Wicomico River (Somerset Court, Judicials, Liber CH, page 57), November, 1738, Reverend Patrick Glasgow, a Presbyterian Minister, qualifying to preach in the county, certified among other "Meeting Houses" the *"Meeting house near the ferry of Capt. John Handy."* (Somerset Court, Judicials, 1738-40, page 33). This was the so-called "Upper Ferry" and the land on which the "Meeting House" stood near that ferry was the land as conveyed on April 3, 1738, by Benjamin Venables to John Handy. While "Manokin" and "Wicomico" were separate congregations it is evident that they were served by the same minister for many years. The exact date of the Wicomico Congregation's abandoning this "Meeting House" we do not know, though by August, 1742, another "meeting house" had been erected further inland from the river.[1] August 19, 1742, Levin Gale, of Somerset County, conveyed (for 5 shillings currency) to John Caldwell, James Cathell and William Brown, of Somerset County, to them and their heirs forever "more especially in regard to the Congregation of the Presbyterian Preswasion in Wicocomoco in the afd County of Somerset and for their erecting a house for Religious Worship in that place . . ." one acre of land on the *north* side of Wicomico River and on the *west* side of the head of a creek called Mill Creek, about one-fourth of a mile above Captain George Paris' Grist Mill *"and whereon was lately erected a meeting house by the said congregation"* (Somerset Court, Deed Liber O 20, page 311). The mill here designated as Captain George Paris' grist mill was formerly known as Hitches, or Rockawalkin Mill, and was on a branch called Cottingham's Creek. The mill and lands adjoining were purchased by Levin Gale in March, 1730/1, and February, 1735/6, from Mary Cordry and William Elgate, respectively, (Somerset Court, Deed Liber O 17, page 299, deed Gale from Cordry; and Deed Liber O 19, page 36, deed Gale from Elgate). July, 1743, Levin Gale sold this mill and the lands to Captain George Paris, (Somerset Court, Deed Liber O 21, page 73). Paris had evidently been operating the mill prior to the time of this conveyance. The site of this "Meeting House" of 1742 was about a mile and half up Rockawalkin Creek from its mouth, and to the west side of that creek. The "Mill Creek" of 1742 and "Cottingham's Branch or Creek" of an earlier

---

[1]Somerset Court, August, 1742, Thomas Winder petitioned that "Whereas the main road that leads from Thos. Humphryses down to the *Old Church* runs through his land" he is willing to make a new road. The petition was granted and the said petitioner was to turn the road as he requested.

day are clearly one and the same creek and are identical with the Rockawalkin Creek of the present time.

In 1767 the Wicomico congregation erected a new (and its third) "Meeting House." May 18, 1767, Thomas Standford and Rachel, his wife, and John Reid, all of Somerset County, conveyed (for 5 shillings) to Isaac Handy and William Venables, of Somerset, and John Henry, of Dorset [Dorchester] County, 3 acres called "Newberry," to them and their heirs forever *"and more especially in Regard to the Congregation of the Presbyterian Perswasion in Wicomico in the afd. County of Somerset and for their erecting a House for religious worship in that place."* This 3-acre tract is described as being on north side Wicomico River and on the west side of a creek called Mill Creek and as beginning at a marked oak standing close on the south side of the main road leading from head of Wicomico [Salisbury Town] to Quantico (Somerset Court, Deed Liber O 25, page 98). This site is today located about four miles west of Salisbury, Maryland, immediately to the south (and visible therefrom) of the highway from Salisbury to Nanticoke. The remaining record book of the Session of Wicomico Presbyterian Congregation, beginning in 1753,[1] gives several items relative to the congregation's action in regard to the erection of this "Meeting House." From these items we learn that there was considerable discussion about whether to attempt repairs to the Meeting House which had been erected about 1742. Finally, however, the erection of a new building was determined on and the order therefor we discover in the following records of the Session of Wicomico Congregation entered under date of February 9, 1767:

> "The Session taking into consideration the ruinous situation of their Meeting House & the Necessity of doing something for the Honor of God & the Promotion of Religion have unanimously agreed to set aside all their former Determinations about repairing the old House & determined to build a new one at or near the Place where it now stands & it is agreed upon that the members of Session put about papers in order to take subscriptions as soon as possible."

In May, 1773, there is record in the Session book of sums paid towards the erection of this new Meeting House which was built on the "Newberry" tract of three acres purchased from Thomas Stanford and Rachel, his wife, and John Reid on May 18, 1767. In the back of the old Wicomico Session record book there is a plat of this "Newberry" tract made in 1842. It was from this

---

[1] While we know that the Wicomico Presbyterian Congregation was in existence at an early date and had erected a "Meeting House" prior to June, 1706, yet no records of the Session of that congregation remain prior to 1753. However, there is a record book of the proceedings of the Session beginning with April, 1753. This record book for some time believed to have been lost has within the past few years come again to light and is the property of the Session of the Wicomico Presbyterian Church, Salisbury, Maryland. This old record book carries on its first page the entry that in January, 1750, the Session of Wicomico in conjunction with Broad Creek [now Laurel, Delaware] called the Reverend Hugh Henry to be pastor. Mr. Henry accepted and was ordained and installed, November, 1750. The further entry appears that the records of the Session of Wicomico while in conjunction with Broad Creek, 1750, 1751, 1752, and to April, 1753, being the time Mr. Henry continued half his labors at Broad Creek had been "lost so cant appear on record." The first record of Session of Wicomico Congregation is given under date of April 30, 1753, when those present were Hugh Henry [minister], John Flint, James Cathol, Benjamin Venables, William Venables, William Moor, and William Winder, elders.

location that the Wicomico Presbyterian Congregation moved into the town of Salisbury, erecting there another (and its fourth) "Meeting House," or church building. The site of the "Meeting House" (erected after May, 1767) on the "Newberry" tract is today marked by a brick pillar bearing a tablet and inscription commemorating the old building which has long since disappeared.

Meeting House, 1697, "at the Road Going Up Along the Sea Side" and in 1705 at "Sea Side"

As we have stated in the text, nothing of definite nature as to the exact location of this Presbyterian Meeting House of 1697 and 1705 has so far been discovered. However, a reference to an *"old Meeting House Branch"* (near the village of Newark, Worcester County) discovered by William B. Marye, of Baltimore, and generously contributed to this present work by him, may eventually prove to be the key to the solution of the problem of the location of this Meeting House of 1697 and 1705.

The present village of Newark, in Worcester County (until 1742 a part of Somerset County), is situated on the state highway about eight miles northeast of the town of Snow Hill and about eight miles southwest of the town of Berlin (both in Worcester County) and at the headwaters of the middle branch of Marshall's Creek, which has been identified as the "Assateague Creek" of ancient records. The present state highway at this point (and for many miles north and south) is easily identified as formerly a part of *"the road going up along the sea side."* In November, 1676, John Smock had a survey for 200 acres of land called "Batchellor's Lot," in Somerset County, lying on the seaboard side, between Poquetonorton and Assateage about two miles in the woods from salt water (Land Office, Annapolis). In May, 1683, a tract of 200 acres, called "Conveniency," was laid out for Colonel William Stevens; the land described as lying on the seaboard side at the head of Assateague [now Marshall's] Creek, back in the woods from the water side. In June 15, 1683, Colonel Stevens assigned his certificate for this land to John Smock (Land Office, Annapolis, Patents Liber XXII, folio 53). In his will, dated January 13, 1692, John Smock, of Somerset County, devised to his son, Henry Smock, "five hundred acres of land two hundred whereof is the land on wch I now live called Batchellors Lott and one hundred acres more being part the moiety of two hundred acres called Yorkshire bought of Coll Stevens between Robert Cad[e] and mee and two hundred more called Conveniency wch said five hundred acres of land I give and bequeath unto my said son." (Land Office, Annapolis, Wills Liber VI, folio 32). Henry Smock, of Somerset County, in his will dated July 20, 1740, probated November 6, 1747, devised to his son, John Smock, certain land situated on the north side of the Main Road and west side of the branch *"called ye Meeting House branch,"* being part of Batchelder's [Batchellors] Lott and part of Yorkshire, and along as the road leads to Queponcoe (Worcester

Registry of Wills, Liber JW 2, page 45).[1] On November 10, 1752, there was laid out for one John Smock (and patented to him September 29, 1763) a tract of 472 acres called "Partnership" (in Worcester County), it being a resurvey on 64 acres, part of an old tract called "Conveniency," and begins "at a marked red oak standing on a ridge to the westward of a county road near a branch *called The old Meeting house branch* about one perch distant from the said road." (Land Office, Annapolis).

The tracts of land referred to above, "Yorkshire," "Batchellor's Lott" and "Conveniency," adjoined each other. The village of Newark as it is today stands on a part of the "Yorkshire" tract, while the land, (part of "Batchellor's Lott" and part of "Yorkshire"), devised by Henry Smock to his son, John Smock, was on the *west* side of *"ye Meeting house branch"* and on the *north* side of the *"Main Road"* and ran *"along as the road leads to Queponcoe."*[2] As further evidence of the location of this *"Meeting House Branch"* we find the tracts of "Batchellor's Lott" and "Conveniency" referred to in 1756 as *"bounded by the Main road and Branch"* and described as *"on main county road that directeth to Snow Hill Town."*[3] This road is now covered by the highway as it runs from Berlin through Newark to Snow Hill.

From the records quoted above we can locate a designated *"Meeting House Branch"* in July, 1740 (date of Henry Smock's will) as being certainly a branch of Marshall's Creek, and as being near the *"road going up along the sea side"* as that road is referred to in 1697. In 1752 and 1763 we have references to this identical branch as *"The old Meeting house branch."* The references which we have to this specific branch in connection with the tracts of "Batchellor's Lott," "Yorkshire" and "Partnership" (which was a resurvey of "Conveniency") certainly locate this branch as being in the immediate vicinity of the present village of Newark in Worcester County (formerly Somerset County).

We have quoted the few records which have been discovered relative to this *"Meeting house branch"*—*"The old Meeting house branch"*; and through investigation we are able to locate it as being only a short distance to the south,

---

[1] Henry Smock's will dated July 20, 1740; probated Nov. 6, 1747, devised to son John Smock (lands as recited above); to son William Smock, land that lies on other side of Queponcoe road and the said side of the main road being part of Batchellor's Lott; being all remainder of my land on that side of the road; to son Samuel Smock, my old plantation whereon I formerly lived being part of Batchellor's Lott and part of Conveniency, bounded on the main road and down the branch to a place called the slash; to son Henry Smock, plantation I now live on being part of Yorkshire and part of Conveniency binding along by the slash and so on down the Savannah to the Beare Swamp and from thence to the main road; son Thomas Smock, remainder of my land called Conveniency joining the Beare Swamp and so right across the maine branch; wife Elizabeth, whole right of my dwelling plantation during life and ⅓ of personal estate; should son John Smock die with his present sickness his land to go to my son Thomas and the land bequethed to Thomas to go to my son Henry; remainder of estate to be divided between all my children; wife Elizabeth, sole executrix. (Worcester Registry of Wills, Liber JW 2, page 45.)

[2] The section just west and northwest of the present village of Newark was evidently the Queponcoe section and what is known today as the Old Mill Branch (a creek of Pocomoke River) about 2 miles northwest of Newark is probably identical with the Queponcoe Creek given on Griffith's Map of Maryland, 1792. Griffith's Map places a Meeting House at the head of Marshall's Creek, immediately to the west of the creek. What Meeting House this was in 1792 we have not been able to discover. The Maryland Geological Survey Map of Worcester County, 1902, gives a village of *Queponcoe*, at or near the site of Newark. The United States Topographic Map—Maryland. Snow Hill Sheet gives Queponcoe and Newark side by side.

[3] See deed of Samuel Smock to William Smock, Aug. 5, 1756, conveying the parts of "Batchellor's Lott" and "Conveniency" devised to said Samuel by the will of his father, Henry Smock, dec'd. (Worcester Court, Deed Liber D, page 124.) See will of Henry Smock, *ante*.

or southeast, of the present village of Newark, in Worcester County, at the head of the south branch of Marshall's Creek. From the positively ascertained location of this branch we can but ask (though we cannot answer) the question: *Was this the location of the Presbyterian Meeting House referred to in 1697 as "at the road going up along the Sea Side," and in 1705 as the "Meeting House at Sea Side"?*[1]

BUCKINGHAM CONGREGATION AND MEETING HOUSE

Bowen in his *Days of Makemie,* page 522, gives this note: "I fail to find any clue to the date of the organization of the ancient Buckingham church . . . near Poplar Town; it was first built on the Buckingham tract and thence deriving its name, thus pointing back to the native [English] Shire of Judge Stevens.[2] Some are inclined to think that this was the meeting house described in the sheriff's report of 1697 as 'at the road going up along the sea side'."[3]

The definite facts in regard to the origin of the Buckingham Congregation of the Presbyterian Church and the date of the erection of its first Meeting House are as much a mystery at this present time as they were when Doctor Bowen wrote the above quoted note nearly a half century ago. The site of what is designated as the *first* erected Meeting House of the Buckingham Congregation is certainly on, or near, the road described in 1697 as "the road going up along the sea side." But there is no evidence so far available by which to identify this Buckingham Meeting House with the Meeting House of 1697, described as located on that road and with "Meeting House . . . at Sea Side," referred to in 1705, which was evidently one and the same with the sacred edifice of 1697. References in 1740, 1752 and 1763 to *"ye Meeting house branch"* and *"The old Meeting house branch,"* identified as the headwater of the south branch of Marshall's Creek in Worcester (then Somerset) County, to the south of the present village of Newark, and very near the "road going up along the sea side," leads to the belief that the Meeting House of 1697 and 1705 may have been at, or near, that point. The site described as the *first* site of the Buckingham Meeting House is about 4 miles north of the location of this "Meeting House Branch" of Marshall's Creek; though on the same "road going up along the sea side," and at this present time a part of the state highway from Snow Hill to Berlin. While the source of origin of the Buckingham Congregation may have been the congregation which worshipped in the Meeting House of 1697 and 1705, and this "Meeting House" may have been the

---

[1] The location of the *"Meeting House Branch"* (of Marshall's Creek), as above described, is about midway between the towns of Snow Hill and Berlin and only a trifle over 4 miles south of the first site of old Buckingham Meeting House which was located (at a later day) on this same road at the place called Buckingham, later Poplar Town, and now Ironshire, in Worcester County, which was until 1742 part of old Somerset.

[2] "Judge Stevens" here referred to is of course Colonel William Stevens, of "Rehoboth" in Somerset County, for many years a magistrate and presiding judge of Somerset Court, and a native of Buckinghamshire, England. The Buckingham tract of land unquestionably derived its patent name from this source.

[3] For the Sheriff of Somerset's report of 1697, see *ante,* page 236.

forerunner of the *first* Meeting House of the Buckingham Congregation, we cannot from references so far discovered prove them to have been identical.[1]

Unfortunately no records remain of the Session of Buckingham Church for this early period; but we are fortunate in having been able to obtain several valuable references to this congregation and its "Meeting Houses" from the court records and the records of the Presbyteries of Philadelphia and New Castle. The "Buckingham" tract of land on which the so-called first "Meeting House" of the Buckingham Congregation was erected, and from which the name is derived, was a tract of 1,500 acres surveyed for John White and resurveyed July 27, 1679, and patented to him under the name of "Buckingham."[2] The immediate site of the *first* Buckingham "Meeting House" was a piece of ground out of this Buckingham tract, which today lies immediately west of the village of Ironshire, formerly called Poplar Town, in Worcester County (prior to 1742 Somerset County).[3] This location is on the state highway (immediately west thereof) leading from Snow Hill to Berlin and about 11½ miles north of Snow Hill and about 2¼ miles south of Berlin, and is at the headwaters of the southwest branch of Newport Creek (the branch of Newport Creek, which appears today on maps as Beaverdam Creek). John White, for whom the Buckingham tract was surveyed and to whom it was patented, and Colonel William Stevens, of "Rehoboth," married sisters.[4] White was a large land owner and prominent official in Old Somerset and lived at "Cordicall" a plantation on Pocomoke River near Stevens "Rehoboth," and appears to have been a friend of the Reverend William Traile, the Presbyterian minister who was at Rehoboth Town from 1683-1690.[5] At John White's death in 1685 the Buckingham tract passed under his will to his children.

It was on the "Buckingham" tract at the location stated above that the Buckingham Congregation's Meeting House was erected.

Though we are able to locate definitely the site of the so-called first erected Meeting House of the Buckingham Congregation, we have been unable to discover the date of its erection or the date of the organization of the Buckingham Congregation. The question, therefore, arises as to how far back this congregation can be traced under the name of "Buckingham."

The earliest recorded reference to this congregation under the name of *"Buckingham,"* so far discovered, is in January, 1735, when Captain William Fassitt made the following bequest in his will: *"I give and bequeath to the dissenting minister of the Congregation and meeting of Buckingham five pounds*

---

[1]For discussion of probability of the "Meeting House branch" of Marshall's Creek as the site of 1697 and 1705 "Meeting House," see *ante*, the note on "Meeting House 1697 at the road going up along the Sea Side, and in 1705 at Sea Side."
[2]"Buckingham" 1500 acres surveyed for John White and resurveyed 27th July, 1679, at the seaboard side at Assateague Point on the north side of Marsh Creek; 350 acres possessed by Mr. Francis Thorowgood; 350 acres possessed by Mr. William Massey; 400 acres possessed by William White; 400 acres possessed by Stephen [Stevens] White [total 1500 acres]. (Somerset Rent Rolls, 1663-1723, page 100, in Maryland Historical Society, Baltimore.)
[3]This location appears as Poplar Town on the Luke, Griffing & Stevenson *Atlas of Wicomico, Somerset and Worcester Counties, Maryland* (1877) in the section entitled *East Berlin District No. 3, Worcester County.* On recent maps this location is marked "Ironshire."
[4]See *post* for note on John White and his family.
[5]John White, in his will dated June, 1685, probated October, 1685, bequeaths "To Reverend friend William Traile" one young mare. (Somerset Registry of Wills, Liber EB 5, page 125-6.)

· 259 ·

currant money to be paid at my death."[1] Captain William Fassitt (1662-1735) was a distinguished official of Somerset County and a wealthy merchant of his day and resided on a plantation in Sinepuxent Neck about four miles east of the location of the Buckingham Meeting House, which was near the present village of Ironshire.

The name of Fassitt (which is the correct spelling) is variously given in the records as Fassitt, Fosett, Fossett, etc. This Captain William Fassitt who made the bequest to the "minister of the Congregation and meeting of Buckingham" in 1735 is easily identified with one William Fosett who appears as a commissioner to the Presbytery of Philadelphia in 1709.[2] Webster in his *History of the Presbyterian Church in America,* page 322, states that the Reverend John Hampton was pastor of the Snow Hill Presbyterian Congregation from 1707-1718, that he also served the "Pitts Creek Congregation," and that the "united congregation" [i. e. Snow Hill and Pitts Creek] were represented in Presbytery of Philadelphia 1709-1715, and the Synod of 1718 by the following commissioners: 1709, William Fossett [Fassitt]; 1710, Benjamin Aidlett [Aydelotte]; 1711, Adam Spence; 1714, Samual Hopkins; 1715, Nathaniel Hopkins; 1718, Edmund Cropper. We believe that Webster's statement in regard to Snow Hill and Pitts Creek as *"united congregations,"* at the dates given, is incorrect;[3] while the names of the commissioners given as representing these "united congregations" in Presbytery 1709-1715 and Synod in 1718 are of men all of whom were identified with the Snow Hill and Buckingham Congregations. Aydelotte, Spence and the Hopkinses were members of the Snow Hill Congregation, and William Fassitt and Edmund Cropper are proved to have been members of the Buckingham Congregation at later dates: Fassitt in 1735, and Cropper in 1747/8. Fassitt and Cropper both lived in Sinepuxent Neck,[4] immediately east (some four or five miles) from the site of the first erected Buckingham Meeting House on the Buckingham tract of land near the old Poplar Town, now (1934) called Ironshire. The homes of William Fassitt (from 1709-1735) and of Edmund Cropper (from 1714/15-1753) were not so far distant from the probable site of the Meeting House "at the road going up along the sea side," referred to in 1697 and 1705, and the site of the first erected Meeting House of the Buckingham Congregation. William Fassitt, as we have seen, was a commissioner to Presbytery in 1709. Edmund Cropper was commissioner to Synod in 1718. Cropper also appears to have been commissioner to the Presbytery of New

---

[1] Will of William Fassitt, of Somerset County, dated January 22, 1734/5; probated May 30, 1735, in Worcester Registry of Wills, Liber MH 3 [1680-1742] page 322-7, and *Maryland Calendar of Wills,* Vol. VII, page 139-141.

[2] *Records of the Presbyterian Church in the U. S. A. Embracing Minutes of the Presbytery of Philadelphia, 1706-1716* . . . [Published 1841].

[3] For Pitts Creek Congregation, see *post.*

[4] The house of William Fassitt is yet standing in Sinepuxent Neck in Worcester (formerly Somerset) County. See Forman, *Early Manors and Plantation Houses of Maryland . . 1634-1800.* At Somerset Court, Mar. 2, 1714/15, a petition of Edmund Craper [Cropper] "who liveth in Sinepuxent Neck" about a road going out of Sinepuxent Neck (Somerset Court, Liber O 12 [Judicials] page 164). In 1731, Edmund Cropper bought of William Turvill, Jr., a plantation of 450 acres called "Wellbeck" on the seaboard side of Sinepuxent Neck and west side of Roach Creek, and also 53 acres called "Tompkin's Meadows" on Roach Creek on east side of Sinepuxent Neck (Somerset Court Deed, Liber O 18, page 18). Edmund Cropper was living at "Wellbeck" at the time of his death in 1753.

Castle in March, 1726/7, when the Reverend Hugh Stevenson was called to the pastorate of the Snow Hill Congregation.[1]

In view of the above recited facts placing the locations of the residences of William Fassitt and Edmund Cropper, the fact that these two men were commissioners to Presbytery and Synod, and that they were both during later days members of Buckingham Congregation; it seems only a reasonable deduction that the congregation to which they belonged (whatever name that congregation may then have borne) and the Snow Hill Congregation were "united congregations" and so represented in Presbytery and Synod, and ministered to by the same pastor. It is not at all improbable (and we think it to have been a fact) that Fassitt and Cropper belonged to the congregation of the Meeting House of 1697 and 1705 "at the road going up along the sea side"; that this congregation, at a date at present unknown, moved the location of its Meeting House, rebuilding at the old Poplar Town (Ironshire) site on the Buckingham tract and taking the name of "Buckingham Congregation." Therefore, the congregation of the Meeting House of 1697 and 1705 "at the road going up along the sea side" became the "Buckingham Congregation" (when the Meeting House was relocated on the Buckingham tract) and *this* congregation and Snow Hill were "united congregations," both ministered by the same pastor and represented together in Presbytery during these earliest days by men first from one congregation and then the other.

We have noted Captain William Fassitt's bequest in 1735 to the "dissenting minister of the congregation and meeting of Buckingham." We find another bequest to the Buckingham Congregation in February, 1747/8, in the will of Edmund Cropper, which recites: "I give and bequeath five pounds to be deliver^d by my Executrix to the Elders of Buckingham Congregation for repairing the said house as they see Conveniant."[2]

The date of the erection of the first Meeting House on the Buckingham tract we do not at present know; however, it was probably erected sometime prior to Captain Fassitt's bequest in 1735 and was certainly old enough to be in need of repairs when Edmund Cropper made his will in February, 1747/8.

We do not know at what date the Meeting House erected on the Buckingham tract was abandoned; however, by June, 1757, the Buckingham Congregation was contemplating the erection of a new Meeting House. On June 21, 1757, William Franklin, of Worcester County, conveyed one acre of ground out of the tract called "Burley" to Hugh Henry, Clerk, of Somerset County,[3] for 20 shillings "as well as in consideration of having the preaching of the Gospel continued heare in this place for the Benefit of the Present and Coming Generation." The conveyance was made to the said Hugh Henry and his successors "to and for the use of the Congregation of Presbyterian Dissenters in the county

---

[1]Records of the Presbytery of New Castle, March, 1726/7, give Edmund Cropper as commissioner from the Snow Hill Congregation (*Journal of the Department of History* [*The Presbyterian Historical Society*] *of the Presbyterian Church in U. S. A.*, Vol. XV, page 166.
The Reverend Hugh Stevenson married Comfort, daughter of Capt. William Fassitt.

[2]Will of Edmund Cropper, of Worcester County, dated Feb. 26, 1747/8; probated Mar. 27, 1753, recorded Worcester Registry of Wills, Liber JW 2, page 121-2.

[3]Rev. Hugh Henry was pastor of Buckingham Congregation from 1751-1758.

of Worcester which goes by the name of the Congregation At Buckingham and their heirs and successors to be a place of Attending divine service . . ." The one acre of ground thus conveyed is described as being part of the tract called "Burley," in Worcester County, on the seaboard side "upon the main road that leads from Snow Hill Town to the head of Indian River." The acre of ground thus conveyed is today found situated at the southern end of the town of Berlin, Worcester County. The "Meeting House" erected on the site just described was some years later destroyed and Buckingham Church was rebuilt in the town of Berlin where it stands today. The old acre of ground at the southern end of the town, conveyed in 1757 by Franklyn to Stevenson and his successors, is reserved as a cemetery.[1]

It has not been our intention to go into the matter of the history of Buckingham Presbyterian Church in any detail; but only to set forth the few facts obtainable from the records relative to the "origin" of this celebrated old congregation and the erection of its earliest church buildings. The Reverend I. Marshall Page, pastor of the Buckingham Presbyterian Church, Berlin, Maryland, has a history of Buckingham Congregation in course of preparation. Mr. Page's work will deal fully with the subject and will no doubt develop many features of Buckingham's history not within the province of this note.[2]

"Meeting House Near Mrs. Edgar's," 1706; and the Congregation, 1718 and 1744 on "South Side of Pocomoke Near the Ferry"

During the early years of the eighteenth century another "Meeting House" of a congregation of the Presbyterian Church appears in Somerset County. At Somerset Court, June 12, 1706, when the Reverend John Hampton and the Reverend George McNish (Presbyterian ministers) qualified before the court to preach in Somerset "The Court did allow that ye aforesaid Hampton & Macknish should preach att ye meeting house near Mrs. Edgar's, the meeting house at ye head of Monocan ye meeting house att Snow Hill & ye meeting house on Mr. Joseph Venables Land as p^r ye Dissenting preachers required" (Somerset Court, Liber AB [09], Judicials, 1705-1707, page 33). We have given accounts of the "meeting houses" at Manokin, Snow Hill and at Mr. Joseph Venables. We now turn to a consideration of the *"meeting house near Mrs. Edgar's."* This "meeting house" was situated on the north side of the Pocomoke River (probably very near the river side) about a half mile above the present Pocomoke City (which is on the south side of the river). In August,

---

[1] Worcester County Court, Deed Liber D, page 187. The "Burley" tract was granted in July, 1683, to William Tompkins for 300 acres. In May, 1684, sold "Burley" to William Fassitt. In Aug., 1715, William Fassitt sold 100 acres of "Burley" to Thomas Collings, and Collings by his will devised the said acreage to his son Thomas Collings, Jr., who in 1738 sold the same to Elias Evans, and the said Evans in turn sold the 100 acres to William Franklyn, who in 1757 conveyed the one acre out of this tract to Hugh Stevenson (Somerset Court, Deed Liber O 6, page 719; Deed Liber O 12, page 372; Deed Liber O 20, page 38; Worcester Court, Deed Liber A, page 284.)

[2] Another, though later bequest to Buckingham Congregation, was as follows: Adam Bravard, of Worcester County, in his will dated Nov. 9, 1782; probated Feb. 15, 1783, wrote, "I will and order fifteen pounds to be given toward building a house of worship for the use of Buckingham Congregation." (Worcester County Registry of Wills, Liber JW 4, page 510-11.)

1686, James Round patented a tract called "Good Success," 300 acres, on northwest side of Pocomoke River. In 1700 James Round died, having by his will devised the tract "Good Success" to his widow, Mary Round. About 1702 Mrs. Mary Round married John Edgar, who, dying about 1705, left his widow, Mrs. Mary Edgar, still in possession of the tract of land called "Good Success." June 24, 1707, Mrs. Mary Edgar, relict of James Round, of Somerset County, deceased, sold and conveyed to William Noble 150 acres, part of the tract called "Good Success," and to Robert Mitchell the remaining 150 acres of the said tract of land. The portions of this tract conveyed to Noble and Mitchell lay respectively to the east and west of a certain (unnamed) branch which divided the acreage conveyed to them. Mrs. Edgar's deed to Noble gives the first bounder of the tract called "Good Success" as a "marked pine on the northwest side of the said [Pocomoke] River by a parcel of land lately belonging to Edward Stevens deceased and now in ye possession of Richard [sic: Ruth] Stevens Relict of ye said Edward." The 150-acre part conveyed out of this tract to William Noble was specified to begin at the *first bounder* of the tract "Good Success" and thence "running up ye river to a certain branch," etc., etc. (For the facts just recited see Somerset Court, Deed Liber O 10, pages 46 and 49, the deeds of Mary Edgar to William Noble and Robert Mitchell; *Maryland Calendar of Wills, Vol. II, page 221,* for the will of James Round, dated April 5, 1700; probated May 26, 1700). There are two facts mentioned above to which we would call specific attention at this point in our deduction. *First:* the statement that the "meeting house" in question is described by record as "ye meeting house *near* Mrs. Edgar's." *Second:* that the tract of land called *"Good Success,"* which was owned by Mrs. Edgar and conveyed by her in June, 1707, to William Noble and Robert Mitchell, is stated to have had as its first bounder a certain marked pine tree "on the northwest side of the said [Pocomoke] River by a parcel of land lately belonging to Edward Stevens deceased and now [June, 1707] in ye possession of Richard [sic: Ruth] Stevens Relict of ye said Edward." The 150 acres of the land conveyed by Mrs. Edgar to William Noble is specifically stated to have its beginning at the *first* bounder of the tract and thence *to run up the river,* which made this course an easterly, or northeasterly one.

Our conclusion in the matter of the location of *"the meeting house near Mrs. Edgar's,"* in June, 1706, is that it was situated on the Edward Stevens' tract, which was to the west and southwest of the Edgar tract. This Edward Stevens' tract, called "Blake's Hope," and containing 700 acres, was purchased by Stevens from Henry Smith, June, 1679, and was described as on the west side of Pocomoke River, "beginning at a marked pine standing north and running down the said river by a marsh called the Broad marsh by a line drawn south 210 perches for breadth to a marked oak." (Somerset Court, Deed Liber O 6, page 56). May 12, 1684, "Edward Stevens, of Pocomoke, in the county of Somerset, planter," made his will (probated September 29, 1685), devising to wife, Ruth, one-third tract called "Blake's Hope" (with personality) during her life and at her death said third part to return to testator's estate, and then the said 700-acre tract called "Blake's Hope" to be equally divided between the three sons of one Florence Tucker, commonly called by the names of Edward Stevens (eldest son), William Stevens and John Stevens (Somerset Registry of Wills, Liber EB 5, page 187). We have seen that in June, 1707, when Mrs. Mary Edgar conveyed 150 acres of the "Good Success" tract to William Noble that the land was described as adjoining "land lately belonging to Edward Stevens, deceased, and now [1707] in possession of Richard [sic: Ruth] Stevens Relict of said Edward." The date of Mrs. Ruth Stevens' death is not now known, but it appears that Edward Stevens, William Stevens and John Stevens (sons of Florence Tucker, and devisees under the will of Edward Stevens, dated May 12, 1684; probated September 29, 1685) entered upon the said land called "Blake's Hope," improved it and built their homes thereon without making any division thereof. In 1705 Edward, William and John Stevens (the devisees as named) sold 100 acres out of the "Blake's Hope" tract to John Broughton. This 100 acres was evidently taken out of that portion of the tract back from the river (Somerset Court, Deed Liber O 8, page 138). This left 600 acres of the said tract and hereon—though still undivided—Edward, William and John Stevens continued to make their homes. William Stevens and John Stevens both dying, their undivided interests (200 acres each) in the "Blake's Hope" tract were finally sold by their heirs.[1] Edward Stevens (the eldest of these three devisees under the will of Edward Stevens, who died in 1685) also made his home on this "Blake's Hope" tract, and we find that in December, 1695, he was named by the court to be ferryman of Pocomoke River and in 1697 was keeper of what was then called "Pocomoke Ferry" (Somerset Court, Judicials, 1695-6, p. 102, and Judicials, Liber DD 17, p. 266). The course of this ferry was from Edward Stevens' farm on the "Blake's Hope" tract on the north (called west) side of Pocomoke River to a landing on the south side of the river, which was near the east end of the site of the present Pocomoke City. This ferry was also designated as "Stevens Ferry." This Edward Stevens died in 1716, and by his will (dated August 11, 1715; probated December 18, 1716) we discover that his dwelling plantation was on "Blackshop" ["Blake's Hope"]. He devised to his daughter, Mary Wharton, the part of the dwelling plantation on which she lived, and to his daughters, Cattron Dormond [Dorman], Sarah Wheller [Wheeler] and Elizabeth Stevens land he had purchased from Robert Cole; and bequeathed to [daughter] Tabbiter Stevens his dwelling plantation called "Blackshop" ["Blake's Hope"] after the decease of her mother, with the proviso that should his unborn child prove to be a son he was to inherit this dwelling

---

[1]William Stevens died in 1709, devising his plantation to his sons, William and Samuel Stevens, with ⅓ to their mother, Eleanor Stevens, during her life; and with provision for the testator's mother, Florence Maliur [Melvin] during life (Somerset Registry of Wills, Liber EB 5, page 152). On January 12, 1727, William and Samuel Stevens, sons of William Stevens, deceased) and Eleanor Stevens (widow and relict of said William Stevens, deceased) sold to Thomas Hayward the ⅓ undivided part of "Blake's Hope" tract which William Stevens, deceased, had inherited under the will of Edward Stevens, deceased (Somerset Court, Deed Liber O 16, page 133). John Stevens died intestate, and in November, 1730, John Stevens (son and heir of John Stevens, deceased) sold to Edward Cluff the ⅓ undivided part of "Blake's Hope" tract which John Stevens, deceased, had inherited under the will of Edward Stevens, deceased. (Somerset Court, Deed Liber O 17, page 295.)

plantation, and should this unborn child be a daughter she was to share equally in the plantation with the said Tabbiter, etc. By this will Edward Stevens bequeathed, *"To the public ½ acre for use of meeting house, where it now stands,"* and appointed his wife executrix and residuary legatee (*Maryland Calendar of Wills, Volume III, page 86*).

In this bequest by Edward Stevens in his will dated August 11, 1715, of *"half acre for use of a meeting house where it now stands,"* we believe that we have the location of the *"meeting house near Mrs. Edgar's"* referred to in 1706. This half acre where the meeting house stood, as devised by Edward Stevens, was certainly on the "Blake's Hope" tract, which today may be located on the north side of the Pocomoke River, about opposite to Pocomoke City. This location of the "Blake's Hope" tract, and that portion thereof which was inherited by Edward Stevens (the testator of the will dated August, 1715) is proved by a deed January 26, 1737/8, when William *Stephens* (son and heir of Edward Stephens, late of Somerset County, deceased) conveyed to Thomas Hayward 1 acre and 9 square perches out of "Blake's Hope" tract on *north* side Pocomoke River, the said acre and nine square perches to begin "at a marked red oak standing near and on the Left of the road as goes to the ferry Landing over Pocomoke Comonly Called or known by the name of Stephens Ferry the said oak standing just by the said Landing and River aforesaid," etc., etc. (Somerset Court, Deed Liber O 19, page 228). From this deed we also infer that William Stephens [Stevens], the grantor, was the unborn child referred to in the will of his father, Edward Stevens, dated August, 1715, who, if a son, was to inherit the "Blake's Hope" dwelling plantation of the testator. This William Stevens' portion of "Blake's Hope" tract is set forth in a survey and defining of boundaries thereof made by William Lane in February, 1734, and recorded July, 1735 (Somerset Court, Deed Liber O 18, page 237; see also bond of William Stevens to Thomas Hayward, dated August, 1743, in Somerset Court, Deed Liber O 21, page 118).[1]

Bowen, in *Days of Makemie*, page 537-9, notes and comments upon the *"meeting house near Mrs. Edgars"* in 1706, the question of whose location we have so fully discussed. Bowen, however, in his note gives the reference as *"Mr. Edgars,"* while the original record (Somerset Court, Liber AB [O9], page 110) which we have examined is clearly *"Mrs. Edgars."* Bowen locates the Round-Edgar tract, "Good Successes," on the north side of Pocomoke River about a mile above Pocomoke City (south side of the river), though he does not trace the location of the "meeting house" to the Stevens' tract, "Blake's Hope," nor did he know of the bequest in Edward Stevens' will (dated August 11, 1715; probated December 18, 1716): *"to the public one half acre for use of meeting house where it now stands."* It is at present impossible to say at what date the *"meeting house near Mrs. Edgars"* was erected; we only know that it was in use in June, 1706; while we are confident that it was identical with the

---

[1]William Stevens continued to live on this land until his death in 1759, and by his will dated Oct. 30, 1758, probated March 21, 1759, devised to "son John Stevens the plantation I now live on with the Ferry and all the appurtenances thereunto belonging after the marriage of my wife hereinafter mentioned," etc. (Somerset Registry of Wills, Liber EB 4, page 68.)

"meeting house" referred to in Edward Stevens' will in 1715. We cannot say when this "meeting house" was abandoned or demolished.

Doctor Bowen in his account (referred to above) also recites the interesting tradition which locates a very early Presbyterian "meeting house" (the tradition even carries it back to the early days of Makemie's ministry) on the site of the present Pocomoke City, which, says he, *"was the old Stevens ferry, at one time called 'Meeting House Landing'."* We will not enter into a discussion of the various elements in this tradition as Bowen recites them. However, the records certainly prove that in November, 1718, there was evidently a congregation of Presbyterian faith located on *"South side of Pocomoke near the ferry."* At Somerset Court, November 18, 1718, "Mr. John Clement Minister was Sworne and Qualified to be Minister of Rehoboth in the Parish of Coventry, *South side of Pocomoke near the ferry.* (Somerset Court, Deed Liber O 13, page 177, Judicials recorded in back of this volume). The obvious meaning of this record entry is that John Clement was holding services on the *"south side of Pocomoke [River] near the ferry"* for the members of his congregation resident in that vicinity. "The ferry" referred to was unquestionably the Pocomoke Ferry, or Stevens' Ferry, of which the southern terminus was certainly located about the east end of the site of the present Pocomoke City, about a mile above the bridge which now spans the river at this point. John Clement appears to have come to America as a probationer from Great Britain and his credentials were approved by the Synod of Philadelphia in September, 1718. He received a call from the then designated Pocomoke Presbyterian Congregation and was ordained at Rehoboth in June, 1719. In 1720 complaint was made against him by some of the elders of his congregation and not being able to satisfactorily meet it he was suspended from the ministry in September, 1721. (Webster, *History of the Presbyterian Church in America, page 371;* see also *Records of the Presbyterian Church in the United States of America, embracing Minutes of Presbytery of Philadelphia, 1706-1716; Minutes of Synod of Philadelphia, 1717-1758 . . . Philadelphia: Presbyterian Board of Publication . . . 1841*). We can but wonder if the *"meeting house near Mrs. Edgars"* in 1706; and mentioned in the will of Edward Stevens in 1715 (as above discussed), on the *north* side of Pocomoke River, was about this time abandoned, or destroyed, and a place of meeting for worship established on the *south* side of Pocomoke River near the ferry? We have discovered no evidence by which to prove this; but certainly a Presbyterian congregation had formed, or was forming, on "south side of Pocomoke near the ferry" in November, 1718, to which John Clement at that date qualified to minister.

From the reference in November, 1718, to John Clements ministering to a Presbyterian congregation on "south side Pocomoke River near the ferry" we find no item throwing further light upon the matter until May, 1744, when the Reverend James Scougal of "the Presbytery of Paisley in North Britain [Scotland]" accepted "a call drawn up by the people of Snow Hill, Buckingham and *the Ferry in Worcester in Maryland."*[1] The fact that *"the Ferry"* is re-

---

[1] Minutes of the Synod of Philadelphia.

ferred to as in Worcester County certainly locates it as on the south side of Pocomoke River as the Pocomoke River became the dividing line (at this point) between Somerset and Worcester Counties when Worcester was set apart in 1742 from Somerset.

In this item of May, 1744, of the Reverend Mr. Scougal's call to Snow Hill, Buckingham and *the Ferry* in Worcester County we believe that we have reference to the Pocomoke Ferry (or Stevens' Ferry), the southern terminus of which was at the east end of the present site of Pocomoke City, and that the congregation at (or near) *the Ferry* was the continuation of the congregation on *"south side of Pocomoke near the ferry"* to which we find reference in November, 1718, in the record of the ministrations of the Reverend John Clement.

Many years later, in 1774, Littleton Dennis bequeathed to his son, Henry Dennis, "one-half of the Cypress Swamp I purchased of Levi Brittingham, to begin for his part next to *the old Meeting House Landing*."[1] Brittingham's deed to Littleton Dennis for this land, July 22, 1755, so describes the acreage conveyed that it is easily identified as lying just to the east of the present site of Pocomoke City, whose forerunner, (on the same site), called Newtown, was built up at the *"old Meeting House Landing."*[2]

We give the above items for the benefit of any one who may be interested in working out to its conclusion the exact location of the Meeting House of the Presbyterian congregation on the "south side of Pocomoke River near the Ferry." J. Paul Ewell, Esq., of Pocomoke City, Maryland, has gathered some interesting items relative to an old Meeting House which was on the site of Pocomoke City and which he believes was on the lot of ground now (1935) occupied by the Parker House. It is to be hoped that some day Mr. Ewell will work out this matter to a definite conclusion.

Pitts Creek Congregation and Meeting House

The date of the "beginning" of the Pitts Creek Congregation and of the erection of its first Meeting House has not yet come to light. There is a "tradition" which has been handed down relative to these matters, but our interest here is concerned only in giving items of record.

The first item of record which seems to refer to this Pitts Creek Congregation and its Meeting House is as follows:

At Somerset Court, November 6, 1735, "The reverend Henry Hunter a presbiterian dissenting Minister came into Court & took the Severall oaths to the Government with the test and Subscribed the Oath of abjuration & test with the articles of the Church of England, accept [except] what part is Expected by act of Parliament &c. Somerset Sc. Wee the Subscribers Members of the dissenting Congregation of Pocomoke in the County aforesaid do hereby humbly

---
[1]Will of Littleton Dennis, of Worcester County, dated Feb. 10, 1774, recorded in Worcester Registry of Wills, Liber JW 4 (1769-1783) pages 231-237. Our attention was first called to this item by William B. Marye, of Baltimore.
[2]Worcester Court, Deed Liber C, page 389.

Certifie to the Generall or quarter Sessions for the said County of Somerset according to the form of the Statute in such case lately made and provided that the Meeting house at Rehoboth Town *and the Meeting house on the Eastermost side of Pocomoke river* both in the aforesaid County are places set apart by the said Congregation as places for their religious worship of which said Congregation the Revd Henry Hunter is at present Minister or teacher as witness our hands this twenty six day of Novr Ann Dom 1735. Pat. Allison, Francis Porter, Robert Geddes, Robt Jenckins Henry" (Somerset Court, Judicials, 1734-1736, page 93).[1] Certainly the *"Meeting house on the eastermost side of Pocomoke River"* referred to in the above record is the "Meeting House" of the Pitts Creek Presbyterian Congregation. This "Meeting House" was on the north side of the headwaters of Pitts Creek, a branch called Beaver Dam, in the present county of Worcester, which was up to 1742 a part of Somerset County. This location is certainly on the *"eastermost side of Pocomoke River,"* the river making a decided turn and running for several miles in an almost due southerly course, and is about three and one-half miles to the east of the river. The Pitts Creek Presbyterian Congregation and its first "Meeting House" have been the subject of much speculation as to "origin" and "erection." Record evidence is lacking, but a persistent "tradition" assigns them to the Reverend Francis Makemie's time, 1683-1708, "Pitts Creek" being designated as one of the "Makemie Churches." We wish to be very guarded in any statement of theory as to the "origins" of this congregation and the time of erection of its first "Meeting House," for we have discovered no positive evidence relative thereto; but we tentatively offer the following as a suggestion towards the solution of this interesting problem. The first Rehoboth Presbyterian Congregation (certainly "organized" by Francis Makemie on his arrival in 1683) drew its membership from residents on both sides of Pocomoke River. The congregation seems to have been designated both as the Rehoboth and Pocomoke Congregation. As years passed this congregation grew and the members to the south of Pocomoke River and towards the Maryland-Virginia boundary line, evidently on the increase, required a place of worship nearer at hand—more accessible to them than the one at Rehoboth Town. No doubt Mr. Makemie during the latter years of his ministry held services *south* of Pocomoke River. Makemie's successors at Rehoboth no doubt did likewise, and then in November, 1735, we find the Reverend Henry Hunter with specified "Meeting Houses" at Rehoboth Town and one *"on the eastermost side of Pocomoke River."* From this date the Pitts Creek Congregation doubtless made steady progress. We do not know when the first "Meeting House" for this congregation was erected, nor its exact location; but we are confident that the *"Meeting house on the eastermost side of Pocomoke river"* in November, 1735, had been erected sometime before that date and that it was probably on the site yet occupied by the well-known old Pitts Creek Presbyterian Church, about four miles south of Pocomoke City, in Worcester County, at the head of Pitts Creek.

---

[1]The discrepancy in the dates of entry in the court record of these items, Nov. 6, and the date of the certificate of the "meeting houses," Nov. 26, 1735, we are at a loss to explain.

We do not know exactly the date at which this congregation was first designated the "Pitts Creek Congregation." In the records of the Session of the Snow Hill Presbyterian Church, May 4, 1753, we find that the Reverend Mr. Donelson was acting as pastor of both Snow Hill and Pitts Creek;[1] while at a meeting of the Session held in Snow Hill Town, June 7, 1753, Smith Mills and Joseph Stevenson [Stephenson], two members of Pitts Creek Congregation, were present. In April, 1755, the Session of Snow Hill agreed to send Thomas Martin to Synod to apply to the Presbytery of New Castle for supplies [pastoral supply?] and that Captain Spence write to said Presbytery in behalf of the Sessions of Snow Hill *and Pitts Creek;* that the Sessions collect money from the congregations to bear said Thomas Martin's expenses; adjourned to May 9, 1755, the Session of Snow Hill *and Pitts Creek* met according to adjournment: Present of Snow Hill Session, Capt. Adam Spence, James Irving, William Nelson, Matthew Hopkins, Thomas Milbourn, Thomas Martin; *of Pitts Creek Session,* Robert Stephenson, Joseph Stephenson, Smith Mills, Moses Mills, Elijah Brittingham.[2]

No early Session records of the Pitts Creek Congregation have so far been discovered and we have had to depend upon court records and the records of the Session of Snow Hill Presbyterian Church for the few items given relative to Pitts Creek Congregation and Meeting House. This further item is of interest. John Mills, Senior, of Worcester County, in his will, dated November 24, 1799, probated December 24, 1799, made this bequest: "First I give and bequeath unto the Session of Pitts Creek Congregation and their Successors one acre of land where the meeting House now stands which is called Pitts Creek meeting the said acre of land to be laid out as the said Session shall think proper, to the said Session and their Successors so long as the same shall be occupied for a place of Presbyterian b[p]ublic worship."[3] The acre of ground on which the Pitts Creek Meeting House stood, devised by John Mills in 1799 to the Session of Pitts Creek Congregation, is today the property of this congregation and upon it stands the old "Meeting House." This ancient church is situated on the west side of the state highway about 4 miles south of Pocomoke City. While the old Pitts Creek "Meeting House" has been restored and the grounds surrounding it beautified, the congregation, some years ago, erected a church building in Pocomoke City, where they now regularly worship.

It is hoped that the fragmentary notes given here will lead someone to make a thorough investigation of the history of the Pitts Creek Congregation and to write the story of this celebrated old church.

---

[1]Nevin, *Enclyclopaedia of the Presbyterian Church in the U. S. A.,* page 1215, (column 1), says: 1753 "Rev. Mr. Donelson was supplying the [Snow Hill] Church at this time; and Pitts Creek for the first time appears on the record asking Presbytery to send him back."

[2]These items referring to Pitts Creek Congregation are from the manuscript record of the Session of the Snow Hill Presbyterian Church, 1751-1762, which volume is in the Presbyterian Historical Society, Philadelphia, Pennsylvania. This manuscript volume bears the inscription "The Presbyterian Dissenting Congregation near Snow Hill Town in the County of Worcester their Session's Book of their Proceedings as a Session Commencing from the [——] day of ——— Anno Dom ———17———."

[3]Worcester Registry of Wills, Liber JBR 1, 1799-1803, page 34-5.

Some Other Early Presbyterian Ministers and Places of Worship

At Somerset Court, March 9, 1718 [1718/19], "Mr William Stewart Qualified himself as a dissenting Minister to preach in the Meeting houses at the head of Manokin & on the north side of Wiccocomico, by taking the usual oaths" (Somerset Court, Judicials, Liber CH [1718], page 57).

Somerset Court, March 18, 1728 [1728/9], "Hugh Stevenson, of Somerset County Gentleman a presbitarian Minister present here in Court Prays that he may be admitted to take the Severall oaths appointed by act of assembly to the Government &c. Whereupon the said Hugh Stevenson took the severall oaths appointed by act of Assembly to the Government and Subscribed the oath of abjuration and test &c." (Somerset Court, Judicials, 1727-30, page 153).[1]

Somerset Court, November, 1738, "Patrick Glasgow a presbyterian Minister Came here into Court in his proper person and moves to be qualified according to act of Parliament in such Case provided Whereupon the said Patrick Glasgow took the Severall Oaths appointed by act of parliament and Subscribed the oath of abjuration & test and declaration and Subscribed the Severall articles of the Church of England except such and such part of them as excepted by Act of Parliament and recorded his places of Meeting (or worship) as followeth viz: I the Subscriber being a protestant dissenting Minister and preacher doe hereby Certifie to the Worshipfull the Justices of the Peace for Somerset County in their Generall Quarter Sessions now sitting the Meeting house at the head of Manokin,[2] meeting house near the ferry of Capt John Handy[3] the meeting house near the Dwelling house of William Oliphant[4] and the dwelling house of Richard Wallis[5] all lying and being in the County afd. as severall places of my meeting to teach and preach to my Congregation According to the form of the statute in that case lately made and provided. Given under my hand this XXII day of November Anno Dom: MDCCXXXVIII. Pat. Glasgow" (Somerset Court, Judicials, 1738-40, page 33).

Somerset Court, August 11, 1747, "Whereas the Reverend Mr Charles Tennent a presbiterian Minister personally appeared here in his Lordship's the Right Honorable the Lord Proprietary of Maryland his Court of Somerset and did then and there before his said Lordship Justices in Court Individually Setting take the Oaths appointed by an act of Parliament made in the first year of King William and Queen Mary And repeated the declaration directed by the Act of Parliament made in the Thirtyeth [thirtieth] Year of King Charles the

---

[1] On March 28, 1744, bond was given in Worcester Court for administration on estate of Hugh Stevenson, late of Worcester County, deceased; Comfort Stevenson, administratrix; Rouse Fassitt and Lambert Fassitt, sureties; bond £250 sterling. (Worcester County Registry of Wills, Liber JW 1, [bonds 1742-53], page 62-3.)

[2] This is now (1934) the Manokin Presbyterian Church at Princess Anne.

[3] This was the Wicomico Congregation's "Meeting House" on Wicomico River. See *ante*, note on "Wicomico Presbyterian Congregation and Meeting Houses."

[4] William Oliphant (or Olliphant) lived on a tract of land (part of "Cox's Fork" tract) situated on head of Rockawalkin River (now Wicomico River) on west side of Wilton Branch. See deed 1726 Disharoon and Stevens, and their wives, to William Oliphant, of Somerset County, and deed 1702 Thomas Cox and wife to John Stevens. (Somerset Court, Deed Liber O 7, page 716, and Deed Liber O 16, page 9.)

[5] Richard Wallis lived in the Dame's Quarter neighborhood in Somerset County.

Second and Subscribed the same and declared his approbation to the articles of faith in the Church of England and subscribed the same Except those articles and part of an article that is disallowed of by such dissenting Ministers &c. I desire that you will register the Severall places within mentioned for public Service and preaching of the Gosple of Jesus Christ the places are as followeth at the meeting house at Rokawalkin on the head of Wickacomoco River,[1] and at the meeting house at Olliphants[2] and also at broad Creek Bridge[3] and also at the dwelling house of Joshua Caldwell and also at Wilson Riders[5] and also at the house of James Polk in Princes Anne Town on his Lot No. 2.[6] Sep^t 23, 1747. P^r me Charles Tennent" (Somerset Court, Judicials, 1747-9, page 22).

Somerset Court, June 21, 1748, "Reverend Mr John Rogers a presbaterian Minister personally appeared"; prayed he might qualify himself agreeable to the Toleration Act of Parliament. He qualified by taking the regular oaths and repeating and subscribing the appointed declaration; and subscribed the articles of the Church of England "except such as disallowed of by such protestant discenting Ministers." "S^r I desire you will record these places of meetings of worship Viz Ben Venables and Wm. Venables att his Saw Mill.[7] John Rodgers." (Somerset Court, Judicials, 1747-9, page 80).

An early eighteenth century item which probably relatest to the Presbyterian Congregation in the vicinity of the town of Snow Hill is found in the will of one Martin Curtis, of Somerset County, dated September 17, 1712; probated January 28, 1712/13. Curtis bequeathed to Sturgis and John Dixon, sons of William Dixon, decd., a tract of land called "Friendship" on, or near, the Indian River, (alias Baltimore River), containing 500 acres, provided that said Curtis and his heirs have peaceable possession of 2 tracts of land on, or near, the Pocomoke River, one tract called "Lymsome," containing 200 acres, and the other tract being part of "Lynneth" [or "Lymneth"], containing 50 acres and adjoining to "Lymsome." These two tracts the said Curtis devised to William Greare and Grizzle, his wife, or the longest liver of them, being the land where they lived; and after the deaths of the Greare's the said lands "unto such minister of the Gospel as shall be chosen by the elders of our society usually meeting at the home of James Stevenson near Snow Hill Town and to his successors to be chosen as aforesaid" (Worcester County Registry of Wills, Liber MH 3, page 103-4).

[1] This was the Wicomico Congregation's "Meeting House" erected about 1740-42.
[2] This was William Olliphant referred to before.
[3] Broad Creek Bridge was at, or near, the present site of Laurel, Sussex County, Delaware. In 1747 this section was claimed as part of Maryland.
[4] We have not attempted to locate Joshua Caldwell's house.
[5] Wilson Rider lived on the south side of Quantico Creek in what is now Wicomico County, but in 1747 Somerset County. In later years the first Methodist Congregation in Somerset County was formed at Wilson Rider's near Quantico. For the Rider lands and their location see Somerset Court Deed Book O 10, page 960, a deed Feb. 28, 1700, William Merrill to Richard Rider; Somerset Registry of Wills, Liber EB 9, page 168, will of Richard Rider, who died in 1734; and Liber EB 1, page 191, will of Wilson Rider who died in 1784. For notes on Rider family, see Richardson's *Sidelights on Maryland History*, and Truitt's *Salisbury*.
[6] Col. Levin Handy's manuscript account of Manokin Presbyterian Church recounts the above, adding, "Mr. Polk's house on Lot No. 2 was the corner (S. E. corner) of Main and Water Streets in Princess Anne, and why Mr. Tennent should preach there instead of the Meeting House, which was then built and quite near, seems strange; but there is nothing to explain it."
[7] William Venables' land was on south side of the head of Wicomico River and is today (1935) within the limits of the city of Salisbury. Venable's mill stood near where the bridge today crosses the head of the river in Salisbury on Division Street.

VI

ORIGINS

HUMAN—PROFESSIONAL—MERCANTILE—INDUSTRIAL

The Northampton-Accomack background of Somerset's first settlers—Social and economic status in Virginia—Names of the first settlers of Somerset—European origins of these settlers—Status of families in Somerset—The first doctors, teachers, attorneys, traders, merchants and tradesmen.

THE remarkably interesting foundations of "Old Somerset," which have been disclosed by our exploration and exacavation of the ground of the past, quite naturally raise the question of the origins of the people by whom they were laid. As we examine these foundations we find as it were graven in the imperishable stuff of which they were made the names of certain human beings whose method in laying them has left ineradicable impress of certain characters on the substance out which they were fashioned. Who were these founders and first settlers of "Old Somerset"; whence did they come and out of what conditions of living?

Certain it is that the early settlers—founders in truest sense of this historically fascinating colonial community—were people alive with a spirit for arduous undertaking and with a power to sustain such an adventure. Stout hearts, as well as strong hands; able minds governed by a will to accomplish, as well as strong bodies, were required for making and laying such imperishable foundations as we find in the soil of Somerset's history.

The county of "Northampton otherwise called Accomack in Virginia" gave to Maryland the first settlers for the section of "the Eastern Shore below Choptank River," from whose southernmost area (south of Nanticoke River) the county of Somerset was erected in August, 1666. The section of Virginia from which these founders of Somerset came was immediately south of the Maryland-Virginia boundary line on the "Eastern Shore." "Northampton otherwise called Accomack," an ancient settlement dating back to very beginnings of Virginia, was a section noted for the hardihood of its inhabitants; not only physical, but mental and moral as well. Separation from the mainland and center of the Virginia colony's life by the wide reach of Chesapeake Bay developed in the inhabitants of this eastern outpost section a markedly independent spirit of living. They were fearless in meeting current issues, in thought, and had a courageous method of dealing with current events. The very geographical position of this section, with open seacoast to the east and comfortable harbors furnished by the quiet western water-boundary of Chesapeake Bay, with its wide creek inlets to the land, seemed to invite contacts with the traveling and trading public of the day. First and last, "Northampton-Accomack" drew to its shores men who were constantly in touch with the life of the world outside. In such an environment it was not unnatural that the people should develop an attitude both liberal and receptive towards experiments in religious faith and practical politics with which the mid-seventeenth century world was teeming. In "Northampton otherwise called Accomack in Virginia" we find among "the people" a cordial attitude towards "non-conformity," questioning as it were the declared sacrosanct nature of an established Church and "the divine right of kings." When rebellion rose against these theories and their accompanying practices in the mother country, in the mid-seventeenth century, "Northampton otherwise called Accomack in Virginia" was not long in feeling its effects. Here, indeed, were to be found stout loyalists; but among the people of all social classes there were degress of liberality in the matter of thinking about these things and the life of the section was honeycombed with "non-conformity."[1]

In such an environment, which we are able barely to suggest, but which is an inescapable atmosphere to him who delves among the recorded transactions of this section's past at that time, the first settlers of the area which later became Somerset County in Maryland were nurtured. The founders and first settlers of "Old Somerset" were truly *of the people* of this "Northampton otherwise called Accomack in Virginia" settlement; and as the restored "Stuart government" in Virginia attempted by law to eradicate the most radical non-conformist element of that day—the Quakers—from the population, certain rebellious spirits led an exodus from this section to that area across the Maryland-Virginia boundary line and became the founders of Somerset County in Maryland. Lord Baltimore desired the lands in this section of his province settled and the tradition and law of his province was congenial to such non-conformist spirits. There was mutuality of appeal.

While it is true that certain rebellious non-conformists from "Northampton otherwise called Accomack in Virginia" were the leaders in establishing the settlement which developed into Somerset County, in Maryland, we also know that there were many people among the first settlers whose attitude towards religious conformity differed from that of the leaders; and though the body of first settlers was made up of the more liberal, or at least tolerant, element from the Virginia area, yet all of them were not impelled to leave Virginia by motives of conscience in matters of religion. Some of these people could have remained there. Nor will we say that Lord Baltimore bid the incoming Virginians welcome from the ground of an unmixed motive:—the motive to give refuge to people hampered by law in the exercise of conscience in matters of religion. The lower Eastern Shore of Maryland had been opened up by the Lord Proprietor for settlement as part of his policy to insure and protect this area of his province adjoining the boundary line between Maryland and Virginia, and the fertile lands in this area appealed to settlers not alone because they were within a government where "religious toleration" was both tradition and law, but also because of the greater economic and industrial advantage of obtaining such lands in an unsettled area at most reasonable "quit rents."

So it is that we find men of varied motives joined together as a body of founders and first settlers in establishing "Old Somerset." Tolerant towards each other; these people worked together; submerging their differences in the will to accomplish one end—the developing of a community in which they would have freedom of conscience in matters of religion while gaining substantial economic independence. In the laying of the foundations of Somerset we find Quakers with other non-conformists whose sectarian predilections we cannot discover; and "Churchmen" (certainly of a liberal type) working side by side, all seemingly mindful of but one thing:—the success of the adventure in which they were engaged.

Once for all, let it be said that the first settlers and founders of Somerset were, with rare exceptions, recruited from what may be called, by way of distinction, the "middle class." They were not (again with the few exceptions which may be noted) men of the office-holding, governing element, in the population of Virginia. These men were not possessed of large means, though some of them were in comfortable circumstances. They were small farmers, or planters, traders and tradesmen; some were merchants, some probably had training in professions. They were evidently people of vigorous mentality and progressive spirit. By far a large majority of them appear to have been people of sound stock and character. Though the English backgrounds of but few of them are known, yet in those few instances we find them issuing from good stock:—even the so-called minor gentry and merchant class. We cannot doubt that this would prove true of the majority of the first settlers of Somerset if we could but find their English origins. Whatever may have been their "social status" in "Northampton otherwise called Accomack in Virginia" (or other parts of Virginia from which a bare minority among them came), they were people who laid hold on advantages which came to them and proved their ability by advancing.

Of course, we find among these first settlers both men and women who belonged to the "indentured servant" class, some of whom were indeed of mere "field-hand" status, while some of them having fallen into this class through the exigencies of life, worked out their freedom, exchanging their status of "the possessed" for that of "possessors."

Then, too, we have no reason to doubt that from the first the even meagre population of this new community carried such a population's normal burden of industrial and moral delinquents:— "neer do wells," who were a tax on the industrial life of the settlement; and men and women whose moral characters were a menace to the life of the community. There were "high ones who were low," as well as "low ones who were high," in character.

Whatever the so-called "social status" in the place from which they came, there is one marked feature about these first settlers, these very founders of Somerset:—the character and spirit to "advance." It is not long after their arrival on the Eastern Shore of Maryland that we find these substantial middle-class people advancing to the gentry class; becoming officials in the settlement and substantially increasing their estates by intelligent use of the new advantages which they possessed.

By May, 1662, the settlement on the lower Eastern Shore of Maryland was apparently well established, at which date an official report states that the two sections thereof—Manokin and Annemessex—numbered fifty tithable persons.[2] We have not been able to discover the names of the fifty tithable persons thus referred to, though later records afford evidence as to who some of them were. Certainly Stephen Horsey, Ambrose Dixon, Thomas Price, Henry Boston, Robert Hart, Alexander Draper, with their families, were settled along the south side of Annemessex River by May, 1662, and Randall Revell, John Elzey and William Thorne, with their households, were settled along the Manokin River by the same date. The fifty tithable persons referred to in the report of May, 1662—whoever they may have been—certainly made up the group of the very first settlers in this area which in time was erected into the county of Somerset. Then from this date, May, 1662, on to the erection of Somerset County in August, 1666, we find the population steadily increasing year by year. No records remain of the transactions of the local courts of this area for the period between May, 1662 (when the court was first established) and December, 1665 (the first date in the oldest remaining local record book), but from remaining records of land warrants and patents (which give the names of patentees of land and "headrights") and local court records of a later period, we have gleaned the names of many of the first settlers of "Old Somerset." The following list contains the names—so far discovered—of these "first settlers" (from 1661/2 to the erection of Somerset County, August, 1666), classified according to the sections of the area in which they apparently settled.[3]

Annemessex: Stephen Horsey and his family (including his step-children, Michael, Thomas and Sarah Williams); John Roach; Benjamin Summer; Ambrose Dixon and his family; Philip Adams; Henry Boston and his family; John Richards; Thomas Price and his family; John Marcam (Marcum) and his son, John Marcam, Junior; Edward Dickeson; Robert Hart; Alexander Draper; Henry Peddington; George Johnson and his family; William Coulbourne and his family; John Rhodes and his family; Thomas Cottingham; Charles Hall; George Hasfurt; Ambrose London and his family; Daniel Curtis and his family; John Crew and his family; Cornelius Ward; Thomas Tull; Richard Tull; Robert Catlin and his family; Edmund Beauchamp; Henry Miles; William Planner.

Manokin: Randall Revell and his family; John Elzey and his family; William Thorne and his wife; John Odbur; Nicholas Fountaine (Fontaine); Thomas

Poole; John Cooper; George and Margaret Mitchell; Edward Surnam; Edward Southern and his wife; John Hobbs; John, Frances and Mary Vincent; John and Susan Johnson; William Furnish (Furnis, Furnes) and his wife; Edward Hazard; Thomas Carnee (Carney); Peter Calloway; William Bosman and his family; Alexander and Lazarus Maddox; James Barnabe and his family; John Westlock and his family; Thomas Walley and his family; Edward Lun; William Boyss (Boyce, Boice) and his family; William, Richard and James Davis; Philip Barre and his family (including Margaret and Mary Ivery); George Lane; Richard Ackworth; Roger Woolford and his family (including several of the Denwood children, who were sisters and brother of Mrs. Woolford); John Nelson; George Betts; John Lawes; John Winder and his family; John Goldsmith and his family; Christopher Nutter; Owen Magra (Magraw, Macraw); Thomas Gillis; Charles Ballard; Thomas Bloyce; Thomas Duparke and his wife; Richard Darling and his wife; Samuel Jones and his wife; Gideon Tillman; Anthony Johnson (the free Negro) and his family.

Monie: Nehemiah Covington and his family; Thomas Covington; Henry Hayman and his family; John Painter (or Panter); John Waller; Cornelius Johnson; William Jones; Robert Ingram.

Pocomoke: Jenkin Price and his family; Edward Wale (Whaley); William Stevens; John White; Donnock Dennis; John Hilliard; Mark Manlove; John Ellis.

Morumsco: John King; Daniel Quillane; Robert Hignett; Jeffrey Minshall; Henry Hudson; John Townsend; Samuel Long.

Wicomico: James Jones; Nicholas Rice; David Spence; James Dashiell; Daniel Haste; Richard Stevens; Thomas Shiall; John Okee; Richard Whittee (Whitty); Peter Elzey; George Booth; James Nicollson.*

With few exceptions the persons named in the above list came from Northampton-Accomack County, in Virginia, viz: Horsey, Dixon, Thomas Price, Boston, Hart, Draper, George Johnson, Coulbourne, Curtis, Hasfurt, London, Williams, Minshall, Tull, Catlin, Revell, Elzey, Thorne, Anthony Johnson, Furnish (in later records Furnis and Furnes), Bosman, Westlocke, Barnabe, Boyes (Boyce), Nutter, Gillis, Covington, Waller, Jenkin Price, Walley, Wale (later Whaley), Dennis, Manlove, Quillaine, Townsend, James Jones, and Rice. From

---

*No doubt there were others who settled in this area between November, 1661 (when the commission authorizing its settlement was issued), and August, 1666 (when Somerset County was erected), whose names have escaped us. Certainly a reading of the names of headrights to patents granted prior to August, 1666 (see *post* Appendix IV), would seem to indicate that others than those named above had come to reside here. But the appearance of a name as a headright to a patent is not positive evidence that such parties actually "settled" in the area; it may be that they came for a short time but were merely "transients." The parties whose names are given in the above list as "first settlers" can be positively proved by extant records to have been *actual* settlers in this area prior to August, 1666. Some of them, it is true, died without having issue, and two or three of them, after a few years, moved out of the county; but the large majority of them became founders of families which have supplied succeeding generations to the population of Somerset County.

Nansamond County, in Virginia, came John Winder and William Davis; from Gloucester, in Virginia, came Henry Hayman, and from Northumberland came James Dashiell and probably David Spence and George Betts; while Richard Stevens (of Wicomico) and Edmund Beauchamp apparently came direct from England. It is not improbable that William Stevens (of Rehoboth) and John White (Pocomoke) also came into this area from Northampton-Accomack, having gone there first on arriving from England, tarrying but a short time, and then moving on into the area which became Somerset County, Maryland. Of the remaining persons whose names are given in the above list we cannot say with certainty whether or not they came from Northampton-Accomack in Virginia.

As to the "status" in Northampton-Accomack in Virginia of the men who came from that quarter, the records reveal some very interesting facts. Stephen Horsey and Randall Revell were "coopers" by trade, Ambrose Dixon, a "caulker," and Thomas Price, "a leather-dresser." Horsey, Revell and Dixon were also planters. Randall Revell, it appears, also participated in the political life of Northampton County; was at one time a member of the Virginia House of Burgesses from Northampton and later a magistrate of the Accomack Court. Jenkin Price was engaged in trading with the Indians; Nehemiah Covington and George Hasfurt were certainly at one time under "indentures" (though the nature of their service is not revealed). Nicholas Rice was a "carpenter" and planter. George Johnson was evidently engaging in trade, probably as a "factor" for English and New England merchants with whom he was connected; John Elzey was a planter with "merchandizing" connections; Roger Woolford, John Winder, William Davis, James Jones, James Dashiell, David Spence and Thomas Poole were planters; Thomas Walley, John Rhodes and George Hasfurt were "chirurgeons" (physicians) as well as planters. William Bosman and William Thorne were planters.

While we cannot positively identify the vocations of the remaining persons whose names are given in the above lists, the majority of them were no doubt small planters, traders and tradesmen, while some of them were no doubt also working under "indentures." It is interesting to note that Anthony Johnson, whose name appears as one of the early settlers, is proved by later records to have been a member of the family of the first free Negroes in Northampton-Accomack in Virginia and Somerset in Maryland. Anthony Johnson appears to have been a successful small planter.[4]

Of these early worthies, Stephen Horsey, Ambrose Dixon, William Coulbourne, Henry Boston, Robert Hart, Alexander Draper, Jeffrey Minshall, John Marcum, Ambrose London and James Jones all had clashes, because of their "non-conformist" principles, with the authorities in Northampton County, Virginia. Some of them refused to pay "ministers and parish dues" and consequently were summoned before the court; some found themselves in more serious difficulties because of open affiliation and sympathy with Quakerism. Stephen Horsey was a recognized leader in Northampton County in causes relating to "the rights of the people," and was once elected to the General Assembly of Virginia on what was evidently "the people's ticket."

While we cannot positively identify the European ancestral origins of all of these first settlers of "Old Somerset," there are some items of record which suggest interesting features of such background. These first settlers were certainly of English, Scotch, Welsh, Irish and French "origins." While as yet the exact "connections" have not been made with English families of their names, we cannot doubt that Stephen Horsey, Ambrose Dixon, Randall Revell, James Barnabe, Ambrose London, Robert Catlin, Nehemiah Covington, Roger Woolford, Henry Hayman, George Betts, and William Thorne were of English "origins." Daniel Quillane and Donnock Dennis are unmistakably Irish, as was also probably Robert Hignett. Thomas Gillis was Scotch, as was also David Spence; and Nicholas Rice and James Jones were undoubtedly Welsh.

Of the European origins of some of these early settlers there is positive proof. Those of English connection were George Johnson, of Annemessex, who was from a family of the name resident in Kent; William Coulbourne was certainly of the Somersetshire family of his name; John Rhodes lived (before coming to America) in both Southamptonshire and Somersetshire; Edmund Beauchamp was of a London branch of an ancient Northamptonshire family; John Elzey was of a Southamptonshire family; William Stevens was from Buckinghamshire; James Jones was from Monmouthshire in Wales;

and Jeffrey Minshall unquestionably came from the Minshall, or Minshull, family of Devonshire, which was derived from Cheshire. Of Frenchmen born the early settlement finds a representative in Nicholas Fountain (also Fontaine), while James Dashiell, though a Scotchman by birth and maternal ancestry, was by paternal descent a grandson of a Huguenot refugee from Lyons in France to Edinburgh in Scotland.

So these men came to the lower Eastern Shore of the province of Maryland between 1662 and 1666—"all sorts and conditions of men" —and settling in this area along the waterways of Pocomoke, Annemessex, Manokin and Wicomico Rivers, and their creek tributaries, became the founders of "Old Somerset." Randall Revell and John Elzey were charged by the proprietary government with establishing the settlement. William Thorne soon joined them in the capacity of "military commander," and commissioner of the peace, and John Odber in the capacity of "commissioner." Then in February, 1662/3, we find the Maryland authorities recognizing the "body of the settlers" in this area by including in the "commission for the Eastern Shore below Choptank River" the name of Stephen Horsey, of Annemessex. Then in October, 1663, came the attempt by Colonel Scarburgh, acting as he alleged in his capacity as "his Majesty's Surveyor General and Treasurer for Virginia," to annex this area to the colony of Virginia. We find the sturdy, valiant and successful resistance made by the settlers, and the Maryland authorities, against this attempt. It is in November, 1663, under a commission from Accomack, Virginia, Court, attempting to extend jurisdiction to this area under semblance of protection to the inhabitants against certain reported uprisings, that we find William Bosman and John Rhodes as residents of the settlement at Manokin-Annemessex. In March, 1664, we find William Coulbourne, of Annemessex, coming to the fore as lieutenant of the military establishment of the settlement, and in May, 1664, Stephen Horsey appears with priority in the commission for granting land warrants and administering justice in the settlement. In August, 1665, we find George Johnson (of Annemessex), William Stevens and John White (of Pocomoke), John Winder and James Jones (of Wicomico) and Henry Boston (of Annemessex) added to the commission for the "Eastern Shore," with

Stephen Horsey (of Annemessex) and William Thorne (of Manokin) continuing in office. A year later, in August, 1666, Somerset County was erected from the area of the "Eastern Shore" from Nanticoke River (north) to the Maryland-Virginia boundary line (south) and from the Atlantic Ocean (east) to Chesapeake Bay (west), with Stephen Horsey, William Stevens, William Thorne, James Jones, John Winder, Henry Boston, George Johnson and John White as commissioners of the peace; while Horsey, Thorne and Stevens were named as "of the quorum" of the court. Stephen Horsey became the first sheriff of Somerset; Edmund Beauchamp, first clerk of the county, and William Stevens, "chief judge," of the court.

After the erection of Somerset County in August, 1666, we find, as years go by, the Woolfords, Dashiells, Ballards, Dennises, Dixons, Williamses, Planners, Ambrose London, William Jones (of Monie) joining the Horseys, Elzeys, Bosmans, Winders and Coulbournes in the commissions of the peace for Somerset, in occupying other local civil and military offices, and in representing Somerset County in the Lower House of Assembly. The later Revells, Beauchamps and Bostons did not follow official life, but became landholders and planters of very substantial means; while some of them engaged in trade of one nature or another. The Covingtons, being Quakers, did not apparently seek office, but with the acquisition of fertile lands and well applied industry in trade became people of ample means. The Whites (of Pocomoke), forsaking the official tradition, became extensive planters. The Prices, Minshalls, Ackworths, Adamses, Roaches, Tulls, Catlins, Fontaines, Furnises, Wallers, Nutters, Gillises, Davises, Spences, Tillmans, Cottinghams, Haymans, Whaleys (originally Wale), Manloves, Townsends, Stevenses (of Wicomico), Curtises, Wards, Magraws, Surnams, and Quillanes were all planters or farmers of comfortable means, apparently devoting themselves wholly to cultivation of the land.

Of these "first settlers and founders" George Johnson (of Annemessex), William Davis (of Back Creek, of Manokin), Ambrose London (of Annemessex) and Daniel Haste (of Wicomico) left no sons surviving them to carry on their names.[5] William Stevens (of "Rehoboth" on Pocomoke) had no children. James Jones (of Wicomico) died childless; as did also Nicholas Rice (of Wicomico), John Westlocke (of Manokin), William Thorne (of Manokin). James Barnabe's only son, James, Junior, was (in his seventeenth year of age) accidentally killed by Marcy Fountaine. John Nellson apparently left no son to continue the name; neither did George Hasfurt. John Rhodes, Thomas Walley, Edward Lun and Robert Hignett all removed from Somerset County before their deaths, as did also David Spence's sons.

* * * *

In the list of the first settlers of this "Eastern Shore" area, which became Somerset County, appear the names of three men who are of particular interest in that they were the founders of the medical profession in "Old Somerset." In November, 1663, John Rhodes appears in the settlement at Annemessex; in August, 1664, Thomas Walley appears in Manokin; and as early as January, 1665/6, George Hasfurt appears in Annemessex. Rhodes, Walley and Hasfurt are specifically designated in the records as "chirurgeons."

John Rhodes was certainly living at Wells in Somersetshire, England, as late as April, 1660, and probably arrived in Northampton County, Virginia, just about the time that Northampton-Accomack men were making their exodus to the lower "Eastern Shore" of Maryland, and certainly he had himself gone thence by November, 1663, while a daughter was born to him and his wife at Annemessex in May, 1664. In deeds and a power of attorney he is designated as "John Rhodes, of Somerset County, chirurgeon," and in an order of court he is referred to as "Doctor Rhodes." John Rhodes made his home on the north side of Annemessex River on a plantation of 200 acres, for which he obtained grant in May, 1668, under the patent name of "Salisbury," and which he sold in February, 1671/2, to Thomas Tull and Richard Tull, of Somerset County (the latter of whom married Martha, the daughter of John Rhodes). John Rhodes disappears from the Somerset Court records shortly after this time, and it is not improbable that he went with his family to the lower part of the present State of Delaware (now Sussex County), but which in Rhodes' day was claimed by Lord Baltimore as part of his Maryland grant. The "Salisbury" tract on which Doctor Rhodes lived in

Somerset County may today be located on the north side of Annemessex River (southeast of the village of Upper Fairmount). We may safely say that John Rhodes, who lived here, certainly from 1663-1672, was the first of the medical profession in this area and may designate him as "first founder" of the long line of physicians of the body in "Old Somerset."

It is August 5, 1664, that we pick up our first reference to Thomas Walley—"shirurgeon"—in remaining records relative to "Old Somerset." At this date he appears as a witness to the will of William Bosman, of Manokin, to whom he was no doubt attending physician during the testator's last illness. Doctor Walley was himself a resident of the Manokin section of the settlement, where a daughter was born to him and his wife in April, 1665. Thomas Walley patented in June, 1665, a tract of 300 acres of land, called "Walley's Chance," on the south side of the present Wicomico Creek (at that date called "river") near the head thereof. It was doubtless on this land that he made his home and the plantation may today be located as part of the farm lands of Miss Edna J. Davey, inherited by her under the will of the late Doctor Edward Tull, about five miles north of the town of Princess Anne. Walley is specifically designated as "Thomas Walley, of Somerset County, chirurgeon," in powers of attorney given by him to Randall Revell and Edmund Beauchamp in 1667 and 1668. About the spring of 1668 Thomas Walley removed from Somerset to Calvert County, Maryland, where he died during the late summer of 1670.

The third of the trio of earliest Somerset physicians was George Hasfurt, whose name is variously spelled in the records: Hasfurt, Hasfort, Horsfoord, Hosfoord and Hosforte. George Hasfurt appears in Northampton County, Virginia, in August, 1664, as an indentured servant to John Custis. Hasfurt was then twenty-four years of age and apparently interested in the practice of medicine. In January, 1665/6, he appears as "George Hosfoord of Enemessicke [Annemessex] on ye Easterne Shore in Maryland, Chirurgeon," and in September, 1669, as "George Horsfoord of Somerset County, Chirurgeon," he was appointed and qualified as "under sheriff" to George Johnson, High Sheriff of Somerset. The exact location of Hasfurt's home has not been discovered; but it is evident from references in the records that he lived in Annemessex Hundred, Somerset. In 1675 he purchased a plantation on Morumsco Creek and the record remains that his wife, Clemence Keene (whom he married in 1674) "dyed and was buried at Morumsco" in September, 1677. Hasfurt married a second time, Mrs. Elizabeth Hudson, and was living in Somerset as late as December, 1683. He died prior to February, 1686/7.[6]

* * * *

While we have been able to quote records somewhat extensively in regard to the honorable practice of medicine in the earliest days of "Old Somerset," references to that most highly valued of the professions—teaching—are virtually microscopic because of their rareness and brevity in the ancient records.

The first item which we have discovered relative to "teaching" appears in August, 1671, and the "teacher" was a woman—Mrs. John Avery. At Somerset Court, August 8, 1671, John Avery entered a complaint against Edward Jones to recover Mrs. Avery's fee for having instructed the children of Mrs. Mary Barnabe. Avery, in his petition, recites "That yor peticioners wife made A bargaine with Mary Barnabe to School her Chilldren one Summer and for consideracon yor peticioner was to have one two-year-old heifer which before was formerly delivered to yor peticioner; your peticioner let the said heifer run at the house of the sd Barnabe until she had a calfe; yor peticconer went to fetch the heifer home when she had Calved; And Edward Jones refused to Let yor peticioner have his heifer without an order of Co^{rt}; yor peticioner therefore Craves ord^r of Co^{rt} for his heifer & Calfe." The court recognized the petitioner's right and ordered that "Edward Jones doe deliver unto John Avery the said heifer appointed him by the widowe Barnaby deceased, with her increase."[7]

We are not informed as to the nature of the "schooling" which Mrs. Avery gave to the Barnabe children; but we may rest assured that it was effectively given. The Barnabe children whom Mrs. Avery was to "schoole" were Elizabeth (born in 1661); Rebecca (probably younger than Elizabeth) and James (who was born in 1664); and they were children of one James Barnabe, of Manokin, in Somerset (who died in February, 1666/7), and Mary, his wife. In 1669 the widow, Mary Barnabe, married Edward Jones and was evidently dead when John Avery made his petition to the court in August, 1671. The record does not state the year of the "one Summer" in which Mrs. Avery taught Mrs. Mary Barnabe's children, but from the fact that the record refers to the employing party as "Mary Barnabe" and "the widow Barnabe, deceased" (though at the time of her death she was the wife of Edward Jones), we cannot but wonder if this "schooling" took place during the Summer of 1669 before the widow Mary Barnabe's marriage to Edward Jones. The Barnabes lived on lands called "Barnabe's Lot" on the south side of Back Creek in Somerset County. John Avery and his wife (whose baptismal name was Sarah) probably also lived in this same locality.

The next item we have been able pick up in the records relative to education is in 1674, when Somerset Court summoned "George Hasfurt, Schoolmaster, late of ye county," to answer to Josias Seward in an action of debt of 350 pounds of tobacco. George Hasfurt, who in this complaint appears as "schoolemaster," is the same person whom we have previously met as a "chirurgeon." Hasfurt lived near Morumsco Creek, which is a tributary of Pocomoke River. We can but wonder if—in addition to his medical practice—he conducted a school in this neighborhood. This bare reference is the only one which we have discovered to "George Hasfurt, Schoolmaster." From the wording of the summons describing him as "late of ye County" it is not improbable that he was temporarily out of the county.[8]

In the estate account of Captain Walker, of Wicomico Hundred, Somerset County, admitted to record October 8, 1685, we find this item: *"Paid James Osborne Schoolmaster for one years Schooling of Thomas & Susannah Walker & for his accom[od]acons . . . 1,500 [pounds tobacco]."* Captain Thomas Walker (who died in February, 1680/1) was a very wealthy planter, merchant and ship-owner, for years one of his Lordship's justices of the peace for Somerset and at one time High Sheriff of the county, who lived on a plantation on the south side of Wicomico River at the mouth of Dashiell's Creek. Thomas (born March, 1675/6) and Susannah Walker (born March, 1676/7, were the only children of Captain Thomas Walker and Jane Coppinball, his wife. No doubt, "James Osborne, Schoolmaster," instructed other children in this same neighborhood.[9]

In 1686 Richard Wallton, of Somerset, who lived in Indian Cabin Neck, on the seaboard side of the county, directed that the produce from a plantation be by his executor "Imployed for my Loving Children's Education and Learning" and that "one young horse and Mare may in the like manner disposed of to & for that end and purpose."[10] Then on April 10, 1686, we find that valiant old worthy, Ambrose Dixon, of Annemessex,—whose character is one of the choicest stones in the foundation of Somerset—but who never signed a document other than with "A D," bequeathing property to his grandson, Thomas Potter, adding "And further it is my Will and desire that the sd Thomas Potter be put to School there to learn Reading, Writing & Arithmatick."[11]

* * * *

The only reference, so far discovered, to a school building (though, of course, there must have been others of like nature) in "Old Somerset" prior to the year 1700, is to one such building which stood "about the year sixteen hundred ninety-six" near "the head of Crane Creek," which issued out of Annemessex River (south side) and on or near the dividing line of "Dixon's Choice" (once the dwelling plantation of Ambrose Dixon) and Major William Planner's lands. The "Crane Creek" here referred to does not appear on the Somerset County maps of today, but may be located as a small creek on the south side of Annemessex River next below the present Gale's Creek (which in the early days bore the name of Red Cap Creek).[12]

The references to education during the early days of "Old Somerset" are far too rare and brief from which to do more than faintly outline the "foundation" of that most important aspect in a community's life. Such as they are, however, we transfer them from the fading records, offering them as a suggestion at least that the basic "three R's" were not absent from this field of human endeavor.

* * * *

While authentic items of information afforded by the ancient records relative to education in "Old Somerset" are marked by their rareness and brevity, there is even less information in the records relative to the "practice of law" in the early days of the county. As a matter of fact, we arrive at a comparatively late period in the county's history before we have certainty that men educated to the practice of law were qualifying in Somerset Court.

The early court was evidently one where simple justice between man and man was dispensed. Differences between parties were brought before the bench of "commissioners" (otherwise designated as "justices of the peace"), the causes heard by them and judgment rendered in strict accordance with the evidence produced and in keeping with the provincial law in regard thereto.

Though we have not found the names of any men actually educated "to the law" and licensed and commissioned as practicing "lawyers" in the earliest Somerset courts, yet several times we find the names of men who appeared in the court "pleading" as "attorneys." No doubt there were men who were better informed in the matter of legal procedure than the majority of their fellow citizens and who from experience and a power of judgment were esteemed by them as good advisers in such matters and as better able to present causes before the court.

Thus it is that we find several persons acting in the capacity of "attorney"—and so designated—in the records of proceedings of the early courts of "the Eastern Shore below Choptank" and of "Old Somerset." The very first of these "attorneys" who appear in the earliest local records as "pleading" the cause either for plaintiff or defendant, and appearing as early as December, 1665, were Patrick Flemman, Edward Southern and Henry Lewis. Somewhat later we find the names of Thomas Poole and Randall Revell appearing as "attorneys."[13]

* * * *

It is very true that "man does not live by bread alone"; but man must have "bread" by which to live. In every adventure there is the problem of the means of subsistence and man is so constituted that he inevitably seeks material protection and through and by his labor would gain not only a sense of satisfaction in his work but also increasing economic independence. Varying degrees of material means are sought by various degrees in human nature; though all seek to establish themselves in economic independence; in relative comfort and convenience.

The basic industry of "Old Somerset" was, of course, farming. Every man lived by the produce of the land. The large majority of the people were farmers after one fashion or another: small, medium or large farmers. Then there were other means whereby men added to their incomes: some engaged in trading, some in the pursuit of trades and others became real merchants.

Farming aside, we come next in our study of "economic origins" in "Old Somerset" to the "trader": the man who was engaged in obtaining from the Indians the profitable furs and skins of wild animals. The authorities of Maryland retained the right to grant commissions to white men who would engage in this trade with the Indians. Very early in the life of this lower Eastern Shore of Maryland settlement we find John Nuttall, trading with Indians here under commission from the provincial authorities. Nuttall held commission as a "trader" from January, 1661/2-June, 1665, trading first out of Northampton County, Virginia, with the Indians of the Eastern Shore of Maryland. In 1664 he apparently moved to St. Mary's County, Maryland, but continued his trading work with the Indians. In February, 1663/4, we find Jenkin Price (who for many years had been a resident and "trader" in Northampton-Accomack in Virginia) and James Jolley (also of Northampton) obtaining commissions to trade with the Maryland Indians.[14] Both Jenkin Price and James Jolley moved into Maryland and settled on the Pocomoke River.

As early as October, 1663, we find the Manokin-Annemessex settlement in trading contact with vessels from the northern colonies. In that month there is reference to "one Hollinsworth Merchant of a Northern Vessel came & presented his request for liberty to trade." George Johnson, of Annemessex, was a merchant who had come trading from England to Virginia and the province of Maryland, settling at Annemessex in 1662 or 3, and had three brothers living in New England. John Elzey had been engaged in merchandizing while resident in Virginia and there is trace there of his connection with New England mercantile matters and no doubt he continued his trading interests after coming to Manokin in Maryland. Between

1665 and 1670 we find William Smyton, Charles Ballard and Thomas Freeman, all of Manokin; and James Weedon, of Pocomoke, each one specifically referred to in the records as "merchant." During this period we find also that Edward Martindale, of Bristol, England; and Thomas Jones, of Bristol, both "merchants," were trading with Somerset County people, and that Devorax Browne, of Accomack County, Virginia, was represented in Somerset by Roger Woolford as his "attorney." Ambrose Dixon appears to have represented Edward Martindale, of Bristol. James Powell, of Bristol, England, Mariner; Matthew Armstrong and Stephen Bond, of Boston, in New England, Mariners, evidently engaged in the shipping trade with many Somerset people. Thomas Jones referred to above as "of Bristol, England, Merchant," was identical with Thomas Jones, who settled south of Manokin River in Somerset County at an earlier day, established himself as a merchant—also becoming a prominent official in Somerset. Thomas Freeman, referred to above, was a Bristol, England, merchant, who established himself "at the house of Mr. Randall Revell, where ye said Thos. Freeman kept his store in ye County of Somersett." It appears that "Thomas Freeman of Bristol, Merchant, died and was buried at the Plantation of Randall Revell Called the Double Purchase in Manoakin in the Month of July Annoque Domini One Thousand Six Hundred Sixty and Eight."

From the year 1670 on we find the merchant class increasing in Somerset County, not only in numbers but also in wealth. With the arrival of David Brown from Glasgow, in Scotland, in 1670, we find marked advance. Brown settled on Manokin River and there conducted an extensive trade. Levin Denwood (the Quaker) on the Great Monie Creek seems also to have engaged extensively in merchandising; while Captain Thomas Walker, who established himself on Wicomico River, became a man of large wealth for his day through operating as a merchant. It was at about this time that Somerset men engaged in merchandising seem to have begun ownership of shipping vessels; a practice which steadily increased with the passing years. At the town of Snow Hill, established in 1686, we find Archibald Erskine, another Scotch merchant, settling and engaging in extensive trading operations before his death in 1687.[15]

From the "merchants" we pass to the element engaged in the "trades" as we say: the carpenters, coopers, tailors and the like. A reading of the remaining records has afforded some interesting items bearing on this line. In 1664 we find Nicholas Rice, of Wicomico, designated as "carpenter." Rice, while evidently trained to his trade, no doubt employed himself, so far as its exercise was concerned, in superintending building work and not improbably as something of a "contractor" for such work. He appears to have been, in addition to his "carpenter's trade," a quite well-to-do planter and was at one time (in later years) one of his Lordship's justices of the peace for Somerset. In September, 1669, we find "George Day, Carpenter"; while other Somerset men who appear designated as "carpenter" are Jeremiah Hooke (in 1670), Thomas Davis (in 1672), William Horvison (in 1673), John Kibble and John Tyler (in 1676). Of men designated "tailor" we have found several mentions: William Johnson (in 1671), Thomas Davis (in 1672), James Robinson (in 1673), John Jenckins (1676), John Aleward (1677), Richard Higginbotham (1677) and William Horseman (1683). Cornelius Johnson appears in 1672 as a "cooper" (he also appears as "mariner" in 1672), while other "coopers" were George Phoebus (1673), John Dorman (1675), William Walstone (1676) and William Dedecker (1683). John Anderson appears as "a sawyer" in 1667 and 1671. Then of other trades there appear John Tizard, Shoemaker (1672); Thomas Hemming, Hatter (1675); Richard Chambers (Black)smith (1677); Thomas Evans, Boatwright (1673), and George Holland, "Butcher by profession" (1675).[16]

VII

FOUNDERS

Stephen Horsey—Ambrose Dixon—Randall Revell—John Elzey—William Thorne—John Odber—Thomas Price—George Johnson—Henry Boston—William Coulbourne—William Bosman—William Stevens—James Jones—John White—John Winder—Edmund Beauchamp.

Stephen Horsey

STEPHEN HORSEY was born about the year 1620.[1] That he was a native Englishman seems beyond question, though the shire and locality of his nativity have not been discovered.[2] As Stephen *Horse* his name appears in 1643 as a headright to a patent for land granted Obedience Robins, of Northampton Count, Virginia.[3] Horsey settled in Northampton County, on whose records his name frequently appears during the course of the succeeding eighteen years. Prior to December, 1650, Stephen Horsey married Sarah, widow of Michael Williams, deceased, in Northampton County.[4]

Stephen Horsey is described as a "cooper" by trade; though the fact that he was a tradesman seemed in no way to affect his exercising a vigorous influence in popular affairs in Northampton County. On March 25, 1652, he signed (with 116 other persons) the "engagement tendered to ye Inhabitants of Northampton County," thereby subscribing a promise "to be true and faithful to the Commonwealth of England as it is now Established without King or House of Lords." This "engagement" was one which the strongly "royalist" Eastern Shore of Virginia was asked to subscribe to upon the surrender of Virginia to the Parliamentary Commissioners on their arrival in that colony in March, 1651/2, after the dethronement and execution of Charles I.

The Parliamentary Government in England, which of course extended to the colony of Virginia, "at first found much support in Northampton County, especially among the middle class and tradesmen." However, this favor towards Parliament did not last long, owing to certain hardships which resulted to the tobacco trade from the enforcement of the Navigation Acts. Then, too, "for sometime the belief had been quite general among the inhabitants ... that Northampton County had become a separate province, the conviction being heightened by the failure of the Governor to call for Burgesses. An intense spirit of independence had therefore grown up among the people and nothing in common was felt to exist between Northampton and the Western Shore." The Royalist Party, which had become very strong, took advantage of this situation and bringing its influence to bear "appealed to the people to resist the unjust burdens imposed upon them by the Assembly at James City and to assert their independence of a government in which their sole participation was to defray its expense." There were repeated popular meetings in Northampton and the agitators were successful in their work. As the result of this agitation a committee of six citizens was "selected by vote of the people to draw up a protest against their present condition and to act in all things as the best interests of the people might demand." This committee consisted of Stephen Charlton, Levyne Denwood, John Nuthall, William Whittington, John Ellis and *Stephen Horsey*. This committee drew up, signed and presented to the Virginia authorities the celebrated "Northampton Protest" of March 30, 1652; a protest in fact against "taxation without representation." Thus it is that we find Stephen Horsey, in 1652, in the very thick of the fight for "popular rights" and esteemed by the people a man worthy of their confidence to represent them in presenting their grievances.

In July, 1653, Stephen Horsey appears upon the records as challenging a certain decision of the Northampton Court embodied in an order relative to the reprisal of a ship. In a popular meeting held in "Doctor Hack's old field" Horsey violently assailed the members of the court, calling them "asses and villanes."[5] In this same year, 1653, we find Stephen Horsey returned as a Burgess from Northampton County to the Virginia Assembly with Thomas Johnson and William Mellin as the two other Burgesses from that county.[6] Ten years later Colonel Edmund Scarburgh in a bitter attack on Stephen Horsey, referring to the fact that he had been "once elected a Burgess by ye Comon Crowd & thrown out by ye Assembly for a factious and tumultuous person; A man repugnant to all Govm^t."[7] We indeed have Horsey's record as that of an agitator in behalf of the people's rights; we know that he was indeed "one of the people." It is no doubt true that Horsey was prevented from taking the seat in the Assembly to which he had been elected by "the people." But in our appreciation of the man we should not fail to throw into the scale of judgment as we weigh him, the facts that Scarburgh was always contemptous of the "Comon Crowd" (except when he could bend them to his own will), and that the Virginia Assembly was not particularly lenient towards those who were deemed in opposition to the government. Stephen Horsey was a man who possessed an independent spirit and never once do we find him failing to exercise it.

Aggressively independent in matters political, we find that Stephen Horsey was vigorously non-conformist in matters religious. His enemy, Scarburgh, referred to him in 1663 as "of all sects yet professedly none, Constant in nothing but opposing Church Govm^t his children at great ages yet unchristened . . ." While this is intended as a biting item of criticism, yet underlying it is evidently the fact that Stephen Horsey was interested in the liberal movements in religion which were prominent at the time, and yet was not content to give his allegiance to any one of them. From his intimate association with the Quakers and the item relative to his children not having been baptized leads one to think that he may have affiliated with these "followers of the Inner Light." Yet there is no evidence to this effect; and Scarburgh's statement that he professed membership in no sect certainly excludes Horsey from membership in "Friends Meeting."

Though we cannot "religiously denominate" Stephen Horsey, yet we do find him most intimately associated with the Quakers and we can prove beyond doubt his absolute non-conformity in relation to the Church of England. As early as November, 1658, Stephen Horsey (together with Ambrose Dixon, Levin Denwood, and Captain William Mitchell) was before Northampton Court at the suit of the Reverend Thomas Teackle, rector of Hungar's Parish, for non-payment of minister's and church dues, having been formerly ordered by the vestry to pay them. The court sustained the vestry's order. On January 28, 1661/2, several delinquents in Hungar's Parish in the payment of minister's and other parish dues belonging to the church were brought before the court and "ordered that they make present payment of what shall be due by them from the year 1654, and the following persons, still owing dues to the minister and church in Hungar's Parish, were returned *non est inventus,* viz: Stephen Horsey, Ambrose Dixon, Alexander Draper, Robert Hart and William Smith.[8] Certainly these items leave no uncertainty in the mind as to Horsey's stalwart non-conformity in relation to the Established Church and of his stout resistance in the matter of meeting the law's demand for his financial support thereof.

Through the last item quoted from the Northampton Court records we find Horsey's point of departure from Virginia for Maryland. We find that Stephen Horsey was returned *non est inventus* by the authorities in Northampton County, Virginia, January, 28, 1661/2, and also we find that on February 27, 1660/1, Stephen Horsey entered a survey for 1,000 acres of land on south side Annemessex River on the Eastern Shore of Maryland.[9] In this survey headrights were named as: Stephen Horsey, Sarah Horsey, his wife; Stephen Horsey, Junior, John Horsey, Abigail Horsey, Samuel Horsey and Mary Horsey (who were children of Stephen and Sarah Horsey), Michael Williams, Thomas Williams and Sarah Williams (who were children of Mrs. Sarah Horsey by her first husband, Michael Williams, deceased), John Roche [Roach], Benjamin Summer and Thomas Whitfield. The land for which this survey was entered by Stephen Horsey was patented to him September 3, 1663, by the name of "Coulbourne," the tract containing 650 acres. This plantation consisted of splendid, fertile river side lands and was located on the south side of the great Annemessex River, beginning at the mouth of Coulbourne's Creek and running in a northeasterly direction up the river, 250 poles to the mouth of Ipsewansey Creek. The plantation had this splendid frontage on the river and extended some distance inland to the heads of both Ipsewansey and Coulbourne's Creeks. It was to this location that Stephen Horsey moved with his family when he left Northampton County, Virginia, prior to January, 1661/2.

So it was that Stephen Horsey, the rebellious and tumultuous nonconformist of Northampton County, Virginia, came with his family to Maryland and settled on the south side of the Annemessex River on the "Eastern Shore." We cannot give the exact date of his arrival at Annemessex (by which name the settlement in that locality came to be officially designated); but certainly he had left Northampton County by January 28, 1661/2, and we strongly suspect that he had taken up his abode on the Eastern Shore of Maryland sometime during the Autumn of the year 1661. This is as definite as we can be in relation to the time of Horsey's settlement at Annemessex.

In the province of Maryland Stephen Horsey found that freedom which his seething non-conformist spirit craved; and becoming, as we believe, the actual *first* settler of the newly created territorial area of "the Eastern Shore below Choptank River"; his settlement formed the nucleus from which Somerset County developed. It was not long before Horsey was joined here by other men whose non-conformist spirit made them also *persona non grata* in Northampton County, Virginia. Ambrose Dixon, Thomas Price, Robert Hart, and Alexander Draper, if they did not in fact arrive at Annemessex at the same time that Horsey did, certainly followed him shortly.

Almost from the beginning of the Annemessex settlement on the Eastern Shore of Maryland, Stephen Horsey occupied a prominent position. On February 4, 1662/3, he was named a member of the commission of the peace for this area, continuing to hold this office until August, 1666, when that part of the area south of Nanticoke River and extending to the Maryland-Virginia boundary line was erected into the county of Somerset. In the commission of the peace, named in May, 1664, Horsey was named as first, thus given priority and the *de facto* chief magistracy in the settlement. During the trying times which overtook the Manokin-Annemessex settlement in the Fall of 1663, when Colonel Edmund Scarburgh tried with all his power to reduce the settlers to submission to the Virginia authorities and annex the area to Accomack County in Virginia, Stephen Horsey became a valiant leader in opposition to Scarburgh's scheme and has the honor of having been described by Scarburgh as an "ignorant yet insolent officer . . . that left ye lower parts [i. e. Northampton-Accomack in Virginia] to head Rebellion at Amanessicks [i. e. Annemessex on the Eastern Shore of Maryland]." Horsey's part in opposing Scarburgh's scheme and his accompanying invasion of Manokin-Annemessex, we have fully set forth in the early chapters of this book. When Somerset County was erected, August 22, 1666, Stephen Horsey was named as first in the commission of the peace and he was directed to administer the oath to the other commissioners named "afore they act as Justices for ye County." Horsey was commissioned, and qualified, as first High Sheriff of Somerset County, retaining the office from August, 1666, to June, 1668. He was also a deputy surveyor of the province of Somerset. In 1668 he again became a member of the court, and on June 30, 1668, signed the court orders as "Stephen Horsi, chiefe Judge of ye Court." Stephen Horsey and William Stevens were the first representatives, or burgesses, elected by the people of Somerset County to the General Assembly of Maryland (under writ of February 18, 1668/9), which met April 19, 1669. Owing to the fact that the people of Somerset, after the election, refused to send but one representative to the Assembly the selection went to William Stevens by an unauthorized action of the sheriff. This action of the sheriff later brought him a reprimand from the chancellor of the province and a fine from the Assembly. It appears, however, that Horsey had written to a member of the Assembly that he "was sick & could not attend." Nevertheless, it remains a fact that Stephen Horsey was duly elected to the Lower House of Assembly as a member of Somerset's first representation in that body, and his name was duly returned by order of the chancellor.[10]

"Stephen Horsey, Sen[r] died and was buried at his plantation in Annemessex 8 August 1671."[11]

Stephen Horsey (1620-1671) married (prior to December, 1650) Sarah (whose surname is unknown), widow of Michael Williams, of Northampton County, Virginia. Stephen Horsey and Sarah, his wife, had issue: (1) Stephen Horsey, Junior, married Hannah Revell; (2) John Horsey, who died April, 1678; (3) Samuel Horsey (died 1736), married Ann ———; (4) Nathaniel Horsey (1664/5-1721), married Sarah Revell; (5) Isaac Horsey (1665—circa 1750), married ——— ———; (6) Mary Horsey, died unmarried, 1678; (7) Abigail Horsey, married, *first,* John Kibble; *second,* Richard Stevens.

AMBROSE DIXON

Ambrose Dixon appears in 1649 as having been transported to Virginia by Richard Bayly, of Northampton County;[1] and it is certain that he became a resident of Northampton County, for in March,

1651/2, we find that he signed "The Engagement tendered to ye Inhabitants of Northampton" by which promise was made "to bee true and faithfull to the Commonwealth of England as now Established without Kings or House of Lords."[2] In 1652 we find a Mary Dixon transported into the colony of Virginia by Ambrose Dixon and Stephen Horsey, of Northampton County.[3] This was evidently Ambrose Dixon's wife, whose baptismal name we know to have been Mary.

Ambrose Dixon was a "caulker" by trade,[4] no doubt finding extensive demand upon his abilities in a section of country where watercraft were so numerous. However, his life was evidently a quiet one, given to the pursuit of his trade, until the exercise of his religious principles brought him into conflict with the colonial authorities, and thence quite prominently into the records.

Ambrose Dixon, with the rise of Quakerism in Virginia, gave whole-hearted allegiance to the faith of the "Inner Light," whose guidance brought him to the insurmountable barricade of the Virginia law against Quakers.

In November, 1660, Ambrose Dixon, Thomas Leatherbury, Henry White, Henry Voss, and Levin Denwood, were brought before the court of Northampton County for breach of the law concerning Quakers. Ambrose Dixon was arraigned for having met with and spoken amongst the people called Quakers, while fearlessly (and perhaps stubbornly) he "acknowledged the same." Leatherbury and White also in conflict with the authorities "for breach of ye law concerning Quakers" were "found guilty." Voss, while professing to be transporting Quakers out of Virginia and "up ye Bay [i. e. to Maryland] delusively causes ye sd Quakers to be sett ashore at Nuswattocks [in Northampton County]." The court proved the charge against Voss. Denwood was also brought in for "breach of ye law concerning Quakers."

The tender-hearted court "remitted executing ye rigor of ye law" and for the present discharged Dixon, White and Leatherbury from payment of sheriff's and clerk's fees in the cause, but "left them to ye Marcy of ye Honble: Govr & Council for ye present." Voss, for his offence was "referred to ye Censure of ye Honble Govr." Denwood was ordered to give security for his good behavior in the future and to pay sheriff's and clerk's fees "and for further Censure is referred to ye Honble ye Govr & Council."⁵

So it was that Ambrose Dixon had the distinction, for "conscience sake," of being before the highest tribunal of a temporal power there to "witness" to his faith in the supremacy of the "King of Kings."

That Ambrose Dixon (with his fellow religionists) was carried before "ye Honble: Govr & Council" of Virginia there can be no doubt; but the nature of "ye Marcy," or lack thereof, extended by that highest court of the colony to these offending religionists does not appear as the records of the General Court for the period have long since disappeared. No doubt, however, the censure which Dixon (and his companions) received was, in quality, thoroughly in keeping with the law against Quakers, and the spirit of a tribunal thoroughly in sympathy with the terms of that law.

As early as November, 1658, Ambrose Dixon, in company with Levin Denwood, Captain William Mitchell, and Stephen Horsey, were subjects of an order of vestry in Northampton County demanding that they pay to the Reverend Mr. Teackle, minister of the parish, the usual dues. The refusal of these persons to do this had caused Mr. Teackle to complain of them to the court which granted him judgment against them, except in the case of Captain Mitchell, "who pleads his privilege as a Burgess." In January, 1661/2, when the delinquents in payment of minister's and other parish dues, in Hungar's Parish, were ordered by the Northampton Court to make payment of amounts that appeared to be due by them from the year 1654, Ambrose Dixon was among those who were returned by the authorities as *non est inventus*.⁶

Before this January, 1661/2, when he was returned to the court as *non est inventus*, we believe that Ambrose Dixon had made his exit from Northampton County in Virginia through the open door of the province of Maryland's toleration of such dissenters and religious rebels, and had entered, with his companion, Stephen Horsey, the settlement at Annemessex on the lower Eastern Shore of Maryland. At any rate, we henceforth find Ambrose Dixon living at "Dixon's Choice" in Annemessex, loyal and undaunted in his spirit of Quakerism.

Ambrose Dixon's home on "Dixon's Choice," on the south side of the Great Annemessex River, on the Eastern Shore of Maryland (in later years Somerset County), was the center for Quaker activities in this area at the time of its settlement. Dixon was "a receiver of many Quakers his house ye place of their resort and a Conveyor of our ingaged persons out of the County [i. e. Northampton-Accomack]," writes the caustic Colonel Scarburgh.

Ambrose Dixon was truly the guide and guard of his brother "Friends" seeking refuge in Annemessex. He was a rugged soul, absolutely loyal to the faith which he embraced and an imcomparable leader among the Quakers in the Annemessex settlement, and later in Somerset County. The "Inner Light" unquestionably led him by a steep and rough way through this earthly life. Let us hope that "beyond this life" the Light guided him to more pleasant paths. It is interesting to note that what was evidently the first Quaker "Meeting House" erected in Somerset County was built on Dixon's land (see *ante*, page 91) and that in the "God's Acre" surrounding it Dixon's body was interred when his earthly journey came to an end. "Ambrose Dixon, Sen[r] died and was buried at the meeting house in Anemessix the 12th day of Aprill Annoq Do[m] one Thousand Six hundred eighty & Seaven."[7]

Ambrose Dixon married Mary (whose surname is now unknown), who was evidently a widow Pedington, as Dixon, in his will (dated April 7, 1686) devises property to "my wife's son, Henry Pedington." Ambrose Dixon and Mary, his wife, together with their children, lived at "Dixon's Choice" on the south side of the Great Annemessex River, and adjoining Stephen Horsey's plantation, "Colebourne." For years "Dixon's Choice" remained in the Dixon family and in the old graveyard on the place many generations of the Dixon connection have been buried. This old graveyard, which has been carefully preserved by the family up to the present time (1935), is located about a mile west of Marion P. O., in Somerset County.

Ambrose Dixon, during the course of his life, amassed a comfortable property in Somerset County in fertile lands and several Negroes. He evidently devoted his time to farming and his religious interests, avoiding political and official life. In November, 1666, Ambrose Dixon appears as one of the first "surveyors for ye highways" in Somerset (see *ante,* p. 72). In November, 1666, Ambrose Dixon, Ambrose London, Paul Marsh, and Roger Woolford, were elected delegates to represent Somerset County in the Lower House of the General Assembly of the province to be convened March-April, 1671. However, when the Assembly met only Marsh and Woolford appeared as Somerset's delegates.[8] No explanation has been found as to why Dixon and London did not attend and qualify as members of the Assembly.

Ambrose Dixon and Mary, his wife, had issue: (1) Thomas Dixon (died 1720), married Christian Potter; (2) Elizabeth Dixon (died 1687), married Robert Dukes; (3) Sarah Dixon, married Edmund Beauchamp; (4) Grace Dixon, married John Richards; (5) Mary Dixon, married Thomas Cottingham; (6) Alice Dixon, married Henry Potter; (7) Hannah Dixon (1666-1667).

RANDALL REVELL

Randall Revell was a man nearly fifty years old and well seasoned through experience in the ways of colonial life when he became the head resident executive of the Manokin-Annemessex settlement on the Eastern Shore of Maryland in 1661-1662. Revell was born about 1613 and appears in the original Accomack County on the Eastern Shore of Virginia as early as January-February, 1633/4. His name again appears in the Accomack court records in September, 1636, and October, 1637. Circumstantial evidence seems to indicate that Randall Revell, whose name appears in the Accomack records at the dates noted, was identical with a certain Randall Revell who was in St. Mary's County, Maryland, between 1636 and 1644.[1]

Randall Revell was certainly in Accomack County, Virginia, at the early time referred to above, and after the original Accomack County's name was changed to Northampton County in 1642 we find, in course of time, that he was again resident in that area. In March, 1652 he appears (with many other persons) as having signed the engagement tendered by the Parliamentary Commissioners to the inhabitants of Northampton County "to be true and faithful to the Commonwealth of England as it is now established without King or

House of Lords."² In October, 1653, Randall Revell, together with Hugh Yeo and John Jenkins, were subjects of complaint to the Northampton Court by "the Great Men of Onancock [i. e. the Onancock Indians]" because they had refused to give them satisfaction for their lands on Pungoteague Creek. The court ordered Revell, Yeo and Jenkins to pay these Indians their due in the matter, and in failure thereof to appear at the next court.³ At the Session of the General Assembly of Virginia held 1657/-1658 we find that Randall Revell was one of the Burgesses from Northampton County; while in July, 1661, Revell was commissioned a justice of the peace for "the county of Accomack," which was at that date in process of formation out of the northern area of Northampton County.⁴

Randall Revell, who is designated in the records as a "Cooper" and as "Wine-Cooper," by trade,⁵ seems from his first appearance to have been a man of vigorous and energetic nature, endowed with considerable ability, which he apparently used to great advantage in advancing himself both politically and economically. The offices of trust which were successively held by Revell and the large and comfortable estate which he accumulated are unquestionable evidences of the man's ability. Then there is a persistent tradition to the effect that Mrs. Katherine Revell, the wife of Randall Revell, was a sister of Colonel Edmund Scarburgh, of Accomack. While this tradition is probably true, yet no record evidence in its support has so far been discovered. Certainly there seems to have been a very close and abiding intimacy existing between Colonel Scarburgh and Randall Revell, which may be accounted for by the fact that Revell married Scarburgh's sister. Furthermore, there was certainly the relationship at least of close friendship existing between Randall Revell, his wife, Katherine, and their children, and one Mistress Anne Toft, of Accomack, a person evidently of rare charm and power. Mistress Toft was joint patentee in 1662 with Revell of the extensive "Double Purchase," tract of land between Manokin River and Back Creek on the Eastern Shore of Maryland (later Somerset County), finally disposing of her interests in these lands by deed of gift to Mrs. Katherine Revell, wife of Randall Revell, and their daughters, Hannah Revell and Katherine Revell, Junior.⁶ This Mistress Anne Toft, we may say in passing, is revealed by the Accomack, Virginia, court records to have occupied a very close relationship (the nature of which the records fail to reveal) to the powerful Colonel Edmund Scarburgh, the beneficiary of whose munificence she most certainly became.

It is from the background of experience in local affairs in Accomack-Northampton County, Virginia, and the connection with the powerful and socially prominent Colonel Edmund Scarburgh and Mistress Anne Toft, as sketched above, that Randall Revell enters the scene of affairs on the Eastern Shore of Maryland.

In answer to the petition of certain residents of Northampton-Accomack in Virginia for the privilege of settling in the province of Maryland, Lord Baltimore directed that the petitioners take up their lands in the area of the lower Eastern Shore of his province near the boundary line between Maryland and Virginia. The proclamation of the provincial governor, November, 1661, directing this settlement also created the territorial area of "the Eastern Shore below Choptank River" and named Colonel Edmund Scarburgh, Randall Revell and John Elzey as commissioners to effect this settlement and grant land warrants to the settlers. At least two of these commissioners were to be resident in the province. Randall Revell and John Elzey fulfilled this requirement by settling within the area on the Manokin River.

The exact date of Randall Revell's settling at Manokin (which appears to have been the early designation of the settlement) is not known, though it was probably late in the Fall of 1661 or early in the Spring of 1662, for in May, 1662, he reported that the settlement was well established. Revell was the first resident executive officer of the settlement (taking priority of John Elzey, the other resident commissioner) holding this position from the date of the commission in November, 1661, until he was relieved of further duty in February, 1662/3. Revell was unquestionably an effective factor in the establishment of this settlement, and his retirement by action of the Lord Proprietor's Council for Maryland was no doubt the result of his sympathetic association with Colonel Edmund Scarburgh's scheme to annex the Manokin-Annemessex area of the Eastern Shore of Maryland to the County of Accomack in Virginia. We have related in the early sections of this book Scarburgh's scheme to bring this section of Lord Baltimore's province into the colony of Virginia. It was to Randall Revell that Colonel Scarburgh wrote in January, or early February, 1662/3, alleging Virginia's claim to the land, and the quit rents on the lands, at Manokin. Information of the fact of this communication from Scarburgh to Revell was sent by John Elzey to the Council of the province almost immediately after Scarburgh's demand had been received (see *ante,* page 30). On February 4, 1662/3, the Governor of Maryland had issued a new commission of the peace for the "Eastern Shore" settlement, naming John Elzey, Randall Revell and Stephen Horsey as commissioners; thus giving Elzey priority over Revell. When this commission came before the Council for confirmation on February 20th, that body evidently having in hand the information relative to Scarburgh's communication to Revell and suspecting Revell's sympathy with Scarburgh's demand, "Ordered . . . That Randall Revell bee out" (see *ante,* pages 20-21). Thus Randall Revell's official connection with the "Eastern Shore" settlement of Manokin-Annemessex ceased. His name does not again appear in the record of proceedings in regard to the settlement until November, 1663, when the Accomack County, Virginia, court illegally extending jurisdiction over the Manokin-Annemessex area in Maryland appointed Randall Revell, with several others, to act for them in an official capacity at Manokin. However, this commission seems not to have been called upon for action (see *ante,* page 43-44). In August, 1670, we find that Randall Revell was High Sheriff of Somerset County.[7]

Randall Revell, from his first settlement on the "Eastern Shore" of Maryland, apparently lived on that part of his "Double Purchase" tract of land which forms the point between Manokin River and Back Creek. Here he erected his dwelling house (which has long since disappeared) and here continued to reside until his death in 1686/7. The "Double Purchase" tract, which was the home of Randall Revell and many of his descendants after him, finds its identity today in the well-known "Revells' Neck" in Somerset County.

Randall Revell was certainly married twice, if not thrice. Edward Revell (*circa* 1638-1691), of Accomack County, Virginia, was a son of Randall Revell by his first (?) wife. Randall Revell, Junior, Katherine Revell (wife of John West), Ann Revell (wife of William Coulbourne, Junior), Sarah Revell (wife of Nathaniel Horsey), and Hannah Revell (wife of Stephen Horsey, Junior), were children of Randall Revell by his last wife, Mrs. Katherine (Scarburgh?) Revell.

JOHN ELZEY

We find reference to John Elzey in Northampton County, Virginia, as early as 1655/6. On February 28, 1655/6, the Northampton Court granted "John Elzye" certificate for 200 acres of land "per rights vizt John Elsye, Arnold Elsye, Ann Shaw, Danl Mickley." The variation in the spelling of the name in no wise affects the matter of identification. From certain items of record that remain to us it is evident that John Elzey derived descent from the Elzeys of Southampton, England, and that he was drawn to Northampton County, Virginia, through relationship to Ralph Barlowe, who had settled there at an early date and had become prominent in the affairs of that county. Records prove that John Elzey was a nephew of Ralph Barlowe; Barlowe and Elzey's father having been half-brothers. Ralph Barlowe died in 1652 naming John Elzey, "my kinsman," a residuary legatee and executor. Thus it was that Elzey came to Northampton County, where his name several times appears in the records with the designation of "merchant." John Elzey and Sarah, his wife, conveyed lands in Northampton County, October, 1658, and in Accomack County in October, 1663.[1]

Lord Baltimore did not enlist a more faithful and upright officer in the "Eastern Shore" adventure than John Elzey. The very fact of Elzey's having been named a member of the original "commission" of November, 1661, to effect the settlement of the Manokin-Annemessex area is evidence of his ability. Surpassing this quality of ability, however, was the man's spirit of loyalty to his charge in guarding the best interests of both the settlers and the Lord Proprietor. The remaining records of the transaction of affairs in the Manokin-Annemessex settlement during the period of its establishment give every evidence of Elzey's able conduct in office.

Under the proclamation of November 6, 1661, directing the establishment of "the Eastern Shore below Choptank" settlement, John Elzey was named as the third among the three "commissioners" (Edmund Scarburgh and Randall Revell being the other two) to grant warrants for land in this area and administer the oath of allegiance to the settlers. Becoming one of the two resident commissioners, Elzey established his home on the north side of the Manokin River on a thousand-acre tract, which he called "Almodington." On May 2, 1662, he was again commissioned (with Scarburgh and Revell) to issue land warrants, and was also named (with Revell and Thorne) in the first "Com^{on} [commission] to keepe the peace" in this Eastern Shore settlement. In February, 1662/3, Elzey was named first in the Commission of the Peace and for issuing land warrants "for that part of the Eastern Shore newly settled and adjoining Virginia," thus becoming the chief officer of the settlement. This office Elzey continued to hold until his death.

When Colonel Edmund Scarburgh first made his "demand for obedience and acknowledgment to his majestie in payment of rights for land from the people inhabiting at Manoakin and Annamessex, as well as submission to his majesties government of Virginia," it was John Elzey who refused to accede thereto and who immediately informed the Governor and Council of Maryland of the perilous position of the Manokin-Annemessex settlement. And, finally, when the undisciplined Scarburgh made his invasion of the settlements with an armed force in October, 1663, in a further pursuit of enforcing his demands, "Mr. Elzey & Capt William Thorne who being officers of ye Lord Baltimore desired respite of time untill they could returne their commissions wch they engaged their words and Reputations to performe as soon as possible." So Scarburgh reported the attitude of John Elzey, Chief Commissioner of the Peace, and Captain William Thorne, the military commander (and also a magistrate) of the settlement. There is no evidence that Elzey (or Thorne) resigned his office or showed further wavering in allegiance to Lord Baltimore; while in the renewal of his Lordship's Commission of the Peace for the settlement in February, 1663/4, we find John Elzey again given first place in the Commission.

We cannot but feel, in view of the evidence afforded by the recorded transactions of affairs in the settlement at that time, that John Elzey's consistently wise course in conducting those affairs, and his unyielding allegiance to Lord Baltimore's government went far towards saving the Manokin-Annemessex area from the rapacious clutches of Colonel Edmund Scarburgh. Elzey's staunchness throughout this whole affair must indeed have been an inspiration to the valiant Annemessex men who openly defied Scarburgh and all of his pretentions.*

"John Elzey died at Manoakin & was buried at his plantation in May A° D° one thousand six hundred sixty and [four]."[2]

John Elzey, married (prior to 1658) Sarah (whose surname is unknown) and by her had at least two sons. (1) Arnold Elzey (died 1716), married Major Waller; and (2) John Elzey, Junior, who died 1667. Mrs. Sarah Elzey, married, *second,* Thomas Jordan; *third,* Charles Ballard; *fourth,* Stephen Luffe.

WILLIAM THORNE

Fleeting references to William Thorne in the records of Northampton County, Virginia, show him to have been resident there in January, 1653/4, and November, 1658, while in 1654 he appears with his wife, Winifred Thorne.[1]

William Thorne came into the Manokin section of the Eastern Shore of Maryland settlement either with the first settlers there or very soon after the settlement was made, and in May, 1662, was commissioned captain of militia at "Manokin" and "Annemessex" and a member of the Commission of the Peace (see *ante,* page 19). The esteem in which Thorne was held by the provincial authorities is indicated by these appointments. Thorne continued in office in the area designated as the "Eastern Shore" from 1662 to 1666, when it was, in the latter year, divided and the counties of Somerset and Dorchester erected therefrom. At this division of the area in 1666 Thorne's residence fell within the limits of Somerset, of which county he became the first military commander, under commission dated August 22, 1666, and a member of the first Commission of the Peace. Thorne held these offices until his death, which occurred about 1669 (see *ante,* page 69, *et seq.*).

---

*For the commissions naming John Elzey as a commissioner to issue warrants and as a Commissioner of the Peace; and for the part taken by him in the establishment of the settlement see Chapters I and II of this book.

In October, 1663, when Colonel Edmund Scarburgh, acting allegedly on behalf of the Virginia government and the Crown, demanded obedient submission of the Manokin-Annemessex settlement on the Eastern Shore of Maryland, Captain William Thorne (with John Elzey), "being officers of ye Lord Baltimore," refused compliance with Scarburgh's demand "untill they could return their commissions." Though Scarburgh says that Thorne and Elzey "engaged their words and Reputations" to return their Maryland commissions as soon as possible, there is no evidence to the effect that these gentlemen fulfilled their promises. Both Thorne and Elzey were continued as Commissioners of the Peace in the settlement in later commissions. It is true that in November, 1663, the Accomack County, Virginia, Court, in an order then issued, refers to "Capt Wm. Thorne, an officer under Coll: Scarburgh"; however, this "attachment" could not have been binding as in February, 1663/4, Thorne was re-commissioned as member of the Commission of the Peace for the Eastern Shore Maryland settlement of Manokin-Annemessex (see, *ante,* pages 41, 43 and 58).

Through the truly trying infant years of the settlement we find Captain Thorne always occupying offices of trust and honor therein; while his record bears marks of faithful and wise service in the positions which he occupied.

Captain William Thorne and Winifred, his wife, lived at "Thornton," a plantation on the north side of Manokin River. Captain Thorne was alive as late as September 29, 1669, when he and his wife, Winifred, conveyed land to Francis Roberts.[2] William Thorne's will, dated February 12, 1665/6 (date of probate missing), devised to one John Richards 300 acres of land provided he remained in the service of testator's wife until he was 21 years old; testator's wife, Winifred, was named executrix and given residue of the estate, both real and personal.[3] There is no evidence that Captain William Thorne left any issue; while the surname of his wife is as yet unknown. Mrs. Winifred Thorne (the widow of Captain Thorne) contracted a second marriage with Colonel David Brown, who came to Somerset County about 1670. Thus the estate of "Thornton" passed into Colonel Brown's hands and there he made his home. Mrs. Winifred Thorne-Brown died about 1696, having had no issue by Colonel Brown.

John Odber

Captain John Odber became a member of the Commission of the Peace for "the Eastern Shore below Choptank" in February, 1663/4.

Captain Obder was one of Maryland's most trusted commanders against the Indian enemy. He first appears in the provincial archives in July, 1658, as commanding the forces from St. Leonard's Creek to the coves on the north side of the Patuxent River and from George Reade's to Cedar Point on the south side of that river. In November, 1660, he was directed to raise a company of soldiers for duty, and in February, 1660/1, we find him again commanding along the Patuxent River as in 1658. In April, 1661, Captain Odber was sent by the provincial authorities (in accordance with articles of a treaty) in command of a detachment of 50 selected men to the aid of the Susquehannaugh Indians at their fort in the upper part of the province. He was engaged in this mission until the Fall of that year, when he appeared before the Council of the province to give account of his expedition. The records of the Council's proceedings at this time give evidence that Odber's conduct of affairs had not been altogether satisfactory and his name disappears from the records for a season.

Then in February, 1662/3, Captain Odber comes again into view, this time a member of the Commission of the Peace for the "Eastern Shore." In April, 1663, August, 1663, and February, 1663/4, he is again named in the commissions for "the Eastern Shore." When the commission of May, 1664, was issued Odber's name is missing. Whether after this brief service of a year Captain Odber continued to live in the section near Manokin-Annemessex, or removed to other regions we do not know. For several years he is again lost to sight. After a period of three years, however, the archives of the Provincial Council and Assembly bring to us, under date of August 6, 1667, this tragic fact: "Captain John Odber and his servant being lately murdered by some of the Wiccomeses Indians."

Investigation on the part of the government led finally, in May, 1669, to the disclosure of the murderer of Captain Odber and his servant. The murderer proved to be one Anatchcomo, "a Wicomis Indian," who was delivered up to the authorities by one "King Ababco" of the "Ababcos Indians."

Thus was brought to a close the brief career of Captain John Odber, a commander against Maryland's Indian enemies, and one of the early commissioners for the direction of affairs in the settlement on the lower Eastern Shore which became Somerset County.[1]

Thomas Price

Though truly one of the "founders" of the Annemessex settlement on the "Eastern Shore" of Maryland, later Somerset County, we have discovered very few items of record about Thomas Price.

Thomas Price was in Northampton County, Virginia, as early as November, 1651, when he made a deposition as "aged about 27 years."[1] He was, therefore, born about the year 1624; though where, or of what parentage, we do not know.

Thomas Price was by trade a "leather dresser,"[2] and embracing Quakerism (though at what time we do not know), came from Northampton County, Virginia, to Annemessex, on the Eastern Shore of Maryland, sometime in 1662, or early in 1663. He was one of the defiant Annemessex men who resisted Colonel Scarburgh's attempt to reduce that settlement to subjection to the Virginia government in October, 1663 (see *ante,* pages 40 and 86). Thomas Price and his wife, Katherine, lived on the south side of Great Annemessex River on a 500-acre tract patented under the name of "Cheap Price." This tract of land Price and his wife sold and conveyed to William Planner by two deeds, dated January 11, 1665/6, and September 21, 1685.[3] In these deeds Price is designated as "planter." Though he may have continued to follow his trade (that of "leather dresser") after coming to Annemessex, it is evident that he was engaged in farming. There is no evidence that he ever held any office of any nature in Somerset.

It was probably at the time that Thomas Price sold the last acreage of his "Cheap Price" tract to William Planner in September, 1685, that he removed with his family to Sussex County in Delaware, where he possessed himself of lands and making his will in March, 1694/5, describes himself as "Thomas Price, Senr of Slater Neck in the county of Sussex, planter." He died between March 14 and 25, 1695.[4]

Thomas Price and Katherine (whose surname is unknown), his wife, had issue, a son, Thomas Price. He was apparently the only child (certainly the only surviving one) of his parents.

George Johnson

George Johnson was born about the year 1627.[1] He was the son of Edward Johnson and grandson of William Johnson, who lived at Canterbury in Kent, England.[2] George Johnson married (when she was twenty years old) Katherine, daughter of John and Katherine Butcher. It is a matter of record that George Johnson and Katherine Butcher were married at the Cathedral in Canterbury by the Reverend John Player, "minister and pastor of a congregation called 'Independents'," and that Mrs. Katherine Johnson was a native of Felling in Kent and had, during her childhood, lived for a time at Maidstone, Kent, with her mother, who had married, as her second husband, Peter Swan, of Maidstone. On the death of her mother, Mrs. Katherine Johnson was taken by her father's brother, Francis Butcher, to live at Garnton, parish of Adsum, Kent. This Francis Butcher, in making his will, in March, 1661, describes himself as "of the Precincts of the Cathedral, called Christ's Church, in the Citty of Canterbury," and by his will bequeathed certain property in Wickhambruex, Kent, to his niece, Katherine Butcher, who married George Johnson. After their marriage George and Katherine (Butcher) Johnson lived for a time in the parish of St. George the Martyr (in Kent?), later moving to London. Two children were born to them while they were living in the parish of St. George, viz: (1) George Johnson; (2) Katherine Johnson. The daughter, Katherine Johnson, married John Goddin, of Bogerternorton Hundred, Somerset County, Maryland, and was dead in 1696, leaving two daughters, Katherine Goddin and Margaret Goddin.

George Johnson was a merchant and went trading to the colony of Virginia and the province of Maryland, finally settling at Annemessex on the Eastern Shore of Maryland (later Somerset County), where his wife, Mrs. Katherine Johnson, joined him in the year 1663, going from England, by way of New England, to Maryland, taking with her their daughter, Katherine, but leaving their son, George, in

England, where he was later apprenticed to a watchmaker.³ George Johnson, it appears, had a brother, John Johnson, who lived at Woburne in New England, and brothers, Edward Johnson and William Johnson, both described as living in New England (though the locality is not given), and a sister, Susanna Prentice.⁴

The exact date of George Johnson's arrival in Northampton County, Virginia, is not known but there are references in the local records indicating that he was living there in January, 1660/1, and June, 1661, and he is named in the list of tithables in that county in 1662. He appears to have been still resident in Northampton County in March, 1662/3.⁵ Johnson was a merchant and it was apparently his trading venture which brought him to Northampton County, Virginia. He does not appear to have been at all conspicuous in the life of the community but quietly engaged himself in mercantile pursuits, thereby laying the foundation of the comfortable estate which was his in later years.

The item of greatest importance which we have discovered relative to George Johnson is that he was evidently associated with the religious element in England known as "Independents" (or Congregationalists). This religious bias Johnson no doubt brought with him to Virginia, where, in Northampton County, his predilection found a more or less congenial atmosphere. From this then liberal "Independency" (or Congregationalism) the step to Quakerism was not a long one. Johnson, in course of time, gave himself over completely to membership in the Society of Friends, thereby subjecting himself to the provisions of the Virginia Assembly's law against Quakers.

The exodus of Northampton-Accomack, Virginia, Quakers, and other non-conformists, and their seeking refuge at Annemessex on the lower Eastern Shore of Maryland in 1661/2 drew Johnson into its van. We do not have the exact date of his settling at Annemessex, but he was certainly established there by the Fall of the year 1663.

From his first appearance in Annemessex on the lower Eastern Shore of Maryland, George Johnson occupied a prominent place in that settlement and throughout the remainder of his life, which lengthened considerably into the history of Somerset County, we find him taking part in affairs as one of the leading citizens.

When Colonel Edmund Scarburgh made his raid upon the Manokin-Annemessex settlement in October, 1663 (see *ante,* page 40) he made of George Johnston a particular target for his scurrilously abusive descriptive powers.[6] "Ye proteus of hersey" (as Scarburgh introduces him), George Johnson was absolutely defiant in his resistance to the Scarburghian attempt to intimidate the Annemessex settlers and reduce them to subjection to a government other than that of the Lord Proprietor of Maryland. George Johnson (regardless of Scarburgh's attempt to wholly discredit his character) will ever stand as one of that valiant small group of Annemessex men whose fearless defiance of Scarburgh's pretentions secured the Manokin-Annemessex area on the lower Eastern Shore to the province of Maryland.

As "the Eastern Shore below Choptank" settlement progressed we find George Johnson taking an increasingly prominent part in local affairs. He became a member of the Commission of the Peace in August, 1665, and in the following December he was appointed by the court "to keep ye records." Thus he became clerk of the court, an office which he held until the arrival of Edmund Beauchamp in the Summer of 1666 (see *ante,* pages 59-60 and 62). When Somerset County was established, August 22, 1666, George Johnson was named as a member of the first Commission of the Peace. When the commissioners assembled to organize the first Somerset Court in September, 1666, George Johnson and James Jones (whose Quakerism we know) "desired time to consider the oath." Time was granted them until the next court, which was to be held the last Tuesday in September. We find, however, that Johnson and Jones took the oath before Governor Charles Calvert at St. Mary's City, September 11, 1666 (see *ante,* pages 68, 70 and 71). Johnson continued as a member of the Somerset Court until June, 1668, when he became High Sheriff of Somerset County (see *ante,* page 74). In 1670 Johnson again became a member of the court, continuing to serve under several commissions until 1680.

George Johnson's home in Somerset County was on the south side of the Great Annemessex River on a tract of land called "Straights," which was near the headwaters of the river, and may today be located about a mile north of the village of Kingston, Somerset County. This tract called "Straights" was sold by Johnson's granddaughter to Colonel Robert King, under whose will (in 1750) it descended to his grandson, Thomas King, becoming part of the original "Kingston Hall" estate.[7]

Notwithstanding his many and varied interests, there were two which carried through to the end and which we find ever to the fore in the life of George Johnson. Johnson came out from England to the colonies evidently on a trading adventure. He was first, last and always a merchant. So he appears time and again in the records and his merchandising was the principal source of the comfortable estate which he acquired during his lifetime. The other prominent interest of George Johnson's life was his religion. He never wavered in his loyalty to Quakerism. He indited his will "In the Name of that Light which enlightneth every Man that Cometh into ye World that was my Condem[n]er but no my savior so be itt"; while by his will, Johnson, after making bequests to his wife, his daughter, a granddaughter, several relations and friends, directed certain trustees to make disposition after her death of the residue of certain estate left his wife, by distributing the same to "such Poor friends [Quakers]" as the said trustees should select. In case of death of the trustees named before the death of the testator's wife then "ye Meeting" [i. e. the Quaker Meeting] was to have the naming of the beneficiaries under this trust.[8]

George Johnson (*circa* 1627-1681) and his wife, Katherine (Butcher) Johnson, had issue: (1) George Johnson, Junior, who became a "watch maker," in London, and died leaving an only child, Ann Johnson; (2) Katherine Johnson, married John Goddin; (3) Gershom Johnson, who was born and died in 1664; (4) Gershom Johnson, who was born and died in 1667.

Mrs. Katherine (Butcher) Johnson married, *secondly,* Thomas Evernden, a prominent Quaker who came to Annemessex to live, and who afterwards removed to Dorchester County, Maryland.

Henry Boston

We have discovered nothing about the origin of Henry Boston. Of the place and date of his birth, his parentage, and whence he came to the colony of Virginia we must plead ignorance. The first item of record which we have discovered about him is that in March, 1655/6, the Northampton County, Virginia, court ordered that "Henry Boston to have the child of Augustine Moore in his charge." Again his name appears on the records of the court in April, 1657.[1]

It is evident that Henry Boston frequented the company of religious and political rebels in Northampton County, Virginia, and got himself into serious trouble by his too "free speech." Major William Andrews testified in open court, April 30, 1660, that "this Day ye late Acts of Assembly being published hee heard Henry Boston say they were simple foolish things whereupon Major Jn° Tilney Reprimanded him & Henry Boston demanded wheither hee did it out of envy & further Saith not." Upon this testimony the court of Northampton County, on May 28, 1660, "ord^d y^t Henry Boston shall for his contempt of Authority & speaking Reproachfull words w^{en} ye Acts of Assembly were publishing bee fined two thousand pounds of tobb: & Remaine in ye Sherr^s Custody tell hee enter into bond wth Sufficient Security for his good behavior to ye Grand Assembly & all ye free people of this Country & pay Court charges."[2]

From this incident we can veritably place Henry Boston's association with the rebellious Quakers and other non-conformist elements in Northampton County; for "ye late Acts of Assembly ... published" in that county on April 30, 1660, and about which Boston was so frankly contemptious, were the Acts passed by the Assembly in March, 1660, one of which was a drastic law against Quakers (see *ante,* page 12).

In August, 1661, we discover that Henry Boston's wife was named Anne, and that they were living in Northampton County.[3]

We do not know the date of Henry Boston's leaving Northampton County, Virginia, to settle at Annemessex on the lower Eastern Shore of Maryland; however, he was established at Annemessex by the Fall of 1663. Boston appears as one of the immortal Annemessex men who, in October, 1663, offered stalwart defiance to Scarburgh's invasion.

When the Commission of the Peace for the "Eastern Shore below Choptank River" was augmented in August, 1665, to meet the needs of a rapidly increasing and expanding population, Henry Boston's name appears in the commission then issued; and he was also named as one of the members of the first court of Somerset when the county was established in August, 1666 (see *ante,* pages 59 and 68). He was again named in the Commission of the Peace for Somerset issued in March, 1675/6.

In March, 1671/2, Henry Boston became the object of the Somerset Grand Jury's indictment because of his action in a rather interesting proceeding. The record reads that on March 12, 1671 [1671/2], the grand jury presents

> "Henry Boston for entertaining of the wife of Thomas Davis and Thomas Davis for disposing of his said wife to the said Boston."

Writs of arrest were then issued against the said Boston and Davis, returnable to June court, 1672.

At a court held for Somerset County, June 11, 1672, suits in his Lordship's name were entered against Boston and Davis on their former presentments by the grand jury and the cases brought to trial. Boston

> "appears & pleades & saith that he hired her [i. e. Judith Davis] with the consent of her husband [i. e. Thomas Davis] and Craves A nonsuite. Tho: Davis, Taylor [i. e. Tailor] appeares and Saith he gave Consent to it. Whereupon the Co^{rt} ord^{rs} A Nonsuite."

Thomas Davis appearing in the suit against him in this cause made plea,

> "saying that for want of sufficiency for maintainance he gave consent that she [i. e. his wife, Judith Davis] shoulld Live at Mr Bostons & craves A Nonsuite. Whereupon the Co^{rt} orders a nonsuite."

The question involved in the indictment of Henry Boston and Thomas Davis and the legal proceedings against them was that of a man's having the right to so dispose of his wife and of the right of another to receive the wife so disposed of. On the face of it the matter looks like a simple trading in human flesh by two men. Evidently there was an illegal as well as an inhuman aspect to this Boston-Davis matter shocking to the moral sensibilities of the community and forcing the authorities to take cognizance thereof. However, the court, when the matter came to trial, accepted Boston's explanation that he had simply hired Judith, the wife of Thomas Davis and Thomas Davis' explanation that he had given consent that his wife should live at Mr. Boston's because he, Davis, was not able to support her. The court, as we have seen, cleared both Boston and Davis of their indictments. However, other records prove that Henry Boston was the father of an illegitimate child by Mrs. Judith Davis before she became the wife of Thomas Davis, the tailor. That child, one Richard Boston, was born early in 1670 while his mother, Judith Best, married Thomas Davis in November, 1670, and as Judith Davis, wife of Thomas Davis, was living at Henry Boston's in March, 1671/2, when the indictments recited above were returned by the Somerset Grand Jury.[5]

Henry Boston lived on a plantation called "Boston Town" on the South side of the Great Annemessex River. This plantation adjoined Ambrose Dixon's home place, "Dixon's Choice," and was sold, in November, 1677, by Henry Boston (son and heir of Henry Boston, deceased) to Captain Thomas Walker, and later sold by Walker to William Planner.[6]

Henry Boston died at his plantation in Annemessex on September 24, 1676.[7]

Henry Boston married, *first,* Ann (whose surname is unknown); *second,* March 19, 1673 [1673/4], Elizabeth Rogerson.[8]

Henry Boston had issue by his *first* wife, Ann, the following children: (1) Henry Boston, Junior, born August 13, 1656;[9] (2) Rebecca Boston, married _____ Millner; (3) Ann Boston.

Henry Boston had issue by his *second* wife, Elizabeth Rogerson: (4) Isaac Boston; (5) Esau Boston.

Henry Boston had issue by Judith Best, an illegitimate son: (5) Richard Boston, born 1670.

Mrs. Elizabeth (Rogerson) Boston married, *secondly,* Henry Lewis, of Anne Arundel County, Maryland.

WILLIAM COULBOURNE

William Coulbourne, evidently of an old Somersetshire, England, family,[1] was in Northampton County, Virginia, certainly as early as March 25, 1652, when he signed (with 116 other persons) the "Engagement tendered to ye Inhabitants of Northampton County," by which they promised "to be true and faithful to the Commonwealth of England as it is now Established without King or House of Lords."[2]

Coulbourne had two patents for land in Northampton County, each for 350 acres, the first granted to him March 4, 1652 [1652/3], the second on February 28, 1662 [1662/3].[3]

We have discovered no record evidence which proves that William Coulbourne ever became a Quaker; but that he manifested marked sympathy with the Quaker movement is well attested. In Northampton Court, April 12, 1661, it was recorded that

> "This day Wm Colborne & his wife came to ye Court & made acknowledgem^t of their error for entertaineing of Quakers making their Recantacon according to Order of ye Right hon^{ble} Gou^{nor} S^r Wm Berkeley denying ye Quakers & their faction and have thereunto sett their hands."

The most significant entry appears in the record by the side of this order of court:

> "This refused to bee subscribed by
> Wm. Colborne."[4]

It does not appear what Mrs. Coulbourne's action in this matter was; but Mr. Coulbourne's defiance of the court's mandate is very clear. One of his descendants is authority for the statement that William Coulbourne (together with Henry White, Thomas Leatherbury and Ambrose Dixon) was arrested and ordered sent to James City for a hearing before the Governor and Council of Virginia charged with giving succor to Quakers in disobedience to the Act of Assembly.[5] About eleven years later, when Coulbourne had become a distinguished resident of Somerset County, we have record that the celebrated George Fox, the founder of the Society of Friends, while on his visit to that county called on William Coulbourne and held a service at his house (see *ante,* page 96).

William Coulbourne certainly had not made his settlement at Annemessex on the lower Eastern Shore of Maryland in October, 1663, for he is not referred to by Colonel Scarburgh in his report of invasion of that territory in that month. But certainly between October, 1663, and January 27, 1663/4, Coulbourne, his wife, and several children, had settled in Annemessex, for a record recites that his son, Solomon Coulbourne, was born at Annemessex, January 27, 1663/4.

William Coulbourne was not long in entering the official life of the territorial unit of "the Eastern Shore below Choptank." On

March 26, 1664, he was commissioned as "Lieutenant under Captain William Thorne of the Foot Company at present and to be raised by him between Choptank River and a line drawne east into the Mayne Ocean from Watkins Point" (see *ante,* page 58). In February, 1669 [1669/70], Coulbourne was commissioned "to be Captain of a company of foot from Manokin to Pocomoke," and in October, 1673, as "captain and commander of a troop of horse to be raised from among the residents of Somerset County." In 1681 the official statement is made that "Colonel William Coulbourne, a Protestant, commands the foot [troops] raised in Somerset and Dorchester Counties." As late as December, 1688, Coulbourne was "Coll: of the foot in said county." In March, 1667/8, William Coulbourne, Stephen Horsey and William Thorne were recommended by the court of Somerset to the proprietary authority that one of them might be appointed sheriff of Somerset for the year 1668. Coulbourne failed to receive the office at this time; however, in October, 1673, and November, 1675, we find him occupying the office of High Sheriff of the county. William Coulbourne became a member of the Commission of the Peace for Somerset County in February, 1670, and continued therein until 1673. He was again a member of the Commission of the Peace from March, 1676, and continued in office until his death in 1689. In July, 1687, Colonel William Coulbourne was designated by the Lord Proprietor of the province to head a commission to draw up a treaty with the Nanticoke Indians. The commission was successful in its undertaking and the treaty was jointly signed on August 11, 1687.[7]

The above record of William Coulbourne's "official career" speaks for itself, evidencing the confidence and esteem in which he was held by the provincial authorities and the people of Somerset County. William Coulbourne was throughout his life a man of manifestly sound and high character. Not once do we find him exercising his offices in other than the most approved fashion; while there is never once the slightest intimation, in record or tradition, that he lived his life throughout its broad range of activity other than with the dignity befitting his station as a gentleman. Unhesitatingly we pronounce him to have been altogether one of "Old Somerset's" finest possessions in the way of a man.

When William Coulbourne came to the Annemessex settlement on the lower Eastern Shore he settled on the south side of the Great Annemessex River on a tract of 1,400 acres of land, located between Jones' Creek (west) and Coulbourne's Creek (east). This tract he patented in June, 1679, under the name of "Pomfret." Here he made his home throughout his life in "Old Somerset," and here, ever since his day, certain of his descendants have continued to reside on parts of the original tract.[8]

"Coll: William Coulbourne departed this life the two and twentieth day of January att Animessex anno Domini one thousand six hundred and eighty nine."[9]

William Coulbourne married, *first,* Anne (whose surname is unknown); secondly, Margaret Cooper.

William Coulbourne had issue by his *first* wife, Ann, the following children: (1) William Coulbourne (1658-17), married Anne Revell; (2) Mary Coulbourne (1661-, *ante,* 1689), unmarried; (3) Solomon Coulbourne (1663-, *ante,* 1689), unmarried; (4) Ann Coulbourne (born 1665), married John Taylor; (5) Robert Coulbourne, married Rebecca Revell.

William Coulbourne had issue by his *second* wife, Margaret Cooper, a daughter: (6) Penelope Coulbourne, who married Michael Holland.

WILLIAM BOSMAN

William Bosman appears in Northampton County, Virginia, as early as 1649, when his name appears as a headright to a patent for land granted to Ralph Barlowe in that year.[1] He apparently continued his residence in Northampton until sometime in 1663, when we find him at Manokin on the Eastern Shore of Maryland. William Bosman was one of the men named by the court of Accomack County, Virginia, to "call together and command" the settlers between Manokin and Pocomoke River for defensive measures in November, 1663 (see *ante,* pages 43-44). In May, 1664, Bosman (with Stephen Horsey and William Thorne) was named by the Maryland authorities on the commission for granting land warrants and administering justice in the "Eastern Shore below Choptank River" (see *ante,* page 58).[2]

William Bosman's home was on the tract of land patented under the name of "More and Case It"; located on the north side of the Manokin River immediately east of Goose Creek. He died between August 5, 1664, which was the date of his will, and December 11, 1665, at which date a guardian was chosen by "John Bossman, aged fifteene years, sonne to William Bossman deceased."

William Bosman married, *first,* Bridget (whose surname is unknown), who died July, 1660. William Bosman married, *second,* February 15, 1661/2, Eleanor Maddox, widow of Alexander Maddox, of Northampton County.

William and Bridget Bosman had issue: (1) John Bosman (1650-1716), married Blandina Risdon; (2) Bridget Bosman, married George Betts; (3) William Bosman; (4) Anne Bosman, married George Downes; (5) George Bosman; (6) Katherine Bosman, marred, *first,* John Nelson; *second,* John Lawes; (7) Mary Bosman.

It may be that Mary was a child of William Bosman by his second wife, Mrs. Eleanor Maddox.

William Stevens

William Stevens was not among the very earliest settlers on the lower Eastern Shore of Maryland. He did not arrive until late in 1664 or early in 1665. From his first appearance we find him taking an active part in the affairs of the settlement, while the exercise of his abilities through the twenty-two years of his residence at "Rehoboth" on the Pocomoke River won for him the unquestioned honor of "first citizen of Somerset."

William Stevens was born in the year 1630 in Buckinghamshire, England. He was the son of "John Stevens, of Llebourne in ye Parish of Mealemore of ye county of Buckingham in England."[1] It is not improbable that William Stevens lived for at least a brief period in Northampton County, Virginia, before finally settling on the lower Eastern Shore of Maryland.[2] William Stevens first appears in the records for "the Eastern Shore below Choptank," August 25, 1665, when he was named in the Commission of the Peace issued on that date. His name appears again in the Commission of the Peace issued February 23, 1665/6 (see *ante,* page 59). When Somerset County was established, August 22, 1666, we find that Stevens was named in the first Commission of the Peace for Somerset and designated as one of the three "judges" of the court (see *ante,* pages 67-68). The office of a judge (and frequently presiding judge) he continued to occupy until his death in 1687—a period of twenty-two years. Stevens was elected, and returned, as the first representative from Somerset County, to the Lower House of the General Assembly of Maryland, which was convened April 13, 1669. This was the first Assembly which met after the establishment of Somerset County in August, 1666 (see *ante,* page 77). He was again elected a member from Somerset to the Lower House of the General Assembly which met October 20, 1678,[3] and on October 7, 1679, he took the oath as a member "of his Lordshipps privy Councill." The office of a member of Lord Baltimore's Council for Maryland Stevens continued to hold through the remainder of his life. "When Charles, Lord Baltimore left for England in 1684 to defend his charter before the Privy Council, he made his son, Benedict Leonard Calvert, governor of the province. Since, however, Benedict Leonard was a minor, the Proprietary appointed a board of Deputy Governors."[5] William Stevens was named as one of these Deputy Governors, or Deputy Lieutenants, as the members of this board were called.[6] Not only was William Stevens called into the high service of the civil offices above referred to but we find him with the rank of colonel, commanding the cavalry force of Somerset and Dorchester Counties.[7]

Besides his various civil and military activities, William Stevens engaged in large real estate and merchandising ventures, through which he built up a handsome fortune. By patent and purchase he obtained thousands of acres of land in Somerset County, disposing by sale of large quantities thereof, unquestionably thereby increasing his wealth. To all appearances he was a wise investor. Facetiously he has been called "the Land Office of the Eastern Shore.[8] That he engaged in merchandising, another profitable source of income (in his time) is evidenced by his designation as "merchant" in the records of Somerset.[9]

But above all of his activities we place William Stevens' interest in the religious life of his times. That he was "born and bred" a member of the Church of England there can be no doubt; nor can there be any doubt that he continued to be a "Churchman," certainly up to May, 1682, when he signed a defence of the policies of the Roman Catholic Lord Proprietor of Maryland, subscribing himself (with others) as *"professing the gospell of Jesus Christ, according to the Litturgy of the Church of England* and Protestants against the Doctrine and Practice of the Church of Rome . . ." (see *ante,* page 135). We believe that Stevens also died in the faith of the Church of England. That Stevens, in 1680, petitioned the Presbytery of Laggan, in the north of Ireland, to send a "godly minister" of Presbyterian faith and order to Somerset County (see *ante,* page 215) has led to a belief in some quarters that he had become a Presbyterian. It is well to note that Stevens' appeal to the Presbytery of Lagga nwas made late in 1680, while in May, 1682, he could subscribe himself as "professing the gospell of Jesus Christ *according to the Litturgy of the Church of England."*

The truth about William Stevens, in relation to matters religious, is that he was liberal and tolerant in the best sense of those terms. The name—"Rehoboth"—which he gave to his home, which he established on the Pocomoke River at his immigration into Maryland in 1664 or 5, is significant of Stevens' liberal attitude towards the various expressions of religious belief. Stevens, a Church of England man, encouraged the "county evangelistic" preaching of Robert Maddox, (whose denominatial connection we do not know), in 1671/2 by establishing one of the four preaching stations at his home. His friendship with the Quakers in the settlement is evident. Though there is no direct evidence to that effect; yet we cannot be wrong in ascribing to Stevens at least a respectful interest in George Fox, the Apostle of Quakerism, during that great man's Somerset itinerary in 1672. Then we have evidence of the exercise of his influence in establishing Presbyterianism in Somerset. It was as the result of his appeal to the Presbytery of Laggan, in 1680, that the Reverend Francis Makemie was sent to Somerset County about 1683. Last, but not least, we have the evidence of William Stevens' friendship with, and loyalty to, the Roman Catholic Proprietor of the province of Maryland. Have we in William Stevens only a man of profound shrewdness, and of ability to "put over" an attitude of "all things to all men," that he himself might profit thereby? Frankly, this has been intimated of Stevens by a disciple of today's so-called "realistic school" of historians. From such an estimate of the man's character we strongly dissent. Having thought upon the things which our study of the man through the wide range of his varied activities has disclosed, we acclaim him a true and great liberal, the choicest product of the spirit of his times in Maryland. Even further than this we acclaim him one of the choicest spirits of American colonial life. As jurist, statesman, community builder, Christian gentleman, William Stevens, of "Rehoboth," in Somerset, ranks with the ablest men who laid the very foundations of this nation.

William Stevens married Elizabeth (whose surname was probably Keyser); but left no issue. He died at his home, "Rehoboth," December 23rd, and his body was there buried on December 26, 1687. The record of the passing of this truly great man has been preserved for us in the ancient register of such happenings in Somerset County, and by the simple slab above his grave:

> "Coll° William Stevens Esq one of his Lopp^s L^{ts} deputies for Maryland died and was buried at his owne plantation Called rehoboth 26th December one Thousand Six hundred eighty & Seaven."[10]

On the "Rehoboth" plantation, beside the wonderfully beautiful and graceful Pocomoke River, there remains to this day the tomb of William Stevens with this inscription:

> "Here lyeth the body of William Stevens Esqr who departed this Life the 23 of December 1687 Aged 57 years, he was 22 years Judge of this County Court one of his Lordships Councill, and one of ye Deputy Lieutenants of this Province of Maryland. Vivit Post Funera Virtus."[11]

Mrs. Elizabeth (Keyser?) Stevens (widow of William Stevens) married, *secondly,* Colonel George Layfield, of Somerset County.

JAMES JONES

James Jones, evidently a native of Monmouthshire, Wales, appeared in Northampton County, Virginia, as early as May, 1660, where he came into conflict with authorities because of conduct strongly savoring of Quakerism.[1] From Northampton County he removed, about 1663 or 4, to the settlement on the lower Eastern Shore of Maryland and settled on a plantation called "Jones Hole" on the west side of the Wicomico River. He became a member of the Commission of the Peace for the Eastern Shore, August, 1665, and was named as one of the first magistrates for Somerset County in the commission of August 22, 1666. He, with George Johnson, requested "time to consider the oath" of office before qualifying, evidently owing to Quaker scruples about taking oaths. These "scruples" were, however, overcome, for we find record that Jones (together with Johnson) took the oath, September 11, 1666, before Governor Calvert at St. Mary's City. James Jones continued to hold office as a magistrate from August, 1665, until his death in 1677, at the same time faithfully abiding in Quakerism (see *ante,* pages 71 and 94).

James Jones acquired a considerable estate in lands in Somerset County which, with his personalty, he devised at his death in 1677 to his wife, Sarah Jones, and "to my cousin Andrew Jones."[2] It does not appear that James Jones left any children. The major portion of James Jones' estate finally passed into the possession of his "cousin, Andrew Jones." It is not improbable that Andrew Jones, designated as "cousin," was in reality a nephew of James Jones. The term "cousin," as used in colonial times, usually signified nephews and nieces. This Andrew Jones came to Somerset County, Maryland, and dying there in 1684, his estate was administered by Thomas Brereton in May, 1686. Andrew Jones married, January 13, 1680/1, Elizabeth Winder. Mrs. Elizabeth (Winder) Jones married, secondly, Thomas Brereton. Andrew and Elizabeth (Winder) Jones left no issue. It appears that in October, 1686, Thomas Jones, the elder, of the Parish of Trevethin, in county Monmouth [Wales], Gentleman, Howell Jones, Gentleman, his only then living son, gave power of attorney to Stephen Luffe and Reverend John Huett, of Somerset County, Maryland, to sell the plantations which were formerly the property of Andrew Jones, late of Wickacomoco River, Somerset County, Gentleman, deceased, except the right therein of the wife of said Andrew Jones, who is now the wife of Thomas Brewerton [Brereton]. It further appears that Andrew Jones, of Somerset County, was a brother of the above mentioned Howell Jones and a son of Thomas Jones, the elder, of the parish of Trevethin, county Monmouth, Wales. It is not improbable that James Jones was a brother of this Thomas Jones, the elder, and hence uncle to Andrew Jones, whom he made his heir.[3]

John White

No evidence has so far been discovered which gives clue to the "origin" of John White, who figured so prominently in the life of "Old Somerset." Neither have we been able to "place" him as having come into the Eastern Shore of Maryland settlement from Northampton-Accomack County in Virginia.

John White apparently did not come to the Eastern Shore of Maryland settlement until about 1664, or 1665, associating himself from the first with the Pocomoke River section. He is first mentioned as a member of the Commission of the Peace for the "Eastern Shore" on August 25, 1665; appearing again in the commission of February 23, 1665/6 (see *ante,* page 59). He is also named as a member of the first court for Somerset County, commissioned August 22, 1666 (see *ante,* page 67). Though thus commissioned White does not appear to have qualified by taking the usual oath of office and there is no record of his having sat as a member of the courts held between September, 1666, and October, 1668. John White's name appears in successive commissions to the court, February 9, 1669/70, February 22, 1672/3, March 2, 1675/6, June 6, 1676.[1] On February 9, 1669 [1669/70], John White was commissioned captain of a company of horse for the whole of Somerset County,[2] and was a representative from Somerset in the Lower House of the Maryland Assembly, October-November, 1678. In 1681 John White appears to have been Sheriff of Somerset County.[3] "John White of Pocomoke, Gent. died and was buried the 3ᵈ day of June 1685 at the plantation of Collº William Stevens, called Rehoboth."[4]

John White, as appears from his will, was possessed of a large landed estate (beside a comfortable personal estate) and lived on a plantation called "Cordicall," near the Pocomoke River, and in the neighborhood of "Rehoboth," in Somerset County. John White and Sarah Keyser were married by Mr. Robert Maddox, Clerk, June 27, 1672.[5] Sarah Keyser appears to have arrived in the province of Maryland in 1671.[6] Mrs. Sarah (Keyser) White was evidently a sister of Madam Elizabeth Stevens, wife of Colonel Williams Stevens, of "Rehoboth." Mrs. Sarah (Keyser) White married, *secondly,* Lawrence Crawford.

John and Sarah (Keyser) White had issue: (1) William White (1673-1708), married Catherine Powell; (2) Elizabeth White, married Francis Thorowgood; (3) Tabitha White, married, *first*, Lawrence Riley; *second*, Robert Hill; (4) Priscilla White, married, *first*, George Layfield; *second*, John Watts; (5) Stevens White (1679-1718), married Katherine Fassitt; (6) Sarah White, married, *first*, William Massey; *second*, Francis Hamlin; (7) Frances White (1682-1683); (8) John White.

John Winder

John Winder came to the Manokin section of the "Eastern Shore" settlement from Nansamond County, Virginia, in the year 1665. He was living in Nansamond County as late as Decemmber, 1664, and received a patent for a tract of land called "Winder's Purchase" on Back Creek of Manokin River on the Eastern Shore in Maryland, July 10, 1665.[1] Winder evidently lived in the Manokin section from his first appearance in 1665 until about 1670, when he moved to the Wicomico section and settled on a plantation on the south side of Wicomico River and north side of Cuttymocktico Creek.[2] This plantation on the Wicomico River continued to be Winder's home through the remainder of his life.

John Winder appears in the Commissions of the Peace for the "Eastern Shore," August, 1665, and February, 1665/6; and was also named in the first Commission of the Peace for Somerset County, August 22, 1666 (see *ante*, pages 59 and 67). He continued a member of the court of Somerset County for some years. John Winder not only served with distinction in a magisterial capacity; but we find him occupying, at different times, offices in the local military establishment of Somerset County. In 1678 he was a sergeant in an expedition against the Nanticoke Indians. In 1680 he appears as a lieutenant in the militia, and in 1682 as a captain. In 1689 he was named as "captaine of a troop of horse." The "treaty meeting" between Colonel William Stevens (representing the Maryland government) and the Great Men of the Nanticoke Indians, in 1687, was held at the house of Captain John Winder on the Wicomico River. In conveyances made in 1697 Winder is styled "lieutenant-colonel." John Winder died in September, 1698.[3]

John Winder married Bridget (surname unknown) and had issue: (1) Susan Winder (1664-1674); (2) Thomas Winder (1666-

1705), of Northumberland County, Virginia; (3) Elizabeth Winder, married Joseph Venables; (4) Miriam Winder, married Simon Perkins; (5) John Winder (1676-1716), of Somerset County, married Jane Dashiell; (6) William Winder (1679-1710) of Northumberland County, Virginia.

Edmund Beauchamp

Edmund Beauchamp was evidently sent to the "Eastern Shore" by Governor Charles Calvert in the spring of the year 1666 as a person whom he considered well qualified to exercise the office of clerk to the court there. This local court "entertayned" the gentleman on this high recommendation with hope that he would carefully discharge the duties of so responsible an office (see *ante,* pages 62-63).

Beauchamp occupied the office of clerk of court of the "Eastern Shore" from June, 1666, until August 22 following, when he was named and commissioned, first, "clark & Keeper of the records of proceedings" of the court of Somerset County, which was established by proclamation, August 22, 1666. Anyone who has had occasion to make careful study and investigation of the records of Somerset Court from its beginning throughout Beauchamp's years of service as clerk will fully realize the care and thought which this early worthy bestowed upon the duties of his office. A more splendidly kept set of records of court proceedings and deeds cannot, we believe, be found elsewhere during the early colonial period. He was a veritable master of his craft.

From his appointment as clerk of Somerset in August, 1666, Beauchamp continued to serve in this office, with the exception of a few months, or perhaps a year, until his death in 1691; a period of practically a quarter of a century.[1]

On June 11, 1668, Edmund Beauchamp married Sarah, daughter of Ambrose and Mary Dixon, of Annemessex, and on June 30, 1668, purchased (from Edmund Dickeson) 300 acres of land called "Contention" lying at the head of the Great Annemessex River. In October, 1669, conveyed this land to his wife, "Sarah Beauchamp, alias Dixon, daughter of Ambrose and Mary Dixon," as a "joynture to her and her heirs forever."[2] It was here on this tract called "Contention" that the Beauchamps made their home.

On January 15, 1689/90, Edmund Beauchamp, clerk of the court, "being very lame," petitioned the court that it was a very great inconvenience to him that the records were kept at Captain Coulbourne's, being at such a distance from his assistant's, John West's, and requested that the records be removed to Mr. West's house. This petition was "denied" at the time it was presented, but on reconsideration two days later (January 17th) it was granted. A further order of court recites that Edmund Beauchamp, owing "to his age and defitiency," was allowed by the General Assembly of the province to choose an assistant, or deputy clerk, and this he did on November 5, 1689, appointing John West, who was approved by the court and was sworn as deputy clerk, and Edmund Beauchamp having died September 26, 1691, the court on September 29, 1691, named John West clerk of the county.[3]

Edmund Beauchamp, in making his will (dated April 10, 1691; probated 12th 9ber 1691), describes himself as "Edmund Beauchamp, Mercer, of London, and at the writing hereof County Clerke of Somerset in the Province of Maryland."[4] This item furnished the clue to Beauchamp's ancestry. Research in English record publications shows Edmund Beauchamp to have been a son of John Beauchamp, of London, Merchant, and his wife, Alicia, daughter of Edmund Freeman, of Pulberry, Sussex; and grandson of Thomas Beauchamp, of Cosgrave, Northamptonshire, and his wife, Dorothy, daughter of Edward Clarke, of Rode, Northamptonshire.[5]

Edmund and Sarah (Dixon) Beauchamp left issue: (1) Thomas Beauchamp; (2) Alice Beauchamp; (3) Edmund Beauchamp; (4) John Beauchamp; (5) Dogett Beauchamp; (6) Edward Beauchamp; (7) Robert Beauchamp.

VIII

SOMERSET IN THE
PROTESTANT REVOLUTION AND THE
ROYAL PROVINCE

With notes on David Brown, Robert King, Francis Jenckins, George Layfield, William Whittington, William Brereton.

RADICAL changes marked the government of Maryland between the years 1689 and 1692. Certain elements in the province which for sometime had manifested opposition to the proprietary regime of the Calverts finally marshaled the strength necessary to deprive Charles, 3d Lord Baltimore, of all authority in the government of his province.[1] Economic conditions in the province were certainly causing distress; there was also an uneasiness among the settlers about the Indian situation; while a powerful element in the population made much of what they deemed objectionable features in his Lordship's method of appointing officials. These so-called "administrative defects" were shaped by clever minds into a powerful weapon for the hand of the Protestant opposition to the Roman Catholic proprietor; a weapon by means of which that opposition was enabled to completely sever the governmental bond. The leaders of the opposition to Lord Baltimore in Maryland were Protestants of strongly anti-Roman Catholic spirit, and they did not hesitate to inject into their movement the serum of religious bias, thereby inflaming the spirit of political and economic discontent, raising it to the fever height of open rebellion. This successful provincial revolution was in spirit (on the religious side) an extension of the Revolution in England in 1689, and has been not unfittingly called "The Protestant Revolution in Maryland."

Though interesting in its every detail, it would be outside our purpose to enter on a general discussion of the matter. We are concerned here only with Somerset County's specific part therein.[2]

Somerset County cannot be accused of any bias in favor of Charles, Lord Baltimore's Roman Catholic religious affiliation. Ultra-Protestant in the spirit of her founding, settlement, and throughout her population (which was composed of Quakers, Presbyterians and manifest evangelical Church of England men), yet Somerset owed her very existence to the fact that liberty of conscience in matters of religion was the tradition and law of the Roman Catholic proprietors' province of Maryland. Somerset's Protestant admixture would not have been peaceably countenanced elsewhere in colonial America at the time of which we are writing.

Only a few years before "The Protestant Revolution" Somerset seems to have had no complaint against Charles, Lord Baltimore, and (as a political unit) certainly did not countenance the factional charges brought against him by a prominent Protestant element in the province. We recall that William Stevens, of "Rehoboth" (markedly liberal in matters religious), who was at the time a member of his Lordship's Council of State; and James Dashiell, Roger Woolford and Henry Smith, elected by the people to serve as the county's representatives in the Lower House of Assembly, (all of them Protestants and members of the Church of England), signed, in May, 1682, a defence of Lord Baltimore against certain partisan charges that he had favored the Roman Catholic religion and in appointment to office had favored men of that faith (see *ante,* pp. 134-5).[3] What development in opposition to Charles, Lord Baltimore, occurred in Somerset County between 1682, when certainly the county's "representatives" defended him, and the final outbreak in 1689 which was successful in his overthrow, in which Somerset County figured conspicuously, we have not been able to trace in remaining records.

The troublous years moved on, every one of them strengthening the opposition to Lord Baltimore's policies. Wise heads attempted to exercise wisdom in the necessary adjustment of affairs but "other men of other minds" offset such measures by inflammatory propaganda.

"In April, 1689," writes Scharff in his *History of Maryland* (Volume I, p. 309), "An Association in arms for the defence of the Protestant religion and for asserting the right of King William and Queen Mary to the province of Maryland and all the English dominions, was formed, at the head of which was placed John Coode . . ."[4]

In July, 1689, the "Associators" seized the government, taking posession of all records. An address of loyalty was sent to the new sovereign in England, and in the name of that sovereign, Coode called an Assembly, to consist of four delegates from each county, to convene at St. Mary's City, August 22, 1689.[5] A paper sent to the sheriffs of the respective counties directed the continuation of all officers save those who were "Paptists" and such as had declared against King William and Queen Mary.

When the "Assembly" convened on the appointed day all of the counties, save Anne Arundel and Somerset, were represented; with two of the members of the Cecil County delegation also reported absent. Anne Arundel County, it appears on good authority, "would not choose Burgesses at Coode's command."[6] But Somerset, though for once not on time, came sailing "over the Bay" in the persons of Francis Jenckins and his associates (whose names we have not discovered) and into port on the last day of the session (in September, 1689). In a letter to Lord Baltimore, drastically describing the Associators' Assembly of August-September, 1689, written by his warm friend and supporter, Peter Sayer, sheriff of Talbot County, we find this quaint reference to the Somerset County delegations' delayed arrival: "Somerset came over the last day and excused their delay, saying, they heard all things were done in your Lordship's name, but indeed they intended to own no other power but their Majesties, which excuse was readily accepted neminine contradicente. Little Jenkins was chief whom your Lordship may remember, and I hope will."[7] Thus the Somerset County delegation with Francis Jenckins—("Little Jenkins"—we can but wonder why Sayer so contemptuously described him!)—as its leading member responded to the "Associators'" summons. The Calvert regime was now anathema in Somerset, and all hats were in the air to their Protestant Majesties! According to "summons" there must have been four delegates from Somerset to the Associators' Assembly of August-September, 1689. "Little Jenkins was chief"; but the records do not disclose the names of the other three.

This Assembly passed, on September 4th, just before its adjournment, an "ordinance for regulating of Offices Military and Civill and other necessary affairs for the present settlement of this province ..." which was to remain in force "till their Majesties further pleasure be made known." In each of the counties men well affected toward the new government, and who would take the oath of allegiance to King William and Queen Mary (instead of to the Lord Proprietor), were appointed to office. On September 10th William and Mary, and the Protestant succession to the throne of England, were proclaimed with great demonstration in Maryland.⁸

In the "ordinance" of regulation (above referred to) we have preserved to us the names of the men whose loyalty to the Associators' Government, and to the King and Queen, warranted their appointment to offices in Somerset County:

> "1689 ... *For the regulating of the Affairs in the Militia in Somersett County:* Mr. William Coulbourne, Col: of foote; Mr David Brown, Capᵗ of a Company of foote; Mr Charles Ratcliffe, Capᵗ of a Company of foote in the roome of Capt Osborne deceased; Mr Robert King, capt. of a Company of foote in the roome of Capt Smith; Mr. John Winder, Capt: of a troope of horse.
>
> ... *That for Regulating Affairs Civill in Somersett County:* Collº. William Coulbourne, Capt: David Brown, Mr Francis Jenkins, Capt: John Winder, Mr William Brewerton [Brereton], and Mr Robert King, justices of the Quorum; Mr James Dasheete [Dashiell], Mr Roger Woolfred [Woolford], Mr Thomas Newball [Newbold], Mr James Round, Mr Samuel Hopkins, Mr Edmund Howard, Mr Stephen Luffe and Mr Thomas Jones, justices.
>
> Capt: David Brown, Mr William Brewerton [Brereton], Mr James Round, Mr Edwᵈ [Edmund] Howard, Coroners, and Mr. Edmund Beauchamp, Clarke."⁹

In the appointments for the province made by this Assembly of August-September, 1689, we find that "Mr Robert King" was named as Naval Officer for Somerset County.¹⁰

The last court for Somerset County *"held for the Rᵗ honᵇˡᵉ Charles Absolute Lord and propᵉʳʸ of the Province of Maryland"* sat June 11, to 13, 1689, on which last date the court adjourned to "August next." On September 24th, following, the court was assembled as *"a Meeting of their Majesties Justices of the Peace."* Present: Colonel William Coulbourne, Captain David Brown, Mr. Francis Jenckins, Captain John Winder, Mr. William Brereton, Captain Robert King, Mr. James Round, Mr. Samuel Hopkins, Mr. Stephen Lufte, Mr. Thomas Jones. The usual business was transacted, concluding with the order that the sheriff summon every justice of the peace *"to meet on 2 Tuesday in Nov[r] next at the Court house there to sitt in Court on their Majesties service."* It appears from the records that Captain William Whittington was high sheriff of Somerset in September, 1689; an office to which he had been previously commissioned by Lord Baltimore, and in which he was continued by the Associators' government.[11]

Students and lovers of Maryland's colonial history cherish the story of the indomitable resistance offered by Michael Taney, the Protestant, who was high sheriff of Calvert County, to the Associators' Government in September, 1689. Taney, though evidently not opposed to the establishment of the Protestant succession to the English throne, nor to the sovereign power, of William and Mary, was not in the least satisfied with the authority assumed by the Associators in the government of the province. For his defiance of their mandates he was arrested and brought before their Assembly. Declaring his loyalty to "their Majestyes in England" he absolutely refused to disown Lord Baltimore's authority, by which he held his commission as sheriff, "until their Majestys pleasure should be otherwise lawfully made knowne."

The thrilling story of Taney's defiance of the Associators' Government is well known.[12] But we find no reference made by historians to the refusal of William Whittington, the Protestant, and high sheriff of Somerset, to deny Lord Baltimore's authority (by which he, like Taney, held his commission) and to summon the court of Somerset County in the name of the Associators' Government. The sheriff of Somerset, like the sheriff of Calvert, wished a more valid assurance than he had received that their Majesties in England had deprived Lord Baltimore of his governing power in Maryland and had duly constituted the Provisional Government of the Associators. Whittington, of Somerset, and Taney, of Calvert, Protestants— Church of England men—were of the same mind in regard to the Associators' Government. There are Protestants who are not reeds shaken by the winds of religious prejudice. Such men were Whittington and Taney, and both of them were staunch in their loyalty to the authority under which they held their commissions. Taney, arrested for his defiance and carried before the Assembly, fared unpleasantly. Why Whittington, of Somerset, was not seized by the provisional authority is not revealed, though his views and his open expression of them were well known at the seat of government in St. Mary's. John Coode, "the commander in chief," satisfied himself with a written reproof of Somerset Court for not having called the high sheriff to account for his behavior, and a warning to that august body regarding its responsibility in the matter.

The records of Somerset Court lay bare the whole of the proceedings in regard to Whittington. The letters of John Coode, "the chief commander," and of Kenelm Cheseldyne (Coode's right bower in his game of governing the province); the action taken by Somerset Court in regard to Whittington's defiance and Whittington's reply to the court's demand, are given in full in the local records. They are far too interesting and important not to be allowed to speak for themselves.[18]

[*John Goode to the authorities of Somerset County*]
October 8th 1689.

Gentlemen I have recd Severall letters from yo: County of some Considerable obstructions of ye civill government Constituted by the late Convention of the Assemblye under King William occasioned principally I understand by Mr Whittington. I know not what pretence he has for soe great a fayline and neglect of his duty wch I understand he has a sufficient notice of upon sight of the late ordinance if his maiesties Interest Suffers here by his meanes or yor Neglect by not takeing notice of itt all men know who will be accountable yors I doe assure you is the only County yt hath been soe prejudiciall toward a generall settlement if Whittington refuses after fair summons from the Court you must put in one of the Coronrs you shall Judge most convenient as the Lawes requires in such Cases if the sd Whittington or any other act or say anything against the Publique Peace or any way in derogation of the King's Authority or Interest you know what to doe according to their respective misdemeanors; wee are all here unanimously resolved to keep the Countrye in the present settlement till order from his Majestye wch wee are very sure according to our repeated Peticons will be for a *protestant* government under which alone wee recon ourselves only safe and to noe other will wee submitt faithfully beleevings his Maiesties reiterated Declarations of his great zeale for the Protestant Interest with his royall undertakings have made good I am glad to understand his Maiesties particular service as to or prsent defence is not neglected with you In order to which have sent for Captn Browne what powder and shott can possible spare Wee are all here very confident that the idle vaine discourses of some Lost & undone Men will not Slaken yor Loyaltye upon which supposicon thinke needless to add but that I am gentlem yor most faythfull servant

JNO COODE

if none of the Coron^rs be fitt or shall refuse the Service Capt^a Smith or some other must be constituted   J^no Coode

 Superscription of the aforesaid Letter vizt
To Coll^o Wm Coleburne and other his Maiesties
officers Military & Civill in Somersett County
for the Kings Service p^rsent.

[Kenelm Cheseldyne to Somerset Court]

 Gentlemen Yo^rs by Capt^a. Browne I have perused and wonder that both Civill & Military officers of yor County being armed with soe ample authority (by the Ordinance of Assembly) to suppress all disloyall practices against their Maiesties you have so long neglected the Calling to account Capt^a. Whittington whose practices of y^t nature are here [i. e. at St. Mary's] too frequently discoursed of to the ill example of others as you have hitherto beene very Loyall soe hope you will still continue the wch you cannot better manifest then by giveing a speedy check to his disloyall practices & removing him from his office & placing one more Loyall in his roome which if the Commissione^rs Soe approve of I cannot advise to a better then Cap^ta Smith understanding ye Cheefe Military officer here [i. e. John Coode] hath writt at Large to you Shall ad noe further but that I am Gentlemen

       Yo^r Humble Servant
         Kenelm Cheseldyn

October ye 18th 1689.

 Superscription of the aforesaid Letter vizt.
To the Worshipfull the Commission^rs of
Somersett County These present.

[An order of Court]

 Somerset County in Maryland this 29th day of October 1689 Capt^a Wm Whittington This day was a meeting of his Maties Justices of the Peace wherein they have consulted this County's concerns and finding you are the onely person y^t. impeads there proceedings Therefore these are in theire Maties Name to will & require you to Meete theire Maties Justices of the Peace at Mr Andrew Whittington's upon Tuesday next p^rcisely at ten of y^e Clock forenoon then & there to give yor reason for yor. Delinquency.

 Signed by order of his Maties Justices of ye Peace by me Edm Beauchamp Cl'ke Cur. P^r[e]sent: Coll^o Colebourne, Capt^a David Brown, Mr Francis Jenckins, Mr Robt King, Mr Edmund Howard, Mr Stephen Luste [Lufte],

Ordered y\[t] the Comm\[rs] meet at the house of Andrew Whittington the 5 day sennight [5th. November 1689].

To Mr Edmund Howard, or Mr James Round, Coroners; returne made by Mr Edmund Howard, Coron\[r] vizt.
Somersett County
In Maryland Ss
November ye first 1689

By vertue of ye within written Capt\[a] Wm Whittington high sheriffe of this County was Summoned to make his appearance at the time & place within mentioned

P\[r]mee EDMUND HOWARD, *Coroner.*

[*William Whittington to Somerset Court*]

Gent: I have a summons from A Suprem\[e] Authority so y\[t] I might have all this Province I cannot attend although at this time I have small intermission to write this but so Confused through the major part of the last nights misery & want of rest it is a great doubt whether there may be any sence &c Yet so far am Capable to answ\[r] what i laid to my Charge thus in brevity So soone as I came from Proclaiming theire Ma\[ties] &c I was by good Informacon toulld their Maj\[ties] had Sent a A Packett to this Province wherein I Concluded So much of their Royall pleasure was much known as wee might know how ye Governm\[t] shoulld continue The Contents whereof wee have not bin thought worthy to know but if any thing had beene Contained that might have Tantamounted to the subversion of y\[t] authority formerly noe doubt but it had bin published w\[ch] if to the contrary I Cannot see well how I can bee discharged from the trust formerly imposed more Especially if y\[t] Clause inserted in ye late ordinance in y\[t] part relating to ye Continuance of the officers bee Considered nither was it ever known That A Sheriff Coulld serve without takinge the usuall oath ye law provides soe y\[t] to be conclude Since their most gracious Ma\[ties] hath not dissented to the late governmt under ye Lord Baltimore (by any wayes as wee Can understand) they assented for (coulld I doubt w\[th] safety) I had rather Secure the precepts bearing the Stile Royall then any other w\[ch] I think in Conscience I cannot doe without an Authority Springing from him the head fountaine of all Lawes &c I mean the King but notwithstanding if you make not me ye Butt to arrive (?) at such measures might be taken as might bring & hold up Creditt to all Authority by causing my Sub Sheriff to Summon the Co\[rt] to Swear &c and so adjourn which hath done upon trivialler [trivialer?] occasion & I may God saying Amen be capable by health to officiate &c before ye time wee may expect Certaine informacon but if this [is?] unsavory in Gods name take yo\[r] Methods which can in no wis p\[r][e]iudice yo\[r] Servant

W\[M] WHITTINGTON

9^{br} y^e [___1689?]

>Superscripcon of the aforesaid Letter vizt
>To his Maties Justices of the Peace of
>Somerset County to be left with Mr Andrew Whittington.

>[*Final action of Somerset Court in regard to William Whittington, High Sheriff*]

>At a meeting of their Majesties justices of the peace for Somerset County, at Mr Andrew Whittington's, in the first year of King William and Queen Mary, November 5th. 1689; The names of the justices of the peace then sworn Colonel William Coulbourne, Captain David Brown, Mr Francis Jenckins, Captain John Winder, Captain Robert King, Mr James Dashields [Dashiell], Mr James Round, Mr Samuel Hopkins, Mr Edmund Howard, Mr Stephen Lufte, Mr Thomas Jones.—"Mr Roger Woolford not sworne, but craved time for consideration. Mr Thomas Newbold did not appeare." At this court the following order was entered:

>>"And whereas Mr William Whittington having been delinquent in Officiating his office of high sheriffe of this county; Therefore the above said Justices have appointed Mr William Brereton high Sheriffe in his stead and place," and thereupon William Brereton took oath of office.

These letters and orders, long buried in an ancient court record book of Somerset County, bring to light a very interesting page in Somerset's history. William Whittington was one of the most distinguished of Somerset's worthies of all times; while the offices held by him, both under the Proprietary and Royal Governments, make up a roll of honorable achievement: magistrate, high sheriff, collector of tobacco export tax in Somerset for Lord Baltimore, assemblyman, treasurer of the Eastern Shore, militia officer and finally a member of the Council of State. Whittington, Protestant though he truly was, (a Church of England man), seems to have been strongly pro-Lord Baltimore and anti-"Associator," and though he apparently worked well in harness with the Royal Government of William and Mary, there is from the pen of a contemporary the cristalization of the opinion of his time: *"Major William Whittington [was] always accounted a Jacobite."* Persistent in his opposition to the Associators' Government there was nothing left for Somerset Court to do but remove him from office. So it was that William Whittington was relieved of his duties as high sheriff of the county, and William Brereton appointed his successor.*

William Brereton was named to the office of high sheriff of Somerset by the county court sitting November 5, 1689, while the court of November 12th and 13th ordered that when a certain address of loyalty (which is to be discussed later) should be "sent over the Bay [i. e. to St. Mary's City] that it should be certified that the Court had appointed and made Mr William Brereton high Sheriffe of the county instead and place of Capt William Whittington."[14] Brereton's appointment was confirmed by the chief authority in the province and he gave bond as high sheriff in Somerset Court June 10, 1690, with John King and John West, his sureties.[15] Brereton barely completed a year in office, for we find that he died between September 4 (the dating to his will) and November 11, 1690 (the date of the probate thereof). Stephen Lufte succeeded Brereton as high sheriff, appearing to have continued in that office from the Fall of 1690 to 1692 or 3.†

* * * * *

The court of Somerset, which on November 5, 1689, relieved William Whittington of his sheriff's office and appointed William Brereton as his successor, also admitted other officers to their positions in the county. Roger Burkam took oath as sub-sheriff, and Edmund Beau-

---

*It will be noted that Coode, "commander-in-chief" under the "Association" in his letter to Somerset Court, October 8, 1689 (see *ante*), calling attention to Sheriff Whittington's policy of "obstruction," told the court that should Whittington not submit then he should be replaced by one of the four "coroners" of Somerset County, "as the lawes requires in such cases," adding in a postscript that should none of them "be fitt or shall refuse the service of Capt^a Smith or some other must be constituted." Kenelm Cheseldyne in his letter to the court, October 18, 1689 (see *ante*) unqualifiedly recommends the appointment of "Capt^a Smith" to replace the "disloyal" Whittington. Captain Henry Smith had figured conspicuously in Somerset's official life as magistrate, member of the General Assembly and militia officer. Just what was the reason for Coode's and Cheseldyne's "preference" of Smith is not made clear; but that these chief authorities preferred his appointment to succeed Whittington is manifest. However, the court found William Brereton, who was one of the "coroners," evidently "fitt" for the office of High Sheriff and willing to serve and so appointed him.

†See *post,* Appendix IV, "Somerset County Officials, 1662-1700."

champ, the county clerk, presented John West as his deputy and assistant, the court agreeing to the arrangement, while Beauchamp agreed to give the said West half the fees received during Beauchamp's incumbency.[16] It appears also that by order of August 13, 1689, the records and papers of the county had been turned over to Captain David Brown, William Brereton, Roger Woolford and Stephen Lufte and "it is now ordered said Brown shall deliver said records and manuscripts to Edmund Beauchamp." "The same day [November 5, 1689] was sworne Edmund Beauchamp, clerk of this county, and John West, deputy clerke." At a court held 12th 9ber, 1689, "Mr James Sangster was admitted and sworne their Maties attorney att Law. Mr Edward Jones and Mr Peter Dent were sworne attorneys at law." Constables were appointed for the ensuing year (and took the oath) as follows: Nicholas Tyler, for Wicomico Hundred; Benjaman Nesham, for Nanticoke; James Langrel, for Mony [Monie]; William Law, for Manokin; James Curtis, for Annemessex; John Waltham, for Pocomoke; George Russell, for Mattanpony, and William Wouldhave, for Bogaternorton.

* * * * *

The revolution in the affairs of the province brought about by the Associators seizure of the government in the name of King William and Queen Mary, and their appeal to the new sovereigns for confirmation of their action in ousting Lord Baltimore's officials and inaugurating a loyally Protestant regime, elicited many addresses of loyalty, from sympathizers with the movement, to the sovereign power in England. In addition to these addresses of loyalty there were also numerous memorials from supporters of Lord Baltimore's cause which, though not lacking in avowed loyalty to the Protestant succession to the throne of England, yet by no means voiced approval of the methods of the "Associators," or of their leaders.

Steiner, in his *Protestant Revolution in Maryland,* commenting upon the fact that memorials from both sides were freely circulated for signatures in the counties of the province states that "Somerset County was a stronghold of Presbyterianism,* and as such men would naturally be opposed to any Roman Catholic, like the Proprietary, we are not surprised to see that the only petition from this county is

---

*See *ante,* page 211, *et seq.,* for account of Presbyterianism in Old Somerset.

one in favor of the so-called Protestant party signed by no less than 238 names."[17]

Steiner is correct in his reference to Somerset as a "stronghold of Presbyterianism"; and though it is true that only a *small minority*—some 15 or 20 at most—of the 238 signers of the Somerset address can be identified as Church of England men, while a *large majority* of those whose religious affiliation is positively known (or from circumstantial evidence reasonably surmised) were Presbyterians (some 100, or more); yet the *first signer* was "John Huett"—*only minister of the Church of England in Somerset County*. The names of Revell, Dixon, Coulbourne, Horsey, Chambers, Dent, Elzey, Tull, Waller, Smith, Dashiell, Brereton and Bozman,* all staunch "Churchmen," appear as signers of the address; yet it is preponderantly a Presbyterian document and of course we find among its signers William Traile, Thomas Wilson and Samuel Davis, the eminent Presbyterian divines at the time residing, and holding charges, in Somerset County. There was no Roman Catholic element in Somerset at the time; and we have been unable to identify any of the signers as Quakers.

It was to the court of Somerset, held "12th 9^{ber}" and "13th 9^{ber}, 1689" [November 12th and 13th] that the matter of this address of loyalty to William and Mary and the Protestant religion and succession to England's throne was brought, and we find in the court record reference thereto in the following terms:

"This same day viz the 13th of 9^{ber} There was an Address presented by the Grand Jury to the Wor^{ll} Court humbly craving there [their] Wor^{ps} and freemens concurrence therein and that it may be with Speed sent to there Majesty^s —Immediately after ye Justices of ye Court signed the Address,† and so did many others that attended the Court. Then the Court Ordered that the aforesaid Address when finished should Be sent over the bay, in order to be presented to there Maties. It was then likewise Ordered by the Court that when ye said

---

*The Coulbournes, Dixons and Horseys were originally most sympathetic with the Quaker and other "non-conformist" elements in the founding of Somerset County; but in the *second* generation transferred their loyalty to the Church of England, which was indeed their "mother church."

†The 12 names, Brown, Jenckins, Brereton, Winder, King, Dashiell, Luff, Newbold, Round, Hopkins, Howard and Jones, signed at the end of the "Address," represent 12 of the 14 "Justices of ye Court"; the name of William Coulbourne, another "Justice," appears also in the body of the list of signers. Roger Woolford seems to have been the only "Justice" commissioned who did not sign the "Address."

Address was Sent over the Bay that it should be certifyed there that the Court had appointed and made Mr William Brereton high Sheriffe of this County instead and place of Cap[t] William Whittington."[18]

The "address" of loyalty, signed as stated in the above court record, was sent "over the Bay" and was no doubt thence transmitted "to there Majesty[s]." In the provincial archives we find a paper entitled: "Address of the Inhabitants of the County of Somersett Nov[er] th 28th 1689," with its signatories, which reads as follows:[19]

"To the King and Queen most Ex[t] [excellent] Maj[ty] [majesty] Wee your Majesty's subjects in the County of Somersett and Province of Maryland being refreshed and encouraged by your Majestys great and prosperous undertakings, and by your late gracious letter to those of this Province, do cast ourselves at your Majesty's feet humbly desiring and hopefully expecting the continuance of your Maj[tys] care of us, as our Case and Circumstance doe or may require, in the confidence whereof wee resolve to continue (by the Grace of God) in the Profession and defence of the Protestant Religion and your Majesty's Title and interest against the French and other Paptists that oppose and trouble us in soe just and good a cause not doubting but your Majestys wisdom and clemency will afford unto us all needful suitable Aid and Protection for securing our Religion lives and liberty under Protestant Governors and Government, and for enabling us to defend ourselves against all Invaders. Thus praying for your Majestys long and happy Reigne over us. Wee know ourselves to bee (with due Reverence and sincerity) Your Majestys Loyall Obedient and humble Subjects. John Huett, Wm. Coulbourne, jun[r]., Thomas Wilson,* Henry Phillips, John Parsons, Thomas Shild [Shiall?], Thomas Stivenson, James Knox, John Brown, Wm. Alexander, Randall Revell, Peter Elzey, James Smith, Epraem [Ephraim] Wilson, Thomas Smith, John Knox, Thomas Wall[r] [Waller?], John Knox, Thomas Wall[r],† Alexander Knox, Alexander Proctor, John Renshaw, James Conner, William Wilmot, Micayah [Micajah] Sadler, John Chanceleer, John Smocke, Nicholas Cornwell, Robert Cade, John Miller, Adam Spence, Tho: Midgley, John Baron, John Deale, Martin Curtis, Clement Giles, Robert Johnson, William Bowen, Devoraux Dregas, Robert Simson, Edward Evans, Hugh Jingle [Tingle], John Colston, Richard Warren, Matthew Jones, Richard Hill, John Goldsmith, John Browne, Wil[m] Owen, Malcolm Knox, William Knox, William Hacaland, Richard Jarrett, Nathaniel Clark, George Boyman [Bozman], John Nelson, William Waller, George Phebus, John Rawley, John Jones, George Park, Wm. Polk, Wm. Wilson, Edward Surnam, Charles Ratclife, William Melvell, William Smith, Richard Macklure, John White, John Rowell [Powell?], John Killam, John More, Sam[l] Hopkins, jun[r]., Benjamin Keyar [Keysar?], Ralph Milbourne,

---

*This Thomas Wilson was either: (1) Thomas Wilson, son of the Reverend Thomas Wilson, pastor of Manokin Presbyterian Congregation; or (2) a certain Thomas Wilson who lived in the upper part of Somerset County (in what is now Wicomico). The name of *the Reverend* Thomas Wilson appears later in this list as signed between the names of his clerical brethren, William Traile and Samuel Davis.

†The repetition of these names is probably due to inadvertance on the part of the first copyist.

Henry Hale, Francis Heap, John Pope, Thomas Oxford, William Hearne, Richard Pepper, John Saunders, Nathaniell Abbott, William Coard [Cord?], William Hale, William Davis, Joshua Light, John Rust, Nathaniel Vesey, Richard Woodcraft, Tobias Pepper, Walter Read, John Peterfranck, Stephen Page, Thomas Edwards, Alexander Mackcullah, George Beniam [Benjamin?], Andrew Miller, Patrick Read, John Steell, William Browne, Thomas Bromley, William Wouldhave, Richard Wildgoose, John Lucas, John Johnson, Richard Cole, William Oswell, John Snow, George Latham, William Law, William Alexand[e]^r, Junr., John Gray, Robert Polk, Thomas Pollett, Charles Mullen, Arnold Elzey, Alexander White, William Nelson, Michael Hannah, William Lawrence, John Swaine, Ambrose Archer, William Stevenson, James Barber, Sam^{ll} Showell, William Jurvill [Turvill], John M^{ck}nitt, Wm Coulbourne, James Murrah, John Roach, Owen M^{ck}graw, William Round, Richard Farwell, Alexander Kyll [Kyle?], Thomas Poynter, John Strawbridge, Adam Fitch, William Burch, Thomas Gordan, Nicholas Carpenter, John Henderson, John Tarr, Richard Hill, Edm^d Beauchamp, Allen Ross, Geo: Nobell, Richard Britten, Peter Whaples, William Layton, William Boyman [Bozman], George Lane, John Crawley, Sam^{ll} Worthington, Robert Peny [Perry?], Moses Fenton, John Porter, Ninian Dulap, James Henderson, James Duncan, John Barber, John Hicks, William Mead, Robert Neame [Nearne?], Henry Mills, Richard Dennis, Thomas Morgan, Humphrey Read, William Shankland, David Dresden [Dreaden, Dryden?], John Watt, John Ellis, Thomas Ellis, John Starret, William Fossit [Fassitt], Thomas Delahide, Arthur Hanley, John Christopher, Philip Askew, Roger Phillips, Robert Crouch, George Bayley, Lazarus Maddox, John Davis, Henry Hamon [Haymon], Miles Harrison, Tho: Dixon, Alexander Maddux, John Frankland, W^m. Coulbourne, Francis Joice, Robert Boyer, Nicholas Jodvin [Todvin, Toadvin], Geo: Layfield, Com^{tr}., Michael Clugstone, Lawrence Crawford, W^m. Traile, Thomas Wilson, Sam^{ll} Davis,* Peter Dent, John West, John Boyman [Bozman], James Sangster, John Tayler, Edward Jones, Thomas Poole, Roger Burkham, John Emmit, John Kine, William Planer, William Planer, junr., Richard Tull, Thomas Tull, Robert Hall, John Broughton, William Nobell, John Coulbourne, John Williams, Richard Chambers, John Trupshaw, Matthew Dorman, James Langreene, Nathl Horsey, Alexander Thomas, John Mackbride, David Brown, Francis Jenkins, William Brer[e]ton, John Winder, Robt King, James Dashiell, Stephen Luff, Thomas Newbold, James Round, Sam^{ll} Hopkins, Edm^d Howard, Thomas Jones, Henry Smith.

This is a true Copy taken from the Original examined and signed by the Order of the Respective Persons above named.

    PETER DENT *dep^{ty} Coll^r of his Majestys Customes in the County of Somersett."*

---

*William Traile, Thomas Wilson and Samuel Davis were the three Presbyterian ministers at the time resident in Somerset County.

* * * * *

It was in January, 1689/90, that John Payne, collector of customs, a prominent member of the Associators' Government, and one of the captains of its military establishment, was killed while attempting to take a vessel belonging to Nicholas Sewall, which was at anchor in the Patuxent River. Sewall was a Roman Catholic, a high official of Lord Baltimore's government (and of course deprived of all office by the Associators), and himself a stepson of Charles, Lord Baltimore.* Sewall, however, was away from the vessel and at his home at the time of the tragic affair, while on board the vessel were John Woodcock, Cecilius Butler, George Mason, William Ayleworth, William Burleigh, George Joseph Freeman and other "Paptists," according to the records.[20]

Our concern with this matter is from the fact that the member of this party whose name appears as *Ayleworth,* was William Ayleward, who had recently been clerk of Somerset County, having been sworn in that office in June, 1688.[21] William Ayleward, if he were in fact a Roman Catholic (as the record in regard to Payne's killing certainly indicates), was the only official of Somerset County at any time during the colonial period who was of that faith. It is not clear from the records why William Ayleward was appointed, commissioned and sworn in as clerk of Somerset County. Edmund Beauchamp had been continuously clerk of Somerset from the organization of the county in August, 1666; and then is suddenly dropped from office, while Ayleward comes into the county and into the clerkship. Of course, he was an appointee of Lord Baltimore, and qualifying to office in June, 1688, was evidently ousted by the "Associators" when they came into power in the Summer of 1689; the clerkship being restored to Beauchamp. Ayleward was no doubt a supporter of Lord Baltimore, and a Roman Catholic.

The outcome of the killing of John Payne, the officer of the Associators' Government, by the party on Sewall's boat, was that Sewall, Woodcock, Mason, Burleigh, Ayleward, "together with other Popish Confederates ... unknowne," were presented by a Grand Jury at St.

---

*For Sewall family, see *IV Md. Hist. Mag.,* p. 292. Scharf, *Maryland,* Vol. I, p. 289, in a footnote refers to the killing of Payne "by the servants of Mr. Sewall." Nicholas Sewall (1644/5-1737) was son of Henry Sewall and Jane Lowe. Madam Jane (Lowe) Sewall married, *second,* Charles, 3d Lord Baltimore.

Mary's, charged with murder. Sewall could not be found; but Woodcock, Mason, Burleigh and Ayleward were delivered to the Maryland authorities by the authorities in Virginia, whence they had fled. They were tried by the Provincial, or Superior, Court of Justice, of which Robert King, of Somerset, had been named a member. Woodcock, Mason and Burleigh were found guilty and were sentenced to be hung. Woodcock was executed; though Mason and Burleigh were reprieved until further orders. William Ayleward was, however, acquitted and released under bond for his good behavior.

The unfortunate affair of the killing of John Payne, an official of the Associators' Government, evidently produced a strong reaction in Somerset County; a condition which was of sufficient gravity (with Captain William Whittington again to the fore) to warrant the court's sending a letter in regard thereto to the authorities at St. Mary's City.

On January 17, 1689/90, the following letter from the Somerset Court to the chief authorities was recorded as having been sent by the hand of William Brereton:

"Gent: We have lately understood of some transactions happenned in your parts and likewise of Mr Paines untimely end, as also that a Proclamacon was Issued out after some persons inhabiting in our parts which said Proclamacon we have not yet recd. There is many disaffected persons here which absolutely denyes this present power dayly making it their studdy to involve others into their factious humours Capt. Will: Whittington has publicly read at Snow Hill Towne three letters in the audience of many persons viz: One from Major Sewall or the late president Joseph, one from Coll Diggs and another from William, Aylward, late Clerke of this county in which letters are inserted that the Lord Baltimore is coming in to enjoy this country as formerly his Charter being confirmed by King and Parliament to confirme which reports, tis likewise said by many here that Mr Keneline [Kenelm] Cheseldyne has quite revolted from that loyall designe he lately pretented to and to which inviolably we shall endeavor to preserve and also that he had rather have given five hundred pounds then been concerned in this Resolution of government—these and such like reports are the occasions of many disturbances what further may bee added we leave to the bearers Signed p^r order of Court

JNO WEST, Dep^t Clk Somerset County Court."[22]

It is a rather interesting view that we obtain of Protestant Somerset from this official document. Evidently the Associators' Government found no rose-leaf-strewn way even here; while certainly "Will: Whittington" was a constantly pricking thorn.

* * * * *

The Associators' Convention (or Assembly), which met in April, 1690, continued John Coode as "Principall or Commander in chiefe of all his Majesties forces within this province, and with the advice and consent of a Committee of 20 persons . . . to continue & remaine till next convention or Assembly or other Lawfull Power sooner Determining the same . . ." This "Committee of 20 persons" was charged with the government of Maryland between the meetings of "Convention" and was composed of two members from each of the counties of the province. Somerset County's representatives on this "Committee of Twenty" were David Brown and Robert King,[23] two men of recognized ability in the affairs of the county and now outward bound on the sea of provincial politics. Both of these men were of gigantic Protestant, and Presbyterian, character-statue. In a communication of John Coode to Governor Nicholson, of Virginia, in June, 1690, we find it stated that George Layfield had been appointed revenue collector for the district of Pocomoke.[24] Layfield had come to Somerset County about 1685-6, where establishing himself, he married Madam Elizabeth Stevens, widow of the Honorable William Stevens, of "Rehoboth."

In July, 1690, the "Committee of Twenty" met and drew up an address to King William, which was deemed of such importance as to warrant the appointment of a personal representation of three men from the "Committee" to take the address to England. The three men appointed for this mission were "John Coode commander in chief of your Majestie's forces here, Mr Kenelm Cheseldine, speaker of the late convention of the Representative body of this Province and Major Robert King one of the said Representatives, whom for their knowledge, loyalty and integrity we humbly commend to your Majesties gracious reception as our agents and deputies . . ." Robert King was from Somerset County. Coode and Cheseldyne sailed for England the latter part of August, 1690; though it does not appear that Robert King accompanied them.²⁵ In September, 1690, the "Convention" was again in session.²⁶

* * * * *

In December, 1690, there is evidence in the court records of further demonstration of a spirit of dissatisfaction and unrest by a certain element in the population of Somerset County. It appears that this dissatisfaction was finding expression in the use of rather drastic methods by those whom this spirit possessed, and though none of the offenders are mentioned by name, an order of court shows that the gentlemen of the Bench were taking every means to protect their dignity and their persons.

> "Xber 10, 1690 [December 10, 1690] . . . Whereas their Maties Justices of the Peace for this County have received divers affronts and injuries at Mr Andrew Whittington's house in their publick concerns by unworthy disafected persons It is therefore Ordered that during the time of Court dayes no person whatsoever shall attempt or be admitted into the Room where the Justices are without leave or Order from some of their Worp^s. The room appointed for the Justices is above the Celler."²⁷

* * * * *

We have evidence that Somerset County was represented in the "Convention" (or Assembly) of the Associators' Government, which met in April, 1691,²⁸ by Colonel David Brown, Major Robert King and Mr. Samuel Hopkins. This evidence comes to us through the record of Somerset Court, at whose session, November 12, 1691, when upon the reading of "A proclamation from ye Convention . . . Co^{ll} Brown, Maj^r King & Mr Hopkins declared to the people present that they did not understand that anything but Indian Corne was the last Convention prohibited for being transported out of the Province they being Burgesses for this County and of the Committee of ye last Convention . . . Then was the Publick Ordinance Read & Ordered to be Recorded."²⁹

Retracing our steps a bit and entering Somerset Court, September 29, 1691, we find two interesting items. The honorable clerk of Somerset, Edmund Beauchamp, who had served in that office for a quarter of a century (lacking some months, when William Ayleward was clerk), had died, September 26th, and was succeeded by his deputy clerk, John West. Then there was returned to this meeting of court of September, 1690, an account of the government's fire-arms kept in Somerset County. Specific accounts of these arms were returned by Colonel David Brown, Edward Day and Captain William Coulbourne. Day's account shows that four guns were kept *"at Mr John Huet's."*[30] Have we here a "fighting parson"—the first Church of England minister resident in Somerset County—one whose home was as it were an arsenal of defence for the Associators' Protestant Government in Maryland? At least the Parson's home appears as a storage place for the government's arms in Somerset. The homes of these men, Brown, Day, Huet, Coulbourne, who had the keeping of these arms, were advantageously situated. Captain Coulbourne lived at "Pomfret," on the south side of the Great Annemessex River, near its mouth; Colonel Brown (who now commanded the militia in Somerset County, and was a member of the province's governing "Committee of Twenty") was at "Thornton," on the north side of the Manokin River; Edward Day's home plantation was on the north side of Wicomico River, just below the present site of old Green Hill Church; and the Reverend John Huet (or Huett) also lived on the north side of the Wicomico River on a plantation immediately joining (and below) Edward Day's.

* * * * *

However drastic may have been the measures employed by the "Associators" in overthrowing Lord Baltimore's authority in the province of Maryland and in establishing their own, whatever the motives which may have governed the leaders in the "Protestant Revolution in Maryland," the "Associators" emphasized the provisional nature of their governmental set up. Their government was holding Maryland in the name of the Protestant sovereigns, William and Mary,

King and Queen of England, and their government was to hold only until the Crown decided the question of the nature of the government that should succeed that of the Calvert Proprietorship; for Charles, Lord Baltimore's cause and claim went down in ignominious defeat before the Protestant opposition's onslaught.

The outcome of the proceedings in England for dispossessing Lord Baltimore of his governing power in Maryland and for a settlement of a government for the province was that the King was advised to send a royal governor to replace the "Associators." Finally, after much discussion and debate, in which every suggestion advanced by Lord Baltimore was completely ignored, the King, in March, 1691, gave a commission to Lionel Copley as the first royal governor of Maryland, which now became a royal province. Copley's commission, in the absence of the King, was signed by Queen Mary, and passed under the Great Seal, June 27, 1691. On March 12, 1691, a royal letter had been sent to the Associators' Provisional Government in the province announcing Copley's appointment as royal governor. Among the twelve members of the Council chosen for Governor Copley we find the name of Colonel David Brown, of Somerset County, whom we have come to known through his prominence in the high councils of the Associators' regime. It was not until March, 1692, that (after many harassing delays) Governor Copley arrived in Maryland. On April 9th he called together the "Convention" for the last time and dissolving it brought the Associators' Government to an end.[81]

Copley expeditiously went about organizing Maryland as a royal province; on April 6, 1692, meeting with his Council and administering to them the oath of office, and calling a General Assembly to convene at St. Mary's City, May 10, 1692. This Assembly opened its session with an address of thanks to the Crown "for delivering them from 'a tyrannical Popish government under which they had long groaned'." The implications intended to be inferred by the addressors in the use of the term "tyrannical Popish government" are debatable, their "long groaning" is not! The tenor of the "Address" and the "grievances" which were made to the Crown clearly reveal this Assembly as controlled by the revolutionary party. Not a scintilla of fairness was shown to the now dispossessed Calverts.

The second act of this first Assembly under the royal government was *"An Act for the Service of Almighty God and the establishment of the Protestant Religion in this Province."* By this Act the Church of England became the established church of the province of Maryland.[82] Under its terms the counties of the province were divided into parishes; vestries elected and organized, Parish Churches and Chapels of Ease erected, and the support of the Establishment provided for by taxation.* Without discussing the details of this Act, or the principle involved in this piece of legislation, we cannot but state the fact that this "Act of Establishment" (no doubt justifiable under the extension of royal government to the province) was the transplanted root from which sprung and luxuriantly developed that many, and strongly, tentacled growth which bound fast the "exercise of conscience in matters of religion." The Presbyterians, and other so-called "sectarians," who were Protestants, doctrinally speaking, were of course safeguarded in the practices of their respective faiths by the Acts of Parliament. But the Roman Catholic, under the development of the principles contained within this Act carried over into later legislation and applied by Protestant magistrates, became anathema, and was virtually made "a man without a country" —save that heavenly one whose maker and builder is, not man— Protestant or a Catholic—but, God. No historian has yet arisen who has been able to prove a good effect upon the glorious Church of England by thus making it the *Established Church* of the province. He who investigates and studies the facts as records disclose them finds an increasing tendency through the colonial years in the legislation and exercise of jurisdiction by the state to shackle and bind the Church, dwarfing its growth both in spirit and in truth. For the support of the Established Church in Maryland the Presbyterians, other nonconformist Protestants, Roman Catholics, and "Churchmen" were taxed equally.

* * * * *

So Maryland became a "Royal Province," completely organized as such, and the royal government established by June, 1692, when the

---

*See *ante*, p. 152, for organization of the Church in Somerset County under this Act.

first General Assembly under the royal governor adjourned. And what of Somerset County as Maryland entered upon the estate of a "Royal Province"?

Evidently the members of the court who had been holding office under the Associators' Provisional Government, from July, 1689, until the arrival of Governor Copley in March, 1692, continued to hold over until a new commission should be issued. In April, 1692, we find Colonel David Brown, Mr. Francis Jenckins, Major Robert King, Captain John Winder, Mr. George Layfield, Captain John King and Mr. Stephen Horsey "on the bench" in Somerset.

The occasion of this session of court at which these gentlemen sat in April, 1692, is interesting. "The Court being called" in session the sheriff read the summons of the royal governor, Copley, to call together four, or more, members of the county court, with their clerk, "who are to sit as a Court and during their sitting" the sheriff was to read the governor's proclamation directing that a special court be convened which should call before it the freemen of the county (who are entitled to vote) for the purpose of electing four deputies, or delegates, to serve for the county at a General Assembly to be held at St. Mary's City, May 10th, ensuing. The sheriff thereupon made proclamation of notice of an election of "Burgesses" to be held Thursday, April 28th, following, at the Court House of the county. The court ordered the clerk to send notice to this effect to each constable and the constables to give notice of this election to the freeholders entitled to vote therein.

The special court so ordered convened for this election April 28th with "Com[s] [commissioners of the peace] Present in Court viz" Mr. Francis Jenckins, Major Robert King, Captain John Winder, Mr. James Dashiell, Mr. James Round, Mr. Samuel Hopkins, Mr. Thomas Jones, Captain John King, Mr. George Layfield. The governor's "precept" for the election was read and the freemen qualified proceeded to vote with the result that the majority voted for *Mr. John Huett, Captain William Whittington, Mr. Thomas Evernden and Mr. John Goddin "to be their Burgesses or delegates to serve the county at next General Assembly to be held at the city of St. Maries 10 May next ensuing hereof which said electors did then sign the two Indentures and seal the same for confirmation thereof."*[33]

These four men, Huett, Whittington, Evernden and Goddin, constituted one of the most remarkably composed delegations ever sent by a county to represent it in a General Assembly. Leading the ticket was the Reverend John Huett, minister of the Church of England in Somerset County*; while following him is that same William Whittington who, through the years of the Associators' Government, we have found to have been such a resolute and stalwart defender of Lord Baltimore's authority. These two men were Church of England men. Thomas Evernden and John Goddin were Quakers. As we shall presently see William Whittington was the only member of this delegation who, under the law, could qualify as a member of the Assembly.

When the Assembly convened, May 10th, and the delegates, or burgesses, took the oath appointed by Act of Parliament, before the Council, we find that "Mr John Huet [Huett] takes the oath as a delegate Mr Thomas Everdine [Evernden] one of the delegates from Somerset and Mr John Edmondson from Talbot County being Quakers refuse to take the oath." On the following day, May 11th, when the roll of members of the Lower House of Assembly was called, Somerset County "returned" Captain William Whittington, Mr. John Huett, Mr. Thomas Evernden and Mr. John Goddin. Captain Whittington and Mr. Hewett [Huett] were *"present."* Mr. Evernden and Mr. Goddin were *"absent."* On May 12th the committee of the House on elections and privileges of members reported having "inspected the election of Mr John Hewitt [Huett] who was elected for the county of Sumersett" and that as they found him to be "a man in sacred Orders is thought not fitt to sitt as a member of the Lower House." On May 14th Mr. Huett was informed of the findings and recommendation of the committee and was "dismissed [from] the house by reason of his Ministeriall function, the Laws in that case ... [being] read in the house, rendering him in the opinion of the whole house unqualified."† However, "they [i. e. the House] desire

---

*See *ante*, p. 140, *et seq.*, for sketch of the Reverend John Huett.
†On the subject of ordained ministers of the Gospel being excluded from membership in the Maryland Assembly, see Andrews, *Tercentenary History of Maryland*, Vol. I, p. 212.

Mr Hewett [Huett] to give them a sermon tomorrow being Sunday." On May 16th the Reverend John Huett, of Somerset County, and the Reverend John Clayland, of Talbot County, were named as chaplains to the Assembly.

At the same time that the Lower House of Assembly disposed of the "election and privileges" of the Reverend John Huett, that august body also settled the question of the right of Thomas Evernden and John Goddin, of Somerset, and other Quakers, to take seats in the House without taking the oath prescribed by law. Evernden and Goddin, being Quakers, refused to take the oath because of religious scruples, but were willing to "affirm" after the Quaker method. George Warner, of Cecil County, and John Edmondson, of Talbot County, who had also been elected to the Assembly from their respective counties, found themselves in like predicament with Evernden and Goddin, of Somerset. On May 11th Evernden and Goddin (together with Warner and Edmondson) appeared in the House and declining to take the oath were refused their seats, whereupon they "Desire to know what account they shall give to their Countyes for ... they were chose to serve & Mr Speaker returned for Answer that they ... draw up in Writeing their Reasons of their not takeing the Oathes and then the House would consider them." Thereupon these gentlemen set forth their reasons in writing; though the record thereof which has come down to us is greatly damaged and very difficult to resupply with its missing words and sentences. However, the substance was evidently in regard to religious scruples about taking oaths and yet willingness to "affirm" to the substance of the oath, and a desire to be so placed as to be able to serve the government and country in an official capacity. On May 12th the House requested that all its members give serious consideration to the petition of Evernden, Goddin, Warner and Edmondson to see "if any expedient can be found out in which Case the usuall Declaration made by persons so principled will be satisfactory to the house ... and the Advice of their Maj[ties] hon[rble] Council herein is by this house desired in the p[r]emises." On May 13th the Council sent its reply to the House saying, that though they would be glad "to give that satisfaction to the house and those persons themselves principally concerned who for tenderness of conscience cannot comply with the Lawe in taking the Oathes in such formality as is required" they could not (after serious deliberation) "find out any expedient for that purpose without violation of the Lawes of England." To permit the petitioners to take their seats on "declaration" as desired, but without the oath, would be in express disobedience to the terms of the governor's commission and his directions in his speech at the opening of the Assembly. The Council refers the House to the governor's speech for their "further and better satisfaction."

Immediately on receiving this message from the Council the Speaker of the House informed Messrs. Evernden and Goddin, of Somerset County, Warner, of Cecil, and Edmondson, of Talbot, that the House concurred in the Council's opinion and that the gentlemen would not be permitted to take their seats in the Assembly without taking the prescribed oaths, and therefore "they were dismissed the house."

The rejection of Huett, Evernden and Goddin by the Lower House of Assembly left Whittington as sole representative of Somerset County in that House, and so another election was required to fill the three vacancies thus created in Somerset's delegation. On May 14, 1692, on request of the Speaker of the House, the governor issued "writts of election of Burgesses to serve" in the places of the men who had been "dismissed." The court of Somerset County received the writs on May 23rd and ordered elections to be held at the Court House, May 27th following. Though we could find no record of this election in the Somerset Court records, yet the records of the General Assembly, under date of Thursday, June [16?], 1692, show that Roger Woolford, John Bosman and Lazarus Maddux had been elected "to supply the vacancies" and that "The said Mr Woolford, Mr Bosman, & Mr Maddox enter the house & were ordrd to be p^{r}sented to the Council by Capt Whittington to be sworne." So was Somerset County's delegation in the first Assembly of the royal province of Maryland finally completed.[34]

Under date of April 11, 1692, Governor Copley issued a Commission of the Peace for Somerset County, naming Francis Jenckins, John Winder, James Dashiell, Roger Woolford, Thomas Newbold, James

Round, Samuel Hopkins, Edmund Howard, Thomas Jones, George Layfield, John King and Stephen Horsey as justices of the county, with Jenckins, Winder, Dashiell and Woolford to be "of the quorum." At a court held for Somerset, June 14, 1692, "the Commission to the Justices and Com^{rs} were [sic] read" and Jenckins, Winder, Woolford, Round, Hopkins, Howard, Jones, Layfield, King and Horsey "took the oaths prescribed by Act of Parlim^t as also the oath of a Justice of the Peace." On September 13th Thomas Newbold qualified as a justice of the peace. At the Somerset Court, held June 14, 1692, John West was sworn as clerk of the court; Stephen Lufte took the oath as sheriff (under commission dated April 11, 1692); James Sangster took the oath and qualified to "the office of Attorney for their Maties"; Peter Dent, Edward Jones and John Strawbridge took the oath as attorneys; Samuel Worthington and Robert Perrie took the oath as sub-sheriffs; Roger Burkum qualified as "Cryer to this Court" and George Noble took the oath as "Deputy Clerk to John West, the clerk of the court."[35]

Other officials of Somerset County commissioned by the royal government, and who qualified to their commissions, were Francis Jenckins and Samuel Hopkins, deputy commissaries* (under commission dated August 9th and recorded September 13, 1692); Joshua Barkstead, surveyor of Somerset County (commission dated October 14, 1692); Edward Greene, chief ranger in Somerset,† and the said Greene (under commission dated October 18, 1692) became "the Chief and only Officer" under the governor, for taking up and utilizing all "drift whales or other fish" and "all other drifts, wastes or wrecks whatsoever as shall at any time ... come or be cast on shore

---

*A "deputy commissary" was one before whom wills were admitted to probate, by whom administrations on estates of intestates were granted, and inventories and estate accounts admitted to record.

†The commission to Green to be "chief ranger in Somerset" directed him to take up all wild horses and mares running at large and "to turn horses and mares upon Assateague Island." Could these "wild" horses and mares turned onto Assateague Island be the "parent stock" of the celebrated Chincoteague (Virginia) Island "ponies" of the present day? Assateague Island and Chincoteague Island are very near each other. It is said that the present day "Chincoteague Pony" comes across, at low tide, from Assateague to Chincoteague.

on the seaboard side . . . of this Province."* A commission, dated October 22, 1692, was issued by the secretary of the province to John West to be clerk of Somerset County, and a commission, dated October 24, 1692, by the attorney-general of the province, to Peter Dent to be clerk of the indictments in Somerset.

* * * * *

And so we trace Somerset County's record through the "Protestant Revolution in Maryland" and the ancient county's entrance into the "Royal Province."

David Brown

Of her many choice sons contributed to Maryland's early provincial life Scotland gave none of worthier mould than David Brown, who came from Glasgow, or its vicinity, to Somerset County about the year 1669 or 70. The earliest record of his name in Somerset is in April, 1670, when he appears as a witness to a bill of sale given by one James Davis to Randall Revell.†

Somerset County was a veritable land of opportunity to David Brown. As we follow him through the years of his life in the county, we find innumerable evidences of his miracle-like touch upon the interests in which he engaged himself. No doubt he came into the county well fitted both intellectually and financially to meet the opportunities which presented themselves. There is an indication in his will that he was "college bred"—he refers to his "formour College of Glasgow." He no doubt came to Somerset to establish trading relations between that fertile and growing section and certain houses of Scotch merchants. Then not many years after his arrival in Somerset—three years at most—he wisely brought his affections to rest in a lady—not only of high social connection—but of a neat and advantageously situated landed estate. Moreover, she was a childless widow and sole heir of her first husband. Before December, 1672, David Brown married Winifred, widow of Captain William Thorne, of "Thornton" on Manokin River,‡ late military commander of Somerset and a most highly esteemed magistrate. David Brown by his marriage not only won Madam Winifred, but the "Thornton" estate as well. Then at "Thornton" he settled and there is evidence of his having developed at this place a good mercantile business. "Thornton" was only the beginning of David Brown's landed possession, for he added acres to acres.

---

*Andrews, *Tercentenary History of Maryland*, Vol. I, pp. 379-380, under the caption "The First Coast Guard and Survey," treats this commission to Edward Greene at some length, stating that it "contains what may be called the beginnings of our modern Coast Guard."
†Somerset Court, Judicials, Liber DT 7, 1670-1, p. 86.
‡Somerset Court, Deed Liber O 3, pp. 133-4.

But, domesticity and business were not Brown's only interests. He manifested equally strong tendencies toward religion and politics, which as a matter of fact he did not seem averse to mixing, and that with deepest sincerity. It was unquestionably David Brown's ardent Protestant—and Presbyterian—spirit which made him such a force in opposition to the government of the Roman Catholic proprietor, Charles, Lord Baltimore; and such a power in the Associators' provisional government which overthrew Lord Baltimore, and ran the province until affairs were finally taken over by their Protestant majesties, William and Mary. It was certainly through his interest (perfectly sincere and honorable from the point of view of his religious convictions) in the Protestant Revolution in Maryland, which opened the outward, upward way in official life for David Brown.

From first to last David Brown occupied office after office in his county—both civil and military—at last becoming a member of the royal governor's council in Maryland.

First, we find David Brown in an official capacity as foreman of that Somerset Grand Jury of March, 1671/2, which recommended to the court the advisability and necessity of establishing four preaching stations in the county for the propogation of the Gospel (see *ante*, p. 118). As juryman and grand juryman Brown always responded to his obligation in such concerns. Then he ascended "the Bench" in 1675, as one of "his Lordship's Justices of the Peace for Somerset," in this capacity having a long and honorable service which continued through the days of the Associators' government. We then find David Brown (with others) representing Somerset County in the "Conventions" of the Associators' provisional government, 1689-1692, and (with Robert King) representing Somerset on the "Committee of Twenty" which from the Spring of 1690 composed the executive governing body of the province until the provisional government was disbanded. At last we find him as "the Hon[ble] Coll David Brown," named as a member of the Council of Maryland (both under Governor Copley and Governor Nicholson) and as a justice of the Provincial Court, 1694-6.* David Brown was barely less distinguished as an officer of militia. We find him first with the rank of captain; then as colonel in the Somerset militia.

We have referred to David Brown's manifest interest in religion. His Presbyterianism can not be questioned; nor can his charitable inclination towards the minister of his beloved church. The first item of David Brown's will (after providing for the payment of his debts) is "that Mr Thomas Wilson, Sen[r] for his better support have Ten Thousands pounds of Tobacco to be paid of my best debts." This "M[r] Thomas Wilson, Sen[r]" was the first minister of the Manokin Presbyterian Congregation in Somerset County; the congregation to which David Brown belonged. Only the absence of the early records of the Session

---

*VIII *Arcv. Md.*, pp. 280, 282-3; XXIII *Arcv. Md.*, p. 540; XX *Arcv. Md.*, pp. 106, 110, 130.

of Manokin prevents our tracing what no doubt was a fact—his close connection with the affairs of that congregation.

When David Brown died in 1697 Somerset County lost a most valuable citizen. It is evident that Mrs. Winifred Brown (David Brown's wife) died only a short time before her husband, for in an account presented by one Ursula Lokey against "The Estate of Coll: David Brown" two items charged as of "An° '96 [1696]" appear:

"To attending his Wife in her Sickness eight days 100 [lbs. tobacco]
To dressing the Coll: Wives [wife's] funerall dinner 100 [lbs. tobacco]."*

There is no record of the births of any children to David and Winifred Brown; and certainly no issue survived them at their deaths. Colonel Brown's handsome estate (by will dated July 19, 1697; probated 7ber. ye 17th 1697) was divided among relatives and friends, with a gift of £100 sterling "to Formour College of Glasgow as a Memorial And support of any of my relations to be educated therein." David Brown's principal legatees were John Brown and Alexander Brown (though no relationship is mentioned); he also leaves small sums to "My Sisters daughters Margaret and Mary Eriskin"; "to my sister Elizabeth." He also bequeathed 6,000 pounds of tobacco to "the Civilized Poore of the County" and also to them "my Town lands in this county."†

Various items in the records of Somerset County make it clear that David Brown was uncle of Alexander Brown (Deed Liber O 20, p. 76); that David Brown's sister Jenet [or Janet] Brown married Archibald Erskin, a Scotch merchant in Snow Hill Town, having issue: (1) Margaret Erskin married, *first,* Alexander Brown; *second,* William Skervin; (2) Mary Erskin married Reverend Thomas Brown, of Paisley, North Britain. Alexander and Margaret (Erskin) Brown had issue: (1) Thomas Brown, of Somerset, who married Sarah (surname unknown) and died without issue; (2) Mary Brown married John Woolford, of Somerset County; (3) Margaret Brown, who died unmarried; (4) Elizabeth Brown, who married William Skervin (who was her stepbrother).

* * * * *

Robert King

Tradition brings Robert King to us as an "Irish baronet" and gives him the title of "Sir"; however, tradition remains unverified and his true origin is unknown. Though we have no doubt that he was indeed of gentle and honorable parentage (which certainly we should like to trace), yet the title to character which the man livingly established for himself in the ancient "Order of the Sons of Men" makes one feel that his patronimic is of far deeper significance than that of a mere name.

---

*Somerset Court, Judicials, Liber DF, 1698-1700, p. 38.
†The will of David Brown is recorded, Somerset Registry of Wills, Liber EB 5, pp. 128-9.

Robert King, of "Kingsland," in Somerset, first appears in the county in 1682 and purchased from Randall Revell, on March 12, 1682/3 (for £17 sterling and two servants) a tract of 300 acres of land on the south side of the Trading Branch (which later became "King's Creek") and to which land was given, at the time of purchase, the name of "Kingsland."* There is no indication in the contemporary records from "whence" Robert King came. This first deed of his simply designates him as "Robert King, of Somerset County, Gent."

The purchase of "Kingsland" in March, 1682/3, was the beginning of the King family's acquirement of a landed estate which for richness and fertility, if not acreage, was truly a regal possession.

Robert King, I, of "Kingsland," apparently devoted his best energies to the development of the "Kingsland" acreage, on which he made his home. By what pursuits, other than his planting and his official employments, he increased his income has not been discovered. By the time of his death, in 1696, he was possessed of a very comfortable estate.

It is in his official capacity, however, and in the establishment of a distinguished family, that Robert King, of "Kingsland," in Somerset, comes prominently before us. In September, 1687, we find him named in the commission of the peace for Somerset County, and one of "Quorum" of the court. Thus he served as one of "his Lordship's Justices of the Peace."† In September, 1689, Robert King was naval officer for Somerset County and again appears as a commissioner of the peace, and of the "Quorum" of Somerset Court under commission from the Associators' provisional government. At the same time there appears this record: "Mr Robert King, Capt: of a Company of foote in roome of Captain Smith."‡

Robert King's sympathies were with the movement which resulted in the "Protestant Revolution in Maryland." He was certainly anti-Lord Baltimore; and we suspect that his Protestant faith was of the Presbyterian order. He appears in the van of the "Revolutionary" movement as a man deeply trusted and highly esteemed by the Associators' provisional government. Robert King (with David Brown and others) represented Somerset in the "Conventions" of this provisional government and (with David Brown) he represented Somerset County on the celebrated executive "Committee of Twenty" which originated in the "Convention" of April, 1690. The high mark of the provisional government's esteem is found upon Robert King in his appointment by the "Committee of Twenty" to accompany John Coode, the commander-in-chief of the Associators' government, and Kenelin Cheseldyne, "second in command," to England, to present by personal representation, the "Committees" address of July, 1690, to King William; though King's failure to make the voyage with Coode and Cheseldyne (who sailed in August) remains unexplained.§

---

*Somerset Court, Deed Liber O 6, p. 330. For notes on "Kingsland," "Kingston Hall" and "Beverly," homes of the King family in Somerset, see *post*, Appendix IX.
†Somerset Court, Judicials, Liber AW, Commission of Peace, dated September 30, 1687.
‡XIII *Arcv. Md.*, pp. 244 and 246.
§Steiner, *Protestant Revolution in Maryland*, p. 334; VII *Arcv. Md.*, p. 195.

Robert King was unwavering in his loyalty to the Associators' government in Maryland and continued to represent (with others) Somerset County in the "Conventions" and on the "Committee of Twenty" of that government, until its dissolution on the arrival of the royal governor, Copley, in the Spring of the year 1692.

With the establishment of the Royal Government in Maryland in 1692 Robert King continued his official life under that regime. In July, 1694, we find him as "Major Robert King" in the military establishment of Somerset County"* while from 1694-1696 he served as naval officer [collector of duties] for Pocomoke District, Somerset County.† Robert King was one of the members of the Provincial, or Superior Court, of Justice which tried the parties indicted for murder in the killing of John Payne, an officer of the Associators' government in 1690. Again, we find that Major Robert King was a justice of the Provincial Court, 1694-1696,‡ and that he had died prior to October, 1696.

Robert King, I, of "Kingsland," Somerset County, married Mary (whose surname is unknown), who, with three children survived him. Robert and Mary King had issue: (1) Mary (1674-1744) married, *first*, Francis Jenckins; *second*, Reverend John Henry; *third*, Reverend John Hampton; (2) Robert King, II (1689-1755) married, *first*, Priscilla Covington; *second*, Ann Makemie; (3) Eleanor King married Charles Ballard.

* * * * *

Facetiously described as "a King who became a Queen" Madam Mary (King) Jenckins-Henry-Hampton was a person of undoubted regal quality. That she was a queen of hearts is manifest when we consider the question of *quantity* involved in her matrimonial companionships; that she possessed true queenly intellectual capacity is evident as we consider the *quality* in those same companionships. Moreover, in the record of this woman's life there is every evidence that she also possessed remarkable business sense which she exercised with true ability.

Born the child of Robert and Mary King, of "Kingsland," in Somerset, (though born October 16, 1674, before her father had established himself in Somerset), Mary King was the inheritor of a splendid tradition; while the domestic and social realms of her earthly activity were alive with the best thought and interests of the times. There is every indication that Mary King reacted most favorably in her contacts with the powerful elements in both her tradition and environment. Though three times taking as husbands men of marked ability in their respective fields of endeavor, men who were ever in the public eye, never once does this woman give the impression of being just the wife of "so and so." She is always a personality within herself. "Madam Jenckins,"

---
*XX *Arcv. Md.*, p. 110.
†XX *Arcv. Md.*, pp. 258, 296 and 521.
‡XIX *Arcv. Md.*, p. 260; XX *Arcv. Md.*, p. 106.

"Madam Henry," "Madam Hampton" were but names and positions through which the ably versatile *Mary King* expressed herself. Never once—though she was indeed truly wife to Francis Jenckins, John Henry and John Hampton—and one with them in their endeavors—never once is she merely "Jenckins"—"Henry"—"Hampton"—but *Mary King* Jenckins—Henry—Hampton.

Mary King was hardly more than eighteen years of age when she was married to her first husband, Francis Jenckins, of Somerset. We shall presently review this gentleman's life in full measure; but here it is only necessary to say that he was a man of marked position and means and many years (probably twenty-five years) Mary King's senior. With her marriage to Francis Jenckins, Mary King went to reside with her husband on a plantation on the Pocomoke River just below the town of Rehoboth. Jenckins was living on this plantation at this time evidently by "right of courtesy," his first wife (he was twice married prior to his marriage to Mary King) having been the widow of one James Weedon, who owned this land. In the year 1700 Francis Jenckins purchased the 400-acre tract from Weedon's heirs, and gave to it the name of *"Mary's Lot,"** obviously in honor of his then wife, Mary King, and doubtless as indicative of his intention (which he carried out by his will) to bestow the plantation upon her. When Francis Jenckins died in 1710 he left (by his will) to his wife, Madam Mary Jenckins and her heirs, personal and real estate which constituted a comfortable fortune. The landed property was situated in various parts of Somerset County and included the home plantation, "Mary's Lot," on the Pocomoke River, where Madam Mary continued to make her home and where she brought her successive husbands, the Reverend John Henry and the Reverend John Hampton, to live with her. This home plantation—"Mary's Lot"—was later inherited by Robert Jenckins Henry, Madam Mary's son by her second husband, the Reverend John Henry. In after years this specific estate came to be known as "Hampton," and was the elegant residence of the descendants of Robert Jenckins Henry.

With Francis Jenkin's death in 1710, Madam Mary (King) Jenckins was left a childless widow, with one of the amplest fortunes in Somerset County. It is now that her remarkable ability for administering affairs develops as she becomes mistress of this handsome estate. But, with Madam Mary, the principal "heart-function" has not in the least diminished and soon we find her responding to the plea of a new lover.

Madam Mary, now certainly in her late thirties, is a prominent and active member of the Rehoboth Presbyterian Congregation. She and Francis Jenckins were certainly intimate and trusted friends of the great Makemie, organizer of the Rehoboth Congregation and for some years its pastor.† Madam Mary, now at least in her thirty-seventh year, enters upon the role of "parson's wife"; though by her worldly possessions mercifully freed from the tragic element

---

* For the title to "Mary's Lot, see *post*, p. 374.
† Makemie, in his will named Francis Jenckins and Mary, his wife, to be guardian of his children and trustees of estate in event of the death of Mrs. Makemie, the children's mother. Nottingham, *Wills and Administrations of Accomack County, Virginia, 1663-1800*, Vol. I, p. 29.

which too frequently enters into the lot of the "parson's wife."

There had come, in the course of Divine Providence, to Somerset County (as successor to the Reverend Francis Makemie), a Presbyterian minister (a graduate of Edinburgh and ordained by the Presbytery of Dublin), Reverend John Henry, who was admitted to the pastorate of the Rehoboth Congregation in September, 1710. In Snow Hill Town, the Presbyterian Congregation had as its settled pastor, since 1707, the silver tongued and able minded Reverend John Hampton, also a Scotchman. Madam Mary King Jenckins, of "Mary's Lot," below Rehoboth Town, widow fair of face and charming disposition, and ample fortuned, was a notable person! First among the two brethren "of the cloth"—Henry and Hampton—the Reverend John Henry, pastor at Rehoboth, laid siege to Madam Mary's heart, and won! Life at "Mary's Lot" took on another aspect. The statesman in the realm of earthly affairs was succeeded by the statesman in the realm of affairs heavenly; the magistrate of earthly courts was succeeded by the herald of the heavenly courts. And now a once childless house echoed the coos and cries of babyhood. Madam Mary became the mother of two children—both sons—by her second husband, the Reverend John Henry. Life at "Mary's Lot" with John and Mary (King) Henry was bright and beautiful—just as the mid-day of life should be—(and it was life's mid-day with John and Mary Henry). But—at "high noon" the shadow of death eclipsed love's light. The Reverend John Henry died in the Spring of 1717, leaving his widow Mary, and their "dear babes," Robert Jenckins Henry and John Henry. Mr. Henry obtained full possession of all the landed estate which Francis Jenckins had devised to his wife Mary and her heirs; however, he graciously redevised the same to Mary (now his—Henry's wife) during her life, and then to their sons, Robert Jenckins Henry and John Henry; thus keeping the "title clear" as established by Mr. Jenckins. As "counsellors" to his wife Mary (whom he named executrix of his will) in her education and raising of the two sons, Mr. Henry names his brother[in-law], Robert King, and Ephraim Wilson and should either die then Robert Wills and the Reverend John Hampton are to supply their places.* And so "passed on" the Reverend John Henry. Again Madam Mary takes up the management of the great estate; with added interest of administering affairs for the benefit of her sons. Then again love comes her way—love irresistible! The Reverend John Hampton, pastor of the Snow Hill Presbyterian Congregation, comes "a wooing" to "Mary's Lot," and wins the heart of the chatelaine. The Reverend Mr. Hampton was a widower, and evidently a man of property in his own right, as evidenced by the bequests in his will. So the Reverend Mr. Hampton and Madam Mary (King) Jenckins-Henry were married, probably late in 1718 or early in 1719. There is certainly romance in this marital adventure of Hampton and Madam Mary. Mr. Hampton, greatly beloved by his congregation at Snow Hill, a

---

*Somerset Registry of Wills, Liber EB 9, pp. 52-4. John Henry's will, dated October 1, 1715, probated June 20, 1717, names wife Mary sole executrix; sons, Robert Jenckins Henry and John Henry; brother, Hugh Henry, and sisters, Jannet and Helen, who evidently lived in Dublin.

pastor superior, a preacher supreme, fine and faithful "in all things pertaining to the Spirit," and as excellent in the things pertaining to this earthly life, became broken in health and in 1717 made a visit to his native country in hope of recuperation. Evidently this hope was not well founded and on his return to Somerset County the Synod of Philadelphia, to which he ecclesiastically belonged, in the Fall of 1718, accepted his dismission of pastoral care for his people because he could not perform his duties "without apparent hazard of his life through bodily indisposition."* But, in his infirm condition, the gentle hands and tender heart of Mary King (now twice become a widow) ministered to Hampton in his declining days. In October, 1719, "John Hampton . . . Minister of the Gospel" indited his will, and a trifle over two years later, in January, 1722 [1721/2], he died. His will names his wife Mary whole and sole executrix of his estate in America, and leaves her (after a few simple bequests of personal effects) the remainder of his estate in America, whether money, plate, goods, chattels or credits, and ⅓ part of his money in Europe, whether in London, or elsewhere. He names his brother, Robert Hampton, Merchant, in Londonderry [Ireland], executor of that part of his estate which is in Europe, and leaves to him (after Madam Mary's death) all "my real estate in lands, lots, houses or tenements." To brother Robert Hampton and to sisters Marjory and Frances Hampton he devised ⅔ of his estate in Europe to be equally divided between them. To "cousins" [probably nephews] James and William Round,† he bequeaths a silver tankard, a silver pint cup, and spoons. "My gold buttons" he leaves to his brother-in-law Robert King [Madam Mary's brother]. "Turkey leather gilt Bible in quarto" to "my sister-in-law" Eleanor, wife of Captain Charles Ballard [Mrs. Ballard was Eleanor King, sister of Madam Mary]. To his "sons-in-law" [stepsons] Robert Jenckins Henry and John Henry, a Negro each.‡

With the death of the Reverend John Hampton in 1722, Madam Mary became for the third—and we hasten to say, for the *last*—time a widow. Now for the remaining twenty-two years of her life she occupies her realm as "Madam Hampton." She quite evidently continued the management of her own affairs, no doubt as time went on accepting the assistance of her male relations. Her brother, Robert King, II, of "Kingsland" (fifteen years her junior), outlived her by some ten years. At the time of her death in 1744 her two sons, Colonel Robert Jenckins Henry and Colonel John Henry, were just entering on their distinguished careers. Colonel Robert Jenckins Henry inherited "Mary's Lot," the home plantation on the Pocomoke River; married Gertrude Rousby, of the celebrated Rousby family of St. Mary's County; himself rose through successive offices to great distinction; and by his management of his affairs amassed a fortune. He established a line which continued to reside at "Mary's Lot," which

---

*Webster, *History of Presbyterian Church in America*, p. 322.

†The Round family was prominent in the Snow Hill neighborhood in Somerset County. John Hampton's *first* wife was Mary, widow successively of James Round and John Edgar, both of Somerset County.

‡Will of John Hampton, Somerset Registry of Wills, Liber EB 9, folio 85.

estate came to be known, in later years, as "Hampton." Of course, the "Jenckins" in his baptismal name was derived from his mother's *first* husband, Francis Jenckins.* Colonel John Henry (Madam Mary's second son) was not less distinguished than his elder brother. He married Dorothy Rider, of Dorchester County, an heiress, and of distinguished lineage, and went to "Weston," an estate in Dorchester, to live. Colonel John and Dorothy (Rider) Henry were parents of John Henry, Governor of Maryland in 1797.

So, the regal pathway of "a King who became a Queen" led through the years, numbering seventy (lacking three days), until at length the great lady relinquished the jeweled sceptre of her earthly reign and passed into the realm where we doubt not a crown adorns the spirit that was hers—a crown whose jewels are her virtues perfected. In the year 1744 Madam Mary (King) Jenckins-Henry-Hampton died at her home, "Mary's Lot," on the Pocomoke River, and there her body was interred. In these later years a descendant of hers has had the stone which covered the grass, and what "dust" the earth beneath it afforded, removed from the old family burying ground and placed within God's Acre surrounding the ancient Rehoboth Presbyterian Church. And there today beside "Rehoboth Church" we find a stone whose inscription reads:

> "Underneath this stone lyeth the body
> of Madam Mary Hampton who
> departed this life the nineteenth
> day of October one thousand
> seven hundred forty and four
> aged seventy years wanting
> three days."

Robert King, II, of "Kingsland," Somerset County (the only son of Robert King, I, and Mary, his wife) was born at "Kingsland," August 29, 1689;† died, and was buried there, in 1755. His father died intestate and so, as heir-at-law, Robert King, II, inherited his father's landed estate (as well as part of the personalty), which included "Kingsland," where Robert, II, continued to make his home. Robert King, II, was like his sister, Madam Mary (King) Jenckins-Henry-Hampton, a person of distinction; though the marks of his distinction are more tangible. Born to a goodly estate, by the exercise of a fine business sense, Robert King, II, increased tremendously the measure of his wealth. Purchasing adjoining acreage eastward along the Trading Branch (which became

---

*Madam Mary (King) Jenckins-Henry-Hampton was *third* wife of her first husband; and *second* wife of her third husband; while her *third* husband (John Hampton) had been also *third* husband to his *first* wife. Therefore, John Hampton had the singular distinction of having been the *third* husband in both of the marriages he contracted. Nothing has been discovered about the marital adventures of John Henry, other than to Madam Mary.

†Robert King, son of Robert King and Mary, his wife, born at Manokin, August 29, 1689 (Somerset Court, Liber IKL). "Manokin" is descriptive of Manokin Hundred, Somerset County, in which the King home, "Kingsland," was located.

King's Creek) he extended his land holdings in the immediate vicinity to nearly a thousand acres. Then a few miles to the southwest he purchased lands on the south side of the Annemessex River (near its headwaters), out of which, in after years, the celebrated "Kingston Hall" estate of his grandson, Captain Thomas King, was created. There were other landed holdings of this second master of "Kingsland" which it is not necessary to enumerate here; though by the cultivation of which he added to his income. Of course, these holdings in tillable lands meant the acquirement of slaves for their cultivation, and of these servants Robert King, II, possessed a number. There is every evidence that this gentleman lived with all the comforts and conveniences that wealth afforded in his day and time.

Then, too, this Robert King, II, of "Kingsland," gave himself to the service of his community in both civil and military positions. We find him occupying for many years the honorable office of a Justice of the Peace in Somerset County; while, for a period of thirty years—from 1722-1752—he was a representative from Somerset County in the Lower House of the Maryland General Assembly. From 1724-1726 he held the office of captain in the military establishment of Somerset; from 1727-1733 he appears as a major; and from 1734-1755 as colonel. In 1733 Robert King, II, was (with Levin Gale, George Dashiell, Henry Ballard and George Gale) appointed by the Assembly a member of the commission to establish a town at the head of the Manokin River. This town was laid out and established as Princess Anne Town. In 1744 Colonel King (together with Edmund Jenings, Thomas Colville, and Philip Thomas) was appointed by the Governor of Maryland as a member of the commission to treat with the Indians of the Six Nations claiming lands on the Susquehanna and Potomac Rivers.*

Not only the state but also the church claimed Robert King's services. He was an ardent Presbyterian in faith and a very active member of the Manokin Presbyterian Congregation, in which he was a ruling elder for many years.

Robert King, II, of "Kingsland," married, *first*, Priscilla Covington; *second*, Anne Makemie. Mrs. Priscilla (Covington) King was the daughter of Nehemiah and Rebecca (Denwood) Covington, of "Covington's Vineyard," on Great Monie Creek. Mrs. Ann (Makemie) King was the daughter of the Reverend Francis Makemie, founder of organized Presbyterianism in America. Robert King had no issue by his second wife, Ann Makemie. Mrs. Ann (Makemie) King married, *secondly*, George Holden, of Accomack County, Virginia.

Robert King, II, and his *first* wife, Priscilla Covington, had issue: (1) Nehemiah King (who died 1766), of "Kingsland," sheriff of Somerset and deputy commissary for the county, married Frances Barnes; (2) Robert King, III, of Somerset and Worcester Counties, died prior to June, 1750; (3) Mary King (born 1715; died October 25, 1739) married Major Abraham Barnes.

---

*Somerset Court, Judicials; *Arc. Md., Proceedings and Acts of Assembly* (volumes covering the period 1720-1752) and *Proceedings of the Council, 1732-1753*, p. 335.

Francis Jenckins

Francis Jenckins (born *circa* 1650 (?); died 1710) first appears in Somerset about the year 1670. From the very first he took a position of prominence in the affairs of the county; later rising through successive offices to membership in the Council of the royal governor of the province of Maryland.

The Somerset County records for the period show Jenckins' constant activity in the life of the community. In June, 1672, he was named as an official for the then proposed county of Worcester (see *post,* p. 424) and first appears as a member of the Commission of the Peace for Somerset in June, 1676, continuing to serve as one of his Lordship's Justices for several years. From 1683 to 1688 he appears to have been High Sheriff of Somerset; while from 1689-1692 we find him active in the affairs of the Associators' provisional government, and as the "chief" of Somerset County's delegation to the Assembly, or Convention, held August-September, 1689.

With the organization of Maryland as a Royal Province in 1692 we find Francis Jenckins again a member of the Court of Somerset County (and of the Quorum thereof) with an ensuing service of several years on "the Bench." There is a reference in the provincial archives in 1697 to Francis Jenckins as "chief justice of the county court of Somerset."* From 1696 to 1698 Francis Jenckins (with Matthew Scarborough, John Bosman and Thomas Dixon) represented Somerset County in the Lower House of Assembly of the province, being elevated to the Council in 1699. In June, 1697, he had been made a member of the Provincial Court (succeeding his father-in-law, Major Robert King, I), on which he continued to serve until 1698.†

When Colonel David Brown, of Somerset County, who had been a member of the Council in Maryland, since 1692, died in the Summer of 1697, a contemporary wrote that "Francis Jenckins—a man of the best sence and Estate &c in Somerset County, who hath born[e] all offices there . . . is proposed in the room of David Brown, deceased."‡ On April 4, 1698, Jenckins was recommended by the Maryland Governor and Council to the authorities in England to be made a member of the Council; while on June 30, 1699, before the Governor and Council in Maryland "Came Mr Francis Jenckins who by his Maty's Royall Instructions is Appointed of his Council here," and took oath of office.§ Jenckins evidently continued a member of the Council until his death. In October, 1709, "Colonel Francis Jenckins offering that he ought to preside at the Board as Eldest of her Majesty's Council is told by the members of the Board that he had relinquished his right thereto & desired that the honble Major Genl Lloyd might take upon him the Presidency and that upon Col. Jenkins not taking any notice of the Governmt after the Governor's death the Board had advised Major General Lloyd to Execute that Duty and do not now think fit to

---

**XXIII Arcv. Md.,* p. 134.
†*Ibid.,* pp. 126, 234, 256.
‡*2 Md. Hist. Mag.,* p. 170, a statement of Sir Thomas Lawrence, secretary of the province, in a note relative to men whose names had been proposed for the Council.
§*XXIII Arcv. Md.,* p. 406; and *XXII Arcv. Md.,* p. 294.

recede from their former Resolves in this matter."* Thus did Francis Jenckins forfeit his right to presidency of the Council and "acting-governorship" of the province at Governor Seymour's death in 1709.

Francis Jenckins settled on the Pocomoke River in Somerset County, living on a plantation which he evidently held for sometime by "courtesy," having married, in April, 1672, Lucy, the widow of James Weedon, deceased, a prominent merchant, who had purchased the plantation from William Stevens, of "Rehoboth." This plantation of 400 acres, which Francis Jenckins finally purchased of Weedon's heirs in 1700, was part of the original grant of "Rehoboth" (1,000 acres) to William Stevens in 1665. The site of this plantation may be located today immediately south of the village of Rehoboth in Somerset County. At his purchase thereof in 1700 Jenckins gave the land the name of "Mary's Lot," in honor of his then wife, Mary King. In after years the place was called, (as it is today), "Hampton." Francis Jenckins amassed a fortune for his day in lands and personal property. His will, dated July 9, 1708, was probated in Somerset County, June 7, 1710, devised the bulk of his handsome estate to his wife, Mary (King) Jenckins, and her heirs, after having made several nominal bequests to "mother Mary King [i. e. his wife's mother]"; "brother Robert King [i. e. his wife's brother]"; to "Captain Charles Ballard and to Eleanor, his wife [who was sister to Jenckins' wife]"; to John Smith, of Virginia, John Croush, and to his servants, Eliza: Denby and Eliza: Bray.†

Francis Jenckins was elected to the first vestry of Coventry Parish (Church of England), Somerset, in 1692, though his religious interests seemed to have been strongly inclined towards the Presbyterian faith. We do not know positively, though there is strong circumstantial evidence to the effect that though doubtless "born and bred" a member of the Church of England, Francis Jenckins became a member of the Presbyterian Church under the influence of the Reverend Francis Makemie during his pastorate of the Rehoboth Presbyterian Congregation. It is certain that Francis Jenckins was an intimate and trusted friend of Mr. Makemie, who directed in his will that should his wife, Naomi, die, that then Francis Jenckins and his wife, Mary Jenckins, should succeed to the executorship of his estate and the guardianship of his children (see *ante*, p. 159).

Francis Jenckins was married three times: *first*, April 12, 1672, Lucy, widow of James Weedon;‡ *second*, Rozanna (whose surname is unknown); *third*, Mary King (1674-1744), daughter of Major Robert King, I, of "Kingsland," Somerset County. There is no evidence whatsoever that Francis Jenckins had

---
XXVII Arcv. Md., pp. 377-8.
†*Maryland Calendar of Wills*, Vol. III, p. 172; Somerset Registry of Wills, Liber EB 5.
‡Somerset Court; liber IKL, p. 119, records "Francis Jenckins and *Henry* Weedon's widow were married by Mr. Robert Maddock, Clerke, ye Twelfth day of April Anno Domini one thousand six hundred and seventy two." The name "*Henry* Weedon" is incorrect (doubtless a clerical error), for in the record of execution of *scire facias* against Stephen Cannon, alias Thomas Davis, by *James* Weedon, January 10, 1670/1, it appears that at Somerset Court, November 9, 1675, "the court orders execution issue thereon to satisfy Francis Jenckins and Lucy Jenckins, his wife, the executor of *James Weedon*, deceased" (Somerset Court, Judicials, 1675-1677, in back of Deed Liber O 7, p. 21). James Weedon's will, probated January 12, 1670 [1670/1], names wife, *Lucy* Weedon, executrix (*Maryland Calendar of Wills*, Vol. I, p. 67).

any children by his *first* wife, Lucy Weedon, or by his *third* wife, Mary King. Jenckins had at least one child by his *second* wife as the record (Somerset Court, Liber IKL, p. 123) shows "Francis Jenckins Son of Francis Jenckins born of Rozanna his wife the tenth day of December One thousand six hundred eighty and eight." This child, Francis Jenckins, son of Francis Jenckins by his *second* wife, Rozanna, probably died in infancy, or early youth, as no evidence has been found of his survival. Certainly Francis Jenckins had no issue surviving at the time of his own death in 1710.

George Layfield

Colonel George Layfield, who was appointed revenue collector for the Pocomoke district in Somerset County in the Summer of 1690 by the Associators' provisional government in Maryland, had arrived in Maryland about 1685, going at once, or very soon thereafter, to Somerset County. Layfield had been commissioned on March 19, 1684/5, "comptroller and surveyor of his Majesties duties in the province of Maryland"; and we find him continuing to hold this office as late as 1688.* He was in fact customs officer of the Crown in Maryland. On November 19, 1686, he was sworn as deputy notary.†

George Layfield was no doubt a man of substantial means at the time of his arrival in Somerset County; and of course a man of prestige in his capacity of royal customs official. Then some four years later, about 1689, Layfield married Elizabeth, the widow of the Honorable Colonel William Stevens, of "Rehoboth," and his position was made doubly secure.

When the government of the province of Maryland was being taken over by the Crown in 1691 and recommendations were made of men for places in the forthcoming royal governor's council we find that Layfield's name was proposed: "Mr George Layfield that married Coll° Stephens [Stevens'] widow; a man well affected to the government that lives in Somerset County in Maryland."‡ Layfield failed to receive an appointment to the Council, the Somerset County representation in that august body going to Colonel David Brown. George Layfield, however, appears in the commissions of the peace for Somerset July, 1692, October, 1694, and October, 1697, when he was "of the Quorum" of the court. In 1697 we find that George Layfield was again his Majesty's Collector of Customs for Pocomoke District and in June of that year was directed to turn over all papers relative to his office to David Kennedy, who had been commissioned to succeed him.§ In August, 1697, Layfield is referred to as a "Notary and Tabellion Public dwelling in Pocomoke, Somerset County."** In 1692 George Layfield was elected a member of the first vestry of Coventry Parish on the organization of the Established Church in the province of Maryland.

**XX Arcv. Md.*, p. 166; *VIII Arcv. Md.*, p. 47.
†*XX Arcv. Md.*, p. 171.
‡*VIII Arcv. Md.*, p. 281.
§*XXIII Arcv. Md.*, pp. 103 and 141.
***Ibid.*, p. 353.

George Layfield married, *first, circa* 1690-2, Elizabeth (Keyser?) Stevens, widow;* *second,* October, 1697, Priscilla White, daughter of John and Sarah (Keyser) White, and niece of his first wife. George and Elizabeth (Keyser-Stevens) Layfield had no issue. George and Priscilla (White) Layfield had issue, an only child, Elizabeth Layfield, who married Peter Collier. Mrs. Priscilla (White) Layfield married, *second,* Captain John Watts, of Accomack County, Virginia.†

George Layfield died in May, 1703. It appears that he had a brother, "Samuel Layfield, of ye city of London, Goldsmith," who was living there in 1705 and 1706 and who came to Somerset County, Maryland, where he died in August, 1709, leaving considerable property to his wife, Mary, and his children, Thomas Layfield, Mary Layfield, and "my honored Mother Margaret Nottle." In the bequest to his wife, Mary, Samuel Layfield, refers to "gold watch and all her gold locketts & rings & Juells she used to ware." In the bequest to his son, Thomas Layfield, is reference to "my Silver Tobacco Box with my Cote of Armes on ye [lid?]." (See Somerset Court, Deed Liber O 7, pp. 5 and 7; Somerset Registry of Wills, Liber EB 5, pp. 157-8).

* * * * *

Colonel George Layfield became, towards the close of his life, one of the principals in what was at the time a case of open defiance of ecclesiastical law which—because of the establishment of the Church of England in Maryland—became a matter for discipline by the civil court. The other principal in this *cause celebre* was the charming Mistress Priscilla White, then just in her twenty-first year of age.

With the establishment of the Church of England in the province in 1692 the ancient ecclesiastical law which forbade the marriage of persons within certain specified degrees of relationship became law of the land. In 1697 Colonel Layfield, who, about 1695, had become a widower, and was now at least nearing fifty years of age, became enamoured of the Somerset beauty and heiress, Priscilla White, who was less than half his age. What constituted the supposed horrible unlawfulness of a marriage between Layfield and Priscilla White was the fact that the young lady was a niece of Layfield's deceased wife.‡ George Layfield's first wife was Madam Elizabeth (Keyser) Stevens, widow of the Honorable William Stevens, of "Rehoboth." Mistress Priscilla White was the daughter of John White and Sarah Keyser, his wife, who was a sister of Madam Stevens Layfield.§

---

*Deed Liber O 7, p. 75, first deed of George Layfield, of Somerset County, Esqr., and Elizabeth, his now wife, relict and executrix of Col. William Stevens, deceased. This deed is dated January 4, 1692 [1692/3].

†Somerset Court, Deed Liber O 17, p. 31.

‡The "Table" specifically prohibited the marriage of a man with his deceased wife's niece and the marriage of a woman with her deceased aunt's husband.

§See *post,* Appendix X for White family.

It seems unnecessary to say that the Layfield-White marriage created a furor in Maryland colonial society, bringing the parties to the marriage to presentment by the Grand Jury of Somerset County and trial of the case by court, and presentment by "the Juro^{rs} of our Sovereigne Lord the King for the body of this Province" and the clearing of Layfield of the charge and indictment against him.

The substance of this celebrated case was as follows: The Grand Jury of Somerset County on March 8, 1697/8, did "present . . . George Layfield Esqr for Cohabitting with Mrs. Priscilla White notwithstanding they by ord^r of Coventry Parish Vestry have been Legally forewarned & forbidden soe to doe it being Contrary to an Act of Assembly of this Province and the evill example of others the good people of this County &c." One June 8, 1698, the presentment was heard in Somerset Court, when Layfield plead not guilty to the charge. A jury, chosen to try the case, found the defendant "guilty of the Indictm^t"; whereupon the court fined him 20 shillings sterling, or 400 pounds tobacco, and costs. Then Priscilla White, who had been indicted by the same Grand Jury, on March 8, 1697/8, "for cohabitting with George Layfield after she was Legally forewarned and forbidden to doe by ord^r of Coventry parish Vestry it being contrary to an act of Assembly of this Province and the evill example of others," was arraigned before the court and "pleads not guilty." Her case was then tried by the same petit jury, who found her "guilty of the Indictment"; and the court fined her 400 pounds tobacco and costs. George Layfield promised to pay the fines and costs.

The evidence produced shows that the Reverend James Brechin, minister of Coventry Parish, repeatedly advised Layfield against proceeding with his marriage to Priscilla White. The Reverend Samuel Davis, a Presbyterian minister, offered to officiate at the marriage if Layfield and Miss White would accompany him into Delaware, whither he was going. Layfield, however, perfectly clear in his own conscience about the lawfulness of the intended marriage, persisted in having it celebrated in Somerset County, and acceded to a Quaker "ceremony" at the suggestion of one William Dennis, master of a vessel, who was then at Layfield's home. Layfield and Priscilla White thereupon married each other according to the Quaker practice and order, the Reverend James Brechin, rector of Coventry Parish, the Reverend Samuel Davis, the Presbyterian minister, William Dennis, and others being present. Mr. Brechin, it appears, wrote a "certificate" of what had occurred, which all parties signed, and Brechin "witnessed" the paper. It further appears that Brechin warned Layfield against consummating the marriage until the consequences [i. e. the legal consequences] thereof were known. Layfield encouraged thereto, and "also being overtaken in drincke" totally disregarded Brechin's advice. The consequences were that Francis Jenckins, a member of the Provincial Assembly from Somerset County, was informed of all the circumstances by the Reverend Mr. Brechin in letters dated October 6 and 8, 1697. These letters were placed before the Governor and Council and "the King's Lawyers" were requested to examine into the matter and suggest proper proceedings. On October 14th George Plater, William Dent and R[obert] Goldsborough, "the King's Lawyers," reported that there had been no legal marriage in the case and that the vestry of the parish (Coventry) should warn Layfield to desist from living "with that woman," and that if he proceeded therein he must be prosecuted and fined. Plater and Dent rendered the further opinion that "the ministers approving off and the others present and consenting to the said pretended marriage" should be summoned before the Governor "to answer such their contempt." This report was approved by the Governor and Council and ordered sent to the vestry of Coventry Parish for them to take action therein as directed. The sheriff of Somerset was ordered to summons the Reverend Messrs. Brechin and Davis and William Dennis, the Quaker, master of the vessel Mary, to appear before the Governor and Council in February, 1697/8. On October 25, 1697, Samuel Worthington, an attorney of Somerset Court, who was reported to have been "a great promoter and instigator of the late pretended marriage," was suspended and debarred from that court by the Governor and Council. Brechin, Davis and Worthington made their peace with the authorities in February, 1697/8, and were discharged from further discipline in the matter; Worthington being restored to his office as an attorney. On Febuary 16, 1697/8, Francis Jenckins, of Somerset, wrote the Governor and Council that *"Mr Layfield still prersists on the Marrying of his Niece and is resolved to endure the Shock of all that can fall &ca."* Action by the Somerset authorities soon followed. Colonel Layfield had been moved according to order by vestry of Coventry Parish, (John Outen, warden, acting for the vestry), to desist from living with Priscilla White; while Priscilla White had been given like warning by the vestry through Isaac Horsey (doubtless also a member of the vestry). The Grand Jury, meeting March 8, 1697/8, made the presentments before recited. The court on June 18, 1698, tried the cases with the verdict and judgments which we have related.* From the Somerset Court's verdict the case of "His Maj^{ty} vs Geo: Layfield & Priscilla White" was carried to the Provincial Court, where George Layfield was indicted and the indictment tried, Layfield pleading "not guilty." The evidence given in this trial of the cause consisted of two depositions, one made by Reverend James Brechin, October 5, 1697; the other by James Standfield, October 12, 1697; both of which Layfield presented to the court. These depositions proved that the marriage of George Layfield and Priscilla White had taken place according to the Quaker custom and all had been said and done and witnessed according thereto. Whereupon the Provincial Court rendered the decision: "And now here this day to Witt the 23^d day of Aprill 1700 Came as well Wm Dent the Attorney for our Lord the King as the said George Layfield and the aforesaid P^{r}sentm^t being here read and all other matters and things thereto relating being by the Court here fully heard and understood and by them inquired into

---

*The Grand Jury for Somerset County, March 8, 1697/8, was as follows: Samuel Collins, Henry Dorman, George Balis, Robert Burrage, Philip Askue, Joseph Benton, Wilis Gray, Thomas Tull, Senr., George Betts, Junr., John Cuvinoe, William Hall, William Henderson, John Patrick, William Killum, John Walton and John Lawes.

doe finde the said George Layfield not guilty of what in the Presentment afd set forth again him Therefore is considered that he goe [free?], there of without day [delay?] And is by the Courte here thereof acquitted paying his fees."*

"And so they lived"—George Layfield and Priscilla White—"happily ever after." On February 4, 1701/2, a daughter Elizabeth is recorded as having been born to George Layfield and Priscilla, his wife. Then, in May, 1703, these two, whom "no man could put asunder," were called upon to part when George Layfield was "gathered to his fathers" by the "divine decree" of death.

WILLIAM WHITTINGTON

Scion of a distinguished family, William Whittington was born in Northampton County, Virginia, about the year 1650. His father, Captain William Whittington (born *circa* 1616; died 1659-60), first appeared in Northampton County in 1640-1, where he was lieutenant and captain of militia and a member of the court. It appears from his will that he was interested in the furtherance of education in his county as he devised "unto ye use of a free School if it go forward" the amount of 2,000 pounds of tobacco. Captain William Whittington was at least three times married, though we are unable to state positively which wife was the mother of his son, William Whittington.†

The exact time of the younger William Whittington's removal to Somerset County, Maryland, is not known, though in September, 1684, he is found described in a document as "of Somerset County, Merchant." Certainly by the Summer of 1689 he was well established in the county, for at that time we find him occupying the office of High Sheriff of Somerset. His career as sheriff, his clash with the authorities of the Provisional Government of the Associators and his final removal from office have been reviewed at length in the foregoing chapter. That Whittington was a stormy petrel in office is quite evident; but his ability, trustworthiness and popularity are equally manifest.

William Whittington's sympathy with Lord Baltimore's cause was no doubt the reason for his appointment in 1691, as collector, on behalf of his Lordship, of the tobacco export tax in Somerset County.‡

With the establishment of the royal government in Maryland William Whittington was elected a representative from Somerset County to the first General Assembly under that regime, which met in May, 1692. He continued a member of the Lower House of Assembly until 1695, when he again became High Sheriff

---

*For records in the matter of the marriage of George Layfield and Priscilla White, and the action taken by the authorities, see *XXIII Arcv. Md.*, pp. 280-2, p. 385, and pp. 390-1; Somerset Court, Judicials, Liber DD (1696-8), pp. 311-312 and pp. 323-325; Provincial Court Judgments, Vol. WT (Hall of Record, Annapolis); and Bowen, *Days of Makemie*, p. 283.

†We are greatly indebted in compiling this note on William Whittington to the scholarly study of the Whittington family by Mrs. Milnor Ljungsted, published in her *County Court Note Book*, Vol. VII, pp. 43-4, and Vol. VIII, pp. 1-2 and 9-11.

‡Somerset Court, Judicials, Liber BWZ, 1690-2, p. 164.

of Somerset. In 1695 he appears as treasurer for the Eastern Shore of the province, and as a member of the court of Somerset County 1693, and 1694.

The office of High Sheriff of Somerset seems to have been a center of attraction for William Whittington and we find him again serving in that capacity from 1695-1698. In June, 1697, George Layfield and Thomas Dixon, members of Somerset Court, complained to the Governor and Council against Whittington, asking for his removal because of "misfeasance of his office." The specific charges do not appear in the Council record. However, this complaint was strongly offset by "a certain representation sent from the Grand Jury of that county court concerning the good behavior of said Whittington in the management of his office during his Shrivalry and wherein they pray he may be continued in said office." There was "much ado" about this matter with reference back and forth from Council to court, and court to Council, with the final vindication of Whittington, whom we find continuing to hold the office of High Sheriff of Somerset in July, 1698.*

In 1699 William Whittington was again returned from Somerset as member of the Lower House of Assembly† in succession to Francis Jenckins, who had been advanced to the Governor's Council. Whittington continued as a representative from Somerset in the Lower House for several years. It is during this period that in a description of members of the House we find the item: . . . "Somerset County. *Major Wm. Whittington always accounted a Jacobite.* Mr. Walter Lane and Mr Samuel Collins are silly drunken fellows easily persauded by Whittington."‡ Lane and Collins were at this time two other representatives from Somerset in the Lower House.

As William Whittington, when he became High Sheriff of Somerset in 1689, succeeded Francis Jenckins in that office, and ten years later, 1699, was elected to the Lower House as successor to Jenckins, who had become a member of the Governor's Council; so, likewise, at the end of another decade Whittington was advanced to the Council, in 1709, taking the seat vacated by Francis Jenckins. To the Governor and Council in Assembly at Annapolis, on October 26, 1709,

> "The hon^{ble} Col: Wm Whittington produced her Majesty's Letter directing he should be sworn of her Council which was done and the said Col: Whittington took his place at the Board."§

Whittington continued as a member of the Council certainly until May 31, 1717, when the Governor informed that body (sitting as the Upper House of Assembly) that he had received a letter from Colonel Whittington telling of his "indisposition and desiring to be excused from his attendance this Assembly."** The Council minutes do not record Whittington as again in attendance between this date and the time of his death in the early Spring of 1720.

---
*XXIII *Arcv. Md.,* pp. 134, 155-158, 445.
†XXII *Arcv. Md.*
‡Jones, *History of Dorchester County,* pp. 50-51, quoting an analysis made of members of the House made by William Smithson for the Reverend Dr. Bray prior to vote on an Act relating to the Established Church.
§XXVII *Arcv. Md.,* p. 377.
**XXIII *Arcv. Md.,* p. 13.

In addition to the various civil offices of responsibility and honor held by him we find Whittington from time to time occupying the milita offices of captain, major and colonel.

William Whittington (*circa* 1650-1720) lived in the southern section of Somerset County below the Pocomoke River.* He became an extensive landholder and owner of a large and valuable personal estate. His will, dated February 28, 1719 [1719/20], with codicil, March 13, 1719 [1719/20], and probated April 11, 1720, is an interesting document. Among its many items are two which show the charitable disposition of the man: (1) he gave part of his Cedar Neck and Sandy Wharf tracts of land to certain trustees for maintainance and teaching of six poor children at a time "to reade and learn the fundamentals of the Christian Religion"; (2) he directed his sons and daughters "to make a payment to the Justices [of the court] for the use of the poor."†

William Whittington (*circa* 1650-1720) was married five times: *first*, Tabitha, daughter of John Smart; *second*, Esther, daughter of Colonel Southy Littleton; *third*, Atalanta, widow of John Osborne, and daughter of Mistress Ann Toft; *fourth*, Hannah [Hopkins?]; *fifth*, Elizabeth (surname unknown). Mrs. Elizabeth Whittington survived her husband and married, *secondly*, the Reverend Samuel Davis, pastor of the Snow Hill Presbyterian Congregation. William Whittington had children (by *first* wife): (a) Smart Whittington; (b) Tabitha Whittington, married Edmund Custis; by *second* wife: (a) William Whittington, married Elizabeth Taylor; (b) Esther Whittington, married, *first*, William Skirven; *second*, Isaac Morris; (c) Hannah Whittington, married Edmond Hough; (d) Southy Whittington, married Frances Fassitt; by *third* wife: (a) Atalanta Whittington, married Stevens White.

WILLIAM BRERETON

William Brereton belonged to a family of distinction in Northumberland County, Virginia, whence he came to Somerset County, Maryland, about 1672. Brereton settled on a plantation in the fork of Wicomico and Passadike Creeks in Somerset County which contained some 500 acres of the tract called "Smith's Adventure." The patent for "Smith's Adventure" (containing in the whole 1,000 acres) was granted in June, 1667, to Colonel Samuel Smith, of Little Wiccocomoco, Northumberland County, Virginia, and a "full half" thereof deeded by the said Smith, on June 8, 1672, "for and in respect of the love and affection which I beare to my son in law William Brereton, of Wiccomoco, afsd., and Sarah, his now wife, . . . to the said William Brereton and Sarah, his wife, and the heirs of the said Sarah, forever."‡ Mrs. Sarah Brereton was probably the daughter of Colonel Samuel Smith.

---

*This section of Somerset County became, in 1742, Worcester County.

†Will of William Whittington, Worcester Registry of Wills, Liber MH 3, p. 172; abstract given in *Md. Cal. Wills*, Vol. V, p. 15.

‡Somerset Court, Deed Liber O 3, p. 116. In May, 1676, Samuel Smith conveyed to "My son in law Peter Presley, Junior, of Northumberland County," Virginia, the remaining 500 acres of "Smith's Adventure" tract. Deed Liber O 5, p. 25-9.

William Brereton evidently first settled on coming to Somerset County on this "Smith's Adventure" tract; though at the time of his death he appears (by his will) to have been living on a plantation called "Brereton's Chance" in Somerset. Brereton is found frequently in the records as a party in various transactions, and appears as one of "his Lordship's Justices of the Peace" for Somerset in the commission of June, 1676. He continued as a member of the court to the year 1690, being of "the quorum" of the court from 1687. In 1689 he was one of the coronors for Somerset County.* It is quite clear that William Brereton's sympathies lay with the "Associators'" Provisional Government which continued him in office. In June, 1690, Brereton was named High Sheriff of Somerset County† in succession to William Whittington, who was removed by the court because of his steady resistance to the provisional government.

The will of William Brereton, dated September 4, 1690, was probated November 11, 1690, when his wife Sarah qualified as executrix. Brereton named "my friend Francis Jenckins, Gent., to oversee and look over my papers books and be an assistant to my wife after my decease."‡ An inventory of the estate of Mrs. Sarah Brereton, deceased, was made October 11, 1703, and an account of her estate returned by William Brereton, administrator, April 12, 1705.§

William Brereton and Sarah, his wife, had issue: (1) William Brereton, who inherited the "Smith's Adventure" tract. He married Diana (whose surname is unknown);** (2) Hannah Brereton (b. February 9, 1676/7), married John Waltham;†† (3) Judith Brereton (b. November 19, 1678), married Jonathan Raymond, who went from Somerset to Queen Ann's County, where he died in 1728;‡‡ (4) John Brereton (b. December 22, 1680); an inventory of his estate returned in Somerset Court, October 11, 1703; (5) Thomas Brereton (b. March 7, 1682/3); (6) Henry Brereton (b. August 3, 1685); (7) Sarah Brereton (b. February 4, 1687); (2) Grace Brereton.§§

---

*See *Post,* Appendix IV, "Somerset Officials Before 1700."

†Somerset Court, Judicials, 1690-2, p. 12.

‡Will of William Brereton, and executrix bond, etc., Somerset Court, Judicials, 1690-2, pp. 53-54 and 112-113.

§Somerset Registry of Wills, Liber EB 14, p. 295, and Liber EB 13, p. 14.

**William Brereton is named in his father's will. In March, 1718/19, William Brereton sold his interest in "Smith's Adventure" to Reverend Alexander Adams, rector Stepney Parish, the said Adams having purchased the interest therein of John Waltham and Hannah, his wife (Somerset Court, Deed Liber O 14, pp. 8, 13 and 27, and Deed Liber O 19, p. 83).

††See deed, August, 1698, William Brereton to "my brother in law John Waltham and Hannah, his now wife"; lease of part of "Smith's Adventure"; Somerset Court, Deed Liber O 7, p. 483. John Waltham probably went to Kent County, Maryland; see *Md. Cal. Wills,* V, p. 151.

‡‡See will of Jonathan Rayman [or Raymond] in *Md. Cal. Wills,* VI, p. 90, and Liber PP, folio 426, Hall of Records, Annapolis, in survey of tract called "Daintry."

§§Dates of births of Hannah, Judith, John, Thomas and Sarah Brereton given in Somerset Court, Liber IKL. Grace Brereton is named in will of John Persons [or Parsons], 1712, *Md. Cal. Wills,* III, p. 227. The inventory of John Brereton's estate, 1703, is recorded in Somerset Registry of Wills, Liber EB 14, p. 289.

OLD SOMERSET
ON
THE EASTERN SHORE OF MARYLAND

PART II

APPENDIXES

APPENDIXES

I. Governor Calvert's Commission for Settlement of the Eastern Shore Below Choptank River, November 6, 1661.
II. Randall Revell's Report on Conditions at Manokin-Annemessex, May, 1662.
III. Colonel Edmund Scarburgh's Report of His Proceedings at Manokin-Annemessex, October, 1663.
IV. Somerset County Officials Before 1700.
V. Somerset Marriages.
VI. First Court House Sites and First Towns.
VII. A Proposed County on the Seaboard Side, 1671.
VIII. Formation of Worcester County, 1742, and Wicomico County, 1867.
IX. The King Homes in Somerset County: "Kingsland," "Kingston Hall," "Beverly."
X. (a) Patents for Land in the Old Somerset Area, 1661-1666.
(b) Names of Settlers in Somerset County, 1666-1700.
(c) First Settlers' Families, 1662-1666: Genealogical Notes.
(d) Names of Quaker, Church of England and Presbyterian Families.

Appendix I
Governor Calvert's Commission for Settling the Eastern Shore Below Choptank River
November 6, 1661

Philip Calvert Esqr Lieuetenn^t and Chiefe Governor of the Province of Maryland under the Right hono^{ble} Caecilius lord and Proprietary of the same to all persons to whome theis p^{r}sents shall come Greeting in our lord God Everlasting knowe yee that takeing into Considera^{con} the peticon of divers persons well affected to this Province now or late Inhabitants of Northt^{on} [Northampton] County otherwise called Accomack in Virg^a who are desirous to transplant themselves and familyes into this Province And for the more speedy and Effectual prosecu^{con} of his said Lo^{ps} Comand to me to see that parte of this Province next adjoyneing to the County aforesaid peopled and for the ease and benefitt of all such persons whoe shall transplant themselves into this Province from Accomack afores^d I have nominated constituted and impowred and Doe by theis p^{r}sents nominate constitute and impower Coll Edmund Scarburgh Randall Revell and John Elzey Gent or any two of them being within this Province to grant warr^{ts} for land (During the terme of six moneths next ensueing the date hereof) upon the Easterne shoare of this Province in any parte below the Choptanck River that is to say fifty acres for every person transplanted upon such Condi^{cons} & tearmes as are Expressed in his Lo^{ps} condi^{con} of planta^{con} now remayning upon Record regulated according to his lo^{ps} Declara^{con} of the 22th Septr 1658 now upon Record alsoe Provided that every pson claymeing any land by vertue of the Condi^{cons} aforesaid for or in respect of the transporta^{con} of any pson or psons into this Province doe before the said Edmund Scarburgh Randall Revell & John Elzey or any two of them and being within this Province take the oathe of fidelity by the said Condi^{cons} of planta^{con} required which said oathe the said Coll Edmund Scarburgh Randall Revell and John Elzey or any two of them are hereby impowred to administer to all or any the persons desirous to transplant themselves as aforesaid before they shall have any warrants granted unto them respectively And also provided that all such persons as shall have any warr^{ts} granted be accomptable to the Secretary for the tyme being for all such fees as for the said Warr^{ts} and Entryes shall become due And the said Edmund Scarburgh Randall Revell and John Elzey are hereby required to keepe a booke of all such Rights and warr^{ts} as shall be by them or any of them granted distinctly reciting the name and surname of every person for or in respect of whose transporta^{con} they have allowed any land And the same at the End of the six months aforesaid to retourne into the Secretary's office Signed with their hands Given at St Marys under the lesser Seale of this Province this sixth day of November in the thirtyth yeare of his lo^{ps} dominion over the said Province Annoq domini 1661

C: Baltimore   Signed Philip Calvert

(*III Archives of Maryland. Proceedings of the Council, 1636-1667*, pp. 435-6.)

Appendix II

Randall Revell's Report of the Manokin-Annemessex Settlement

May, 1662

At a Councell held at   Lieuten^t Generall
St Johns ditto die   Present   Deputy Lieut. &
                                                             Secretary

May 2^0 1662 This day came Randell Revell and represented the State of the plantation seated at Manoakin; and desired that Course might bee taken for the supply of the plantation or continuance of the Comm^{on} to himselfe and others Granted for Grantings of warrants and survey of lands in that Parte of the Province dated 6th of November last past, his relation thereof is in his verbis.

(viz) that there weare now at this present seated there fifty tithable psons viz at Manokin and Anamessicks a place distant som fower miles from Monokin, that they had made an agreem^t with their neighbour Indians viz: the Emperor of Nanticoke which they desired mought be by the Governor and Councell confirmed, which is as followeth. viz that the Emperor and his Indians weare to have for every plantation six match coates to be payd by them that seates each plantation. That they weare to bringe in all runaways for which they weare to receave a matchcoate p. pole for every runaway delivered. that they should not kill nor murthur any the English, neither should any English murthur any of theirs. That if the Indians stole any thing from the English they should pray for: as alsoe the English should pay for anythinge they stole from the Indians. that I [in] case the English lick [like] not the Dutch trading with them that they would prohibit the Dutch trading with them Provided they might be supplyed with necessarys from the English. That noe English man whatsoever should pass through their Quarters without a pass from the Governor or som Magistrat thereunto authorized.

Whereuppon it was ordered first that som fitt person be authorized to conclude a peace with the Emperour of Nanticoke uppon the forementioned Articles to bee entred upon Rec^d. [record] and that the Comissin for Granting warr^{ts} for land dated 6° november last be renewed to Coll Edmund Scarburgh, Randall Revells, and John Elzey Gen^{tls} to continue till his L^{op} or his Heirs, or his or their Lieut. or Chiefe Governor of this Province for the tyme being shall recall the same, uppon the same tearmes as the sayd Commission was to the s^d Edmund Scarbragh, Randall Revells and John Elzey Granted as aforsayd.

And uppon consideration of the two Proclamations the one for Prohibiting trade with the Indians and exportation of Corne Dated the 7° day of December 1661 And the other for the better observation of the Act for Navigation and increase of shipping dated 31 January 1661 ordered that Coppys of the sayde Proclamation bee delivered to the s^d Revell, and that Com^{on} be graunted unto him and Elzey or any of them to seize upon any shipps, boates, vessels or truck of any persons offending against any the Proclamations, or the Acts to which they doe relate.

Ordered further that a Comision bee Graunted to William Thorne to comaund the Company of foote to bee leavyed and raised at Manokin in usuall forme, and that hee choose his Lieut and Ensigne Ordered further that a Commission be graunted to Randall Revell, John Elzey and William Thorne to heere and determine any Causes to the vallue of 2000[1] of tobacco or under and that they make choyce of som man who may serve in the mature of a Sheriff or Martiall to bringe such people before them as shall be delinquent or in debt till a County bee Erected and further order taken therein.

(*III Archives of Maryland. Proceedings of the Council, 1636-1667*, pp. 452-3.)

APPENDIX III

COLONEL EDMUND SCARBURGH'S REPORT OF HIS PROCEEDINGS AT ANNEMESSEX AND MANOKIN IN OCTOBER, 1663

To ye Honble Govn^{or} & Councell of Virginia—Emd: Scarburgh humbly presenteth ye account of proceedings in his Maties affaires at Anamessecks and Manoakin on ye Eastern Shoare of Virginia:

Accompanied wth Coll Stringer foure of ye Co^{m}ission & about fourty horsemen whom I tooke wth me for pomp of Safety, and to repell y^t Comtempt wch I was informed some Quakers & a foole in office had threatened to obtrude: wee came to Anamessecks on Sunday neight being ye 11th of October last past [1663], on Monday morning at ye house of Stephen Horsey an officer of ye Lord Baltimore, I began to publish ye Comands of ye Assembly, and for y^t ye officer could not reade, I often read ye Act unto him, who made me noe Reply but brought a pattent instead of his Comission, and tould us their was his Authority, and y^t hee was put in trust by ye Lord Leif^t: of Maryland and he would not be false to his trust, wth more like that. Hee was answered that their could bee no trust where there was no interest, that it was evident by ye Lord Baltimore's bounds he had noe land to ye Southward of Watkins point, and y^t that question was determined by a power beyond private mens controverting, wherefore all that was Required of him was, that he would please to subscribe his obedience to his Maties according to ye Act of Assembly & peaceably enjoye his Lands, goods &c. which his Maties Govno^r would protect as his Maties Subjects, But if he refused to conforme his obedience I should arrest him to answer before his Maties Govon^r for his Contempt & Rebellion, At this ye said officer something startled, and said but case I doe underwrite my obedience & many more, The Govno^r of Maryland will Come so soone as you are gone and Hang me & them at o^r doores, It was answered him, That hee thought so unworthely of ye Lord Leif^t: and y^t it was a tiranny not imaginable to be done, The officer answered such things has bin done in Maryland, and therefore I dare not subscribe. Then having spent much time, and consulting wth our Military & Civill officers, it was resolved as ye best expedient to arrest him and take some of o^r selves for security for his appearance before ye Honble Govon^r & Councell and sett ye broad arrow on ye doore. So thus proceeding wee went to ye house of Ambrose Dixon a Quaker where a boat & men belonging to Groomes Shipp and two running quakers were, also George Johnson & Thomas Price inhabitants & Quakers.

Their publishing ye Act of Assembly wth a becoming Reverence wch ye quakers scoft & dispised. George Johnson filled wth ye Spirit of Nonsence talked till hee forgott w^t hee said, and speaking much from ye purpose I thought not my part to spend time as he did, But briefly demanding their obedience and they all Refusing, I proceeded to arrest them to appeare before ye Honble Govno^r & Councell to answer their Contempt & Rebellion, offering to take one for ye other as securities for their appearance, But they refusing I sett ye broad arrow on the doore, and so marched of to Henry Bostons, where publishing ye Act hee desiered Consideration a day or two, and then hee would attend, so wee departed thence to Manoakin where I sent Sumons for all ye housekeepers & freemen to appeare, who coming most willing & Cheerfully they all subscribed except Mr. John Elzey & Capt. William Thorne, who being *officers* for ye Lord Baltimore desired respite of time untill they could return their Comissions wch they ingaged their words and Reputation to performe so soon as possible. Their I held his Maties Court of sirvey and had assistance of ye comission^rs therein, then all the people made entries of their Lands & acknowledgements of Conveyances of Land, they all desiring ye Honble Govno^r of Virginia protection as his Maties subjects, which wee did assure them of, so farr as was in o^r powers They also complained of a late invasion from ye Indians, and great danger of being cutt of, and said they sent to Maryland to ye Lord Leif^t: for aid, who after about fourteene daies delay had a letter of advise to stand on their owne guard, for they had more than enough to doe in Maryland, soe that these people said they were owned for profit and deserted in distress. That if a Report of Coll. Scarburgh's coming wth troopes of horse had not prevented together wth a sloope of his full of armed men, seeking Runawaies had not hapned their in y^t juncture of time to ye terror of ye Indians, they had undoubtedly bin cutt of, therefore desired course to be taken therein wch accordingly was done—They further desired y^t in regard of ye remotnes of officers, and ye intermixed neighborhood of quakers, together wth ye frequent access of boats full of quakers, and the Confusion they did & might produce, That officers might be their appointed, wch they were also assured to expect so soon as I could give ye Honble Govon^r & Councell account of ye affaires: som of them also discoursed of ye Lord Leif^t of Maryland's claim to Manoakin & also ye other places to Anancock, to wch it was answered that whilst ye erronious proclamation was uncontroled that declared Anancock to be Maryland's Southern bounds, it might not be so received, But since occasion made ye Govment of

Virginia not only reverse that proclamation, But also by this p^rsent Act of Assembly ye certaine bounds of ye Lord Baltimore's pattent was declared, and that if ye Lord Leift had ought to pay, Hee was refered by ye Act to persons & place, Therefore they might not trouble themselves therein, for ye Question apertained to higher powers and above private mens controverting, at wch they were well satisfied & desired protection of their persons & estates from any pretenders under ye s^d Lord, wch being assured them, they departed well sattisfied: At that time one Hollinsworth, Merchant of a Northern Vessel, came & presented his Request for Liberty to trade, wch I doubted was some plott of ye Quakers, and y^t it was their hopes to interupt ye Compliance of those at Manoakin by imagining I would demand Customs & other Charge, upon wch hee should take occasion to depart, and then ye Quakers to upbraid ye obedient wth this lost trade, by Reason of Impositions, and therefore urge them to receede in tyme, but to defeat this designe, I presumed in their Infant plantation to give freedome of trade w^thout impositions, wch when ye people perceived some said ye Quakers were lyers, for they had prophesied otherwise, I hope this will not be ill taken if the time place & occasion be considered, it may bee otherwise ordered hereafter when it shall bee thought fitt, Then came Stephen Horsey & Henry Boston, who appeared according to promise, & ye said Horsey pretended he would visitt us next morning, and pass upon ye same Resolves, as Mr Elzey and Capt. Thorne had done, that was to lay downe his Comission & then subscribe his Conformity, But hee never saw us more & as wee are informed carried away Boston wth him & advised others to Rebellion & to this Day wth the Quakers bid defiance to ye Govm^t of his Maties Country of Virginia boasting their insolence & forgeries.

    The Number & Quallification of this Rout I shall Account.

    Stephen Horsey, ye Ignorant, yet insolent officer, a Cooper by profession who lived long in ye Lower parts of Accomack, once elected a Burgess by ye Comon Crowd & thrown out by ye Assembly for a factious and tumultuous person, A man Repugnant to all Govm^t, of all sects yet professedly none, Constant in nothing but opposing Church Govm^t, his Children at great ages yet uncristned, That left ye lower parts to head Rebellion at Amanessicks, where hee now liveth, and stands arrested, but bids defiance untill by stricter order delt w^th:

    George Johnson ye proteus of heresy who hath bin often wandering in this County where hee is notorious for shifting scismatticall pranks At length pitched at Anamessicks where hee hath bin this yeare and made a plantation, A known Drunkard & Reported by ye neighbors to be ye father of his Negro Wenches bastards, suspected to be made away privately, & wth stands Govm^t: feare of Justice, hee now professeth quaking and to instruct others, who is himself to learne good manners, calling ye obedient subjects villians Rogues & forsworne persons for their subscribing, stands arrested to appeare before ye Honble Govn^r and bids defiance untill stricter course be taken.

    Thomas Price a creeping quaker by trade a leather dresser, whose conscience would not serve to dwell amongst ye wicked, and therefore retired to Anamessicks, where he heares much & saith nothing else but y^t hee would not obey Govm^t: for wch hee also stands arrested.

Ambrose Dixon a caulker by profession that lived longe in ye lower parts, was often in question for his quaking profession, removed to Anamessicks, there to Act what hee could not be here permitted, Is a prater of nonsense, and much led by ye spirit of Ignorance, for wch he is followed, A receiver of many quakers, his house ye place of their Resort, and a Conveyor of o^r ingaged persons out of the County, averse to Govm^t, for wch hee stands arrested, and ye broad arrow on his doore, but bids defiance until severer course reforme him.

Henry Boston an unmannerly fellow y^t stands condemned on o^r records slighting & condemning ye Lawes of ye Country, a Rebell to Govment & disobedient to authority, for wch hee received a late reward wth a Rattan and hath not subscribed: hid himselfe & so scaped arest.

These are all except two or three loose fellows y^t follows ye quakers for scrapps whome a good whipp is fittest to Reforme.

Some daies since ye people of Manoakin & ye parts adjoining made Request to ye Court for meanes of Safety in respect y^t severall strange speaches were spread by ye Quakers and their adherents, whereupon the Court of Accomack made ye following order:

At a Court held in Accomack County ye 10: Day of November by his Maties Justices of ye Peace for ye s^d County &c. And in ye yeare of o^r Lord God 1663

Present	Capt: Geo: Parker	Mr Dvorx Browne
	Maj^r Jno Tilney	Mr Hugh Yeo
	Mr Jno West	Mr Jno Wise
	Mr Edm: Bowman	

Whereas his Maties good subjects inhabiting Manoakin and other Remote parts of this County haveing lately conformed their obedience by subscription to ye Act of Assembly wch ye quakers & some other factious people for their owne ends have Refused, and doe persist in that Rebellion broaching & reporting as from the Lord Leif^t: of Maryland many mutinous & factious speeches tending to breach of peace, and disturbance of ye peoples quiet in these parts, which wee rather believe to arise from their owne Inventions, Then so Honble a person as ye Lord Leif^t of Maryland, Nevertheless to prevent ye designes of these people Quakers whom his Matie hath declared to endeavour the subversion of Govm^t: and to secure those good subjects who by their Requests have sought this Court for meanes of protection, The Court have thereupon ordered That until his Maties Govno^r can be fully informed of this affaire & provide a fitter expedient, That Capt. Wm Thorne an officer under Coll Scarburgh, Mr Randall Revell, Mr Wm Bosman and Mr Jno Rhodes, all or any of them be qualified wth sufficient Authority to call together & Comand all his Maties good subjects at Manoakin & all other parts of this County so farr as Pokomock River to come togeather and arme themselves only for defense, against any person or p^sons y^t shall invade them, to ye disturbance of ye people or their estates, & breach of his Maties peace, wch to conserve the Court hath taken this Care & course, and y^t it may appear absolute necessary, wee have anexed ye Rumors that ye Quakers & factious fooles have spread to ye disturbance of ye peace and terror of ye less knowing, wch wee are assured doth arise from ye Quakers desires more than ye Lord Leif^t: of Maryland, or any other Civill or Ingenious person, And y^t ye wicked plotts & contrivances of ye said quakers & factious fooles may be prevented, have taken this Course for ye safety of his Maties good subjects.

Some of ye Reports are these:

That ye Lord Lef^t: of Maryland will hang all those his Maties subjects that have subscribed their obedience to his Maties Govno^r of Virginia.

That ye Govno^r of Virginia for medling hath a piece of Green Wax sent for him.

That one Jolly intends to settle at Pokomoke River on some of ye peoples land of this County, and to hold it vi et armis.

That Coll; Scarburgh for executing ye Govno^r of Virginia & Grand Assembly's comands deserves to be hanged, and more stuff like.

This is ye full account of ye proceedings to this Day, as concerning ye performance of ye Grand Assembly's comands & ye consequences thereof—It Resteth wth yor Hono^rs to direct w^t further course is to be taken. I writt to ye Lord Lef^t: of Maryland & sent ye Copy of ye Act to wch I aded my readiness to attend wth Mr Catlet & Mr Lawrance if his Hon^r did desire it, but have received now other answer But a capittulatory letter wch I have sent herew^th: p^rsumeing ye Lord Leif^t: hath personated his afaires wth ye Honble Govno^r at James Towne though I suppose according to ye Act of Assembly, their ought to have bin a meeting on ye Easterne Shoare, wch ye Quakers say is contemned, Whatever my owne person may bee, I p^rsume ye office I p^rsent is not so unworthy nor ye persons of those joyned wth me, nor when I come to tryall shall they finde y^t affaire negotiated wth less Repute then becomes such a concerne, Wee only now expect either some particular orders or leave it to ye Court of Accomack to proceed as occasion shall serve for ye peace & safety of his Maties subjects. I suppose ye Lawes of o^r Country put in Execution will order ye Quakers, whose interest will never permit their Consciences to comply wth y^t Govm^t wch is inconsistent wth their affaires, Therefore Strictest course must be taken, and if Commanded though they are not free to come, they shall be brought before yor Hon^rs by yor most humble servant

EDM: SCARBURGH.

(From Accomack, Virginia, Court Records, Vol. I, p. 43. This report is also printed in *Virginia Magazine of History and Biography,* Volume XIX, pp. 173-180; and in *Report and Accompanying Documents of the Virginia Commissioners Appointed to Ascertain the Boundary Line Between Maryland and Virginia . . . Richmond . . . 1873;* (Part II Documents), pp. 73-78.)

APPENDIX IV

SOMERSET COUNTY OFFICIALS BEFORE 1700

High Sheriffs

1666 and 1667—Stephen Horsey (*III Arcv. Md.*, p. 555; *V Arcv. Md.*, p. 4).
1668—George Johnson (*V Arcv. Md.*, p. 33; Somerset Court, Deed Liber, O 1, p. 114).
1669 and 1670—Randall Revell (Somerset Court, Judicials, Liber AZ, 1671-5, p. 494; and *V Arcv. Md.*, p. 70).
1671—Thomas Walker (*V Arcv. Md.*, p. 104).
1672—Thomas Jones (*V Arcv. Md.*, p. 111).
1673-1675—William Coulbourne (*V Arcv. Md.*, p. 121; and Somerset Court, Deed Liber O 7 [reverse], p. 26).
1676-1678—Thomas Walker (Somerset Court, Deed Liber O 7 [reverse], p. 43; and *XV Arcv. Md.*, pp. 162 and 232).
1679—John White (*LI Arcv. Md.*, p. 287).
1681—John White (*VII Arcv. Md.*, p. 134).
1682-1683.
1684-1689—Francis Jenckins (Somerset Court, Deed Liber O 7 [front], p. 14; *V Arcv. Md.*, pp. 470 and 545; Somerset Court, Judicials, Liber AW, p. 41; *XIII Arcv. Md.*, p. 225; *VIII Arcv. Md.*, p. 22).
1689—William Whittington (Somerset Court, Judicials, EFG, 1689-90, p. 19).
1689-1690—William Brereton (Somerset Court, Judicials, Liber EFG, 1689-90, p. 19; and Judicials, 1690-1, p. 12).
1690-1693—Stephen Luffe (or Lufte) (Somerset Court, Judicials, Liber BWZ, 1690-2, pp. 58, 94 and 214; *VIII Arcv. Md.*, p. 554).
1694—Ephraim Wilson (*XX Arcv. Md.*, p. 77).
1695-1699—William Whittington (*XIX Arcv. Md.*, p. 242; Somerset Court, Judicials, Liber DD 17, 1696-8, p. 41; *XXIII Arcv. Md.*, p. 155; *XX Arcv. Md.*, p. 572).
1699—John West (*XXIII Arcv. Md.*, p. 332).

Clerks of Somerset Court

Edmund Beauchamp, August 22, 1666, to June, 1688, when he was replaced by one William Aylward, who was sworn as clerk in June, 1688; we find, however, that Aylward was out of the clerkship by November 5, 1689, when Edmund Beauchamp again took oath as clerk of Somerset County, continuing to hold the office until his death in 1692. (See *ante,* Chapter VII, "Founders," sketch of Edmund Beauchamp).

John West (who became deputy clerk under Beauchamp in November, 1689) was commissioned as clerk of Somerset October 22, 1692, continuing to hold office through 1694 and being succeeded by Peter Dent. (Somerset Court, Judicials, Liber 1692-3, p. 104; Liber 1693-4, pp. 2 and 157).

Members Lower House of Assembly

1669—William Stevens, Stephen Horsey (*II Arcv. Md.*, p. 156).
1671, 1674, 1674/5—Paul Marsh, Roger Woolford (*II Arcv. Md.*, pp. 239, 241, 311, 345, 422, 439).*
1676—William Stevens (?) (*II Arcv. Md.*, pp. 481, 485, 493, 495, 496).
1678-1681—William Stevens, John White, Roger Woolford, James Dashiell (*VII Arcv. Md.*, pp. 5, 6, 7, 125, 134 and 147).
1682—James Dashiell, Henry Smith, Roger Woolford (*VI Arcv. Md.*, p. 301; Scharf, *Maryland I*, p. 289).
1683-1685—Henry Smith, John Osborne (*VII Arcv. Md.*, pp. 462, 468, 551; *XIII Arcv. Md.*, 56 and 57).
1686-1688—Stephen Luffe (or Lufte), James Round, ... Jones (?) (*XIII Arcv. Md.*, pp. 147, 153, 196).
1689-1692 (Associators' Provisional Government).—Francis Jenckins, David Brown, Robert King, Samuel Hopkins (see references for Somerset delegates in Associators' conventions and on "Committee of Twenty," as given *ante*, Chapter VIII, "Somerset in the Protestant Revolution and into the Royal Province."
1692 (May-June Assembly)—John Huett, Thomas Evernden, John Goddin, William Whittington. Huett, Evernden and Goddin were excluded (see *ante*, Chapter VIII, "Somerset in the Protestant Revolution and into the Royal Province"). Roger Woolford, John Bozman and Lazarus Maddox were elected, and qualified, in room of Huett, Evernden and Goddin (see *ante*, Chapter VIII, for references).
1693—William Whittington, Roger Woolford, John Bozman, Lazarus Maddox (*XIX Arcv. Md.*, p. 3).
1694-1695—John Bozman, Matthew Scarborough, Thomas Dixon, William Whittington (*XIX Arcv. Md.*, pp. 30, 37, 172 and 271).
1696-1697—Francis Jenckins, Thomas Dixon, John Bosman and Matthew Scarborough (*XIX Arcv. Md.*, pp. 287, 329, 332, 475).
1697/8-1699—Francis Jenckins, John Bosman, Samuel Collins, Walter Lane, William Whittington (*XXII Arcv. Md.*, pp. 13, 84, 86, 94, 117, 121 and 126. Walter *Lane's* name several times is erroneously given as *Lowe*).

Justices of the Peace

Stephen Horsey, 1666, 1669; William Stevens, 1666-1687; William Thorne, 1666-1668; James Jones, 1666-1676; John Winder, 1666-1698; Henry Boston, 1666, 1675; George Johnson, 1666-1681; John White, 1666-1680; Henry Smith, 1669, 1683; Edward Smith, 1672, 1675; James Weedon, 1669; William Coulbourne, 1669-1672, 1676-1689; Charles Ballard, 1669-1676; David Browne, 1672-

---

*An election for delegates held at Somerset Court, January 10, 1670/1, resulted in election of Ambrose Dixon, Ambrose London, Capt. Paul Marsh and Roger Woolford to serve for Somerset County. (Somerset Court, Judicials, Liber DT 7, 1670-1, pp. 49 and 52). However, the Assembly proceedings show that only Marsh and Woolford took their seats.

1689; Nicholas Rice, 1672-1675; James Dashiell, 1672-1694; Thomas Walker, 1676; William Jones, 1676-1687; Francis Jenckins, 1676-80, 1689-96; William Brereton, 1676-1689; Roger Woolford, 1676-1697; William Ennis, 1676; Thomas Newbold, 1683, 1689-97; Ambrose London, 1683; Robert King, 1687-1689; James Round, 1687-1699; Stephen Lufte, 1687-1689; Samuel Hopkins, 1687-1699; Edward Day, 1687; Thomas Jones, 1687-1699; Stephen Horsey, 1692-1699; George Layfield, 1692, 1694-1697; John King, 1692-1694; William Whittington, 1692-1694; Edmund Howard, 1687-1697; Arnold Elzey, 1693-1699; Thomas Dixon, 1694-1699; Matthew Scarborough, 1694-1699; John Bosman, 1694-1699; John Francklin, 1697-1699; John Goddin, 1680.

The sources from which the justices names have been obtained, with dates of service, are: *V Arcv. Md.*, p. 61; Somerset Court, Judicials, Liber AZ, 1671-5, p. 217; *XV Arcv. Md.*, pp. 69, 77 and 332; Somerset Deed Liber O 7 [front], pp. 19, 39 and 51; and Deed Liber O 7 [reverse], pp. 3, 4, 6, 11 and 20; Somerset Court, Judicials, Liber AW, November, 1687-June, 1689, and June, 1690-October, 1691; *XIII Arcv. Md.*, p. 224; Somerset Court, Judicials, Liber LD, 1692-3, pp. 78, 154; Judicials, 1692-3, p. 225; Judicials, 1693-4, p. 3, *et seq.;* Judicials, Liber DD, No. 17, 1696-8, pp. 5, 261.

Some Militia Commissions

February 9, 1669—Capt. John White, troop of horse for whole of Somerset; Capt. Paul Marsh, company of foot from Nanticoke to Manokin Rivers; Capt. William Coulbourne, company of foot from Manokin to Pocomoke Rivers (*V Arcv. Md.*, p. 61).

July 11, 1672—Capt. Paul Marsh, of Somerset, to raise and muster company (*Ibid.*, p. 111).

October 25, 1673—Capt. William Coulbourne, of Somerset, captain and commander troop of horse to be raised in Somerset (*Ibid.*, p. 120).

[1682]—Col. William Coulbourne, a Protestant, commands foot troops in Somerset and Dorchester.

Col. William Stevens, a Protestant, commands the horse forces in Somerset and Dorchester (*Ibid.*, pp. 309 and 310).

December 2, 1688—Commissions issued at request of Col. William Stevens, as follows: Capt. Francis Jenckins, Lieut.; Thomas Newbold, Cornet John King, Cornet Thomas Winder (under Capt. John Winder); Charles Ratcliff, Capt.-Lieut. to Col. Stevens; William Coulbourne, Jr., Capt.-Lieut. under Col. Wm. Coulbourne, of the foot forces (*Ibid.*, p. 568).

1689—William Coulbourne, colonel of foot; Charles Ratcliff, captain of foot in room of Capt. Osborne, deceased; Robert King, captain of foot in room of Captain [Henry] Smith; John Winder, captain of horse (*XIII Arcv. Md.*, p. 244).

1694, July—Military Officers of Somerset Co.: David Browne, colonel; Robert King, major; John Winder, John King and Charles Ratcliff, captains of horse;

William Coulbourne, Benjamin Saucer, William Whittington, Arnold Elzey, captains of foot (*XX Arcv. Md.*, p. 110).

October, 1694—David Brown, colonel; John Winder, lieutenant-colonel; William Whittington, major, for Somerset County; appointed under order of Governor and Council that there be three field officers appointed for each county, a colonel, lieutenant-colonel and major, with power to appoint and constitute all officers under them and enlist soldiers in such and so many divisions as they deem proper and convenient; a troope to consist of captain, lieutenant, cornet, quartermaster, clerk, 3 corporals, 36 private troopers and a trumpeter; a company of foot to consist of a captain, lieutenant, ensign, clerk, 3 sergeants, 4 corporals, 2 drummers and 72 private soldiers; where convenient Dragoons to be raised, each troop to consist of a captain, lieutenant, cornet, quartermaster, clerk,—sergeants, 4 corporals and 45 troopers. The colors of horse, foot and Dragoons to be for Somerset County: the union, or Jack flag (*XX Arcv. Md.*, p. 153).

1696—Military Officers of Somerset County (as their names appear signed to address of the province of Maryland to King William and Queen Mary), vizt: David Browne, John Winder, William Whittington, Thomas Winder, Nicholas Evans, Benjamin Lawser [Sawser; Saucer, etc.], James Dashiell, John McClester, Samuel Worthington, Joseph Venalles [Venables], Thomas Dixon, Arnold Elzey, Peter Dent, Edward Hamond [Hammond] (*XX Arcv. Md.*, p. 544).

Appendix V
Somerset County Marriages

(The following list of marriages in Somerset County has been derived from the register in Liber IKL, Somerset Court):

George Andrew and Thomason Hurt [Hart?] September 22, 1672. Richard Ackworth and Sarah Hardy, December 6, 1683. Philip Adams and Anne Crew, July 9, 1670. Richard Allingsworth and Margaret Covington, October 22, 1672. Philip Adams and Mary Barry, September 1, 1691. William Keen, Jr., and Sarah Ackworth, July 14, 1692.

John Browne and Sarah Minard, September 16, 1668. George Betts and Bridgett Bossman, November 7, 1669. Rowland Bevens and Mary Bewry (?), August 4, 1672. John Bishop and Mary Bowen, December 31, 1672. Richard Barnes and Susanna Searle, February 1, 1672. Henry Boston and Elizabeth Rogerson, May 19, 1673. Stephen Bond and Jane Sewell, June 6, 1673. John Barber and Anne Winne (?), August 31, 1680. Roger Berkum and Lucia Jones, December 10, 1681. William Banes and Anne Phesey, December 26, 1684. Pasque Barleigh and Hannah Keene, August 21, 1684. Peter Body and Frances, daughter of Stephen Cannon, December 28, 1686. John Broughton and Elizabeth, daughter of William Bradshaw, February 26, 1684. Anthony Bell and Abigaill Roatch, December 25, 1687. George Benson and Anne Roberts, May, 1682. John Bennett and Sarah Furnis, February 6, 1683.

Daniel Curtis and Mary Greene, July 1, 1666. Thomas Cottingham and Mary, daughter of Ambrose Dixon, July 8, 1666. Nehemiah Covington and [Anne] Ingram, July, 1667. George Cullen and Avis Grottin, October 1, 1673. Richard Chambers and Mary Ivery, May 24, 1676. Philip Connard and Mary Dance (?), December 17, 1677. Robert Cattlin, Jr., and Elizabeth Curtis, February 15, 1676. Leonard Campison and Margaret Morgan, December 26, 1677. John Colehoune and Jane Carter, June, 1676. George Carter and Mary Nichollson, September 4, 1677. Robert Collier and Elizabeth Dashiell, March 2, 1675. Edward Carey and Katherine Ferrill [or Fervill], December 10, 1680. John Covan and Elizabeth Carr, March 8, 1680. John Chissam and Abigaile Bell, August 31, 1678. James Conniew (?) and Dorothy Bundick, September 18, 1673. Samuel Collins and Margaret Hodson, September 3, 1680. James Curtis and Sarah, daughter of Charles Hall, February 2, 1685. William Coulbourne and Anne Revell, June 15, 1678. William Colebourne Curier and Elizabeth, daughter of John Ellis, Jr., June, 1683. Thomas Carroll, Jr., and Rebecca Walton, October 19, 1686. Edmund Collins and Honora ....; entered 16th 9ber, 1692. John Cullen and Mary ...., October 12, 1694.

George Day and Ellianor Ditty (?), June 10, 1669. William Davis and Anne Hooper, August, 1667. Thomas Davis, carpenter, and Judith Bloyes, September, 1671. Matthew Dorman and Phillipa Gillman, August 19, 1672. John Dorman and Sarah Percell, December 31, 1672. Thomas Dixon and Christiana Potter, August 12, 1672. Thomas Dias and Jane Pelingham, September, 1674. Robert Dukes and Elizabeth Dixon, April, 1674. Edward Day and Jane Walker, April, 1681. Thomas Davis, of Annemessex, and Sarah Guy, May 7, 1687. Richard Davis and Elizabeth Barry, [circa 1675?].

Edward Evans and Mary Daniell, May 22, 1677. James English and Sarah Bee, September, 1681. John Ellis, Jr., and Mary, widow of Thomas Shiletto, September, 1686. Thomas Everton and Ann Wood, April, 1686.

John Freeman and Rachel Moodey, July 7, 1671. William Flutcher and Mary King, November 16, 1672. Joseph Freeman and Mary Robbins, February 14, 1673. Marcy Fountain and Mary, daughter of John Bossman, September 14, 1686.

William Greene and Elizabeth, widow of Mark Manlove, February 2, 1666. William Gullett and Susanna Mills, November 1, 1674. George Goddard and Judith Goodin, July 4, 1679. Thomas Gillet and Jane Blades, October 17, 1685.

Henry Hooper and Elizabeth Denwood, July 4, 1669. Edward Hassard and Anne Carr, February, 1671. William Herne and Katherine Mallis, December 31, 1672. John Harrison, Jr., and Judith Godfrey, February 18, 1670. William Howard and Mary Hobday, January 4, 1673. Thomas Humphry and Mary King, April 29, 1674. George Hasfurt and Clements Kerne [Keene?], October 8, 1674. John Hill and Alce Brangeman, September, 1674. George Hasfurt and Elizabeth Hudson, November 29, 1677. Thomas Horssman and Jane Edgar, September 19, 1681. Edmund Howard and Margaret Dent, May 26, 1681. Daniel Haste and Sarah Rogers, August 2, 1680. Robert Hall and Elizabeth

Mackettrick, October 18, 1682. Edward Harper and Lydia Huttson, May 13, 1682. Samuel Handy and Mary Sewell, March, 1679. John Hinderson and Elizabeth Barnabe, July 1, 1680. William Henderson and Sarah Bishop, August, 1684. Timothy Harvey [Harney?] and Elizabeth Greene, December 26, 1682. Richard Harris and Susanna Richardson, January 17, 1682. Henry Hayman, Jr., and Mathewe, daughter of Thomas Standridge, August 24, 1687. Samuel Heyden and Ruth Miver (?), January 23, 1679. William Harris and Alce Roberts, March 5, 1676. Isaac Horsey and Sarah _____, August 7, 1688. Edward Harper and Lydia Hudson, April 4, 1682. Charles Hall, Jr., and Martha Davis, October 31, 1693.

Edward Jones and Mary Barnabe, widow, 1669. Francis Jenckins and Henry Weedon's widow, April 12, 1672. William Jenkins and Ann Stadley, August 26, 1674. Richard James, a Manny Indian, and Honor _____, August 28, 1688. Andrew Jones and Elizabeth Winder, January 13, 1680. Charles Jones and Grissegon Barre [Berré], December 8, 1681. Samuel Jones and Mary Flannakin, Nevember, 1691.

John Ingram and Sarah Prince (?), October 20, 1680. James Ingram and Mary Askewe, August, 1682.

William Keen, Jr., and Sarah Ackworth, July 14, 1692. John King, of Morumsco, and Elizabeth Crew, February 11, 1672. John Kibble and Abigail Horsey, February 27, 1672. Richard Kimble and Jane Jemison, October 18, 1674. John King and Elizabeth Ballard, April 6, 1687.

Samuel Long and Jane Michell [Minshall?], February 15, 1667. Henry Lawrence and Elizabeth Williams, July 4, 1672. William Loudridge and Katherine Jones, March 20, 1674. Timothy Lane and Mary Ball, April 11, 1674. David Lindsey and Sarah Conard, October 5, 1676. George Lane and Dennis Fountaine, October 20, 1678. John Light and Elizabeth Greene, 1680. Thomas Laremore and Katherine _____, August 4, 1680. Thomas Lister and Abigail London, September, 1682. Samuel Lluellen and Anne Kelly, March 30, 1684. Henry Lake and Mary Cooke, December 25, 1683. James Langreene and Alce Primme (?), December 1, 1684. Walter Lane and Sarah Gunby, April 16, 1684. Walter Lane and Sarah Wilson, September 24, 1689. Samuel Long and Elizabeth King, February 22, 1693/4. Thomas Lewes and Anne Parsons, June 3, 1695.

Martin Moore and Margrett Cornelius, April 13, 1667. John Marritt and Hannah Manlove, June 5, 1667. John Marrett and Hannah Manlove, June 25, 1667. Thomas Manlove and Jane Dillamas, 1667. Thomas Moolson and Ann Taylor, 1669. Mark Manlove and Elizabeth Greene, April 4, 1672. John Melson and Elizabeth Painter, April 4, 1672. John Manlove and Elizabeth Lee, August 9, 1672. Lewen [Julien?] Mesex and Sarah Convention, April 29, 1674. William Manlove and Alce Robins, November 1, 1676. Owen Maccrah and Mary Benderwell, April 23, 1676. William Mason and Anne Deane, August 18, 1680. George Marsh and Elizabeth Davis, August 15, 1681. Manus Morris and Elizabeth Ellis, April 23, 1680. Samuel Marchment and Mary Wharton,

March 25, 1685. Griffin Morris and Sarah Vaus, July 23, 1684. John Moore and Anne Mitchell, October 25, 1685. Francis Martin and Mary Roatch, November, 1683. Randolph Minishal and Alice Potter, 169___. John McKnitt and Jane Wallis, March 28, 1693.

James Nicholson and Mary Price, 1663. William Noughton and Katherine Newgent, December 12, 1672. Isaac Noble and Mary Robinson, May 9, 1676. Benjamin Nesham and Elizabeth Jemison, May 10, 1680.

John Oke and Mary Vincent, October 2, 1666. Thomas Owen and Mary Turner, 1669.

Roger Phillips and Dorothy Clarke, October 22, 1672. Richard Partridge and Margaret Lee, November 18, 1671. Henry Pedington and Margaret Griffith, August 25, 1674. John Prout (?) and Mary Wilkinson, September, 1674. William Prentice and Elizabeth Johnson, April 6, 1678. James Pearle and Mary Glover, April 2, 1682. John Puckham [an Indian] and Jone Johnson, Negro, February 25, 1682. George Phebus and Anne Streete, October 14, 1678. John Perkins and Sarah Roatch, March, 1683. Robert Poyer and Rose Bayley, March 4, 1687. Alexander Price and Rebecca, daughter of Alexander Thomas, January 29, 1680. Thomas Phillpot and Mary Goldsmith, July, 1686. John Porter and Elizabeth Gray, January 25, 1688.

John Roch [Roach] and Sarah Williams, February 4, 1663. William Right [Wright] and Frances Bloyse, December 27, 1670. John Rixon and Ann Davis, January 10, 1672. Teauge Riggin and Mary London, 1667. William Robinson and Elizabeth Hady, January 8, 1680. Thomas Relfe and Ann Hoston [Houston?], March 12, 1680. John Rowell and Margarett Gra_____, May, 1686. James Rawley and Jane Wilson, August 15, 1685. Randall Revell and Sarah Ballard, October, 1682.

Edward Surnam and Ann Frowin, _____ 26, 1664. George Smith and Martha Gibbs, October 3, 1671. William Stewnes [Stevens?], formerly called Robert Lewin, and Ann Nolton, August 17, 1668. Richard Shockley and Ann Boyden, October 4, 1674. Thomas Seawell and Jeane Boist, October 8, 1677. Thomas Shiletto and Mary Rogers, January 31, 1678. James Sangster and Mary Benston, November 13, 1679. George Sturges and Frances Nicolls, April 22, 1680. William Steele and Frances Bowzer, November, 1687. William Summer and Margaret Butler, September 18, 1691. Andrew Speer and Priscilla _____, March 10, 1690. John Sargent and Sarah Carne, October 2, 1692. Edward Stockdell and Jane _____, August 9, 1693.

Alexander Thomas and Cicell Shaw, 1678. William Turpin and Margaret Ivery, January 6, 1668. Richard Turner and Elizabeth Teague, March 8, 1672. Thomas Tull and Mary Minshall, October, 1666. George Treherne and Anne Cammeday, August 29, 1676. Nicholas Toadwin [Toadvin] and Sarah Lowry, November 15, 1675. Hugh Tingle and Elizabeth Powell, December 22, 1683. Alexander Trice and Bridgett Eley, September, 1687. Gydeon Tillman and Margurett Maneux, February 15, 1681. John Tyler and Alice Butter, March 8,

1693/4. Richard Tull and Elizabeth Turpin, January 26, 1695/6. John Turpin and Rebecca Bainton, January 23, 1695/6.
Cornelius Ward and Margaret Franklin, January, 1666. Edward Wale [later Whaley] and Elizabeth Ratclife, January 9, 1668. Thomas Wingod and Elizabeth Cooper, January 1, 1669. John White and Sarah Keyser, June 7, 1672. William Walston and Ann Catlin, November 9, 1672. Michael Williams and Ann Williams, February 7, 1672. William Wright and Frances Bloys, December 7, 1669.* Christopher Wright and Isabell Gradwell, June 1, 1673. Richard Webb and Mary Jeferies, May, 1672. Charles Williams and Mary Watson, September 24, 1675. Thomas Wolston [Walston] and Ruth London, April 16, 1677. Thomas Walker and Jane Coppinhall, December, 1674. James Willis and Rebecca Barnabe, March 13, 1679. Edward Wooten and Cullett Southern, January 5, 1679. John Waltham and Peerse Manlove, May 25, 1681. Edward Wheeler and Margaret Hardy, February 10, 1682. Thomas Williams and Frances Robinson, June 10, 1674. William Wilson and Mary Cotman, October 29, 1688. George Wilson and Jane Cooper, April 4, 1692. Abell Wright and Katherine Clarke, January 12, 1695/6.

* * * * *

(The following are records of Marriage Banns "published" in Somerset County Court and record made thereof in the court minutes):
Deed Liber O 1 (including court proceedings): September 4, 1666—John Okee and Mary Vincent, both of Manokin; Thomas Tull, of Annemessex, and Mary Mitchell [Minshall], of Morumsco (p. 29). November 27, 1666—William Greene and Elizabeth Manlove, both of Pocomoke; Cornelius Ward and Margaret Frankling, both of Annemessex; Robert Dorman and Elizabeth Knight, both of Manokin; Anthony Taylor and Alce Bassett, both of Annemessex (p. 41). January 29, 1666 [1666/7]—Benjamin Sumbler and Isabel Wale, both of Somerset (p. 51). March 26, 1667—Martin Moore and Margarett Cornelius; John Panter and Mary Williams; Peter Calloway and Elizabeth Johnson; William Davis and Elizabeth Hooper, all of Somerset (p. 62). May 28, 1667—John Mackettrick and Mary Allen, widow; John Marlett and Hannah Manlove; John Cooper and Susanna Brayfield; John Sterling and Alce Basset, all of Somerset (p. 68). July 30, 1667—Thomas Manlove and Jane Lamas; Teege Riggin and Mary London, all of Somerset (p. 79). November 26, 1667—David Williams and Jane Covington (p. 90). January 28, 1667 [1667/8]—Henry Miles and Mary Barnabe, widow (p. 107). April 26, 1668—Arthur Evitt and Mary Gray; James Davis and Ann Marckum; William Canneday and Anne Pisher, all of Somerset (p. 112). June 30, 1668—Thomas Covington and Susanna Cooper; Robert Lewen and Anne Nolton, all of Somerset (p. 116). September 29, 1668—George Mitchell and Izabell Higgins, of Somerset; William Cockee, of Severne [Anne Arundel County], and Frances Vincent, of Somerset (p. 136).

---

*Also entered as Wm. *Right* and Frances Bloyse, *December 27, 1670* (see above).

Liber DT, No. 7 (Judicials, 1670-1): September 14, 1670—John Tyferd and Barbara Lawrence, both of Somerset (p. 18). November 8, 1670—Thomas Davis, taylor [tailor], and Judith Best, both of Somerset (p. 37). December 27, 1670—Rowland Bevend and Margaret Price, both of Somerset (p. 49). January 10, 1670/1—John Harrison and Judith Godfrey; John Walker and Rachel Moody,* all of Somerset (p. 68). March 14, 1670/1—George Hamblin and Margaret Pepper, both of Somerset (p. 122). June 13, 1671—John Freeman and Rachel Moody; John Lawes and Katherine Nelson, widow, all of Somerset (p. 133). April 10, 1671—John Pepper gives permission to marriage of his daughter [name not entered] to George Hamill, and prays "certificate" may be sent by bearer (p. 160). August 8, 1671—James Nicholls and Martha Popley; Richard Turner and Elizabeth Teague, widow; David Bishop and Sarah Persill, all of Somerset (p. 182). August 9, 1671—William Herne, of Mattapony, Somerset County, caused his banns of matrimony with Katherine Maltis, widow, to be set up at courthouse. The court being informed that said Katherine "goes under the notion of John Pikes' wife, of Mattapony," orders same taken down and orders said Herne to be taken into custody until he give security for his good behavior (p. 193).†

Liber AZ, No. 8 (Judicials, 1671-5): December 8, 1671—Edward Hassard and Ann Carr, of Somerset (p. 26). January 9, 1671/2—Richard Tull and Martha Rhoades; John Melson and Elizabeth Painter, all of Somerset (p. 43). May, 1672—Richard Webb and Mary Jefferies ; April, 1672—Henry Lawrence and Elizabeth Williams; April 5, 1672—Mark Manlove and Elizabeth Greene (p. 84). [1675?]—Charles Williams and Mary Watson; John Winsar and Elizabeth Gager, all of Somerset (p. 551).

Deed Liber O 7 [reverse: court proceeding, 1675-7]: January, 1675/6, Isaac Noble and Mary Robeson (p. 27). March 14, 1675/6—Joseph Taylor and Margaret Rollens; John Richards and Grace Dixon; Richard Davis and Elizabeth Berre; Richard Chambers and Mary Ivery; Richard Lawe and Anne Smith, all of Somerset (p. 39). April 18, 1676—Benjamin Summers and Deborah Wooldridge, both of Somerset (p. 42). June 16, 1676—John Colehoune and Jane Carter, both of Somerset (p. 43). August 8, 1676—Thomas Holbrook and Alce Leverton; Tobias Piper and Mary Empson; William Manlove and Mary Robbins; Thomas Roberts and Ann Webb; John Rickards and Elizabeth Trevett, all of Somerset; Anguish Morroe, of Dorsett [Dorchester County], and Rose Daniel, of Somerset (p. 45). 1676—George Treherne and Anne Cameday; Nicholas Silvero and Elizabeth Barnett; David Lindsey and Sarah Connard;‡ Thomas Davis, planter, of Manokin, and Mary Nicholson, all of Somerset

*John Freeman in behalf of Rachel Moody "underwrites" these banns: "Rachell Moody hath nothing to say to John Walker in the way of matrimony, therefore its no effect." The banns of John Freeman and Rachel Moody were "published" June 13, 1671, and they were married July 7, 1671.
†Whatever may have been the validity of this "notion," it appears that William Herne and Katherine Mallis [Maltis] were married December 31, 1672.
‡September 17, 1676, Philip Connard, "naturall fathr" of Sarah, forbade these banns; then gave consent to the marriage (p. 59).

(p. 54). October 24, 1676—Nicholas Toadvine and Sarah Loury; John Chancellour and Abigail Harringdon, all of Wicomico Hundred (p. 60). November 14, 1676—Isaac Hilliard and Mary Thomas; John Hilliard and Alce Roberts; Alexander Mitcheller and Anne Surnam; John Aleward and Mary Dixon; Francis Gunby and Sarah Kirke, all of Somerset (p. 62). January 9, 1676/7—John Robeson and Tanzine Prideaux; Jacob Jones and Elizabeth Stevens; Robert Catlin and Elizabeth Curtis; Evan Williams and Mary Periman, all of Somerset (p. 70). February 5, 1676/7—William Yalding and Mary Wilson (p. 85). June 12, 1677—John Wright and Mary Fox; John Rowell and Mary Owen; George Downes and Anne Bossman, all of Somerset; Henry Lewis, of Anne Arundel County, and Elizabeth Boston, of Somerset (p. 100). August 14, 1677—Richard Higgenbothem and Dennis Fountaine; Samuel Jones and Mary Davis; George Carter and Mary Nichollson; Richard Prim and Alce Wilson; Daniel Shealy and Elianor Harris (p. 121).

Deed Liber O 7 [front: court proceedings, November, 1683-March, 1683/]: November 13, 1683—John Barnett and Alce Taylor; Henry Lake and Mary Cooke (both servants of Thos. Cottingham), all of Somerset (p. 11). January 8, 1683/4—John Bennett and Mary Furnis; John Cowdry and Mary Nuttley, all of Somerset (p. 18). February 5, 1683/4—Hope Taylor and Margaret Doricks (? by any possibility intended for Daniels?) (p. 23).

Appendix VI

First Court House Sites and First Towns in Somerset
(A) First Court House Sites in Somerset

The earliest record for *"A Court helld . . . on ye Easterne Shore in ye province of Maryland . . ."* (i. e. for the territorial area between the Choptank River and Watkins Point at the mouth of the Pocomoke River, designated by proclamation, November 6, 1661, as "the Easterne Shore") bears date *"Monday ye 11th december 1665"* and carries the specific statement *"At a Court helld att Thomas Poole['s] . . . in Manoakin . . ."* (see *ante*, p. 61, *et seq.*, and Appendix I; see also Somerset Court, Deed Liber O 1, p. 1).

The place thus specified as that at which the court was held was the home of Thomas Poole, situated on a tract of land called "Poole's Hope" on the south side of the Back Creek of Manokin River, near the head of the creek and in the settlement called Manoakin, which later became Manokin Hundred, after the creation of Somerset County in 1666. On March 30, 1669, Thomas Poole sold and conveyed 200 acres of the "Poole's Hope" tract to one James Davis, designating the acreage so conveyed as "Davis' Change" (Deed Liber O 2, p. 6), and there is a reference to *"A Co*rt* helld in Mr Revell's Neck* at the house . . .*

---
*Randall Revell claimed all the lands in this vicinity as part of his survey of "Double Purchase." However, the Poole-Davis tract was not in "Revell's Neck."

James Davis did live in In the yeare one thousand six hundred and Sixty Nine" (Judicials, Liber AZ, 1671-5, p. 364, a statement in testimony of one Edward Dickinson, August 11, 1674).

It is quite evident from these data that the courts for "the Eastern Shore below Choptank River," and for Somerset County, were held at this designated location from December, 1665 (and probably before that date), up to and including the year 1669.

While the *regular* place for holding court appears to have been at "Poole's Hope" (the Thomas Poole, later the James Davis house), there are extant items of record which make it evident that at certain times sessions of court were held at the houses of certain commissioners, or justices, of the peace for the county. The following entries in the records are evidence of this fact: "21 Jany. 1669 [1669/70] To Mr John Winder for Trouble & Charge of *keeping Co^{rt} at his house* . . . 300 [pounds of tobacco]" and "*Court held at the house of Mr Stephen Horsi [Horsey] 15 June [1671]*" (Judicials, Liber AZ, 1671-5, p. 68; and Judicials, Liber DT 7, 1670-1, p. 155). Winder was a commissioner of the peace for Somerset and was living at the date referred to on "Winder's Purchase" tract on the Back Creek (see *ante,* p. 332). Stephen Horsey, a prominent official of the county, lived on the south side of the Annemessex River, near Coulbourne's Creek (see *ante,* p. 300).

The exact date of the abandonment of the Poole-Davis house as the *regular* place of holding court for Somerset County has not been discovered. It appears, however, that by *August, 1670,* the "now Court house" was located on the south side of the Manokin River at some place (whose situation is not definitely stated) below the mouth of "the Trading Branch (at this time, 1935, King's Creek). The evidence of this fact appears in depositions made in August, 1670, relative to the location of this so-called Trading Branch. The exact location of this "now Court house' 'of 1670 has evaded us in our research but certainly it was on Randall Revell's land in what is familiarly called "Revell's Neck" and at most only a distance of a mile or two (maybe less) below the mouth of the Trading Branch, which records surely identify as the present King's Creek, and on the Manokin River. It is not improbable, and we believe it true, that this "now Court house" of 1670 was a house in, or near by, the old Somerset Town (or Sommerton), which had been established in 1668 on Revell's land at Deep Point on the Manokin River (see *post* for Somerset Town). In a deposition made on August 9, 1670, one German Gillett refers to "the Trading Branch . . . which is the second branch from the now Court house"; while one Richard Bundick in a deposition made on the same date refers to the Trading Branch as being "the second branch on the south side of Manoakin River from the now Court house upwards."* This designation of the site of the "now

---

*These depositions appear in Somerset Court, Judicials, Liber DT No. 7, 1670-1, p. 6, *et seq.,* at a court held September 13, 1670, as evidence in plea of trespass, Randall Revell vs. Richard Ackworth. Ackworth it appears had cut down two oak trees which Revell claimed were on land included in his patent for the tract called "the Double Purchase," of which the northeastern boundary called for was *"the Trading Branch."* The question at issue was the correct location of this so-called *Trading Branch.* Revell was at this time contending that it was the "uppermost fork"

Court house" in August, 1670, definitely places it as below (southwest) of the mouth of the Trading Branch (now King's Creek).

While this 1670 reference says the *"now Court house,"* it is evident (from records presently to be quoted) that the house so used and designated was one that had not been specifically erected as a "Court House." It was no doubt a house conveniently situated for such usage and which had been designated by the county authorities as a place for holding sessions of court.

Though Somerset County had been created by proclamation, August 22, 1666, yet no definite decision appears to have been made as to the most convenient location for the "county seat" and no "Court House" had been erected prior to the Spring of 1671. On April 19, 1671, the governor of the province issued an order to Somerset Court calling attention to the necessity for erecting a permanent court house for the county and stating that he had been informed that no agreement had been reached as to where the court house should be situated. This order emphasized the necessity for locating the court house as conveniently as possible to the inhabitants of the county and directed that James Jones, Stephen Horsey and George Johnson (three of the justices for Somerset) should determine on some spot of ground near the center of the county and to encourage some one to erect the necessary buildings thereon (Judicials, Liber DT 7, 1670-1, p. 132). On September 13, 1671, James Jones and George Johnson, two of the justices* named in the governor's order of April 19th, preceding, and in compliance with the said order, reported to the court that they "doe pitch upon the eastmost side of the branch or Creeke called Trading Branch or creeke near unto the place where John Westlock is now seating to be the hart [heart] of the county"† (Judicials, Liber DT 7, 1670-1, p. 211). We have not been able to ascertain this reported location with any degree of exactness.

As early as January 10, 1670/1 the commissioners of Somerset County were

---

of the *Manokin River.* There was much befogging in the evidence; but the matter was finally cleared. This case was decided in favor of the defendant Ackworth.

Records abundantly prove that *the Trading Branch,* whose location Revell called in question, is identical with the *King's Creek* of this present time (1935) and is the *lower fork* of the Manokin River. The *"upper fork"* of the river is identical with the Jones' Creek of this present time (1935). The *Trading Branch* was also called *Mudford,* and later *King's Branch.* In March, 1682, Randall Revell conveyed to Robert King a tract of 300 acres (now to be called Kingsland), which said 300 acres is stated in deed to "begin . . . on eastmost side of a small branch . . . called Surnam's Branch which trendeth out of an arm of Manokin River called *Trading Branch alias Mudford"* (Somerset Deed Liber O 6, p. 630). This "Kingsland" acreage can today be located on the south side of the present *King's Creek.* In 1734 a deed of Whittington King to Daniel Long refers to *"King's Branch alias Trading Branch"* and *"King's Branch commonly called Mudford or Trading Branch"* (Somerset Deed Liber O 21, p. 103).

The name Trading Branch was given to this stream, owing to the fact that the Manokin Indians (who lived in the neck of land just north—in that day called "the Indian Neck" and today [1935] called "Stewart's Neck") did their trading here with incoming white traders. It has not been discovered how it obtained the name of Mudford. The present name of King's Creek is derived from the fact of the extensive ownrship of lands along the crek by the families of Maj. Robert King, of "Kingsland," and Capt. John King, of "Oxhead" plantation (which was at the very headwaters of the creek).

The Trading Branch, alias Mudford, and now King's Creek, enters the Manokin River on the south side thereof about midway between the mouth and headwaters of the river.

*Stephen Horsey (the other jusice named in the governor's order) had died, August 8, 1671 (see *ante,* p. 302).

†We have not been able to locate the tract where John Westlock was "seating" or settling at this date.

negotiating with Henry Smith in regard to providing a proper house for a court house for the county in a location which would be approved by the court. Smith proposed to the court, January 10, 1670/1, that in consideration of certain specified amercements he would (at his own charge) "finde A convenient house to keepe Co^{rt} in or to use for any other publicke meeting so long as the Co^{rt} for this County shall thinke fitte to make use of the same." The court acceded to this proposition (Judicials, Liber DT 7, 1670-1, p. 62, for date of this court,* and p. 92 for the record). Whatever may have occurred in the way of discussion as to the most convenient location for the "court house" we find on November 16, 1671, that the justices entered into further agreement with Henry Smith to erect stocks, ducking stool, etc., and also provide a convenient house for meetings of court *"at the head of Back Creek, at Manoakin, upon plantation of [where] Tho: Poole, lately lived and where the Co^{rs} [courts] for this County was formerly kept."* This record of November 16, 1671, refers to the "order of a Court held for this County in January last past [i. e. January, 1670/1]" and the agreement then made as to Smith's receiving certain amercements for his work (Judicials, Liber AZ, 1671-5, pp. 27-8). At this date, November, 1671, Henry Smith had acquired possession of the whole of the "Poole's Hope" tract at the head of Back Creek, where this order of court directed him to erect stocks, ducking stool, etc., and provide a house for holding court and other public meetings.†

So it is that we have the direction of the court in November, 1671, that Smith utilize the site *where Thomas Poole formerly lived and where the courts of the county were formerly held.* What Henry Smith did in the way of carrying out the court's order in regard to building operations on this specified tract we cannot say. However, there seems to have been further consideration of the matter of a site for the hourt house.

On April 6, 1675, a warrant was granted for laying out 50 acres of land for the use of Somerset County, and on April 22nd the deputy surveyor for Somerset County made return that he had laid out for the county's use a tract of 50 acres, to be called *Ilchester,* "near the head of Manokin River about three miles back in the woods from the said river . . . beginning at a marked red oake standing on the southwest side of a branch of Manoakin River called Smith's branch

---

*Liber DT, No. 7, 1670-1, gives this court as "At a County Cort helld the 10 day of Jan. in the XXXIX year of . . . the Rt honble Cæcilius . . . Lord Proprietary . . ." In Testamentary Papers, 1671 (12-8), in Hall Records, Annapols, there is a paper dated January 19th, *40th year* of Cecil Calvert, Lord Baltimore, *1671* [i. e. 1671/2]. If January 19, *1671,* was the 40th year of Cecil, Lord Baltimore then the *39th year* of his Lordship would be January, *1670* or *1670/1.*

†Somerset Court, Deed Liber O 2, p. 6, deed March 30, 1669, Thos. Poole to James Davis for 200 acres of "Poole's Hope"; *Ibid.,* p. 7, deed March 30, 1669, James Davis to William Thompson, reconveying 100 acres of this same tract; Deed Liber O 3, p. 65, deed, 1671, William Thompson to Henry Smith, reconveying the same 100 acres; Judicials, Liber DT, No. 7, 1670-1, p. 166, deed March 23, 1670 [1670/1], Thos. Poole to Henry Smith, for 100 acres of "Poole's Hope," of which Poole had sold 200 acres to James Davis in 1669. To continue the "descent" of the title to "Poole's Hope" we find that in November, 1674, Henry Smith sold to Gidion Tillman the 100 acres of "Poole's Hope" which Smith had formerly purchased of Wm. Thompson, and now to be called "Thompson's Advnture" (Deed Liber, O 4, p. 112). On May 30, 1678, Jas. Davis sold to Gideon Tillman 100 acres of "Poole's Hope," then known as "Davis Change" (Deed Liber O 5, p. 323). In 1674 Henry Smith sold to Wm. Furniss 100 acres of "Poole's Hope" which he bought of Thos. Poole in 1670/1 and then called "Smith's Chance" (Deed Liber O 4). Therefore, the original 300 acres of "Pool's Hope" tract was by 1678 in the hands of Gideon Tillman and William Furniss.

..." This return of order and survey was made to Somerset Court August 10, 1675* (Judicials, Liber AZ, 1671-5, p. 554). At Somerset Court, November 10, 1675, "It is ordered that the Tobacco in the hands of Cap^{ta} William Colebourne Sherife of this County wch was Levied towards the building of *A Court house & prison*† be paid unto Mr David Browne of this county, gent^l the same to be paid by the Said Mr David Browne to ye Workemen for the building of the said Court house & Prison" (Deed Liber O 7 [back], Judicials, 1675-6, p. 27).‡ Then on June 15, 1676, it was "Ordered by his Lordship that Two ac[res of land] adjacent to *the Court house new e[rected] for Somerset County* never y[et taken] up [i. e. not patented] be reserved and confirm[ed to the] Commission^{rs} of the said County for [the use] of the said Commission^{ers} and county [aforesaid]" (*II. Arcv. Md.*, p. 515). Whether this *"Court house new Erected for Somerset County"* and thus referred to under date of June 15, 1676, was on the "Ilchester" tract before referred to we cannot definitely say. We have found neither deed nor patent for the tract called "Ilchester" issued to Somerset County, and no record appears of the reservation of the 2 acres on which *"the Court house new E[rected]"* in June, 1675, was situated. We have found no details of record relative to the erection of this court house, though its use may be evidenced by the record that a court was held *"At the Co^{rt} house* the 13th day of June . . . 1676" (Deed Liber O 7 [back], Judicials, 1675-6, p. 43). Whether the erection of the court house was on the "Ilchester" tract, which certainly seems to have been contemplated by the warrant and survey in April, 1675, we cannot say. It is not impossible that it may have been erected on the "Poole's

---

*Though we have found no record of patent or deed to the Somerset County authorities for the 50-acre tract to be called "Ilchester," we find a survey under warrant, April 5, 1683, for a tract called "Ilchester," 900 acres on south side Manokin River, back in the woods from the water side, the first bounder being "a white oak standing on south side Smith's Branch" and one of the lines extending to "westermost side of the head of King's Branch." (Patent Liber 22, p. 31, Hall of Records, Annapolis). This 900-acre "Ilchester" tract was certainly in the head branches of the upper fork of the Manokin River—the branches of what is now (1935) called *Jones' Creek*. The tract owned by Henry Smith was sold off in parcels by certain trustees appointed to dispose of his estate. In June, 1707, Whittington, West and Dent, commissioners, sold to James Strawbridge 500 acres out of a tract called "Ilchester" granted to Henry Smith, deceased, and now sold for a debt due Arnold Elzey and Richard Chambers. The said tract described as "beginning at a white oak standing in a swamp on ye south side of a ridge called *the Court House Ridge*" and a line thereof ran to "westermost side the head of King's Branch." (Somerset Court, Deed Liber O 10, p. 43-4). Here we crtainly have an indication of a *Court House* in close proximity to a tract called "Ilchester." We do not attempt to explain the matter; but simply state the record for future investigators. The Somerset and Dorchester Rent Rolls (Maryland Historical Society, Baltimore), p. 46, give: "Ilchester [in Manokin Hundred, Somerset County] surveyed May 25, 1683, for Capt. Henry Smith; possessors: John Knox, 150 acres; James Strawbridge, 500 aacres; Margaret Goldsmith, 100 acres; Wm. Knox, 75 acres; the other part being 75 acres, in all 150 acres."

†We did not find the record of this "levy."

‡Other records bearing on county buildings at this time are: March 10, 1675 [1674/5], Chas. Ballard and David Brown ordered to take up piece of land to build prison on for Somerset County in some convenient place they shall think fit and make agreement with a carpenter for building said prison. June 8, 1675, at court held June 8, 1675, "Whereas at March Crt upon the debating the business of A Cort house Mr Randall Revell made a proposition to finde a prison built for the use of the county the concluding of which was put off till this Court at which the justices have ordered that the house built near Randall Revell's dwelling house be the prison for this county till the 25th March next ensueing [i. e. March 25, 1676] and do order that five hundred pounds of tobacco be paid to the said Randall Revell for locks and bolts for the same" (Somerset Court, Judicials, Liber AZ, 1671-5, pp. 525 and 539-540). In Somerset Court, Deed Liber O 7 [back], Judicials, 1675-7, we find this entry: "Memorandum. That this day to witt the eleaventh day of Janry Anno Dom 1675 [1675/6] *at the Court house kept at Mr Randall Revells in Manoakin* in the County of Somersett . . ."; the court to be held this day was adjourned to second Tuesday [14th], February, 1675, [1675/6]. In same Liber, O 7 [back], p. 40, at a court held March 31, 1676, proclamation of election for burgesses to be held "at the house of Mr Randall Revell on Tuesday the 18th day of Aprill now next comeing at A Cor then to be holden . . ."

Hope" tract at the head of Back Creek as contemplated in the court order of November, 1671, when agreement was made with Henry Smith. The location of *"the Court house new Erected,"* which appears in Lord Baltimore's order relative to the reservation of the adjacent 2 acres of land in June, 1676, we cannot positively state; but that court house, whatever its situation, was evidently the first court house, specifically erected as such, for Somerset County. Of this fact we feel assured.

What happened to the court house which appears as "new Erected" in June, 1675, we do not know; but in November, 1683, we find again a reference to a *"New Court house called Unity."* At a court held November 14, 1683, we find the order "That Co^{rt} adjournes till the twenty seaventh day of this present Month of November and all process to stand good that are executed And further ordrd the County Charge then to be Laid *at the New Co^{rt} house called Unity"* (Deed Liber O 7 [front], Judicials, November, 1683-March, 1683/4, p. 8).* Then at a court held by adjournment, November 28, 1683, "Capt^a Henry Smith made a proposall *to finish the Co^{rt} house* for and in consideration of twelve thousand pounds of tobacco to be paid the present year out of ye County Leavy & five hundred pounds of tobacco for the fine of Elizabeth Dornington due to be paid by John Walter as security to be performed in Work of his trade Capt^a John Winder securitie to see the same performed . . ." The court accepted Captain Smith's proposal and directed him *"to finish or Cause to be finished the Court house* well plankt above as also below with good & substantiall sleepers in both the Lower roomes the upper roome to be divided into Two the outermost doores of ye house with hinges Locks and keyes staires glass windowes Carpenters Joyners & Turners worke Barr Seates for Justices pinacles Tables & all other necessaries to ye Compleating of ye said Co^{rt} house." On the same day Captain Smith proposed to build a sufficient dwelling house and stable, with rack and manger, for the use of the county his remuneration to be "the severall fines for spinning of wool unto good yarne." The court accepted this proposal also and directed that Smith "Cause the said Houses to be built accordingly *on the Countries Land where the Court house now is"* (Deed Liber O 7 [front], Judicials, November, 1683-March, 1683/4, p. 14).

These orders of court of November 14 and 28, 1683, relative to *"the New Court house called Unity,"* and to Captain Smith's *finishing "the Co^{rt} house,"* and the erection of a dwelling house and stable *"on the Countries Land where the Court house now is"* inevitably raises the question: Was this *"New Court house called Unity,"* at which an adjourned court was directed to meet on November 27, 1683, and which appears to have been *"on the Countries Land,"* and in such an unfinished and incomplete state of construction at this date, really on the 2 acres of land *"adjacent to the Court house new Erected"* as of

---

*Why this "New Court house" was "called Unity" we do not know. It certainly was not located on one of the several tracts of land in Somerset County which bore the patent tract name of "Unity," but on the tract of land called "Webley." We hazard the guess that the name "Unity" was here applied (and only this once do find the court house so-called) because this court house had been located here as the result of a practical uniformity of opinion that this site was the most convenient one for it.

date June 15, 1676, which land Lord Baltimore ordered (on that date) "be reserved and confirm[ed to the] Commission^{rs} of the said County for [the use] of the said Commission^{ers} and County [aforesaid]"? The circumstances inevitably raise the question; though we cannot answer it.

However, we can certainly "locate" this *"New Court house called Unity"* of November, 1683, as being on a tract of land called "Webley."* On January 12, 1687 [1687/8], the court of Somerset "Or^d that the Clerk draw a conveyance for the tenn acres of land *where the Court house is* from Andrew Whittington and wife to any two of ye Com^s [commissions; i. e. justices of the peace] y^t he shall think fitt and to their successors forever" (Judicials, Liber AW, 1687-9 and 1690-1, pp. 24 and 94). It was several years before this deed was finally made, but on June 18, 1692, Andrew Whittington and Ursula, his wife (for 1,000 pounds tobacco), conveyed to Francis Jenckins, and others, the justices of the peace for Somerset County, "a certain tract or parcel of land containing and laid out for ten acres, being part of a certain tract containing 250 acres called 'Webby' [Webley, or Webly] as by Patent doth apear, which said ten acres being part of the aforesaid 250 acres of land called 'Webby,' now lies situate and being on the south side of Manokin River in the aforesaid Somerset Coun*ty whereon the present Court House now stands* upon the aforesaid ten acres, which as aforesaid is surveyed and laid out but the Plat not herein inserted, To Have and To Hold, &c., &c., the said land for the only proper use of the said Justices *to build a Court House upon*† and to keep Court for the good of this said County of Somerset, and likewise to build a Church upon and Alms House and such like charitable uses.‡ But in no wise for any person or persons whatsoever to keep an Ordinary thereon or to raise a Shoppe or otherwise that may be detrimental and prejudicial to us the said Andrew and Ursula or to our heirs. . . ." This deed was recorded in Somerset Court, June 21, 1692, with the "Memorandum that the inserted Ursula refused to sign and seal the above conveyance" (Deed Liber O 7, p. 28).

Before considering the location of this "Webley" (or "Webby") tract let us return to the matter of the completion of the court house building. No doubt Captain Henry Smith did the work on the building for which he agreed with the court on November 28, 1683; however, more work seemed necessary to

---

*This tract called "Webley" appears in later records also as "Webby"; doubtless a clerical error for "Webly."
†An inference from this wording would be that, after all, the court house had not been built, or completed, at time this deed was made in June, 1692. However, it is certain that Somerset Court held sessions Dec. 10, 1692, in Andrew Washington's house (see *ante*, p. 354).
‡It was in June, 1692, that the Act establishing the Protestant religion in the province of Maryland was passed by the General Assembly, which Act carried provisions for laying the counties out into parishes and erecting parish churches and Chapels of Ease. In acquiring this land of Whittington's for a court house, etc., the erecttion of a parish church at the court house was no doubt contemplated. However, no record has been found that indicates that a church was ever erected on this land in question; while it is known that the church for Somerset Parish was erected on the north side of the Manokin River on an acre of ground of the "Almodington" tract, just west of the mouth of Goose Creek. (See *ante*, p. 163, for provision of the Act of Establishment for building parish churches, and p. 180, *et seq.*, for the church of Somerset Parish). In after years, about 1715-20, a Chapel of Ease for Somerset Parish was erected on the north side of King's Creeek, on the tract called "Chance," which joined the "Webley" tract (see *ante*, pp. 192-3, for "King's Mill Chapel").

make the building what was desired. On November 14, 1688, the court made an agreement with one William Venables "to cover the court house and to remove the stairs that now are and to make a staircase in the next corner and to remove the partition further in and to make a table for the justices as also to make a seat for the justices with agreeable chairs in the middle and a panell overhead, the said chairs with my Lord's [i. e. Lord Baltimore's] coat of arms to be carved in the same and a barr with a table and seat for the clerk and the same and every part thereof to be well made according to plat" and Venables was to furnish the necessary materials for this work and to receive 5,500 pounds of tobacco therefor (Judicials, Liber AW, 1687-9 and 1690-1, p. 94). Thus was completed this court house of Somerset County which was situated on the tract of land called "Webley" (or "Webby").

Now as to the location of the "Webley" tract. On October 14, 1679, a special warrant was granted Henry Smith, of Somerset County, for resurveying and laying out two tracts of land called "Thompson's Purchase" and "Narsworthy's Choice" (with waste lands adjacent) into one or more surveys. By virtue of this special warrant parts and parcels of the said lands were resurveyed and laid out into a tract called "Webley." This tract called "Webley" contained 250 acres and lay in the so-called Indian Neck to south of the main branch of the Upper Fork of Manokin River, extending in a southerly direction to Trading Branch. On December 24, 1679, Henry Smith assigned the said "Webley" tract to Andrew Whittington. This "Webley" tract may today be located about a mile south of the town of Princess Anne, Somerset County, on the main highway leading south.* We cannot say positively on just which section of the "Webley" tract the court house stood.

The court house for Somerset County was not, however, to remain for long on the "Webley" tract site, after the deed finally passed, in June, 1692, from Andrew Whittington to the justices of Somerset.

---

*The survey and assignment of the "Webley" tract are recorded in Liber 21, p. 151, Hall of Records, Annapolis, Maryland. The "Upper Fork" of Manokin River, referred to in the survey, is identified today (1935) in "Jones' Creek." "The Indian Neck" comprised the lands between the Upper Fork of Manokin River (now Jones' Creek) and the Trading Branch (now King's Creek). At Andrew Whittington's death in 1694 "Webley" became the inheritance of his daughter Ursula, who married John King, and so passed to her son, Whittington King. On February 10, 1734 [1734/5], Whittington King conveyed part of the "Webley" tract to his brother, John King; at the same time also conveying to him the tract called "Chance" of 90 acres. The tract called "Chance" also lay on north side of Trading Branch (or King's Creek). "Webley" and "Chance" adjoined each other (Somerset Court, Deed Liber O 18, p. 205, deed of Whittington King to his brother, John King). The tract called "Chance" was granted to Henry Smith in 1675 under warrant of survey, January 19, 1673, and by Smith conveyed to Andrew Whittington in October, 1681, and from Andrew Whittington passed to his daughter Ursula, who married John King, and thence to their son, Whittington King, and from him to his brother, John King (Liber 18, folio 59, Hall of Records, Annapolis, Maryland; Somerset Court, Deed Liber O 6, p. 523, deed of Smith and wife to Andrew Whittington, and Deed Liber O 18, p. 205, deed Whittington King to brother, John King. See also Somerset and Dorchester County Rent Rolls, No. 1, pp. 50 and 52, Hall of Records, Annapolis, for entries relative to "Chance" and "Webley."

It is interesting to note that, in after years, when the ancient and honorable "Washington Academy" was moved from its original site on the "Westover" tract at the head of Back Creek (north side) its new building was erected on a part of the "Webley" tract about a mile south of the town of Princess Anne. This (second) site of "Washington Academy" is well known today. Some years later "Washington Academy" was moved into the town of Princess Anne and a frame structure erected for its building. In more recent years a building was erected for the Washington High School, in Princess Anne ,out of the bricks of the abandoned academy building on the "Webley" tract. Washington High School, Princess Anne, is the successor of "Washington Academy" and stands on the Washington Academy (third site) grounds in Princess Anne.

At Somerset Court, June 15, 1693, we find this order entered: "Whereas all the Justices were Sumoned to this Court to Consult of a New Court House &ca. It was this day (viz) the 15th day of June an° Domini 1693 The opinion of the Justices then in Court to have the new Court house at the Dividing Creek near London Bridge. Justices present Mr Fra: Jenckins, Mr Ja: Round, Mr Saml Hopkins, & Mr Edm^d Howard."*

On March 1, 1694, it was ordered by Somerset Court that Francis Jenckins and William Whittington purchase a tract of land not exceeding 200 acres, near Dividing Creek, Somerset County, and erect thereon a court house, 50 x 20 feet, gable ends of brick and chimney below and above, to be underpinned with brick; the said Jenckins and Whittington to have full charge and direction of the work and the cost to be borne by the county. In pursuance of this order, on June 18, 1694, the justices of Somerset purchased from Edward Stockdell, and Jane, his wife, the tract called "Little Derry," on the west side of Dividing Creek† and north side of the Pocomoke River.‡ At this site a new court house was erected and the courts of Somerset County were held until the division of Somerset County in 1742 and the erection of Worcester County from the area along the seaboard side and to the south of the Pocomoke River. At the time of this division the court house for Somerset County was moved to the town of Princess Anne, where it has remained to this present time. The last court for Somerset was held at Dividing Creek in November, 1742, and the first court for the county held in Princess Anne Town was that of March, 1742 [1742/3]. The new (and first) court house erected in Princess Anne Town was completed for the court held in June, 1747 (Somerset Court, Judicials, 1742-4, pp. 24 and 72; Judicials, 1744-7, record of June Court, 1747).

* * * * *

(B) First Towns in Somerset County

Somerset County having been created in August, 1666, was included in the declaration of the lieutenant-general [i. e. the governor] and Council of the

---

*Somerset Court, Judicials, 1692-3, p. 247.
†The site of the location of this court house at Dividing Creek may be located at this present time (1935) as a lot of ground on the north side of the Pocomoke River and west side of Dividing Creek, very near where the creek enters the river. This site is well known and is about 2 miles east of the highway from Princess Anne to Pocomoke City, Maryland.
‡Though the court house was erected at Dividing Creek, the change from the old site on the "Webley" tract was not effected without considerable disturbance. An influential element in the population of Somerset County did not wish this change; while another element attempted to erect a court house in the extreme southern part of the county within six miles of the Maryland-Virginia boundary line. The provincial authorities were drawn into the controversy, only finally subduing the objectors by threatening to divide the county in half and making two counties, one on the seaboard side and one on the Bay side. See *XX Arcv. Md.*, p. 132; *XIX Arcv. Md.*, pp. 94, 246, 290, 303 and 340; *XXII Arcv. Md.*, pp. 102-103. See also a paper on the court houses of Somerset County, prepared by H. Filmore Lankford, Esq., of Princess Anne, and read by him at the opening of the present court house building in 1905. Mr. Lankford's paper is inscribed on the records of Somerset Court, Minutes, Liber OTB, No. 1, page 59, *et seq*. To Mr. Lankford's paper we are indebted for many items given in this Appendix. For a full discussion of the erection of the court house at Dividing Creek, and the several court house buildings which have been erected in succession in Princess Anne Town, we refer our readers to Mr. Lankford's charming and scholarly paper: a paper which should be given to the public in print. We have presumed to write our note (given in this Appendix) relative to the site of the first erected court house (or court houses) of Somerset simply because of the fact that our research in the ancient county records developed several features of the matter not touched upon by Mr. Lankford.

province of Maryland, June 8, 1668, appointing certain places (as "ports of entry") for unlading and selling goods and merchandise brought into the province. This declaration was "sett forth by special command from the Lord Proprietor." Among the places designated in this declaration was: *"Att Deepe point att Randall Revell's in Somerset County"* (*V Arcv. Md.,* p. 32). In a further declaration to the same effect, dated June 30, 1671, was again specified *"at deep point at Randal Revels in Somerset County"* (*Ibid.,* p. 93).*

As Deep Point, which was on the south side of the Manokin River, was appointed the port of entry for Somerset County it was the practical place for the erection of a town which it was no doubt intended should become the location for the county offices as well as a center for trade. The following items from the Somerset County records relate the transactions which took place in view of this probable intention.

[Somerset Court, Deed Liber O 1, p. 127]

"Mattapenny, Sep^t 16th 1668

George Johnson: You are hereby authorized to take of Randall Revell A Conveyance of so much Land as he thinke fitt to Grant to his Lopp^s for the use of the Contry at Deepe Pointe & when he hath donne the same the same you lay out in Streets for a Towne according to your discretion & Certificatt thereof with platt of the Same you Send to me with all Convenient Speede given under my hand the day & year abovesaid. Signed by ye R^t hon^{ble} Charles Calvert. Recorded at ye request of Mr George Johnson."

In compliance with the above directions Randall Revell and Katherine, his wife, on October 1, 1668, gave and conveyed to "ye R^t hon^{ble} Caecilius, absolute Lord & Proprietor of this Province of Maryland & to his heires Lords & Proprietors forever for ye use of his contry," a parcel of land called *Sommerton,*† on the south side of the Manokin River, at Deepe Pointe, and containing 20 acres; being taken out of a tract called "ye Double Purchase," granted July 22, 1665, to Randall Revell and Anne Toft; the said Anne Toft having by deed, June 19, 1667, conveyed all her share in said tract to Katherine, wife of the said Randall Revell, and to Hannah and Katherine Revell, Jr., their daughters. The said 20 acres of land so conveyed is described as "Beginning for length near a pointe of land called Deepe Pointe at ye south side of Manokin river thence running up to a markt hiccory y^t standeth near ye river side aforesaid & from thence running alongst a hill side southeast easterly 60 perches bounded on ye South

---

*For some unstated reason this "port" for Somerset County was changed in an "ordinance" of the Lord Proprietor to the same effect, dated April 20, 1669, in which the "port" is placed *"in Somerset County above James Jones his plantation"* (*V Arcv. Md.,* p. 47). James Jones' plantation was a tract called "Jones' Hole" on the north side of Wicocomico River, just opposite to the mouth of the present Wicomico Creek. By June, 1671, the "port" was returned to Deepe Point at Randall Revell's, on the south side of the Manokin River.

†"Sommerton" was doubtless a contraction for "Somerset Town." We find that there was, in October, 1672, a "Somerton [in] Somersetshire," England. (See *29 Md. Hist. Mag.,* p. 119.)

with a line drawne from y^t end of ye former line Southwest southerly for breadth fifty four perches bounded on ye west with a line drawne from ye end of ye former line for length northwest westerly 60 perches to a markt white oake & from thence to ye river side aforesaid which said white oake standeth near a Glead of Marsh bounded on ye north with ye aforesaid river of Manokin" (Somerset Court, Deed Liber O 1, pp. 127-130).

In accordance with the above quoted orders and conveyance "Somerset Town" was laid out and established on the 20-acre tract at Deep Point, on the south side of the Manokin River. No plat of the town as laid out has so far been discovered, and the "register of Town lots" which was kept by the authorities and which gave the names of purchasers of lots in the town has disappeared. That "Somerset Town" was laid out and established is evidenced by the appearance of its name on Augustin Herman's map of *"Virginia and Maryland As it is Planted and Inhabited this present year 1670 . . ."**

The port of entry fixed by the governor and council by order, June 5, 1668, was *"Att Deepe point att Randall Revell's in Somerset County."* The governor's letter, September 16, 1668, to George Johnson directs him to receive from Randall Revell "land . . . for the use of the Contry *a Deepe Pointe."* Revell and wife's deed to the Lord Proprietor, October 1, 1668, conveyed 20 acres of land, called "Sommerton" [i. e. Somerset Town], *on south side the Manokin River at Deep Point.* Again in June, 1671, Somerset County's port of entry is designated as *"at Deep Point* at Randall Revels." When we come, however, to consider the *exact location* of this "Somerset Town" we are confronted by the matter of positively establishing the location at that date of the "point" designated as *Deep Point.* That *Deep Point* was on the south side of the Manokin River below (south, or southwest) the mouth of the then so-called Trading Branch (now King's Creek) is certain for *Deep Point* was on "the Double Purchase" tract and this tract did not extend on the Manokin River above the Trading Branch (now King's Creek). We frankly confess to our inability to *positively locate* this *Deep Point* as referred to in 1668-1671. Herman's map of 1670 very certainly places "Somerset Town" on the south side of the Manokin River and a short distance above what is apparently the mouth of Back Creek. Herman's map does not, however, designate either Manokin River, or Back Creek, by name, though the streams in question traced on his map can be identified as such. Yet Herman's map is not very detailed in the section along the south side of the Manokin River. It *may* be that the point marked *Clifton Point* on present day maps of Somerset County, which is on the south side of Manokin River, about a mile above the mouth of Back Creek, can eventually be identified as the *Deep Point* referred to in the records of 1668-1671. The water

---

*For a description of Augustine Herman's map (completed 1670, engraved 1673 and copyrighted 1674), see Mathews, *The Maps and Map Makers of Maryland* . . . p. 368, *et seq.* "A photograph from this rare map was reproduced in a report of the Virginia Commission [on the Maryland-Virginia boundary line] in 1873 . . ." It is this photographic reproduction of the Herman map which we have consulted in our research.

at this present "Clifton Point" is certainly of great depth.* It is certainly with regret that we cannot be more explicit in our statements relative to the location of this *first* Somerset Town; the *first* town venture is Somerset County. There are references of later date to a "Somerset Town"; but these references refer to a town of that name of later erection in a proved different location (see *post,* p. 416). In conclusion we would say, however, that Mr. Benjamin J. Dashiell, of Towson, Maryland, a careful student of ancient sites of homes, towns, etc., in Somerset County, himself a surveyor and civil engineer, thinks that the present *Clifton Point,* on the south side of the Manokin River, is identical with the *Deep Point* referred to in 1668-1671 and that the site of this original "Somerset Town" is just to the northeast of this "Clifton Point."

* * * * *

It was in the session of the General Assembly of Maryland, October 2 to November 6, 1683, that "town building" in the province became a vital question in relation to the advancement of trade, and it is from this session of the Assembly that there issued "An Act for the Advancement of Trade" embodying the policy of the Lord Proprietor as to the erection of "towns, portes and places . . . in the severall Countys within this province . . ." where all goods shipped into the province should be unloaded, the traffic in them be conducted, and from which all "tobacco, goods, wares and merchandise of the growth, production or manufacture of this province," should be brought for trade and export (*VII Arcv. Md.,* pp. 609-619). It is from this Act for "Advancement of Trade," October-November, 1683, that we obtain the reference to the location of "towns" proposed to be established in Somerset County. The passage of interest to us, naming the locations for town sites is as follows:

> "And in Somersett County in Wiccocomoco River on the south side on the land next above the Land of the Orphants of Charles Bollard [Ballard]† & on the Land on the North side of Winford [Mudford] Creeke‡ (vizt) Smith & Glannills [Glanvill]§ Land & on Horsey's Land in Annimessex & on Morgan's Land formerly called Barrowes towards the head of Pokomoke, & on the Land between Mr Jenkins Plantacon & Mr Howards Plantacon on the North side of Pokomoke"

Here we have directions for the establishment of five towns at important locations in Somerset County. Back of the final decision and conclusion as to the locations for these five towns as incorporated in this Act of Assembly lay a considerable amount of procedure in both the Upper and Lower House of the

---

*Herman's map of 1670 does not give *Deep Point;* nor have we been able to find any "point" on the Manokin River so designated on other, and later, maps. It might be, however, that a careful detailed study of deeds for lands along this section of the south side of the Manokin River might possibly disclose more definite information about the location of this *Deep Point.*
†That this name is *Ballard* is attested by items in *VII Arcv. Md.,* pp. 465, 511, 548.)
‡That this is *Mudford* Creek is attested by items in *VII Arcv. Md.,* pp. 460, 511, 548.
§That this name is *Glanvill* is attested by items in *VII Arcv. Md.,* pp. 465, 548.

Assembly. The first four locations were named in the proceedings of the two Houses of Assembly, October 9th, with the fifth location added on October 11, 1683. The bill from which this Act was made appears under discussion in the two Houses of Assembly, October 9th-11th, on which last date it doubtless assumed its final form and was passed (*VII Arcv. Md.*, pp. 460, 462, 465, 541, 548, 609-619).

This "Act for the Advancement of Trade" also specified that 100 acres of convenient land be purchased at the specified places for the erection of the towns, the land to be surveyed by the proper authorities, divided into streets, lanes and alleys "with open space places to be left On which may be erected Church or Chappell & Marckett house, or other publick buildings," the remaining acreage to be divided into 100 equal lots to be marked and numbered from 1 to 100. The matter of securing title to purchasers of these lots was set forth and it was directed that a book be kept by a clerk appointed by the commissioners in which should be entered the sale of the lots and prices paid for them. A purchaser had to erect a sufficient 20-foot house on his lot at least before the last day of August, 1685. The towns were not to be allowed to elect special representatives to the Lower House of Assembly until such time as they were actually inhabited by a sufficient number of persons, or families, to defray the expenses of such elected representatives. "Revenue officers" were directed to be appointed before the last day of August, 1685, in Wicomico, St. Mary's, Patuxent and Anne Arundel, on the Western Shore, and in Talbot and Somerset Counties on the Eastern Shore. Of course, this Act included the whole province. Such were the general provisions of the Act. We give them in order to show the nature of the town building venture. Our quotations refer only to the portions referring to Somerset County.

By this Act the following men were named as commissioners in Somerset County to carry out the provisions of the Act as it related to that county, namely, Colonel William Stephens [Stevens], Catpain Henry Smith, Captain John Osborne, Colonel William Colebourne, Captain William Colebourne, Captain David Browne, Captain John Winder, Mr. James Dashiell, Mr. Edward Day, Mr. Robert King, Mr. Edmond Beauchamp, Mr. Thomas James [Jones?], Mr. Charles Ratliff [Ratcliff], Mr. Thomas Purall [Purnall, Purnell], Mr. Francis Jenckins, Mr. Leven Dennard [Levin Denwood], Mr. John King, Mr. Charles Hall, Mr. William Planner, Mr. Thomas Price, Mr. John Williams, Senj^{or} [Senior], Mr. Thomas Newball [Newbold], Mr. William Walton, Mr. Roger Woolford (*VII Arcv. Md.*, p. 611).

And so the stage was effectively set for the coming of the towns to Somerset County.

The *first* location designated for a town in Somerset County was *"in Wiccomoco River on the south side on the land next above the orphans of Charles Ballard."* In proceedings of the Assembly, April 18, 1684, we find the "inhabitants of Wicocomoco and the Meenyes [Monies]" petitioning for continuance of the Act of Trade (of 1683) as for want of a sufficient number of commissioners they had not been able to lay out their town, and they also desire that their town may be appointed to be located at the place called "Lot's Wife" on the land of William Wright (*XIII Arcv. Md.,* p. 22). In "An Additionall & Supplementary Act to the Act for the Advancement of Trade," passed by the Assembly at its session, April 1-26, 1684, this desired change of location for the town on Wicomico River was made and it was directed that the town be laid out at, or near, the tract called "Lot's Wife" on land which formerly belonged to William Wright (*Ibid.,* p. 113). This location may be identified today (1935) as on the south side of the Wicomico River, in Somerset County, about opposite to the town of Whitehaven,* in Wicomico County, on the north side of the river. Whether this town and port were actually established is uncertain. No items of record in regard to it have been discovered other than those which show an intention to establish a town at this point.

The *second* of the locations designated for a town in Somerset County was *"on the land on the north side of Mudford Creeke (vizt) Smiths & Glanvills Land."* This Mudford Creeke we can identify as the Trading Branch, which is the present King's Creek, on the south side of the Manokin River. When the locations for towns in Somerset County was before the Assembly on October 9-10, 1683, this location is described as *"At the mouth of Mudford Creek in Mannokin River,"* and on October 11th as *"on the land on the North side of Mudford Creek (vizt) Smith & Granviles lands"* (*VII Arcv. Md.,* pp. 460, 465, 541, 548).

We find that there was objection in the county to this site for a town. There was read in the Assembly, April 18, 1684, a petition from inhabitants of Manokin River requesting that body "to vacate the Towne appointed at the land of William Glanfeild [Glanvill] and since the land of Capt Henry Smith, and that it may be appointed near the mouth of the river [Manokin River] below the flatt upon Oyster shell neck and White Hall" (*XIII Arcv. Md.,* p. 22). It appears, however, that when this petition reached the Upper House of Assembly, April 21st, the record of its reception there reads: "Manokin petition endorsed, vizt. Lower House April 19, 1684, Voted that this peticon be rejected this house being well informed that the place where the Towne is, is the most convenient place in the said River" (*XIII Arcv. Md.,* p. 25). The Upper House evidently concurred in the Lower House's rejection of this petition, and so for the time being the town site directed by the Act of 1683 stood as *"on the land on the north side of Mudford Creek (vizt) Smith's & Glanvills Land."*

While there is very little in the way of evidence relative to this town, we have items which incontestably prove that a town was laid out and established near this location and that the town was called "Somerset Town." The location in question was evidently a trifle above the north side of the mouth of this Mudford Creek, which we can identify as the Trading Branch, and today

---

*Whitehaven is an ancient town of Somerset County, but now (by subdivision) in Wicomico County. This town was established near the beginning of the 18th century, doubtless through the influence of Col. George Gale, who came to Somerset County from Whitehaven, Cumberlandshire, England. Doubtless the "Lots Wife" proposition failed, and hence the establishment of Whitehaven.

(1935) King's Creek, and on the south side of the Manokin River and on land at that date (1683-4), the property of William Glanvill, called "Glanvill's Lot." The acreage for the town doubtless extended northward on the Manokin River across the dividing line between "Glanvill's Lot" and "Smith's Recovery" tract, which belonged to Captain Henry Smith.* This location places this specific site in the southwest corner of the present Stewart's Neck on the south side of the Manokin River, in Somerset County. Our brief items of evidence that this town was laid out and established near this specified place, and that it was called "Somerset Town," are as follows: On July 3, 1708, appears a record indited *"Somerset Town on ye Fork of Manocan River,"* Arthur Denwood sells ½ of his lot No. 9 in the said town to Maj. George Gale; copy of entry made in *"Somerset Towne Register"* and signed *"Jn⁰ Fisher, Cl'k Somerset Town."* This item appears in Somerset Court records, Judicials, Liber EFH, 1707-1711, p. 105. The other item is that on January 29, 1739/40, one Heber Whittingham stated in a deposition then made by him "That Alexʳ Hall, Senʳ who was an inhabitant of *Somerset Town* tould this deponent that the bounder of Capell King's land† was then in the water which bounder was also the bounder of *Somerset Town* aforesaid when it was first laid out and further saith not." Heber Whittingham's deposition is recorded in Somerset Court records, Judicials, 1738-40, p. 268.

The *third* location designated for a town in Somerset County was *"on Horsey's Land in Annemessex."* This location was on the land of the Horsey family on the tract called "Coulbourn" on the south side of the Great (or Big) Annemessex River, and south of Coulbourn's Creek. This town was evidently laid out and established, for we find a reference to "Annemessex Town" in August, 1706 (Somerset Court, Judicials, Liber EFH, p. 21), and in 1673, in establishing public warehouses for the inspection of tobacco in Somerset County the General Assembly designated one of them as at Great Annemessex, Horsey's Land, on Coulbourn's Creek, *"at the old Town"* (Acts of Assembly, 1763).

The *fourth* location designated for a town in Somerset County was *"on Morgan's land formerly called Barrowes towards the head of "Pokamoke."* This was land belonging to one Henry Morgan on the south side of the Pocomoke River, near the headwaters.‡ This location was not very far above the present

---

*The Act of 1683 directing the establishment of these towns designated that each town should be of 100-acre size.

†"Glandvill's Lot," 500 acres was granted to William Glandvill, of London, mariner, and passed from him to his son, William Glandvill, of Kent County, Maryland, who in March, 1693, sold the said tract of land to John King, of Somerset County. John King, by his will, dated May, 1696, probated July, 1696, devised this 500 acres of "Glandvill's Lot" to his son, Capell King. Thus it was that Capell King's land adjoined this "Somerset Town." In 1739 Capell King sold "Glandvill's Lot" to the Reverend James Robertson, rector of Coventry Parish. "Glandvill's Lot" is described as being on south side of Manokin River and northeast side of a small creek called the Lower Fork, also Mudford Creek—the Trading Branch, now (1935) King's Creek (see Somerset Court Deed Liber O7, p. 172, Glandvill to King; *Md. Cal. Wills*, Vol. II, p. 124, will of John King; Somerset Deed Liber O 20, p. 71, King to Robertson; Somerset Judicials, 1740-2, p. 72-3, commission establishing boundaries of "Glandvill's Lot" for Reverend James Robertson.

‡On November 26, 1679, Henry Morgan had a patent for 400 acres, called "Sandy Wharf," on south side side Pocomoke River, near the head of the river; and on November 26, 1678, the said Morgan received a patent for 200 acres, called "Land Downe," on south side of Pocomoke River, near the head of the river, a little to the southward of Bogatenorton Landing and adjoining William Stevens' tract, called "Snow Hill." In September, 1694, Henry Morgan (then of New Castle, Kent County, in the territories of Pennsylvania [now Delaware], sold the "Sandy Wharf" tract to William Whittington, of Somerset County, and the "Land Downe" tract to John Webb, of Somerset County (Somerset Court, Deed Liber O 7, pp. 234 and 285).

town of Snow Hill, but was considered after investigation and inspection to be an undesirable location, so the town site was changed to the Snow Hill tract. The site at "Barrowes Landing" (as then it became designated) was held through the session of the Assembly, April 1-26, 1684 (*XIII Arcv. Md.,* pp. 22, 24, 25 and 84). In October, 1684, however, a petition went to the Governor and Council of the province which fully developed the "inconveniences" of the "Barrow's Landing" tract and the greater advantages of the Snow Hill tract, and requesting the Council's permission to make this change in location. The Council assented to the plea of the petitioners and consented to the building of the town on the Snow Hill tract rather than at "Barrowe's Land" if the same can be procured, and promise to join with the petitioners in procuring confirmation of the Lord Proprietor and the General Assembly, at its next session, to this change in location (*XVII Arcv. Md.,* pp. 284-286). The next session of Assembly, October 26, 1686, by Act directed *"In the County of Somersett a towne or port at Snow Hill on the land formerly belonging to Henry Bishop and last to Ann Bishop his widow . . ."** (*XIII Arcv. Md.,* p. 132).

Thus it was that the town of Snow Hill, then in Old Somerset County, now in Worcester County (by subdivision in 1742) had its origin and founding in 1684-1686, and has had a consecutive history of life on the same site for two centuries and a half. The commissioners obtained the necessary acreage for the town of Snow Hill from the Bishop family and soon had their venture well under way. From the beginning the town seemed to attract the thrifty Scotch merchants and we find such men as Alexander Erskine, John Galbraith, John Henry, the Spences, Martins, Rounds, and Donelsons, establishing homes and businesses in and about the town.

The town of Snow Hill became in reality the "metropolis" of Old Somerset and when Worcester County was created in 1742 became the county seat of Worcester. Though the record book of the commissioners of Snow Hill Town which contained the names of original purchasers of lots has disappeared, yet numerous items of interest relative to the town's inhabitants are to be found in the Somerset Court Judicials, deeds and wills between 1686 and 1742, and the Worcester County deeds and wills from 1742 on. During the early part of the 18th century the arrival of Robert and Edward Martin, two brothers, who were Scotch merchants, gave added zest to the commercial activities of Snow Hill Town. The Martins purchased lands adjoining and lots within, the town. They were soon followed by a cousin, James Martin, who, after Robert Martin's death, married his widow, Mrs. Mary (Downes) Martin. It appears from various deeds that Robert Martin had by the year 1721 obtained by purchase most of

---

*On December 10, 1678, William Stevens, of Pocomoke, Somerset County, and Elizabeth, his wife (for 15,000 pounds tobacco), conveyed to Henry Bishop, of Boquetenorton, in Somerset County, 500 acres, called "Snow Hill" tract, on south side Pocomoke River, beginning at a marked cypress standing to southward of the Landing, thence running up the said river and bounded therewith by a straight line, 150 poles, to a marked tree standing by the river side; thence a line southeast by south, ½ point southerly, 534 poles; thence west by west, ½ point westerly, 150 poles; thence northwest by north, ½ point northerly, with a line drawn from the first bounder; the said "Snow Hill" tract having been granted by patent to the said William Stevens, September 29, 1676 (Somerset Court, Deed Liber O 5, p. 396).

the acreage surrounding the town of Snow Hill and all the lots in Snow Hill Town not formerly sold (Somerset Court, Deed Liber O 13, p. 261 and 265, deeds of John Bishop, Jr., and others, to Robert Martin; Deed Liber O 14, p. 50, deed of John Murray to Robert Martin; Deed Liber O 15, p. 182, deed of James Dayley to Robert Martin; Somerset Court, Liber A, Views of Land by Commissioners, pp. 44-46 and 92-94, survey of Snow Hill tract for Robert Martin and James Dayley). With Robert Martin's death in 1725 his Snow Hill properties passed to his son, John Martin (see will of Robert Martin, Worcester Registry of Wills, Liber MH, No. 3, folio 327-8). The records give ample evidence that from this time John Martin (son of Robert) and James Martin (the cousin, who married Mary, widow of Robert Martin, and mother of John) became the controling factors in the development of Snow Hill Town. By the Fall of 1742 such questions had arisen concerning the boundaries of Snow Hill Town that it became necessary to make a new survey of the town area and re-establish the boundaries thereof. This resurvey and re-establishment of boundaries was carried out under an Act of the General Assembly of Maryland passed at the session of September-October, 1742 (*XLII Arcv. Md.*, p. 409, *et seq.*).* In 1793 there was another survey of Snow Hill Town with marking of the boundaries. A plat of this 1793 survey, giving lot numbers, streets and alleys, and the evidence upon which the survey rests, is recorded in Worcester County Court, Deed Liber P, pp. 286-293.

With all the data available for that purpose it is hoped that some day someone will undertake the writing of the story of this interesting and charming Snow Hill Town and its early residents.†

It may be interesting to note that the *first* "Meeting House" of the Snow Hill congregation of the Presbyterian Church and the *first* parish church of Snow Hill (later All Hallows) Parish (see *ante*, pp. 242 and 182) were in all probability erected on the "open space places to be left On which may be erected Church or Chapell . . ." as provided in the "Act of Advancement of Trade," 1683, which provided for the laying out of the towns, of which Snow Hill Town became one.‡

---

*It appears that prior to June, 1728, Snow Hill Town had been "laid out" three times. Somerset Court, Judicials, 1727-30, p. 95-6, depositions of Donelson, Spence, Round, Martin, and Robins, relative to boundaries.

†The will of John Cropper, of Somerset County, carpenter, dated September 25, 1686, probated December 14, 1688, devises to his daughter, Elizabeth Cropper, a tract of 300 acres of land which he describes as being "in Asskimeconson Neke Right over against Harford Town in Somerset County upon Pocomoke River and is called the Indian Landing" (Somerset Registry of Wills, Liber EB 5, p. 167). The "location" of this tract of land places it on the north side of Pocomoke River not far above the site of Snow Hill Town, and in all probability opposite to the first proposed site for the town on Morgan's land called the Barrow's land. It may be that it was at first proposed to call the town "Harfford Town." This is the only reference to this "Harfford Town" which we have come across.

‡On April 18, 1864, there came to the General Assembly a petition from the inhabitants of Pocomoke, in Somerset County, for the establishment of a town at "Chip Landing," in Somerset. The Lower House voted on this petition that a town was necessary at the sea side as the petition desired and that the place appointed should be "betweene the going in of Selby's Bay and Cornelius Innis his land at Assateague Bay at discretion of the commissioners." The Upper House of Assembly concurred in the judgment of the Lower House, and so an Act of Assembly to that effect directed the establishment of such a town (*XIII Arcv. Md.*, pp. 22, 24, 25, 26, 84, 112-113). We have not followed out the history of this "town."

There also went to the Assembly on April 21, 1684, a petition from the inhabitants of Somerset County, more particularly of Nanticoke River, that a town be established at Tipquin [also Tix-

The *fifth* and last location for a town in Somerset County proposed by the Assembly's Act for "Advancement of Trade," October-November, 1683, was designated as *"on the Land between Mr Jenkins Plantacon & Mr Howard's Plantacon on the North side of Pokamoke."* The location thus designated was land between the plantations of Colonel Francis Jenckins and Mr. Edmund Howard and lay along the Pocomoke River side—in reality on the west side of the river as its makes its turn in this vicinity. The town laid out and established at this point was Rehoboth Town, which was doubtless given its significant name by Colonel William Stevens, whose plantation, called "Rehoboth," lay immediately above the town site. The plantation on which Francis Jenckins lived was, as a matter of fact, made up of 400 acres of land immediately south of Colonel Stevens' plantation and which had been sold off of Stevens' original "Rehoboth" tract.* Edmund Howard's plantation lay immediately south of Jenckins' plantation and extended around to the west thereof and so in a northerly direction.† Thus the tract of land on which it was directed that the town should be built lay between the Jenckins and Howard plantations.

We find reference to "Rehoboth" as a town in September, 1686 (*V Arcv. Md.*, p. 503), and in October, 1694, we find the record in the proceedings of the Council of Maryland that "In the Act for Ports wee are of Opinion that *Rehoboth be made a port* & Snow Hill a Towne in Somersett County . . ." In the Reverend Francis Makemie's will, dated April 27, 1708, we find the designation of *"Pcomoke towne called Rehoboth"* (see *ante,* p. 169). Somerset Court, 11th 9ber, 1701, "Ordered on Maj^r John Cornish motion relating to the building a Prison at Rehoboth Towne on his own proper Charge that the said Prison when built and Viewed and found Sufficient shall be Reputed and taken as a County Prison the other Prison being now by the Justices thought Insufficient" (Somerset Court, Liber P, Judicials, 1701-5, p. 42).

Rehoboth Town was quite a place of trade and commerce, and most notable from the fact that it was the cradle of organized Presbyterianism in America (see *ante,* pp. 216 and 234). Within the town were erected both the parish church of Coventry Parish, Church of England, and the "Meeting House" of the Rehoboth Congregation of the Presbyterian Church. It seems clear that in later years the title to the land on which Rehoboth Town stood must have become vested in Colonel Robert Jenckins Henry, for in his will, dated July 21, 1764, probated November 14, 1766, he confirms to their respective authorities title to the grounds on which the Presbyterian "Meeting House" and "the

---

quin], on the south side of Nanticoke River; "this place being a most convenient situation for a town or place of trade and most frequented by shipping of any river in the said county." The Upper and Lower Houses favorably agreed to the petition and an Act was passed in the Assembly of April 1-26, 1684, directing the erection of a town "at or near Tipquin on the south side of Nanticoke River" (*XIII Arcv. Md.,* pp. 28, 30, 89,90, 112-113). We have not followed out the history of this "town." Today (1935) there is a village called Tipquin (or Wetipquin) on the south side of Nanticoke River, in Wicomico (formerly Somerset) County.

*For an account of Francis Jenckins' plantation, see *ante,* Chapter VIII, under note on Francis Jenckins.

†Edmund Howard, and his son, William Stevens Howard, were given this plantation by Col. William Stevens, by whose will it was confirmed to them. The area of this plantation is described in Col. Stevens' will, dated August 29, 1687, probated March 26, 1688. See Somerset Registry of Wills, Liber EB5, folios 171-2.

Parish Church of Coventry" then stood in said town. He also confirmed to that use the ground on which the tobacco "Inspection House at Rehoboth now stands . . . so long as subjected thereto under the Inspection Law of the Province of Maryland" (Will of Robert Jenckins Henry, in Somerset Registry of Wills, Liber EB 4, pp. 119-121).*

* * * * *

In October, 1686, we find that a *sixth* town was proposed for Somerset County. Among the Acts passed at session of the General Assembly, October 26, 1686, there was one called "A Further Additionall Act to the act for the Advancement of Trade [1683] and to the Supplementary Act to the same [1684] . . ." This "Further Additionall Act . . ." directed "In the County of Somersett a towne or port at Snow Hill . . . and *one other in Arnold Erzeys [Elzey's] land & the land adjacent att Oyster Neck att the mouth of Monokin* . . ." (*XIII Arcv. Md.*, pp. 132 and 134).

The site proposed for this town was on the north side of the Manokin River, west of the mouth of Goose Creek, on Arnold Elzey's estate of "Almodington." In April, 1684, there had been a petition to the General Assembly from certain inhabitants of the Manokin River section requesting that the Assembly abandon its proposed site for a town on Glanvill and Smith's land north of the mouth of Mudford Creek (the Trading Branch, later King's Creek) and south side of Manokin River, and substitute therefor a town site "near the mouth of the river [Manokin] below the flatt upon Oyster shell neck and White Hall." However, this petition was rejected by the Assembly (see *ante*, p. 415) and the town erected on the Smith and Glanvill land as the Assembly's Act of 1683 contemplated. Now in October, 1686, we find the Assembly directing the erection of a town on Arnold Elzey's land and land adjacent in Oyster Neck at the mouth of the Manokin River (north side).

Just what transpired in carrying out this direction of the Assembly's Act of October, 1686, we do not know; but, in the Spring of 1695, we find another reference to a town on Arnold Elzey's land. In the General Assembly, on May 13,† 1695, there was a resolution introduced to the effect that "an additionall bill be drawn to the Act appointing Ports and Towns," and on reference to the Assembly of "the Law Concerning Towns" a resolution was proposed that ports be made in Patuxent and Potomac Rivers and "that a port be constituted in Somersett County where Shipps trading thither may enter and clear." Then it was "Resolved *that Mr Arnold Elzeys land where the Towne formerly was in Monnochin River, be the town and Port for Somersett County.*" However, on May 14th "voted whether a bill shall be drawn to make ports in Ptauxent and Monochin River, Carryed in the negative" (*XIX Arcv. Md.*, pp. 178, 180).

---

*Colonel Henry had in June, 1735, deeded to the vestry of Coventry Parish 2 acres of land "in Rehoboth Town . . . on which the Parish Church now standeth and next adjoining . . ." (see *ante*, p. 175). The "Meeting House" of the Presbyterian Congregation had been erected in 1705-6 on a lot at that time the property of the Reverend Francis Makemie (see *ante*, p. 237).

†The date given in the printed journal, May 18th, is erroneous, as is proved by record of adjournment, *Friday, May 10th*, to "*Monday* morning," Monday being, therefore, May 13.

We have found nothing further relative to this town proposed for Arnold Elzey's land near the mouth of the Manokin River. However, we cannot but wonder if there were proceedings looking towards the erection of a town in this vicinity, for it was on Arnold Elzey's land, on the "Almodington" tract, just below the mouth of Goose Creek, that the first Somerset Parish Church was built about 1694-7 (see *ante*, p. 181).

* * * * *

Before concluding this note on the towns in Somerset County there are two other items of record which we wish to note. On November 22, 1692, Somerset Court directing the free-holders of Manokin and Monie Hundreds to meet on December 27th following to elect the first vestry for Somerset Parish (which was composed of those Hundreds) designated that the meetings should be held at *"Somerset Towne"* (see *ante*, p. 154). It is impossible to say whether the *"Somerset Towne"* so designated was the *"Somerset Town"* established in 1668 at Deep Point on the south side of the Manokin River (see *ante*, p. 410, *et seq*), or the "Somerset Town" established in 1683 further up the river, on the south side, on Glanvill and Smith's land above the mouth of Mudford Creek (the Trading Branch, now King's Creek).

The other item of record which we would note here appears in 1708. Somerset Court, November, 1708, directed "a road to be cleared to Monocan [Manokin] Town from Mr John King's Mill . . . as it would be convenient for all persons to go to ye Church in Town & who shall have business at ye offices keep [kept] there. Ordered ye Clk [clerke] to send an order to James Furnace overseer [of roads] of Monokin [Manokin Hundred] y^t he forthwith cleare a road to Monocan Town . . ." (Somerset Court, Judicials, Liber EFH, 1707-1711, p. 152). *"Mr John King's Mill,"* referred to in this court order, was "King's Mill," at the head of the Trading Branch (now King's Creek), on the south side thereof, while *"ye Church in Town"* evidently refers to the parish church of Somerset Parish which stood from about 1694 to 1710, occupied a site on the north side of the Manokin River, just west of the mouth of Goose Creek, on Arnold Elzey's land.* The site of this Somerset Parish Church was just about opposite to the present *Clifton Point* (south side the river), which is most probably identical with the *Deep Point*, at which the first *"Somerset Town"* was established in 1668 (see *ante*, p. 410, *et seq*. That the court order refers to *"Monocan [Manokin] Town"* does not effect the matter as these towns were not infrequently alternately called by the name of the "Hundred," in which they were located or the river on which they were situated.† The road ordered, November, 1708, "to be cleared to Monocan Town from Mr John King's Mill . . ."

---

*There has been no trace discovered of any evidence whatsoever (direct, circumstantial, or even in "tradition") of there having ever been a "church" at the *"Somerset Town"* above the mouth of Mudford Creek (Trading Branch, now King's Creek) on Glanvill and Smith's land.
†Rehoboth Town, on Pocomoke River, was evidently also called "Pocomoke Town" (see *ante*, p. 169).

was evidently what is known at this present time (1935) as the "old Revell's Neck Road," which extends from the head of the present King's Creek (not far from the old King's Mill site) and so through the length of Revell's Neck (on the south side of King's Creek) direct to the present "Clifton Point." There was no doubt at this early day a ferry from "Somerset Town" (or "Monocan [Manokin] Town") across to "ye Church." This we believe is the most probable explanation of the court order of November, 1708. What may have been *"ye offices keep [kept] in town,"* as referred to in the court order, we cannot now say.

* * * * *

The General Assembly of April 2-19, 1706, in an "Act for the Advancement of Trade and Erecting Ports & Towns in the Province of Maryland," declared the towns and ports to be

> "In Somersett County on the Northwest side of Wicomico River on the woodland reach below Daniel Hast creek; At Rehoboth In Pocomoke River, and at Snow Hill where the towns were formerly erected and on a point of Land lying in the fork of Manokin River where Captain Henry Smith formerly lived sometimes called the White House and at Colebournes Creek in Annemessex" (*XXVIII Arcv. Md.*, pp. 636-7).

We have considered the Rehoboth, Snow Hill and Annemessex towns. The town directed to be established on the northwest side of Wicomico River below Haste's Creek became the town and port of *Green Hill*. There is in the Maryland Historical Society, Baltimore, a drawing (evidently a copy of the "original") of the "Plat of the Town and Port of Green Hill as laid out in 1707."*

The town now directed to be established, on "a point of land lying in the fork of Manokin River where Captain Henry Smith formerly lived sometimes called the White House," was on the south side of the Manokin River and just southwest of the mouth of the present Jones' Creek, and was doubtless just a slight change in the location of the "Somerset Towne on ye fork of Monocan River," which appears of record in July, 1708. The town as first laid out, about 1683-4, being partly on "Glanvill's Lot" above the mouth of the present King's Creek, was now evidently carried over onto Smith's land ("Smith's Recovery" tract) below the mouth of the present Jones' Creek. We believe that whatever may have been the "history" of this town of 1706 directed to be established on "a point of land lying in the fork of Manokin River where Captain Henry Smith formerly lived sometimes called the White House," it is virtually in succession to the town directed to be established near this location in 1683-4. At any rate the "town" disappeared ages ago. Records in the year 1740 show that Captain John Tunstall was then living on the plantation where Captain Henry

---

*Salisbury, at the head of the Wicomico River, was established in 1732, and Princess Anne Town, at the head of Manokin River, was established in 1733.

Smith had formerly lived, and that he was operating a "shipyard" there (Somerset Court, Judicials, 1740-2, pp. 72-3, commission and evidences establishing the boundaries of "Glanvill's Lot" for the Reverend James Robertson).

APPENDIX VII
A PROPOSED COUNTY ON THE SEABOARD SIDE

The charter for the province of Maryland granted to Cecil, Lord Baltimore, June 20, 1632, specifically included (besides the territory west of the Chesapeake Bay) that of the peninsula between the Atlantic Ocean and Delaware Bay (east) and the Chesapeake Bay (west) and extending from the Maryland-Virginia boundary line (south) in a northerly direction along the ocean side up through Delaware Bay to the 40 degree north latitude. Lord Baltimore, regardless of other claimants to this territory, continued his assertion of right thereto, and in 1669, in order to try and stop encroachments thereon by others, directed his provincial authorities to encourage (under liberal terms) settlers to take up lands "upon the Seaboard side of the Eastern Shore and on Delaware Bay within the degree forty northerly latitude and particularly the Whorekill . . . (*V Arcv. Md.*, pp. 54-5). On October 22, 1669, the Council of Maryland, acting on his Lordship's instructions, "Ordered that from the hore kill [Whorekill] to the degree forty north latitude be erected into a county called by the name of Durham and from the hore kill [Whorekill] to Mount Scarborough be likewise erected into a county and called as the Lord Proprietary shall hereafter direct (*Ibid.*, p. 56).

The "Whorekill" is a creek ("kill" in the Dutch language means "creek"), known also as Lewes' Creek, near Lewes, Sussex County, Delaware (present time), and Mount Scarborough lay south of the town of Snow Hill in Worcester County, Maryland (present time), while the 40 degree north latitude was shown on the maps of the period in question as being a little north of New Castle, Delaware (present time). Roughly speaking, then the counties thus created on the Seaboard side, in 16669, along the Atlantic Ocean and Delaware Bay (west side) were created out of territory which was under jurisdiction of the counties of Somerset, Dorchester, Talbot and Baltimore as the areas of those counties extended eastward to the eastmost limits of Lord Baltimore's patent (i. e. the Atlantic Ocean and Delaware Bay to the 40 degree north latitude).

In October, 1669, therefore the "County of Durham" was set up north of the Whorekill, and in June, 1672, the county of Worcester was set up as "beginning at the southermost branch of the Bay called Rehoboth Bay and from thence running northerly up the Seaboard side to the south cape of Delaware Bay and thence to the Whore Kill Creeke and up the Bay to the fortieth degree northerly latitude . . ." (*Ibid.*, p. 56). By comparison of the specified boundaries of this Worcester County of 1672 it will be seen that it included virtually the area mentioned in the boundaries for Durham County set forth in 1669, extending in a southerly direction below the Whorekill only about halfway to the former reefrred to limit at Mt. Scarborough. The land included in the southern part of this area, set up as Worcester County in June, 1672, was taken from the Seaboard side of Somerset County, as that county was in 1669, and is at this present time (1935) included in Sussex County, Delaware. The area included in these so-called counties of Durham and Worcester later became New Castle, Kent and Sussex Counties (the three present counties of the State of Delaware), and were referred to as the "Three Lower Counties on Delaware." The transfer of this territory by the Duke of York to William Penn in 1682 did not effect the Lords Baltimore in trying to maintain and substantiate their claim. However, as we know, this territory was finally entirely lost to Maryland.

It is the county of Worcester, set up in June, 1672, which is of interest to us. The officers appointed for this county were Somerset County men; many of the settlers who took up lands about the Whorekill and to the south thereof went from Somerset County and certainly Somerset Court had jurisdiction over this section south of the Whorekill until 1742, when a later Worcester County was created in Maryland, after which the court of this later Worcester County had jurisdiction over a considerable part of what is now the lower part of Sussex County, Delaware, until 1767, when the boundary line was finally settled between Maryland and Delaware.

In referring to the county of Worcester, which was created out of territory along the seaside (Rehoboth Bay, the Whorekill, etc.) in June, 1672, it should be noted that this county evidently consumed the territory specified as the county of Durham in 1669, and that it is doubtful just what procedure was followed towards organizing the county after its creation and the commissioning of its first officers. No records of proceedings have been so far discovered. On June 19, 1672, the Maryland authorities commissioned Henry Smith,* Francis Jenckins,† Thomas Jones,‡ John Winder, Thomas Walker, Alexander Draper and Richard Whitty, gentlemen, to be his Lordship's commissioners and justices o fthe peace for Worcester County in the province of Maryland. Smith, Jenckins, Jones and Winder were named as judges of the said court (in absence of a member of his Lordship's Council). Smith and Jenckins were directed, after taking oath of office themselves, to administer the oath to the other justices (*LI Arcv. Md.*, p. 78). Francis Jenckins was commissioned on June 20, 1672, to take proof of rights of those persons desiring land in the county of Worcester and to grant warrants of survey therefor, and "to keep a fair Book of all such Rights before

---

*Captain Henry Smith occupied a prominent place in the early life of Somerset County. We find him first in Accomac County, Virginia, where his unsavory conduct resulted in his wife's, Joanna Smith, petition to the court for separate maintenance from him. The record in this case, February, 1668/9, furnishes one of the rarely discovered suits for separation of husband and wife, in the colonial records of Virginia (Accomac, Virginia, Court Order Book, 1666-70, pp. 103-108). Henry Smith came to Somerset County, Maryland, in 1669 and we find him as one of the justices of the peace for Somerset, 1669 and 1683; captain in the militia, and a representative from Somerset County in the Lower House of the Maryland General Assembly, 1682-1685. He figured prominently in the matter of locating and erecting the first court house for Somerset County (see *ante*, page 405 *et seq.*). In 1672 Smith appears as first named in the commission of the peace for the newly created county of Worcester. Henry Smith patented large tracts of land in Somerset County, principally on the south side of the Manokin River, about the mouth of what is now (1935) called Jones' Creek. Extant records show that Smith lived on a tract of land called "Smith's Recovery," on the southeast side of the Manokin River, south of the present Jones' Creek, and that his house stood near the point of land made by the confluence of Jones' Creek and the Manokin River (Somer-

you proved or such warrants thereupon or otherwise by you Granted a Copy of which as oft as Conveniently you may you shall transmit to the Secretaries office at the city of St. Maries to be recorded" (*V Arcv. Md.*, p. 109).* One June 20, 1672, the Governor of Maryland commissioned Thomas Jones to be "Captain under me of all the forces horse and foot that are or shall be in the said county of Worcester" (*Ibid.*, p. 110).† July 12, 1672, Thomas Jones, one of the justices

set, Judicials, 1740-2, p. 72-3, commission and affidavits establishing the boundaries of "Glanvill's Lot" for Reverend James Robertson). Captain Henry Smith died intestate prior to the year 1703 (*XXIV Arcv. Md.*, p. 318; Somerset Registry of Wills, Liber EB 14, p. 328, inventory of Captain Henry Smith, and Liber EB 13, p. 29, account of administrators of said Smith.
Captain Henry Smith was the father of: (1) Henry Smith, Jr.; (2) William Smith, born in Manokin, Somerset County, January 20, 1676; (3) John Smith, born same place, November 4, 1680; (4) Tomasen Smith, born September, 1682. Whether Henry Smith, Jr., was a child by Joanah, first wife of Captain Henry Smith, we cannot say; but William, John and Tomasen Smith are stated in Liber IKL (Somerset Court Register of Births, etc.) to have been children of Captain Henry Smith by his wife Ann; evidently a second wife.
†For note on Francis Jenckins, see *ante*, Chapter VIII, "Somerset County in the Protestant Revolution and into the Royal Province"; for John Winder, see *ante*, p. 332; Thomas Walker, *ante*. p. 139; Alexander Draper, *post* Appendix X.
‡Captain Thomas Jones was an influential merchant and official in Somerset County. His home was on the south side of the Manokin River and just north of the present Jones' Creek, which evidently derived its name from his family. The site of his home was on the tract of land called "Bridger's Lot," which he acquired by purchase. In 1675 Jones patented the tracts of land called "Nasworthies Choice" and "Friends Choice" on the south side of the Manokin River, which he conveyed to William Stevens in 1679.
The Thomas Jones, whose record we are here relating, was no doubt he who, as "Thomas Jones, of St. Mary's County, Merchant," was licensed in April, 1672, with exclusive right to trade with the Indians "on the seaboard side, the Whorekeil or on the western side of the Bay [Chesapeake] or within any other place within the province" (*V Arcv. Md.*, p. 196). Thomas Jones probably about this time moved to Somerset County and in 1672 we find him as a justice of the peace and captain of militia (virtually military commander) of the newly created Worcester County (as stated in the text above). While commissioned as an officer for this newly created Worcester County, we find also that he appears as "Captain Thomas Jones, High Sheriff of Somerset County in July, 1672, and as collector of revenue duties in Somerset at the same time" (*V Arcv. Md.*, p. 111). In May, 1675, and April, 1676, he appears in the Somerset County records as "Thomas Jones, of Bristol [England], Merchant," and is clearly identified by items in the record as "Captain Thomas Jones, of Somerset County" (Somerset Court, Judicials, Liber AZ; 1671-5, p. 528, and Deed Liber O 7 [reverse], p. 40, court proceedings for April 18, 1676). In the record of April 18, 1676, Jones' dwelling house on Manokin River is referred to. In 1677 the beligerent nature and violent, uncontrolable temper of Captain Thomas Jones is exhibited in the court records (Liber O 7 [reverse], pp. 123-129). Jones appears as a justice of the peace for Somerset County, 1687-1699. He died in the year 1701 (Hall of Records, Annapolis, Will Liber 11, folio 164, and Inventories and Accounts Liber 21, folio 219).
Captain Thomas Jones may have been married more than once. However, the records of Somerset County show that he was married before 1690, to Martha, daughter of William and Ann (Hooper) Davis, of Somerset County (Somerset Court, Deed Liber O 7 ,p. 671). Mrs. Martha (Davis) Jones married, second [prior to January, 1703/4], Robert Catherwood (Somerset Court, Judicials, 1702-1705 [back of Deed Liber O 8], p. 107).
Thomas and Martha (Davis) Jones had issue: (1) Sarah Jones, born September 20, 1691; married Levin Woolford; (2) Thomas Jones, born February 11, 1693; (3) William Jones, born *circa* 1695; died 1745/6; married, *first*, Elizabeth (surname unknown); *second*, Mrs. Elizabeth (nee ....) Campbell; (4) John Jones (Will of Thomas Jones, dated April 5, 1700; Liber IKL [Somerset Court, Register of Births, etc.]; deeds in Somerset Court).
*There is in the Pennsylvania Historical Society, Philadelphia, Pennsylvania, a manuscript entitled "Warrant Book, 1671-1682, of Somerset County, Maryland." An examination of this manuscript (the volume contains a variety of items) shows that it embodies a list of warrants granted, evidently by Francis Jenckins, for lands in the area under discussion.
†Neill, in his *Terrae Maria*, p. 164, writes that "In 1671 a person by the name of Jones, with others from Somerset County, surprised Lewistown [Lewes?], on the Delaware, and Governor Lovelace, of New York, who claimed jurisdiction [under the Duke of York], remonstrated." In the records of the Maryland Provincial Court, complaint by Thomas Jones against Henry Smith, and Henry Smith against Thomas Jones, in 1672. The gentlemen did not pass compliments, but each tried to paint the character of the other as black figures. Among other items Smith stated that "Captain Thomas Jones did with six or seven men go up to the Horekeele [Whorekill] where he first caused all the Dutchmen to be bound then opened their Chests taking severall furres and two Blankets, and some powder the which he ordered to be thrown into the River and Dranke their Anniseed water . . . we did see him bring into the Guard (with others he employed) Deer skins, Wampum Peake, Blankets, Trading Cloth, Powder, knives, pipes, looking glasses, with severall fures suppose to the vallue of sixty pounds sterling . . ." The said Jones was sheriff of Somerset County and was reported as having been rather contemptuous in his conduct towards the court. We have not followed this matter farther.

for Worcester County, was authorized to appoint and depute some proper person to be clerk for the said county (*Ibid.*, p. 112). No record has so far been discovered of the name of this appointee. Evidently trouble was anticipated in the settling of this area under Lord Baltimore's government, for on July 11, 1672, Captain Paul Marsh was commissioned to raise and muster such a party of men as shall be desired ... by Captain Thomas Jones, commander of the forces in Worcester County and with him the said Jones to go unto the said Worcester County with said party of men and all enemies that shall be shewed you by said Jones to encounter fight with overcome and destroy or take prisoners and them to secure; also you are to press men horses provisions ammunition and all other things necessary for this designe and an account of your proceedings herein you are to render to me [the Governor] by all opportunities, and for your said proceedings this shall be your sufficient warrant" (*Ibid.*, p. 111). No account of Captain Marsh's proceedings under this commission has been found. June 19, 1672, Daniel Brown was commissioned to be high constable of Worcester County (*Ibid.*, p. 107).

All of the men named in the above referred to civil and military commissions were Somerset County men. Francis Jenckins, Thomas Jones,* John Winder and Thomas Walker continued their residence in Somerset County, as did Henry Smith until some years later, when he apparently went to the Whorekill section, where he died. Alexander Draper certainly went to the Whorekill to live, where he became a man of prominence. Richard Whitty may have gone there for a while, though some of his family are later found in Somerset County. We have not traced Daniel Brown's record. As time went on we find a number of Somerset County people taking up lands south of the Whorekill and going there to reside.

The situation as relates to the "Three Lower Counties on Delware" territory which was claimed by the Lords Baltimore under the charter to Cecil Calvert, 2nd Lord Baltimore, June, 1632, is well summed up by Walter A. Powell in his *Fight of a Century Between the Penns and the Calverts Over the Three Lower Counties on Delaware, which resulted in Making the State of Delaware a Separate Commonwealth.* Mr. Powell writes: "Both before and after the Duke of York assumed jurisdiction of the Three Lower Counties [on Delaware] in 1664 Lord Baltimore continued to assert his right to these counties against the Duke, Swedes and Dutch. A few grants of land were made along the near coast by the governors of the Duke of York ... Penn, except along the coast, exercised no authority,† nor made any grants of land in Sussex [County] until after the boundary lines had been established in 1767. In Kent and New Castle

---

*In December, 1672, Captain Thomas Jones, Peter Groenendyck and Harman Cornellinson were granted licenses to trade for furs, skins, etc., with the Indians and other inhabitants at the seaboard side of the Eastern Shore in Worcester, Somerset, Dorchester, Talbot and Baltimore Counties (*V Arcv. Md.*, p. 114-115). In December, 1672, Henry Smith, at his own request, was relieved from his duties as justice of the peace in both Somerset and Worcester Counties (*V Arcv. Md.*, p. 117).

†There is in the Pennsylvania Historical Society, Philadelphia, a manuscript entitled "Sussex County, Delaware, Record Book," which contains records of the "county of Deale" as organized by William Penn, and his commissioners' courts, beginning in 1681-2.

[counties, Delaware] Penn made some grants farther inland, but none on the western part of what is now Delaware. Lord Baltimore, especially in Kent and Sussex, continued making grants of land until the boundary lines were established in 1767. Courts had been established under Lord Baltimore . . . Counties had been organized, the first one in Kent County (Maryland) in 1650, followed by Talbot in 1660, and later, but prior to 1682 [the beginning of the Penn era], Dorchester [1669], Somerset [1666], and Cecil [1674].* The courts in these counties exercised jurisdiction over the whole Peninsula until 1767, except in that part along the River and Bay [i. e. Delaware River and Delaware Bay] settled by the Swedes, Dutch, and Duke of York and William Penn."

That Somerset County and Worcester County (the formation of 1742) continued to exercise jurisdiction over the area now Sussex County, Delaware, is evidenced by items in Somerset Court records directing the laying out and upkeep of roads in parts of what is now Sussex County, Delaware, and deeds recorded for land conveyances in that area. The judicial records, or court orders, of Worcester County (1742) are missing, but among the deeds are various items of conveyances of land in what is now Sussex County, Delaware. What is now Baltimore Hundred, in Sussex County, Delaware, was originally laid off as in Somerset County, Maryland. Broad Creek Chapel (now Christ Church), east of the town of Laurel, Sussex County, Delaware, and erected between 1770 and 1772, was biult as a Chapel of Ease in Stepney Parish, Somerset County, Maryland (see *ante,* p. 191). Prince George Chapel, situated near Daggsboro, Sussex County, Delaware, was erected between 1755 and 1757 as a Chapel of Ease in Worcester Parish, Worcester County, Maryland (see *ante,* p. 206).

We have not attempted to enter into detail in regard to the Lords Baltimores' claim, under the Maryland charter of June, 1632, to the area which is now the State of Delaware. For the interesting history relative to this claim and the proceedings which finally separated it from the province of Maryland, we refer the interested reader to the standard histories of Maryland, Pennsylvania and Delaware, and the large amount of material in monograph form which has grown out of the subject. More particularly we would call attention to the article by Walter A. Powell (published in *Maryland Historical Magazine,* Vol. XXIX, pp. 83-101), entitled *"Fight of a Century Between the Penns and Calverts Over the Three Lower Counties on Delaware Which Resulted in Making the State of Delaware a Separate Commonwealth."* In scholarly fashion, illuminatively, though with brevity, Mr. Powell has treated the abundant data relative to the subject. To us it seems that he views the subject from every angle without prejudice; while his article, by its clarity, places the matter within the grasp of any interested mind. For enlightenment relative to the subject of "Durham County," of 1669, we refer the reader to the able study prepared by Percy G.

---

*For the notes on erecting of Kent, Talbot, Dorchester and Cecil Counties, see Mathews, *The Counties of Maryland, Their Origin, Boundaries and Election Districts.* Cecil County was erected from part of the territory of the original Baltimore County.

Skirven (published in *Maryland Historical Magazine*, Vol. XXV, pp. 157-167), entitled *"Durham County: Lord Baltimore's Attempt at Settlement of His Lands on the Delaware Bay, 1669-1685."* For valuable notes relative to the Delaware area as it refers to Somerset and Worcester Counties, Maryland, see Edward B. Mathews, *The Counties of Maryland, Their Origin, Boundaries and Election Districts*, pp. 543-545 and 566-567.

APPENDIX VIII

WORCESTER COUNTY (1742) AND WICOMICO COUNTY (1867)

Somerset County, created by proclamation, August 22, 1666, was "bounded on the South with a line drawne from Watkins point (being the North point of that bay into which the River Wighco formerly called Wighcocomoco afterwards Pocomoke and now Wighcocomoco [the Pocomoke River] againe doth fall exclusively) to the Ocean on the East, Nanticoke River on the North and the Sound of Chesipeake bay on the West" (see *ante,* pp. 5and 67). In 1668 there was an adjustment of the southern boundary line of Somerset County, which was the boundary line between Maryland and Virginia, through which considerable acreage was lost from the county (see *ante,* p. 54). With this exception Somerset County retained its original boundaries from 1666 until 1742.

In 1742 the General Assembly of Maryland, upon petition of certain inhabitants of Somerset, erected Worcester County from the southern and eastern sections thereof. By this Act the dividing line between Somerset and Worcester Counties was run as follows: "Beginning at Watkins Point and from thence up Pocomoke Bay to mouth of Pocomoke River, and up and with the said River to mouth of Dividing Creek thence up the Westermost side of the said creek and main Branch to the Bridges called Denstones Bridges and from thence West to the main road called Parahawkin Road; thence up and with the said road to John Caldwell, senior's, saw mill, thence up and with the said road over Cox's Branch to Broad Creek Bridge" (*XLII Arcv. Md.,* p. 428). By this Act, therefore, Worcester County, as laid out in 1742 included the area *south* of the Pocomoke River to the Maryland-Virginia boundary line (which became the southern boundary of Worcester County) and the area *east* of Dividing Creek, with a line from the head of this creek, running in a generally northerly direction to "Broad Creek Bridge," which is at this present time (1935) Laurel, Sussex County, Delaware, and from this point a line running easterly to the Atlantic Ocean.* Up to 1867, when Wicomico County was erected from sections of Somerset and Worcester County, Worcester County retained its boundaries as set forth in the Act of Assembly, 1742. It is interesting to note that the east-west boundary line between Somerset and Worcester Counties, from 1742-1867,

---

*With the final adjustment of the Maryland-Delaware boundary line, 1767, the northerly line of Worcester County was made as it is at present (1935) and became the boundary line between Maryland and Delaware.

in the neighborhood of Salisbury, Maryland, followed the present Division Street of that (now) city.*

It may be interesting to students of Worcester and Somerset County history to note here that it is related that "Giovanni de Verrazano, the Florentine navigator, and the first European known to have reached the continent of North America, anchored in Sinepuxent Bay and called the land Arcadia" (note on *Historical and Literary Map of the Old Line State of Maryland,* published by the Enoch Pratt Library [Baltimore], 1931. Jenings C. Wise, in his *Kingdome of Accawmacke, or the Eastern Shore of Virginia in the 17th Century,* pp. 4-7, gives an account of Verrazano's voyage. Louis D. Scissco, in *Maryland Historical Magazine,* Vol. XVIII, p. 130, has an interesting article relative to "Colonel Henry Norwood in Worcester County, 1650." Norwood, a Cavalier, was shipwrecked (with a party) off the Eastern Shore of Virginia while on a voyage from England to Virginia. While on this coast he went up into what later (1666) became Somerset County, Maryland, and still later (1742) Worcester County.

The town of Snow Hill is today the seat of Worcester County.

In 1867 (by Article 13, Section 2, of the Constitution of Maryland) Wicomico County was erected from parts of Somerset and Worcester Counties. The boundaries for Wicomico County were defined as "beginning at the point where Mason and Dixon's line [Maryland-Delaware boundary line] crosses the channel of Pocomoke River, thence following the said line to the channel of Nanticoke River, thence with the channel of the said river to Tangier Sound, or the intersection of Nanticoke and Wicomico Rivers, thence up the channels of the Wicomico River to the mouth of Wicomico Creek, thence with the channel of said Creek and Passedyke Creek to Dashield's or Disharoon's Mills [as located at that date], thence with the mill pond of said mills and branch, following the middle prong of said branch to Meadow Bridge on the road dividing the counties of Somerset and Worcester ... thence due east to the Pocomoke River, thence with the channel of said river to the beginning ... said parts of Worcester and Somerset Counties shall become and constitute a new County, to be called Wicomico County ..." Salisbury is the seat of Wicomico County (Mathews, *The Counties of Maryland, Their Origin, Boundaries, and Election Districts,* p. 562).

Somerset County, of this present time (1935) assumed its present boundaries in 1867, when Wicomico County was formed.

---

*Worcester County was organized at the house of David Murry in Snow Hill Town, December 11, 1742, by virtue of a commission from Lord Baltimore dated December 10, 1742; commissioners, or justices of the peace, being John Henry, John Scott, William Lane, Samuel Hopkins, John Miller, John Scarborough, John Kilby and William Burton; Robert King, Jr., became clerk, and Edmund Hough, underclerk (Worcester Court, Deed Liber A, pp. 1-5).

Appendix IX

The King Family Homes in Somerset County

"Kingsland"

On March 12, 1682/3, Robert King, I, purchased of Randall Revell a tract of 300 acres of land on the south side of the Trading Branch (later called King's Creek, in Somerset County (Somerset Court, Deed Liber O 6, p. 330). Robert King, I, built and established his home on this land, which was given the name of "Kingsland." In 1696 Robert King, I, dying intestate, this "Kingsland" plantation descended to his only son and heir at law, Robert King, II. This Robert King, II, by his will, dated May 30, 1750, probated June 26, 1755, devised to son, Nehemiah King, "my Dwelling Plantation at Manokin in Somerset County whereon my Deceased Father, Major Robert King in his lifetime did dwell containing about 300 acres (and I believe called Kingsland) for and during his natural life and after to his heirs male during his or their lives and so on from heir male to heir male as long as any male issue derived from my son Nehemiah shall happen to continue by way of inheritance according to priority of birth and senority of age; and for want of such issue and heirs then to my grandson Thomas King," etc., etc.* Nehemiah King married Francis Barnes and their eldest son was a certain Robert King. Nehemiah King resided on the "Kingsland" plantation and by his will, dated December 29, 1766, probated January 10, 1767, he devised to "son Robert King, his heirs and assigns forever my *dwelling plantation* including the lands called Foxons and the lands I bought of Spencer Hack and William Thompson," etc., etc.† The *"dwelling plantation,"* so devised, was of course the "Kingsland" plantation. We have not been able to find any will, or administration, on the estate of the Robert King to whom his father, Nehemiah King, devised the "Kingsland" plantation. However, in August, 1808, in valuation of real estate belonging to Charlotte W. King and Robert Jenckins Henry King (who were orphans of Nehemiah King, decd., who was next younger brother of Robert King, who inherited "Kingsland") we find this item: "on the farm called the Old Mansion place . . . there is a brick dwelling house, one story, two rooms and passage below, three rooms above, eighteen sash windows, two porches, covered with cypress shingles, in very bad repair . . ." In the valuations made in 1805 and 1807 this item appears: "On the old Dwelling Place 1 Brick Dwelling House in indifferent repair . . . 12 panels railing around the grave yard . . ."‡ The Kings lands along King's Creek (formerly the Trading Branch) all came into the possession of Nehemiah King (son of Nehemiah King, who died in 1767) and at his death (intestate) in 1802 descended to his two children, Charlotte W. King and Robert Jenckins Henry King, and the said Charlotte W. King, dying at the age of 10 years, the whole

---
*Will of Robert King recorded Somerset Registry of Wills, Liber EB 4, p. 31, *et seq.*
†Will of Nehemiah King recorded Somerset Registry of Wills, Liber EB 4, p. 127.
‡Somerset Registry of Wills, Liber EB 28 (Bonds, 1805-15), pp. 132-3 (Valuation, 1808); p. 7 (Valuation, 1805); p. 45 (Valuation, 1807).

of this landed estate became the property of Robert Jenckins Henry King.* In
1822 there was a commission appointed to determine the boundaries of the said
Robert J. H. King's lands lying between King's Creek and Back Creek, Somerset County, and the commission set forth the boundaries thereof, throwing the
several tracts into one tract, called "Beverly," containing the whole 1,557½
acres.† Finally, in 1857, there was a division of this "Beverly" tract of 1,557½
acres between the children of Robert Jenckins Henry King, viz: Charlotte
(wife of William H. Waters; Laura, wife of Isaac T. Barnes); Anne Maria
(*alias* Aurelia W. White, wife of Edward J. White); Henry N. King, and George
King (represented by guardian). In plat of division of these lands, Lot No. 3 is
stated to contain *the King family burying ground*.‡ May 3, 1880, Gale and
Stewart (trustees of Isaac T. Barnes and Laura, his wife) conveyed to Warwick
those parts of "Beverly" tract known as "Peach Blossom" farm and *"the old
House Place."* In a confirmatory deed (passed later) by Gale and Stewart (trustees) to Warwick, the "King family grave yard" is referred to as being on *"the
old House Place."* In October, 1917, Warwick conveyed to Brittingham the
farm of 217 acres known as *"the old House Tract,"* or part of tract of land
called "Beverly." In December, 1925, the Brittinghams conveyed to Marion T.
Gates 208 acres, being part of a tract of land called "Beverly" on the county
road from Princess Anne to Revell's Neck.§ In 1934 Cassius M. Dashiell and
Clayton Torrence together went onto the farm of Marion T. Gates on the south
side of King's Creek, in Somerset County, and Mr. Gates showed to them the
remains of the King family graveyard,** and a site some 100 yards northeast of
the graveyard (and on a rise in the ground near the creek side) where he (the
said Gates) had from time to time found pieces of brick which indicated that
there had been a house on that site in former days. From the tracing of title to
this land, and the presence of the positively identified King family graveyard
on this tract and nearby the evident site of an ancient house, this tract (referred
to in deeds quoted above as *"the old House Place,"* on which was the King
family graveyard) is identified as "Kingsland," the home of Robert King, I
(died 1696), of his son, Robert King, II (died 1755), and of his son, Nehemiah
King (died 1767).

---

*In old record in a Bible owned by Mr. Henry Barnes, of King's Creek, Somerset County, gives: Nehemiah King (son of Nehemiah King and Frances Barnes), b. August 13, 1755; d. June 12, 1802; married December 26, 1797, Esther Winder Polk; issue: (1) Charlotte Washington King, b. March 24, 1800; d. September 20, 1810; (2) Robert Jenckins Henry King, b. April 3, 1801 [d. April 26, 1873]; married, *first*, August 17, 1826, Aurelia Winder Handy (b. 1808; d. 1833); *second*, December 31, 1834, Matilda Handy (d. 1842); *third*, January 3, 1843, Mary Broughton . The widow, Esther Winder (Polk) King married Alexander Stuart, who d. April 17, 1824. Mrs. Esther W. Stuart, d. Octobe 3, 1832.

†Somerset Court, Judicials, 1822, 1823, 1824, pp. 244-258; on p. 257 is a plat of this whole tract of 1,557½ acres, now called "Beverly."

‡Somerset Court, Equity Record, Liber LW, No. 2, p. 227, *et seq.*; the plat, showing divisions of land, is given on pp. 246-7.

§For divisions, plats of land and deeds referred to, see Somerset Court Chancery Record, BFL, No. 2, p. 32, *et seq.*, description of "Not No. 2," known as "the old House Place," and pp. 40-41, giving plat of division of land; Deed Liber BFL, No. 2, pp. 696-698; Deed Liber BFL, No. 3, p. 295; Deed Liber WJS, No. 73, p. 421; Deed Liber WJS, No. 92, p. 416.

**This graveyard (now covered by a thicket) disclosed on examination a tombstone bearing the inscription "Mary, wife of Abraham Barnes, Mercht * * *, died 25th October, 1739, in the 25th year of her age." There were also apparent fragments of other now broken tombs. Mrs. Mary Barnes was the daughter of Robert King, II, and Priscilla Covington, his wife.

"Beverly"

The well-known "Beverly" estate on the south side of King's Creek, Somerset County, on which stands a beautiful mansion house of brick, was the home established by Nehemiah King, II (born August 13, 1755; died June 12, 1802), son of Nehemiah King, I (died 1767), and Frances Barnes, his wife. The plantation on which Nehemiah King, II, erected his "mansion house" was inherited by him under the will of his father, Nehemiah King, I, described as "lands on King's Branch."* Nehemiah King, II, erected the "mansion house" on the "Beverly" plantation between 1785 and 1795.† From Nehemiah King, II (who died intestate, June 12, 1802), this "Beverly" plantation with its buildings went to his son, Robert Jenckins Henry King. The portion of the "Beverly" plantation on which the "mansion house" stood finally became the property of Isaac T. Barnes, who married Laura, daughter of the said Robert Jenckins Henry King.‡ In more recent years the "mansion house," with its surrounding acreage, was purchased by Lynde Catlin, Esq. The house has been beautifully restored by Mr. Catlin.

"Kingston Hall"

The history of "Kingston Hall" estate, in Somerset County, is most interesting.

Colonel Robert King, II, of "Kingsland," by his will, dated May 30, 1750, probated June 26, 1755, recites that "Whereas my son Robert King hath departed this life intestate§ leaving two sons Thomas and Robert Jenckins King, and as Thomas will inherit as eldest son and heir at law all lands possessed by his said father & his younger brother be deprived of inheriting any part of his deceased father's estate" the testator directs that the land in Worcester County (200 acres) "whereof my said son was seized in fee simple . . . where my said son *last settled*" be sold and the money arising from such sale be put at interest for the benefit of the testator's grandson, the said Robert Jenckins King.** The will of Colonel Robert King then proceeds to devise "to my grandson Thomas King and to his heirs and assigns forever all my lands on the south side Great Annemessex River at the head thereof *where his deceased father first settled* and Marumsco Branch in Somerset County, containing by estimation 1,566 acres . . ."††

There have been so many statements as to the origin of "Kingston Hall" that it may be well to set forth here the ascertainable facts. In May, 1723, Robert

---

*See will of Nehemiah King, will dated December 29, 1766, probated January 10, 1767, in Somerset Registry of Wills, Liber EB 4, p. 31. The King's Creek of this present time (1935) was referred to in 1743 as "King's Branch, alias Trading Branch," and "King's Branch, commonly called Mudford or Trading Branch," in deed of Whittington King to Daniel Long, Somerset Court, Deed Liber O 21, p. 103.

†The house was completed in 1796, according to an iron plate on one of the chimneys.

‡In Somerset Court, Judicials, 1822, 1823, 1824, p. 257, plat of the tract called "Beverly," giving the mansion house; Somerset Court, Equity Record, Liber LW, No. 2, p. 227, *et seq.*, which shows the allotment of this mansion house tract to Mrs. Laura (King) Barnes.

§Somerset Registry of Wills, Liber EB 6, p. 65, gives administrator's account of Robert King, Jr., of Worcester County, July 10, 1750.

**Somerset Registry of Wills, Liber EB 14, pp. 52-4, will of Robert Jenckins King, of Somerset County, dated December 24, 1788, probated March 17, 1789, after disposing of his property, names as executors "my brother, Thomas King, and friend and near relation, Nehemiah King."

††Somerset Registry of Wills, Liber EB 4, p. 31, *et seq.*, will of Robert King, dated May 30, 1750, probated June 26, 1755.

King (II) purchased from a certain Ann Johnson two tracts of land (adjoining each other) on south side Annemessex River, Somerset County; one of these tracts, called "Straights," contained 600 acres, and the other, called "Johnson's," contained 300 acres.* In August, 1724, Robert King purchased from William Kennerly, of Dorchester County, 500 acres, called "Evernden's Lot," patented in 1694 to Thos. Evernden and by him devised to the said Wm. Kennerly. In January, 1728/9, Robert King (II) purchased from William Catlin 66 acres to be called "Closure" out of a larger tract called "First Choice" and adjoining tract called "Johnson's," owned by said King. In October, 1744, King purchased of William Beauchamp a small acreage, then called "Conveniency" (adjoining said King's lands), and in February, 1748, the said King purchased of George Marshall, Samuel Long and Sarah, his wife, and Thomas Cottingham and Mary, his wife, tract called "Lots Purchase," 85 acres, and made up of the two tracts, "Long Lott" and "Leadburn," and adjoining King's lands, called "Conclusion."† These lands evidently went towards making up the 1,566 acres left by Robert King to his grandson, Thomas King, as recited above. Robert King, Jr. (the father of the said Thomas King), had first settled on part of these lands at the head (and on the south side of) the Annemessex River; afterwards moving to a plantation in Worcester County. Thomas King entered into this inheritance and making his home on this land created a great estate therefrom. At Thomas King's death this estate passed to his only child, a daughter, Elizabeth Barnes King, who married Colonel Henry James Carroll, and from them to their son, Thomas King Carroll (afterwards Governor of Maryland). In October, 1835, William Williams recovered judgment against Thomas King Carroll in Somerset Court. Acting under a writ of the court the sheriff of Somerset levied on certain lands and tenements of the said Carroll, and by deed, September 19, 1837, conveyed the said lands and houses to John W. Dennis, of Worcester County. The lands of Carroll thus conveyed were included in and were "consolidated by a patent of resourvey granted to a certain Robert King and called 'Conclusion,' containing 1,500 acres."‡

This estate, no doubt, was given its name, "Kingston Hall," during the lifetime of Thomas King; while the now celebrated "mansion house" thereon is assigned by a recent authority on colonial architecture, because of certain specifically named features in building, *"at the earliest to the middle of the eighteenth century."*§

---

*Deed May 29, 1723, Ann Johnson, of Parish of St. Paul's, Covent Garden, county Middlesex, Kingdom of Great Britain, Spinster (daughter and only child of George Johnson, late of the same place, Watchmaker, decd., who was only son of George Johnson, late of Somerset County, Maryland, decd.), to Robert King, of Somerset County. The lands called "Straights" and "Johnson's," totaling 900 acres, had formerly been patented by George Johnson, the grandfather of said Ann (Somerset Court, Deed Liber O 15, pp. 58 and 129).

†See Somerset Court, Deed Liber O 17, p. 122 (Catlin to King); Deed Liber O 21, p. 118 (Beauchamp to King), and Deed Liber O 22, p. 36 (Marshall and others to King), Deed Liber O 15, p. 173 (Kennerly to King).

‡Somerset Court, Deed Liber O 59, p. 210, deed September 19, 1837, Holbrook, sheriff of Somerset County, to John W. Dennis.

The resurvey patented February 4, 1728/9, by Robert King under the tract name of "Conclusion" calls for 1,500 acres on south side Great Annemessex River, Somerset County, and was made up of three tracts of land, viz: (1) "Straights," 600 acres; (2) "Johnson's," 300 acres (both granted George Johnson in February, 1663/4), and (3) "Evernden's Lot," 500 acres (granted Thos. Evernden in August, 1694). The warrant and patent for King's "Conclusion" are recorded, Hall of Records, Annapolis, Liber PL, No. 7, folio 82, and Liber IL, No. A, folio 864.

§Forman, *Early Manor and Plantation Homes of Maryland*, p. 148.

Appendix X
Early Settlers

(*a*) *First Settlers' (1662-1666) Families: Genealogical Notes.*
(*b*) *Names of Settlers in Somerset County, 1666-1700.*
(*c*) *Names of Quaker, Church of England and Presbyterian Families.*
(*d*) *Patents for Land in Old Somerset Area, 1662-1666.*

(a) First Settlers' (1662-1666) Families: Genealogical Notes

Note.—As this book is a study in Somerset "origins," we offer these brief notes indicating the "origin" of the "first settlers." These notes make no claim to exhaustiveness. They are merely intended to furnish a brief note on the "settler" and to name his wife and children (when these names could be discovered). These notes are intended only as "starters" for research into Somerset County's earliest families. It is hoped that someone will eventually make an exhaustive study of the early family history of Somerset County people.

The records to which reference is made in these notes are the deed, judicial, will and administration records of Somerset County, and the Maryland Calendar of Wills (*Md. Cal. Wills*), by Mrs. Jane (Baldwin) Cotton.

The deed and judicial records of Somerset County are in the office of the clerk of Circuit Court for Somerset County, Princess Anne, Maryland. The references to "O 1," etc., are to the deed books; references to "AW," "DT," "BWZ," "AZ," "BWZ," "EFH" and "O 7 [reverse]" are to the series called "Judicials." The references to "IKL" are to the *liber* bearing those initials which is in the office of the clerk of Circuit Court for Somerset County. This volume includes record of births, marriages and deaths. For a note describing this "IKL" see reference in index thereto.

The references to the series "EB 5," etc., are to will and estate account books in the office of the Register of Wills for Somerset County, Princess Anne, Maryland.

Necessity for economizing with space compelled the use of abbreviations in these notes. Inclusive dates of birth and death of a person are given, *e. g.* "(1642-1723)." The date of a year immediately following a baptismal name, *e. g.* "John, 1682," is the year of birth of that individual; "d." indicates *died;* "m." indicates *married;* "c." indicates *circa.*

Adams. Philip Adams, in Annemessex, 1663 (headright to patent to Ambrose Dixon), and lived in Morumsco section. He m., 1670, Ann Crew (see *post,* Crew); issue: (1) Thomas, 1673; (2) Philip (b. and d. 1675/6); (3) Jacob, 1676; (4) Philip, 1679; (5) William, 1681; (6) George, 1685; (7) David, 1687; (8) Mary, 1683. Philip Adams m., 1691, Mary Barry, and had issue: (1) Anne, 1692; (2) Abraham, 1694 (IKL).

Anderson. John Anderson and wife Eleanor; Pocomoke Hundred, 1666; from Patuxent [Calvert County?]; issue: (1) Sarah, 1664; d. inf.; (2) Sarah, 1666 (IKL). 1673 Anderson deeds to daughters Mary, Sarah and Elizabeth (AZ, 229).

Ackworth. Richard Ackworth (*c.* 1634-1676); wife Anne [Manlove?]; Manokin, 1664; issue: (1) Richard, 1664-1728; m., 1682, Sarah Hardy; (2) Thomas 1666; (3) Henry, 1668-1715; m. Sarah _____; (4) Anne, 1670; (5) [Sarah, 1676; m., 1692, Wm. Keen, Jr.] (DT, 206; *Md. Cal. Wills,* I, 75; EB 9, 121 and 105; IKL).

Avery. John Avery and wife Sarah; mariner; in Somerset, 1667-72 (O 1, 99; AZ, 4, 63, 98 and 205). Mrs. Avery earliest, so far discovered, school teacher in Somerset (see *ante,* p. 287). Averys went to Sussex County, in Delaware (Sussex County, Deeds Liber A 1, p. 10; Sussex record book, 1681; Penna. Hist. Soc., Phila.). John Avery lived on Rehoboth Bay, Sussex County; lieutenant military forces and president of the Whorekill, Delaware, 1675; captain, October, 1675; justice peace, 1672-82 (*Md. Soc. Colonial Wars... Genealogies... Records,* ... p. 138).

Ballard. Charles Ballard, Manokin Hundred, 1665; justice peace, 1672-6; d. *ante* 1672; m. Sarah _____ (widow of John Elzey and Thomas Jordan). Sarah m., *fourth,* Stephen Lufte (see *post,* Elzey). Charles and Sarah Ballard had issue: (1) Henry, 1666; (2) Sarah, 1668; m. Randall Revell, Jr. (see *post,* Revell); (3) Charles (d. 1724/5); justice peace; colonel; m. Eleanor King (see *ante,* p. 367); (4) Elizabeth, m., *first,* 1687, John King (d. 1696); *second,* Thomas Wilson (d. 1702; *third,* Peter Dent; (5) Jarvis, d. 1765; m. Ann _____ (IKL; EB 9, p. 98; EB 6, p. 167).

Barnabe (also Barnaby). James Barnabe, Manokin, 1665 (from Northampton County, Virginia); d. February, 1666/7; m. Mary _____; issue: (1) Elizabeth, 1661/2; m., 1680, John Henderson; (2) Rebecca, m., 1669/70; James Willis; (3) James, 1664/5-1681. Marriage banns, January, 1667/8, Henry Miles and Mary Barnabe [widow of James] (see *ante,* p. 400); evidently marriage did not take place as Mary Barnabe (widow of James) m., 1669, Edward Jones (IKL; EB 9, p. 5; O 1, p. 66).

Beauchamp. Edmund Beauchamp (see *ante,* p. 333) m., 1668, Sarah Dixon (daughter of Ambrose; see *post,* Dixon); issue: (1) Thomas, 1670-1716/17; m., *first,* Mary Turpin; *second,* Sarah _____; (2) Alice, 1674; (3) Edmund, 1674/5-1733; m. Sarah [Traherne?]; (4) John, 1679; (5) Doggett, 1681-1716/17; m. [Sarah?] Gray; (6) Edward, *c.* 1683-1750; m. Neomy [Fontaine?]; (7)Robert, *c.* 1685 (IKL; BWZ, pp. 116-18; EB 9, pp. 19, 59, 64; EB 14).

Boice (also Buse, Buss, Boyss, Boist). Mary, wife of Wm. *Buse,* d. Annemessex, January, 1666. Jane *Buss,* daughter Wm. and Mary *Buse,* b. Manokin, March 5, 1663. Wm. Boyss, w. prob. January 19, 1666, names (among others) sister, Jane Bellams, Northampton County, Virginia; only daughter, Jane Boyss, and Robt. Catlin and Ann, his wife, to hold estate until said Jane is of age. Jane Delemas, wife of Thomas Manlove, in 1672 was sister of Wm. Boist, decd. Jane Boyss (only daughter of Wm.), m., *first,* Thomas Sewell (d. 1692/3); *second,* Edward Stogdell (also spelled Stockdell, Stockdale) (IKL; *Md. Cal. Wills,* I, p. 39, and II, p. 61; AZ, p. 146; EB 9, p. 57; O 10, p. 109, and O 23, p. 83).

Booth. George Booth, in Wicomico Hundred, 1666. A John Booth, w. prob.

June 25, 1698, names children, John, Elinor, Isaac, Daniel, Easter and Eliza Booth, legacy to Bridget, daughter of James Spence (*Md. Cal. Wills*, II, p. 153).

Barre. Philip Barre (also Berre, Bairee), Manokin section, 1662-3 (from Northampton County, Virginia); August, 1662, had warrant for land for transporting himself, wife Olive, Elizabeth *Barie*, George Lane, Margaret Ivery and Mary Ivery. Philip and Olive Barre had issue: (1) Elizabeth, 1659; [? m. Richard Davis; see *post*, Davis]; (2) Grisegon, 1664; m., 1681, Charles Jones (IKL; Hall of Records, Annapolis, Liber 5, pp. 209-211).

Betts. George Betts, in Manokin, 1666; later in Monie section; m., *first*, Margaret _____; *second*, 1669, Bridget Bosman (see *post*, Bosman); issue, *first* marriage: (1) Margaret, d. 1667; (2) Frances, 1666-1670; issue, *second* marriage: (3) William, b. and d. 1670; (4) George, 1671; (5) Anne, 1673; (6) Bridget, 1682 [? m. _____ Shiles]; (7) Frances (1682-*post* 1732); m., *first*, John Irving; *Second*, Ephraim Wilson; (8) Mary, 1687; [? m. James Collier]; (9) William, 1691; (10) John, 1694 (IKL; *Md. Cal. Wills*, III, pp. 222 and 137).

Boston. Henry Boston (see *ante*, p. 139); m., *first*, Ann _____; second, 1673, Elizabeth Rogerson. Henry Boston was father of (1) Henry Boston, Jr., b. Aug. 13, 1656; (2) Rebecca, m. _____ Millner; (3) Anne; (4) Isaac (d. 1701), m. Elizabeth Long (see *post*, Long); (5) Esau (d. 1721), m. _____ _____. Henry Boston, Sr. (d. 1676), had also an illegitimate son, Richard Boston (d. 1707/8), whose mother was one Judith Best, later wife of Thomas Davis, tailor. Marriage banns, June 12, 1677, Henry Lewis, of Anne Arundel County, and Elizabeth Boston [widow of Henry Boston, Sr.?], of Somerset County (see *ante*, p. 402). The settlement of estate of Henry Boston, Sr. (d. 1676), in May-August, 1677, proves wife Elizabeth and sons Henry, Isaac and Esau; daughters Rebecca Millner and Anne Boston.* These estate records call Isaac and Esau Boston "natural sons" to distinguish them (as legitimately born) from Richard Boston, who is described as "bastard child" of Judith Best, begotten by Henry Boston, Sr. (Judicials, 1675-1677 in O 7 [reverse], pp. 62, 75, 98, 99, 112, 113 and 133; *Md. Cal. Wills*, II, p. 212; EB 13, pp. 28 and 131).

Brayfield. Susannah Brayfield, in Manokin section, 1665; indentured servant to Randall Revell and John Cooper. Susannah was before court several times charged with (and fined for) bearing illegitimate children, of whom the fathers were John Cooper and John Griffith. Susannah was mother of "Gabriel Brayfield," b. March, 1665/6, whose father was proved to have been John Cooper (O 1, pp. 1, 5, 11, 12, 34, 42, 52-53; AZ, p. 67; IKL, for birth of "Gabriel Brayfield"). Susannah Brayfield m., May, 1667, John Cooper, the father of Gabriel (see *ante*, p. 400, for marriage banns). Cooper evidently dying soon after we find "Susanna Cooper" m., June, 1668, Thomas Covington (see *ante*, p. 400, for marriage banns). Thomas Covington (d. 1704) left by will "to Gabriel Cooper his Mothers iron pott" (See *post*, Covington). Gabriel Cooper lived in Barren Creek section (now Wicomico County) and dying 1737 left wife Ann,

---

*Liber IKL gives marriage of Thomas Relfe and Anne Boston, March 12, 1680.

sons Gabriel, Samuel, Isaac, Thomas, and James Cooper; and daughters Ann Cottman, Phillis Clarkson, Sarah Taylor and Betty, wife of Jonathan Houfington (EB 9, p. 199).

Bosman (also Bozman, Bossman). William Bosman (see *ante*, p. 326) m., *first*, Bridget _____ (d. July, 1660); *second*, Eleanor Mattocks, widow (Mattox, Maddox; see *post*, Maddox). Eleanor m., *third*, James Caine (see *post*, Caine). William and Bridget Bosman had issue: (1) John (1650-1716); justice peace, and presiding justice, 1713, in Somerset; coroner; high sheriff; member Lower House Maryland Assembly, 1707-10 (*Arcv. Md.*); m. Blandina Risdon; (2) William, 1655; (3) George, 1659-1706/7; m. Jane _____ (widow of Wm. Jones [see *post*, Jones of Monie]. Mrs. Jane Bosman m., *third*, Luke Valentine); (4) Bridget, 1653; m. George Betts (see *ante*, Betts); (5) Anne, 1657; m. (probably George Downes (see *post*, Downes); (6) Katherine (b. prior to February, 1660/1) m., *first*, John Nellson (d. *ante* January 11, 1670/1); issue: (a) John Nellson; (b) Bridget Nellson. Katherine (Bosman) Nellson m., *second*, John Lawes; issue: (a) William Lawes; (b) John Lawes; (c) Robert Lawes; (d) Mary Lawes. (7) Mary Bosman (querry: was she a child by Bosman's *second* wife, Eleanor?) (IKL; *Md. Cal. Wills*, I, p. 31; EB 9, p. 57; O 10, pp. 706-8; AB [in O 9], p. 353; DT, p. 82, and AZ, pp. 177, 216 and 482). Liber IKL gives John, George, Wm., Bridget and Anne Bosman as children of William and *Eleanor* Bosman, but dates of births prove them children of William and *Bridget* Bosman. Katherine Bosman is proved by deed gift, February, 1660/1, from Mrs. Katherine Scarburgh; this gift made at time pre-nuptial contract between Wm. Bosman and Mrs. Eleanor Mattock's (or Maddox) (see Richardson's *Sidelights on Md. Hist.*, II, pp. 264-7. Northampton County (Virginia) records, Vol. IX, pp. 92 and 144, give Mrs. *Eliza Mattocks;* this is clerical error; her name was *Eleanor.*

Bloyce (Bloys, Bloyse). Thomas Bloyse was an overseer of will of Wm. Bosman in 1664. Frances Bloys (daughter of Thomas) m. William Wright, December, 1669 (*Md. Cal. Wills*, I, p. 31, IKL).

Caine. James Caine, in Manokin, August, 1666; m., c. 1666-7, Eleanor, widow of William Bosman (see *ante*, Bosman). James Caine, w. dat. December 12, 1667, prob. April 15, 1670, devised some personalty to John Avery and residue of estate to wife, Ellinor Caine, executrix (*Md. Cal. Wills*, p. 54). Mrs. Eleanor Caine d. November 17, 1694 (IKL).

Calloway. Peter Calloway, in Wicomico section, January, 1664/5; m. Elizabeth Johnson; banns published March 26, 1667 (see *ante*, p. 400), though they were probably not married until some years later, for in May, 1667, Elizabeth Johnson was fined "for bearing a bastard child" and "Peter Calloway for getting a bastard child of Elizabeth Johnson (AZ, p. 67, listed and recorded at court held February 2, 1671/2). Elizabeth Johnson's peculiar conduct of wandering "to and againe amongst ye Indians and layeth in ye Marshes" was reported to court, November 26, 1667, and Thomas Ball was ordered "to fetch her in & deliver her to ye next magistrate," who was to give her "corre^{con} for her idleness alsoe to pvide [provide] her a service that she may worke for her living" (O 1, pp. 69 and 93). Peter and Elizabeth Calloway had issue: (1) Sarah, 1676; (2) Anne, 1678; (3) Peter, 1681; (4) William, 1689 (IKL).

Carr. Anne Carr, in Manokin section, 1665; indentured servant to Randall Revell; presented by Somerset Grand Jury for bearing illegitimate children of whom Edward Hassard (or Hazzard) was father. Hassard attempted to leave Somerset in March, 1670/1, but was prevented from doing so owing to his obligations to his children by Anne Carr. Finally, Anne Carr and Edward Hassard were married in February, 1671/2 (see *ante,* p. 397). The children of Anne Carr by Edward Hassard (born before marriage) were: (1) Elizabeth, b. March, 1668; (2) David, b. July, 1670; after their marriage was born: (3) Susanna, b. June, 1672 (evidently conceived before marriage); and, as we discover later, there was a fourth child, whose name we do not have. Edward Hassard finally fled his responsibilities, for at June court, 1677, we find Anne *Hazard* (as her name is then spelled) petitioning court that Alexander Draper, who had the care of her child David (then seven years old) and to whom she had paid 1,600 pounds of tobacco for the child's maintainance, should no be allowed to take the said David to the Whorekill (on Delaware Bay), outside the limits of Somerset County. Mrs. Hazard states that her husband, Edward Hazard, had left her with four small children and with insufficient maintainance; she pleads "y^t as a mother shee may not be separated from her child contrary to Law & Equity." The court directed the child David to be returned to his mother (AZ, p. 67, and Liber DT, pp. 27, 51, 68, 122 and 137; IKL; O 7 [reverse], p. 101). David *Hazzard* is referred to as "father in law" in will of Robt. Hill, of Somerset, in October, 1719 (*Md. Cal. Wills,* V, p. 70). In later years David *Hazard* is referred to as living in Sussex County, on Delaware (Scharf's *History of Delaware*).

Catlin (also Catling, Catlyn). Robert Catlin, Northampton County, Virginia, 1651; wife Ann, lately indentured servant to Edward Drew (Northampton records). Catlin came to Annemessex, 1663, bringing with him wife Ann, daughter Ann, son Joseph and [son] Robert Catlin, Jr. Robert Catlin, Jr. (son of Robert and Ann), d. 1699; m., *first,* 1676/7, Elizabeth Curtis (d. 1676/7; see *post,* Curtis); *second,* Hannah _____. Ann Catlin (daughter of Robert and Ann) m., 1672, William Walston (IKL; EB 5, p. 118; O 7, p. 243; and Hall of Records, Annapolis, Patents, Liber 6, p. 255).

Cooper. John Cooper, in Manokin, 1665; see *ante,* Brayfield.

Cottingham. Thomas Cottingham, in Annemessex, July, 1666, when he m. Mary Dixon (daughter of Ambrose; see *post,* Dixon), by whom he had issue: (1) Mary, 1668; (2) Thomas, 1670; (3) Sarah, 1673; (4) Charles, 1676; (5) John, 1678; (6) Esther, 1680 (IKL).

Coulbourne. William Coulbourne (see *ante,* p. 322); m., *first,* Anne _____; *second,* Margaret Cooper; issue, *first* wife: (1) William (1650-1701), m., 1678, Ann Revell (see *post,* Revell); issue: (a) Ann, m. Thos. Mitchell; (b) Wm., m. Jane Handy; (c) Solomon, m. Rachel Handy; (d) Mary; (e) Katherine; (f)

Abigail, m. Wm. Eskridge. (2) Mary, 1661; (3) Solomon, 1663/4; (4) Anne, 1665; m. John Taylor; (5) Robert (*c.* 1667?-1698), of Accomack, County, Virginia, m. Rebecca Revell (see *post*, Revell); issue: (a) Robert; (b) Frances; (c) "unborn child." William Coulbourne and *second* wife, Margaret, had issue: (1) Penelope, m. Michael Holland (IKL; BWZ; pp. 5-6; EFG, p. 27; EB 9, p. 80; O 11, p. 221, and O 19, p. 14; O 7, p. 566; O 22, p. 83; *Md. Cal. Wills,* II, p. 222; Nottingham, *Accomack Wills and Adms., 1663-1800,* p. 23).

Covington (also Coventon). Nehemiah Covington (*c.* 1628-1681), in Northampton County, Virginia, 1647 (headright to patent to Horsey and Waddelow); signed "engagement" of loyalty to "Commonwealth of England," March, 1651/2 (Wise, *Accawmacke,* p. 136); was before court (and fined), March, 1652/3, for "incontinency before marriadge," and in April, 1653, appears before court on account of trouble he was having with person to whom he (Covington) was evidently an indentured servant (Northampton Court, OB, 1651-4, pp. 167 and 177). Nehemiah Covington went to Monie section (later Somerset County, Maryland) in 1662; settled 300 a., "Covington's Vinyard," n. side Great Monie Creek; in November, 1674, stated his age as about 46 years; he d. 1681; m., *first,* Mary _____ (d. and buried, Great Monie, April, 1667); *second,* July, 1667, Anne Ingram, widow (see *post,* Ingram). Nehemiah Covington and *first* wife, Mary, had issue: (1) Jeane (Jane), m., 1667, David Williams (see *post,* Williams); (2) John; (3) Katherine, baptized June 10, 1661; d. August, 1681; m. Edward Wright; (4) Sarah, baptized June 10, 1661; m., 1674, Lewen [Julian] Messex [Messick, Mezick, Mesex]; (5) Margaret, m., 1672, Richard Allingsworth; (6) Nehemiah, Jr. Nehemiah Covington, Sr., and Anne, his *second* wife, had issue: (1) Elizabeth, 1668; (2) Thomas, 1670; (3) Anne, 1672; (4) Jeremiah (1675-1676). Nehemiah Covington, Sr., planter, and Anne, his wife, deeded "Covington's Vinyard," on n. Great Monie Creek, to John Covington planter, and Nehemiah Covington, Jr., carpenter, on January 20, 1679. John Covington (son of Nehemiah and Mary), d. 1692/3; m. Mary _____; issue: (1) John, 1667; (2) Abraham, 1683; (3) Mary, 1684; (4) Nehemiah; (5) Philip. Nehemiah Covington (son of Nehemiah and Mary) d. 1713; Quaker (see *ante,* p. 100), general interpreter for government on any treaty with Indians of Eastern Shore (*XIII Arcv. Md.,* p. 251); amassed comfortable estate; m., 1676, Rebecca Denwood (see *post,* Denwood); issue: (1) Nehemiah, 1680; (2) Levin (1685-1725), of Prince George's County; (3) Elizabeth, m. Benjamin Wailes; (4) Priscilla, m. Robert King (see *ante,* p. 372); (5) Sarah, m., *first,* Maj.-Gen. Edward Lloyd, of Wye, Talbot County, Governor of Maryland, 1709-13; *second,* James Hollyday, of Queen Ann's County; member council and judge provincial court. (References: Greer, *Early Va. Immigrants,* p. 80; Hall of Records, Annapolis, Liber 5, p. 209, and Liber 7, p. 562; records of Hungar's Parish, Northampton County, Virginia, given in *XXIV Journal of American History,* p. 212; IKL; O 6, p. 425; EB 5, pp. 125 and 154; EB 9, p. 148; O 16, p. 28; O 28, p. 238; *XXVI Md. Hist. Mag.,* p. 168; Richardson, *Sidelights on Maryland History,* II, p. 309).

Thomas Covington (between whom and Nehemiah Covington no family relationship appears) was in the Monie section in June, 1666. He married, 1668, Susanna (Brayfield) Cooper (see *ante,* Brayfield). Thomas Covington (d. 1704) and Susanna, his wife, had issue: (1) Samuel, 1669; (2) Sarah, 1670; (3) Rachel, 1671; (4) Jacob, 1672/3; (5) Rebecca, 1674; (6) Isaac, 1675; (7) Amy, 1676; (8) Thomas, 1687; (9) Abraham; (10) Susanna, m. Daniel Jones (see *post,* Jones of Monie) (IKL; EB 5, p. 117, will of Thos. Covington, in which, besides naming his own children, he gives to "Gabriel Cooper his Mother's iron pott." This Gabriel was son of Mrs. Susanna (Brayfield) Cooper, who m., *second,* Thomas Covington).

Crew. John Crew, Northampton County, Virginia; buried there August 29, 1660; m. Elizabeth _____; issue: (1) Anne, 1655; m. 1670, Philip Adams (see *ante,* Adams); (2) Elizabeth, 1657; m., 1672/3, John King, of Mormusco (see *post,* King); (3) John, 1660/1. Elizabeth (widow of John Crew, of Northampton), m. Robert Hignett (see *post,* Hignett), and with him and her children by Crew went to Somerset County, Maryland (Hungar's Parish records, Northampton County, in *Journal of American History,* XXIV, p. 211; IKL; O 1, p. 37).

Curtis. Daniel Curtis (d. 1681), in Accomack County, Virginia, 1661; in Annemessex section, 1665 (see *ante,* p. 121); "capt: Lieut" in militia, 1678 (*VII Arcv. Md.,* p. 97); m., *first* _____ _____; *second,* July 1, 1666, Elizabeth Greene; issue, *first* wife: (1) Elizabeth (1661-1677), m., 1676, Robert Catlin, Jr. (see *ante,* Catlin); issue, *second* wife: (1) James, b. November 7, 1666 [*sic*]; d. 1721; m. Sarah Hall (see *post,* Hall); issue: (a) Charles; (b) Catherine, m. Boaz Walston; (c) Esther; (d) Rachel; (e) Eliza, m. _____ Roach; (f) Mary, m. _____ Beauchamp; (g) Sarah, m. Charles Revell (*Md. Cal. Wills,* I, p. 101; EB 9, p. 72; EB 13, p. 146).

Dashiell. James Dashiell (1634-1697); a Scotchman by birth, though of French extraction; came from Northumberland County, Virginia, to Wicomico section (later Somerset County), 1663/4; lived first on s. side Wicomico River at mouth of Dashiell's Creek, and later on e. side Wetipquin Creek(now in Wicomico County); surveyor of highways, 1666; justice peace, 1676-97; member Lower House Maryland Assembly, 1678, 1681 and 1682; customs officer for Somerset County, 1697(see *ante,* pp. 72, 394 and 395); m. Ann Cannon, and had issue: (1) James (*c.* 1660-1708/9), m., *first,* Mary Waters; *second,* Isabel Mitchell (see *post,* Mitchell); (2) Thomas (1666-1755), m. Elizabeth Mitchell (see *post,* Mitchell); (3) George (1669-1733), m. Priscilla Mitchell; (4) Katherine (1672-1696), m., 1692/3, William Jones; (5) Jane, 1675; m., 1696, John Winder (see *post,* Winder); (6) Robert (1677-1718), m. Sarah Haste (see *post,* Haste). The Dashiell connection has been worked out in all branches by Benj. J. Dashiell, of Towson, Maryland, and the genealogy published as *Dashiell Family Records,* three volumes, edited by Mr. Dashiell.

Davis. Three brothers, William, Thomas and Richard Davis, were settled in Manokin section on s. side Back Creek, 1664-5, probably coming from Nansamond County, Virginia. William and Richard Davis continued to reside in Somerset County, though Thomas Davis removed to Nansamond County, Virginia, about 1684. William Davis m., August, 1667, Anne Hooper, and had issue: (1) Elizabeth, 1668; m., *first,* Henry Lynch; *second,* Ephraim Wilson; (2) Martha, 1670; m., *first,* Thomas Jones; *second,* Robert Catherwood (see *ante,* p. 425). (3) Sarah, 1672. Richard Davis m. Elizabeth Barry (see *ante,* Barre), and had issue: (1) Martha, 1676; (2) Richard, 1679; (3) William, 1682; (4) John (1684-1715); (5) Elizabeth, 1687; (6) Rosannah, 1690 (IKL; EB 9, p. 21; O 5, pp. 269 and 285; Halls of Records, Annapolis, Liber 7, p. 312).

Dennis. Donnock Dennis (spelled variously Donnoch, Donach, Donagh) was in Northampton County, Virginia, July 31, 1661, when he married Elice Nehulian, or Nebulian. (Northampton records, Wills, Deeds, etc., 1657-1666, p. 114; *24 Journal of American History,* p. 214.) Donnock Dennis may be identified with one *Tonath* (or Tonnath) Dennis who appears as a headright in November 27, 1657, to a patent granted William Roberts for land in Northampton County. (Nugent, *Cavaliers and Pioneers . . . Virginia Land Patents,* 1623-1800, pp. 353 and 356). The baptismal name *Elice* (wife of Donnock Dennis) also appears later invariably as *Ellis.* The surname appears as Nehulian, or Nebulian. There was one Darman (or Dorman) Neheuallin (also Nehevellin?) who was a headright to a patent granted November 27, 1657, to Thomas Stratton, of Northampton County (*Ibid.,* pp. 353 and 356). From these references in Virginia land patents it looks very much as though the Dennises, Nehulians and other apparently Irish families arrived in Northampton County, Virginia, about the same time.

Donnock Dennis came from "Northampton-Accomack," in Virginia, to Somerset County, Maryland, bringing his wife Ellis, daughter Elizabeth and son Donnock, Jr., about 1668; probably earlier (Hall of Records, Annapolis, Land records, Liber 11, p. 514). Donnock Dennis obtained lands, both by patent and purchase, on the north and south sides of the Pocomoke River, and apparently first settled on Morumsco Creek. In 1672, Thomas Blake, of Galloway, Ireland, gave power of attorney to friend "Donagh Dinis, of Morumsco Creeke," Somerset County, to collect debts due said Blake (AZ, p. 114), November 13, 1683, Donald [Donnock] Dennis was appointed constable of Annemessex Hundred (O 7 [front], p. 1).

Donnock Dennis (d. 1716/17) and Ellis, his wife, had issue: (1) William; (2) Elizabeth, b. November 16, 1665; (3) Margaret, b. February 8, 1667/8; (4) Donnock, b. February 16, 1669; (5) Ellis, b. July 29, 1673; (6) John 1676/7-1741) m., *first,* Sarah Littleton; *second,* Elizabeth Day; (7) Eleanor, m. Jeremiah Morris; (8) Katherine [? m. Hugh Porter] (William Dennis and Elizabeth Dennis were transported to Maryland in 1668 as children of Donnoch Dennis; Liber IKL, gives Elizabeth, Margaret, Donnock, Jr., and John Dennis as children of Donnock and Ellis Dennis. The will of Roger O'Cane, of Somerset County, probated June 6, 1688 (*Md. Cal. Wills, II,* p. 35), devises his property to Donagh [Donnock] and Alice [*sic* Ellis] Dennis, Sr., and to Alice (*sic*) Ellis

· 441 ·

Dennis, Jr., and to Katherine, John and Ellinor Dennis, Donagh [Donnock] Dennis, Jr., executor and residuary legatee. Donnock Dennis (Sr.) was living in 1716/17, (the time of his death) on a plantation called "Dennis' Purchase" on the Pocomoke River. His will dated February 16, 1716/17, probated March 23, 1716/17, names "wife"; son Donnock Dennis, Jr., grandsons William and Theophilus, sons of Donnock Dennis, Jr.; grandson Donnock, son of John Dennis; daughter Eleanor, wife of Jeremiah Morris; son-in-law Hugh Porter; daughter Margaret; son Henry Hudson; son John Dennis (executor); son Donnock Dennis. On March 23, 1716/17, Elizabeth Dennis, widow of the testator, "did revoke the will and fly to her thirds." (*Md. Cal. Wills,* IV, p. 82.) In that Donnock Dennis names "*son in law Hugh Porter*"; and Hugh Porter in his will dated May 28, 1709, probated August 23, 1701/7, names wife *Katherine* Porter (*Md. Cal. Wills,* IV, p. 155), it seems evident that Katherine (daughter of Donnock Dennis) married Hugh Porter. Whether "Henry Hudson" named as son in will of Donnock Dennis was actually son, or whether son-in-law, or stepson, is not clear. Evidently, Donnock Dennis' first wife, Ellis Nehulian, who was living as late as February, 1687/8, (see Roger O'Cane's will above) died, and Donnock married, *secondly,* Elizabeth _____, who was living at the time of his death in March, 1716/17.

Downes. George Downes, in Manokin section, 1666; lived near Back Creek; m., *first,* Anne probably Bosman; (see *ante,* Bosman); *second,* Margaret Mitchell (see *post,* Mitchell); issue, *first* wife, Anne: (1) Bossman [Bosman?], 1677; (2) Elizabeth, 1679 [m.? _____Bennett]; issue, *second* wife, Margaret: (1) Anne, 1683; m., *first* [Samuel?] Covington; *second* [Thomas?] Dixon; (2) Margaret, 1685; (3) Isabel, 1688; (4) Mitchell George, 1690; (5) Sarah, 1693; m. _____ Claggett; (6) Betty, m. _____ Hooper; (7) Priscilla, m., *first,* _____ Derickson; *second,* _____ Robinson; (8) Mary, m._____ Martin; (9) Esther; (10) Robert (IKL; *Md. Cal. Wills,* Vol. VII, p. 233; and Vol. VIII, p. 186; and Worcester Registry Wills, Liber JW 3, p. 101).

Dixon. Ambrose Dixon (see *ante,* p. 302), m. Mary _____, and had issue: (1) Thomas (d. 1720); justice peace; member first vestry Coventry Parish; member Lower House Maryland Assembly, 1694-7 (see *ante,* pp. 155, 394 and 395); m., *first,* August 12, 1672, Christiana Potter; *second,* Susanna _____; issue: (a) Ambrose (1673-*ante* 1718); (b) Adria (1675-*ante* 1718); (c) Thomas (1677-1747), m. Sarah _____; (d) Mary (1683-1687); (e) William 1686-1751), m. Elizabeth _____; (f) Alice, m. Henry Toadvine; (g) Christiana; (h) Abigail; (i) Dianna; (j) Grace.* (2) Mary, m., 1666, Thomas Cottingham (see *ante,* Cottingham); (3) Elizabeth, d. 1686/7; m., 1674, Robert Dukes; (4) Grace, m., 1676, John Richards; (5) Sarah, m. Edmund Beauchamp (see *ante,* Beauchamp); (6) Alice, b. 1663/4; m. Henry Potter; (7) Hannah (1666-1667)—Robert Dukes (d. 1691/2) and Elizabeth Dixon had issue: (a) Elizabeth (b)

---

*Liber IKL, records Ambrose, Adria, Thomas, William and Mary, as children of Thomas and *Christiana Dixon.* The dates of Mrs. Christiana Dixon's death and Thomas Dixon's *second* marriage to Susannah _____ we do not have, so we cannot state positively which wife was mother of Alice, Christiana, Abigail, Dianna and Grace Dixon.

Mary; (c) Robert; (d) John; (e) Sarah. Henry Potter and Alice Dixon had issue: (a) Thomas (d. 1727) (IKL; EB 5, p. 165; EB 9, pp. 68-9).

Denwood. Levin Denwood (*c.* 1648-1726); in Somerset (with brother-in-law, Roger Woolford), 1665; returned to Accomack County, Virginia, then came to Somerset County to live about 1670-1; lived at "Hackland," on s. side Great Monie Creek, at the head thereof; a leading member Monie Friends' Meeting (see *ante,* p. 99); member Somerset Grand Jury, March, 1671/2 (see *ante,* p. 118); overseer highways, November, 1675, and "pressmaster" (for providing provisions for militia) Monie Hundred, August, 1676. Levin Denwood was son of Levin Denwood, of Northampton and Accomack Counties, Virginia (see *ante,* p. 99).* Levin Denwood (*c.* 1648-1726), of Somerset County, m. Priscilla _____, and had issue: (1) Levin (1670-1703), unmarried; (2) Arthur (1671/2-1720), m. Esther Robins; (3) Elizabeth (Betty), b. 1674; d. 1736; m. George Gale; (4) Mary (1676-1735), m. Henry Hill. (This statement based on items of record in Liber IKL; and Somerset judicials, deeds, wills and administrations). The baptismal name *Levin appears* in the records variously spelled as Lyving, Liveinge, Leaven, Levyne, Leveyne, Levinge, Leving, Livinge, Levin; finally assuming the form *Levin.*

Dickeson. Edward Dickeson, in Annemessex settlement, November, 1662; his wife, Elizabeth Denson; issue: (1) John, 1662; (2) Peter, 1664; (3) Edward, 1666; (4) Elizabeth, 1670 (IKL; O 1, p. 46). Dickenson patented 300 a., "Contention," at head Annemessex River, in 1667, and sold same in 1668 to Edmund Beauchamp (Deed Liber O 1, p. 117). In 1673 he purchased part of "Irish Grove" tract on Morumsco Creek from Quillane and sold same to Thos. Owen in 1675 (O 4, p. 339). Will of Peter Dickeson, of Somerset, carpenter, prob. August, 1733, names sons Charles, Edward, John, Peter, Abraham, Isaac, and Teague Dickeson, and daughter Rachel Dougherty and her son Peter Dougherty (EB 9, p. 154).

Draper. Alexander Draper, from Northampton County, Virginia, to Annemessex section late 1661 or early 1662 (see *ante,* p. 86); owned several tracts of land obtained by patent and purchase, all of which he sold in 1676 and 1677; m. Katherine _____. In 1677 Draper went to the Whorekill on Delaware Bay, now Sussex County, Delaware, where we find reference to his being in 1681 (O 4, p. 394, 404 and 413; O 5, p. 70; Sussex County, Delaware, record book, 1681, in Penna. Historical Society, Philadelphia).

Dupark. Thomas Dupark in Northampton County, Virginia, 1660. He married (in Hungar's Parish, Northampton), November 13, 1660, Elizabeth Powell (*24 Journal of American History,* p. 214); he and his wife came to the Manokin settlement in 1662.

Ellis. John Ellis, in Morumsco section, 1665; m. Elizabeth _____; issue: (1) John, 1665; (2) Elizabeth, 1667; (3) Thomas, 1669; (4) Henry (1670-1677);

---

*Levin Denwood (*circa* 1602-*post* 1663), of Northampton and Accomack Counties, Virginia, 1637, m. Mary _____; issue: (1) Thos.; (2) Luke; (3) Levin (see above); (4) Susanna, m. Thos. Brown, of Accomack; (5) Mary. m. Roger Woolford (see *post* Woolford; (6) Elizabeth, m. Henry Hooper, of Dorchester County; (7) Rebecca, m. Nehemiah Covington (see *ante* Covington); (8) Sarah, m. Thos. Hicks, of Dorchester County.

(5) Mary, 1672; (6) Henry, 1677; (7) Anne, 1679; (8) Richard, 1683. John Ellis, Jr., m., 1686, Mary, widow of Thomas Shiletto (IKL).

Elzey. John Elzey (see *ante,* p. 310), m. Sarah _____;* issue: (1) Arnold; (2) John, Jr., d. 1667. Arnold Elzey (son of John and Sarah) inherited "Almodington" tract on Manokin River; was builder of well-known brick mansion house there; justice peace; major in militia; d. 1733; m., 1682, Major Waller (see *post,* Waller), and had issue: (1) Sarah (1683-1753), unm.; (2) Major (a daughter), b. 1685; d. unm.; (3) Anne, 1686; m., *first,* Robert Catherwood; *second,* William Stoughton;† (4) John, 1693; m. Anne Catherwood; (5) Arnold, b. 1695; d. unm.; (6) Alice, m., *first,* Merrick Ellis; *second,* Samuel Worthington; (7) Elizabeth (IKL; EB 9, p. 153; EB 4, p. 19).

Peter Elzey (brother of John), in Somerset County, 1666; d. 1716; m., 1672, Mary Bell; issue: (1) John, 1673; (2) Arnold (1674-1674/5); (3) Arnold (1676-c. 1716); m. Jane, widow of John Fisher; (4) Peter, 1678; (5) Frances; (6) Elizabeth (IKL; EB 9, pp. 15 and 77; EFH, p. 422; and Judicials, 1715-17, p. 485, and 1722-24, pp. 19 and 20).

The brothers, John and Peter Elzey, of Somerset County, Maryland, descended from the Elzeys of Southampton, England, and were sons of Arnold Elzey, who was son of John Elzey (d. 1633), a merchant of Southampton, England, and his wife Joan, widow Barlowe (*XXIX Va. Mag. of Hist. and Biog.,* pp. 345-6, and items of record, Northampton County, Virginia, Court, Vol. IV [1651-4], pp. 131-2, and Vol. IX, pp. 12, 20-1, and 50). There was a John Elzey (Elsey), of Calvert, Maryland (d. 1700); justice peace, 1661 (*III Arcv. Md.,* p. 424); wife Ann (*Md. Cal. Wills, II,* p. 204). We cannot yet identify him.

Fountaine (also Fontaine). Nicholas Fountaine (*c.* 1638 or 40-1708); native of France (*II Arcv. Md.,* p. 282); in Manokin section, 1662; m., *first,* Grace _____; *second,* Joanna _____ (she m., *second,* John Brown). Nicholas and Grace Fountaine had issue: (1) Dennis, 1663/4; m. George Lane (see *post,* Lane); (2) Mercy (1667-1727), m., 1686, Mary Bosman (daughter of John and Blandina [Risdon] Bosman; see *ante,* Bosman) ;(3) Nicholas (*c.* 1692-1743/4), m. Mary _____; (4) Stephen. Mercy and Mary (Bosman) Fountaine had issue: (1) Nicholas; (2) John; (3) Samuel; (4) Thomas; (5) Bridget; (6) Baly; (7) Esther; (8) Grace, m. _____ McClamme; (9) Sarah, m. Daniel Maddox (10) Priscilla; (11) Elizabeth; (12) Hannah, m. _____ Williams. Nicholas and Mary Fontaine had issue: (1) Mary; (2) William; (3) Collier; (4) John; (5) Ann; (6) Mary; (7) Bridget. The name Fountaine (also Fountain) assumed

---

*Sarah (surname unknown) m., *first,* John Elzey (d. 1664); *second,* Thomas Jordan; *third,* Charles Ballard (see *ante* Ballard); *fourth,* Stephen Lufte (or Luffe). These marriages proved by records in Somerset Deeds O 3, p. 192; O 7, p. 121, and O 8, p. 77.

†William Stoughton (b. 1692; d. March 12, 1759), of Somerset County, magistrate, member Lower House of Maryland Assembly, vestryman Somerset Parish. The ancient communion silver (flagon, cup, large and small plates), bearing marks which date it as 1719, also bears on each piece the engraved inscription, *"For the Use of Sommerset Parish in Sommerset County in the Province of Maryland. Per Wm. Stoughton."* This silver was evidently the gift of Stoughton to Somerset Parish. Stoughton's body was interred at "Almodington," doubtless in the "God's Acre" surrounding the first parish church of Somerset Parish (see *ante,* p. 180); but in recent years the tombstone covering the original grave was (with the "dust" beneath it) removed to the church yard of All Saints' Church, Monie, and today may be seen at the west end of the church.

(what was the correct form) Fontaine. The baptismal name "Mercy" also appears as "Marcy" (IKL; EB 9, p. 42; DT, p. 6; AZ, p. 285).

Furnis. William Furnis (d. *ante* June, 1689) and wife Olive, in Manokin section, 1662; issue: (1) Comfort, 1663; m. Stephen Costin; (2) Sarah, 1665; m. John Bennett; (3) William (1668-1732/3), m. Ann _____; (4) Elizabeth 1672; (5) James (1678/9-*c*. 1710), m. Judith _____; (6) Rozannah, 1680; (7) Priscilla, 1683; (8) Katherine. Olive (widow of William), *m.* second, John Strawbridge (IKL; AW, p. 10; EFG, p. 87; EB 13, p. 37; EB 9, p. 149). The name appears variously spelled Furnis, Furness, Furnish, Furnace.

Gilliss (also Gilley, Gillis). Thos. *Gilley* in Northampton County, Virginia, when November 23, 1661, he married Mary, daughter of Mark Manlove (see *post,* Manlove). They went to Manokin section, September, 1665. Thos. Gilliss (as name spelled in Somerset County) d. *circa* 1685. Thos. and Mary (Manlove) Gilliss had issue: (1) John (*c*. 1662-1720), m. Mary _____; (2) Hannah (1665-1667); (3) Thomas, b. 1668; probably died young; (4) Mary (*c*. 1670-1728), m. Graves Jarrett. (We are indebted to Charles J. Gilliss, Haymarket, Virginia, for data contained in this note. Mr. Gilliss and his brother, Rev. W. W. Gilliss, are making a detailed study of Gilliss family history. We look forward with pleasure to the publication of their work at some not distant day).

Goldsmith. John Goldsmith and wife Mary, from Accomack County, Virginia, in Manokin section, 1665. John Goldsmith m. Mary Longo; issue: (1) John, 1660/1; (2) William, 1665; (3) Anthony; (4) Mather [Martha?], 1672; (5) Hannah, 1679. John Goldsmith [evidently son of John and Mary], of Somerset County, carpenter, w. prob. January 19, 1701/2, names wife Margaret; son John (under 18 years old); "my five children"; wife executrix; John Gray, Archibald Smith and Anthony Goldsmith, overseers of will (IKL; Hungar's Parish [Northampton County, Virginia] records in *XXIV Journal of American History,* p. 210; EB 5, p. 113).

Hart. Robert Hart, from Northampton County, Virginia; in Annemessex, 1663 (see *ante,* p. 86-88). He owned "Heartsease," 200 a., s. side Annemessex River at head of Hart's [Jones'] Creek, and in 1679 he and wife Jone sold same to Robert Coulbourne. Robert Hart removed to Sussex on Delaware and was one of the first justices of peace named by William Penn for county of Sussex in 1682 (O 6, p. 254, Sussex County, Delaware, record book, 1681—in Penna. Hist. Soc., Philadelphia).

Hall. Charles Hall (d. 1695), in Annemessex, 1665; m. Alice _____ (d. 1724); issue: (1) Charles (1665/6-1709); m., 1693, Martha Davis; issue: (a) Richard, 1694; (b) Charles; (c) William; (d) John; (e) Alys [Alice]; (2) Sarah, 1668; m. James Curtis (see *ante,* Curtis); (3) Katherine, 1670; [? m. William Planner]; see *post,* Planner); (4) Alce [Alice], 1673; m. John Roach (see *post,* Roach); (5) Mary, 1675; m. _____ Bannister; (6) Rachel, 1677; m. Randall Revell, Jr. (see *post, Revell*) (IKL; EB 5, pp. 129 and 147; EB 9, p. 95; O 7, p. 299).

Haste. Daniel Haste (d. 1701), in Wicomico section, 1665; m., 1680, Sarah Rodgers; issue: (1) Sarah, m. Robert Dashiell; (2) Elizabeth, m. Benjamin Wailes (*Md. Cal. Wills,* III, p. 2; *Dashiell Records,* III, p. 692; Somerset Rent Rolls, p. 33, in Maryland Historical Society).

Hasfurt. George Hasfurt (*c.* 1640-*post* 1683); indentured servant to John Custis; in Northampton County, Virginia, 1664; in Annemessex section, 1665; "chirurgeon [surgeon]," "schoole master" and "undersheriff" (see *ante,* p. 286); m., *first,* Clemence Kerne (d. 1677); *second,* Elizabeth Hudson. George Hasfurt d. prior to February 20, 1686/7 (and after 1683), leaving wife Elizabeth, formerly widow of Nicholas Hudson, decd. Nicholas Hudson (or Hutson) d. Pocomoke Hundred, January, 1676; m. Elizabeth _____; issue: (1) Elizabeth, 1671; (2) Richard, b. and d. 1676; (3) Violetta. It appears that in February, 1686/7, Elizabeth Hudson was wife of John Snow, and Violetta Hudson was wife of Richard Warren (IKL; O 6, pp. 873-4). The name appears variously spelled Hasfurt, Hasfort, Horsfoord, Hosford, Hosforte.

Hassard. Edward Hassard, in Manokin, 1665; see *ante,* Carr.

Hayman. Henry Hayman, in Monie section prior to May, 1664; from Gloucester County, Virginia; lived at plantation called "Second Choice" at head of Great Monie Creek; d. April 16, 1685; m. Ellinor _____; issue: (1) Henry, 1663; m., 1687, Mathewe [Martha] Standridge; (2) Charles, 1664 (3) Anne, 1666; (4) William, 1669 (5) James, 1688 (IKL; O 4, p. 132; O 10, p. 893).

Hignett (also Hignot). Robert Hignett, in Morumsco section, 1666; owned "Hignett's Choice," 300 a., at head of Morumsco Creek; m. Elizabeth (widow of John Crew), and had issue: (1) William, 1665/6; (2) Mary (1667-1668); (3) Thomas, b. and d. 1669; (4) Mary [twin of Thomas], b. and d. 1669; (5) John, 1670; (6) George, 1673; (7) Robert; (8) James (IKL; AZ, 1671-5, p. 344; O 4, p. 314; O 6, p. 746). It appears that in 1682 Robert Hignett was living in what is now Sussex County, Delaware (Sussex County, Delaware, record book, 1681_____; in Penna. Hist. Soc., Philadelphia).

Hilliard (also Hillyard). John Hilliard, in Morumsco section, February, 1665/6; owned "Seaman's Choice," 150 acres, which he sold to Thomas Carrell in 1670; sold "Hackla" (200 a.) and "Coventry" (200 a.), n. side Pocomoke River in Naswaddocks Neck in 1673 and 1677/8. John Hilliard and Mary, his wife, had issue: (1) Jane, 1667; (2) Thomas, 1669/70; (3) Oliver, 1673 (IKL; O 3, p. 254; O 5, p. 229).

Hobbs. John Hobbs, in Manokin section, 1666. A Thomas Hobbs, of Somerset County, will dat. December 10, 1691, prob. October 24, 1692, names son Joy Hobbs; sister Elizabeth Gambrill; wife Elizabeth; legacy to John Price (*Md. Cal. Wills,* II, p. 61).

Horsey. Stephen Horsey (see *ante,* p. 297), m. Sarah (widow of Michael Williams, decd), and had issue: (1) Stephen (d. 1722), m. Hannah Revell (see *post,* Revell); issue: (a) John (1681/2-1744/5), m., *first,* Elizabeth Horsey;*

---

*Elizabeth Horsey was daughter of Nathaniel Horsey (1689-1748), who was son of Nathaniel Horsey (1664/5-1721) and Sarah Revell.

second, Rachel Mitchell; (b) Katherine, 1683/4; (c) Sarah, 1685/6; m., *first*, _____Wheatley; *second*, _____ Roach; (d) Stephen, 1688; (e) Mary, 1690; (f) Anne, 1690/1; m. _____ Stevens; (g) Elizabeth, m. _____ Outerbridge; (h) Abigail. (2) Nathaniel (1664/5-1721), m. Sarah Revell (see *post*, Revell); issue: (a) Revell (1687-1741), m. Mary _____; (b) Nathaniel (1689-1748); (c) Stephen, 1693; (d) Isaac; (e) Randall; (f) William, d. 1736. (3) John, d. 1678; (4) Samuel (d. 1736), m. Ann _____; issue: (a) Smith; (b) Stephen; (c) [daughter] m. John Roach; (d) [daughter] m. Isaac Williams; (e) [daughter] m. Alexander Addams;† (f) [daughter] m. Heber Whittingham. (5) Mary, d. May, 1678; (6) Isaac (b. 1665; d. 1752), m., 1688, Sarah _____; issue: (a) Sarah (b. 1689), m. [George?] Bosman. (7) Abigail, m., *first*, 1672, John Kibble (issue: (a) William; (b) Sarah); *second*, Richard Stevens (see *post*, Stevens) (Hall of Records, Annapolis, Will Liber, No. 1, fo. 458; IKL; EB 9, pp. 82, 85, 163, 254, 92, 195; EB 14, p. 119).

Huttson (also Hudson). Henry Huttson was at morumsco in 1666; m. Lydia _____; issue: (1) Lydia, b. March 8, 1666; (2) Henry, b. July 8, 1666; (3) Robert, b. November 14, 1672. A Lydia Huttson m., May 13, 1682, Henry Harper (IKL). There is doubtless a clerical error in the years entered for births of Lydia and Henry; while Robert's birth is given also as November 13).

Ingram. Robert Ingram was in the settlement (which became Somerset County) and had died before July, 1666. In that month Anne, widow of Robert Ingram, decd., made conveyance to her children by the said Ingram, viz: John, James and Robert Ingram O 1, p. 75). July, 1667, Nehemiah Covington m. [Anne] Ingram, widow (see *ante*, p. 397). In 1675 Nehemiah Covington and Anne, his wife, alias Ingram, appears as guardians to the orphans of Robert Ingram, decd. (AZ, p. 550).

Ivery. Nicholas Ivery was in Northampton County, Virginia, in 1652 (Wise, *Accawmacke*, pp. 135-6). Nicholas Ivery was father of (1) Margaret, b. Hungar's [Parish, Northampton County, Virginia], July 27, 1654; m. in Somerset County, Maryland, January 6, 1668/9, William Turpin; (2) Mary, b. Machepongo in Accomack [Virginia], February 5, 1656/7; m., in Somerset County, Maryland, May 24, 1674, Richard Chambers (IKL). Margaret and Mary Ivery (daughters of Nicholas Ivery) came to the Manokin settlement (later Somerset County) in 1662 with Philip Barre (see Barre, *ante*). Wise, *Accawmacke*, pp. 135-6, gives the name as *Juerye;* but comparison of the name with original source shows it to be Iuerye, while finally the spelling of Ivery was apparently adopted.

Johnson. Anthony Johnson, see *ante*, p. 75, et seq.

Johnson. Cornelius Johnson (late servant of Thomas Savage) presented in Northampton County, Virginia, February, 1662/3, for adultery with Alice Baily (whom he has since married), and March, 1662/3, fined 500 pounds tobacco for incontenency before marriage (Northampton Court, Order Book, 1651-4, pp. 161 and 167). Cornelius Johnson appears in Somerset in 1666 and in June, 1672, January, 1676, and December, 1684, purchased "Sweetwood" and "Man-

---

†Query: Was this Alexander Adams, rector of Stepney Parish, Somerset County, 1704-1769.

nings Resolution" tracts (adjoining), on n. side Great Monie Creek, the former from Charles Ballard and Sarah, his wife (widow of John Elzey, decd.); the latter from John Manning and Sara, his wife (O 5, p. 87; O 6, p. 732; O 8, p. 192). Cornelius Johnson, by will prob. June 17, 1687, devised to Margaret, daughter of William Jones, personalty, and residue of his estate to William Jones, Jr., and Daniel Jones (at 18 years of age) and their heirs (*Md. Cal. Wills*, II, p. 19; see also *post*, Jones of Monie).

Johnson. George Johnson (see ante, p. 316); m. Katherine Butcher, and had issue: (1) George; (2) Katherine, m. John Goddin; (3) Geshom, b. Sept., and d. October, 1664; (4) Gershom, b. June, and d. September, 1667. Mrs. Katherine (Butcher) Johnson m., *second*, Thomas Evernden. George Johnson (son of George and Katherine) resided in England (see *ante*, p. 317); d. *ante* October, 1727, leaving an only child, Ann Johnson, then "of St. Paul's Parish, Covent Garden, Middlesex, England," who sold her grandfather's lands, "Straights" and "Johnson's," in Somerset County, Maryland, to Robert King (see *ante*, p. 433). Katherine Johnson (daughter of George and Katherine) m. John Goddin, of Annemessex, and Bogerternorton Hundreds, Somerset County (d. 1712/13); a prominent Quaker (see *ante*, p. 106); elected to Lower House Maryland Assembly, 1692 (see *ante*, p. 358, *et seq.*); justice peace, 1680 (see *ante*, p. 395). Goddin patented, October, 1687, 2,900 a., called "Rochester," s. Pocomoke River, near the headwaters. Here he made his home.* Parts of this tract he sold off during his lifetime; the residue was sold by his daughters after his death. John and Katherine (Johnson) Goddin had issue: (1) John, b. November, 1681; d. unm.; (2) Katherine (also Catherine), still single in November, 1715 (Liber IKL; Worcester Registry Wills, Liber JW 14, p. 211, bond administratrix of John Goddin, decd., February 20, 1712; Somerset Court, Deed Liber O 11, p. 268, and Deed Liber O 12, p. 348). Mrs. Katherine (Butcher) Johnson (widow of George Johnson, who d. 1681), m. *second* (after May, 1683†), Thomas Evernden, a prominent Quaker, of Annemessex Hundred, Somerset County, and later of Dorchester County, Maryland (see *ante*, p. 90, *et seq.*, and p. 358, *et seq.*). The date of Mrs. Katherine (Butcher) Johnson-Evernden's death we do not know, though she was living as late as February, 1695/6.‡ Thomas Evernden (at a date not known) removed to Dorchester County, Maryland, where he died between May 4 and June 5, 1710. Evernden's will discloses the fact that he had children: (1) Martha Evernden, who m. Joshua Kennerly, and had children: (a) William Kennerly; (b) Martha Kennerly; (c) Hester Kennerly. (2) Nathaniel Evernden.§ Thomas Evernden devised by his will land in St. Dunstan's

---
*Goddin's homeplace was about 5 or 6 miles northeast of the town of Snow Hill (then Somerset, later Worcester County) and adjoined homes of George Truitt (a leading member of Bogerternorton Friends' Meeting) and Rev. Samuel Davis (pastor of Snow Hill Presbyterian Congregation).
†May 25, 1683, Katherine Johnson, widow of Geo. Johnson, decd., deed to Charles Hall (Somerset Court, Deed Liber O 6, p. 663).
‡February, 1695/6, Thos. Evernden and Katherine, his wife, executrix of Geo. Johnson, decd., deed to Wm. Planner (Somerset Court, Deed Liber O 7, p. 342).
§It is not known whether Martha Evernden (wife of Joshua Kennerly) and Nathaniel Evernden were children of Thomas Evernden by Mrs. Katherine (Butcher) Johnson, or by a former wife whose name is now unknown. Thomas Evernden's bequest to his daughter, Martha Kennerly, and her daughters, Martha and Hester, consisted of personalty. His bequest to grandson, Wm. Kennerly, was land in Somerset County. and bequest to his son, Nathaniel Evernden, was a house on Second Street in Philadelphia, Pennsylvania.

Parish [Kent, England?] "now used as a burying place for Quakers, provided it be continued as such a burying place," to John Sims and Henry Wilcox, of Canterbury, Kent, England, as trustees. Evernden also bequeathed £10 towards building a Quaker Meeting House at the head of Transquaking [Creek], Dorchester County, Maryland. He also made bequests to George, eldest son of Abraham Johnson, of Canterbury, Kent, England, and to Joseph Kennerly [of Dorchester County, Maryland] (*Md. Cal. Wills,* Vol. III, p. 17, will Thomas Evernden, dated May 4, prob. June 5, 1710).

Jones of Monie. William Jones, of Monie; in Manokin section, June, 1666; justice peace, 1676; d. 1690; m., *first,* Margret ———— (d. 1683); *second,* Jane ———— (she m., *second,* Geo. Bosman; *third,* Luke Valentine; see *ante,* Bosman). William and Margaret Jones (his first wife) had issue: (1) William, 1666; (2) John, 1668; (3) Mary (1670-1677), (4) Margaret, 1672/3; (5) Ann, 1675; (6) George, 1678; (7) Daniel (1680-c. 1723), m. Susanna Covington* (see *ante,* Covington); (8) Robert, 1681; (9) Elizabeth (IKL; BWZ, pp. 17 and 19, will of Wm. Jones, prob. June, 1690†). August 3, 1703, Wm. and Danl. Jones divided landed estate composed of "Manning's Resolution" and "Cox's Mistake," n. side Great Monie Creek, which had been devised them by Cornelius Johnson (O 10; see *ante,* Johnson, Cornelius). The Joneses added to their lands on north side Great Monie and for generations their descendants in the male line have continued to hold parts of these lands up to this present time.

Jones. Samuel Jones, in Manokin section, August, 1666; d. 1678/9; m. Mary ————; issue: (1) Samuel; (2) John; (3) Mary; (4) Elizabeth. Samuel Jones (son of Samuel and Mary) m. Mary ————; issue: (1) Samuel, 1679/80; (2) Mary, 1682; (3) Lewis, 1683/4. One Samuel Jones m., 1691, Mary Flannikin; issue: (1) Hugh, 1692 (IKL; *Md. Cal. Wills,* I, p. 101).

King. John King was in Morumsco section in 1663. Jeane [or Jane], wife of John King, died March 12 and was buried in Somerset, 1663 (IKL). John King was from Northampton County, Virginia, where he married, October 8, 1660, Jane Bishop (*XXIV Journal of American History,* p. 210). Mary (daughter of John King) m., 1674, Thomas Humphreys (IKL; Richardson, *Sidelights on Maryland History,* II, p. 263). John King m., February 11, 1672, Elizabeth Crew (IKL; see *ante,* Crew).

Lane. George Lane appears to have come into the Manokin section August, 1662 (see *ante,* Barre); m. October 20, 1678, Dennis Fountaine (see *ante,* Fountaine); issue: (1) Elizabeth, 1682; (2) Mary, 1686; (3) Katherine, 1688; (4) Dennis (a daughter), 1690/1 (IKL).

Lawes. John Lawes (see *ante,* Bosman).

London. Ambrose London and Mary, his wife, in Northampton County, Virginia, June, 1659. In February, 1663/4, Ambrose London presented by North-

---

*Susanna, widow of Daniel Jones, evidently m. William Story; for the account of William Story and Susannah, his wife, administratrix of Daniel Jones, of Somerset County, decd., was returned and recorded November 2, 1723 (EB 14, p. 153).

†William Jones' will names "my loving brother George Mitchell and my loving brother George Betts" overseers of his will. How Mitchell and Betts were "brothers" to William Jones has not been discovered.

ampton County Grand Jury "for not coming to church and being brought before the court demeaned himself insolently and appeared under the notion of a Quaker"; fined 1,000 pounds tobacco "for Sabbath breaking and his said Insolent behavior" (Northampton County, Virginia, records, Order Book, 1657-64, pp. 22 and 188). Ambrose London came to the Annemessex section in 1665, bringing with him his wife, Mary London, and Abigail London, Ruth London and Mary London, Jr. (Hall of Records, Annapolis, Liber 9, p. 200). He appears as "major" and justice peace in Somerset, 1683; elected Lower House of Maryland General Assembly, 1670/1 (see *ante*, p. 394, footnote; p. 395), though there is no evidence that he took his seat. London died prior to November, 1706. Ambrose and Mary London had issue: (1) Thomas London (Northampton County, Virginia, records, Order Book, 1657-64, p. 62). Abigail, Ruth and Mary London, Jr., who came to Somerset with Ambrose and Mary London, were their daughters. Abigail London (d. October, 1692) m., September, 1682, Thomas Lidster (also spelled Leister). Ruth London m., April, 1677, Thomas Walston. Mary London m. prior to August, 1670; Teague Riggin (IKL; DT, 1670-1, p. 107).

Long. Samuel Long, in Morumsco section, September, 1665; m., February 15, 1667 [1667/8], Jane Michell (Minshall?; see *post*, Minshall); issue: (1) John (1669-1673); (2) Elizabeth (1670/1-1716/17); m., *first*, Isaac Boston; *second*, _____ Marshall; (3) Daniel, 1673/4; d. infancy (?); (4) John, 1674/5-1718 (?); (5) Daniel (1677-1741); (6) Jeffery 1679-1732); (7) Randolph (1682-1739/40); (8) David (1687-1716/17); (9) William, 1689; (10) Ann, m. _____ Wood; (11) Jane. Jane, wife of Samuel Long, d. December 5, 1692. Samuel Long m., February 22, 1693/4, Elizabeth King (IKL; EB 5, pp. 178-9; EB 9, pp. 13, 18, 137, 211 and 219; EB 13, p. 96). Though the register in Liber IKL gives marriage of Samuel Long to Jane *Michell*, the spelling *Michell*, we believe, to be a clerical error, and that the name should be *Minshall*. The baptismal names of "Jeffery" and "Randolph" (also spelled "Randall") given to two sons of Samuel and Jane Long are distinctively Minshall family names (see *post*, Minshall). Col. John D. Long, of Baltimore, is a student of, and authority on, the Long family history and we hope that he will eventually publish his "findings." We are indebted to Col. Long for the item that Samuel Long was a headright to patent assigned by John Hilliard to Jenkin Price for land in Somerset area, September, 1665 (Hall of Records, Annapolis, Warrants, Liber 9, pp. 210, 211 and 221).

Lunn (Lum, Lunne). Edward *Lum,* in Manokin, January, 1664/5; appears in deeds with wife Mary, 1674, when he is called "Edward Lunne, of Anne Arundel County, carpenter." He also appears in deeds as "of Somerset County," 1675, 1676, 1678 and 1686 (O 2, pp. 8 and 10; O 4, pp. 283 and 307; O 5, pp. 10 and 492; O 6, p. 799; AZ, p. 585). Edward Lum had daughter, Elizabeth, b. Manokin, January 17, 1664 [1664/5]; baptized November 28, 1669 (IKL; see also *ante,* p. 116).

Macrah (also Macraw, Magraw, Macah, Maragh). Owen *Macah* (d. 1692/3) obtained warrant for 300 acres, in Manokin section, August 13, 1662 (Hall of Records, Annapolis, Liber 5, p. 209-11) and had grant for land on n. side Manokin River. Owen Maccrah m., April 23, 1676, Mary Benderwell, and had issue: (1) Owen, 1676; (2) Mary, 1679; (3) William, 1681; (4) John, 1686; (5) Richard; (6) David (IKL; and *Md. Cal. Wills,* Vol. II, p. 64).

Maddox. Lazarus Maddox (*c.* 1656 (?)-1716/17), of Northampton County, Virginia, came to Manokin section, 1663, with mother, Eleanor, and her second husband, William Bosman (see *ante,* Bosman); owned lands called "Maddox's Hope" and "Mother's Care," Somerset County, and was member Lower House Maryland Assembly, 1692 and 1693 (see *ante,* p. 394). Lazarus Maddox m. Sarah _____, and had issue: (1) Mary, 1679; (2) Thomas, 1684; (3) Lazarus, 1690; (4) Alexander, 1693; (5) Daniel; (6) William; (7) Sarah; (8) Eleanor; (9) Elizabeth.

Lazarus Maddox (*c.* 1656?-1716/17) was son of Alexander Maddox (d. 1659/60), of Northampton County, Virginia, who was probably the person of that name, aged 22 years, who came from London to Virginia in 1635 (Hotten, *Emigrants,* p. 138). Alexander Maddox appears in Northampton County, Virginia, records between 1651 and 1659. He married, *first,* _____ _____, by whom he had several children (viz: Thomas, Alexander, Elizabeth m. Philip Fisher, and Ann). Alexander Maddox m., *second,* Eleanor _____, by whom he had Lazarus Maddox. Mrs. Eleanor Maddox m., *second,* 1661/2, William Bosman (see *ante,* Bosman); *third,* James Caine (see *ante,* Caine). Mrs. Eleanor Caine, dying in 1694, refers in her will to Lazarus Maddox as her only son.

Alexander Maddox (half-brother of Lazarus) also came to Somerset County. He was b. *c.* 1654. He may have come to Somerset in 1663 (he was then but about 9 years old) with his stepmother, Eleanor, and her second husband, Wm. Bosman. He certainly was established in Somerset by 1678; issue: (1) Thomas, 1679; (2) Lazarus; (3) Sarah, 1681; (4) Mary, 1682; (5) Alexander, 1688; (6) Anne, 1691; (7) Nathaniel; (8) Elizabeth. (Items on which this note is based supplied by William P. Maddox (a descendant of Lazarus Maddox), Instructor in Government, Harvard University, Cambridge, Massachusetts. Richardson, *Sidelights on Maryland History,* Vol. II, p. 319, *et seq.,* gives note on Maddox family, which states (though we have not verified the statement) that Mrs. Eleanor Maddox-Bosman-Caine was daughter of Lewis White, of Northampton County, Virginia).

Manlove. Mark Manlove, in Northampton County, Virginia, April, 1659, and February, 1661/2 (Northampton records, Order Book, 1656-64, pp. 46, 125); in Pocomoke section (later Somerset County, Maryland), 1664 or 5; lived at "Manlove's Lot," n. side Pocomoke River; m., *first,* Hannah _____; *second,* Elizabeth _____. The following deduction (based on items we have gathered) is merely *tentative* and subject to revision by anyone who may make careful research in order to establish a Manlove pedigree. Mark Manlove (d. 1666) and his *first* wife, Hannah, had issue: (1) John, m., *first,* Ann _____ (d. 1670/1); *second,* 1672, Elizabeth Lee; (2) Mary, m., November 23, 1661, Thomas Gilley (or

Gillis; see *ante,* Gillis); (3) Ann; (4) Thomas, m., 1667, Jane Dillimas (or Delmas; see *ante* Boyce); (5) Hannah, m., 1667, John Marrett; (6) Abia, m. John Parramore; (7) Mark, m., 1672, Elizabeth Greene; (8) Elizabeth, m., 1666, William Greene. Mark Manlove and his *second* wife, Elizabeth, had issue: (1) George, 1660; (2) Peercy, 1663; m., 1681, John Waltham; (3) Luke, 1666; (4) Christopher; (5) William, m., 1676, Alice Robins. Mark Manlove names in will (September, 1666) son-in-law Richard *Hackworth* and grandson Richard *Hackworth*. The name doubtless should be *Ackworth*. Richard Ackworth's wife Ann was probably Ann, daughter of Mark Manlove (see *ante,* Ackworth) (Northampton, Virginia, records, Order Book, 1656-64, pp. 46, 125; Wills and Deeds, 1657-66, p. 14 (marriage of Thos. Gilley [Gillis] to Mary Manlove). *Md. Cal. Wills,* I, p. 37; O 1, p. 42; IKL).

Marcum (also Marcam). John Marcum in Northampton County, Virginia, in 1661/2 (see *ante,* p. 87); came, with his son, John Marcum, Jr., to the Annemessex settlement in 1662.

Minshall. Jeffery Minshall and Frances Carsley, his wife, in Northampton County, Virginia, October, 1651 (Northampton records, Order Book, 1651-4, p. 48). The name variously spelled Minshall, Mentiale, Michell, Mitchell; but identity is clear. The baptismal name Jeffery also appears as Jeffry, Jeofry, Jeffrey (and was doubtless originally Geoffry), while Randolph appears also as Randall. *Jeffry Mentiale* entered rights for land in Somerset, April 12, 1666, viz: Jeffrey and Frances (evidently himself and his wife), Mary, Anne and Jane, his daughters; Jeffrey and Randall, his sons; and Wm. Collett, his servant. Jeffry Mentiale patented (on these "rights") 400 a., at head Morumsco Branch (Hall of Records, Annapolis, Liber I 0, pp. 10 and 133; supplied by Col. John D. Long, Baltimore). Following items from Liber IKL (Somerset Court) refer to Jeffery Minshall and his children: Alce (?), daughter of Jeffery *Mitchell* and Frances, his wife, b. December 27, 1668; Elizabeth *Mitchell,* daughter of same, b. December 28 (*sic*), 1668. Thomas, son of Jeffery *Minshall* and Frances, his wife, b. August 18, 1672 (these children were born after Jeffery and Frances Minshall settled in Somerset). Jeffery *Minshall,* Senr, d. and buried at Morumsco, April 8, 1675. September, 1679, Jeffrey *Minshall,* of Somerset, son and heir of Jeffrey Minshall, decd., and Frances Minshall, widow of said Jeffrey, decd., appear in deed (O 6, p. 289). Jane *Mentiale* (daughter of Jeffrey and Frances Mentiale, or Minshall), who appears as "headright," 1666 (see above), was doubtless she who appears as Jane *Michell,* m. Samuel Long (see *ante,* Long). February 15, 1667/8 (IKL), Mary *Mentiale* (daughter of Jeffrey and Frances) was doubtless the Mary *Minshall* who m. Thomas Tull, October, 1666 (see *post,* Tull). Jeffrey Minshall (d. 1675), of Northampton County, Virginia, and Somerset County, Maryland, no doubt derived descent from the Minshull, or Minshall, family of Cheshire and Devonshire, England, though as yet the connection has not been worked out and proved. The Visitation of Devonshire, 1620 (*Harlein Soc. Pubs.,* VI, p. 184) gives a Minshull pedigree in which the names "Jefferie" and "Geoffrey" and "Randall" appear.

Mitchell. George Mitchell, in Manokin section, 1666; owned lands on Monie Bay between Great and Little Monie Creeks; m. Isabel Higgins, 1668 (see *ante,* p. 400); issue: (1) Margaret, m. George Downes (see *ante,* Downes); (2) Elizabeth, 1670; m. Thomas Dashiell; (3) Priscilla, 1671; m. George Dashiell; (4) Isabel, m., *first,* James Dashiell; *second,* Joseph McClester (IKL; see also *ante,* Dashiell).

Nellson. John Nellson; see *ante,* Bosman.

Nicholson. James Nicholson, in Manokin section, 1663; m. Mary Price; issue: (1) Richard, 1664; (2) James [1665?]; (3) Charles, 1667; (4) Roger, 1668; (5) Elizabeth, 1669; (6) Sarah, 1671; (7) Rachel, 1672; (8) Samuel, 1674. James Nicholson, d. and buried at Manokin, January 13, 1675/6. Mary Nicholson [widow of James] m., September 4, 1677, George Carter (IKL).

Nutter. Christopher Nutter (c. 1636 or 40-1702/3), in Northampton County, Virginia, August, 1662; in Manokin section, 1665-6; lived at "Nutters Purchase," n. side Manokin River (now [1935] in part occupied by northern end of town of Princess Anne), 1666-*c.* 1674; removing thence to "Nutter's Neck," on Quantico Creek (now Wicomico County). He was a government Indian interpreter, 1693 (*XIV Arcv. Md.,* p. 532). He m. Mary [Dorman?], and had issue: (1) John, 1667; d. infant; (2) Sarah, 1669; d. infant; (3) John (1670-1702), went to Sussex County, Delaware; (4) Mary (1672/3-*ante* 1702); (5) Sarah, 1674/5; m. Capt. Wm. Piper; (6) Christopher, 1676/7; d. infant; (7) Charles (1680-1735), went to Dorchester County, Maryland; (8) Thomas (1681-*ante* 1702); (9) Christopher (1683-1729), m. Margaret [Mackmorie?]; (10) Matthew (*c.* 1685-1720), m. Ann Huett, daughter of Rev. John Huett (see *ante,* p. 140); (11) William, *c.* 1687 (IKL; DT, p. 6; EB 9, pp. 37 and 128; EB 14, p. 160-1; *Md. Cal. Wills,* VII, p. 128; Sussex County, Delaware, Wills, Liber A1, p. 36; Northampton County, Virginia, records, Order Book, 1657-64, pp. 141 and 150).

Oke (also Okee, Okey). John Oke, in Manokin section, 1662; m., October, 1666, Mary Vincent; living in Wicomico Hundred, 1667-71, in Somerset County, as late as April, 1680; issue: (1) John, b. and d. 1667; (2) Elizabeth, 1668; (3) John, 1671 (IKL; O 1, p. 29; O 6, p. 555). In 1682 there is reference to John Okay, late constable, in Sussex County, Delaware, record book, in Penna. Hist. Soc., Philadelphia.

Peddenton. Henry Peddenton, stepson of Ambrose Dixon (see *ante,* Dixon), came to Annemessex with him. In June, 1675, Peddenton and Margaret, his wife, "late of Somerset Co. power of attorney to George Hasfurt to acknowledge deed to Joseph Freeman for land on Mormusco Branch" (O 4, p. 211). Henry Pedington (or Peddenton) m. Margaret Griffith, August 25, 1674 (IKL).

Planner. William Planner, in Annemessex section, January, 1665/6, when purchased from Thos. Price 300 acres of "Cheap Price" tract, n. side Annemessex River, to which name of "Planner's Purchase" was given. In 1685 Planner purchased the remainder (200 a.) of "Cheap Price" (O 1, p. 2; O 6, p. 758). July, 1666, Planner and Rebecca, his wife, sold 100 acres called "Planner's Adventure," n. side Annemessex River, to Thos. Cottingham (O 1, p. 20). William Planner was father of William Planner, Jr., who d. 1734 (Somerset Rent Rolls). William Planner [Jr.] probably m. Katherine, daughter of Charles Hall (see *ante*, Hall), but died probably without surviving issue (EB 9, p. 166-7).

Price. Jenkin Price, in Northampton County, Virginia, 1650; trader with Eastern Shore Indians. It was Price who found and guided to safety (January, 1650) the party of Cavaliers, consisting of Henry Norwood, Francis Morrison, Francis Cary and Philip Stevens, whose vessel, the "Virginia Merchant," going from London to Jamestown, in Virginia, was driven by storm into Assoteague Bay and there wrecked. For this service Price was rewarded by the Virginia Assembly. After living in Virginia about 17 years Jenkin Price and his wife went to England in 1656 intending to settle at Canterbury (*XXII Wm. and Mary Quarterly* . . . p. 53; Wise, *Accawmacke,* pp. 111-112). Evidently Jenkin Price returned to Northampton County, Virginia, and his trade with the Indians and went to Somerset County, in Maryland, about the time of its creation in 1666. He owned lands (as shown by patents and and deeds) along the Pocomoke River and finally settled on tract called "Newtowne," on n. side Pocomoke River, near Aquintica Swamp (now in Worcester County), not far from the present town of Snow Hill (O 1, pp. 59, 71 and 96; DT, pp. 100-2). Jenkin Price's wife, Mathew [Martha?], joined in several deeds with him. In 1652 Jenkin Price was "about 30 years" of age and in 1667 stated his age to be "about 50 years." He was born probably between 1617 and 1622 (Northampton Court, Order Book, 1651-4, p. 97; Somerset Court, O 1, p. 55). Jenkin and Mathew Price had issue: (1) Sarah; (2) Margaret; (3) Thomas (*XLIX Arcv. Md.,* p. 34; Somerset, O 1 [reverse], pp. 1-21, list of cattle marks; see under September, 1670).

Price. Thomas Price (see ante, p. 315) lived at "Cheap Price," on n. side Annemessex River, and went from there to live in Slater's Neck, Sussex County, Delaware, where he d. 1695. Thomas Price and Katherine, his wife, had issue: (1) Thomas Price, b. Annemessex, November 9, 1665; went to Sussex County, Delaware; m. _____ _____, and had issue: (a) William; (b) Catherine; (c) Jean; (d) Rachel (Sussex County, Delaware, Registry of Wills, Liber A1, pp. 19-20).

Poole (Pool). Thomas Poole, in Manokin section, 1665; lived at "Poole's Hope," on s. side Back Creek (see *ante,* p. 402); m. Elizabeth _____; issue: (1) Rachel, 1665/6; (2) John, 1666; (3) Thomas, 1667/8; (4) James (1669-*ante* 1676); (5) James, 1676; (6) King, 1678; (7) Andrew, 1680/1; (8) Grace, 1683 (IKL). In July, 1691, Elizabeth, widow of Thomas Pool, of Somerset, decd., and John Pool (son and heir of said Thomas Pool) and Mathew [Martha?], his wife, convey land to Hannah Carpenter. January 20, 1708/9, Thomas Pool, son of Thomas Pool, decd., made deed in which statement is made that Elizabeth Pool and John Pool (widow and son of said Thomas Pool, decd.) were both dead (BWZ, p. 102, and O 10, p. 253).

Quillane. Daniel Quillane and Lydia, his wife, in Northampton County, Virginia, 1661; and by May, 1665, were in the Morumsco section. Quillane had patents in Somerset County for lands called "The Irish Grove," on e. side Morumsco Creek, and "Limbrick," on n. side Pocomoke River, in a neck of land called Nassawaddocks (O 7, p. 536). Daniel and Lydia Quillane had issue: (1) Eliza, 1661/2; (2) Thomas, 1665; (3) Daniel, 1667; (4) Teague, 1669; (5) Judith, 1673; (6) Elizabeth, 1675 (IKL). It appears that "the Almighty God hath so disposed that . . . Daniel Quillane came by misadventure to his death and dyed intestate" (see deed in Somerset Court, October 24, 1691, Thomas Quillane to Thomas Lidster). Thomas Quillane (son of Daniel and Lydia) m., 1685, Sarah Morris; issue: (1) Daniel, 1687; (2) Thomas, 1691 (IKL).

Revell. Randall Revell (*c.* 1613-1686/7), of Accomack County, Virginia; St. Mary's County, Maryland; Northampton County, Virginia, and Somerset County, Maryland (see *ante,* p. 306). Randall Revell appears in Accomack County, Virginia, January, 1633/4; February, 1634/5, and September, 1636 (Northampton County, Virginia, records, Vol. I, pp. 10, 28, 57*). Randall Revell appears in St. Mary's County Maryland, 1636: "Green's Poynt, alias Randall's Point, a freehold, 100 acres land due Randall Revell for transporting himself [into Maryland] in *Ann° 1636;* surveyed for said Randall 17 October 1640, patented same day and year: St. George's Hundred, St. Mary's County" (St. Mary's County Rent Roll, p. 12; and see also Liber ABH, p. 79, Hall of Records, Annapolis). Later (same volume) appears: "300 acres due Randall Revell for transporting [into Maryland] his wife Rebecca and sons John and Richard; surveyed 14 Dec. 1641; patented 6 July 1642." Randall Revell's name appears in the Maryland records between 1636 and 1644 (*IV and V Arcv. Md*). Randall Revell is referred to as *"cooper,"* March 9, 1641/2 (*IV Arcv. Md.,* p .120). After 1644 Revell disappears from St. Mary's County, Maryland, and there is no record of will or administration on any Revell estate until the will of Randall Revell, of Somerset County, in 1686/7. Randall Revell disappears from St. Mary's County, Maryland, after 1644, and about 1650 a Randall Revell appears in Northampton County, Virginia (Wise, *Accawmacke,* p. 136). Randall Revell, of St. Mary's County, Maryland, is designated *"cooper."* Randall Revell, who appears in Northampton County, Virginia, about 1650, is also designated as *"wine cooper"* and *"cooper,"* in April, 1656, and August, 1657, respectively, when he deeds (April, 1656) some cattle to *"my son in law John Nicols,"* and (August, 1657) deeds cattle and horses to *"my only son Edward Revell"* (Northampton records, Wills, Deeds, &c., 1657-66, p. 2, *et seq.*). The records quoted above lead us to think that R ndall Revell, of St. Mary's County, Maryland, 1636-1644, and Randall Revell, of Northampton County, Virginia, from about

---

*The whole of the peninsula of the Eastern Shore of Virginia was one county called Accomack, 1634-1642; then in 1642 the name of the county was changed to Northampton, and so continued from 1642-1663 as Northampton County. In 1663 the peninsula was divided (though greatly unequal as to territory) into the two counties of Accomack and Northampton, as these counties are at the present time (1935). The records of the old Accomack County, 1634-1663, were (on division of the peninsula in 1663) retained by Northampton County Court and are at this present time (1935) in the keeping of the clerk of Circuit Court for Northampton County, Virginia, at Eastville, Virginia. However (by common consent), to simplify matters this series of records is referred to as "Northampton Co. records" by all parties using them for reference. These records begin with the year 1632, before any Virginia county had been actually formed.

1650 on, both of whom were designated as *"cooper"* were identical.* There has so far been discovered no further record of Rebecca Revell (wife of Randall Revell) and John and Richard Revell, sons of Randall Revell, in 1641 (see above). These sons were certainly dead in August, 1657, *if* Randall Revell, of St. Mary's County, Maryland, 1636-1644, and Randall Revell, of Northampton County, Virginia, about 1650 on, were identical persons, because Randall Revell, of Northampton County, Virginia, *cooper,* calls Edward Revell, in August, 1657, "my *only* son" (see above). How John Nicols was *"son in law"* to Randall Revell does not appear. It may be that Revell had married Nicol's mother, as the term "son in law" was commonly used instead of "step son." It may be that Rebecca, wife of Randall Revell, of St. Mary's, in 1641, was a widow Nicols.† Edward Revell (who is called "my *only* son" by Randall Revell in 1657) was born *c.* 1638-40, for he was *"aged about 20 years"* in January, 1658/9 (Northampton records, Order Book, 1657-1664, p. 40). John and Richard Revell, sons of Randall Revell, of St. Mary's County, Maryland, were certainly born prior to 1641. Edward Revell (son of Randall Revell, of Northampton County, Virginia, 1657, and after 1662 of Somerset County, Maryland), dying in 1681, named his only then living daughter, *Rebecca.* Our deduction is that Randall Revell (*c.* 1613-1686/), of Accomack County, Virginia, 1633-1636; of St. Mary's County, Maryland, 1636-1640; of Northampton County, Virginia, 1650 (or earlier) to 1662; and of Somerset County, Maryland, 1662-1686/7; m., *first,* Rebecca ...., and had issue: (1) John Revell; (2) Richard Revell (both died young), and (3) Edward Revell (*c.* 1638 or '40-1687), of Northampton and Accomack Counties, Virginia, m. Frances ...., and had issue: (a) Rebecca Revell, m. Robert Coulbourne (son of William Coulbourne; see *ante,* Coulbourne); (b) John Revell, of Accomack County.* Then Mrs. Rebecca Revell dying, Randall Revell (*c.* 1613-1686/7) m., *second,* Katherine [Scarburgh?†], and had issue: (1) Randall Revell, Jr. (*c.* 1661-1718); (2) Katherine Revell, b. November 14, 1664; d. 1723; m., April 22, 1688, John West, of Somerset County; (3) Sarah Revell, b. October, 1667; m. Nathaniel Horsey (see *ante,* Horsey); (4) Hannah Revell, m. Stephen Horsey, Jr. (see *ante,* Horsey); (5) Anne Revell, m., 1678, William Coulbourne, Jr. (see *ante,* Coulbourne).‡ Randall Revell

---

*A careful examination of the Accomack record books, 1632-42, and Northampton record books, from 1642-1663, might disclose items relative to Randall Revell as would make proof in this matter positive.

†Then again it may be that Rebecca Revell and the sons, John and Richard Revell (of 1641), died. and that Randall Revell then married a widow Nicols, with a son, John Nicols.

*Will of Edward Revell, of Accomack, dated October 6, 1686, probated January 21, 1687 (Nottingham, *Accomack Wills and Administrations, 1663-1800,* p. 12 (Nottingham's January 21, *1681,* should obviously be *1687*).

†An invariable "tradition" states that Randall Revell's wife, Katherine, was a sister of Col. Edmund Scarburgh. The late Stratton Nottingham, the authority on Accomack and Northampton Counties genealogy, told me that while he was inclined to accept this "tradition" as true, yet he had after many years research failed to discover in records any evidence either direct or circumstantial as verifying this tradition.

‡Somerset Court, Liber IKL, Deed Liber O 1, p. 80, Deed Liber O 6, pp. 725, 726, 728, 745 and 666, and Deed Liber O 11, p. 253, prove that Katherine (m. John West), Hannah (m. Stephen Horsey, Jr.), Ann (m. Wm. Coulbourne, Jr.), and Sarah (m. Nathaniel Horsey) were children of Randall Revell and Katherine, his wife, and that they married the parties as stated. *XXIII Va. Mag. of Hist. and Biog.,* p. 428, shows Randall Revell, Jr., to have been "heir at law" to Mrs. Katherine Revell and thus he is proved to have been child of Randall and Katherine [Scarburgh?] Revell. Randall Revell, Sr., of Somerset County, in his will, dated May 27, 1685, probated March 8, 1686, names wife Katherine, son Randolph [*sic* Randall]; daughters Ann, Hannah, Katherine and Sarah; son Edward, of Accomack (Somerset Wills, Liber EB 5, p. 141).

(son of Randall and Katherine [Scarburgh?] Revell) b. *c.* 1661-2; d. 1718; m., *first,* October, 1682, Sarah Ballard (see *ante,* Ballard), and had issue: (1) Randall, 1687; d. young; (2) Ballard, 1689; d. young; (3) Sarah, m. William Bozman (IKL and *XXXVIII Arcv. Md.,* p. 397). Randall Revell, Jr., m., *second,* Rachel Hall (see *ante,* Hall), and had issue: (1) Alice, m. Henry Miles (O 15 [reverse], p. 5); (2) Charles, m. Sarah Curtis (see *ante,* Curtis); (3) Randall (d. 1744), m. Katherine _____; (4) William; (5) Mary, m. William Roach; (6) Sarah (EB 9, p. 22; EB 14, p. 128; O 22, p. 199, and O 10, p. 408).

Rhodes (Rhoades, Roads). John Rhodes, in Annemessex, November, 1663 (see *ante,* pp. 43 and 285). Rhoades lived on land called "Salisbury," n. side Annemessex River, which was patented by him and which he sold to Thomas Tull and Richard Tull in 1671/2, removing at that time, or soon after, to what is now Sussex County, Delaware. Either John Rhodes, or his son by the same name, appears among the first justices of the peace commissioned for Sussex in 1682 (Sussex County record book, 1681-_____, pp. 73-4, Penna. His: Soc., Philadelphia). John Rhodes had children: (1) John, b. Hampshire, Southampton County, England, March 20, 1652; (2) Robert, b. same, June 20, 1656; (3) Martha, b. same, March 6, 1654; m., 1671, Richard Tull (see *post,* Tull); (4) Werenia, b. Wells, in Somerset, England, April 4, 1660; d. [Anemessex, in Maryland] December 10, 1666; (5) Elizabeth, b. Annemessex [in Maryland], May 2, 1664; (6) William, b. same, May 24, 1666.* (IKL). The will of John Roads, of Sussex County, Delaware, prob. 1687, names children Elizabeth, Patience and John Roads; wife Comfort; "my most dear and tender mother" [evidently stepmother, or mother-in-law]; "my brother in law Richard Tull"; Grace White, Nehemiah Field, Sarah, wife of Henry Stretcher, and John How (Sussex County, Delaware, Registry of Wills, Liber A1, pp. 11-12).

Rice. Nicholas Rice, living on n. side Wicomico River, January, 1664/5 (*XLIX Arcv. Md.,* p. 369). His home plantation, "Rice Land," was a short distance above the present town of Whitehaven. Nicholas Rice is designated as "carpenter." He was justice of the peace, 1672-5, and d. 1677/8, apparently without wife or child, devising his comfortable estate to Elizabeth, daughter of Robert Hardy, to Philip Ascue's [Askews] three children, to Mary Bishop and to Richard Crocket and John Evans (EB 5, p. 136, and *Md. Cal. Wills,* I, p. 204).

Richards. John Richards, in Annemessex section, 1666; m. Grace, daughter of Ambrose Dixon (see *ante,* Dixon).

Roach. John Roach (also spelled Roch) was an early settler in Annemessex, coming in with Stephen Horsey.* On February 4, 1663/4, John Roach m. Sarah

---

*The two last named, Elizabeth and William, are recorded as children of John Rhodes and Elizabeth, his wife. John, Robert, Martha and Werenia are simply recorded as children of John Rhodes. Werenia's death is recorded as daughter of John Rhodes and *Katherine,* his wife. Evidently John Rhodes was married twice.

*"Makepeace," the Roach family home established by John Roach, first of the name in Somerset County, 150-acre tract at head of Apes Hole Creek, several miles east of town of Crisfield. This tract was patented by John Roach, February 9, 1663. The brick colonial dwelling house is stated to date "immediately after 1663" (Forman, *Early Manor and Plantation Houses of Maryland,* p. 149). This was the home of John Roach (d. 1717/18), who devised his dwelling plantation, "Makepeace" (after death of wife Sarah), to eldest son, John Roach, who, dying in 1727, devised "Makepeace" to his son, Charles Roach (wills of John Roach, Sr., 1717/18, and John Roach, Sr., 1727, Will Liber EB 9, pp. 66 and 111, Somerset Registry of Wills).

Williams (daughter of Michael and Sarah Williams and stepdaughter of Stephen Horsey; see *post,* Williams, Michael). John Roach d. 1717/18, leaving by Sarah, his wife, issue: (1) John (1664-1727); m. Alice Hall (see *ante,* Hall); (2) Sarah, 1667/8; m. 1683, John Perkins; (3) Mary, 1668/9; m., 1683, Francis Martin; (4) Elizabeth, 1670/1; (5) Abigail, 1672/3; m., 1687, Anthony Bell; (6) William (1674/5-1687); (7) Arabella, 1679; m. ———— Cullen; (8) Nathaniel (d. 1721), m. Elizabeth ————; (9) Michael (d. 1729); (10) Rebecca, 1685; (11) Hannah, 1687; (12) Joseph, 1689; (13) Samuel (1692-1736) (IKL; EB 9, pp. 66, 72, 111, and 182; EB 14, p. 288; EB 15, p. 135).

Shiall. Thomas Shiall was in Wicomico section (north side the river) in August, 1666. His plantation was just south of the present town of Whitehaven, Wicomico County. Thomas Shiall d. November, 1675, leaving sons Thomas and John, and daughter Elizabeth (*Md. Cal. Wills,* I, p. 179). The name also appears as *Shiels, Shiles.*

Southern. Edward Southern, in Northampton County, Virginia, 1647 (Greer, *Virginia Immigrants,* p. 307), and in 1658 accused (though the charge was not sustained by evidence) of having said "y^t God was ignerant, childish & foolish" (Northampton records, Order Book, 1657-64, p. 24). Southern appears in Manokin section, 1664; and he and his wife Mary in 1674 and 5. The Southerns lived on Tomactico Creek, s. side Wicomico River (O 1, p. 140; O 4, pp. 83, 223 and 237). July, 1683, reference to "Edward Southern, late of Somerset County, Maryland, now living at the Horekill [i. e. the Whorekill, now Sussex County, Delaware]." Edward Southern among the justices of peace first named by Wm. Penn in first commission for establishing territories of Pennsylvania on the Delaware [i. e. Sussex County] (Sussex County record book, 1681-————, pp. 73-4, in Penna. Hist. Soc., Philadelphia).

Spence. David Spence, in Wicomico section, 1664/5; lived on "Despence" tract, s. side Wicomico River just below mouth of Wicomico Creek; m. Ann ————; issue: (1) David, 1666/7; (2) Alexander, 1669; (3) John, 1672; (4) James, 1674/5; (5) Ann, 1677. David Spence, d. July, 1679. Alexander, John and James Spence (sons of David) evidently went to Pasquotank Precinct, North Carolina. It does not appear what became of David Spence (eldest child of David). However, there was a Spence family in Northumberland County, Virginia, in early 18th century which carried baptismal name of David. The Westmoreland County, Virginia, family of Spence carried the baptismal name of Alexander (IKL; *Md. Cal. Wills,* I, p. 216; O 10, p. 590, and O 22, p. 258; Grimes, *Abstracts of North Carolina Wills;* Torrence, *Virginia Wills and Administrations, 1632-1800—An Index*).

Stevens. Richard Stevens (*c.* 1641-1713); came from England; in Wicomico Hundred, July, 1666; home on s. side Wicomico River just above Wicomico Creek; d. 1713 (see *ante,* p. 102). Richard Stevens m., *first,* Frances ————; issue: (1) Elizabeth, 1667; m. ———— Emmitt; (2) Frances, 1669/70. Richard Stevens m., *second,* 1676, Mrs. Abigail (Horsey) Kibble (see *ante,* Horsey). Richard Stevens' (so signed) will, prob. November 3, 1713, names wife Abigail;

sons Richard, Isaac and John; daughter Elizabeth Emmitt; daughter Sarah Bounds; daughters Ann, Abigail and Hannah Stevens. Name appears in text of will as *"Stephens,"* but is signed *"Stevens."* While we cannot positively state that all the children (except Elizabeth Emmitt) named in will were by second wife, Abigail, yet it seems likely such was the case. A careful search in Somerset records might produce the needed evidence (AZ, p. 415; O 1 [reverse], p. 7; IKL; EB 9, p. 49).

Summer (also spelled Summers, Sumbler). Benj. in Annemessex, 1662; m. 1666/7, Isabel Wale (see *ante*, p. 400), and had issue: (1) Benjamin (1668-1687/8; (2) William, 1671. Mrs. Isabel Summer d. and buried at her husband's plantation in Annemessex, December, 1675. Benjamin Summer m., *second,* _____; issue: (1) Thomas, 1680 (IKL). Marriage banns of Benjamin Summers and Agnes Wooldridge published, Somerset Court, April 18, 1676 (see *ante,* p. 401).

Surnam. Edward Surnam, in Manokin section, 1664, when he m. Ann Frowin, and had issue: (1) Thomas, b. 1663/4; d. _____; m., 1683, Margaret Jemmison (she m., *second,* Peter Booth); (2) Edward, b. 1666; d. 1668; (3) Edward, b. 1669; (4) Peter, b. 1672; d. 1713 (IKL). Edward Surnam died in 1676, leaving a non-cupative will, naming wife Ann, and three sons, Thomas, Edward and Peter Surnam, and directed that John Johnson, Negro, "bee assistant to my children for may bee if I leave them with my wife they will take them from her." The will was proved in court, January 10, 1676, "by John Johnson, negroe," and Ann, relict of said surnam confirmed the same, giving her son Edward a heifer with calf, and declaring "my three sons bee att age at ye yeares of eighteen yeares old" (O 7 [reverse], p. 78). Marriage banns of Alexander Mitcheller and Ann Surnam published November, 1676 (see *ante,* p. 402). Peter Surnam (son of Edward and Ann) appears in will and estate account, 1713, as Peter *Sermon* (EB 9, p. 39; EB 13, p. 70). Edward Surnam moved from Manokin to Wicomico Hundred, living near Wicomico Creek.

Tillman. Gideon Tillman, in Manokin section, 1666; m., February 15, 1681/2, Margaret Maneux; issue: (1) Gideon, 1682; (2) Solomon, 1685/6; (3) Elner [Eleanor], 1688; (4) John, 1689; (5) Moses, 1692; (6) Elizabeth, 1694/5 (IKL). The name was spelled Tillman by the earlier generations of this family; but later the spelling "Tilghman" was adopted in several branches of the family. Richardson's *Sidelights on Maryland History,* II, p. 448, *et seq.,* carries notes on this family; and we understand that there is in preparation a thorough study of this family.

Townsend. John Townsend (d. 1698), in Northampton County, Virginia, May, 1660; and in Morumsco section, August, 1666; m., *first,* Eliza Whearly (d. December, 1660); *second,* February 9, 1661/2, Elizabeth Danfroy. John Townsend and *second* wife, Elizabeth, had issue: (1) Elizabeth, 1663; m. Robert Smith; (2) John, 1666; (3) Jeremiah, 1669; (4) James, 1672; (5) Mary, 1674; (6) William; (7) Solomon; (8) Charles (*Md. Cal. Wills,* II, p. 161; IKL; Hungar's Parish [Northampton County, Virginia] records in *XXIV Journal of American History,* pp. 210, 211 and 214, the name appearing there as Townsend and Towson).

Tull. Thomas and Richard Tull (probably brothers; and from Northampton County, Virginia), in Annemessex section, 1666. Their homes were on n. side Annemessex River. Thomas Tull m., October, 1666, Mary Minshall (see *ante,* p. 400; and *ante,* Minshall), and had issue: (1) Thomas, 1668; (2) Richard, 1670; (3) John, 1674; (4) Mary, 1677 (IKL). Richard Tull m., 1671/2, Martha Rhodes (see *ante,* p. 401; and *ante,* Rhodes), and had issue: (1) Rachel, 1672; (2) Richard, 1675; (3) George, 1677; (4) John, 1681; (5) William, 1684; (6) Benjamin, 1686; (7) Elizabeth, 1688 (8) Mary, 1690; (9) Sarah, 1694; (10) Richard, 1695/6 (IKL).

Wale (also Whale and, later, Whaley). Edward Wale was in the Pocomoke section when Somerset was created August, 1666. He first owned and lived on lands ("Aquintica" and "Springfield") on Pocomoke River which had been conveyed to him by George Wale and Lewis, his wife. These lands Edward Wale sold to Thomas Newbold and removed about 1678 to the Sinepuxent section on the seaboard side. Edward Wale (d. 1718), m. January 29, 1668/9, Elizabeth Ratcliff (sister of Charles Ratcliff, of Somerset County), and had issue: (1) John, 1669; (2) Sarah, 1671; (3) Charles, 1673; (4) George, 1678; (5) Elizabeth, 1677; m. William Turvile (or Turvill); (6) Bridget, 1681; m. Ebenezer Franklin; (7) William, 1683; (8) Nathaniel, 1686; (9) Rachel, 1688; (10) Elias, 1690-1720) (IKL; O 5, p. 358; O 18, p. 18; *Md. Cal. Wills,* IV, p. 165, and V, p. 44). The Wale, or Whaley, family, of Somerset County, for many years made claim (traditionally) to descent from the celebrated Edward Whalley, "the Regicide," but finally abandoned the claim. In *Penna. Mag. of Hist. and Biog.,* IV, p. 258, appears a letter by Dr. Robert P. Robins, May 24, 1880, in which the evidence against this claim is well summed up.

Waller. John Waller appears in Northampton County, Virginia, about 1654 and was in the Monie section when Somerset County was created in August, 1666. He lived at "Waller's Adventure," a tract on south side Little Monie Creek, and died prior to July 30, 1667 (see *ante,* p. 74). John Waller married Alice Major, and had issue: (1) William, 1661; (2) Major, 1664; m. Arnold Elzey (see *ante,* Elzey); (3) Alice, 1666 (IKL; Somerset Rent Roll; Greer, *Early Virginia Emigrants,* p. 341; Nottingham, *Accomack Wills and Administrations, 1663-1800,* p. 1; Cabell, *The Majors and Their Marriages.*)

Walley. Thomas Walley (see *ante,* p. 286) in Northampton County, Virginia, June, 1661; in Manokin section, 1665; m. Elizabeth _____; issue: (1) Rachel, 1661; (2) John, 1661/2; (3) Rebecca, (1665-1666); (4) Margaret; (5) Elizabeth. Thomas Walley removed from Somerset to Calvert County, Maryland, where he died, 1670 (24 *Journal of American History,* p. 210 and 213; IKL; *Md. Cal. Wills,* I, p. 55).

Whaley (see *ante,* Wale).

Ward. Cornelius Ward in Annemessex section when Somerset County created August, 1666; lived east of Little Annemessex River, near head of Jones Creek; married, January, 1666/7, Margaret Franklin; issue: (1) Alice, 1665 (*sic*); (2) John, 1666/7-1687); (3) Cornelius, 1670; (4) Thomas, 1672; (5) William,

1673; (6) Samuel (IKL) Cornelius and Margaret (Franklin) Ward, and their descendants have been made the subject of a scholarly genealogical article published in *XI, Tyler's Historical Quarterly Magazine*, pp. 51-60 and 241-254.

Westlock (also Westlake). John Westlock (*c.* 1580-1674) trading with Indians along Manokin River, 1620 (see *ante,* p. 7); early resident in Accomack, later Northampton County, Virginia; in Manokin section, 1662; in 1664 patented "Brownstone" (300-a), north side Manokin River, and in 1669 sold same to Richard Ackworth, after which he moved to Wicomico section, where he died, 1674, leaving wife, Magdalen. In November, 1670, "John Westlock, about 90 years of age & poore," was exempted from paying levies for year 1670. Westlock's name is kept in remembrance in Somerset by the name of a small branch called "Westlock's Branch," just west of Mrs. Margaret Fitzgerald's home, "Arcadia," on Manokin River, about four miles west of Princess Anne Town. The diminutive branch so located was pointed out by Cassius M. Dashiell (then in the 86th year of his age) to Clayton Torrence in 1934 and recalled by him in the name of "Westlock's Branch." (Wise, *Accawmacke; Md. Cal. Wills,* I, p. 85; O 2, p. 12; DT, p. 48.)

White. John White (see *ante,* p. 331); married, June 27, 1672, Sarah Keyser (who married, *second,* Lawrence Crawford). John and Sarah (Keyser) White had issue: (1) William (1673-1708) m. Catherine Powell; (2) Elizabeth, 1674, m. Francis Thorowgood; (3) Tabitha, 1677, m., *first,* Lawrence Riley; *second,* Robert Hill; (4) Priscilla (twin), (1677-1730/1) m., *first,* George Layfield (see *ante,* p. 376); *second,* John Watts; (5) Stevens, (1679-1718) m., *first, c.* 1710, Atalanta Whittington (see *ante,* p. 381); *second,* Mrs. Katherine (Fassitt?) Hope, (she m., *third,* James Round); (6) Sarah, 1680, m., *first,* William Massey; *second,* Francis Hamlin; (7) Francis (1682-1683); (8) John, *c.* 1684, probably died young. (Evidence for statements in this note will be found in Somerset deeds, judicials and wills in the following volumes: IKL, pp. 273 and 282; EB 5, p. 125 and 185; O 20, p. 173; O 11, p. 125; O 14, pp. 188, 189 and 209; O 10, p. 5; O 15, p. 21; and *Md. Cal. Wills,* III, p. 161; Ljungstedt, *County Court Note Book,* VIII, p. 18.)

There has always been the tradition in Somerset County of a relationship between Col. William Stevens (1630-1687), of "Rehoboth," and the White family. The most constant form of that tradition is that Sarah, wife of John White, was a sister of Col. Stevens. This is obviously erroneous, as the record (Liber IKL, p. 273) shows that John White married, June 27, 1672, Sarah *Keyser,* and that William, Elizabeth, Tabitha, Priscilla, Stevens, Sarah and Francis White were children of John and Sarah (Keyser) White. Col. William Stevens, in his will dated August 29, 1687, probated March 26, 1688 (Liber EB 5, p. 171-2), devises property to John and Sarah (Keyser) White and several of their children. Col. Stevens calls Mrs. Sarah White *"my sister White"* and John White *"my brother John White,"* and two of their children he calls "cousin" (a term used for nephew or niece). As a matter of fact, the relationship of Col. Stevens to the Whites seems to have been through Stevens' wife Elizabeth. After Stevens' death his widow

Elizabeth married George Layfield, and after *her* death George Layfield married Priscilla White, daughter of John and Sarah (Keyser) White. The marriage of Layfield to Priscilla White created quite a sensation because, as it was said, *"Mr. Layfield ... persists in marrying of his neice...."* Priscilla White, whom Layfield married as his second wife, was not his own blood-niece, but the *niece* of Layfield's *first wife,* Madam Elizabeth Stevens. (For a full account of Layfield's marriages, see *ante,* p. 376). Such marriages were forbidden by ecclesiastical law of the established church. Madam Elizabeth Stevens-Layfield was, before either of her marriages, no doubt Elizabeth *Keyser,* sister of Sarah Keyser, the wife of John White, and therefore aunt to Priscilla White who married George Layfield as his second wife. There was a Benjamin Keizer (or Keyser) of Somerset County (who died in 1691), who in his will names "my father George Keizer," *brothers* Eliazer and John Keizer, *sister* Mary Mould and *"my cousins* [*Nieces and nephews?*] Tabitha White, Priscilla White, Sarah White, Stevens White and William White." He also left small legacies to Lawrence Crawford and George Layfield, and refers to land which Col. William Stevens had left him by his will (BWZ, p. 89). Benjamin Keyser, Madam Elizabeth (Keyser?) Stevens-Layfield and Mrs. Sarah (Keyser) White were no doubt brother and sisters. Col. Stevens, when devising the property to Benjamin Keyser, does not refer to any relationship.

Col. William Stevens, of "Rehoboth," in his will, also devised property to Edmund Howard and his son *William Stevens* Howard, not mentioning any relationship. William Stevens Howard was the son of Edmund Howard and Margaret Dent (IKL). John White, in his will, probated October 3, 1685, calls William Stevens Howard *"my cousin."* The relationship is unexplained beyond the reference. (Liber EB 5, p. 126.)

Stevens White (son of John and Sarah [Keyser] White) inherited Col. William Stevens' "Rehoboth" plantation, and dying in 1718 the plantation descended to his son, William White (d. 1736/7). The "Rehoboth" plantation descended in the White family for several generations, when it was finally sold.

Whitty. Richard Whitty (also spelled Whittee and Whitte) was in Wicomico section when Somerset County was created August, 1666. He owned land south side Wicomico River and north side Cuttymocktico Creek (AZ, p. 139). He was named in commission of peace for proposed Worcester County on the seaboard side, 1672. Sarah, daughter of Richard and Alce Whitte, was born Manokin, March 8, 1679 (IKL). Will of Richard Whitty, of Somerset County, dated July 20, 1690; probated March 15, 1692/3, names wife Dorothy; daughter Sarah. (*Md. Cal. Wills,* II, p. 61.)

Williams. David Williams was in Monie section in August, 1666. The records show clearly that David *Williams* was also called David *Williamson,* for he is, in January, 1699, specifically referred to as *"David Williams, alias Williamson, late of Somerset County, decd."* who had died prior to March 5, 1678/9. (Deed, Liber O 7, p. 531, deed of Walker and Evans to Cowdry.) As David *Williamson* he appears in possession of land called "David's Destiny," on south side the mouth of Manny [Monie] Bay (Judicials, Liber DT, p. 25-6). The marriage banns of David Williams and Jane Covington were published in Somerset court November 26, 1667, (see *ante,* p. 400). Jane was probably daughter of Nehemiah Covington (see *ante,* Covington). David and Jane Williams had issue: (1) Mary, b. Little Manny [Monie], April 15, 1670; (2) Elizabeth, b. same, October 1, 1672; (3) Thomas, b. same, February 15, 1673/4; (4) Sarah, b. Wicomico, May 10, 1676, (Liber IKL). In August, 1674, as David *Williamson,* Williams purchased from James Jones, 200 acres called "Long Acre," on north side Wicomico River, about a mile back in the woods (Deed, Liber O 4, p. 117). David Williams removed to this "Long Acre" tract in Wicomico Hundred, then Somerset (now [1935] Wicomico) County, with his family, and here the youngest child was born in May, 1676. Then, within about eighteen months David Williams and his whole family were brutally murdered in February, 1677/8—so we learn from a letter directed by Capt. Thomas Walker, High Sheriff of Somerset to the Governor of the province. The murder was the work of some Indians, and so the Governor ordered a rendezvous of the military forces of Somerset, Dorchester, Kent and Cecil counties at Chicacone on Nanticoke River, the residence of the "emperor" of the Nanticoke Indians. Col. William Burgess was ordered to take troops from St. Mary's, Calvert and Charles counties and meet Col. William Coulbourne, of the Somerset forces, at the appointed rendezvous. The Indian guilty of the murder of the Williams family was delivered to the authorities by the emperor of Nanticoke and making his escape from his guards was finally located among the Rappahannock Indians in Virginia. His extradition was immediately sought, and on his being brought back to Maryland, his execution was ordered without further delay. (*XV Arcv. Md.,* pp. 142, 145, 162, 164, 171 and 190.) "An Inventory of all the goods and Cattle of David Williams and Jane, his wife of ye County of Somerset in the Province of Maryland lately Murthered by the Indians Appraised by us whose names are hereunto subscribed the twentieth Day of April Annoq^r Domini 1678 . . . " The appraised articles consisting of cattle, clothing, household goods, with a sole an only book "*1 Old Bible,*" amounted to 10,793 pounds of tobacco. Cornelius Johnson and Henry Hayman were the appraisers. (EB 14, pp. 236-7.)

Williams. Michael, Thomas and Sarah Williams were children of Michael Williams (died *ante,* December, 1650) and Sarah, his wife, of Northampton County, Virginia. Mrs. Sarah Williams married, *second,* Stephen Horsey (see *ante,* p. 297) (Northampton records, Order Book, 1651-4, p. 194). Michael and Thomas Williams and their sister Sarah (who married John Roach; see *ante,* Roch) came to Annemessex, 1661 or 2, with their stepfather, Stephen Horsey.

Michael Williams (died 1699) settled at "Williams Conquest," south side Annemessex River, part of which he sold to his brother Thomas in January, 1686/7, and the remainder he deeded to his second wife, Patience Browne, in January, 1696/7. Michael Williams married, *first,* 1672, Ann Williams; *second,* Patience Browne, and had issue, *first* marriage: (1) Elizabeth, 1674; (2) Sarah, 1676; and by *second* marriage: (3) Rebecca, 1688; (4) Michael, 1691; (5) Nathaniel; (6) **Walter.**

Thomas Williams (brother of Michael, above) lived on south side Annemessex River; died April, 1720; married, 1684, Frances Robinson; issue: (1) Thomas, 1684/5; (2) Sarah, 1686; (3) Hannah, 1688, m. .... Turpin; (4) John, 1692; (5) Elizabeth, m. .... Herne; (6) Mary. (O 6, p. 793; O 7, pp. 441 and 452; IKL; EB 5, p. 189, and EB 9, p. 32.)

Winder. For John Winder and his children, see *ante*, p. 332-3. For published accounts of the Winders, see Johnson, *Winders in America*, pp. 87-91, and *Some Records of the Winder Family of Maryland* written by R. H. Winder for P. D. Laird in 1864 or 5, published in Bulletin No. 3 (May, 1913), Maryland Original Research Society of Baltimore.

Woolford. Roger Woolford was in Northampton County, Virginia, March, 1660/1, when he married Mary Denwood (*24 Journal of American History*, p. 211). Mary Denwood was daughter of Levin Denwood, of Northampton and Accomack counties, Virginia, and sister of Levin Denwood, of Somerset, (see *ante,* Denwood). Roger Woolford came to Manokin in 1664 and settled on north side Manokin River, east of Goose Creek; surveyor of highways, and justice of the peace, 1676-1697 (see *ante,* p. 395); member Lower House of Maryland Assembly, 1671, 1674 and 1682 (see *ante,* p. 394). He died 1702. Roger and Mary (Denwood) Woolford had issue: (1) Elizabeth, 1664/5; (2) Rosanna, 1666/7; (3) Roger, 1670; m. Mary ....; (4) Sarah, 1672/3; (5) Ann, 1675; (6) James, 1677; (7) Living (Levin), 1683. (IKL; *Md. Cal. Wills, III,* p. 6; Jones, *History of Dorchester Co., Md.*)

(b) NAMES OF SETTLERS IN SOMERSET COUNTY, AUGUST 1666-1700

(*Note.*—The following list is made up of names taken from deed and judicial records of Somerset Court between August, 1666 and 1700, as these records were read through during our research and are offered as a guide to those who may desire to make further investigation concerning families of these names.)

Philip Askew, John Atkins, Richard and John Allen, John Aylward, William Alexander, Henry Ayres.

John Bounds, Stephen Bond, Henry Bishop, Wm. Bowen, Wm. Bradshaw, John Browne, Roger Bercum (Berkum), John Bennett, David Browne, Thos. Ball, Rowland Bevends (Bevans), Wm. Barker, Robt. Bowditch, Pasque Barleigh, Anthony Bell, Jno. Barber, Saml. Benton, Richd. Britaine, Wm. Broadway, Jno. Briant, Wm. Broadwell, Richd. Blades, Richd. Bundick, Wm. Brereton, Thos. Blake, Jno. Bult.

Robt. Cade, Richd. Chambers, Thos. Carey, Robt. Collier, Wm. Cheeseman, Thos. Carrell, Edwd. Carter, Stephen Costin, Jno. Carter, Philip Carter, Leonard Campison, Robt. Crouch, Nicholas Cornewell, Danl. Cox, Jno. Cropper, Herbert Croft, Saml. Collins, Jos. Crowder, Wm. Coulbourne, currier, Saml. Cooper, Richd. Cole, Nicholas Carpenter, Ellis (Elias?) Coleman, Thos. Camplin, Wm. Cannedy, Edwd. Chicken, Benj. Cottman, Stephen Cannon (see *post,* "Thomas Davis, carpenter"), Jno. Cornish, Danl. Cordry (Corddry, Cordray), Jacob Cheltnam, Jno. Chancellor.

Danl. Dennahoe (Derryhoe, Donehoe), Geo. Day, Thos. Davis, carpenter (*alias* Stephen Cannon),* Wm. Dounin, Robt. Dukes, Jno. Dorman, Jno. de Brulagh, Thos. Davis, tailor, Nathaniel Doughterie (Dougherty), Edwd. Day, Jonas Davis, Saml. Davis, minister, Michael Disharoone, Jno. Dredon (Dreadon, Dryden, Driden), Wm. Daniell, Wm. Duste, Jno. Devorax (Devorix), Edw. Davis, David Dale, John Deale (later Dale), Humphrey Davis, Wm. Davidson, Peter Dowty, Wm. Derickson.

Jno. Evans, Nicholas Evans, Ellis Emperour, Saml. Ennis (also Innis), Stephen Elliott, Arthur Evitt, Geo. Eanes (Eaves, Eves?), Archibald Ereskin, Jno. Emmett.

Jno. Francklin, Arthur Frame, Wm. Flutcher, Jno. Freeman, Jos. Freeman, Edwd. Fowler, Richd. Farewell, Jos. Foxcroft, Thos. Fisher, Wm. Fassitt, Jno. Fassitt, Edwd. Furlong, Arnold Francis.

Wm. Gullett, Jno. Galbraith, Langdon Goddard, Jas. Gadds, Jos. Gray, Jno. Gladstone, Jno. Goslin (Gosling), Wm. Giles, Jr., Geo. Glandenning, Jno. Griffith, Jas. Gill, Jarman (German) Gillett, Miles Gray, Francis Gunby, Wm. Gullick.

Saml. Hopkins, Saml. Handy, Wm. Howard, Edmund Howard, Jno. Harrison, Jno. Hues, Jos. Hues, Thos. Hayward (also spelled Haward), Geo. Hamblin, Robt. Houlston (Holston), Abraham Heath, Jno. Holland, Geo. Harris, Jno. Henderson, Thos. Horsman, David Harris, Jno. Hepworth, Timothy Harney, Adam Heatch (later Hitch?), Michael Hanna, Thos. Humphreys, Jno. Huett, minister, Wm. Harvey, Jno. Haynes, Thos. Hunt, Mathias Holbrook. Thos. Holbrook, Oliver Hale, Jeremiah Hooke, Wm. Hearne (Herne), Jno. Hust (Hurst), Geo. Howell, Thos. Hughes, Stephen Hancock, Robt. Higgenbotham, Wm. Hall.

James Inglish, Saml. Innis (Also Ennis), Wm. Ingle.

Robt. Johnson, Saml. Jackson, Chas. Jones, Gilbert (?) James, Richd. Jefferson, Leonard Jones, Thos. Jones, Francis Jenckins, Alexander Jemison.

Alexander King, John King (Manokin), Robert King (Manokin), John Kirke, Wm. Keene, Benj. Keyser (Keizer), Wm. Kennett, Richd. Karey (Carey), Richd. Kimball, Jno. Kibble.

Jasper Lane, Edwd. Linnis, Robt. Loe, Thos. Larramore, Jno. Lyte, Walter Lane, Thos. Leslie, Henry Leaton, Thos. Leister (Lister, Lidster), Saml.

---

*On October 6, 1664, the Hon. Philip Calvert informed the Provincial Court of Maryland that one Stephen Cannon, servant to Mr. John Pate, [of Gloucester County, Virginia?] had been apprehended by William Nodin at Francis Barnes's, "upon Kent [Island]," and that Cannon had afterward run away from Nodin and was "entertained" by said Barnes. The court directed an order sent up to Kent to said Barnes's for the apprehension of the said Cannon (*XLIX Archiv. Md.*, p. 275). Prior to 1670 one "Thomas Davis, carpenter," appeared in Somerset County, in whose early records we find him frequently mentioned. In September, 1671, "Thomas Davis, Carpenter," married Judith Bloyes (see *ante*, p. 397). On January 10, 1670, a *scire facias* was issued in Somerset Court against "Thomas Davis, Carpenter," because of a debt of 430 pounds tobacco due by him to James Weedon. James Weedon died and his widow, Lucy, married Francis Jenkins, and at the suit of said Jenkins and Lucy, his wife, executors of said James Weedon, deceased, Somerset Court, November 9, 1675, directed execution of the said *scire facias* against "*Stephen Cannon, alias Thomas Davis, Carpenter*" (O 7 [reverse], p. 21). It appears that on January 20, 1674 [1674/5] "Thomas Davis, Carpenter," (appearing before Somerset Court) claimed his real name of *Stephen Cannon*. From this date on there are frequent references to Stephen Cannon and Judith, his wife, and their children, in Somerset records.

Lluellen, Henry Lawrence, Henry Lake, Jas. Langreene, Henry Langley, Stephen Lufte (Luffe), Wm. Lewis, Robt. Lewin, Thos. Lampin, Jno. Langford (later Lankford), Geo. Layfield, Morris Liston, Christopher Little.

Jno. Mackettrick, Alexander Mitcheller, Cornelius Morris, Jenkin Morris, Thos. Moolson, Henry Morgan, Henry Miles, Teage Miskell, Thos. Miller, Paul Marsh, Danl. Moore, Robt. Murdaugh, Wm. Mathews, Francis Martin, Jno. Moore, Geo. Moore, Geo. Marsh, Jas. Mumford, Jno. Macknitt (McNitt), Thos. Milliman, Saml. Marchment, Jno. Mahaun, Thos. Middleton, Jno. Marlett, Thos. Miller, Cornelius Mulla, Jno. Mason, Jas. Milles, Jno. Meech, Martin Moore, Robt. Millner, Jno. Murphee.

Thos. Newbold, Wm. Noble, Geo. Newman, Christopher Newgent, Ben Nesham.

Thos. Owen, Thos. Oxford, Donnan Olandman, Jno. Osborne.

Thos. Pointer, Jno. Panter, Rode (Rory) Patrick, Thos. Purnell, Wm. Prentice, Jno. Peicke, Walter Powell, Jno. Polke (Polk), Peter Parsons, Jno. Parsons, Richd. Pepper, Tobias Pepper, Jno. Price, Thos. Pyle, Wm. Paterson, Jas. Prise (Price), Richd. Prim, Jno. Pope, Geo. Phoebus, Jno. Parramore, Jno. Parker, Jno. Porter, Richd. Pomfrey.

Jas. Round, Wm. Round, Wm. Robbinson, Thos. Robins, Patrick Robinson, Jno. Renshaw, Francis Roberts, Wm. Redelphus, Jno. Richards, Jno. Rogers, Jas. Rawley, Jno. Rogers, Chas. Ratcliff, Jno. Renny, Wm. Rogers, Percifull Read, Wm. Raynbowe, Robt. Richardson, Thos. Row (Roe).

Matthew Scarborough, Danl. Selby, Christopher Snossall, Josias Seward, Jno. Shipway, Jno. Simmons, Edwd. Smith, Thos. Selby (Selbe), Jacob Sheltenham, Thos. Strawbridge, Thos. Standbridge, Jno. Starrett, Edwd. Stevens, Jno. Sterling, Jas. Sangster, Wm. Scott, Benj. Sawser (Sauser, Sawcer), Jno. Sherman, Richd. Small, Saml. Showell, Robt. Smith, Jos. Staton (Stayton), Edwd. Shipham, Benj. Schoolfield, Jno. Smock, Wm. Smyton, Geo. Smith, Henry Smith, Thos. Seawell (Sewell), Edwd. Stockdell (Stogdell, Stockdale), Thos. Shiletto, Edwd. Sidbury, Augustine Standford (Stanford), Vincent Shuttleworth.

Saml. Tomlinson, Geo. Trahearne, Jno. Tyferd, Jos. Taylor, Nicholas Toadvin, Walter Taylor, Wm. Tompkins, Thos. Tyre, Jno. Tucker, Alexander Thomas, Anthony Taylor, Jno. Tyzard, Jno. Thompson, Jno. Tarr, Wm. Turvill (Turvile), Hugh Tingle, Wm. Traile, minister.

Jno. Vigorous, Wm. Vaughan, Jos. Venables.

Jas. Weatherly, Wm. Wouldhave, Jas. Weedon, Jno. Winsar (Winser, Winsor), Thos. Wingod, Jno. Waters, Andrew Whittington, Wm. Whittington, Wm. Warwick, Jno. Waltham, Richd. Wharton, Alexander Williams, Edwd. Wootten, Jas. Willis, Jacob Waring, Richd. Warren, Robt. Willson (Wilson), Geo. Wilson, Thos. Wilson, minister, Thos. Wilson (Wicomico), Richd. Webb, Wm. Walter, Jno. West, Archibald White, Edwd. Wright, Wm. Wright, Jno. Wyne, Edwd. Wheeler, Wm. Whittfeeld, Phenix White, Ambrose White, Phinias White, Thos. Walker, Wm. Woodgate, Philip Wallahane, Wm. Wallis (Wallace), Richd. Wildgoose (Wilgus).

(c) Names of Quaker, Church of England and Presbyterian Families

(*Note.*—It is impossible to identify all of the early Somerset County families in relation to their religious affiliations. However, there is a considerable amount of evidence remaining which shows something of these religious connections. The names of the families whose religious affiliations seem beyond doubt are here listed for the period from 1662 into the early part of the 18th centpry.)

Quakers. Ambrose Dixon, Nehemiah Covington, Levin Denwood, Thomas Price, George Johnson, Richard Stevens (of Wicomico), Walter and William Powell, John Goddin, Thomas Evernden, James Jones, George and John Truitt, Richard Waters, Affradozi Johnson, Mrs. Katherine Johnson (later Mrs. Katherine Evernden), Mrs. Katherine Goddin, Arthur Denwood, Mrs. Betty (Denwood) Gale, Mrs. Walter Lane. There were certainly other Quakers, but the absence of any records of Somerset County "Meetings" prevents discovering their names.

Through the kindness and courtesy of Miss Harriett P. Marme, custodian of records of the Baltimore Yearly Meeting of Friends, we have been able to examine early Friends records of Yearly and Half Yearly Meetings which would throw any light upon the matter of Somerset County Meetings.

The record book of Minutes of West River [Anne Arundel County] and Third Haven [or Tred Avon, Talbot County] from 1677 to 1758 (now in possession of Baltimore Yearly Meeting) show the existence of, and give some brief reports from the Somerset Meetings of Annemessex, Monie (also spelled Munny, Monney, Mony, Monnye) and Bogerternorton (spelled also Poccatynorton, Pockytanorton, Pocatinorton). These Meetings appear as making reports as stated in our accounts of them (see *ante*). However, Bogerternorton appears first in the Minutes as early as 1688 (nine years prior to 1697, which is our statement, *ante,* p. 106). Bogerternorton Meeting became "Mulberry Grove Meeting" in 1699; the latter name evidently derived from the tract of land on which the meeting house was erected (see *ante*, p. 107-9). Annemessex, Monie and Bogerternorton (later Mulberry Grove) were never "flourishing" meetings, but appear to have been steady, persistent ones with "unity and love abiding." As stated in the text of our chapter on the Friends Meetings in Somerset (see *ante*), after a precarious continuance from their beginning up to about 1735-40, they disappear. Though no local records of the Meetings in Somerset County have so far been discovered to be yet in existence, there is evidence in 1690 that Annemessex and Monie Meetings kept records, for it was then directed *"y^t the books be kept att Levin Denwoods."* In 1682 the names of Thomas Price, George Trewett and Levin Denwood (Somerset County men) appear on the Committee of 10 men entrusted with the selection of a site for, and the erection of what is known as Third Haven (or Tred Avon) Meeting House in Talbot County, which is yet standing in Easton, Maryland. These items are from Minutes of West River and Third Haven (Half Yearly and Yearly Men's) Meetings, 1677-1758, beginning on page 5 and continuing through the volume as each year's record appears until the three meetings in question disappear.

Church of England Families

The Elzey, Revell, Bosman (or Bozmans), Beauchamp, Thorne, Brereton, Dennis, Hall, Barnabe, Woolford, Fountain (Fontaine), Furniss, Poole, Jones (of Monie), Mitchell, Dashiell, Downes, Betts, Ballard, Barre (Berre), Renshaw, Nelson, Panter, King (John, of Manokin), Purnell, Tillman (later Tilghman), Ackworth, Winder, Haste, Spence (David Spence's family), Shiall, Maddox, Askew, Noble, Cottman, Rhodes, Ward, Tull, Walker, Evans, Day, Chambers, Whittington, Newbold, Scarborough, Smith (Henry), Hammond, Holbrooke, Howard, families appear from earliest times as connected with the Church of England. After the first generation the Dixon, Coulbourne, Horsey and Boston families appear as Church of England families. There were many more of the early settlers who were no doubt Chuch of England men, but whom we cannot now positively identify as such. The names given here cover the period from 1662-1700. For later periods names of Church of England families may be obtained from the remaining Coventry, Stepney and Worcester Parish registers and a fragment of an old Somerset Parish register.

Presbyterian Families

The Brown (David and Alexander), King (Robert), Erskine, Alexander, Strawbridge, Wilson (Robert), Wilson (Ephraim and Thomas*), Shipway, Stevenson, Hopkins, Fassitt, Cropper, Jones (Thomas), Spence (Adam), Galbraith, Strawbridge, Round, Martin, Aydelotte, Polk, Driden, Fenton, Bray, Handy, Venables, Franklin, Knox, Brevard, Wallis (or Wallace), Caldwell families are certainly identified as Presbyterians who were in Somerset County prior to 1700. From about the middle of the 18th century, names of Presbyterian families are to be found in the remaining Session records of the Manokin, Wicomico and Snow Hill congregations.

*Ephraim and Thomas Wilson were sons of Rev. Thomas Wilson, first pastor of Manokin Presbyterian Congregation (see *ante*, p. 226-32). Ephraim Wilson (b. Ireland, December 2, 1664; d. Somerset County, Maryland, January, 1733), m. *first* Elizabeth Davis (daughter of William Davis; see *ante*, Davis) and widow of Henry Lynch. Ephraim Wilson m. *second* Frances Betts (daughter of George Betts; see *ante*, Betts) and widow of John Irving. By his will Ephraim Wilson directed that if his sons or grandsons should forsake the Presbyterian faith that his bequests should be taken from them. David Wilson (1704-1750), son of Ephraim Wilson, was an elder of Manokin Presbyterian Church.
Thomas Wilson (brother of Ephraim Wilson), b. *circa*, 1666-8; d. 1705; m. Elizabeth Ballard (daughter of Charles Ballard; see *ante*, Ballard), widow of John King of Manokin. Mrs. Elizabeth (Ballard) King-Wilson, m. *third* Peter Dent. Thomas and Elizabeth (Ballard) Wilson had issue: (1) Margaret Wilson (1699-1742) m. James Lindow; (2) Elizabeth Wilson. Mrs. Margaret Lindow finally inherited and became possessed of the tract called "the Turner's Purchase," the home of her grandfather, Rev. Thomas Wilson. In 1742 Margaret Lindow sold and conveyed this land to the Vestry of Somerset Parish for a glebe (Deed Liber O 21, p. 14). In 1747 David Wilson, (son of Ephraim, and cousin of Mrs. Lindow) confirmed the title to this land to the Vestry of Somerset Parish (Deed, Liber O 2, p. 286). This tract remained the glebe of Somerset Parish until 1799 when the vestry sold it to John Bird (Deed, Liber O 33, p. 26).

(d) Patentees of Land in Old Somerset Area, 1662-1666

The list as given below has for its objective a statement of the names of persons who received warrants for lands within the area of Old Somerset (the present Somerset, Worcester and Wicomico Counties) from the time of the origin of that settlement under proclamation of November, 1661 (see *ante,* p. 13), to August 22, 1666, when Somerset County was created (see *ante,* p. 67). This list of "patentees" of lands in this area, together with the list of "rights," proved for transportation into the province (appended hereto) has been made in attempt to obtain from the remaining original sources the names of the early settlers: those persons who were within the area when Somerset County was created and thus were truly "first settlers." The list as here given has been made up from the Lord Proprietor's Rent Roll (in the Calvert Papers, Maryland Historical Society) with additions from the Land Patent books in the Hall of Records, Annapolis. There are variations in the dates of surveys between the Rent Roll and the Land Patent records. These variations are, however, slight, and this list gives the dates as carried by the Rent Roll. The dates here given follow the so-called "old style" with the year beginning on March 25th and ending with March 24th.

Jenkin Price, Glyneath, 400 a., July 23, 1663.
James Jolley, Jolleys Delight, 700 a., July 20, 1663.
Alexander Draper, Little Bolton, 250 a., _____, 1663.
Edward Dixon [Dickeson], Contention, 300 a., September 5, 1663.
George Johnson, Johnson, 300 a., September 5, 1663.
Matthew Armstrong, Skippers Plantation, 600 a., September 20, 1663.
Ambrose Croutch, Croutch's Choice, 500 a., June 20, 1664.
Henry Sewall, Wicomico, 1,000 a., March 12, 1663.
Jenkin Price, Pungatesex, 500 a., March 3, 1663.
German Gillett, Coldharbour, 250 a., March 6, 1663.
Percivall Read, James' Grove, 200 a., March 13, 1663.
Henry Ellery, Ellery's Island, 100 a., March 13, 1663.
Richard Hackworth [Ackworth], Hackworth's Charity, 600 a., March 16, 1663.
Thomas Davis, Davis' Choice, 450 a., March 20, 1663.
Robert Cattlyn [Catlin], Cattlyn's Lott, 300 a., April 9, 1664.
Walter Taylor, Taylor's Choice, 600 a., March 9, 1663.
Richard Davis, Davis' Lott, 300 a., March 5, 1663.
George Nasworthy, Nasworthy's Choice, 1,000 a., March 10, 1663.
John King, King's Lott, 300 a., March 6, 1663.
Stephen Horsey, Jr., Undoe, 200 a., April 2, 1664.
George Wale, Wale's Island, 150 a., August 26, 1664.
Randall Revell, Revell's Grove, 1,500 a., October 1, 1665.
William Whitfield, Whitfield, 300 a., May 2, 1665.
Raymond Stapleford, Stapleford's Neck, 250 a., November 2, 1665.
John Townsend, Townsend's Neck, 150 a., November 5, 1665.

Edward Price, Price's Hope, 200 a., February 13, 1663.
James Price, Price's Vineyard, 200 a., February 14, 1663.
Morris Liston, The Irish Grove, 1,500 a., November 10, 1665.
Stephen Horsey (Tract on Tomatico), 500 a., March 26, 1664.
Stephen Horsey, Horsey's Down, 150 a., March 30 [1664].
Cornelius Ward, Bear Point, 200 a., February 26, 1663.
Thomas Bloyce, Bloyce's Hope, 150 a., March 1, 1663.
Southy Littleton, Pharsalia, alias Littleton's Delight, 736 a., April 6, 1666.
Richard Ackworth, Ackworthy's Folly, 300 a., February 18, 1664.
Richard Whitemarsh, Whitemarsh Chance, 200 a., February 9, 1664.
Richard Whitemarsh, Whitemarsh Delight, 300 a., February 18, 1664.
Stephen Horsey, Wetepkewant, 600 a., July 1, 1664.
Peter Parsons, Bacon Quarter, 200 a., November 13 [1665?].
John Parramour, Parramour's Double Purchase, 1,500 a., _____, 1666.
Stephen Horsey, Coleburn, 650 a., August 18, 1663.
Ambrose Dixon, Dixon's Choice, 550 a., April 19, 1663.
Robert Hart, Hearts Ease, 200 a., _____, 1663.
Thomas Williams, Williamston, 300 a., September 4, 1663.
William Waters, Waters' River, 1,280 a., September 5 [1663?].
George Johnson, Straights, 600 a., September 4, 1663.
George Johnson, Johnstown [Johnston], 300 a., September 5, 1663.
Henry Boston, Boston Town, 350 a., August 20, 1663.
Thomas Price, Cheap Price, 500 a., September 4, 1663.
Michael Williams, Williams' Conquest, 300 a., September 4, 1663.
German Gillett, Ware Point, 100 a., March 13, 1663.
William Wilkinson, Yorkshire, 100 a., June 2, 1664.
Ambrose Dixon, Dixon Lott, 300 a., _____, 1663.
William Boyce, Boyce's Branch, 300 a., April 9, 1664.
Charles Hall, Hall's Choice, 300 a., June 6, 1665.
William Planner, Planner's Adventure, 100 a., April 6, 1664.
John Horsey, Watkins' Point, 150 a., February 20, 1664.
Benjamin Summer, Emesex, 300 a., February 10, 1663.
John Roach, Makepeace, 150 a., February 9, 1663.
John Johnson, Johnson's Lott, 200 a., February 12, 1663.
Henry Boston, Boston's Adventure, 400 a., February 1, 1664.
Stephen Horsey, The Desert, 400 a., March 10, 1665.
· Edward Dickeson, Contention, 300 a., February 1, 1665.
Matthew Armstrong, Armstrong's Lott, 300 a., April 10, 1666.
John Vanhack, Hackland, 1,000 a., October 18, 1662.
Thomas Manning, Manning's Resolution, 800 a., October 16, 1662.
George Mitchell, Mitchell's Choice, 500 a., March 2, 1662.
John Marcomb, Marcomb's Lott, 400 a., March 7, 1663.
John Elzey, Sweetwood, 300 a., February 12, 1663.
Nehemiah Covington, Covington's Vineyard, 300 a., March 3, 1663.

Stephen Horsey, Chance, 300 a., March 1, 1663.
Thomas Bloyce, Success, 300 a., February 26, 1663.
George Betts, Betts' Purchase, 100 a., June 1, 1666.
John Taylor, Noble Quarter, 1,000 a., September 8, 1663.
Nicholas Rice, Rice Land, 1,000 a., September 8, 1663.
David Spence, Despense, 1,000 a., December 8, 1663.
James Jones, Jones' Hole, 250 a., September 8, 1663.
Robert Ingram, Killums Folly, 550 a., June 6, 1665.
John Elzey, Erlindy, 250 a., May 20, 1663.
William Bozman, Tinson, 300 a., June 9, 1665.
Richard Stevens, Stevens' Conquest, 300 a., June 6, 1665.
Richard Bennett, Bennett's Adventure, 2,500 a., June 7, 1665.
Thomas Walley, Walley's Chance, 300 a., June 9, 1665.
William Thorne, Taunton Deane, 300 a., January 7 [1663?].
William Thomas, The Hazard, 400 a., November 2, 1664.
William Thomas, The Adventure, 100 a., November 2, 1664.
George Johnson, Johnson's Lott, 300 a., October 20, 1664.
John Winder, Kikotan's Choice, 300 a., April 2, 1666.
Stephen Horsey, Horsey's Bailwick, 500 a., March 26, 1664.
Robert Hardy, Barber's Rest, 300 a., April 6, 1666.
Thomas Cottingham, Vulcan's Vineyard, 300 a., April 6, 1666.
Daniel Haste, Daniell's Adventure, 300 a., April 2, 1666.
Henry Heman [Haman, Hayman], Heman's Hill, 200 a., April 5, 1666.
Thomas Carny, Jr., Carny's Delight, 300 a., April 6, 1666.
Richard Whitty, Whitty's Later Invention, 300 a., April 10, 1666.
Richard Whitty, Whitty's Invention, 300 a., April 7, 1666.
Alexander Mitchell[er], Mitchell[er's] Lot, 300 a., April 4, 1666.
Samuel Smith, Samuell's [later Smith's] Adventure, 1,000 a., June 7, 1665.
William Thomas, The Lott, 1,000 a., November, 1664.
Stephen Horsey, Tonies Vineyard, 300 a., October 10, 1665.
William Cole, Colebrook, 550 a., October 20, 1662.
William Thorne, Thornton, 600 a., November 2, 1662.
John Westlock, Brownstone, 300 a., March 15, 1663.
William Bozman, More and Case It, 1,200 a., November 11, 1662.
James Barnaby, Barnaby's Lott, 200 a., March 12, 1663.
Owen Macrah, Owen's Choice, 300 a., March 9, 1663.
John Shipway, Deepe, 300 a., March 8, 1663.
James Davis, Davis' Choice, 600 a., March 14, 1663.
James Cane, Cane's Choice, 300 a., March 18 [1663].
John Nelson, Nelson's Choice, 300 a., March 22 [1663].
Philip Berrer [Berre], Berrer's [Berre] Lott, 600 a., March 13, 1663.
William Furnis, Furnis' Choice, 300 a., March 12, 1663.
Stephen Ellard [Elliot], Ellard's [Elliott's] Choice, 200 a., March 14, 1663.
William Glanville, Glanville's Lott, 500 a., March 11, 1663.

William Davis, Davis' Conquest, 300 a., March 14, 1663.
Peter Elzey, St. Peter's Neck, 400 a., May 2, 1663.
John Elzey, Almodington, 1,000 a., November 10, 1663.
Richard Hackworth [Ackworth], First Choice, 210 a., September 10, 1663.
William Thorne, South Betherton, 300 a., September 15, 1665.
Christopher Nutter, Nutter's Delight, 150 a., September 23, 1665.
John Winder, Winder's Purchase, 200 a., April 1, 1663.
Henry Elliott, Wassawomack, 250 a., March, 1663.
German Gillett, Owen Glandore, 300 a., March 1, 1663.
Joel Blake, Blake's Hope, 700 a., March 9, 1663.
William Price, Aracco, 250 a., March 9, 1663.
William Price, Price's Grove, 400 a., March 9, 1663.
John Waughop, Piney Point, 800 a., March 13, 1663.
James Jolly, Cobham, 100 a., March 13, 1663.
William Edwin, Edwin, 350 a., June 3, 1664.
William Elgate, Elgate, 150 a., June 3, 1664.
John Laurence, Laurence's, 200 a., June, 1664.
Thomas Harwood, Golden Lyon, 700 a., March 10, 1663.
Thomas Smith, The Strand, 1,000 a., March 7, 1663.
William Smith, William's Hope, 1,000 a., March 13, 1663.
Christopher Stevenson, Stevenson, 150 a., November 16, 1664.
Richard Gaines [Games?], The Lanam Devory, 300 a., November 18, 1664.
William Smith, Smith's Folly, 1,000 a., March 13, 1663.
George Wale, Aquintica, 200 a., August 26, 1665.
Robert Jones, Greenfield, 300 a., August 26, 1665.
Robert Jones, Accompson, 150 a., August 28, 1665.
Mark Manlove, Pimmo [Pimmore], 300 a., January 20, 1665.
Jenkin Price, The King's Neck, 300 a., November 20, 1665.
Thomas Ball [John Hilliard], The Seaman's Choice, 150 a., July 4, 1665.
William Stevens, Rehoboth, 1,000 a., July 18, 1665.
John Mackitt, Dublin, 100 a., November 5, 1665.
Henry Hudson, Hudson's Fortune, 100 a., November 7, 1665.
Henry Priestly, Thornbury, 1,000 a., August, 1665.
Daniell Quillen, The Irish Grove, 150 a., November 6, 1665.
Morris Liston, The Irish Grove, 150 a., November 10, 1665.
Robert Hignett, Hignett's Choice, 300 a., February 8, 1667.
Francis Hill, Little Town, 300 a., November 7, 1663.
Catherine Price, Cambrooke, 300 a., December 2, 1663.
Edward Carter, Kent, 1,500 a., March 18, 1665.
Jenkin Price, Aquintica, 300 a., October 20, 1665.
Jenkin Price, New Towne, 450 a., October 2, 1665.
Robert Pitt, Chuckatuck, 1,000 a., October 28, 1665.
Jeffery Menshall [Minshall], Adventure, 400 a., February 10, 1665.
Thomas [Phinias] White, King's Norton, 100 a., July 16, 1665.

William Smith, Bringingham, 500 a., June 2, 1664.
Henry Smith, Smith's Chance, 150 a., December 12, 1665.
William Smith, Assicomico, 500 a., June, 1664.
William Stevens, Partner's Choice, 2,000 a., July 17, 1665.
Richard Lloyds, Lloyds' Choice, 500 a., November 18, 1665.
William Stevens, Lebbourn [Ledbourne], 500 a., March 1, 1665.
Jenkin Price, Northfield, 500 a., November 8, 1663.
Hugh Stanley, Stanley's, 1,350 a., July 24, 1663.
William Harper, Middle Plantation, 150 a., May 12, 1663.
Richard Ackworth, Ackworth's Choice, 100 a., February 16, 1664.
Richard Ackkworth, Ackworth's Purchase, 300 a., February 19, 1664.
Nicholas Fountain, Fountain's Lott, 300 a., March 12, 1663.
William Coleburn, Pomfrett, 1,400 a., [March 8, 1663].
Joseph Bridger, Bridger's Lott, 1,100 a., [May 4, 1663].
Charles Hall, Hall's Choice, 300 a., June 6, 1665.
William Bosman, Bosman's Choice, 300 a., March 2, 1663.
Roger Woolford, The Woolfe Ford, November 11, 1663.
William Jones, Jones' Choice, 700 a., [March 20, 1663].

The tracts of land noted in the above list as surveyed for and patented by the parties whose names are given were in the sections of the Old Somerset area along the Pocomoke, Great Annemessex, Manokin, and Wicomico Rivers (with one or two of them in the neighborhood south of Nanticoke River) and about Morumsco, Monie and Back Creeks. In July, 1666, the governor issued a proclamation authorizing the commissioners for "the Eastern Shore" to issue warrants for lands on "the seaboard side" to those who wished to settle there (Somerset Court, Liber O 1). However, it was several years later before there appears to have been any movement towards the section comprehended by this proclamation. In 1670 William Stevens and James Weedon were appointed deputies for granting lands on "the seaboard side" (*Ar. Md., Proceedings of Council, 1667-1687/8,* pp. 79, 90 and 96). The objective of this movement was principally the establishment of settlements in the northeastern section of the Old Somerset area which at the dates given included what is now the lower part of Sussex County, Delaware. By 1672 numerous warrants were issue for lands in this section and a county by the name of Worcester was proposed (see *ante,* p. 423, *et seq.*).

* * * * * *

The following persons were entitled to 50 acres of land each for coming into Maryland to settle. In some instances they assigned their "right" to the 50 acres to others, who received a grant thereof. In other instances the parties were transported by others who therefore received the "right" of 50 acres of land. Those whom we can prove to have been actual settlers in the Somerset area are marked with an asterisk. The names of these "rights" have been obtained from the Land Patent books, Hall of Records, Annapolis, which books contain records of surveys as made on warrants issued and names of those proving "rights" as well as the patents issued. The references given: *e. g.* (5:209-211) refer to volume and page of Land Patent books.

August 12, 1662—Edwd. Southern* and wife Mary*; Wm. Jones*; Michael* and Thos. Williams,* orphans; Phillip Bairee* for himself, wife Olive,* Geo. Lane,* Margaret* and Mary Ivory* and Elizabeth Barie*; Wm. Furnish* for himself and wife Olive*; Roger Woolford* and Owen Macah* for themselves; Jno. Marcam* for self and son Jno., Jr.*; Jno. Worslake [Westlock]* for self, wife Magdalen* and son John.*

September 24, 1662—Thos. Bloyce* for himself, wife Frances* and daughters Judith* and Frances,* Jno. Painter and Emanuel Porting. Nehemiah Coventan* for himself, wife Mary,* sons John* and Nehemiah,* and daughters Jeane,* Margaret,* Katherine* and Sarah*; Robt. Hardie,* John _____ and Elizabeth _____, servants.

October 3, 1662—Matthew Armstrong, Wm. Fisher and Wm. Hadson, to make good rights. Saml. Jones* for himself, wife Mary* and sons Saml., Jr.,* and John*; Thos. Fox and Elizabeth Wood. Wm. Boyst* for himself and wife Mary.* Wm. Planner* for himself. Thos. Duparke for himself and wife Elizabeth. Richd. Darling for himself, wife Abigail and daughter Elizabeth (5:209-211).

August 16, 1662—Stephen Horsey* for himself, wife Sarah*; Jno.,* Saml.,* Mary* and Abigail Horsey* [his children]; Thos.,* Michael* and Sarah Williams* [his step-children]; John Roche [Roach],* Benj. Summer* and Thos. Whittfield (4:580).

August 16, [1662], William Colebourne* for himself, wife Ann*; Wm. Colebourne, Jr.* [his son]; Saml. Jackson,* John Rensha* (4:580-1).

December 16, 1663—Randall Revell and Ann Toft entered rights; Randall Revell* [for himself]; Katherine Revell* [his wife]; Randall, Jr.,* Hannah* and Katherine, Jr.* [his children]; Jno. Nicholls, Robt. Right, Nicholas Fountain,* Susan Willers [or Willis], Jno. Gouldsmith,* Mary Langworth, Elizabeth Poole,* Thos. Poole,* Sarah Grifin, Thos. Fuller [or Fallen], Jno. Haggamore, Jno. Cooper,* Baker Smith, Elias Duggar, Isaac Duggar, Margaret Mitchell,* Edwd. Sudman [Surnam],* Ann Sudman [Surnam],* Geo. Mitchell,* Thos. Smith, Philip Hawkins [or Hawkes], Hannah Lester [or Lister], Jno. Hastings, Thos. Payne [or Pane] (6:171). When patent was issued to Revell and Toft, in 1665, we find the same "rights" named as above with the addition of: Anthony Johnson,* Mary Johnson,' Jno. Cassaugh,* Jno. Hobbs,* Mary Vincent, Frances Vincent,* Mary Williams, Thos. Roche, Wm. Hall, Humphrey Fuller, Jno. Johnson, Susan Johnson, Thos. Williams, Humphrey Hall, Wm. Furnish,* Olive Furnish* (8:495).

September 3, 1663—Jenkin Price* for himself, wife Martha* and his children, John* and Margaret*; and servants Edwd. Whitty, Jeremy Bursted, Thos. Miller (5:441).

October 20, 1662—Wm. Cole for himself, wife Sarah and daughter Susan, and four servants (5:208; 274-5).

February 6, 1663—Henry Boston* for himself, wife Ann*; [sons] Henry, Jr.,* and Isaac*; [daughter] Rebecca Boston*; Saml. Moore,* Wm. and Mary Wilkinson, Robt. Dornewell, Thos. Molson [or Moolson],* Judith Beste* (9:283-4).

April 27, 1664—John Westlocke* for himself, wife Magdalen* and "John Manyott his son in law" (6:302-3).

1663—Ambrose Dixon* for himself, wife Mary,* daughters Elizabeth,* Grace,* Mary* and Sarah Dixon*; son Thomas Dixon* (5:255).

March 10, 1663—Ambrose Dickson [Dixon] for Phillip Adams* and Henry Pennington* (6:255).

March 10, 1663—Robt. Cattling, the Elder,* for himself, wife Ann,* sons Joseph* and Robert,* daughter Ann* (6:255).

March 10, 1663—Stephen Horsey for Reb^a [Rebecca?] Horsey (6:255).

October 26, 1663—Alexander Draper* for himself, wife Catherine* and servant Edward Furlong* (6:22).

March 8, 1663—William Coleburn* for himself, wife Ann,* son Wm., Jr.,* daughter Mary*; Saml. Jackson,* Jno. Rensha,* Geo. Read, Richd. Peacock, Alice Bassett,* Richd. Mills, Elizabeth Taylor, Saml. Jones* (6:157; 239).

June 14, 1665—Arnold Elzey and John Elzey had patent for "rights," viz: Jno. Elzey, Sr.,* decd. (who came into the province, where he died), Jno. Cole, Edwd. Lane, Thos. Floyd, Jacob Jones, John Hust,* Stephen Hill, Saml. Blage, Jno. Cooper, Anthony Williams, Nicholas Prate, Mary Price, Margaret Stradling, Amy Read, Ann Sallaway, Mary Blood, Sarah Lane, Elizabeth Martin (7:605).

June 13, 1665—Charles Ballard,* himself, and for Wm. Johnson, Jos. Harrison, Diana Gidney, Robt. Dixe, Elizabeth Baker, Parnall Jones (7:598).

January 16, 1664—Thos. Harwood for transporting Edwd. Hodson, Jos. Borud, Wm. Pritchett, Robt. Pake, Wm. Bosse, Wm. Fisher, Thos. Tilsley, Swgan Risbrooke, Wm. Skipworth, Margaret Fisher, Jone Penny, Humphrey Michell, Thos. Flaxon (7:500).

1665—John Shipway for himself and Ann Mills (8:449).

October 28, 1665—Robt. Pitt for Jno. Hudson, Mary Allen, Ellis Emperor, Susanna Serle, Jno. Noble, Jno. Wells, Ellen Wells, Elizabeth Jenkins, Thos. Saywells, Wm. Johnson, Ann Morgan, Allen Moyer, John Monkey (?), John Dawes (?) (10:4-5). William Thorn* for himself, wife Winifred,* Jno. Richards,* John Bunnel? (Bird?), Edwd. Lee (6:19).

July 11, 1665—Roger Woolford* for himself, wife Mary,* daughter Mary,* Richard Colmore, Laban [Levin] Denwood,* Sarah Denwood,* and by assignment from Jno. Nutall for transporting Elizabeth Cobb, Elizabeth Cole, Jno. Davis, Robt. Booth, Wm. Lee, William Sutton, William Brittinham, Jno. Austin (8:490).

July 11, 1665—Wm. Planner for himself (8:491).

1663—Robt. Hart for himself, wife and child (6:24). Richard Ackworth for transporting Mary Williams, Wm. Shoares and Ann Manloe [Manlove]in 1663 (6:31).

January 6, 1663—Henry Boston* for himself, wife Ann,* son Henry,* Isaac Boston [son],* daughter Rebecca,* Saml. Moore,* Wm. Wilkinson, Mary Wills, Robt. Dorman, Thos. Blouse (6:125).

[February, 1663]—William Bosman* for himself, wife Ellen,* Catherine,* John,* Wm., Jr.,* John,* Bridget,* Ann,* George* and Mary Bosman* [his children], Stephen [Lazarus] Maddocks [or Maddox*], Stephen Elliott, Jones Davies, Wm. Halso, Jno. Davies, Thos. Layden, Robt. Busbo, Ann Moseley, Gideon Chelse (6:171).

March, 1663—Stephen Horsey entered "rights" for John King,* Jane King,* John King [Jr.?], Mary King, Jas. Davies, James Cane,* George Carter, Wm. Howard (6:255).

1663—William Elgate* for himself, wife Hannah* and sons John* and William* (6:267 and 8:444).

February 10, 1665—John Nelson* for himself (9:172).

February 20, 1665—Mark Manlove for transporting George,* Christopher,* Hannah,* Perce,* and Thomas Manlove* and Ann Williams (9:207).

September 24, 1665—Mark Manlove for transporting Thomas Gille* [Gillis], Mary Gille* [Gillis], John ....; and assignment of Philip Conner's "own right," and rights of Thos. Macom (?) and Katherine, his wife (9:209).

September 30, 1665—Jenkin Price enters "rights," viz: John Hilliard, Sr.,* Mary Hilliard,* John Hillard, Jr.,* Samuell Long* (9:211).

January 15, 1665—Philip Connor, Sr., assigned rights of Philip Conner, Jr.,* Ann Conner* and Sarah Conner* (9:211).

February 24, 1665—Thos. Ball* for himself, Nicholas Webb and Jno. Davies (9:214).

September 20, 1665—Marguerite Edwyn for herself and husband Wm. Edwyn [decd.] (8:444).

November 14, 1664—Richd. Gaines by assignment from Philip Morgan enters Edward Ward, Saml. Gosse, Henry Gillett, Robt. Dickerson (?), Martha Fuller, Jone Sugar (8:296).

September 26, 1665—Owen Mackrue [Macraw]* for himself and Isaac Noble* (8:451).

June 13, 1665—Sarah Jorden by assignment from Danl. Jennifer enters Michael Mason, Thos. Bedford, Wm. Russell, John Williams, Wm. Walker, Thos. Evans (7:599).

George Johnson enters rights transported in 1662, viz: William Poulson; in 1663 Thos. Hunt, Katherine Johnson, Senr.,* and Katherine Johnson, Jr.* (6:154).

January, 1665—Richard Whitty* for himself, wife Elizabeth,* Ann Fisher, George Phoebus,* Patience Porter (9:217).

1665—William Stevens* for himself, wife Elizabeth,* Thos. Phillips, Robert Moore and 40 rights assigned by the Ann Hack (9:216-217).

February 24, 1665—Mark Manlove* for himself, Elizabeth,* John,* Ann,* William* and Mark Manlove, Jr.* (9:205).

January 22, 1665—Ambrose London* for himself, wife Mary,'* Mary,* Ruth* and Abigail London,* "his children"; Wm. Kennedy, Denham Olandman* and George Hasford [Hasfurt]* assigning same "rights" to Stephen Horsey (9:200 and 202).

February 24, 1665—William Stevens for himself, wife Elizabeth, Thos. Phillips and Robt. Moore; by assignment Richard Whitty and wife, Anne Fisher, George Phoebus, Patience Porter, Jacob Cloyse, Wm. Clarke, Thos. Dab, John Seaman, Wm. Seaman, Simon Carpe, Elizabeth Pent, Paul Sereeke, Morgan Abraham, James Ferreby (?), Ann German (9:220).

February 24, 1665—Richard Stevens* for himself, George Booth,* Toby Core; and by assignment for Lucy Wynne, James Wynne and John Sikes (9:222).

February 24, 1665—Thomas Davis* for himself, John Spratt, Richd. Wood, Francis Yonson, Jno. Timbells, Henry Portland, Peter Cole, Prudence Hopkins (9:224).

February 24 [1665]—William Jones* for himself and wife Margaret*; George Mitchell* for himself (9:229).

March 24, 1665—Philip Berrer* [Barre] for Philip,* Griffes [Grisegon?],* Olive* and Elizabeth Berrer*; Nicholas and Elizabeth Barnett; Margaret* and Mary Ivery*; George Lynn [Lane?]* and Ann Taylor (9:297).

December 1, 1665—George Johnson proves "rights," viz: John Johnson, Elizabeth Johnson, Morris Liston,* Evis Foster, Isabell Walle* (9:280).

June 5, 1666—John Winder* enters himself, Bridget Winder,* Susanna Winder,* Daniel Heast* [Hast, Haste], Martin Moore, John Okey,* Richd. Price, John Daw, Mary Gray (9:450 and 10:361).

January 1, 1665—Nicholas Rice enters John Wattson, Thos. Davis, Mary Grove, John Charles, Henry Thomas, Nicholas Rice* and John Wancklen (9:100).

January 1 [1665?]—James Jones* enters himself, wife Sarah,* Elizabeth Meredith, Peter Hellany, Johnson Jones (9:99).

January 1 [1665?]—David Spence* enters himself, James Dashiell,* Ann Dashiell,* James Dashiell, John Thomas, Joell Taylor, Robt. Murdrake, Wm. Laxtone, Geo. Doone, Elizabeth Dashiell,* Isabell Egions (?) (9:99).

October 3, 1665—Randell Revell enters Thos. Bales, Susanna Brayfield,* Edwd. Brayer, Conever Barber, Dorothy Bundick, John Hardidge, Servate Fuller, Jno. Croweley, Thomas Sowell, Symond Millard, Jno. Barnard, Jno. Napenis, Hanna Leach (9:11).

September 4, 1665—Christopher Nutter enters himself and wife Mary (8:204).

August 1, 1665—Thomas Walley* enters himself, wife Elizabeth,* son John* and daughters Margaret* and Rachell* (8:19).

[August 1, 1665]—James Barnaby,* himself, Mary,* Elizabeth* and Rebecca Barnaby* (8:19).

[August 1, 1665?]—George Prouse, Abraham Davis, John Hattfield, Geo. Coggin, Nathaniel Horsey,* Isaac Horsey* (8:19).

1665—Thos. Bloyce* for himself, Frances,* Judith* and Frances* Bloyce, Mary Williams, Manniwell Deas and Richd. Partridge (8:486).

1665—Wm. Boyst* for himself, Mary Boyst,* Jeane Boyst,* Jane Defarmus [Delamus?] (8:486).

1665—William Robinson for himself, Jone Robinson, Wm. Robinson, Mary Robinson, Thos. Cooke (8:486).

1665—Robert Ingram* for himself, Ann Ingram,* John Ingram,* James Ingram,* Anthony Taylor, Edward Hazard* [Hassard] (8:486).

1665—James Davis,* himself, Margaret Lewis, Sarah Davis, Arthur Evitt, Jos. Bruneridge, Elizabeth Hudd, Elizabeth Bennett (8:486).

1665—Richard Davis,* himself, John Griffith, Richd. Mount, Jas. Yarritt, Ann Roagues (8:486).

1665—Roger Woolford enters Leven Denwood,* Sarah Denwood,* John Wells, Martha Robinson, Owen Mackara* [Macrah] (8:486).

1665—William Planner,* himself (8:486).

1665—James Cane,* George Carter, William Howard, Isaac Noble* (8:486).

September 16, 1665—Katherine Price enters Katherine Price,* Rebecca Pollard, Jno. Price, Wm. Kirby, Thos. Hedges, Jos. Taylor (9:454).

[1666?]—Jenkin Price enters Jno. Chares, Phineas White,* John Hudson (9:516).

January 22, 1666—Jno. Price, himself, wife Susan, Jno. Hill, Sarah Ratcliff (10:344).

December 22, 1666—Daniel Curtis,* himself, wife Mary,* daughter Elizabeth* (10:541).

December 22, 1666—Robt. Hignett,* himself, Elizabeth Hignett,* Elizabeth _____, Jno. Crow,* Robt. Hignett, Jr.,* James Hignett* (10:298).

January 20, 1665—Charles Hall,* himself, Ellis [Alice] Hall,* Mary Freake, John Walker (10:343).

April 3, 1666—Richard Davis enters John Sherman, John Sherman [Jr.?] (10:342).

August 10, 1666—George Johnson and Jno. Wynder enter Henry Hayman,* Elinor Hayman,* Henry Hayman, Jr.* (10:190).

June 6, 1665—John Avery* enters himself, wife Sarah,* Francis Rames, Edward Perkins (7:580).

April 12, 1666—Jeffrey Mentiale [Minshall]* enters himself, Frances Mentiale,* Mary Mentiale,* Anne Mentiale,* his daughters; Jeffrey Mentiale* and Randall Mentiale,* his sons; William Collett, his servant (10:10).

May 14, 1662—John Rhodes* enters himself and "sonnes" John Rhodes* (5:73).

July 23, 1663—Charles Ratcliffe* enters himself, and George Johnson* himself (5:412).

September 3, 1663—Jenkin Price enters wife Martha,* John* and Margaret Price,* his children; Edw. Whitty, Jeremy Bursted and Thomas Miller, his servants (5:442).

May 14, 1662—Ambrose Dickeson* enters rights for himself, his son Ambrose Dickeson,* Mary Dickeson,* Thomas Dickeson,* Mary Dickeson,* Sarah Dickeson,* Elizabeth Dickeson,* Grace Dickeson,* Daniel Moore, Margaret Francklen* and Cornelius Ware [sic Ward?]; *all transported in An⁰ 1661* (5:73). Note: the spelling *Dickeson* is evidently a clerical error; the name is *Dixon*.

[April 28, 1663]—Ambrose Dixon* enters his rights, vizt: himself, Mary Dixon,* his wife; Thomas Dixon,* his son; Mary,* Sarah,* Elizabeth* and Grace Dixon,* his daughters; Cornelius Ware [Ward],* Daniel More, Thomas Williams and Margaret Franklin* (5:255).

September 28, 1663—The patent for "Dixon's Choice," 550 a., issued to Ambrose *Dickson,* states that the grant was "for transporting himself, Ambrose, his son; Mary Dickson, Thomas Dickson, again Mary Dickson, Sarah, Elizabeth and Grace Dickson, Daniel Moore, Margaret Franklin and Cornelius Ware, Ann⁰ 1661" (5:608). The spelling of the name *Dickson* is again a clerical error; it should be Dixon. The name given in the above items as "Cornelius Ware" should be *Ward*.

* * * * *

Before the marking in 1668 of the Maryland-Virginia boundary line on the Eastern Shore (see *ante*, p. 53-54) there were certain grants for lands south of the Pocomoke River (within the area of Somerset County) made by the Virginia government. These lands were after the running and marking of this boundary line found to be within Somerset County in the province of Maryland. These grants as noted, *Virginia Commission Report (1873),* pp. 34 and 136-9, were as follows: June 10, 1664, John Wallop, 400 a. October 2, 1663, Robert Pitts, 3,000 a. March 12, 1662, Robert Pitts, 1,000 a. September 10, 1664, Edmund Scarburgh, 2,000 a. April 5, 1666, Robert Holston, 500 a.; John William, 500 a.; Thomas Davis, 400 a.; James Henderson, 400 a.; John Davis, 700 a.; Henry Smith, 1,700 a. November 9, 1666, Charles Ratcliffe, 1,200 a. June 22, 1664, Edmund Scarburgh, 3,000 a.

* * * * *

This note on *Patentees of Land in Old Somerset Area, 1662-1666,* together with the appended list of "rights" proved, is intended as the briefest outline. Any adequate treatment of this matter would require intensive study, while the publication of the results of such a study would require an extensive volume to itself. We are glad to announce that Harry L. Benson, Esq., of Baltimore, has been engaged for some years in preparing a work on the Early Settlers of Somerset County, 1662-1683, giving an account of their lands. Mr. Benson's work, a scholarly one in every sense of the word, will embrace the entire landholding population of the Old Somerset area, and will be illustrated by a series of charts and maps showing the locations of the patented tracts of land. Such a work will be an incomparable contribution to the history of Old Somerset and it is hoped that Mr. Benson will be able to publish his monumental work before so many years.

OLD SOMERSET
ON
THE EASTERN SHORE OF MARYLAND

Part III
References and Index

Abbreviations Used in References

Md. Hist. Mag.—Maryland Historical Magazine.

Wise, *Accawmacke*—Wise, *Ye Kingdome of Accawmacke, or the Eastern Shore of Virginia in the Seventeenth Century.*

Scharf, *Maryland,* Vol. I—Scharf, *History of Maryland from the Earliest Period to the Present Day* [1879], Vol. I.

Va. Mag. Hist. & Biog.—*Virginia Magazine of History and Biography.*

Steiner, *Prot. Rev.*—Steiner, *The Protestant Revolution in Maryland* (published in Report American Historical Society, 1897, pp. 279-353).

Va. Commission Report (1873)—*Report and Accompanying Documents of the Commissioners Appointed to Ascertain the Boundary Line Between Maryland and Virginia* (Richmond ... 1873).

Wise, *Col. John Wise*—Wise, *Col. John Wise, of England and Virginia* (1617-1695).

Morris, *The Early Friends (or Quakers) in Maryland*—The Early Friends (or Quakers) in Maryland. A paper read at a meeting of the Maryland Historical Society, March, 1862, by J. Saurin Morris. Printed for the Maryland Historical Society by John D. Toy.

Somerset Court Deed Liber, or Judicials—The records in office of clerk of Circuit Court for Somerset County at Princess Anne, Maryland.

Somerset Registry of Wills, Wills or Administrations—Will and administration records in office of Registrar of Wills of Somerset County at Princess Anne, Maryland.

Worcester Court, Deed Liber—The records in office of Circuit Court for Worcester County at Snow Hill, Maryland.

Worcester Registry of Wills—Wills in office of Registrar of Wills for Worcester County at Snow Hill, Maryland.

Northampton County, Virginia, Court—Records in office of clerk of Circuit Court for Northampton County, Virginia, at Eastville, Virginia.

Accomack County, Virginia, Court—Records in office of clerk of Circuit Court for Accomack County, Virginia, at Accomack, Virginia.

Arcv. Md.—*Archives of Maryland.* This is a series of published volumes of Maryland Council, Assembly and Provincial Court Proceedings and Acts of Assembly published under the general title of *Archives of Maryland.* The Roman numerals in the references (e. g. *I Arcv. Md.*) refer to the volume numbers of the general series.

I Arcv. Md.—Proceedings and Acts of Assembly, 1637/8-1664.
II Arcv. Md.—Proceedings and Acts of Assembly, 1666-1676.
III Arcv. Md.—Proceedings of Council, 1636-1667.
V Arcv. Md.—Proceedings of Council, 1667-1687/8.
VII Arcv. Md.—Proceedings and Acts of Assembly, 1678-1683.
VIII Arcv. Md.—Proceedings of Council, 1687/8-1693.
XIII Arcv. Md.—Proceedings and Acts of Assembly, 1684-1692.
XV Arcv. Md.—Proceedings of Council, 1671-1681.
XIX Arcv. Md.—Proceedings and Acts of Assembly, 1693-1697.
XX Arcv. Md.—Proceedings of Council, 1693-1696/7.
XXII Arcv. Md.—Proceedings and Acts of Assembly, 1697/8-1699.
XXIII Arcv. Md.—Proceedings of Council, 1696/7-1698.
XXV Arcv. Md.—Proceedings of Council, 1698-1731.
XXVI Arcv. Md.—Proceedings and Acts of Assembly, 1704-1706.
XXXIV Arcv. Md.—Proceedings and Acts of Assembly, 1720-1723.
XXXVIII Arcv. Md.—Proceedings and Acts of Assembly, 1694-1729.
XLII Arcv. Md.—Proceedings and Acts of Assembly, 1740-1742.
XLIX Arcv. Md.—Proceedings of Provincial Court, 1663-1666.
LI Arcv. Md.—Proceedings of Provincial Court, 1669-1679.

I

Break of Day

[1] Lady Mary Somerset (wife of Sir John Somerset) was sister of Anne Arundel, wife of Cecil, 2nd Lord Baltimore. Lady Somerset and Lady Baltimore were daughters of Thomas, Lord Arundel (1560-1639) and his 2nd wife, Anne Philipson. See *XXII Md. Hist. Mag.*, p. 315.

[2] *III Arcv. Md.*, p. 553-5. See also *ante*, p. 67, proclamation erecting Somerset County.

[3] Matthews, *The Maps and Map Makers of Maryland*, p. 347-354. See also Edward Arber's edition of *The Works of Captain John Smith*.

[4] Wise, *Accawmacke*, p. 62, and *XXIV Md. Hist. Mag.*, p. 160.

[5] The Monie Indian Town is referred to in a patent granted Nehemiah Covington in 1662 (Hall of Records, Annapolis, Liber, No. 9, folio 14; and in January, 1679/80, in a deed from Nehemiah Covington to his sons, John and Nehemiah, as the "Indian Towne of Great Monie," on north side Great Monie Creek (Somerset Court, Deed Liber O 6, p. 425).

[6] Somerset Court, Judgments DT 7, 1670-1, p. 6, *et seq.*, Revell vs. Ackworth; case to determine a boundary of Revell's land. "The Trading Branch" was location in question and depositions taken in order to establish identity of this branch. "The Trading Branch," of 1670 (and earlier and later dates) may today be found in the stream called, and known as, "King's Creek" on south side of the Manokin River.

[7] For settlement of Maryland see Andrew's *Tercentenary History of Maryland*, Vol. I, in which the settlements of St. Mary's and the Isle of Kent are fully discussed. See also Claiborne's *William Claiborne of Virginia*, and Thom's *Claiborne and Kent Island in Maryland History*.

[8] For Kent County see Hanson's *Old Kent* and Matthew's *The Counties of Maryland*.

[9] For later settlements east of Chesapeake Bay and origin and development of Talbot and Dorchester Counties see Tilghman, *History of Talbot County;* and Jones, *History of Dorchester County*.

[10] *I Arcv. Md.*, p. 332; Scharf, *Maryland*, Vol. I, p. 260, *et seq.*

[11] *II Arcv. Md.*, p. 327.

[12] Wise, *Accawmacke*, p. 155.

[13] *Va. Commission Report* (1873), pp. 34-35; see also *V Arcv. Md.*, p. 43.

[14] For full discussion of Maryland-Virginia boundary line on the Eastern Shore see Whealton, *The Maryland-Virginia Boundary Line Controversy*, 1668-

1894; Andrews, *Tercentenary History of Maryland,* Vol. I; Wise, *Accawmacke,* Chapters X and XI; *Va. Commission Report* (1873).

[15]*Va. Commission Report* (1873), p. 22. Jones, *History of Dorchester County,* pp. 32, 45 and 104, recites the settlement of Taylor's Island and other patents in 1659 in the area which in 1669 became Dorchester County. There was a patent in 1660 to one Daniel Moore for land on Nanticoke River.

[16]Hening, *Statutes at Large . . . of Virginia,* Vol. I, p. 252-3, *"An act for suppressing of the Quakers,"* passed by Virginia Assembly, March, 1659/60. See also Wise, *Accawmacke,* Chapter X, and Jones, *Quakers in the American Colonies,* and also the standard histories of Virginia and Maryland.

[17]So far all efforts to locate a copy of this petition of Northampton-Accomakians to Governor Calvert have failed. Evidence that the petition was made is contained in Calvert's proclamation, November 6, 1661, by which he granted it. For this proclamation in full see *post,* Appendix I.

[18]*III Arcv. Md.,* pp. 449, 450, for action of Council and John Elzey's deposition. The deposition of Francis Wright, ordered to be taken, has not been discovered.

John Nuttall, who was accused of informing the Wicomico Indians so unpleasantly about the character of the Accomackians was a rather noteworthy person. He may be identified with one "John Nutwell" who as a youth ran away from his master, one Hugh Hays, in Virginia (Northampton County), and going to live among the Indians was purchased from them by one William Jones for "the price of a hoe." Jones was at the time trading in the Chesapeake Bay and brought Nuttall home again "well straped w'th ye hallyards." (*Va. Commission Report* [1873], Part II, p. 79). Nuttall in later life became prominent in Northampton County, Virginia (Wise, *Accawmacke,* pp. 135, 139 and 163, and Northampton Records, Order Book 1651-4, p. 201). Nuttall came into Maryland to reside and had commissions from the governor to trade with the inhabitants and Indians for beaver furs, skins and other commodities, in January, 1661/2 and 1662/3, and so on to June, 1665 (*III Arcv. Md.,* pp. 445, 467, 472, 488, 489, 490, 513 and 526). He was one of his Lordship's justices of the peace for St. Mary's County, September 5, 1664 (*III Arv. Md.,* pp. 503 and 540).

[19]Wise, *Accawmacke,* p. 161, and other references therein to treatment of Indians by Accomackians. For Edmund Scarburgh's hostility to the Indians see Wise, *Colonel John Wise of England and Virginia* (1617-1695), p. 38, *et seq.*

[20]See *post,* Appendix II, for Randall Revell's report, May, 1662, of condition of the settlement of Manokin-Annemessex.

[21]Commission of November 6, 1661, renewed to Scarburgh, Revell and Elzey in May, 1662, see *III Arcv. Md.,* p. 452-3; proclamations of December 7, 1661, and January 31, 1661/2, relative to trade with Indians and Act of Navigation and Increase of Shipping, in *III Arcv. Md.,* pp. 443 and 446.

[22]The published *Archives of Maryland* fail to disclose names of persons chosen

by Thorne to serve as lieutenant and ensign of his company; and name of person appointed by Commission of the Eastern Shore to serve as "sheriff or martiall." There remain no records for this period of proceedings of Commission for the Eastern Shore.

[23]*III Arv. Md.*, p. 443, records these commissions and licenses: "May vt supra (May 2, 1662) Lycence to trade for Francis Wright and Clausen. Com^{on} for Capt to Wm. Thorne to bee Captn. at Manoakin and Anamesick. Com^{on} to seiz all vessels &c; Com^{on} to graunt warr^{ts} &c; Com^{on} to keepe the peace to Revell, Elzey and Thorne. May the 3 Lycence to exporte 40· barrells of corne out of the Province to Randall Revell. Idem to Mr. Wright to exporte 12 barrells. Idem to Mr. Elzey to exporte 12 barrells."

Francis Wright appears as a trader with the Indians. His name frequently appears in the *Archives of Maryland*. He later went to Westmoreland County, Virginia, to live. The man Clauson referred to was Jacob Clauson, an Indian trader.

[24]*III Arcv. Md.*, pp. 469-471.

[25]*III Arcv. Md.*, pp. 476 and 488.

II

A Storm at Sunrise

[1]That the settlement at Annemessex was made probably late in the year 1661 seems attested by the fact that Stephen Horsey had transported into the province of Maryland in the year 1661 himself, Sarah, his wife, John, Mary, Samuel and Stephen Horsey, Junior, and Michael Williams and Thomas Williams (Hall of Records, Annapolis, Liber 4, p. 580); and that Stephen Horsey, Ambrose Dixon, Robert Hart and Alexander Draper had fled the jurisdiction of Northampton County, Virginia, Court by January 28, 1661/2 (Northampton County, Virginia, Records, Order Book, 1657-1664, pp. 123-4).

[2]That the Manokin section of the settlement was made certainly as early as March, 1661/2, seems to be attested by a deposition made by John Elzey on April 2, 1662, about the Indians' attitude towards the settlers from Accomack. See *ante*, pp. 16-17, for Elzey's deposition.

[3]Though the surveys and patents to Revell for "Double Purchase" and Elzey for "Almodington" were not made until a year or so later, all of the official documents given in the *Archives of Maryland* (and quoted in this present study) prove that Revell and Elzey were settled at Manokin in the early Spring, March, 1661/2-May, 1662.

[4]For Scarburgh's conduct in this affair of "locating" Watkins Point, see Wise, *Accawmacke*, pp. 163 and 178; Wise, *Col. John Wise* . . . p. 39; Whealton, *The Maryland and Virginia Boundary Controversy*, 1668-1894; Chapter II, pp. 12-19; Scharf, *Maryland*, Vol. I, p. 260, *et seq.*; Andrews, *Tercentenary History of Maryland*, Vol. I, pp. 341-2.

[5] *III Arcv. Md.,* p. 473-4, Elzey's letter to the Council, dated March, 1662/3, in which he says he had formerly sent this information to them in a letter by John Anderson; adding that since that time of writing (i. e. the letter sent by Anderson) he, Elzey, went to Accomack on business and while there Scarburgh arrested him, demanding obedience and payment for rights of land to the Virginia government. Elzey was in Accomack and received Scarburgh's demand and made reply thereto, February 23, 1662/3. Thus it is that we date Scarburgh's writing to Revell, "concerning their claim to this place," as in January, or early February, 1662/3. For Elzey's letter to the Council, March, 1662/3, see *ante,* pp. 33-4.

[6] *III Arcv. Md.,* p. 473-4; also see *Va. Commission Report* (1873), pp. 24-26.

[7] For Elzey's letter of March, 1662/3, read to Council April 8, 1663, see references under note 6 above.

[8] See Scharf, *Maryland,* Vol. I, p. 261 (fourth paragraph), for comment on Maryland authorities' attitude in matter of protection for settlers against the Indian menace. Scarburgh, in his report of proceedings at Manokin-Anamessex in October, 1663, to the Governor and Council of Virginia, gives the feeling of the settlers at Manokin about neglect of them in their defenceless state before the Indian enemy. For this statement by Scarburgh see *ante,* page 42, and, *post,* Appendix III.

[9] *III Arcv. Md.,* p. 474.

[10] See references under note 4 above.

[11] Hening, *Statutes at Large . . . of Virginia,* Vol. II, pp. 183-4. This act also given in *Va. Commission Report (1873),* p. 92-93.

[12] For Scarburgh's report in full see, *post,* Appendix III.

[13] Wise, *Accawmacke,* p. 178; Wise, *Col. John Wise,* p. 39, where Scarburgh is described as one who "hated Quakers intensely" and "upon these unfortunate people visited the most relentless persecution."

[14] For this action of Accomack County Court see Accomack County Court Records, Vol. I, p. 43; also *Va. Commission Report (1873),* Part II, p. 77. For the record of the Action of Accomack Court given in full see *post,* Appendix III.

[15] *III Arcv. Md.,* p. 496-8, and *Va. Commission Report (1873),* pp. 26-28, where proclamation of Calvert, June, 1664, including commission to Philip Calvert, is given in full.

[16] See *post,* Appendix III, Scarburgh's report of his proceedings (October, 1663) at Manokin-Annemessex.

[17] *Minutes of the Council and General Court of Colonial Virginia, 1622-1632 and 1670-1676; With notes and excerpts from Original Council and General Court Records now lost . . . Edited by H. R. McIlvaine . . .* pp. 493 and 507.

[18] *Va. Commission Report (1873),* Part II, pp. 32, 78-79. See also Whealton, *The Maryland and Virginia Boundary Controversy, 1668-1894,* pp. 12-19.

[19]Patents for lands issued by the Virginia government show nearly 33,000 acres granted in Maryland area by Virginia authorities. These lands, mostly patented in 1664, 1665 and 1666, and situated between southeast bank of Pocomoke River and the Atlantic Ocean, in what is now (1935) Worcester County (formerly part of Somerset County), Maryland, were proved by the survey of the dividing line in June, 1668, to be on the Maryland side of that line. A list of these patents is given in *Va. Commission Report (1873)*, p. 33, and *V Arcv. Md.*, p. 43.

[20]*V Arcv. Md.*, p. 43-45; *Va. Commission Report (1873)*, pp. 36-7, and p. 98; Wise, *Accawmacke*, p. 181; Scharf, *Maryland*, Vol. I, p. 262; Andrews, *Tercentenary History of Maryland*, Vol. I, pp. 341-2; Whealton, *The Maryland-Virginia Boundary Controversy, 1668-1894*, Chapter II.

[21]For later developments and controversy over the Maryland-Virginia boundary line see *Va. Commission Report (1873)*; and Whealton, *The Maryland-Virginia Boundary Controversy, 1668-1894*.

[22]Andrews, *Tercentenary History of Maryland*, Vol. I, p. 342, quoting Lieutenant Michler's United States Coast Survey of 1858.

III

As Clouds Rolled Away

[1]*III Arcv. Md.*, p. 490 (commission to Elzey, Horsey, Thorne and Odbur); p. 491 (commission to William Coulbourne as lieutenant); and pp. 495-6 (commission to Horsey, Thorne and Bosman).

[2]*III Arcv. Md.*, p. 533 (commission to Horsey, Thorne, Johnson, Stevens, White, Winder, Jones and Boston as justices, and to Thorne as captain) and p. 557 (commission to Horsey, Thorne, Johnson, Stevens, White, Winder, Jones and Boston as justices).

[3]Somerset Court Records, Liber O 1. This first and only volume of records of courts of the "Eastern Shore" is now in the office of the Clerk of Circuit Court of Somerset County, at Princess Anne, Maryland, and bears the serial number "Liber O 1." This volume is in a good state of preservation; only that the entries on the first few pages are somewhat faded, though still decipherable. The inscription opening the record is as follows: "1665 The Booke of Records for the County of Sommersett in ye Province of Maryland beginning ye 11th daye of December in the yeare of our Lord God 1665." That this inscription bears the words "County of Sommersett" leads one to believe that the inscription was entered at a later date than the record of the court, December 11, 1665, which is designated "a Courte helld att Thomas Poole ... in Manoakin on ye Easterne Shore ..." It may be, however, that the proposed erection and naming of the county, being already known, the descriptive entry is only anticipatory.

[4]Somerset Court Records, Liber O 1, p. 17.

IV

Then a Perfect Day in Summer

¹*III Arcv. Md.*, p. 553-5.

²*III Arcv. Md.*, pp. 555 and 553, commissions to Horsey and Thorne.

³Somerset Court, Liber O 1, pp. 23-25, where the recited documents are recorded in their entirety.

⁴Somerset Court, Liber O 1, p. 24, and *III Arcv. Md.*, p. 555.

⁵Somerset Court, Liber O1. Records of Courts, September, 1666, to June, 1668, do not give name of Stephen Horsey as present. Stevens and Thorne, alternately, presided at these courts. Horsey, serving as High Sheriff from September, 1666, to June, 1668, when he was succeeded in that office by George Johnson, did not take his seat on the bench until June 30, 1668, when he appears as presiding justice.

⁶Somerset Court, Liber O 1, p. 29, for marriage banns of John Okee and Mary Vincent and Thomas Tull and Mary *Mitchell*. The banns give the bride's name *Mitchell;* the record of marriage in Liber IKL, p. 255, gives her name as *Minshall*. *Minshall* is correct.

⁷Somerset Court, Liber IKL, pp. 196 and 255. Liber IKL, containing register of marriages, births and deaths (though probably by no means a complete record), gives record of marriages of James Nicholson and Mary Price in 1663; John Roch [Roach] and Sarah Williams in February, 1663/4; and of Edward Surnam and Ann Frowin in 1664.

⁸Somerset Court, Liber O 1, pp. 30-31.

⁹Somerset Court, Liber O 1, p. 34.

¹⁰Somerset Court, Liber O 1, pp. 34, 39, 40, 41 and 51.

¹¹See *ante*, p. 402, *et seq.*, for items relative to Somerset County's early court houses.

¹²Somerset Court, Liber O 1, pp. 44-45, for the Orders of court given in the text.

¹³The following order of court, evidently in furtherance of laying out "the highway for the Countie of Sommersett" was entered March 26, 1667: "It is ordered that every man shall marke out and cleare his owne Land (excepting where bridges are judged needful) for A highway by the direccon of the Surveyors. (Somerset Court, Liber O 1, p. 55).

¹⁴The "Hundred" was the first civil division of the province. In after years, with the formation of counties, they became as it were, constabulary districts within the counties. The "Hundred" was analagous to the modern "district" or "precinct." For an account of the "Hundred" see L. W. Wilhelm, *Local Institutions of Maryland.*

¹⁵The "original" five "Hundreds" in Somerset County, laid out by order of court, January 17, 1666/7, were Pocomoke, Annemessex, Manokin, Great and Little Monie, and Wicomico. In the course of years four more "Hundreds" were laid out, though we have not the exact dates of their origin, save that of the

last, viz: Baltimore Hundred. Of these four additional "Hundreds," *Pockerternorton* [also *Bogerternorton*] *Hundred* appears in November, 1670, in a list of tithables ordered to be taken (Somerset Court, Judicials, Liber DT 7, 1670-1, p. 48). *Nanticoke Hundred* appears in August, 1676, in a list of Pressmasters appointed for Somerset County (Somerset Deed Liber O 7 [back of book], Judicials, p. 44). *Mattapony Hundred* appears in November, 1683, in a list of constables appointed (Somerset Deed Liber O 7 [front of book], Judicials, p. 1). *Baltimore Hundred* was erected under proceedings of Somerset Court, November, 1697, with report of boundary line to the court, January 15, 1697/8 (Somerset Court, Judicials, Liber DD 17, pp. 267 and 283).

Nanticoke Hundred occupied the area between Wicomico River and Nanticoke River; Bogerternorton [or Pockerternorton] Hundred occupied the area east of Snow Hill Town and along the sea side. Mattapony Hundred was in the extreme southeastern section of the county, and Baltimore Hundred in the extreme northeastern section of the county. Mattapony and Baltimore Hundreds were set off from Bogerternorton Hundred. Nanticoke Hundred was set off from Wicomico Hundred.

The word Bogerternorten (with its variations in spelling which occur in the records) interested Mrs. Helen Torrence, of Baltimore, who makes the suggestion that it may be a popular corruption of the Spanish *Boca de Norte* (Mouth of [the] North). It will be recalled that Giovanni de Verrazana, the Florentine, navigator, anchored in Sinepuxent Bay and called the land thereabouts Arcadia (see *ante*, p. 429). Verrezano's visit to this region was in 1524. It may be that the entrance to Sinepuxent Bay was alluded to as *Boca de Norte* and the words picked up by Indians and given to the section immediately west of Sinepuxent and thus brought down to the first settlers. Bogerternorten Hundred, Old Somerset, occupied the territory immediately west of and bordering on Sinepuxent Bay.

[16]Somerset Court, Liber O 1, pp. 54, 55, 77, 111, 114 and 118. For Stephen Horsey's commission as high sheriff, dated April 23, 1667, for one year, see *V Arcv. Md.*, p. 4. For George Johnson's commission as sheriff, dated 1668, see *Ibid.*, page 33.

[17]Somerset Court, Liber O 1, p. 74.

[18]The facts given in regard to the Johnson family of "free Negroes" have been compiled from Wise, *Accawmacke*, p. 285, *et seq.*; Northampton County (Virginia) Court Records, Vol. IX, pp. 16 and 47; Revell and Toft patent for "Double Purchase," November, 1662, Hall of Records, Annapolis, Liber 8, folio 495; Somerset Court, Liber O 1, p. 32 (lease of Stephen Horsey to Anthony Johnson); Liber O 2, p. 20 (lease of Stephen Horsey to Mary Johnson); Liber AZ, No. 8, 1671-5, pp. 159 and 161 (Mary Johnson power of attorney to John Johnson; and Mary Johnson's deed to her grandchildren, Anthony, Francis and Richard Johnson). Liber DT, 1670-71, p. 6, *et seq.*, September, 1670, John Johnson, Negro, aged about 37 years, made deposition relative to boundaries of Randall Revell's land. Another "headright" to the patent to Revell and Toft for "Dou-

ble Purchase" in November, 1662, was one *"John Cassaugh."* Could this "Cassaugh" have been identical with the *"John Cazara, Negro,"* who witnessed, September 3, 1672, Mary Johnson's power of attorney to her son, John Johnson? Two other names of "headrights" to the Revell and Toft patent of November, 1662, were *"John Johnson, Susan Johnson."* We have not been able to determine whether this John Johnson was *"John Johnson, Negro,"* or some other party. It appears that a tract of land, 44 acres, called "Angola," in Wicomico Hundred, Somerset County, was surveyed August 29, 1677, for Wm. Green, and assigned to "John Johnson, Negro," on the south side Wiccocomoco. No heir was found for the land and is escheated to the Lord Proprietor (Rent Rolls, Somerset Co., 1663-1723, p. 29, in Maryland Historical Society, Baltimore). Another item relative to "free Negroes" in Somerset County at a later date appears in record of a court held August 14, 1688, as follows: "The peticon of Sarah Driggers and the rest all Negroes desiring that they might be putt out of the list of Tythables from paying any Taxes as being free borne Negroes whereupon it was the same day Ordered that the four women be exempted and that the mn [men pay?] taxes for this yeare and that they bring a Certificate under the Ministers hands where they formerly did live or were borne that they are free Negroes and baptized" (Somerset Court, Liber AW, 1690-1 [Court proceedings, November, 1687-June, 1689, and June, 1690-October, 1691], p. 58). No attempt has been made to trace further this Sarah Driggers and other free Negroes. Wise, *Accawmacke,* p. 287, refers to Immanuel *Driggs,* free Negro servant, in Northampton County, Virginia, in 1647.

"Tonie's Vineyard," where Anthony Johnson, the free Negro, lived may be located today about five miles northwest of Princess Anne, Maryland, and on the south side of Wicomico Creek, just west of where Passadike Creek enters Wicomico, and is probably included in the lands now owned by Mrs. William Burr Cochran and Miss Edna Davye.

The land where "the Negroes Lived . . . called Tony's vineyard," was recalled by one Peter Sermon (aged about 64 years) in September, 1736, when he made a deposition in relation to the boundaries of the tract called "Tony's Vineyard" on Wicomico Creek, which had been bought by the Reverend Alexander Adams. Sermon testified that he heard John Cassadow [John Cassagh, Cazara?] say that he had marked a tree, or saw it marked, as a "bounder of the land that did belong to the Negroes "or was their division tree" between their land and "Horsey's Chance" (which belonged to Stephen Horsey). (Somerset Court, Judicials, 1734-1736, pp. 286-7, Alexander Adams, commission, and affidavits in relation to bounds of part of a tract called "Tony's Vineyard." See also Horsey to Rine, in Deed Liber O 7, p. 657, and Horsey to Adams, Deed Liber O 21, p. 265). For further accounts of Anthony and Mary Johnson, the free Negroes; Emanuel Dregis, Negro, and John Casor [Cassagh, Cazara?] see Russell, *The Free Negro in Virginia, 1619-1865,* pp. 24-26, 27-28 and 32 (in Johns Hopkins University Studies in Historical and Political Science, Series XXXI, No. 3). Wright, *The Free Negro in Maryland, 1634-1860,* p. 31, says "The earliest reference to free Negro [in Maryland] I have found was one in Somerset County . . . John Johnson, Negro."

[19] *II Arcv. Md.,* pp. 155 and 156. The Assembly convened May 13, 1669, was the first Assembly held after the creation of Somerset County, in August, 1666.

[20] *II Arcv. Md.,* pp. 187-188. *Horsey's* name is given *Horsly,* which from the context is clearly a clerical, or typographical, error. The record of this affair, as we have it, is from the journal of proceedings of the Upper House of Assembly, which simply incorporates the proceedings of the Lower House into its record.

V

THE HOUSEHOLD OF FAITH

1. Followers of the Inner Light

[1] From 1634 to 1642/3 the peninsula forming the Eastern Shore of Virginia (from the Maryland-Virginia boundary line on the north to Cape Charles on the south) was one county by the name of *Accomack*. In 1642/3 the name of the county was changed to *Northampton* and so continued until 1663, when the territory was divided into the present counties of Accomack and Northampton. Though the "county" existence of this area dates only to 1634—when counties or "shires" were first laid out in Virginia, the settlements here extend back almost to the beginning of the colony of Virginia. See Wise, *Accawmacke;* and Robinson, *Virginia Counties: Those Resulting from Virginia Legislation* (in Bulletin of the Virginia State Library, Vol. 9, Nos. 1, 2 and 3. January-July, 1916).

[2] For act of Virginia Assembly against Quakers see *ante,* page 12. For an interesting account of the religious and political radicalism in Northampton County, Virginia, see Wise, *Accawmacke,* pp. 124, *et seq.;* 153, *et seq.,* and 251, *et seq.* Wise makes many suggestions as to contacts of Northampton County, Virginia, people with the liberal movements in religious and political matters; their contacts with the "Independent," or "Congregationalist," group in New England; the Dutch in New York. He sets forth fully the later reception of Quaker "missionaries" by elements in the Northampton County population.

[3] Northampton County, Virginia, Records, Order Book, 1657-1664, pp. 123-4.

[4] Northampton County, Virginia, Records, Order Book, 1657-1664, p. 165, George Johnson made deposition in this court, March 2, 1662/3; see sketch of George Johnson, *ante,* p. 316.

[5] That George Johnson, Henry Boston and Thomas Price were settled at Annemessex by October, 1663, is fully attested by Colonel Scarburgh's report of his invasion of that settlement during that month. See Scarburgh's report given, *post* Appendix III.

[6] Somerset Court, Liber IKL, gives record of birth of Solomon, son of William and Anne Coulbourne, *at Annemessex,* January 27, 1663/4. See sketch of William Coulbourne, *ante,* p. 322.

[7] See Minshall family and Marcums, Appendix X.

[8] Northampton County, Virginia, Court, Order Book, 1657-1664, p. 188, shows Ambrose London before the court in February, 1663/4, for his Quakerism.

⁹That the Annemessex Meeting House of the Quakers stood on Ambrose Dixon's land is proved by affidavits taken in Somerset Court, November, 1739, when one Thomas Dixon was establishing certain ancient boundary marks of the tract called "Dixon's Choice" on south side of Great Annemessex River. In a deposition made at that time by Captain Thomas Williams (one of the evidences) there is reference to a *"Gum stood in a valley or branch and Leaned over the Road near to a place where the Quaker Meeting house stood."* Affidavits relating to bounds of "Dixon's Choice" and containing depositions of Captain Thomas Williams recorded in Somerset Court, Judicials, Liber 1738-1740, pp. 201-202. The Thomas Dixon who in 1739 was proving the boundaries of "Dixon's Choice" was a son of Captain Thomas Dixon and grandson of Ambrose Dixon. See also sketch of Ambrose Dixon, *ante*, p. 302.

¹⁰Rufus Jones, *The Quakers in the American Colonies*, p. 305; Mann's *Commemoration Exercises of 200 Anniversary of Friends Meeting House at Third Haven;* and Morris, *The Early Friends (or Quakers) in Maryland*, pp. 26-7. It should be noted that Rufus Jones in his *The Quakers in the American Colonies* states positively that Stephen Horsey was a Quaker. Investigation of all sources available shows that we cannot positively identify Horsey as a Quaker, though he was evidently a "non-conformist" of the most marked type.

¹¹Somerset Court, Liber IKL, p. 56, gives the entries: "Elizabeth Dukes ye wife of Robert Dukes died and was buried at the Meeting house in Anemessex the last day of February one thousand Six hundred eighty seaven." "Ambrose Dixon, Senr died and was buried at the meeting house in Anemessex the 12th day of April Annoq Dom one Thousand Six hundred eighty & seaven." For the proof that Elizabeth (wife of Robert Dukes) was daughter of Ambrose Dixon see Dixon notes, Appendix X.

¹²See notes on John Goddin and Thomas Evernden, under data on George Johnson, of Annemessex, Appendix X. Goddin married Katherine, daughter of George Johnson; and Evernden married Katherine, *widow* of the said Johnson. Thomas Evernden, of Dorchester County, in his will, dated May 4, 1710, probated June 5, 1710 (among other bequests), leaves £10 towards building of Quaker Meeting House at head of Transquaking in Dorchester, and a piece of ground in St. Dunstan's Parish (Kent), England, to certain trustees as a burying place for Quakers. (*Maryland Calendar of Wills*, Vol. III, p. 171).

¹³*Journal of Thomas Chalkley*, pp. 28-30. Chalkley gives date of his arrival "within the capes of Virginia" as "31st 1st mo 1698" (March 31, 1698) and says that next day anchored ship in mouth of Patuxent River in Maryland. "Spent severall days—probably a week and some days over"—in Calvert County holding "meetings" and making visits (which he records) and continues his *Journal:* "and then we sailed over to the east side of Chesapeake Bay with Thomas Everden [Evernden] in his sloop; went to his house and had a meeting where many people came. Here we met our friends Jonathan Tyler, Henry Payton and Henry Payton's sister. While I was at this Friend's house one Robert Cathing [Catling, Catlin] being very ill sent for Thomas Everden, and he, not be-

ing very well, desired me to visit the sick person. So I went and the man was near to death. Howbeit he said he was comforted much with the visit and that he never had received so much benefit by the parish priest, although, said he, it cost me dear for what I had, and if I ever live to get over it, by the assistance of God, I shall have nothing to do with them more. But he said he should not live three days. And before the end of three days he expired. He desired if I were not gone that I would be at his funeral. On notice hereof about ten Friends went; and there were a great many people, among whom we had a good opportunity, and many weighty truths were opened to them in the love of God; and some of them were tender; and wept; and the most if not all, I think I may say, were solid and weighty. From Thomas Everden's we went to George Truit's, at whose house we had a meeting. This Friend and I went to an Indian town not far from his house, because I had a desire to see these people, having never seen any of them before. When we came to the town, they were kind to us, spoke well of Friends, and said they would not cheat them as others did.* From George Truit's in Maryland we went down to Virginia and in Accomack and Northampton counties had large meetings . . ." Then, in returning, Chalkley writes: "went by the seaside the nearest way to Philadelphia and afterwards I had a meeting at George Truit's brother's and on the First day [Sunday?] another near the Court House [at Dividing Creek on the Pocomoke River] and went to Thomas Everden's and so to Levin Denwood's and thence to Nanticoke River and visited Friends up the bay until I came to the river Choptank about which there are many Friends."

[14]*Thomas Story, Journal . . . [published] Newcastle Upon Tyne, 1747,* pp. 227-236, relates itinerary of Thomas Story during his visit to the Eastern Shore of Maryland and Virginia in September and October, 1699. Story visited Great Choptank Yearly Meeting, John Pitts at King's Creek, Widow Elizabeth Bury at Threadhaven [Tredhaven], James Riddel, the meeting at Tuckaho, William Trouth's [Troth's], Choptank River Meeting, William Stevenson, the Widow Stevenson, Widow Alice Kennerly's at Little Choptank, Thomas Hicks' near Chickinacomoco, a meeting appointed at Nanticoke River at Edward Fisher's. These places were in Talbot and Dorchester Counties. From Edward Fisher's place Thomas Story crossed the Nanticoke River, thus arriving in "Old Somerset" (the part that is now Wicomico County) and continuing his journey crossed the ferry on Wicomico [River or Creek] and arrived at Levin Denwood's on Monie Creek, thence to Pocomoke River ferry and on to Widow Johnson's at Muddy Creek in Accomack County, Virginia, and to her son John Johnson and Gerge Drewett [George Truitt, Trewett], of Mulberry Grove. From Accomack County, Virginia, Thomas Story returned to "Old Somerset" County in Maryland, his Journal reciting:

*This was the Askinimikonson Indian Town near the head of Pocomoke River, on the north side of the river, and was only a short distance from George Truit's [Truitt's] home place, "Mulberry Grove," which was on the south side near the headwaters of Pocomoke River. The sites of this Indian town and of George Truitt's home are not far distant from the present town of Snow Hill, Worcester County (formerly part of Somerset County).

"Meeting in Meeting House at Muddy Creek and to Mary Johnson's in evening and next morning 45 miles to George Trewett's [at Mulberry Grove near head waters of the Pocomoke River] where we staid until 1st of the Ninth Month [1st of November] 1699. Next day meeting at Nasawadocks* at house of one Walter Lane about 15 miles off whose wife was a Friend but himself not. Rode 15 miles more to our friend Thomas Evernden's at Annonessicks [Annemessex] where stayed 2 days and had some service in the family. On the 4th [9th Mo. 1699] went to Richard Waters'† about 4 miles over the creek [from Everndens?] and next day 1st of the week had a meeting there which was hard and dry in the main, though we were easy after it, and had some good times in the Friends House, he and his wife not having been long convinced were tender and innocent.

Neill, in *Terra Mariae, or Threads of Maryland Colonial History*, p. 143, says that Thomas Story, who was the Paul among the Friends of America, came from Philadelphia, teaching and preaching in the wilderness of Maryland. He visited in Virginia and then on the Western Shore of Maryland, attending the Yearly Meeting of Friends at West River, 27th 3 mo. 1699. Neill (*Ibid.*, p. 147) continues, "At a later period Story made a tour of the Eastern Shore with Edward Shippen and wife, Samuel Carpenter, Isaac Morris and Griffin Owen." Shippen was a distinguished Philadelphia Quaker and citizen (progenitor of the well-known family of that name) and his daughter, Anna, married Thomas Story. Carpenter was considered the wealthiest man in Philadelphia and was treasurer of the province of Pennsylvania. Morris was chief-justice of Pennsylvania. Owen was a physician, skilled in his profession, and much beloved by William Penn. The "Friends"—Story, Shippen, Carpenter, Morris and Owen—were on the Eastern Shore of Maryland about 1702-5.

[15]See note on location of Annemessex "Meeting House," under note 9 above. Somerset Court Records, Deed Liber O 8, p. 133, gives this item: Somerset Court, June 14, 1704, "To the Worp[ll] Justices of Som[r]sett County now in Court Sitting it is hereby Certifyed by Livin Denwood, Richard Waters and George Truitt on behalf of themselves and the Rest of the people Called quakers and humbly desire y[t] it may be entered upon the Records of the County that the house of Livin Denwood att Mony the house of Richard Waters in Annemessix and the house of George Trewetts upon Pocomoke may be appointed meeting houses for the people Called Quakers to worship god in pursuant to an act of Parliam[t] and the good Lawes of the province. The above petion in open Court was Read and allowed."

[16]See sketches of Horsey, Dixon, Price, Boston, Johnson, Coulbourne, in the section on "Founders," *ante,* Chapter VIII, and London, Appendix X.

[17]For sketch of James Jones see *ante,* p. 94, and p. 329.

*This Nasawadocks (also spelled Nasawaddox) was a neck of land on lower Pocomoke River in Somerset County and should not be confused with Nassawaddox in Northampton County, Virginia.

†For references to Richard Waters, and his wife, in connection with the Annemessex and Monie Meetings in Somerset County see *ante,* pp. 92 and 105.

[18]Fox's *Journal* says the boat "ran aground in a creek of Monaco River." This river we can identify as Manokin; but the creek we cannot identify, unless it is "Back Creek."

[19]This account of Fox's itinerary in Somerset County is from *The Journal of George Fox ... Seventh Edition ... In Two Volumes (edited by) Wilson Armistead ... London ... 1852*, Vol. II, p. 124. While we have used in our text the Somerset County itinerary of Fox as given in Wilson Armistead's edition of the *Journal* we wish to introduce here the Somerset account as given in *The Journal of George Fox, Edited from the MSS. by Norman Penney, F. S. A., with an introduction by T. Edmund Harvey, M.A. ... Cambridge: At the University Press: Philadelphia: The John C. Winston Co., 1911*; Vol. II, pp. 241-243:

"&un the 12th day of ye 12th moth [1672] wee pased by water [from the Cliffs in Calvert County] in the boate aboute 70 milles much of it on the night & wee Run her on grouen neare Manoca River in a Creeke wee being in a open boat & ye weather very bitter & coueld with hard frost that som had like to have lost the use of their hands they were soe frozen & benumbeed with cold & in ye morning when the tyde floated our bote wee got to land & made us a fire to warme us & then came to ouer bote agene & passed about 10 milles to a friendes houis & on ye 14th day wee had a very pressious meeting one of the Justices & a Justices wife was there & when the meeting was done I pased 4 milles to a Justices house by land in Anemessy that is neare ye heade of Anemessy River & un the 15th day the Judge of the County came to mee & was very loving & much satisfied with frinds order [& the did Disier ye same might bee spoken againe there] & on the 16th day wee had a large & pressious meeting at the Justices in his barne for the house would not houlld them & the people was much taken with truth & the Clarke of the Couenty & one that had beene a Justice & a Justice wife was there & an opposer but all was preserved quiete blesed bee the lord ye 17th day wee pased 8 milles to a captains house who is a Justices whose name is [William] Colleburne where wee hade service & on the 19th wee pased aboute 9 milles among frinds & on the 20th day wee had a very pressious & ag[l]orious meeting at the Justices house before mentioned & there was many people of account & the Judge of that Country & Captaine & hee y^t was the late high shirive & the head secretary at whose house the p[r]east used to preach & the was all much taken with the truth & a large meeting it was & ye lords power was much seene & there was 4 new England men masters of shipps and marchants: the truth spreeads blesed bee the lord, & on the 22^d day wee pased through the woods & boggs aboute 16 miles & wee headed anemesse River & wee headed amoroca River & went over it in a Cainoe & a man got over ouer horsses & wee came to manoke to frindly womans house & un the 24th day wee had a glorious meeting in a barne & the lords liveing presence was with us & among the people blesed bee his name for evermore & frinds had never ameting beefore in those partes, & on the 26th of ye 12th month wee passed aboute 9 milles over a grete River wicocomico to a frinds house called James Jones hee is a Justice [wee headed Ani River] & very bad & watrie swampes & marshey way, & on ye 27th of ye 12th month wee had a very glorious meeting at James Jones the Justice & it was large praysed bee the lord god & on the 28th of ye 12th mo: wee pased over ye water in aboate & carried ouer horsses in it & Road through the woods & swamps & Crecks tedious way aboute 24 miles to a Justices house & had a very lardge & prescious meeting theere & John Cartwrite wente with another frind to [Acomake in] virginia where there was Disiers after the truth & on ye 3th of ye 1 month wee had a pressious & a glorious metinge & the liveing presences of the lord was amongst us praised bee the lord & there was many people of account & som came fare to it & it was at the Justices houes as beefore & the Judge & the Captaine came to it & there was three Justices wifes & many other of account & a very large meetinge it was & after the meetinge was done wee pased 4 milles to a frinds houes, & there was a woman at Enemessy which had beene many yeares in trobell & wouelld sometimes sitt moping neare 2 month togeather & hardly speake nor minde any thing, so I was moved to goe to heare & tell her that Sallvation was come to heare house & did speake other wordes to here & for here & that hower Shee mended & passed up & downe with us to meetings & is well blessed bee the lord [& on the 5th of the first month wee had a heavenly & liveing meeting & ther was two Justices of the peace & there wifes & many others—blesed bee the lord god over all whose truth is over all & doth Rule] and now wee are Cleare wee waite for winde & went from anemesse on 7th of the 1 mo: & pased by water aboute 50 milles & came to hunger river to afrindly womans houes—in ouer passage the wether was very Rough & the giveing the saylers over the bote struck of my hat & cap & wee had like to have turned the boate over but at the laste wee got them gaine with much adoe . . ."

* * * *

This Norman Penney edition of *The Journal of George Fox*, as quoted above, while not differing in the substance of any statement of facts, with the Wilson Armistead edition of *The Journal*, which we have used in our account (see *ante*, pp. 96-97), yet makes several interesting addition in the way of dating certain "meetings," affording at least two other items and giving a statement which aids us in identifying the section to which Fox returned from James Jones' on Wicomico River, as certainly being Annemessex and the "Justice's house," at which he arrived (by the 24-mile route from Jones' house), as being George Johnson's house at the head of Annemessex River (see for further comment *post* note 27).

It is unnecessary to comment on the additional items in Penney's edition of the *Journal* which date certain "meetings" referred to in the Wilson Armistead edition of the *Journal*. The reader may make the comparison of the two editions.

The "new matter" afforded by the Penney edition of the *Journal*, however, calls for comment.

The *first* additional item of interest which we find in the Penney edition of the *Journal* is in the statement about the "meeting" held on the 16th day 12 mo [February 16, 1672/] "at the Justice's in his barne." The item is: "*& the Clarke*

of the Couenty & one that had been a Justice & a Justice wife was there . . ."
We are unable to identify the *"one that had been a justice & a Justice wife"*; but we can certainly identify *"the Clarke of the Couenty"* of Somerset at this date. He was Edmund Beauchamp, who lived on the plantation called "Contention," which was located at the head of Annemessex River and adjoining George Johnson and Robert Catlin. Edmund Beauchamp married Sarah Dixon, daughter of Ambrose Dixon, of "Dixon's Choice," on Annemessex River, who was one of the founders of the settlement; an ardent Quaker, and at whose house the first Quaker Meetings in the settlement were held and on whose land the first Quaker meeting house in Somerset was erected (see *ante,* pp. 333 and 302, for sketches of Edmund Beauchamp and Ambrose Dixon). Edmund Beauchamp evidently remained a Church of England man (though doubtless interested in Fox and his teachings). Beauchamp's wife, Sarah, and three of their children were baptized in 1671, 1674 and 1677, respectively (see *ante,* p. 132). Certainly the Beauchamps did not become Quakers.

The *second* additional item given in the Penney edition of the *Journal* is that on 20th day 12 mo: [February 20, 1672/3] at the meeting at the same justice's [i. e. George Johnson's] *"there was many people of account & the Judge of that Countrey & Captaine & hee y^t was the late high shirive & the head secretary at whose house the p[r]east used to preach . . ."* Of course, "the Judge of that Countrey" was William Stevens, of "Rehoboth" on Pocomoke River (see *post* note 22). The "Captaine" was William Coulbourne, at whose house Fox had visited and held a meeting. *"Hee y^t was the late high shirive"* was either Randall Revell, who was high sheriff of Somerset in 1669 and 1670, or Captain Thomas Walker, who was high sheriff 1671-2. *"The head secretary at whose house the p[r]east used to preach"* must have been Edmund Beauchamp, whom we have identified as *"the Clarke of the Couenty"* to whom Fox referred as being present at the "meeting" on 16th day 12 mo. [February 16, 1672/3]. Why Fox should use different terms in referring to the same official we do not know, yet the fact cannot be questioned that the terms of clerk of a county and "head secretary" of a county are analogous. The reference made by Fox to the fact that *"the p[r]east [priest] used to preach"* at the house of this "head secretary" of Somerset County throws light upon the problematical question, the holding of religious services by a minister of the Church of England in Somerset County before the time that there was such a minister *resident* in the county. We have fully discussed the probability that the Reverend Thomas Teackle and the Reverend Henry Parkes, both of Northampton and Accomack Counties in Virginia, may have come into Somerset on occasions to minister (see *ante,* pp. 116 and 133 for "tradition" of Teackle's ministering in Somerset County; and p. 138 for Parkes being in Somerset for a marriage in 1678). From Fox's statement that *"the p[r]east used to preach"* at *the head secretary's house,* it is evident that prior to February, 1672/3, Edmund Beauchamp's house was a place at which services were (at least occasionally) held by a minister of the Church of England; for such a clergyman Fox would designate *"the preast."* This circumstantial evidence also lends weight to our "belief" (fully set forth, *ante,* page 132-3) that Mrs. Sarah Beauchamp and her three children who were recorded as having been baptized in 1671, 1674 and 1677, respectively, were baptized by a minister of the Church of England, and our "belief" that the minister who baptized them may have been the Reverend Thomas Teackle, of Accomack County, Virginia.

The *third* additional item given in the Penney edition of the *Journal* helps considerably in positively identifying the place of the last "meeting" held by Fox in Somerset County. The Wilson Armistead edition of the *Journal* quoted by us, *ante,* p. 96, says that Fox on leaving James Jones' on Wicomico River "traveled about twenty-four miles through woods and troublesome swamps and came to another justice's house where we had a very large meeting . . . This was on the 3d of 1st. [March 3] 1672/3 and on the 5th we had another living heavenly meeting . . . Being now cleare of these parts we left Anemessy on the 7th [March 7, 1672/3] . . ." The Penney edition of the *Journal* gives the record that from James Jones, on the 28th 12 mo [February 28, 1672/3] Fox crossed the water [Wicomico River] "and Road through the woods & swamps & creeks . . . aboute 24 milles to a Justice's house and had a very large & precious meeting there . . . & on ye 3th of ye 1st month [March 3, 1672/3] wee had a pressious & glorious meeting . . . & it was at the Justices houes as beefore . . . & after the meeting was done wee pased 4 milles to a frinds houes . . . [& on the 5th of the first month [March 5, 1672/3] wee had a heavenly & liveing meeting . . . and now we are cleare we waite for wind & went from anemesse on 7th of the 1st month [March 7, 1672/3] . . ." The context shows that Fox returned by a roundabout way from James Jones on Wicomico River to Annemessex, and his use of the words "& it was at the Justices houes as before," in regard to the "meeting" on "3th of the 1st month," seems to indicate that he was again at the house of George Johnson in Annemessex, where he had held meetings previously (see *post,* note 27).

[20]George Fox must use the term "Friend" as signifying a member of the Society of Friends. We cannot identify the friend here referred to by Fox. He may have been Ambrose Dixon, whose home was just about four miles southwest of George Johnson's. See next note for Johnson.

[21]This "Friend," residing at the head of Annemessex River (called Anamessy by Fox), was George Johnson, a distinguished Quaker and an official of Somerset County. Johnson's home was on the south side of the river, near the headwaters thereof, on lands called "Straights" and "Johnsons" (adjoining tracts), which were later purchased from Johnson's heirs by Robert King and included in the now celebrated "Kingston Hall" property. These lands were left by Robert King to his grandson, Thomas King (see *ante,* p. 432). The site of George Johnson's home may today be located about three-quarters of a mile north of the present village of Kingston in Somerset County. See sketch of George Johnson, *ante,* p. 316. George Johnson was at the time (February 1672/3) a justice of the court.

[22]The "judge" of the county here referred to was certainly the worthy William Stevens of "Rehoboth." Stevens appears as "presiding magistrate" of the

courts, sitting from March 12, 1671/2, to March 11, 1672/3 (Somerset Court, Judicials, Liber AZ, 1671-5, records of court sessions for period named). The justice referred to by Fox was evidently George Johnson, for in Penney's edition of the *Journal of George Fox* (see *ante,* note 19), the passage reads Fox "pased 4 miles to a Justice's house . . . neare ye head of Annemessy River . . . and on the 16th day wee had a large & pressious meeting at the Justices in his barne for the house would not houlld them . . ." (see *ante,* note 21).

On returning to England after his visit to the American colonies, George Fox sent to certain persons of importance whom he had met there copies of the works of the late Edward Burroughs, a celebrated Quaker. The sending of these books was entrusted by Fox to Friends in Bristol, England, who forwarded them accompanied by a message. On Fox's list of persons to whom these books were to be sent we find (among others) the names of *"Judge Stephens at Annemessy"* and *"Justices Johnson and Coleman* [sic Coulbourne] *at Annemessy"* and *"Lt.-Col. Waters in Accomack"* (Bowden, *History of the Society of Friends,* Vol. I p,. 358, and quoted by Neill, *Founders of Maryland,* p. 146). These parties named were William Stevens, of "Rehoboth," Somerset County, George Johnson and Capt. William Coulbourne, justices of the peace in Somerset. *"Lt.-Col. Waters in Accomack"* was William Waters, a prominent official in Northampton County, Virginia, and father of Richard Waters, of "Waters River," in Somerset, a faithful member of Annemessex Friends' Meeting (see *ante,* p. 92).

[23]This was William Coulbourne, a marked sympathizer with the Quakers, and one of the most distinguished officials of Somerset. Coulbourne's home was on south side of the Annemessex River, and south of Coulbourne's Creek.

[24]Fox evidently went around the headwaters of Annemessex River, Back Creek, King's Creek, and Manokin River. We are unable to identify "Amoroka River," unless it be a misspelling of Manokin. His reference, *"and came to Manoake,"* is evidently to *Manokin Hundred.* The exact location in Manokin Hundred to which Fox refers we cannot now determine, though probably in that portion north of Manokin River.

[25]Fox refers to the meeting of "24th 12th mo" (February 24, 1672/3) at the "friendly woman's house" at Manokin, as the first meeting which "Friends" in this section of the county had held for them. His use of the term "Friends" would indicate that there were now Quakers in this section where he held this meeting. Levin Denwood had settled at the head of Great Monie (south side) about 1671; the Covingtons were just across that creek. Denwood and Covington later became the leading Quakers in this section of Somerset.

[26]James Jones' home was on the northwest side of Wicomico River (about a mile above the present town of Whitehaven) and just opposite to the mouth of the present Wicomico Creek. Here he lived from 1664 until his death in 1677.

[27]It is not clear what direction Fox took after crossing Wicomico River from James Jones' house, and taking horse and traveling 24 miles "through woods and troublesome swamps and came to another justices house." Who this "jus-

tice" was we cannot now positively make out. It seems certain, however, that Fox, after leaving James Jones' and recrossing Wicomico River again traveled in the direction of Annemessex. The presence at a meeting of the "woman that lived at Annamessy," and the later reference, "being now clear of these parts we left Anamessy on the 7th" [i. e. 7th 1st mo. 1672/3: March 7, 1672/3] certainly indicate that Fox had returned to points in Annemessex Hundred after his visit to James Jones' home. The account of these last meetings as given in Penney's edition of the *Journal of George Fox* seem to indicate that this "justice's house" in Annemessex was the house of George Johnson (see *ante* under note 19).

[28]Fox leaving Annemessex in Somerset County, now went up the Bay to Dorchester County. Hungar's River is on southwest coast of Dorchester County and empties into Hooper's Straights. Honga River [as the spelling now is] separates Hooper's Island from the mainland of Dorchester County.

[29]George Fox in his *Journal,* (Norman Penney edition, *The Journal of George Fox* . . . Vol. II, p. 243), writes: "Now we are Cleare wee waite for winde & went from anemesse [Annemessex] on 7th of the 1 mo: [March 7, 1672/3] & *pased by water aboute 50 milles & came to hunger* [Hungar, Honga] *river to a friendly womans house* . . ." Here is definite and positive statement which proves that George Fox left Annemessex in Somerset County, March 7, 1672/3, and went up Chesapeake Bay by boat to Honga [as it is now spelled] River in *Dorchester County.* From this point in the *Journal,* March 7, 1672/3, to April 8, 1673 ("8th of ye 2 mo:"), the record of events proves that he was in *Dorchester, Talbot and Kent Counties.* (*Ibid.,* Vol. II, pp. 243-245). We call particular attention to this fact because of a correction which we wish to make of an erroneous statement which has been perpetuated by three writers on early events in Somerset County's history.

Doctor L. P. Bowen, *Days of Makemie (1885),* p. 58, and followed by Reverend J. S. Howk, *Rehoboth by the River (1897),* p. 6, and H. P. Ford, Esq., *History of Manokin Presbyterian Church (1910),* p. 93, definitely assign a certain meeting which Fox states that he held, March 23, 1672/3 (23th 1 mo.), at the house of one "Wm. Stephens" to the home of William Stevens at "Rehoboth" in Somerset County, while the context of Fox's *Journal* proves that this meeting (i. e. of March 23, 1672/3, or 23^{d} 1 mo 1673) was held at the house of one William *Stephens* (as Fox spells the name) in, (we believe), Talbot County. This William Stephens (or Stevens, as the name is also spelled) lived on a plantation on Dividing Creek, Talbot County, and was prominent in the affairs of that county and an ardent Quaker. He was the son of a certain William Stephens (or Stevens), of Dorchester County, who lived on a plantation on the south side of Great Choptank River in Dorchester, about the neighborhood of Horn's Point, and who was a distinguished official in Dorchester and a Quaker. William Stephens (or Stevens), of Talbot County, lived almost directly across Great Choptank River from the plantation of his father, William Stephens (or Stevens), in Dorchester. A digest of Fox's *Journal,* March 23, 1672/3, to April 8, 1673, shows: March 23, 1672/3 (i. e. 7th 1 mo) left Annemessex and arrived in Honga River, Dorchester County, at a friendly woman's house; March 10th (i. e. 10th 1 mo.) meeting; March 14th (i. e. 14th 1 mo.) went by water 4 miles to head of Little Choptank to Dr. Winsmore's and *from there went by land 2 miles to one William Stephens* [this was William Stephens, or Stevens, on south side the Great Choptank in Dorchester County] and *"on the 16th day [March 16, 1672/3] we pased by water aboute 4 milles to a meeting which was without doores . . . & on the 18th day of the 1 month [March 18, 1672/3] we passed 4 milles by water to a frind's house Wm. Stephens* [this was the son, William Stephens, or Stevens, on Dividing Creek, Talbot County] where frinds mete that hade bee[ne] abrode & we went a mille or two & vissited som frinds & the 23th day [i. e. March 23, 1672/3] we had a glorious meeting," at which were present the judge and his wife, three other Justices, the High Sheriff and his wife and the Indian Emperor, an Indian King and "there speaker" [i. e. their spokesman]; March 24, 1672/3 (i. e. "24th of the first mo:") "wee went by water 10 milles to the Indian towne wheare the Emperour dwells." [This Indian town was in Dorchester County; Fox had recrossed the Great Choptank River from Talbot into Dorchester County.] Fox held a great meeting at this Indian town. March 25, 1673 (i. e. 25th 1 mo:), Fox went 5 miles by land and rowed across "fusher creake" [i. e. Fishing Creek, Dorchester County, which empties into Little Choptank River]; March 26, 1673 (i. e. 26th 1 mo), Fox went back 5 miles through the woods; March 27, 1673 (i. e. 27th 1 mo), "wee had a blessed meetinge & large at William Stephens at grete choptanck [Great Choptank] . . . & it was a generall monthly meeting . . . & when the meting was done we went by water 4 milles [i. e. he crossed the Great Choptank River from William Stephens near Horn Point in Dorchester to the Talbot County side of the river] & one by land; March 28, 1673 (i. e. 28th 1 mo), "wee pased about by land to trade haven creecke [Tred Avon Creek] aboute 14 milles and held a large meeting on March 30th [this site was doubtless about where the Friends' Meeting House now stands just outside Easton, Talbot County, Maryland]. From here Fox crossed Miles River and Wye River thence back to Tred Haven River and to Reconow Creek and on April 4, 1673, he went 14 miles by water and 2 miles by land to Kent Island, where he held several large meetings, and on April 8, 1673, Fox crossed the Chesapeake Bay from Kent Island "to the western shore."

We have gone into this matter at length and in detail in order to try and authoritatively correct the erroneous statement (originally made by Bowen, *Days of Makemie,* p. 58, and followed by Howk, *Rehoboth by the River,* p. 6, and Ford, *History of Manokin Presbyterian Church,* p. 93) that Fox held his great meeting of March 23, 1672/3, at the home of William Stevens, of Rehoboth, Somerset County, and later visited and preached to the Indians at Askiminiconson Indian Town at the head of the Pocomoke River. The *facts* are that Fox held his meeting, March 23, 1672/3, at William Stephens (or Stevens) in Talbot County, on Dividing Creek, and from there went by water (the Great Choptank River) back across to Dorchester County, and on March 24, 1672/3, held the great meeting at the Indian Town, in Dorchester, which appears by Herrman's

Map of Maryland and Virginia (1673) as being in the fork made by the Little Choptank River and Fishing Creek (?); and from here going 5 miles he crossed Fishing Creek.

For an account of the family of William Stevens (or Stephens), of Dorchester County, and that of his son, William Stevens, of Talbot County, see Tilghman, *History of Talbot County*, Vol. I, p. 622, *et seq.*, and Jones, *History of Dorchester County*. In passing, we cannot but comment on the singular omission from Jones, *History of Dorchester County*, of any reference to the great George Fox's sojourn in that county.

[80] Wise, *Accawmacke*, p. 156; and for notes on Covington, Denwood and Woolford families see Appendix X.

[81] Jones, *The Quakers in the American Colonies*, p. 305, and *Commemorative Exercises of the 200th Anniversary of Friends' Meeting House at Third Haven*.

[82] Morris, *The Early Friends (or Quakers) in Maryland*, p. 26-7.

[83] Richardson, *Sidelights on Maryland History*, Vol. II, pp. 311-12.

[84] *Journal of Thomas Chalkley*, pp. 28-30; *Journal of Thomas Story*, p. 233. For excerpts from Chalkley and Story *Journals*, relative to their visits to Somerset County, see above, under notes 13 and 14.

[85] Neill, *Terra Mariæ*, p. 154, says that William Edmundson, on a second tour in America, "visited the lower counties of the Eastern Shore going from Choptank to Nanticoke crossing the Vienna ferry to Mulberry Grove and from thence to the Widow Gale's at Monay [Monie]. Then he journeyed to Annamessex and Virginia."

[86] The facts given in regard to Richard Stevens (1641-1713) are from the Somerset Court Records, as follows: Liber AZ, 1671-5 (Judicials), p. 415, deposition of Stevens (then aged about 33 years), made November 11, 1674, in which he says: "I being at the house of Mr. Winder soon after I came out of England," etc., etc. Deed Liber O 1 (back of volume), p. 7, a cattle mark is recorded, July, 1666, for "Richard Stevens of Wiccocomoco." Deed Liber O 2, p. 2, deed of Daniel Haste to Richard Stevens, and Deed Liber O 6, p. 309, deed of Richard Stevens and Abigail, his wife, to Richard Hull. See also deeds of the Stevenses to other parties in Deed Liber O 6, p. 778; Deed Liber O 7, p. 485; Deed Liber O 11, p. 306, and Deed Liber O 14, p. 233. That Richard Stevens married, first, Frances (surname unknown), see Liber IKL, pp. 241 and 242. For the marriage of John Kibble to Abigail Horsey see Liber IKL, p. 142. The evidence that Abigail (Horsey) Kibble married (as his second wife) Richard Stevens, see Deed Liber O7 (back), p. 58, deed of gift, October 20, 1676, Abigail Kibble, widow, to her children, William Kibble (under 16 years old) and Sarah Kibble (under 14 years old) for cattle and a mare which are "to run in a stock amongst Richard Stevens of this county of Somersett," and if the said animals "increase to many it shall be at ye pleasure of myself and Richard Stevens afterwards to convert them to the use and benefitt of my said children as the said Richard Stevens shall thinke convenient without any let or molestation of mee ye said Abigail Kibble," etc., etc. We then find Richard Stevens with wife, Abigail. The inference is clear that the widow, Abigail Kibble, married Richard Stevens.

In Somerset Court, Liber A, Views of Land Commissioners, p. 84, in a survey for determining the boundaries of "Bennett's Adventure," March, 1719/20, the question arose as to the boundary line of the land of Richard Stevens, deceased, called "Conquest," and William Kibble gave evidence in relation to the first bounder of "Stevens' Conquest" as follows: "that he heard *his father Richard Stevens say,*" etc., etc. Richard Stevens was stepfather to Kibble. The will of Richard Stevens (not dated; probated November 3, 1713) containing the item as given in the text may be found in Somerset Registry of Wills, Liber EB 9, pp. 49-50.

[87] Somerset Court, Deed Liber O 8, p. 133, in record of Court Proceedings, June 14, 1709. See this record given above in full, under note 15.

[88] Somerset Court, Liber GH (Judicials), 1711, p. 107.

[89] Somerset Court, Deed Liber O 10, p. 803, for deed of Daniel Jones to Levin Denwood. The acre of land on which the Monie Quaker Meeting House and Burying Ground were situated was taken out of a 70-acre tract sold March 6, 1709 (1709/10), by Emanuel Husk to Daniel Jones (Husk's name is also written Hurst and Hust), which 70-acre tract was conveyed to Emanuel Hust by his father, John Hust, the said John Hust having bought this land by deed, August 18, 1686, from Thomas Cox. The 70-acre tract was out of a larger tract called "Cox's Choice," granted Thomas Cox by patent. This 70-acre tract (as well as the larger one) is described as on "south side Wicomico River in the woods." When Daniel Jones conveyed the one acre to Levin Denwood for the meeting house and burying ground, it is described as follows: "beginning at a cedar post marked on each of ye four sides with four notches standing in an old field where John Hurst did formerly live and from thence running east sixteen poles thence with a line drawn south ten poles thence with a line drawn west sixteen poles thence with a line drawn north ten poles to ye first bounder." The exact date at which this meeting house disappeared we do not know, but in 1746 we pick up two references to the site. Thomas Holbrook, Junior, was proving the boundaries of his land called "Privilege" which depended on the first bounds of a tract called "Coxe's Choice," then in possession of Daniel Jones. At that time Thomas Holbrook, Senior, in an affidavit about a boundary marker of "Coxes Choice," refers to *"a cedar post which post was set up on account of an Ancient Quaker Meeting house about thirty strides to the westward of the afsd post."* At the same time Thomas Covington, in an affidavit, says that "the first bounder of the afsd Coxes Choice stood in a low swamp *near where the Quaker meeting house did stand."* As nearly as we have been able to locate this old "meeting house and burying ground" site today, is to place it in the neighborhood of a mile to a mile and a half north of the Somerset County Alms House (the old Waggaman mansion), and about half way between Great Monie Creek and Wicomico Creek. (See Somerset Court, Deed Liber O 6, p. 807, Cox to Hust; Deed Liber O 8, p. 105, Hust to Hust; Deed Liber O 10, p. 523, Hust to Jones; Deed Liber O 10, p. 803, Jones to Denwood. Somerset Court, Judicials, 1744-1747, p. 205-206, depositions of Thomas Holbrook, Senior, and Thomas Covington, Senior, November Court, 1746).

⁴⁰Somerset Registry of Wills, Liber EB 9, pp. 103-4, will of Levin Denwood.

⁴¹See under Appendix X for notes on Jenkin Price. He was a celebrated Indian trader of the early days of both Accomack County, Virginia, and Somerset County, Maryland. His home was on the north side of Pocomoke River (not far above the site of Snow Hill Town) and in close proximity to the Aquintica Indian Town of Askiminiconson.

⁴²For John Goddin's exclusion from a seat in the Lower House of Assembly in 1699 see *ante,* p. 360. For note on Goddin and his home see Appendix X, under "Johnson, George," whose daughter, Katherine, married John Goddin.

⁴³Somerset Court, Liber DT, No. 7, pp. 41-3, deed, July, 1670, from Thomas Walker to Walter Powell for the three tracts of land, "Greenfield," "Middle," and "Exchange"; see wills of Walter and William Powell in *Maryland Calendar of Wills,* Vol. II, p. 102, and Vol. IV, p. 76. Walter Powell was evidently not a Quaker when he came into Somerset County to reside in 1669 or 1670. We find that John Powell, son of Walter and Margaret Powell, was born at Pocomoke [Pocomoke Hundred], September 27, 1674, *"and baptized ye 25 day of October next following"* (Somerset Court, Liber IKL, p. 209), and that Elizabeth Powell (who was daughter of Walter Powell) was married December 22, 1683, to Hugh Tingle, *"by William Traile, minister"* (*Ibid.*). William Traile was a Presbyterian minister. Now we know that Quakers did not submit their children to "baptism," nor were they married by ordained ministers. Evidently Walter Powell and his household became "convinced" later than 1674, when his infant son, John, was baptized. The date of his "conviction" and becoming a "Friend" is not known. That his daughter, Elizabeth, was married to Hugh Tingle by a Presbyterian minister is not evidence that Walter Powell may not have become a "Friend" before that date. Parents who are "Friends" cannot be held accountable for the acts of their children any more than parents who are "non-Friends." Ladies in marrying—even gentle Quaker ladies—sometimes make choice "out of meeting"!

⁴⁴Somerset Court, Liber BWZ, 1690-2, p. 27, deed July 17, 1689, Elizabeth Stevens, widow, of Somerset County, to George Trewett, of same, planter. The name is spelled in the deed variously as Trewett, Truit and Truitt.

⁴⁵Morris, *The Early Friends (or Quakers) in Maryland* . . . p. 26-7, referring to the then Weekly Meetings of Friends in Somerset County, in 1697, as Annemessex, Monie and Pocotynorton.

⁴⁶*Journal of Thomas Chalkley,* pp. 28-30. See above, under note 13. Chalkley's reference to the Indian Town, near George Truit's house, is to the town of the Askiminiconson Indians, which was on the north side of Pocomoke River, occupying lands along and back from the river and nearly opposite the town of Snow Hill.

⁴⁷*Journal of Thomas Story.* See above, note 14.

⁴⁸Somerset Court, Deed Liber O 8, p. 133, in record of court proceedings, June 14, 1704. See above for this record given in full, under note 15. The location of George Truitt's house may today be found on a tract of land about four and

a half miles northeast of the town of Snow Hill in Worcester County (formerly Somerset), on the road from that town to Berlin.

[49] The will of George Truitt (dated August 15, 1720; probated November 21, 1721, in Worcester County, Registry of Wills, Liber MH, No. 3, pp. 212-214. See also for abstract *Maryland Calendar of Wills*, Vol. V, p. 80-1.

[50] Neill, *Terra Mariæ*, p. 147, *et seq.*; Bowen, *Days of Makemie*, p. 509. Bowen refers to this Quaker burying ground as "the only monument of the sect in those counties where George Fox and Story and Keith and Chalkley once preached." Doctor Bowen is doubtless here confusing the great Keith with a "lesser light," the Reverend Robert Keith, who was at one time rector of Coventry Parish, Somerset. There is no evidence that the celebrated George Keith (once a Quaker, and later a missionary of the Society for the Propagation of the Gospel) ever came to Somerset County. Doctor Bowen is in error also in saying that this Quaker Burying Ground is "the only monument of the sect in those counties where George Fox and Story . . . and Chalkley once preached." One has but to recall the wonderfully beautiful old Quaker Meeting House of Tredhaven (also called Third Haven), near Easton, in Talbot County, on the upper Eastern Shore of Maryland. This is only one instance of the presence of such a remaining memorial; and must suffice; though doubtless others on the "upper Shore" might be named. We call attention also to the fact that the sites of the Annemessex and Monie Meeting Houses and burying grounds have been located in this present work (see above, under notes 9 and 39).

In a conversation with Doctor Jones (Register of Wills for Worcester County), in 1932, he "located" the old Quaker burying ground for this present writer, whose privilege it has been to visit the sacred spot. This burying ground is on the old "Mulberry" tract, which was once George Truitt's, and may be found on the road from Snow Hill to Berlin, about four and a half miles northeast of Snow Hill. This Truitt place and Quaker burying ground were also located for me by Edward P. Davis, Esq., of Snow Hill, now (1932) in his 85th year of age. Mr. Davis is a descendant of Affradozi Johnson.

[51(a)] Another man whom we can identify as a member of Bogerternorton Meeting was Affradozi Johnson, who came to Somerset County, about 1710, evidently from Accomack County, Virginia. He was doubtless related to George Johnson, of Annemessex, and to George Johnson, of Muddy Creek, in Accomack. It may be that Affradozi Johnson was of the New England branch of this family. George Johnson, of Annemessex, had two brothers who settled in New England (see sketch of George Johnson, under "Founders"). Affradozi Johnson signed the inventory of George Truitt, deceased, of Somerset County, on January 17, 1721/2, as "*Approved by me as one of ye nearest of kin. Affradozi Johnson.*" (Worcester Registry of Wills, Liber MH 3, pp. 142-3). How Johnson was related to Truitt has not been discovered. Affradozi Johnson, calling himself of Somerset County, purchased in July, 1710, from John Goddin, 200 acres of the tract "Rochester," on south side Pocomoke River, near headwaters (Somerset Court, Deed Liber O 10, p. 632). On this land Johnson made his home, bequeathing the same, at his death, to his son, George Johnson. Affradozi Johnson married Sarah, daughter of Thomas Purnell, and had issue: (1) George Johnson; (2) Thomas Johnson; (3) Samuel Johnson; (4) Sarah Johnson; (5) Purnell Johnson. (Somerset Court, Deed Liber O 18, p. 214, deed of Affradozi Johnson and Sarah, his wife, daughter of Thomas Purnell, to their son, Purnell Johnson, in 1730; Worcester Registry of Wills, Liber JW 2, pp. 18-19, will of Affradozi Johnson, dated May 3, 1743; probated October 5, 1744, names children as above, and in addition "my grandson Samuel Dennis"). Johnson's home place may be located today about five miles northeast of Snow Hill, Worcester County. In his day his plantation joined those of John Goddin and George Truitt. Affradozi Johnson was for some years a prominent member of the Bogeternorton Meeting of Friends, and his body is doubtless buried with those of the Powells, Goddins, Truitts, in the old Quaker burying ground in that vicinity.

Certainly as late as 1763 we find reference to Isaac Morris, a Quaker, as living in the vicinity of the town of Snow Hill, Worcester (formerly Somerset) County. Isaac Morris was from the Anthony Morris family of Pennsylvania and was connected, in some way (now unknown) with the Hough family of Worcester County. (Authority for this statement is William B. Marye, Esqr., of Baltimore). A branch of the Fooks family which came to Somerset (later Worcester) County, from Accomack County, Virginia, was apparently also of Quaker connection, or affiliation.

51(b) We wish to introduce here for future students of religious life in Somerset in colonial days the following items relative to the Baptist Church. Somerset Court, Judicials, 1734-1736, pp. 62-3, August Court, 1735: "The Reverend Paul Palmer a dissenting Baptist minister came here into Court in his proper person & prays that he may be admitted to preach and teach the Severall Congregations that Shall Come to hear him in the County of Somerset to wit at Michael Robinsons, Robert Gauts, Geo: Trewitts, Henry Jermans, Capt John Walker's and at William Burton's which is granted him he Complying with the act of parliament in such Case made and provided &c whereupon the said Paul Palmer took & Subscribed the oath of fidelity as by the said act of Parliament is directed and Subscribed to the articles of religion Except what part of the said Articles is Excepted against in favour of Such dissenting Ministers by said act and Likewise took the severall oaths to the Government as by act of Assembly is directed with the test and Subscribed the Same Oath of abjuration and Declaration as is by the afsd act of Assembly required &c. Somerset Court, Judicials, 1738-1740, p. 266, Somerset Court, March, 1739/40: "Somerset County the first day of May 1740 Worthy Sir I hope you remember that when I was Qualified at your Court that I made mention of the following places to be recorded for our meetings (to witt) William Burtons at Indian River* and Michael Robinsons, Robert Golts, George Truets, Henry Garmans (Jarman's) at Snow Hill and Capt John Walkers on Swann Gutt* and further I Humbly pray that on (one)

---

*The Indian River, which in 1735 was counted as in Somerset (after 1742 Worcester) County, was at the final determination of the Maryland-Delaware boundary line, cut off into Sussex County, Delaware.

*This "Swann Gutt" may be identified in the present day "Swan Gut," immediately below Welbourne Post Office in the extreme southeastern section of Worcester County, Maryland, and flowing across the Maryland-Virginia boundary line.

half acre of land on the Land of Luke Watson adjoining on the healing Spring on the west side of Swann Gutt† and the House of James Houston may be recorded for our Assembly of Worship to God and your Humble S^r (servant) and he your assured friend as he hopes shall learn to be thankfull to God and yourself now and at all times—Paul Palmer—to Mr Thomas Howard [Haward, Hayward] at his Office in Somerset County in Maryland These—." These items were given to Clayton Torrence by the late Stratton Nottingham, Esquire, who, knowing his interest in religious history in Somerset, picked them up in his reading of Somerset Judicials.

51(c) We would like to enter here a note of the fact that in a careful reading and study of the Somerset Court Records, 1665-1700, we did not discover a single item by which a single Roman Catholic could be identified as living in Somerset County between those dates. It may be that one "Anthony Machaee, Portugez [Portuguese] of the Island of Tersara" (who also appears as "Anthony Machare, alias Asher"), who was an indenture servant finally assigned to Miles Gray, of Somerset County, was a Roman Catholic. It is nowhere stated that he was such in religion; but his "nationality" would lead one to think that he may have been a Roman Catholic. Machaee was indentured to Arthur Mason, of Boston, November 20, 1685, to serve 8 years, and assigned by Mason to Joseph Thaxter, of Boston, and by the said Thaxter to Miles Gray, of Somerset County, Maryland; and the question of the "indentures" came up in Somerset Court in 1692 (Somerset Court, Judicials, Liber 1692-3, pp. 110 and 112). Bowen, *Days of Makemie,* p. 181, refers to Walter *Lowe,* who appears in the Somerset Court Records in 1690 as having been called a "Papist" by Colonel Francis Jenckins. We investigated this "charge" and found that the man designated as a "Papist" by Colonel Jenckins was not named *Lowe,* but was one *Walter Lane,* who had made rather violent charges against Colonel Jenckins as a member of the court. Colonel Jenckins, resenting the matter, referred to Lane as an "Irish Papist." However, the irate, and outraged official's "charge" proves nothing as we find Walter Lane considerably intermixed with the Quakers (see *ante,* p. 91). The case of Jenckins against Lane is given in Somerset Court, Judicials, Liber EFG, September, 1689-November, 1690, p. 115.

Only a few years after the beginning of the 18th century we find, however, that an official report, 1708, credits Somerset County with 81 Roman Catholics. Only the number of Catholics is given; no names being recorded. (See Thomas, *Chronicles of Colonial Maryland,* p. 172; footnote, quoting London Public Record Office, Maryland, BT, No. 4, H, p. 79, and Scharf, *Maryland,* Vol. I, p. 370). If it be a correct statement that in 1708 there were 81 Roman Catholics in Somerset County, we believe there certainly must have been some of them there prior to the year 1700. However, as much as we should like to have identified some Catholics among the Somerset population prior to the year 1700, we have not been able to do so.

†This reference to "one half acre of land" on Luke Watson's place looks very much as though these early Somerset Baptist's contemplated the erection of a "meeting house" at this place for their congregation.

⁵¹⁽ᵈ⁾It is to be hoped that some day there will appear a historian who will charge himself with the interesting undertaking of a history of the Methodist Church in Somerset County. Of course, Methodism, from its late appearance, is precluded from our study. Richardson, *Side Lights on Maryland History*, Vol. II, p. 435, writes that the first Methodist meeting in Somerset County was held in the home of Wilson Rider on Quantico Creek. Truett, *Historic Salisbury, Maryland*, pp. 30-34, has many interesting items about Methodism in Salisbury. Wallace's *The Parson of the Islands, A Biography of the Rev. Joshua Thomas* (published, Philadelphia, 1861) gives completely the life of that great minister of the Methodist Church in vivid detail. Wilson Rider's home on Quantico Creek was in Somerset County up to 1867, when Wicomico County was erected from the northern portion of Somerset. Salisbury is the county seat of Wicomico County.

⁵²Morris, *The Early Friends (or Quakers) in Maryland*, pp. 26-27. This pamphlet, by J. Saurin Morris, gives Doctor Ethan Allen's statement. For the report of the Sheriff of Somerset, 1697, as to Quakers in Somerset: *"none as I know particularly"*; see Perry *Papers Relating to the History of the Church in Maryland, 1694-1775*, p. 22. Various writers on the subject of Maryland history have quoted this document and some have made comment thereon.

2. Voice of the People

¹The records of Elizabeth Lum's birth and baptism by Mr. George Moonerow are given in Somerset Court, Liber IKL, p. 150. No other references has been found to the name of *George Moonerow*. It has been suggested that *Moonerow* is a corruption of Monroe (oftentimes spelled *Munroe* in old records). The will of Robert Cager, of St. Mary's County, Maryland, dated August 10, 1667, probated September 5, 1667, leaves property to his son, Robert Cager, Junior (to be at age at 21 years old), and daughter, Dorothy, wife of George *Monnroe* (*Maryland Calendar of Wills*, Vol. I, p. 41). Then one *"Geo: Monrow"* witnessed the will of Richard Collett in January, 1667/8 (*Ibid.*, p. 43). The Reverend G. M. Brydon, D.D., Historiographer of the Diocese of Virginia, to whom we appealed for assistance in regard to solving the problem of *George Moonerow* "the baptizer," writes that he has never come across his name. There was a John *Munro,* Senior, a minister of the Church of England, resident in Virginia *circa* 1650 (at Pamonkie [Stratton-Major Parish?] in old York County); and John Monro, Junior (son of John Munro, Senior), who was minister of Hungar's Parish, Northampton County, Virginia, in 1692 (Goodwin, *The Colonial Church in Virginia*, p. 294, and *William and Mary Quarterly, Second Series*, Vol. XIII, pp. 231 and 233).

²See *ante*, pp. 133 and 135 for reference to, and comment on, the "tradition" that Reverend Thomas Teackle, of Northampton, and Accomack, in Virginia, ministered to Church of England people during the early days of Somerset County's life.

³For the Church of England in Somerset County see *ante*, p. 129, *et seq.*

⁴For the Presbyterian Church in Somerset County see *ante,* p. 209.

⁵It should be borne clearly in mind in this connection that the Society of Friends has always most emphatically denied and rejected an "ordained ministry of the Word and Sacraments." Their "ministry"—to which all honor and praise for its reality and power—is purely a "lay-ministry," depending solely upon "inner call and guidance." See a very remarkable tribute paid to the Quakers by Charles Gore, Bishop of Oxford, "highest" and most "sacerdotally minded" of Anglicans in his *Basis of Anglican Fellowship in Faith and Organization,* p. 44.

⁶These presentments were three in number: (1) against a woman for bearing a bastard child; (2) against the surveyor of highways of Manokin Hundred for not repairing the bridge at Goose Creek and at the head of Manokin River called Mr. Smith's bridge; (3) against Henry Boston for hiring the wife of Thomas Davis; and against the said Thomas Davis "for disposing of his said wife to the said Boston." This Thomas Davis, so "presented" by the grand jury, must not be confused with *"Thomas Davis, Carpenter,"* who was a member of this grand jury. The man whom the grand jury presented was "Thomas Davis, Taylor," who married Judith Best in 1670. See for further references sketch of Henry Boston, *ante,* p. 319.

⁷Somerset Court, Judicials, Liber AZ, October, 1671-1675, pp. 78-9.

⁸The province of Maryland had no established Church until 1692. Whatever may have been the intention of the Crown in regard to the promotion of the Church of England in the province under the charter to Cecil, Lord Baltimore, the province of Maryland was certainly a "land of sanctuary" for Roman Catholics, whose religion was prosecuted in England. Maryland was in the beginning and for years afterwards,—whatever means were employed to that end and whatever may have been the power exercised for that purpose,—a province of "religious toleration." Men were left free in the exercise of conscience in matters pertaining to religious affiliation. Maryland became a "land of sanctuary" not only for Roman Catholics, but for Quakers, Presbyterians, Independents, liberal Church of England men, and almost every sect and denomination under the seventeenth century sun. This Somerset County Grand Jury's "county-wide" evangelization program of March, 1672/3, under "Mr. Matix," when Church of England men, Presbyterians, Quakers joined together in recommending the matter as their "opinion" is a splendid illustration of Maryland "toleration." Then came the Established Church in 1692, followed by deprivation of the Roman Catholics; the taxation of all people, regardless of religious affiliation, to give financial support to the Church of England in the province. The "Churchmen" became relentless; the Presbyterians horrified by "Popery"; both "Churchmen" and Presbyterians were scandalized by the thought of Quakerism. These two joined in their attack on the then Lord Baltimore and with a plus of strong political jealousy of a certain powerful element against Charles Calvert, 3rd Lord Baltimore's chartered rights (their cause no doubt strengthened by his own weak management of affairs) succeeded in overthrowing the Lord Proprietor in

his governing power. A later Calvert only recovered the government because of his forsaking the Roman Catholic Church for the Church of England. To the present writer, nothing could have been more unfortunate for all concerned, including the Church of England, than the "establishing" of the Church of England by law in the province of Maryland, thereby bringing true religious toleration to an end.

[9 and 10]For proof that William Stevens was a "Churchman" and liberal in his attitude towards other forms of expression of the Christian faith see sketch of Stevens, under "Founders."

[11]*"The house of William Stevens at Pocomoke."* On February 24, 1664/5, William Stevens received a patent for 1,000 acres of land, in Somerset County, lying along the Pocomoke River, and when the "Hundreds" were laid out this fell in Pocomoke Hundred. The tract of land thus granted was given the patent name of "Rehoboth." In 1668 Stevens sold 400 acres from the lower part of this tract to James Weedon, retaining as his home place the 600 acres of the upper part, which continued under the name of "Rehoboth." It was at this place that William Stevens' house stood in March, 1671/2, when the Grand Jury of Somerset designated it as the first of the "preaching stations" for "Mr. Matix." Here Stevens lived and here died and was buried in 1687. His tomb is still to be seen at this place. The site of *"the house of William Stevens at Pocomoke"* of March, 1671/2, may today be located on a farm on the north side of the Pocomoke River, in Somerset County, immediately on the river, something over a mile northeast of the present village of Rehoboth, Maryland.

[12]*"The house of Daniel Curtis in Anemessicks."* Somerset, Judicials, Liber AZ, 1671-5, pp. 64-5, January 21, 1671 (1671/2), document showing that Daniel Curtis had purchased one moiety or one-half (being 250 acres) of two parcels of land, called "Armstrong's Purchase" and "Armstrong's Lott," both containing 500 acres as by grant June 20, 1665. This purchase was made by Curtis from Sampson Waters, attorney for Hannah Armstrong, relict and executrix of Matthew Armstrong, of Boston, New England, Marriner, deceased. Curtis agrees by bond with Stephen Bond to a division to be made between them. Somerset Court, Deed Liber O 1, p. 150, shows that on May 16, 1665, Stephen Bond had purchased from Matthew Armstrong one moiety or one-half of tract called *"the Sckipers (Skipper's) plantation,"* on north side Annemessex River. *Ibid.,* p. 21, power of attorney from Matthew Armstrong, of Boston, to Randall Revell, of Somerset County, Maryland, dated September 20, 1670, shows that Daniel Curtis then had possession of Matthew Armstrong's plantation on north side of Annemessex River, *"commonly knowne by name of Scipers [Skipper's] plantation but in the patent granted me ... called Armstrong's Lott and bond's (Bond's) Purchase."* These documents make it clear that Daniel Curtis was living in March, 1671/2, on the north side of Annemessex River, Somerset County, on a plantation made up of parts of "Armstrong's Lott" and "Armstrong's Purchase" (commonly called the Skipper's plantation at one time). Deed Liber O 3, pp. 71-74, shows that in February, 1671 (1671/2), John Rhodes sold to Thomas and Richard Tull a tract called "Salisbury" on north side Annemessex River,

which ran from a point west to mouth of Swanny Creek, thence up the side of this creek to Major Waters' land, thence east to line of *Matthew Armstrong's land,* etc. Judicials, 1752-1754, p. 128, *et seq.,* shows that a creek issuing out of north side Annemessex River is *"called Tull's Creek, otherwise called Swanny Creek."**

According to deductions, Swanny Creek, or Tull's Creek (both names have become lost from record and tradition), is a small creek on north side Annemessex River, being the first creek to the east of the present Hall's Creek. By these deductions we are able to practically locate today (for our purpose) the place designated by the Somerset Grand Jury of March, 1671/2, as the second named of the "preaching stations" for "Mr. Matix," being *"the house of Daniel Curtis in Annemessicks."* This Daniel Curtis property remained for some years in possession of his descendants, and is now included in the farm of Mr. Cameron, a short distance southeast of the village of Upper Fairmount.

[13]*"The house of Christopher Nutter in Manoakin."* Somerset Court, Deed Liber O 3, p. 206, shows that on August 5, 1667, Christopher Nutter received patent for 300 acres, called "Nutter's Purchase," in Somerset County, north side Manokin River between lands of Owen Macrah and John Nelson. Here Nutter made his home until he sold it by deed, November 12, 1672, to Charles Ballard. Nutter evidently continued to live here, certainly until February, 1672/3, for there is record that his daughter, Mary Nutter, was *"born at Manokin"* in that month. Between February, 1672/3, and February, 1674/5, Nutter moved to his plantation in Nanticoke Hundred, for there is record that his daughter, Sarah Nutter, was *"born at Nanticoke,"* February 18, 1674/5 (Somerset Court, Liber IKL, Nutter entries under letter "N"). Christopher Nutter sold "Nutter's Purchase," in November, 1672, to Charles Ballard, and the land descended to Ballard's eldest son and heir at law, Charles Ballard, who conveyed ¼ acre thereof to Reverend William Stewart, and the Elders of the Presbyterian Congregation of Manokin, August 19, 1723, for the use of "Meeting House for the worship and service of Almighty God according to the Presbyterian PrSuasion" (Somerset Court, Deed Liber O 15, p. 71).

This "Nutter's Purchase" tract is today largely included in the town limits of Princess Anne, Maryland, just north of the bridge across Manokin River. On this tract stood *"the house of Christopher Nutter in Manokin,"* designated as the third of the "preaching stations" for "Mr. Matix" by the Somerset Grand Jury in March, 1671/2.

[14]*"The house of Thomas Roe at Wiccocomoco."* It appears that on November 8, 1670, James Dashiell, of Somerset County, acknowledged in court a deed to **Thomas Roe, of Somerset, for 500 acres** on southernmost (east) side of Wicomico River, which said land begins at mouth of Dashiell's Creek (running north up the said river) and was part of 1,000 acres called "Despence," granted to

---

*Somerset County Rent Rolls, 1663-1723, p. 1 (a manuscript in the Maryland Historical Society, Baltimore), proves that the plantation called "Waters River," surveyed September 5th, ..., for William Waters, was "on north side Annemessex River between Assateage Creek and Swansey [Swanny?] Creek" and that the *"possessors"* (at date rent roll was made up, which date is not given) were: "150a. Thos Tull, Senr., 700a. John Waters, 430a. Richard Waters."

David Spence, February 8, 1663/4, and the said 500 acres sold by said Spence to Dashiell in June, 1668 (Somerset Court, Liber DT, No. 7, 1670-4, pp. 34-7). On June 4, 1672, Thomas Roe and Ann, his wife, sold 258 acres of this tract of 500 acres to Thomas Holbrook and John Holland (Somerset Court, Deed Liber O 3, p. 220), then on June 1, 1675, Roe conveyed to Thomas Walker, of Somerset County, the remaining 240 acres of the said 500-acre tract (Somerset Court, Deed Liber O 4 p,. 231). From Thomas Walker, dying in 1681 (see his will, Hall of Records, Annapolis, Will Liber No. 2, folio 127-9), this land descended by his will to his son, Thomas Walker, Junior, who by his will (1744) directed it sold for the benefit of the children of his daughter, Elizabeth, by her husband, Jacob Sarley (will of Thomas Walker [1744/5], Somerset Registry of Wills, Liber EB 9, pp. 252-3). Sarley, some years later, sold this land to his wife's sister, Mrs. Jane Lucas. (Somerset Court, Deed Liber O 26, p. 135). Mrs. Jane Lucas, dying intestate, the land descended to her three daughters: (1) Jane, wife of Robert Dashiell; (2) Matilda Bounds; (3) Margaret, wife of Thomas Waters. In 1786 Dashiell and Bounds sold their two-thirds interest to Thomas Waters (Somerset Court, Deed Liber O 29, p. 170). Thomas Waters by his will left his property to his second wife, Mrs. Susanna Waters, who by her will devised it to her nephew, Thomas Waters Stone. (Somerset Registry of Wills, Liber EB 23, p. 252, will of Thomas Waters; Liber JP 4, p. 195, will of Mrs. Susanna Waters). The property now belongs to the heirs of Daniel W. White, deceased, and extends from the mouth of Dashiell's Creek up the east side of Wicomico River.* Thus are we able to locate today the plantation on which *"the house of Thomas Roe at Wiccocomoco"* stood in March, 1671/2, when the Grand Jury of Somerset County designated it as the fourth of the "preaching stations" for "Mr. Matix."

[15]For the record that "Mr. Matix" was chosen as the preacher in this early evangelistic adventure in Somerset County see record of Somerset Grand Jury's action, March, 1671/2, given in full *ante*, p. 118. Records of marriages at which Robert Maddox (and other various spellings of the name) officiated are preserved for us in Somerset Court, Liber IKL.

There was a family of Maddox resident in Somerset County at this same time, but a careful examination of the records has failed to disclose any connection whatsoever between this family and the Reverend Robert Maddox. In an attempt to definitely settle the question of Robert Maddox's "orders of ministry," the published lists of Oxford and Cambridge University graduates were consulted to try and discover if he was a graduate of either of these universities and, if so, if he was ever ordained in the ministry of the Church of England. The result of investigation in these sources was negative. Then, no list which we have seen of early Presbyterian ministers gives this man's name. As a last resort, we appealed to the Reverend Willard P. Sperry, of Harvard

---

*The old Roe-Walker-Waters-Stone-White plantation on Wicomico River, at the mouth of Dashiell's Creek, was the birthplace of Judge Samuel Chase (1741-1811), of Maryland, who was son of Reverend Thomas Chase and his wife, Matilda Walker, daughter of Thomas Walker (died 1744/5). The evidence in this matter has been collected and compiled in a paper (yet in manuscript form) by Cassius M. Dashiell, Benjamin J. Dashiell and Clayton Torrence.

University, to see if Robert Maddox's name, in any of its variations of spelling, could be found among the early New England Congregational ministers. Doctor Sperry referred the matter to the Reverend Owen H. Gates, of Andover-Harvard Theological Library, Cambridge, Massachusetts, who replied to our inquiry that he could not find the name of Maddox in the lists of New England Congregational ministers.

We are indebted to Miss Louise E. Magruder, of Annapolis, Maryland, for consulting the list of "Early Settlers" of Maryland (in Hall of Records, Annapolis) in an attempt to discover at what date Robert Maddox came into Somerset County, Maryland. Miss Magruder's kindly contributed research failed, however, to disclose any item in regard to this specific Robert Maddox. The only even vague approach to a reference to a name in Somerset County anything like *Robert Maddox* (or *Maddock*) prior to his designation as preacher by the grand jury in March, 1671/2, appears in "An Act for payment of the Public Charge of this Province (Maryland) Assembly of April-May 1669 . . . Somerset County . . . Robt Mordick 00100 [pounds tobacco]" (*II Arcv. Md.*, p. 232). Who this *"Robt Mordick"* was, or why he was paid this amount, does not appear. We have not so far been able to pick up any other reference to him. In the Sussex County, Delaware, Record Book, 1681 (in the Pennsylvania Historical Society, Philadelphia), p. 35, at court held March 14, 1681 [1681/2], at Deale, for the town and county of Deale by the King's Authority, among the persons fined by the court for not working the highways after being legally warned thereto was "Robert *Medock* . . . 050 lbs. tobo." Could this Robert *Medock*, in Delaware in 1681, have been in any way connected with our Robert *Maddock* (or Maddox)?

[16]"Liber IKL" of Somerset Court *contains* a register of births, marriages and deaths entered for Somerset County and a few entries of baptisms. Some of these entries appear to be dates of births of residents of Somerset County who were born outside the county and brought into the county by their parents at the time of their immigration. On p. 1 of this book appears the inscription, "Alphabett of Somersett County Register of Births Marriages & Bu[rials]." Then follows an index giving the page number for the initial letter of surnames; i. e. "The surname of A begins in folio 1, the surname of B begins in folio 12," etc., etc., following the whole alphabet through. The entries are not always contemporaneous with the events, for there are records dated from 1650, 1661 on. The latest of entries seems to have been 1719/20. This register was doubtless begun under authority and direction of "An Act for Registering Births, Marriages & burialls," which was "revived" under recommendation of a "Comitee of both houses" of Assembly, May-June, 1674, session. This "register," though it contains some entries after 1692, when the Church of England was established by Act in the province, was followed by the regular "Parish Registers" provided for by Acts of the Assembly. This "Liber IKL," which was evidently begun as a register for entering births, marriages and deaths, after discontinuance of its use as such, was filled in on its blank pages with records of deeds and cattle marks. The register of births, marriages and deaths is by no

means a complete one for Somerset County during the time that it was kept as a register of such events. But such as it is it is an invaluable record and a priceless heritage of the county. A manuscript copy of this register (though by no means a "letter perfect" copy) was made some years ago and is in the Maryland Historical Society, Baltimore. The "original" Liber IKL is in the office of the Clerk of Circuit Court for Somerset County, Princess Anne, Maryland.

[17]These references to Benjamin Salisbury, Morgan Jones and Robert Richardson as Ministers of the Gospel officiating, at the respective dates, at weddings in Somerset County, have been gleaned by reading through the marriage records contained in the "Register of Births, Marriages & Burrials" in Liber IKL, Somerset Court. The one reference is all that we have to "Benjamin Salisbury, Clerke," January, 1673/4. There was, somewhat later, a family by the name of Salisbury on the upper Eastern Shore of Maryland and in Delaware. No attempt has been made to trace connection. We cannot "identify" the "Robert Richardson, Minister." There was a *Robert Richardson* who lived at a plantation called "Mt. Ephraim" on the seaboard side of Somerset County, in the neighborhood of St. Martin's River. However, he died and was buried at "Mt. Ephraim," September 10, 1682 (Liber IKL, p. 232), while *"Robert Richardson, Minister,"* officiated at the wedding of William Henderson and Sarah Bishop in *August, 1684.* We wonder if, by any possibility, the record, *"Robert Richardson, Minister,"* is a clerical error and that the minister was *David* Richardson, whose history we have been able to fully trace (see *ante,* p. 126). It has also been impossible to identify "Morgan Jones, Minister," who officiated in 1678 at the wedding of Alexander Thomas and Cecil Shaw. In the Northampton County (Virginia) Records, Order Book, 1657-1664, p. 144, there is record that certificate for land rights was granted Maj. William Waters on the names of *Morgan Jones* and Richard Tull. *Maj. Waters* owned the large plantation, "Waters River," on the north side of the Annemessex River in Somerset County, Maryland. We know that Richard Tull came from Northampton County, Virginia, to Somerset County, Maryland, and settled there. May not also this Morgan Jones have come to Somerset? In September, 1671, Richard Ackworth made deposition in Somerset Court that "the mare wch I Soulld *Morgan Jones* which was transported in Mr Stevens Sloope had no other marke then Crop^t A little of ye top of the ear & branded with RA on the buttocks" (Somerset Court, Judicials, Liber DT 7, p. 206). We have not been able, however, to identify Morgan Jones in Northampton County and Morgan Jones in Somerset County in 1671 with "Morgan Jones, Minister," who appears in Somerset in 1678. McConnell, *History of the American Episcopal Church,* pp. 82-3, gives an account of one Morgan Jones, a Welshman, who was chaplain of the colony of English adventurers which landed at Port Royal, South Carolina, in 1660, and who had quite an experience with the Tuscarora Indians, finally being freed from them and making his way north. "In 1680 this same Morgan Jones was officiating at Newtown, Long Island," says McConnell. Though the story of the adventure (which McConnell quotes from *The Gentleman's Magazine* for 1740) may con-

tain apochryphal elements, yet Morgan Jones, the Welshman and chaplain (evidently a clergyman of the Church of England), was a reality; as was the Morgan Jones who in 1680 was on Long Island. Though we have no way in which to identify the "Morgan Jones, Minister," who appears in Somerset County in 1678, with Morgan Jones, the chaplain of the English expedition of 1660 and later on Long Island, we cannot but wonder if there was any connection between the two ministers of the same name. Could Morgan Jones, the chaplain, have passed through Somerset County on his way to the north? Of course, we have no data relative to the church to which "Morgan Jones, Minister," in Somerset in 1678 belonged.

[18] Somerset Court, Deed Liber O 6, p. 590, for deed of Henry Smith to David Richardson, Minister, and Deed Liber O 6, p. 574, for deed of William Stevens to David Richardson, Clarke. For record of indictment and trial of David Richardson for drunkenness and the court's dismissal of the action see Somerset Court, Judicials, Liber 1692-3, pp. 184 and 242, and Liber 1693-4, p. 38. The will of David Richardson, dated December 23, 1695, probated April 28, 1696, devised to his eldest son, John Richardson, and his heirs, 500 acres, called "Wiltshire," purchased by testator of Captain Henry Smith; to son William Richardson, and his heirs, tract called "Weamouth" [this land is identified as the tract "Weymouth," which Richardson bought of Colonel William Stevens]; to eldest daughter, Elizabeth, youngest daughter, Ann, and daughter Hannah, and to sons aforesaid, personalty; executor, son William Richardson; overseers of will, Samuel Hopkins, John Sonhill and Thomas Parramore (*Maryland Calendar Wills*, Vol. II, p. 103). On April 28, 1696, William Richardson, administrator of David Richardson, deceased, late of Somerset County, gave bond as administrator in the sum of £213 sterling. Matthew Scarborough and Samuel Hopkins, sureties (Worcester County Registry of Wills, Liber JW, No. 14 [Bonds 1667-1742], pp. 40-1). William Richardson (son of David Richardson) married Elizabeth Scarborough, daughter of Matthew Scarborough (Somerset Court, Deed Liber O 9, p. 52).

There was a very interesting character in Northampton County, Virginia, one *Daniel* Richardson, who was employed by the vestry, and ministered to the Church of England Congregation in Hungar's Parish, prior to 1676, though he was not *episcopally ordained*. On objections raised by the Governor of Virginia, Sir William Berkeley, the vestry of Hungar's Parish, finally discharged him in May, 1676. Wise, *Accawmacke*, p. 275, says: "The ousted Richardson moved to Maryland and was living in Somerset County in 1680." Mr. Wise evidently confuses *Daniel* Richardson, of Northampton County, with *David* Richardson, whose record of ministerial service in Somerset County we know. Of course, it may be that the "ousted" *Daniel* moved across the line into Somerset, there becoming *David*. However, evidence of this identity is totally lacking. The minister in Somerset invariably appears as *David* Richardson. The only reference we have discovered to the name *Daniel* Richardson as connected with Somerset County is in the will of one John Custis, of Somerset County, dated 1706, who devised personalty to one Daniel Richardson (*Maryland Calendar of Wills*, Vol. III, p. 88).

3. Of Ancient and Apostolic Lineage

[1] Somerset Court, Liber IKL, p. 150, for record of birth and baptism of Elizabeth Lum.

[2] The first *recorded* appearance of Robert Maddox (or Maddock) in Somerset County is in *November, 1671* (see *ante,* p. 125). However, Maddox may have come to Somerset County some little time prior to that date. Mrs. Beauchamp and her infant son, Thomas, were baptized in April, 1671, eight months prior to the first recorded mention of Maddox's name in the Somerset records. Maddox was certainly in Somerset in May, 1674, when Alice Beauchamp was baptized; but the *last reference* in Somerset records of Maddox's appearance there was in March, 1674/5—*two years and five months* prior to the baptism of Edmund Beauchamp, Junior, in July, 1677. For a further statement of circumstantial evidence that a Church of England minister was occasionally ministering in Somerset County at the time of these baptisms see *ante,* under note 19, in references for "Followers of the Inner Light."

We note three other baptisms recorded in Liber IKL of Somerset Court, but without reference to the name of the minister who baptized the infants: (1) William Walston (son of William), born December 15, 1673, *"baptized ye 24 January following* (Liber IKL, p. 275); (2) John Powell (son of Walter and Margaret), born at Pocomoke, September 27, 1674, and *"baptized ye 25 day of October next following (Ibid.,* p. 209); (3) Ambrose Dixon (son of Thomas and Christiana), born at Annemessex, November 13, 1673, and *"was Baptized the 17th day of May following. Annoq Domini 1674" (Ibid.,* p. 52). This Ambrose Dixon was a first cousin of Alice Beauchamp, who was also baptized in May, 1674. Alice's mother, Mrs. Sarah (Dixon) Beauchamp, was sister to Thomas Dixon, father of the said Ambrose who was baptized May 17, 1674.

[3] For Reverend Thomas Teackle's rectorships in Accomack County, Virginia, see Wise, *Accawmacke,* and Goodwin, *The Colonial Church in Virginia,* pp. 310, 321 and 334.

[4] The document here referred to as signed (among others from various parts of the province) by Stevens, Dashiell, Woolford and Smith, is the declaration in defence of Lord Baltimore against certain interests by which he was being attacked on account of his Roman Catholicism. These interests were attempting to prove that his conduct of affairs in the province was strongly biased by his own personal religious attitude: in fact, was discriminating against Protestants in his government in appointments to both civil and military offices. The document bears date May 13, 1682 (*V Arv. Md.,* pp. 353-5; Scharf, *Maryland,* Vol. I, pp. 287-9. Of course, as we know, Lord Baltimore finally lost the government of his province.

William Stevens, of "Rehoboth" on Pocomoke River, Somerset County, left no children at his death, but had practically adopted his wife's kindred, to several of whom he left handsome properties. For sketch of William Stevens see *ante,* p. 326. For notes on James Dashiell, Roger Woolford see Appendix X, and Henry Smith see *ante,* p. 324. Cassius M. Dashiell and Henry Filmore Lankford, to whom this present work is inscribed, are descendants (respectively) of James Dashiell and Henry Smith. Roger Woolford has many descendants in Somerset, among whom the author numbers some of his dearest friends. Benjamin J. Dashiell, of Towson, Maryland, is another descendant of James Dashiell, to whom the author is indebted for most loyal encouragement and much assistance towards completing this work. It has been through Mr. Ben. Dashiell's guidance that he has been enabled to work out the location of many of the historic spots referred to in this work. Mr. Benjamin J. Dashiell is the author of the monumental genealogical work: *Dashiell Family Records,* 3 volumes.

[5] For the Northampton-Accomack "background" of the liberal type of "Churchmanship," which was a distinguishing mark of Church of England people in the early days of "Old Somerset," see interesting items given in Wise, *Accawmacke,* p. 269, *et seq.*

[6] The only recorded evidence so far discovered showing that Reverend Thomas Teackle, of Accomack, was ever on Somerset County soil is the fact that he officiated at the marriage of "John Cullen and Mary his wife," October 12, 1694, as recorded in the Somerset Court Register of "Births, marriages and burials," in Liber IKL. There is also evidence that the Reverend Henry Parkes, rector of Accomack Parish, Accomack County, Virginia, officiated on June 15, 1678, at the marriage of Captain William Coulbourne and Anne Revell, of Somerset County (Somerset Court, Liber IKL).

[7] It is needless to say that there are no remaining "Church records" for the early period of the history of "Old Somerset." There was no organized congregation; no resident minister. There were no "parishes" and no vestries with their clerks until the law established the Church of England in Maryland in 1692, at least in so far as regular organization is concerned. No doubt in some parts of the province, before this date, congregations and ministers of Church of England faith and order did keep records after a fashion; but "Old Somerset" at this very early period had no congregation of this Church and no minister. Even for years after the Establishment of the Church of England in the province of Maryland in 1692, the organization of parishes and vestries, there are no "parish records" remaining for the four parishes of "Old Somerset."

Somerset Parish has a mere fragment of a seventeenth century "Register," only a few pages, evidently from an old book, giving some baptisms and burials. The dates in this fragment represent various years from 1690 on to 1750. Into a later "register" have been copied from an older register, now gone, records of some baptisms and burials between 1690 and 1720. The earliest Vestry Book for Somerset Parish begins in 1766. There is a register for Stepney Parish giving births, marriages and deaths with dates beginning in 1733. Coventry Parish has a register with dates beginning in 1738. The Worcester Parish Register, containing dates as early as 1727 (while the Worcester Parish area was still included in All Hallows [or Snow Hill] Parish), and Vestry Book, 1753-65, are both in existence.

[8] James Barnabe's will, "original," filed among "original wills" in the Somer-

set Registry of Wills, Princess Anne, Maryland; also recorded in Somerset Court, Liber O 1, p. 66 (Clerk's Office), and Reigstry of Wills for Somerset County, Will Liber EB 9, pp. 5-6. The record of James Barnabe's death and burial is from Somerset Court, Liber IKL, p. 3. For note on James Barnabe see Appendix X.

⁹Somerset Court, Liber IKL, p. 17, for record of birth and baptism of Hannah Brereton. Reverend John *Fransele,* who baptized Hannah Brereton—"at Wiccomico in ye County of Northumberland in Virginia," remains a mystery. Goodwin, *The Colonial Church in Virginia, Part II, A List of the Colonial Clergy from 1605-1785,* gives no reference to any clergyman by the name of John *Fransele.* However, the rector of Fairfield Parish, 1672-1702, and Boutracey Parish, 1690, in Northumberland County, Virginia, was Reverend John *Farnifold. Fransele* may be a perpetuated misreading of the name *Farnifold.* The Reverend G. MacLaren Brydon, D.D., historiographer of the Diocese of Virginia, whom we consulted in regard to solving the mystery of John *Fransele,* could throw no light upon the matter. It may be, however, that Wicomico Parish, in Northumberland County, Virginia, had at the date in question a temporary minister by the name of *John Fransele,* the record of whose service is now lost. It is worth noting that in after years part of this tract of the Brereton home place (including the house tract) on the north side of Wicomico Creek (present designation), became part of the dwelling plantation of the Reverend Alexander Adams, for 65 years (1704-1769) rector of Stepney Parish. This old and interesting place, on which Hannah Brereton was born, and later the Reverend Mr. Adams' home, is now (1935) the home of Doctor George W. Jarman, a vestryman of Somerset Parish. This place is situated about 5 miles north of the town of Princess Anne. Immediately south (and across the Creek) from the present house on this Brereton-Adams-Jarman place is the site of an old Chapel of Ease of Stepney Parish, called "Goddard's Chapel." (See *ante,* p. 186 for note on "Goddard's Chapel").

¹⁰Somerset Court, Liber IKL, p. 40.

¹¹Will of Captain Thomas Walker, dated May 1, 1680, probated March 10, 1680/1, recorded Hall of Records (Annapolis), Liber 2, folio 127; Somerset Registry of Wills, Liber EB 13, pp. 1-5, for estate account of Captain Thomas Walker, the specific item in regard to John Huett being on p. 4. The record of Walker's death and burial is from Somerset Court, Liber IKL, p. 282. See also Richardson, *Sidelights on Maryland History,* Vol. II, p. 459, *et seq.*

¹²The Reverend John Huett's name appears in the Somerset County and Maryland provincial archives spelled variously as Huett, Huet, Huitt, Hewett, Hewitt, but most commonly *Huett,* which was the spelling used by him in witnessing the will of John Evans, of Somerset County, dated May 6, 1686, probated July 12, 1686, the *original* of which will is on file in the Registry of Wills for Somerset County at Princess Anne, Maryland. As a witness to this will we find the signature *"J^{no} Huett, C'k* [Clerk]." Reverend John Huett, of Somerset, was not less distinguished in his birth than in his life. Born *circa* 1640, John Huett was the eldest son of the Reverend John Huett (born September, 1614; died June 8,

1658), of Pembroke College, Cambridge, and Doctor of Divinity of Oxford; minister of St. Gregory's by St. Paul's, London; a royalist divine; published devotional works; said to have harbored Ormond in 1658 when that nobleman went into England under disguise to obtain intelligence as to the chances for an uprising in behalf of Charles Stuart—later to come to the throne as Charles II. Huett, involved in this royalist plot, though interceded for by Mrs. Claypoole, was finally beheaded in June, 1658. The Reverend John Huett (1614-1658) married, *first,* Miss Skinner, daughter of Robert Skinner, a merchant-tailor of London; *second,* Mary, daughter of Bertie, 1st Earl of Lindsay. The father of John Huett (1614-1658) was Thomas Huett, a merchant-tailor of London. The eldest son of the Reverend John Huett (1614-1658) and his *first* wife, Miss Skinner, was John Huett (born *circa* 1640), who was granted, February 19, 1661, an annuity of £100 on account of his father's beheading. This eldest son, John Huett (born *circa* 1640), has been identified as the Reverend John Huett, of Somerset County, the first Church of England clergyman who came there to reside. John Huett (who came to Somerset County) is believed also to have been identical with one John Huett, who was transported to Virginia in 1663 by Captain Adam Thorogood, afterwards returning to England, studied for "holy orders," was ordained deacon, came to Somerset County in Maryland, and returning to England again, was ordained priest by the Bishop of London in 1682, coming again to Somerset, where he remained during the rest of his life. For these facts in regard to John Huett's ancestry, we are indebted to Mr. Benjamin J. Dashiell, of Towson, Maryland, who has made extensive search into Somerset County parochial and family history. The matter given herein is stated just as Mr. Dashiell gave it.

[13]In "An account of the Parishes . . . as also of the Clergyman of the Church of England within this his Majesty's Province of Maryland . . . ," recorded in the *Journal of the Board of Trade,* October 15, 1697, appears: "Somersett Parish . . . The Reverend Mr. John Hewett who hath been in the Country about 20 year." (*Journal Board of Trade,* p. 157. Public Record Office, London, C. O. 5, 725). This item has also been given in *V Md. Hist. Mag.,* p. 291. If Mr. Huett (or Hewett) had been in Maryland about 20 years in 1697, then he must have come in about 1677. Of course, the term "about" may extend over the year 1680/1, at which date we have the *first* mention of Huett's name in the Somerset records. Somerset Court, Liber IKL, p. 15, gives the earliest reference to John Huett's presence in Somerest County, January 29, 1680/1, when he officiated at the marriage of Alexander Prise and Rebecca Thomas.

[14]Careful research in remaining records has failed to disclose a single reference to a church building in Somerset County save the one reference to "Pocomoke *Church*" in 1692, in which building (so designated) the freeholders of Pocomoke and Annemessex Hundreds, Somerset County, were directed to meet for electing the first vestry of Coventry Parish. For note on "Pocomoke Church" see *ante,* p. 169.

[15]Somerset Court, Liber IKL, p. 18, gives the record of birth and baptism of Thomas Brereton; and on p. 210 is the record of the baptism and marriage of

"John Puckham, an Indian." The location of the Monie Indian Town is attested by deposition of Thomas Dashiell (aged about 87 years), made October 13, 1753, when he is proving the location of a branch called "King's Creek" flowing into the north side of Great Monie Creek. Dashiell said he knew there was an Indian Town to the east of the said King's Creek. (Somerset Court, Judicials, Liber 1752-4, p. 185, *et seq.*, commission and affidavits offered to establish boundaries of tract called "Covington's Folly"). In a deed, January 20, 1679/80, Nehemiah Covington conveys to his sons, John and Nehemiah, a tract called "Covington's Vineyard," described as being on *north* side of Great Monie Creek, beginning at a small gut, dividing it from *the Indian Town of Great Monie* (Somerset Court, Deed Liber O 6, p. 425).

The record of the marriage of "John Puckham, an Indian," specifically states that he married "Jone Johnson, *negro.*" Bowen, in *The Days of Makemie,* p. 60, makes a singular error in describing the marriage of this "John Puckham, an Indian," to "Jane Johnson," whom he calls a *white* maiden and describes this marriage as a union between the white settlers and the Indians. Doctor Bowen's interpretation is in no way upheld by the record, in which the bride is specifically designated as *"negro."* The name of Puckham continued in the vicinity for some years. In 1723 and 1729 there were suits against Abraham Puckham, of Stepney Parish, and Abraham Puckham and Honour, his wife, who had been Honour Norgate, an indentured servant to Philip Covington (Somerset Court, Judicials, 1722-24, p. 155; Judicials, 1727-30, p. 205, and Judicials, 1730-33, p. 46).

[16]John Huett was in Somerset County certainly as early as January 29, 1680/1, when he officiated at marriage of Alexander Prise and Rebecca Thomas (see note 13 above). Mr. Benjamin J. Dashiell, of Towson, Maryland, makes the statement that "John Huett was ordained in 1682 by the Bishop of London for Somerset County, Maryland." If this be correct, then John Huett was ordained *deacon* before his appearance in Somerset on January 29, 1680/1. As in "deacon's orders" in the Church of England he could officiate at marriages, baptize persons, bury the dead, and have any service of worship of the Church other than a celebration of the Holy Communion and he could not pronounce the declaration of absolution of sins. It may be that Huett was ordained deacon, came to Somerset, later returning to England for priest's orders, then coming again to Somerset. *The fact to be borne in mind is that we have record evidence of his presence in Somerset, acting in a ministerial capacity, on January 29, 1680/1.* He had at this time to be at least in "deacon's orders."

[17]See *ante,* p. 153, for account of organization of parishes in Somerset County; and Chapter VIII for Somerset County in the Protestant Revolution and in the Royal Province.

[18]*XXII Arcv. Md.,* p. 113. March 28, 1698, Mrs. Rachel Hewitt, widow of Mr. John Hewitt, minister, petitions the assembly about arrearages in her late husband's salary from Stepney and Somerset Parishes.

[19]Skirven, *First Parishes of the Province of Maryland,* pp. 106, 150, 152 and 157, quoting Ethan Allen's MS. history of the parishes.

[20] For references to sources for the election of Reverend John Huitt to the Lower House of Assembly and the Assembly's action in debarring him see Chapter X, *ante*, p. 359, *et seq.*

[21] Scharf, *Maryland*, I, pp. 350-1; *XIX Arcv. Md.*, p. 78 and pp. 420-26. We find among the members of the Lower House of Assembly contributing to the fund for this school, Captain William Whittington and Matthew Scarborough, 1,000 pounds of tobacco each, and Thomas Dickson (Dixon) and John Bozman, 400 pounds of tobacco each. These four men represented Somerset County in the Lower House of Assembly in 1694. Whittington and Bozman were both "Churchmen." Matthew Scarborough lived in Mattapony Hundred, on the seaboard side (now Worcester County), was a "Churchman" and a member of the first vestry of Snow Hill Parish. Thomas Dixon (son of the uncompromising old Quaker, Ambrose Dixon, of Annemessex) had become a "Churchman" and was a member of the first vestry of Coventry Parish.

[22] *XXXVIII Arcv. Md.*, p. 27, for the Act of 1696; see also Scharf, *Maryland*, Vol. I, p. 352.

[23] *XXXIV Arcv. Md.*, p. 740. "An Act for Encouraging of Learning and Erecting Schools in the Several Counties within this Province . . . Visitors for Somerset County School: the Reverend Alexander Adams, the Reverend James Robertson, Mr. Joseph Gray, Mr. Robert Martin, William Stoughton, Esq., Mr. Robert King, Mr. Levin Gale."

Mr. Adams was for 65 years (1704-1769) rector of Stepney Parish (Mr. Huett's old charge); Mr. Robertson was rector for some years of Coventry Parish (and purchased Mr. Huett's old home on Wicomico River); Mr. Martin was a Scotch merchant, who settled at Snow Hill (then Somerset County; now Worcester), and with Mr. King (an elder of Manokin Congregation) represented the cream of Presbyterianism in Somerset of their day. (Mr. King's sister, Mary, had for her first husband Colonel Francis Jenckins, who, with Reverend Mr. Huett, was on the board of the proposed school of 1696. Mr. King's *first* wife was Priscilla, daughter of Nehemiah Covington, and maternally a niece of Levin Denwood, of Monie. Covington and Denwood were the heart and soul of the Monie Quaker Meeting. Mr. King's second wife was a daughter of the Reverend Francis Makemie, founder of organized Presbyterianism in this country). Joseph Gray was an elder in the Presbyterian Church in Somerset County. William Stoughton was a vestryman of Somerset Parish and married a daughter of Arnold Elzey, who (in 1705) gave the ground on which the first church of Somerset Parish had been built about 1695. Mr. Levin Gale was a "Churchman" and the son of that very staunch "Churchman," Colonel George Gale (died 1712), and his wife, Madam Betty Gale (one of the first "Trustees" of Monie Quaker Meeting House), who was the daughter of Levin Denwood, of Monie—a moving spirit in the "Monie Meeting."

[24] Ethan Allen, MS. history of Somerset Parish.

[25] Considerable research was required to exactly locate the home place of the Reverend John Huett. However, the definite location as given by us here is attested by items of record in Somerset Court. We are indebted to Benj. J.

Dashiell, of Towson, Maryland, for going onto the ground indicated by the records which we unearthed, and making such measurements and calculations as only a surveyor could make, thus "certifying" the location of Huett's home place and burial place as here stated.

The record upon which statement made will be found in Somerset Court, Judicials, 1744-7, pp. 169-171, August Court, 1746, commission and affidavits in relation to boundaries of "Rice Land"; see particular deposition of Thos. Dashiell; *Ibid.*, p. 233-3, November Court, 1746, deposition of John Evans, Sr. Liber IL, No. A, folio 498 (Hall of Records, Annapolis) survey of tract called "Contention" for Alex. Lecky and Ann, his wife. Somerset Court, Deed Liber O 8, p. 85, deed (1699) Rachel Huett to daughter Ann Huett, for land said Rachel lived on; Deed Liber O 17, p. 345, deed (1731) Johnson and wife to Nutter conveying land ". . . at or near the plantation . . . wherein one the Revd John Huett, deceased, lived . . ." These references are to the primary documents in the mass of items constituting evidence upon which our statement of location of Huett's home, and burial place, rest.

Reverend John Huett (*circa* 1640-1698) m. Rachel Battian and had issue: (1) Ann Huett m., *first,* Matthew Nutter (d. 1720), of Somerset; *second,* Alexander Leckey (Lecky, Lackie, etc.), of Somerset; (2) Susanna Huett m. Joseph Johnson, of Charles County, Maryland (see Somerset Court, Deed Liber O 17, pp. 345 and 348) . Mrs. Rachel (Battian) Huett m., *second, circa* 1700, Nicholas Evans, of Somerset. The will of Mrs. Rachel (Battian) Huett Evans, dated April 26, 1726, probated July 4, 1726, is recorded in Somerset Registry of Wills, Liber EB9, p. 104.

[26]For Somerset County in the "Protestant Revolution," which was successful in overthrowing Lord Baltimore's power, and for Somerset in the Royal Province, see Chapter VIII of this book.

[27]Skirven, *First Parishes of the Province of Maryland,* p. 37, *et seq.,* quoting VIII *Arcv. Md.,* pp. 271 and 276. See also Andrew's *Tercentenary History of Maryland,* Vol. I, pp. 370-1.

[28]XIII *Arcv. Md.,* p. 425, *et seq. "An Act for the Service of Almighty God and the Establishment of the Protestant Religion in this Province."* Skirven, *First Parishes in the Province of Maryland,* p. 49, gives an abstract of this Act with splendidly prepared sub-titles for each section.

[29]The few references discovered have been incorporated in the account of John Huett's ministry from 1680-1692; see *ante,* pp. 140-150.

[30]"Freeholder" entitled to vote, or represent county in General Assembly must have a "freehold" of 50 acres of land or visible estate of £40 sterling at least. "Principal Freeholder" was one of the most substantial and prominent among the freeholders in his "district." Skirvin, *First Parishes of Maryland,* p. 51, footnote; also XXVII *Arcv. Md.,* p. 352.

[31]See list of vestrymen given, *ante,* p. 155.

[32]VIII *Arcv. Md.,* p. 366.

[33]Somerset Court, Judicials, Liber 1692-3, p. 99. The name of Bogerternorton Hundred does not appear, nor names of any freeholders as appointed therefrom in this matter.

[34]Somerset Court, Judicials, Liber 1692-3, p. 154. For boundaries of the "hundreds" here combined into parishes see *ante,* p. 73.

[35]*XX Arcv. Md.,* p. 110.

[36]*XXIII Arcv. Md.,* pp. 4, 17 and 22. We cannot say positively at what date the elections of vestries for the four parishes in Somerset County were held. The date set by order of court was December 27, 1692 (St. John Evangelist's Day). It may be that the meetings of freeholders and elections of vestries took place on that day and no "return" thereof made until some time later. The date of first return which has been found, *"Somerset County has ffour parishes laid out; but never a church"* (see *ante,* pp. 162-3), was July 30, 1694. This return of boundaries and vestries of the four parishes was certainly not presented in Council until February, 1696/7.

[37]Public Record Office, London, C. O. 5. 725. *Journal Board of Trade B.,* 312, pp. 150, *et seq.* 1697, Oct. 15, "An Account of the Parishes with their Bounds; Vestrymen and Taxables of every Parish, as also of the Clergymen of the Church of England within this his Majesty's Province of Maryland." Items for Somerset County as quoted in text are given on pp. 157-158 of "Journal." A copy of document obtained for us by Reginald M. Glencross, 176 Worple Road, Wimbledon, S. W. 20, London, England, through the courtesy of Cassius M. Dashiell, of Princess Anne, Maryland. This document reads as follows: "Sommersett County is divided into four Parishes vizt Sommersett, Coventry, Stepney, Snow Hill. Sommersett Parish consists of Monoikin and Mawny Hundreds. The Reverend Mr. John Hewett who hath been in the country about 20 year. Vestrymen for the said parish as by returne viz. John Hewett, Rich, Chambers, John Panter, Nath: Horsey, Miles Gray, Peter Elzey. Taxables 304—Coventry Parish consists of Pocomoke and Annamesex Hundreds. The Reverend Mr. James Breechin who came into the Countrey in the year 1696. Vestrymen for the said parish as by Returne, vizt. M[r] Fra: Jenkins, Mr. Geo. Layfield, Mr. Tho. Nuball, Mr. Wm. Planner, Sen., Mr. Tho: Dixon, Mr. Wm. Coleburne. Taxables 369. Stepney Parish consists of Wicocomoke and Nantecoke Hundreds. Vestrymen of the said parish as by returne Vizt M[r] John Hewett, Clk., Mr. James Wetherly, Mr. John Bounds, Mr. Ph: Carter, Mr. Rob: Collier, Mr. Theo: Holdbrook, Mr. Ph: Askew. Taxables 362. Snowhill parish consists of Poquedenorton and Mattapany hundreds. Vestrymen for the said parish as by returne Vizt M[r] Matthew Scarborough, Mr. Wm. Round, Mr. John Franklin, Mr. Tho: Pointer, Mr. Thomas Selby, Mr. Edw. Hammond. Taxables 353. A true copy. Hen: Denton, Clk. Councill."

[38]See *ante,* p. 213, for connection of Stevensons, Alexanders, Wallises and Strawbridges with Presbyterianism in Somerset.

[39]For Coulbourne and Dixon, respectively, see under "Founders" and Appendix X.

[40]For first Parish Church of Somerset Parish see *ante,* p. 180.

[41]For Nutter see Appendix X. The quotation is from William Piper's will, dated February 3, 1733/4, probated May 16, 1734, Somerset Registry of Wills, Liber EB 6, p. 169.

⁴²For David Brown see *ante,* p. 363.

⁴³For Dashiell, Woolford, Winder see Appendix X; for Jenckins and Layfield see *ante,* pp. 373 and 375.

⁴⁴For "Somerset Town" see *ante,* p. 410.

⁴⁵For "Pocomoke Church" see *ante,* p. 169.

⁴⁶For "Mr. John Huett's" see *ante,* note 25.

⁴⁷For Snow Hill Town see *ante,* pp. 416-17.

⁴⁸For references to Francis Jenckins and Mary, his wife, as the trusted friends of Reverend Francis Makemie see *ante,* p. 374.

⁴⁹For Layfield's marriage to Priscilla White see *ante,* p. 376.

⁵⁰Somerset County records afford an abundance of material about the Chambers, Panter, Elzey, Newbold, Planner, Weatherley, Collier, Bounds, Askew, Scarborough, Round, Francklin, Pointer and Selby families.

⁵¹Accomack County, Virginia, Court, Vol. II, p. 107; Somerset Court, Judicials, Liber AZ, Judgments, 1671-1675, pp. 467 and 490. This last named volume (on p. 136) that Miles Gray was an overseer for Colonel Edmund Scarburgh, in Accomack County, Virginia, in January, 1671 (1671/2).

⁵²Somerset Court, Judicials, in Deed Liber O 9, pp. 70 and 77, March Court, 1705/6, presentment and case against Captain Edward Hammond.

⁵³In February, 1690/1, in a case of criminal assault tried in Somerset Court, a deposition made by Mrs. Sarah Saunders, February 11, 1690/1, there is the statement: "about the month of August last was two years [i. e. August, 1688] ... that he [Thomas Oxford] came to her house upon a Sabbath day as he was either *going to church or looking for a horse in order to go."* The parties involved in this case, the Saunderses and Oxfords, lived in Mattapony Hundred, which was in the extreme southeastern section of Old Somerset County (now in Worcester County) along the seaside and the Maryland-Virginia boundary line. We are not willing to assume from the reference, *"going to church,"* that the service was being held in a regular *church building.* The passage so framed may simply be used as referring to divine service held in any building (dwelling, barn, etc.) where people were accustomed to gather for worship, or even to a religious service held out of doors. The reference given above will be found in Somerset Court Records, Liber AW, 1690-1, p. 40.

⁵⁴For all items relative to this "Pocomoke Church" see *ante,* p. 169, *et seq.*

⁵⁵Will of Reverend Francis Makemie (the Presbyterian minister), dated April 27, 1708, probated August, 1708, there is reference to *"Pocomoke Towne called Rehoboth."* Accomack County (Virginia) Records, Wills, &c., 1692-1715, p. 443.

⁵⁶*XX Arcv. Md.,* p. 110, for this report, and p. 130 for evidence of Colonel David Brown's presence "at the Board" on this date.

⁵⁷*XIII Arcv. Md.,* p. 425, *et seq.* "An Act for the Service of Almighty God and the Establishment of the Protestant Religion in this Province," passed June 2, 1692.

⁵⁸Reverend John Huett's ministry in Stepney and Somerset Parishes, 1692-1696, is attested by return of parishes, vestrymen, taxables and clergymen of the Church of England in the province of Maryland, made to the Governor and

Council, February, 1696/7; and Mrs. Huett's petition to the Assembly, March, 1698/9, for arrears of her late husband, Reverend John Huett's, salary due from Stepney and Somerset Parishes. (*XXIII Arcv. Md.*, pp. 17-22, and *XXII Arcv. Md.*, p. 113). See also notes 13, 18 and 37 above.

[59]Reverend George Trotter's "incumbency" in Stepney and Somerset Parishes from 1696-1703 is noted as follows: (a) for 1696 in *XII Md. Hist. Mag.*, p. 119, and Skirven, *First Parishes of the Province of Maryland*, p. 169; (b) in 1700 Mr. Trotter was present, as incumbent in Stepney and Somerset Parishes, at the "visitation" held in Annapolis by Reverend Thomas Bray, Commissary of the Bishop of London in Maryland. See Ethan Allen, Manuscript Histories of Stepney and Somerset Parishes; (c) Mr. Trotter appears several times as baptizing infants in Somerset Parish during the years 1700-1703. See fragment of Old Somerset Parish Register in possession of the vestry and registrar of Somerset Parish, Somerset County, Maryland.

Reverend James Brechin's "incumbency" in Snow Hill Parish in 1696 is noted in *XII Md. Hist. Mag.*, p. 119, and Skirven, *First Parishes of the Province of Maryland*, p. 169. Mr. Brechin's ministry in Coventry Parish, 1696-1698, is noted in Ethan Allen's Manuscript History of Coventry Parish, p. 18; see also Skirven, *First Parishes in the Province of Maryland,* and an historical sermon on Coventry Parish, entitled *Sermon by the Reverend Samuel F. Hotchkin . . . August 21, 1892. Addenda by Reverend Oliver H. Murphy, rector of Coventry Parish,* p. 2. Reverend James Brechin, rector of Coventry Parish, 1696-1698, was doubtless identical with one Reverend James Brechin, of Cople Parish, Westmoreland County, Virginia, 1702 and 1714, and St. Paul's Parish, New Kent (later Hanover) County, Virginia, 1704, and who died in Westmoreland County, Virginia, in 1722 (see Goodwin, *The Colonial Church in Virginia*, p. 254).

Reverend Robert Keith's rectorship of Coventry Parish, 1703-1707, is fully attested by references to him in the Somerset County records and the Maryland Provincial Archives. For these references see *ante*, p. 237, *et seq*. Keith's rectorship is also noted by Ethan Allen, Manuscript History of Coventry Parish.

* * * *

The objective of the present work is simply to unearth, as it were, the foundations" of "Old Somerset," but we cannot forbear reference here to one who labored in remarkable fashion in erecting the "superstructure" of the Church of England in Somerset. When the Reverend George Trotter, incumbent in Stepney and Somerset Parishes, 1696-1703, left this field he was succeeded as rector of Stepney Parish by the Reverend Alexander Adams (1680-1769). The Reverend Mr. Adams was veritably one of the most remarkable men whom the ministry of the Church of England contributed to the work in the province of Maryland and it is hoped that at some future day he will find a biographer who will contribute to Maryland's ecclesiastical history a sketch worthy of so interesting and truly fine a subject. The Reverend Alexander Adams was born *circa* 1680; ordained deacon and priest by the Bishop of London and came to Somerset

County, Maryland, as rector of Stepney Parish in 1704. At one time, during the early years of his ministry, he "served as Presbyter of the Church of England the whole of Somerset County," from about 1707 to 1711. This ministry included the four parishes, Stepney, Somerset, Coventry and Snow Hill (or All Hallows). Mr. Adams retained his rectorship of Stepney Parish for 65 years. He died in 1769.

4. Children of the Covenant

[1]Ninian Beall (born *circa* 1625; died 1717), from Fifeshire, Scotland, settled in Calvert County, Maryland, 1668; distinguished as both civil and military officer in the government of the province; and likewise in the affairs of the Presbyterian Church on the Western Shore of Maryland, in which he was a ruling elder for many years, and to which he made munificent gifts. For references to Ninian Beall see (for his civil and military service) the *Archives of Maryland*. For his connection with Presbyterianism see McIlvaine, *Early Presbyteranism in Maryland*, p. 12-13; and Barber, *The Cradle of Presbyterianism: Upper Marlboro's Claims Gain New Support from the Facts,* pp. 11-12, in Magazine Section, "The Baltimore Sun," Sunday, March 23, 1930. Mr. Barber's article is an excellent presentation of the story of the congregation founded by Ninian Beall; but, unfortunately, he has been led into the error, in one instance, of quoting from Bowen's *Days of Makemie,* as a fact stated by the Reverend Francis Makemie, a bit of Doctor Bowen's own imaginative treatment of his subject. A reading of Doctor Bowen's reference to Ninian Beall clearly reveals the error into which Mr. Barber has fallen. See also for an account of Colonel Ninian Beall and some of his descendants, McKenzie's *Colonial Families of the United States.*

In our reference to Ninian Beall as "the first thus far identified Presbyterian in Maryland," we wish to safeguard ourselves against the possible identification, through later more particular research, of Presbyterians resident at an earlier date in the province. We cannot be unmindful of the prohibitory clause in regard to the opprobrious use of certain terms of religious designation—among them *"Presbyterian"*—contained in the famous Maryland "Act Concerning Religion" of 1649: the so-called "Toleration Act." Were there avowed Presbyterians resident in Maryland in 1649; or was the term Presbyterian included in this Act in anticipation of later arrivals? We have not gone into research to definitely settle this question; therefore, we have no evidence from which to speak. For the "Act Concerning Religion" (the so-called Toleration Act) of 1649 see Andrews' *Tercentenary History of Maryland,* Vol. I, p. 361, *et seq.,* and p. 930, where the full text of the Act is given.

For an interesting note on what had hitherto been considered an early congregation in Charles County of the Presbyterian Church see *XXII Md. Hist. Mag.,* p. 7 (footnote), and *XXIII Md. Hist. Mag.,* p. 157, Scisco's *The First Church in Charles County.*

[2]Steiner, *Presbyterian Beginnings,* in *XV Md. Hist. Mag.,* p. 305, refers to the Reverend Matthew Hill as laboring in Charles County in 1670; McIlvaine,

Early Presbyterianism in Maryland, p. 7, *et seq.*, for references to Matthew Hill; Bowen, *Days of Makemie*, p. 513; Briggs, *American Presbyterianism*, and particularly Appendix VII, XL-XLI, of that work where certificate of ordination of Matthew Hill, ordained June 3, 1652; certificate made June 24, 1654, shows Hill to have been ordained by Nathaniel Jackson, Edward Bowles, Thomas Calvert, "ministers of Christ called to watch over part of his flock in the city of York, with the assistance of others." This certificate states that Hill was "set apart unto the office of Presbyter and work of the ministry by laying on of hands with fasting and prayer." This is obviously Presbyterial ordination. See also Neill, *Terra Mariæ*, p. 139.

While we have referred in the text only to Matthew Hill as ministering among the Presbyterians in Southern Maryland, we would call attention to the ministry of Reverend Francis Doughty, who, though Episcopally ordained and a minister of the Church of England, became more or less of an "Independent," affiliating with both the Reformed Church of the Netherlands, and Congregationalism. Doughty ministered both in New England and Flushing, Long Island. Doughty (a brother-in-law of William Stone, the Protestant Governor appointed for Maryland by Lord Baltimore in 1649) was for several years in Northampton County, Virginia, and later in old Rappahannock County, Virginia, marked as a "Non-conformist." He was in Charles County, Maryland, 1659-1661 (?). Mr. Scisco shows clearly in his article (to which we refer) that Doughty cannot be considered, ecclesiastically speaking, as a minister of the Presbyterian Church. See Scisco, *The First Church in Charles County*, in XXIII *Md. Hist. Mag.*, p. 155. Wise, *Accawmacke*, p. 269; Goodwin, *The Colonial Church in Virginia*, p. 265. There was another early so-called "Presbyterian" minister in Maryland in 1669, Reverend Charles Nicholet; see Steiner, *Presbyterian Beginnings*, in XV *Md. Hist. Mag.*, p. 305; and Andrews' *Tercentenary History of Maryland*, Vol. I, p. 289.

[3]Somerset Court, Liber DT 7, Judicials, 1670-1, p. 86. David Brown witnesses a bill of James Davis to Randall Revell. Somerset Court, Deed Liber O 2, pp. 22-23, David Brown and Jacob Chiltnam witnesses to deed of Jones and Wingod to Bradshaw, July 20, 1670.

[4]For sketch of David Brown see *ante*, p. 363.

[5]For references to these families see the index.

[6]It is unfortunate that none of the early records of the Sessions of these Somerset County Presbyterian Churches are in existence. The earliest Session records for these respective churches are: Snow Hill Session record, 1745-1801 (in the Presbyterian Historical Society, Philadelphia); Wicomico Session record, beginning 1753 (in possession of the Session of Wicomico Presbyterian Church, Salisbury, Maryland); Manokin Session records, 1747-1800 (in possession of the Session of Manokin Presbyterian Church, Princess Anne, Maryland). No records for periods earlier than early 19th century seem to remain for Buckingham and Pitts Creek churches. The records of Philadelphia and New Castle Presbyteries, of which the Somerset Presbyterian Churches were members, are in existence from nearly the beginning of these Presbyteries.

[7]Briggs, *Rise of Presbyterianism in America,* and Craighead, *Scotch and Irish Seed in American Soil,* both make reference to the arrival of emigrants from the North of Ireland and Scotland coming to Maryland at this period.

[8]Briggs, *American Presbyterianism,* and Reid, *History of the Presbyterian Church in Ireland.*

[9]It is interesting to note in this connection the statements relative to nonconformists in the province of Maryland made by Charles, Lord Baltimore, to the Lords of Trade and Plantations, July 19, 1677, in his "Paper setting Forth the Present State of Religion in Maryland." He refers to some Church of England Clergymen who are "maintained by voluntary contributions of those of their own persuasion, as others of the *Presbiterians* [italics ours], Independents, Anabaptists, Quakers & Romish Church are." He also states that "the greatest part of the Inhabitants of that Province (three of four at least) do consist of *Presbiterian,* Independents, Anabaptists and Quakers . . ." Thus in 1677 we know that there was a strong Presbyterian element in the population of Maryland. The "Western Shore" certainly had its "quota." We cannot doubt that on the "Eastern Shore" in Somerset County there were at this date a reasonable gathering of Presbyterians. It was only three years later, December, 1680, that we find Colonel Stevens' request going from Somerset to the Presbytery of Laggan, for "a godly minister." See *V Arcv. Md.,* p. 133, for Lord Baltimore's "Paper." See also Skirven, *First Parishes of the Province of Maryland,* p. 29; Scharf, *Maryland,* Vol. I, p. 362; Andrews' *Tercentenary History of Maryland,* Vol. I, p. 345; McIlvaine, *Early Presbyterianism in Maryland,* p. 5.

[10]The modern sceptic of the sincerity of the motives of "the fathers"—and of the motives of men in general—will unquestionably see how well accommodated to his pecuniary interest in the development of Somerset County was Colonel William Stevens' attitude of tolerance in matters of religion. Of course, some modern enlightened critic of the motives of men will make a disquisition bearing upon Stevens' methods of "enlightened self-interest." So it may be. We will let it pass. Really no man of today can, upon the assumption of any hypothesis, "throw stones" at Stevens of "Rehoboth." We have indeed tried the game, but always with the result that the stones of criticism have been shattered as they struck his character: his character remaining unbroken and unmarred. For a sketch of William Stevens see *ante,* p. 326.

[11]Say what he please, argue as he may, the stiff Churchmen of the Anglican or of the Roman succession, if he truly knows the glorious heritage of the "Children of the Covenant" knows his own "high doctrine" matched by Presbyterianism's doctrines of the Church of God, of Ordinance, of the Word, and of the Ministry. For those who are ignorant of these great doctrines of the faith as held by the Presbyterian Church, we would recommend that they "read, mark, learn and inwardly digest" that little masterpiece by Witherspoon and Kirkpatrick, *A Manual of Church Doctrine,* an exegetical work on Presbyterian doctrine, of great power and beauty. McConnell, *History of the American Episcopal Church,* p. 159, says in a footnote that "The definition of the Sacraments in the 'Confession of Faith' are such as would satisfy the very highest Churchman."

¹²Bowen, *Days of Makemie,* p. 516, quoting Minutes of Laggan Presbytery, p. 247. A copy of this entry sent Reverend L. P. Bowen by Professor Thomas Witherow, of Magee College, Derry, Ireland, May, 1880. Students of "religious foundations" laid in America during colonial days owe to the late Reverend Littleton Purnell Bowen, D.D., of the Presbyterian Church, a debt of gratitude for his charming presentation of the establishment of the Presbyterian Church in Somerset County. Doctor Bowen presents his subject under the guise of a contemporary relating events then transpiring, and his work must be judged according to the limitations imposed by the adoption of such a method. However, he incorporates in his work results of wide research in original records, and by a series of appended notes gives references for many of the facts upon which his conclusions are based. We had the pleasure of meeting this charming gentleman and scholar, this true minister of Christ and of the Presbyterian Church, just two years before his death, and discussing with him many of the points made by him in his *"Days of Makemie."* We are not able to agree with some of Doctor Bowen's conclusions, and certainly think some of his judgments passed upon ministers of the Church of England and comments upon Roman Catholicism more harsh than facts in the respective cases warrant. However, we wish to pay tribute to a work which has proved an inspiration and from which we have gleaned facts of utmost importance to our study and for the knowledge of which we are wholly indebted to Doctor Bowen's work. Above all, we pay tribute to the Christian gentleman and scholar who so graciously with his wisdom of years, experience, and scholarship, received and encouraged the work of one so many years his junior, who counts as one of the treasures of his life an afternoon spent with this veritable "man of God."

¹³Bowen, *Days of Makemie,* p. 516, quoting letter of Professor Thomas Witherow, of Magee College, Derry, Ireland, May 28, 1880, says "no minutes [of Laggan Presbytery] are preserved from July, 1681, till after 1689." There are no references to the Somerset appeal made through Colonel William Stevens, from the entry in December, 1680, to the record of meeting of the Presbytery in July, 1681, when the gap appears between that date and 1689. On p. 514 of his *Days of Makemie,* Bowen, quoting further from the letter of Professor Witherow, gives the territory covered by the Presbytery of Laggan in 1681 and a list of the ministers of that Presbytery in 1681. Professor Witherow said that the Presbytery of Laggan in 1681 covered a district which, omitting the Presbytery of Linwardy, was about co-extensive with all the Presbyteries comprised in the modern synod of Derry and Omagh: viz., Derry, Glendermot, Letterkenny, Strabane, Raphoe, Omagh and Donegal. The following were the ministers of Laggan Presbytery in 1680, viz.: Robert Rule, of Derry; John Hart, of Taboyn; William Liston, of Letterkenney; Robert Campbell, of Ray; James Alexander, of Raphoe; John Hamilton, of Donaheady; Robert Craighead, of Donaughmore; Thomas Drummond, of Ramelton; David Brown, of Urney; James Tailazor, or Taylor, of Glendermot; Robert Wilson, of Strabane; William Traile, of Lifford; William Hampton, of Burt; Adam White, of Ardstraw; Samuel Haliday, of Omagh; William Henry, of Drumholm; John Rowatt, of

Cappaph; Thomas Wilson, of Killybegs; Fannet Congregation, vacant; Enniskillen Congregation, vacant.

[14](a) Bowen, *Days of Makemie,* Chapter IV, accepts the year 1683 as the time of Francis Makemie's arrival in Somerset County. See also Ford, *History of Manokin Presbyterian Church,* pp. 94-99, for an ably prepared "Makemie Chronology" based on authorities. The weight of evidence quoted by Mr. Ford gives 1683 as the time of Makemie's arrival. (McIlvaine, *Early Presbyterianism in Maryland,* p. 16; Roberts, *History of the Presbyterian Church, A Sketch,* p. 6; Howk, *Rehoboth by the River,* p. 8, as quoted by Ford.) Craighead, *Scotch and Irish Seeds in American Soil,* p. 287, quoted by Ford, says Makemie arrived "either in 1682 or 1683." The consensus of opinion among historians in the Presbyterian Church today is that Makemie arrived in Somerset County in 1683, and that Chuch celebrated the 250th anniversary of his arrival in October, 1933.

(b) That the Reverend William Traile was in Somerset County by June, 1683, we know from the recorded evidence of his having in that month officiated at the marriage of William Coulbourne Currier and Elizabeth Ellis (Somerset Court, Liber IKL, p. 383).

(c) Reverend Samuel Davis had a patent for tract of land called "Inch" on St. Martin's River, Somerset County, September 11, 1684 (Somerset Court, Deed Liber O 18, p. 138), and officiated, February 26, 1684/5, at the marriage of John Broughton and Elizabeth Bradshaw (Somerset Court, Liber IKL, p. 20).

(d) Reverend Thomas Wilson purchased, by deed dated January 20, 1685/6, land from Jacob Waring in Somerset County (Somerset Court, Deed Liber O 6, pp. 774-6). This is the first recorded reference we have found to Reverend Thomas Wilson as actually having arrived in Somerset County. McIlvaine, *Early Presbyterians in Maryland* (and followed by Ford, *History of Manokin Presbyterian Church,* p. 12), by erroneously identifying Reverend Thomas Wilson with another Thomas Wilson, also resident in Somerset (but a "layman" to all appearances), places the Reverend Thomas Wilson as being in Somerset County in May, 1681. In May, 1681, Colonel William Stevens assigned to one Thomas Wilson a tract of 350 acres of land, called "Darby"; but by tracing the descent of title to this land we have proved conclusively that Thomas Wilson, to whom the said tract was assigned, was an entirely distinct person from the Reverend Thomas Wilson.

Somerset records afford the following interesting item: Somerset Court held January 8, 1683 (1683/4), "Whereas this Co^{rt} is informed y^t John Roch of this County hath reported that there was four Thousand pounds of tobacco raysed out of ye County for incouragem^t of Ministers lately arrived here The said John Roch appearing ownes the report but saith his author is John Barnett ordered y^t John Barnet be summoned to appear to answer ye p^{r}misses next County Co^{rt} & y^t John Sterling Also his wife & Francis Martin be sumoned agt next County Co^{rt} & y^t John Roch give securitie to prosecute ye allegacon then Francis Martin appears & became security for app^a of John Roch in ye Summe of 5l. money Sterl. to y^t end & purpose pble to ye Lord Proprietary.

(Somerset Court, Judicials, November 16, 1683-March 11, 1683[4] in Deed Liber O 7 (front), p. 18).

[15] See for references about persecutions of Presbyterians in North of Ireland, above note 8.

[16] The facts in regard to the life of Francis Makemie are drawn from the "Chronological Outline of the Life of Francis Makemie," given in Ford's *History of Manokin Presbyterian Church*, pp. 94-102, and a study of references to Makemie in Bowen, *Days of Makemie*, p. 515, *et seq.*, and pp. 539-40 (note on date of first Presbytery); Briggs, *American Presbyterianism;* Webster, *History of the Presbyterian Church in America;* McIlvaine, *Early Presbyterianism in Maryland;* Wise, *Colonel John Wise of England and Virginia;* Wise, *Accawmacke;* McIlvaine, *The Struggle of Protestant Dissenters for Religious Toleration in Virginia;* Nottingham, *Accomack Tithables, 1663-1695;* Nottingham, *Accomack Wills and Administrations, 1663-1800*. Records of the Presbyterian Church in the U. S. A., Embracing Minutes of the Presbytery of Philadelphia, 1706-16 . . . Philadelphia: Presbyterian Board of Publication . . . 1841.

[17] The Reverend Francis Makemie's home in Accomack County, Virginia, was situated west of the now village of Temperanceville, Accomack County. A suitable memorial monument marks the site. Naomi (Anderson) Makemie married, *secondly,* James Kemp. See Bowen, *Days of Makemie*, p. 543, and Ford, *History of Manokin Presbyterian Church*, p. 101.

[18] This sketch of the Reverend William Traile is based upon the notes given in McIlvaine, *Early Presbyterianism in Maryland*, p. 19; Briggs, *American Presbyterianism*, pp. 116-117; and in Bowen, *Days of Makemie*, p. 522, *et seq.*, and obtained by him from Reid's *History of the Presbyterian Church in Ireland . . . Continued by Kellen . . . Belfast . . . 1867*, and correspondence with Professor Witherow, of Derry; Doctor Robert Anderson, of Glasgow, and Doctor Killen. Bowen enters the year 1684 as his first discovered reference to William Traile in the Somerset Court Records; however, Liber IKL, p. 38 (Somerset Court), records that William Traile officiated at marriage of William Coulbourne Currier and Elizabeth Ellis, June, 1683. Somerset Court, Deed Liber O 6, pp. 815 and 936, give the deeds to William Traile from Mark Manlove and Josiah Seward for the tracts of land "Brother's Love" and "Killelah." It was in opening up the last named tract of land that Traile found the main road in that direction required changing and so petitioned Somerset Court on June 11, 1689, "shewing that he is Setling of a New plantation on Pocomoke" and requesting "leave to alter the said Road by his plantation at his owne Charges a nearer and better way for the Inhabitants thereabouts who are likewise willing thereto." The petition was granted (Somerset Court, Judicials, Liber AW, p. 107). Traile's power of attorney to his wife, Eleanor Traile and Mrs. Eleanor Traile's deed to Archibald White, are given in Somerset Court, Liber EFG, p. 191, and Liber O 7, p. 12. Suit of Margaret, Lady Baltimore, against James Traile, son and heir of the Reverend William Traile, deceased, given in Somerset Court, Judicials, 1722-4, p. 97.

[19] The sketch of the Reverend Samuel Davis, based upon notes formerly pub-

lished in regard to him; see McIlvaine, *Early Presbyterianism in Maryland*, pp. 20-21; Briggs, *American Presbyterianism*, p. 124, *note;* Bowen, *Days of Makemie,* p. 523; *Records of the Presbyterian Church in the U. S. A., Embracing Minutes of Presbytery of Philadelphia, 1706-1716 . . . Philadelphia: Presbyterian Board of Publication . . . 1841;* Webster, *History of the Presbyterian Church in America,* p. 310; Ford, *History of Manokin Presbyterian Church,* p. 13. Somerset Court, Liber IKL, p. 20, gives evidence of Davis' presence in Somerset County, February, 1684/5, when he officiated at marriage of John Broughton and Elizabeth Bradshaw. Reverend Samuel Davis had a patent for tract called "Inch" on St. Martin's River, Somerset County, September 11, 1684 (Somerset Court, Deed Liber O 18, p. 138). The deed by which Samuel Davis acquired the lands called "Grove," on which he made his home, conveyed to him by William Round and Martha, his wife, in 1687, is recorded in Somerset Court, Deed Liber O 6, p. 853. June, 1703, a deed refers to Davis as "Samuel Davis formerly of Somerset and Province of Maryland, alias Doctor, now of Lewis Town in the Territory of Pennsylvania [i. e. Delaware]." May, 1705, he is designated, "Mr. Sam[ll] Davis of Lewis Town in County of Sussex, Territory of Pennsylvania Doctor." (Somerset Court, Deed Liber O 8, pp. 83 and 141). Inventory of Reverend Samuel Davis' estate, 1725, recorded in Worcester County Registry of Wills, Liber JW 15 (Inventories, 1688-1742), pp. 148-51.

[20] This sketch of the Reverend Thomas Wilson, based upon notes in Bowen, *Days of Makemie,* p. 524, containing the references in the Minutes of the Presbytery of Laggan relative to Wilson's connection with the charge of Killybegs in Donegal, Ireland, searched out by Professor Witherow, of Derry, and sent by him to Bowen; Ford, *History of Manokin Presbyterian Church,* p. 12; McIlvaine, *Early Presbyterianism in Maryland,* pp. 19-20 (McIlvaine, however, is in error in identifying the Reverend Thomas Wilson, of Somerset, and first pastor of Manokin Congregation, 1685-1702, with one Thomas Wilson, to whom Colonel William Stevens assigned in May, 1681, a tract of land in Somerset called "Darby." By tracing the title of descent of the tract called "Darby," we have been able to prove that the Thomas Wilson to whom it was granted was an entirely different person from the Reverend Thomas Wilson. McIlvaine also is in error in stating that Ephraim Wilson, Sheriff of Somerset, was a brother of Reverend Thomas Wilson. (Ephraim was the eldest surviving son of Reverend Thomas Wilson.) For the deed of Jacob Waring (a turner by trade) to the Reverend Thomas Wilson in January, 1685/6, for the land which became Wilson's "home-place," see Somerset Court, Deed Liber O 6, pp. 774-6, and for Wilson's deed of division of property between his sons, Ephraim Wilson and Thomas Wilson, Junior, in 1700, see Somerset Court, Deed Liber O 8, pp. 60-1. That the "home-place" (the tract of 130 acres called "The Turner's Purchase") of the Reverend Thomas Wilson finally became the Glebe of Somerset Parish and the residence of the rectors of that parish is attested by several conveyances recorded in Somerset Court. We wish to acknowledge here our debt of gratitude to Miss Louise Magruder, of Annapolis, Maryland, who most kindly investigated records in the Hall of Records there in an attempt to ascertain more definitely the

date of the Reverend Thomas Wilson's arrival in Somerset. No record, however, could be found by Miss Magruder which indicates Wilson's arrival earlier than our dating of 1685.

[21] Research in Somerset County records for evidence of the presence in the county, prior to 1700, of any other Presbyterian minister than Makemie, Traile, Wilson and Davis, disclosed but one item which would seem to indicate such a fact. In Somerset Court, Liber IKL, p. 173, is the entry that John McKnitt and Jane Wallis were married March 28, 1693, by *"Mr Burnett, minister of ye Gospell."* We have not been able, so far, to discover any further reference to this *"Mr Burnett."* Lists of clergymen of the Church of England in Maryland and Virginia at the date in question do not give his name as of that "faith and order." There is no list of Presbyterian ministers prior to 1706; and the "Index of Presbyterian Ministers, 1706-1881" does not give any Burnett for the early period. The *"Mr Burnett minister of ye Gospell,"* of the record quoted, may have been a Presbyterian minister visiting or sojourning in Somerset County for a brief period.* John McKnitt (McKnitt, McNitt) and Jane Wallis (also Wallace, as the records show) were most certainly of Scotch descent, and their families doubtless came to Somerset County from the North of Ireland—of "Scotch-Irish" stock. We can only place them as Presbyterians. The McKnitt-McNitt family was most certainly in later years markedly identified with the Presbyterian Church.

[22] *VIII Arcv. Md.,* p. 366; see *ante,* p. 152, for quotation in full of this record.

[23] See *ante,* p. 419, for note on Rehoboth Town.

[24] Bowen, *Days of Makemie,* p. 90, under "Chapter V, A. D. 1684": "Here, upon our own Pocomoke, we now raise our little sanctuary . . ." Bowen is here introducing this tradition imaginatively as he writes the story of Makemie; casting it in the form of a contemporary observer. Bowen does not—nor has any other writer upon this subject after whom we have read—attempt to trace the "source," or the backward extent in time of this tradition of the date of the erection of the first house of worship used by the Presbyterian Congregation at Rehoboth.

The Reverend Samuel McMaster (1744-1811), for 32 years pastor of Rehoboth Presbyterian Church, states in a fragment which remains of his account of early Presbyterianism in Somerset that "the first congregation [of Presbyterians] which worshipped at Rehoboth . . . formed themselves into a religious society for the public worship of God. A house for public worship was built on the west side of the [Pocomoke] River at a place called 'Rehoboth'." McMaster (who was pastor of Snow Hill, Pitts Creek and Rehoboth Presbyterian Churches, 1779-1811) does not give any date for the construction of this first house of worship erected by Presbyterians at Rehoboth. This statement is quoted by Irving Spence, *Letters on the Early History of the Presbyterian Church in America,* p. 97. For an account of McMaster and a note on

---

*Our friend, the Reverend Paul Trout, of Manokin Presbyterian Church, Princess Anne, Maryland, querries: "Could *Mr. Burnett, minister of ye gospel* be the *Mr. Thomas Barret,* a minister who lived in South Carolina, who, when he wrote to Reverend Francis Makemie from Ashley River, was to take shipping for New England. Barret is mentioned in a letter of Makemie to Mather in July, 1685, to whom he wrote also a letter."

his now extinct historical paper on Rehoboth Church see *A Sketch of Reverend Samuel McMaster (1744-1811)*, by John Stevenson McMaster; A. J. Doan, Printer, Jersey City, N. J., 1900. Andrew's *Tercentenary History of Maryland*, Vol. I, p. 361, describes Rehoboth as [in 1683] "then in Somerset, now Wicomico County." "Rehoboth" is now (1935), and always has been, in Somerset County.

[25] Bowen, *Days of Makemie*, p. 529, quotes this record stating the fact that Makemie (spelled in this record Mackemy) preached a funeral sermon at "Rehoboth Church," April 2, 1691. The statement of the fact appears in deposition made by John Vigorous before justices of Somerset Court as to certain blasphemous language used by one William Morris at the house of Mr. Edmund Howard, near Rehoboth Town, on "toward the night on the day aforesaid" [i. e. April 2, 1691, on which Mr. Makemie preached the funeral sermon in Rehoboth Church]. Vigorous' deposition was introduced as testimony i ntrial of William Morris for blasphemy; and record of this trial, including the Vigorous deposition, is given, Somerset Court, Judicials, Liber AW (1687-89; 1690-91), p. 90.

[26] For the probable identity of "Rehoboth Church" of 1691 with "Pocomoke Church" of 1692 see *ante*, p. 169, for a note on "Pocomoke Church."

[27] *Papers relating to the History of the Church in Maryland, 1694-1775* . . . by W. S. Perry . . . (1878), p. 22. This item, in regard to the three "Dissenting" houses of worship in Somerset, has been quoted by various writers on this subject: McIlvaine, *Early Presbyterianism in Maryland;* Bowen, *Days of Makemie;* Ethan Allen, *Who Were the Early Settlers of Maryland?;* Scharf, *Maryland*, Vol. I; Hodge, *History of the Presbyterian Church;* Ford, *History of Manokin Presbyterian Church*, etc., etc. We must note, however, that Ford (p. 14) gives the date of this report incorrectly as *1687,* ten years prior to its correct date of 1697.

[28] The following record in Somerset Court proves that the Presbyterian Congregation of Rehoboth was using, in March, 1702/3, the house of Peirce Bray (where the Reverend William Traile had lived) as their meeting place. Somerset Court, March 10, 1702 [1702/3], the following letter was presented and recorded:

> "Mr Dent, S^r pray be pleased to Record my house on the maine road wherein Mr Traile formerly Lived the psent meeting house for Mr Mackimme or others of his perwasion to preach in all at psent from
> S^r your humble servant   PEIRCE BRAY."
> March 18th. 1703.
> Recorded the 6th Day of May An^o Domij 1703 pr Peter Dent, Clke."
> (Somerset Court, Liber GI (O 8), Judicials, November 10, 1702—7ber 11th, 1705, p. 35).

Peter Dent was clerk of Somerset County. Pierce Bray was an elder of Rehoboth Congregation, and married Mary, widow of Archibald White, the said White having purchased in 1691 the home of the Reverend William Traile.

[29] The petition of the Coventry Parish Vestry presented by Reverend Robert

Keith and the Reverend Alexander Adams, and the petition of the Reverend George McNish, together with Somerset Court's action thereon, are given in Somerset Court, Liber AB (O 9), Judicials, 1705-1707, pp. 3-4. The justices composing the court at this session, November 14, 1705, were Captain John West, Major John Cornish, Mr. Thomas Newbold, Captain John Franklin, Captain Charles Ballard and Mr. Joseph Venables. See also Bowen, *Days of Makemie*, pp. 397-398.

[30] The records (as quoted of action of the Governor and Council in this matter of the petitions of Keith, Adams, McNish and Makemie are contained in proceedings of that body, February, 1705/6, April, 1706, February, 1706/7, and April, 1707, and are published in *XXV Arv. Md.*, pp. 200, 211 and 212, and *XXVI Arcv. Md.*, p. 528.

[31] The Church of England was the Established Church in the province of Maryland, and the provincial and parochial authorities were in duty bound to exercise every care in the protection of that Church's interest. The orders of the governor and Council (1706 and 1707) were an attempt to keep "Dissenters" from erecting "Meeting Houses" near buildings of the Established Church. However, a more liberal spirit prevailed and the order did not hold.

[32] Petition of Moses Fenton and Pierce Bray, the objection thereto by Captain John West and Joseph Gray, and final order registering the "New Meeting House" in Rehoboth Town, recorded Somerset Court, Liber EFH, Judicials, 1707-1711, pp. 106 and 140.

[33] The Reverend Francis Makemie by his will, dated April 27, 1708, probated in Accomack County, Virginia, Court, August 4, 1708, directed his executrix to sell certain properties, among them "my lot Joyning to the new meeting House Lott in Pocomoke Towne, called Rehoboth, empowering my executrix afterwards named to make over and Alienate that Lott on which the meeting house is built, in as ample manner to all intents and purposes, as shall be required for the ends and uses of a Presbyterian Congregation, as if I were personally present, and to their successors forever, and none else, but to such of the same perswation in matters of Religion." The testator's wife, Naomi, was named as executrix. (Accomack County, Virginia, Court, Wills, &c, 1692-1715, p. 443). A search in Somerset Court records for the deed of Makemie's executrix Naomi Makemie (who married, secondly, James Kemp) has failed to discover her deed conveying the "meeting house lot" as directed. The title to the Rehoboth Town lands in later years, however, became involved in the properties of Colonel Robert Jenckins Henry, and he by his will, dated July 21, 1764, probated November 14, 1766, cleared the title to the lot on which the Presbyterian Church stood by the following devise: "It is my will and desire that the Land whereon the Presbyterian Meeting House and retireing house in the Town of Rehoboth now stand and a convenient small quantity of Ground about the same may be forever quietly and peaceably used and without Interruption enjoyed by the People of the Presbyterian Congregation of Pocomoke for their Assembling for Divine Worship as they have heretofore done." (Somerset Registry of Wills, Liber EB 4, p. 119-121).

[34]'That the Reverend Samuel Davis resided on the "Grove" tract, about two miles northeast of Snow Hill Town, is evidenced by a record in January, 1689/90, of the names of certain persons dwelling at that date, "some very near and others some farther off from the Indian Town." Among the names of persons appearing in this list are those of Samuel Davis, George Truitt, John Goddin, and William Round (Somerset Court, Judicials, Liber EFG, p. 33). The Indian Town referred to was on the north side of Pocomoke River, above the town of Snow Hill (which is on the south side of the river). John Galbraith, a Scotch merchant, residing in Snow Hill Town, in his will, dated August 12, 1691, makes (among others) a bequest "to Mr. Samuel Davis minister at Snow Hill." (Somerset Court, Liber BWZ, 1690-2, p. 94).

[35]*Papers relating to the History of the Church in Maryland, 1694-1775* . . . by W. S. Perry . . . (1878), p. 22.

[36]Somerset Court, Liber A B (O 9), Judicials, 1705-1707, p. 12, a court order was directed to be "published at the Churches and *meeting houses at Snow Hill* and Sea Side" prohibiting persons to drive or catch horses on the "great bridge" on Pocomoke River. On February 19, 1718/19, John Bishop, Junior, and William Henderson and Elizabeth, his wife, conveyed to Robert Martin "Two lots in Snow Hill Town . . . Lying & being along the head of the Lotts between the lot now belonging to Thomas Robins and the Alley between *The Meeting house Lott* and the Lott belonging to Edward Martin being numbered by the Last Survey or Laying out of the said Town Number twenty three & Number twenty four [Lots Nos. 23 and 24]." On August 18, 1721, Robert King and Priscilla, his wife, conveyed to Robert Martin a lot and house in Snow Hill Town described as "standing at this day upon ye East side of the Street *opposite to ye Church* having ye Lott of Edward Martin lying upon ye South side & *ye Meeting house of desenters above it.* (Somerset Court, Deed Liber O 13, p. 265, and Deed Liber O 14, p. 156).

The description of the location of the lot conveyed August 18, 1721, by the Kings to Robert Martin certainly places the *"Meeting House of desenters"* (which was the "Meeting House" of the Presbyterian Congregation of Snow Hill) very near to *"ye Church"* (Church of England building). *"Ye Church"* certainly stood on the lower part of the original lot No. 9, and next to the Pocomoke River. (See Worcester Court, Deed Liber P, p. 293, plat of Snow Hill Town, 1793). The lot of Edward Martin was certainly lot No. 11.* This lot No. 11, as shown by several deeds and wills in Somerset and Worcester Court and Worcester Registry of Wills, descended in the Martin family for some years. This lot No. 11 is shown by the plat of Snow Hill Town, 1793 (Worcester Court, Deed Liber P, p. 293), to have been bounded by Green Alley, Strawberry Alley and the Pocomoke River. The "Meeting House of desenters"—the first Meeting House erected by the Presbyterian Congregation of Snow Hill—probably stood somewhere along Green Alley, near Strawberry Alley, and in the vicinity of lot 10 of the above referred to plat of Snow Hill.

---

*Somerset Court, Liber EFH, 1707-1711, page 149, Edward Martin takes up Lot 11 in Snow Hill Town, October 21, 1706; *Ibid.*, Deed Liber O 21, page 16, John Martin sells Lot No. 11 to James Martin; see also *XLII Arcv. Md.*, page 417, Act of Assembly confirming title to Lot No. 11.

[37] and [38]Record of Session of Snow Hill Presbyterian Church, 1751-1801 (original manuscript in the Presbyterian Historical Society, Philadelphia, Pennsylvania), gives facts relative to erection of this new "Meeting House" and its completion. Worcester Court, Deed Liber B, p. 78, gives the deed, 1748, of John Martin to Adam Spence, Thomas Milbourne and Matthew Hopkins for Lot 32 in Snow Hill Town "on which the Protestant Presbyterian Dissenting Meeting House hath been lately built and now standeth." The Session record refers to agreement with William Nilson in 1745 for building the "Meeting House" in Snow Hill Town and in September, 1747, to a meeting about building seats in the "Meeting House," and January 11, 1752, there is record of allotment of seats to members of the congregation. In January, 1762, William Nilson, John Irving and Adam Spence were appointed to settle with Samuel Hopkins for building [addition to?] Meeting House and to make return to the next meeting of Session, and July 3, 1762, there is record of having paid Samuel Hopkins £1:17s. 6d. currency, being balance due him for *"building addition"* to Meeting House as appears p^r receipt." Then on May 13, 1795, appears the subscriptions to be taken to build a "Meeting House" on Lot 32.

[39]Record Book of Session of Manokin Presbyterian Church, July 20, 1747-1800; manuscript in possession of the Manokin Presbyterian Church, Princess Anne, Maryland. See also Ford, *History Manokin Presbyterian Church (1910)*, p. 50. Ford relates, by his excerpts from Session records, and other sources, the various modifications made from time to time in the original "Meeting House" building of 1765, resulting in the present modernized building as supported by the original foundation and walls.

[40]*Papers relating to the History of the Church in Maryland, 1694-1775* . . . by W. S. Perry . . . (1878), p. 22.

[41]Somerset Court, Judicials, Liber P, 1701-1702, p. 26, in an order about laying out the Pocosan Road, which can be identified as the road leading through the back country from head of Wicomico Creek to headwaters of the Manokin River, directs that the said road be laid out from Archibald Smith's path at the branch down by Alexander Brown's door and thence by John Gray's and through William Polk's pasture and "from thence away by William Smith's *by the C[h]urch."* (Somerset Court, Liber AB (O 9), Judicials, 1705-1707, p. 110, Somerset Court, held June 12, 1706, "This day appeared Mr. John Hampton and Mr. George Macnish Exhibited an order from his Ex^{ny} the Govr & honourable Councill* for their Qualification to preach in this County in obedience thereunto the Court did administer ye Oath appointed pr Act of Parliament to ye sd Hampton & M^{c}nish who did Comply therewith and did Likewise subscribe ye Declaration whereupon this Court did allow ye aforesaid Hampton & Macknish should preach att ye meeting house near Mrs. Edgars, the meeting house att ye head of Monocan, ye meeting house at Snow Hill & ye meeting

*In Somerset Court, Liber AB (O 9), page 110, and immediately following the above quoted order of the court, is the record of the governor's and Council's order: "By his Exncy the Govr March the 13th 1705 [1705/6] Ordered yt ye Worpfull Justices of Somerset County take ye oaths of ye Dessenting Ministers according to ye Act of Parliamt of ye first of King Wm. & Queen Mary Exempting her Matyes protestant Subjects from Certain penaltys &-ca. Signed pr Order W. Bladen Cl[erk] Councell. Indorst to Somerset Court."

house on Mr. Joseph Venables Land as pr ye Desenting preachers required." This "order of court" is also given in Bowen, *Days of Makemie,* p. 411, but there modernized as to spelling; and the Edgar item is given as "near *Mr.* Edgars," while the original record gives the item quite clearly as "near *Mrs.* Edgars." Our reading of the "original" has been verified by H. Filmore Lankford, Esq., of Princess Anne, Maryland, and the Reverend Paul Trout, pastor of Manokin Presbyterian Church, Princess Anne. Ford, *History Manokin Presbyterian Church,* p. 34, also refers to the above court order in so far as it pertains to the Manokin "meeting house."

[42] Somerset Court, Liber EFH, Judicials, 1707-1711, p. 106, petition of George McNish for registration of "Meeting House" near Manokin River bridge; and the court's order therein. This document also given in Bowen's *Days of Makemie,* p. 493, but modernized as to spelling.

[43] Somerset Court, Deed Liber O 15, p. 71, deed August 19, 1723, Charles Ballard, of Somerset County, Gentleman, to the Reverend William Stewart, John Tunstall, Robert King, John Gray, Robert Wilson, Mark Smith, Richard Wallace, William Alexander and James Strawbridge, Elders of the Presbyterian Congregation of Manokin. The title is recited as by grant to Christopher Nutter, August 5, 1667, 300 acres, called "Nutter's Purchase," in Somerset County, north side the head of Manokin River, between lands of Owen Magraw and John Nelson; said land became property of said Ballard's father by purchase, and descended to him; "and the said Charles Ballard out of Good will and respect which he hath for the service of God as allso for the consideration of five shillings to him in hand paid hath freely given and granted to the above named persons being the Present Pasture [pastor] and Elders of above said Congregation and to their successors forever for the use Support Mentainance and Continuance of a Meeting House for the worship and Service of Allmighty God according to the Presbyterian pSwasion and for no other use whatsoever Being Bounded as followeth Beginning at a marked red oake with Sixteen Notches Six poles [?] and 3 yards north five degrees West from the East side of the End of the Casway [causeway] thence running north by west Six perches thence with a line drawn South Six perches and from thence East to the first bounder Containing and thought to be fourth of an Acre of Land . . ."

[44] "Manokin Bridge" is referred to at various times in the Somerset records. It was located in these early days either at the point where the bridge at present time (1935) crosses "headwaters" of the river on Main Street, Princess Anne (some 50 yards south of Manokin Presbyterian Church), or some 100 yards east of the present (1935) bridge at a point on the river familiar as the site of the old Bombay-hook Bridge. On "12th 9ber 1689" Somerset Court ordered Captain David Browne, Mr. Roger Woolford and Mr. Stephen Lufte to employ workmen to build a bridge over the wading place at the head of Manokin River (Somerset Court, Judicials, Liber EFG, p. 10). In January, 1696, a court order refers to road from the Courthouse to Manokin Bridge (Somerset Court, Juidcials, Liber DD 17, p. 174). November, 1697, repairs ordered to Manokin Bridge (*Ibid.,* p. 267). After this date frequent references to Manokin Bridge occur in court orders about road overseers.

[45] The title to the Manokin Presbyterian Church site is set forth in the deeds of Somerset Court; a deed November, 1672, from Christopher Nutter to Charles Ballard (Senior), Deed Liber O 3, p. 206, and the deed August 19, 1723, Charles Ballard (Junior), to the Reverend William Stewart, and others, Elders of the Manokin Presbyterian Congregation, Deed Liber O 15, p. 71. The residue of the "Nutter's Purchase" plantation was devised by Charles Ballard (will dated February 24, 1723/4; probated January 21, 1724/5) to his son, Henry Ballard. Charles Ballard, who deeded the land on which the Meeting House of Manokin Congregation stood (and the Church now stands), married Eleanor King, daughter of Major Robert King, of "Kingsland," and sister of Colonel Robert King, of "Kingsland," an elder of Manokin Congregation in 1723 and later. Mrs. Eleanor (King) Ballard's sister, Mary King, married, *first,* Colonel Francis Jenckins; *second,* Reverend John Henry; *third,* Reverend John Hampton. Henry and Hampton were pastors, respectively, of Rehoboth and Snow Hill Presbyterian Congregations (see King family, *ante,* p. 367, *et seq.*). The final perfecting of title of the Manokin Presbyterian Church site was made by deeds October 16, 1812, Elizabeth Jackson to Samuel Ker and George Handy (Somerset Court, Deed Liber O 42, pp. 26-27), and July 31, 1827, Samuel Ker and Elizabeth Handy (widow and relict of George Handy, Senior, deceased) to William Jones, Senior, Samuel Ker, William Stewart, Henry P. C. Wilson, George Handy and Robert Patterson (Somerset Court, Deed Liber O 53, p. 556).

[46] *Papers relating to the History of the Church in Maryland, 1694-1775* . . . by W. S. Perry . . . (1878), p. 22.

[47] The following item, in regard to roads in Old Somerset County, will be of interest in this connection. At Somerset Court, January 16, 1696 (1696/7): "And for the better asserting what are Publick Roads are as followes from Penfex Point to the Co^{rt} house the former road continued and from the Indian River the ancient Road to the Court house continued & from the line of Accomack [Maryland-Virginia boundary line] to meet at George Trewett's Plantacon from Pocomoke ferry to meet the said Road &c and from Pocomoke ferry the road over Littleton's Creeke to Snow Hill as formerly cleared from the Court to Manoakin Bridge the old Road from thence to Wiccocomoco ferry and from thence to Nanticoke ferry (vizt) John Rusells, and all other Roads not expressed to be cleared by the overseers as formerly according to Act of Assembly &c." (Somerset Court, Liber DD 17, Judicials, p. 174).

It will be noted that the center of this "road system" was the Courthouse of Somerset County. The Courthouse was at that time—January, 1696/7—situated on the north side of the Pocomoke River and west side of Dividing Creek, immediately in the fork where the creek enters the river. The *"road going up along the sea side,"* as referred to by the sheriff of Somerset County in 1697 as the location of one of the "meeting houses," seems unquestionably to have been the road referred to in this court order as running *from the line of Accomack* [the Maryland-Virginia boundary line] *to meet at George Trewett's plantation."* Trewett's [Truitt's, Truit's] plantation was about four and a half miles north of Snow Hill Town and on the south (really the east) side of the Pocomoke

River (see *ante,* p. 108, for Trewett's plantation). The meeting of this *"sea side road"* with the road at George Trewett's plantation was probably made by a road run in a westerly direction (about 2 or 3 miles) from the main "sea side road" to unite with the road at Trewett's plantation. We certainly pick up the main "sea side road" again at the present railroad station at Newark in Worcester County (which was prior to 1742 Somerset County).[*] From this point (Newark) the "sea side road" runs in a northerly direction, crossing the head of Newport Creek and on to the town of Berlin, thence north, crossing the Middle and Burch branches of St. Martin's River and through the town of Bishopsville, Maryland, thence crossing the Maryland-Delaware line and into Delaware and across the Indian River. In January, 1696/7, when the above quoted court order about roads was entered, the Indian River (now in lower Sussex County, Delaware) was counted as being in Somerset County, Maryland. The Maryland-Delaware boundary line had not at that date been settled. The road referred to in the court order of January, 1696/7, as *"from the Indian River the ancient road to the Court house continued,"* was probably the road which at present turns west from the present main highway, just north of the present St. Martin's Church (north of the town of Berlin), and, running westerly, crossed the headwaters of the Pocomoke River (in what is now Wicomico County), thence turning south and running in a southerly direction (along the west side of Pocomoke River) to within a few miles of Snow Hill Town, thence turning again in a westerly direction continued across the Nasawango Creek and on to Dividing Creek and the then Somerset County Courthouse.

"Pocomoke Ferry," referred to in the above court order of January, 1696/7, was situated on the Pocomoke River, crossing the river from the north side thereof, from the plantation of one Edward Stevens, called "Blake's Hope," to the south side of the said river and landing at a point about a quarter of a mile east of the present (1935) Pocomoke City. This ferry was also called "Stevens' Ferry" and was kept by one Edward Stevens (see *ante,* p. 264, for this Stevens' Ferry, or Pocomoke Ferry). The road from "Pocomoke Ferry" (to meet "the ancient road" at the courthouse), as referred to in the court order above, ran from the ferry landing on the north side of the Pocomoke River (at Edward Stevens' plantation) in an easterly (or northeasterly) direction to the Courthouse.

"Penfex Point," referred to in the above court order, is on the north side of the Pocomoke River and is now called Williams Point. The ancient "Penfex [or Penfax] Point" evidently derived its name from one Daniel Penfax, of London, Mariner, who purchased the tract of land called "Glyneath," on which the "point" is located, from Jenkin Price, of Somerset County, June 14, 1671 (Somerset Court, Liber DT 7, Judicials, 1670-1, pp. 155-162, deed of Price to Penfax). The road "from Penfex Point to the Co^{rt}house" ran from the "point" in a northeasterly direction and along the west side of the Pocomoke River.

---

[*]William B. Marye, of Baltimore, who has made a careful study of sites of old Indian towns on the seaboard side of Somerset (now Worcester) County, writes us: "I no longer have the slightest doubt that the 'road up the sea side' is the road which runs through [the villages of] Wesley, *Newark* and Ironshire up to Berlin and beyond."

The road referred to as "from Pocomoke Ferry, the road over Littleton's Creek to Snow Hill," was a road evidently beginning at the ferry landing on the *south* side of the Pocomoke River and running thence to Snow Hill Town. "Manoakin Bridge" referred to was a bridge at the head of the Manokin River at the present site of the town of Princess Anne. See note 44 above.

[48]Somerset Court, Liber AB (O 9), Judicials, p. 12, for references in 1705 to "church and *meeting houses* at Snow Hill and Sea Side."

VI

Human Origins

[1]Wise, *Accawmacke,* see especially Chapter VI, "Origin of the People," from p. 73-80; Chapter IX, "The Dutch War, The Eastern Shore [of Virginia] Under the Commonwealth, The Northampton Protest," and Chapter XIV, "The Early Church on the Eastern Shore, Puritan Ministers, Makemie."

[2]For report of Randall Revell in May, 1662, on state of Manokin-Annemessex Settlement, numbering 50 tithables, see *post* Appendix II.

[3]References to authoritative sources for all facts from this point on, in regard to individuals who appear as "first settlers," will be found in notes given under their respective surnames in Appendix X.

[4]See *ante,* p. 75, for Anthony Johnson, free Negro.

[5]George Johnson and Katherine, his wife, had three sons, two of whom died in infancy, and the other, named George, who remained in England, where he died leaving an only child, a daughter, Ann Johnson. See *ante,* Johnson in Appendix X.

[6]The Somerset Court records contain references to several physicians in the years succeeding the time of John Rhodes, Thomas Walley and George Hasfurt, who appear as the earliest of Somerset County "chirurgeons." *Doctor John Vigorous* appears as early as July, 1670, in the Pocomoke River neighborhood. At this date he appears as witnessing a deed from Thomas Walker to John Powell (Somerset Court, Judicials, Liber DT 7, pp. 41-3). In August, 1677, "Anne ye daughter of *John Vigorous, Chirurgeon,* was borne of Anne his wife att Pocomoke" (Somerset Court, Liber IKL, p. 263). In the estate account of Capt. Thomas Walker, decd., recorded October 8, 1685, there is reference to accounts paid *Doctor John Vigorous* and *Doctor William Stevens* (Somerset Registry of Wills, Liber EB 13, pp. 1-5). In June, 1689, there is a reference to *"a Doctor by name James Steward"* who treated one Thomas Weatherhead, and in March, 1690/1, reference appears to *"Mr Walter Lodge, of Somerset, Chyrurgeon"* (Somerset Court, Liber AW, 1688-9, and 1690-1, pp. 74 and 107). In November, 1683, *James Pearse, of Somerset County, Chirurgeon,* appears in court (Somerset Court, Liber O 7 [reverse, Judicials, 1683], p. 7). The above are

just references to "chirurgeons" on which the eye fell as we were reading through the early Somerset records. For Rhodes, Walley and Hasfurt notes see *post* Appendix X.

[7] For complaint of John Avery against Edward Jones, and Avery's petition, and the decision of court in this matter, see Somerset Court, Liber DT 7 (Judicials), pp. 185-6.

[8] The reference to "George Hasfurt, Schoolmaster," is in Somerset Court, Liber AZ, Judicials, 1671-5, in the back of the volume where some entries are made on reversed unnumbered and torn pages.

[9] See references to "James Osborne, Schoolmaster," in the estate account of Capt. Thomas Walker, decd., recorded Somerset in Registry of Wills, Liber EB 13, pp. 1-5.

[10] Richard Walton's will, dated April 10, 1686, probated August 14, 1686, is recorded in Somerset Registry of Wills, Liber EB 5, pp. 180-1.

[11] Ambrose Dixon's will, dated April 7, 1686, probated August 10, 1686, is recorded in Somerset Registry of Wills, Liber EB 5, pp. 165-6.

[12] For reference to school held in 1696 at head of Crane Creek, south side of the Annemessex River, see deposition of Capt. Thomas Williams (aged about 55 years), made November 10, 1739, in relation to boundaries of "Dixon's Choice" tract, which Thomas Dixon was re-establishing; the said deposition by Williams is given in Somerset Court, Judicials, 1738-1740, pp. 201-202.

[13] Somerset Court, Liber O 1, pp. 1 and 5.

[14] *III Arc. Md.,* pp. 445, 467, 472, 488, 489, 490, 513 and 526, for commissions to John Nuttall; and same volume, p. 490, for commissions to Jenkin Price and James Jolley.

[15] For reference to "Hollinsworth, Master of a Northern Vessel," see *post* Appendix III in Col. Scarburgh's report of his proceedings at Annemessex-Manokin, October, 1663. For the references to George Johnson and John Elzey see under "Founders." For references to Thomas Freeman, Charles Ballard, William Smyton, James Weedon, Edward Martindale, Thomas Jones and Devorax Browne, as "Merchants," and to James Powell, Matthew Armstrong and Stephen Bond, as "Mariners," see Somerset Court, Deed Liber O 1, pp. 17, 51, 89, 113, 123, 126, 131, 147 and 148, and Liber AZ, 1671-5 (Judicials) p. 528. For reference to Thomas Freeman, of Bristol and Somerset, see Somerset Court, Deed Liber O 1, p. 126, and Liber IKL, under letter "F" in register of births, marriages and deaths. For reference to David Brown and Archibald Erskine see under Chapter X, *ante.* Archibald Erskine married Janet, sister of David Brown.

[16] For references to names of the men mentioned as carpenters, tailors, coopers, sawyer, shoemaker, hatter, blacksmith, boatwright and butcher see Somerset Court, Deed Liber O 1, p. 107, and Liber AZ, 1671-5 (Judicials), pp. 19, 31, 48, 58, 73, 84, 93, 110, 112, 116, 119, 125, 141, 182, 215 and 251. The reference to Nicholas Rise as "carpenter" is in *XLIX Arcv. Maryland,* p. 369.

VII

Founders

Stephen Horsey

[1] Stephen Horsey, born *circa* 1620; a deposition made September, 1670, by Stephen Horsey, *"aged about 50 years"* (Somerset Court, Liber DT 7, 1670-1, p. 6, *et seq.*).

[2] Though the parentage and birthplace of Stephen Horsey (*circa* 1620-1671), of Somerset County, Maryland, have not been discovered, he no doubt came from one of the branches of the Horsey family which resided in Warwickshire, Dorsetshire, and Hertfordshire, in England.

[3] Greer, *Early Virginia Immigrants, 1623-1666*, p. 167.

[4] Stephen Horsey, who intermarried with Sarah, relict of Michael Williams, decd., confirms gift made by said Sarah during her widowhood to her three children, Michael, Sarah and Thomas Williams; deed dated December 28, 1650, recorded June 21, 1654, Northampton (Virginia) Court, Order Book, 1651-4, No. 4, p. 193.

[5] Wise, *Accawmacke*, pp. 137-143 and 153-4.

[6] *Journals House of Burgesses of Virginia, 1619-1658/9*, p. 21.

[7] For Scarburgh's statements about Horsey see *ante*, Appendix III.

[8] Northampton (Virginia) Court, Order Book, 1657-64, p. 36.

[9] The date *"27 Feby 1660"* which appears in Land Patents, Liber 4, p. 580 (Hall of Records, Annapolis), over the two items: "Warrant to Stephen Horsey," each for 600 acres *"return the last of Jan."* and the date *"16 Aug^t"* appearing in the margin opposite the entries of these "warrants" to Horsey are indeed confusing. The volume, Land Patents, Liber 4, is a composite manuscript book, the photostatic copy (which is in use for reference) and the "original" (from which the photostatic copy was made) having both been examined by us. Land Patents, Liber 4, from p. 541 to p. 627, contains the record of certain warrants for land, with the caption *"Anno 1661 Record for Land."* The left-hand margin of the pages, also the center of the pages above each warrant, or group of warrants, issued on the same date, carry dates for the year 1661. When we come to pages 580 and 581 we find the singular entries for Stephen Horsey and William Coulbourne as follows: in the left-hand margin the dates *"16 Augst,"* (obviously 1661), with in the center of page (and following immediately a warrant on "8th August [1661]" to one Marcome) the items: *"27 Feby 1660 Warrant to layout for Stephen Horsey"* 600 acres, *"return the last of Jan";* and warrant to Horsey for 600 acres more, *"return the last of Jan,"* and the warrants to William Coulbourne (under same date), two tracts, one of 500 acres, *"return the last of Jan,"* the other, 400 acres, *return the last of June next."* Horsey entered the names of 13 "rights" and *"the rest he is to enter last of June next."* Coulbourne entered the names of 51 "rights" and *"the rest to be made good by last of June next."*

· 545 ·

The date *"27 Feby 1660"* is February, 1660/1, while *"the last of Jan'* would be January, 1661/2, and *"the last of June next"* would be June, 1661, provided the reference is back to *"27 Feby 1660."* However, if the reference is to the date in the margin, *"16 August* [1661]," *"the last of Jan'* would refer to January, 1661/2, and *"the last of June next"* would refer to June, 1662. The area in which the lands granted on these warrants of survey to Horsey and Coulbourne was not opened to settlement until November, 1661 (see *ante,* p. 13), so it was certainly after that time that the surveys and grants were made. The only explanation of the date "27 Feby 1660 [1660/1]" seems to be that Horsey and Coulbourne at that date made application to the Provincial authorities for grants of land in Maryland in anticipation of the opening up of this lower Eastern Shore area to settlement (a matter which had been under consideration since 1651-1656; see *ante,* pp. 11-12). Then, when warrants for land in this area were actually issued Horsey and Coulbourne had surveys and patents for their respective tracts on the south side of the Annemessex River.

[10] See *ante,* Chapter I and III, for Horsey in commissions of peace for "the Eastern Shore below Choptank"; Chapter IV for his offices in Somerset County.

[11] Somerset Court, Liber IKL.

Ambrose Dixon

[1] Greer, *Early Virginia Immigrants, 1623-1666,* p. 96. Nothing is indicated about Dixon's forbears.

[2] Wise, *Accawmacke,* pp. 135-7.

[3] Greer, *Early Virginia Immigrants, 1623-1666,* p. 96.

[4] See Scarburgh's statement about Ambrose Dixon, *ante,* Appendix III.

[5] Northampton (Virginia) Court, Order Book, 1657-64, pp. 82 and 83.

[6] *Ibid.,* pp. 36 and 123.

[7] Somerset Court, Liber IKL.

[8] Somerset Court, Judicials, Liber DT 7, 1670-1, p. 52; *II Arcv. Md.,* pp. 239, 241.

Randall Revell

[1] Northampton (Virginia) Court, Vol. I (Order Book, 1633-40), p. 28, deposition February 19, 1634/5, Randall Revell, *aged 21 years or thereabouts;* that Revell was in Accomack County January, 1633/4, September, 1636, and October, 1637, see *Ibid.,* pp. 10, 57 and 85. Somerset Court, Judicials, Liber AZ, No. 8; 1671-5, p. 286, a deposition by Randall Revell, *aged 60 years or more.* For circumstantial evidence that Randall Revell, of Accomack and St. Mary's, were identical see *ante,* Appendix X, "First Settlers."

[2] Wise, *Accawmacke,* p. 136.

[3] *Ibid.,* p. 122.

[4] *Journals of the House of Burgesses of Virginia, 1619-1657/8,* p. 23; Wise, *Accawmacke,* p. 122; Northampton (Virginia) Court, Order Book, 1657-64, p. 40.

⁵For Revell as "cooper" and "wine-cooper" see deeds in Northampton (Virginia) Court, Wills and Deeds, Vol. IX, 1657-62, p. 2.
⁶Somserset Court, Deed Liber O 1, p. 80.
⁷Somerset Court, Liber DT 7, 1670-1, p. 6; *III Arcv. Md.*, p. 70.

John Elzey

¹The rights for land, February 28, 1655/6, given in Northampton (Virginia) Court, Vol. V, p. 142. For references to Elzey's in Southampton, England, see *XXXIX Va. Mag. Hist. and Biog.*, pp. 345-6. For deeds John Elzey and Sarah, his wife, see Appendix X.

²Liber IKL (Somerset Court), which records the death of John Elzey, gives the date as *May, 1663*. There is every evidence that Elzey was still alive as late as *February, 1663/4* (see *ante*, p. 58). The entry in Liber IKL as *1663* is obviously a clerical error.

William Thorne

¹Northampton (Virginia) Court, Order Book, 1651-4, p. 219; Order Book, 1657-64, pp. 37 and 77; Deeds and Wills, &c., 1654-5, p. 74.
²Deed Thorne and wife, to Roberts, Somerset Court, Deed Liber O 1, p. 138.
³Will of William Thorne, *Maryland Calendar of Wills*, Vol. I, p. 51.

John Odber

¹*III Arcv. Md.*, pp. 347, 394, 402, 411, 417, 434, 471, 476, 488 and 490; *V Arcv. Md.*, p. 195.

In Dorchester (Maryland) Court, Land Records, No. 5 Old, 1692-1701, folio 35 appears a deed May 10, 1686, describing Ababco as "native of the Province of Maryland and King of the Natives, or Indians, of the Lower Found, or Nation of Indians, in Choptank River in the said Province called in my langauge Transquakins."

Thomas Price

¹Northampton (Virginia) Court, Order Book, 1651-4, pp. 42 and 45.
²Price is called "leather dresser" by Col. Edmund Scarburgh; see *ante*, Appendix III.
³Somerset Court, Deed Liber O 1, p. 2, and Deed Liber O 6, p. 758.
⁴Sussex County, Delaware, Registry of Wills, Liber A 1, pp. 19-20, the will of Thomas Price, dated March 14, 1694 [1694/5], probated March 25, 1695.

George Johnson

¹Northampton County (Virginia) Court, Order Book, 1657-64, p. 165. On March 2, 1662/3, George Johnson, aged about 35 years, made deposition relative to a bargain between Henry Smith and Henry White.

²Will of George Johnson, dated November 30, 1680, probated December 23, 1681, recorded in Somerset Registry of Wills, Liber EB 5, pp. 137-8.

³Somerset Court Judicials, Liber DD 17, 1696-8, pp. 189-190, a statement filed in Somerset Court, March 9, 1696/7, by Mrs. Katherine (Butcher) Johnson-Evernden, of Somerset County, Maryland, widow of George Johnson, Merchant, in Annemessex, Somerset County, and now wife of Thomas Evernden, of Annemessex. The statement was made to prove a question of heirship to property in England. "March 9, 1696, attested in open court according to allowance by Act of Parliament to the People Call^d Quakers. Test. P. Dent, Clerk." This shows Mrs. Katherine (Butcher) Johnson-Evernden to have been a member of the Society of Friends.

⁴Will of George Johnson; reference as above.

⁵Northampton County (Virginia) Court, Order Book, 1657-1664, "List of [owners] of sheep...Northampton County," January 28, 1660 [1660/1], among names: George Johnson, James Jones at George Johnson's house, John Goddin, Goddin, in after years married Katherine, daughter of George Johnson; *Ibid.,* p. 102, list of tobacco received January 26, 1661; Tithables in Northampton County, 1662; *Ibid.,* p. 165, deposition of George Johnson, aged about 35 years, deposition made March 2, 1662 [1662/3].

⁶For Scarburgh's description of George Johnson see Appendix III.

⁷Title to "Straights," see Appendix IX, conveyance of property by Anne Johnson to Robert King.

⁸Will of George Johnson, dated November 30, 1680, probated December 23, 1681, Somerset Registry of Wills, Liber EB 5, pp. 137-8, last clause for bequest to "poor Friends."

Henry Boston

¹Northampton County (Virginia) Court, Deeds, Wills, &c., 1654-5, No. 5, p. 74. Querry: Did Henry Boston marry the widow of Augustine Moore, or some member of Moore's family? A search in Northampton records would probably show (Northampton County, Virginia, Order Book, 1657-1664, p. 14.

² and ³Northampton County (Virginia) Court Order Book, 1657-1664, pp. 69-71 and 109.

⁴Record of presentment by Grand Jury, and of the suits, Somerset Court, Judicials, Liber AZ, 1671-5, pp. 79, 121 and 126.

⁵March 8, 1669 [1669/70], fine of 500 pounds tobacco placed on Judith Best for having a bastard child (Somerset Court, Judicials, Liber AZ, 1671-5, p. 67. March 13, 1669 [1669/70], Henry Boston deeded cow and calf to Judith Best "for and in consideration of her three barrells of Indian corne which was her freedome corne." (Evidently Judith Best was an indentured servant of Henry Boston). (Somerset Court, Judicials, Liber DT, No. 7, 1670-1-, p. 127. November 8, 1670, marriage banns published between Thomas Davis, Tailor, and Judith Best, both of Somerset County (Somerset Court, Judicials, Liber DT 7, 1670-1, p. 37. August 11, 1677, Robt. Catlin, Jr., petition to have Richard Boston,

bastard child of Henry Boston, begotten on the body of Judith Best, now wife of Thos. Davis, Tailor. Said Jude Davis, mother of said Richd. Boston, gives consent; said Richd. Boston showed his willingness to serve said Catlin until he is of age (Somerset Court, Judicials, November 9, 1675, to August 15, 1677, in back of Deed Liber O 7, p. 133).

[6] Somerset Court, Deed Liber O 5, p. 151, deed November 13, 1677, Henry Boston to Thos. Walker; Deed Liber O 6, p. 1, deed of Thos. Walker to Wm. Planner.

[7 and 8] Somerset Court, Liber IKL, register of Births, Marriages and Deaths under letter "B."

[9] Somerset Court, Deed Liber O 5, p. 133, Henry Boston, Jr.'s, statement and proof of his age.

William Coulbourne

[1] While we cannot, as yet, positively identify William Coulbourne, of Somerset County, Maryland, as a member of the Coulbourne family of Somersetshire, England, yet it is not unlikely that such was his "origin." Harlein Society Publications, Vol. XI, p. 26, visitation of county of Somerset, England, 1623, give the following significant pedigree. William Colborne, of Wythehill, county Somerset, was father of John Colborne, who was father of Thomas Colborne, who was father of William Colborne, of Braton, county Somerset, living in 1623, and who married Mary Topp and had issue: (1) Charles Colborne, born 1603; (2) William Colborne, born 1604; (3) Edward Colborne, born 1609; (4) John Colborne, born 1611. The coat of arms of this family are given as "Argent, on a chevron sable between 3 bugle horns or, stringed of the second, 3 mullets of the third. Crest, Out of a ducal coronet, a stag's head attired or."

[2] Wise, *Accawmacke*, pp. 137, 141.

[3] Land Office, Richmond, Va., Patent Book 3, p. 30, and Patent Book 5, p. 237.

[4] Northampton County (Virginia) Court, Order Book, 1657-1664, p. 93.

[5] W. Coulbourne Brown, of Philadelphia, in his excellent paper (yet in manuscript form) on the Coulbourne family. Mr. Brown kindly allowed me to read his paper and to quote therefrom.

[6] Somerset Court, Liber IKL, record of Solomon Coulbourne's birth.

[7] *V Arcv. Md.*, p. 61 (capt. foot); p. 120 (capt. horse); pp. 309-10 (colonel commanding foot, Somerset and Dorchester); p. 568 (colonel foot in Somerset); Somerset Deed Liber O 1, p. 54, recommended high sheriff, March, 1667/8. *III Arcv. Md.*, p. 121 (high sheriff, October, 1673); Somerset Deed Liber O 7 (back), p. 26 (high sheriff, November, 1675); *V Arcv. Md.*, p. 61 (commissioner of peace, 1670-3); *XV Arcv. Md.*, pp. 69, 77, 216, 279, 328, and Somerset Court, Deed Liber O 7 (back), pp. 3, 4, 6, 11 and 20; Judicials, Liber AW, and EFG, p. 8 (commissioner of peace, 1676-1689); W. Coulbourne Brown's paper (Wm. Coulbourne heads commission, July, 1687, to make treaty with Nanticoke Indians.)

[8] W. Coulbourn Brown, Esq., of Philadelphia, Pennsylvania, has made a detailed study of the "Pomfret" estate and the descent of these lands in the Coul-

bourne family. The result of Mr. Brown's study is, however, yet in manuscript form.

A plat of the "Pomfret" tract, made under a survey, March 14, 1722, and recorded January 27, 1725/6, is recorded in Somerset Court, Deed Liber O 15, p. 298.

[9] Somerset Court, Liber IKL.

William Bosman

[1] Greer, *Early Virginia Immigrants, 1623-1666*, p. 39.

[2] *A Memoir of John Leeds Bozman, the First Historian of Maryland*, by Samuel A. Harrison (Fund Publications, Maryland Historical Society, No. 16), says the Bozman "family was of Dutch origin, having had for its founder in America William Bozman, the immigrant . . . He is said to have been in the Chesapeake as early as 1627. He was later seated in that portion of the peninsula which afterwards became Somerset County and this may be regarded as the home or *solar* of the family."

William Stevens

[1] The tombstone over the grave of William Stevens states that he was 57 years old at the time of his death, December 23, 1687. The record of the death and burial of Richard Stevens, April 22, 1667, given in Somerset Court, Liber IKL, p. 241, states that said Richard Stevens was youngest son of John Stevens, of Llebourn [Lidbourne?], in the parish of Mealmore [Millmore?], county of Buckingham, England, and that said Richard Stevens was brother of William Stevens, of Somerset County, and that he had died April 20th at the house of his said brother William, and was buried at his brother William's plantation, called "Rehoboth," in Somerset County, April 26, 1667.

[2] William Stevens seems to have invariably signed his name: *"Will: Stevens."* In Northampton County (Virginia) records, Order Book, 1656-1664, p. 206, we find one *"Will: Stevens"* as a member of a petit jury, February 15, 1664 [1664/5]. Jennings Wise, in his *Ye Kingdome of Accawmacke, or the History of the Eastern Shore of Virginia in the 17th Century*, pp. 111-112, confuses William Stevens, of Rehoboth, Somerset County, Maryland, with a certain Major Philip Stevens, a Cavalier refugee to Virginia in 1649 with Col. Henry Norwood. The identity of "Major Stevens," the companion of Colonel Norwood, as being Major *Philip* Stevens is clearly proved by a statement in the *William and Mary Quarterly Historical Magazine*, Vol. XXIII, p. 53.

[3] *VII Arcv. Md.*, pp. 5 and 7.

[4] *XV Arcv. Md.*, p. 260, October 7, 1679, "Then was Col William Stevens, Esqr, sworne one of his Lordshipps Privy Council."

[5] Andrews, *Tercentenary History of Maryland*, Vol. I, p. 324.

[6] Richardson, *Sidelights on Maryland History*, Vol. II, p. 175. William Stevens' tombstone states that he was "one of ye Deputy Lieutenants of this Province of Maryland" (see *ante*, p. 329).

[7] *V Arcv. Md.*, pp. 309-310 (Stevens as commander of horse in Somerset and Dorchester Counties).

[8]For patents and deeds of land to William Stevens proving his really vast land holdings and transactions see records of Land Patents in Hall of Records, Annapolis, Maryland, and Somerset County deeds in office of clerk of Circuit Court, for Somerset County, at Princess Anne, Maryland.

[9]Somerset Court, Judicials, 1692-3, p. 198, a bond dated November 17, 1687, from John Colston to William Stevens, of Rehoboth, Merchant.

[10]Somerset Court, Liber IKL, p. 247.

[11]The tombstone over the grave of Col. Wm. Stevens with the inscription intact may be seen today in a walled space in a field of the old "Rehoboth" plantation on the Pocomoke River, about a mile east of the present village of Rehoboth in Somerset County, Maryland. This tomb was restored some years ago after having lain in a neglected condition for many years. Evidently the site of Colonel Stevens' grave was the old family burying ground of the Rehoboth plantation, though today there is no appearance of any other graves. It might be that "sounding" and excavation in the immediate area would show the location of other graves and develop fragments of tombstones. The inscription from Col. Stevens' tombstone has also been published in Bowen's *Days of Makemie*, p. 163.

Rehoboth plantation of 1,000 acres was granted by patent to William Stevens, February 24, 1665. In September, 1668, Stevens sold 400 acres from the lower end of this tract to James Weedon (Somerset Court, Deed Liber O 1, pp. 123-5). Out of the remaining 600 acres William Stevens developed his celebrated "Rehoboth" plantation, where he resided throughout his life. The nature of the first erected dwelling house on the "Rehoboth" plantation we do not know; but there is evidence that Stevens had a brick mansion house erected here in 1674 by one John Lenham. A question as to Lenham's contract brought the whole matter into Somerset Court in January, 1675/6 (Judicials in Liber O 7 [reverse], p. 30). Unfortunately the plan and size of the house are not stated in the court proceedings. This brick mansion house, erected not far from the Pocomoke River side (north side) on "Rehoboth" plantation, was Stevens' home place. It has been stated that the old cellar and foundation of this house were still to be seen in 1884-5 about some 30 to 50 yards from the graveyard (Bowen, *Days of Makemie*, pp. 512 and 524). This "Rehoboth" plantation Col. William Stevens devised to Stevens White (Somerset Registry of Wills, Liber EB 5, pp. 171-2, will of William Stevens, dated August 29, 1687, probated March 26, 1688). The "Rehoboth" plantation descended for several generations in the White family.

Madam Elizabeth Stevens, widow of Col. William Stevens, remained a widow certainly as late as June, 1689 (Somerset Court, Judicials, Liber AW, 1690-1, June Court proceedings, 1689. She later married Col. George Layfield, and was living, as Layfield's wife, as late as September, 1695 (Somerset Court, Deed Liber O 7, pp. 481-2). Madam Elizabeth Stevens-Layfield died somewhat prior to 1697, when Colonel George Layfield had married Priscilla White, a niece of Madam Stevens-Layfield (see Chapter VIII for note on Col. George Layfield).

James Jones

[1] Northampton County (Virginia) Court, Order Book, 1657-1664, pp. 69 and 72, James Jones "for moveing into ye Court in an Irreverent Manner wth his hatt on his head" was committed to the sheriff's custody until he entered into bond and security for his good behavior, according to Act of Assembly and pay court charges, and he was ordered to remain in the sheriff's custody until he give security "for payment of that part of y^e [parish?] Leavie for himself and family wch should have been leavied last year." On July 30, 1660, James Jones was "released from his imprisonment, the Crt think fitt to release him, Mr Revell being security for his good behavior and paying his fees and crt. charges."

[2] Will of James Jones, of Somerset County, Planter, dated October 27, 1673, probated November 13, 1673 (Somerset Registry of Wills, Liber EB 5, p. 127).

[3] Somerset Registry of Wills, Liber EB 14, p. 239, inventory of Andrew Jones, decd., December 22, 1684, Liber EB 13, p. 5, account of Wm. Brereton, attorney of Thos. Brereton, administrator of Andrew Jones, decd., recorded May 8, 1686. Liber IKL, marriage of Andrew Jones to Elizabeth Winder.

Somerset Court, Deed Liber O 6, p. 848, power of attorney, October 13, 1686, from Thomas Jones and his son, Howell Jones, to Stephen Luffe and Rev. John Huett. Deed Liber O 7, pp. 193 and 196-7, which shows that Thomas Jones, the Elder, of Trevithan, was father of Howell Jones and Andrew Jones, of Somerset County, Maryland.

John White

[1] *V Arcv. Md.*, p. 81 (commission of peace, February 9, 1669/70); *XV Arcv. Md.*, pp. 69 and 77 (commissions of peace, March 2, 1675/6, and June 6, 1676).

[2] *V Arcv. Md.*, p. 61 (captain).

[3] *VII Arcv. Md.*, pp. 5 and 7 (member Assembly).

[4] Somerset Court, Liber IKL, p. 284 (date of John White's death).

[5] *Ibid.*, p. 273 (marriage of John White to Sarah Keyser).

[6] Hall of Records, Annapolis, Liber 16, folio 304 (Sarah Keyser, headright, 1671).

John Winder

[1] It appears that Susan, daughter of John and Bridget Winder, was born "att Nansimun [Nansamond]," December 9, 1664 (Somerset Court, Liber IKL). The patent to John Winder, for "Winder's Purchase," on Back Creek of Manokin River, July 6, 1665, is recorded in Hall of Records, Annapolis, Liber 8, folio 486, and Liber 9, folio 450; the first record gives headrights as Bridget Winder, Susan Winder, Daniel Hast, John Okey, Richard Pikes, John Day and Mary Gray; the second record gives headrights as John Winder, Bridgett Winder, Suzanne Winder, Daniel Heast, Martin Moore, John Okey, Richard Price, John Daw, Mary Gore.

[2] In June, 1671, Richard Whitte [Whitty] conveyed to John Winder 600 acres of land in Somerset County, on north side Cutty Mocktico River [creek],

bounded on land formerly George Johnson's and now Daniel Haste's and "the lands said Winder now lives upon on the said River" (Somerset Court, Judicials, Liber AZ, 1671-5, p. 139).

³*Winders of America* . . . Compiled by Winder Johnson . . . pp. 87-91; see also *Wilson Miles Cary Genealogical Collection,* Vol. I (manuscript), in Maryland Historical Society, Baltimore. The offices held by John Winder are all stated in the Archives of Maryland.

Edmund Beauchamp

¹Somerset Court, Liber O 1, pp. 23-5; *III Arcv. Md.,* pp. 553-5; also *XV Arcv. Md.,* p. 35; records of Somerset Court, 1666-1691. June 8, 1688, Wm. Aylward sworn clerk of Somerset, see Somerset Court, Liber AW, 1690-1 (court proceedings, November, 1687-June, 1689, and June, 1690-October, 1691), p. 41.

²Somerset Court, Liber IKL, p. 13 (marriage of Edmund Beauchamp to Sarah Dixon); Deed Liber O 2, p. 11, deed of Beauchamp to his wife Sarah; Deed Liber O 1, p. 117, Beauchamp to Dickenson; Judicials, Liber BWZ, 1690-2, p. 47, deed September, 1690, Edmund Beauchamp and Sarah, his wife, conveying 100 acres of "Contention" tract to their son, Thomas Beauchamp.

³Somerset Court, Liber EFG, p. 33, Beauchamp about removal of records from Capt. Coulbourne's; Liber AB (1690-1), p. 157, Beauchamp names John West, deputy clerk; date of Beauchamp's death and West as his successor. John West was sworn deputy clerk, Liber BWZ, folios 7-8.

⁴Will of Edmund Beauchamp in Somerset Court, Liber BWZ, pp. 116-118.

⁵*Harlein Society Publications,* Vol. XV, p. 59 (*Visitation of London, 1633-4*); see also Baker, *Northampton,* II, p. 218, for Beauchamps; see *Edmund Freeman of Sandwich* [*Massachusetts*] *Genealogy,* for reference to John Beauchamp as brother-in-law to Edmund Freeman, and *Boston Transcript,* January-March, 1930, for letters on Beauchamp-Freeman connection.

VIII

Somerset County in the Protestant Revolution and the Royal Province

¹Charles, Lord Baltimore, was by the action which deprived him of governmental authority in the province of Maryland "reduced to the status of a landlord entitled only to the rents of his estates, the quitrents of the tenants and import duties on tobacco" (Andrews, *Tercentenary History of Maryland,* Vol. I, p. 354).

²For a full discussion of this movement in its every detail see Steiner, *The Protestant Revolution in Maryland,* published in *Report of the American Historical Association, 1897,* pp. 279-353. See also Scharff, *Maryland,* Vol. I; Andrews, *Tercentenary History of Maryland,* Vol. I, and his *History of Maryland: Province and State;* Hall, *The Lords Baltimore and the Maryland Palatinale,* and Russell, *Land of Sanctuary.*

[3]For the charges against Lord Baltimore, and his reply, and the "declaration" of prominent Protestants in his defense see *V Arcv. Md.*, pp. 133-4 and p. 354. See also Scharff, *Maryland*, Vol. I, and Andrews, *Tercentenary History of Maryland*, Vol. I, Chapter VI.

[4]For remaining official documents relative to the Associators' Provisional Government in Maryland, 1689-92, see *XIII Arcv. Md.*, pp. 231-247, "Papers relating to Associators' Assembly," and *VIII Arcv. Md.*, pp. 99-301, "Records and other documents illustrating history of Maryland, 1689-92."

[5]Steiner, *The Protestant Revolution in Maryland*, p. 307.

[6]Andrews, *Tercentenary History of Maryland*, Vol. I, p. 352, and footnote quoting *VIII Arcv. Md.*, p. 149.

[7]*VIII Arcv. Md.*, pp. 158-62. Scharf, *Maryland*, Vol. I, pp. 325-6, also gives the Peter Sayer letter.

[8]Steiner, *Prot. Rev.*, pp. 311 and 312.

[9]*XIII Arcv. Md.*, p. 244.

[10]*Ibid.*, p. 246.

[11]Somerset Court, Judicials, Liber AW [front], p. 105, and *Ibid.* [reverse], pp. 1 and 3.

[12]Steiner, *Prot. Rev.*, p. 315; also Scharff, *Maryland*, I.

[13]The letters of Coode, Cheseldyne, the order of Somerset Court concerning William Whittington, Whittington's reply, and the record of appointment of William Brereton to supercede Whittington in the sheriff's office are recorded in Somerset Court, Judicials, Liber BW, 1689-90, pp. 3-8.

[14]Somerset Court, Judicials, Liber EFG (1689-1690), p. 19.

[15]Somerset Court, Judicials, Liber 1690-1, p. 12.

[16]In 1689 the Assembly authorized Edmund Beauchamp, clerk of Somerset County, "to make choice of an assistant or Deputy Clerk in regard to his [i. e. Beauchamp's] age and defitiency [i. e. his physical incapacity?]," and on November 5th Beauchamp presented John West, who, being approved by the court, was at that time sworn as "deputy clerk (Somerset Court, Judicials, Liber EFG, pp. 7-8, and Liber AW, 1690-91, p. 157).

[17]Steiner, *Prot. Rev.*, pp. 319 and 321. See also Scharff, *Maryland*, Vol. I, p. 328, *et seq*.

[18]Somerset Court, Judicials, Liber EFG (1689-1690), p. 19.

[19]*VIII Arcv. Md.*, pp. 139-142. The paper was endorsed "Maryland 1689 Address of the Inhabitants of the County of Somersett to their Maj[ties]. Recd. from my Lord Shrewsbury 7th Feby. 1689 [1689/90]."

[20]Steiner, *Prot. Rev.*, pp. 323, 345; *VIII Arcv. Md.*, pp. 163 and 246.

[21]Somerset Court, Judicials, Liber AW, p. 41.

[22]Somerset Court, Judicials, Liber EFG, p. 41. Somerset Court, January 17, 1689 [1689/90], William Brereton "offers to go over the bay [i. e. to St. Mary's City] on the Countyes courses and he is ordered by the court to go with such letters and other precepts as shall be thought requisit. Ordered that William Brereton and William Round go over the bay directly to Mr Cheseldyne, or

to them in present authority and receive a particular answer to the therein written * * * leaving the whole to be discovered by the said Brereton and Round as they shall think requisit not forgetting the late insolences of our Indians, to call for what shott arms and ammunition can be had. The following letter was sent by ye said Brereton and a speedy answer was required to be returned." The letter, which followed this court order, we have given in the text.

[23] *VIII Arc. Md.*, p. 198. See Steiner, *Prot. Rev.*, p. 333; Scharf, *Maryland*, Vol. I, and Andrews, *Tercentenary History of Maryland*, Vol. I, for the "Council of Twenty" of the Associators' Government.

[24] Steiner, *Prot. Rev.*, p. 333.

[25] *Ibid.*, p. 334, and *VIII Arcv. Md.*, pp. 193-5.

[26] *Ibid.*, p. 336.

[27] Somerset Court, Judicials, Liber AW (1690-1), p. 22.

[28] Steiner, *Prot. Rev.*, p. 345, lists a session of "Convention" as held in April, 1691.

[29] Somerset Court, Judicials, Liber BWZ, 1690-2, p. 133.

[30] Somerset Court, Judicials, Liber AW (1690-1), pp. 157 and 158.

[31] For the final proceedings in dispossessing Lord Baltimore of his governing power in Maryland, the commissioning and sending of Lionel Copley as first royal governor, and Copley's reorganization of Maryland as a royal province, see Steiner, *Prot. Rev.*, p. 341-351; Andrews, *Tercentenary History of Maryland*, Vol. I, Chapter VII; Scharf, *Maryland*, Vol. I.

[32] *XIII Arcv. Md.*, p. 425.

[33] Somerset Court, Judicials, Liber BWZ, 1690-2, p. 211.

[34] The proceedings of the General Assembly in regard to the refusal to seat Huett, Evernden and Goddin are set forth in *XIII Arcv. Md.* (*Proceedings and Acts of Essembly, 1684-1692*), pp. 252-3, 267-8, 350-2, 354-5, 358-9, 361, 364, 366-7, and 404.

[35] Somerset Court, Judicials, Liber BWZ (1690-2), pp. 215 and 221.

[36] Somerset Court, Judicials, Liber 1692-3, pp. 22, 100, 102, 104 and 105.

INDEX

ABBOTT, NATHL., 350.
ABRAHAM, MORGAN, 477.
ACCOMACK, Va., court issues commission for Manokin settlers protection, 43-4; formation of county and records, 455, 493.
ACKWORTH FAMILY, note, 435; Ann, Henry, Jno., Richd., Sarah, Thos., 435; Richd., 118, 120, 131, 280, 396, 468, 469, 470, 472, 473, 475; Sarah, 396, 398.
ADAMS FAMILY, note, 434; Anne, Abraham, David, Geo., Jacob, Mary, Philip, Thos., Wm., 434; Alexander, 175, 187, 188, 237, 282, 447, 527-8; Philip, 440, 475; Wm., 189.
ADULTERY, 447.
ALEXANDER, Wm., 153, 332, 349, 350, 464, 468.
ALLEN, Jno., 464; Mary, 400, 475; Richd., 464; Wm., 198.
ALL HALLOWS PARISH, see Snow Hill Parish.
ALLINGSWORTH, Richd., 396, 439.
ALL SAINTS CHURCH, Monie, 182.
"ALMODINGTON," 16, 27, 311, 421.
ANDERSON FAMILY, note, 434; Eleanor, Elizabeth, Jno., Sarah, 434; Jno., 34, 293; Wm., 218.
ANDREW, Geo., 396.
ANDREW, Jedediah, 219.
ANNEMESSEX, Chapel (Coventry Parish), 197, et seq.; Friends' Meeting, 89, et seq.; 467; Meeting House location, 494; Hundred, boundaries designated, 73; area settled, 26; settled by Quakers and other non-conformists, 26; invaded by Scarburgh, 39, et seq.; settlers defy Scarburgh's demands, 41; Town, 416.
ACHER, Ambrose, 350.
ARMSTRONG, Matthew, 469, 470, 474.
"ARMSTRONG'S LOTT" (tract), 121.
"ARMSTRONG'S PURCHASE" (tract), 121.

ARUNDEL, Anne, 485; Thos. Lord, 485.
ASKEW (also ASCUE), Mary, 398; Philip, 118, 120, 154, 350, 378, 457, 464, 468.
ASKIMINICONSON INDIAN TOWN, note, 495.
ASSATEAGUE CREEK, 256.
ASSEMBLY, Lower House, members from Somerset (1669-1700), 394.
ATKINS, Jno., 464.
ATKINSON, Angelo, 200.
ATTORNEYS, 290.
AUSTIN, Jno., 475.
AVERY FAMILY, note, 435; John, Sarah, 287, 435, 475.
AYDELOTTES, 223, 468; Benj., 260.
AYLEWARD (also ALEWARD, AYLEWORTH), Wm., 293, 351, 355, 402; Jno., 464.
AYRES, Henry, 464.

B

BACK CREEK, 27.
BAILY, Alice, 447.
BAINTON, Rebecca, 400.
BAKER, Eliz., 475.
BALES, Thos., 477.
BALIS, Geo., 378.
BALL, Mary, 398; Thos., 437, 464, 472, 476.
BALLARD FAMILY, note, 435; Chas., Eliz., Henry, Sarah, 435; Chas., 105, 131, 232, 241, 280, 312, 367, 370, 374, 394, 444, 448, 468, 475; Eleanor, 370, 374; Eliz., 398; Henry, 372; Levin, 195; Sarah, 399, 448, 468.
BALTIMORE, Caecilius, Lord, 67; Charles, 351.
BALTIMORE HUNDRED, 74, 491.
BANES, Wm., 396.
BANNISTER, 445.
BAPTISMS, 132.
BAPTISTS IN SOMERSET (1739) and their "meetings," 508-9.

BARBER, Conover, 477; Jas., 350; Jno., 396, 464.
BARKER, Wm., 464.
BARKSTEAD, Joshua, 362.
BARLEIGH, Pasque, 396, 464.
BARLOWE, Joan, 444; Ralph, 310.
BARNABE (also BARNABEE, BARNABY) FAMILY, note, 435; Eliz., 287, 398; Jas., 131, 136, 280, 287, 435, 468, 471; Mary, 287, 398, 400, 435; Rebecca, 400, 435.
BARNARD, Jno., 477.
BARNES, Abraham, 372, 431; Frances, 372, 430, 431; Francis, 465; H. T., 431; Isaac, 432; Laura, 432; Mary, 431; Richd., 396.
BARNETT, Eliz., 401, 477; Jno., 402; Nicho., 477.
BARON, Jno., 349.
BARRE (BERRE, BAIREE, BERRER) FAMILY, note, 436; Eliz., Grisegon, Olive, Philip, 436, 477; Eliz., 401, 474; Grisegon, 398; Olive, 474; Philip, 131, 280, 447, 468, 471, 474.
BARROWES LANDING, 417.
BARRY, Eliz., 397; Mary, 396, 434; Richd., 441.
BASSETT, Alce, 400, 471.
BASTARDY, see illegitimate child.
BARTON, John O., 197.
"BATCHELLORS LOTT" (tract), 257.
BATTAIN, Rachael, 148.
BAYLEY, Geo., 350; Richd., 302; Rose, 399.
BEALL, Ninian, 211, 528.
BEARE SWAMP, 257.
BEAUCHAMP FAMILY, note, 435; Alice, Doggett, Edmund, Edwd., Jno., Robt., Thos., 435; Alice, 132; Edmund, 62, 63, 76, 132, 279, 306; sketch of, 333, et seq.; 343, 350, 351, 355, 393, 414, 442, 443, 468; Church of England services at home of, 499; Jno., 334; Sarah, 132; Wm., 132, 334.
BEDFORD, Thos., 476.
BEE, Sarah, 397.
BEETE (BESTE), Judith, 475.
BELL, Abigaile, 397; Anthony, 396, 458, 464; Hamilton, 194; Mary, 444.
BELLAMS, Jane, 435.
BENDERWELL, Mary, 398, 451.
BENJAMIN, Geo., 350.
BENNETT, Eliz., 478; Jno., 396, 402, 442, 445, 464; Richd., 471.
BENSON, Geo., 126, 396; Harry L., 479.
BENSTON, Mary, 399.
BENTON, Jos., 378; Saml., 464.
BERCUM (also BERKUM, BURKHAM), 350, 362, 396, 464.
BERKELEY, Sir Wm. (governor of Va.), 12, 45; disclaims giving authority to Scarburgh to invade Annemessex-Manokin, 47.
BEST, Judith, 321, 401, 436.
BETTS FAMILY, note, 436; Anne, Bridget, Frances, Geo., Jno., Margaret, Mary, 436; Frances, 488; Geo., 131, 153, 378, 380, 326, 396, 431, 444, 468, 471.
BEVANS (BEVENS, BEVANS), Rowland, 396, 401, 464.
"BEVERLY," 432.
BEWRY, Mary, 396.
BIRCH BRANCH, St. Martins River, 203.
BIRTHS, register of; see "I. K. L."
BISHOP, David, 401; Henry, 417, 464; Jno., 396; Mary, 457; Sarah, 126, 398.
BLACKSMITH (tradesman), 293.
BLADES, Jane, 397; Richd., 464.
BLAKE, Joel, 472; Thos., 441, 464.
"BLAKES HOPE" (tract), 263, 265.
BLASPHEMY (charge against Edwd. Southern), 458.
BLOOD, Mary, 475.
BLOUSE, Thos., 476.
BLOYCE (BLOYES, BLOYSE, BLOYS) FAMILY, note, 437; Frances, 399, 400, 437; Judith, 397, 437, 474, 478; Thos., 280, 470, 471.
BOATRIGHT (tradesman), 293.
BLOYSE, see Bloyce.
BODY, Peter, 396.
BOGERTERNORTON HUNDRED, 74, 491; landing, 416; Friends' Meeting, 106, et seq., 467.

BOICE (BOYCE, BOIST, BUSE, BUSS) FAMILY, note, 435; Jane, Mary, Wm., 435, 478; Jeane, 399; Wm., 280, 470, 474.
BOND, Stephen, 396, 464.
BOOTH FAMILY, note, 435; Danl., Easter, Eliza, Elinor, Geo., Isaac, Jno., 435, 436; Geo. 280, 477; Peter, 459; Robt., 475.
BOQUETENORTON, BOGOTEE NORTON, POCKYTENORTON; see Bogerternorton.
BORUD, Jas., 475.
BOSMAN (BOSSMAN, BOZMAN) FAMILY, note, 437; Ann, 326, 402, 437, 442, 476; Bridget, 326, 396, 436; Blandina, 444; Eleanor, 437, 476; Ellen, 437, 476; Geo., 437, 476; Jno., 118, 120, 397, 326, 437, 444; Katherine, 326; Mary, 326, 397, 444; Wm., 44, 58, 59, 131; sketch of, 325, *et seq.*; 391, 437, 451, 457, 468, 471, 473, 476.
BOSSE, Wm., 475.
BOSTON FAMILY, note, 436; Ann, Esau, Henry, Isaac, Rebecca, Richd., 436, 475, 476; Ann, 320, 322; Eliz., 402; Esau, 322; Henry, 6, 26, 40, 59, 62, 63, 67, 68, 86, 87, 88, 93, 279, sketch of, 319, *et seq.*; described by Scarburgh, 391, 394, 396, 468, 470; Isaac, 322, 450; Rebecca, 322.
BOSTON, Richd., 322.
"BOSTON TOWN" (tract), 322.
BOUNDARY LINE, settlements ordered for protection of, 9, *et seq.*
BOUNDS, Jno., 153, 154, 464; Sarah, 458.
BOWDITCH, Robt., 464.
BOWEN, L. P., 228; Mary, 396; Wm., 349, 464.
BOWMAN, Edm., 391.
BOWZER, Frances, 399.
BOYDEN, Ann, 399.
BOYER, Robt., 350.
BOYES, Wm., 72.
BOZMAN, Geo., 349; Jno., 350, 394, 395; Wm., 280, 350; see also Bosman.

BRADSHAW, Eliz., 222, 396; Wm., 396, 464.
BRANEGAN, Alce, 397.
BRAVARD, Adam, 262.
BRAY, 468; Eliza., 374; Pierce, 241; house meeting place of Rehoboth Presbyterian Congregation (1703), 536.
BRAYER, Edwd., 477.
BRAYFIELD, Gabriel, 436; Susanna, 400, 436, 440, 477.
BRECHIN, Jas., 165, 377.
BRERETON, 131, 468; Diana, Grace, Hannah, Henry, Jno., Judith, Sarah, Thos., Wm., 382; Hannah, 137; Sarah, 137, 143, 381; Thos., 143, 330; Wm., 137, 143, 340, 345, 350; sketch of, 381, *et seq.*; 393, 395, 464; home of, 520, 524.
BREVARD, 468.
BRIANT, Jno., 464.
BRIDGER, Jos., 48, 49, 473.
BRISCOE, Abraham, 203.
BRITANIE, Richd., 464.
BRITTEN, Richd., 350.
BRITTINGHAMS, 431; Elijah, 269; Wm., 475.
BROAD CREEK, 191; bridge at, 428; Presbyterian Meeting House at, 271; chapel (Stepney Parish), 191.
BROADWAY, Wm., 464.
BROADWELL, Wm., 464.
BROMLEY, Thos., 350.
"BROTHER'S LOVE" (tract), 221.
BROUGHTON, Elijah, 177; Jno., 222, 350. 396; Mary, 431.
BROWN, 468; Alex., 365; David, 118, 120, 212, 213, 292, 313, 340, 343, 353, 356; sketch of, 365, *et seq.*, 373, 394, 395, 396, 414, 426, 464; Eliz., 365; Janet, 365; Jno., 232, 349, 396, 444, 464; Margt., 365; Mary, 365; Thos., 99, 365, 443; Wm., 254, 350; Winifred, 363.
BROWNE, Devorax, 292, 391; Patience, 463.
BRUFF, Thos., 176.
BRUNERIDGE, Jos., 478.

"Buckingham" (tract), 259.
Buckingham Presbyterian Congregation and "Meeting House," 258, et seq.
Buckinghamshire, Eng., 326.
Bult, Jno., 464.
Bundick, Dorothy, 397, 477; Richd., 464.
Bunnel, Jno., 475.
Burch, Wm., 350.
Burgess, Wm., 463.
Burgesses; see Delegates to General Assembly.
Burleigh, Wm., 351.
"Burley" (tract), 261, 262.
Burnett, Rev. Mr., note, 535.
Burrage, Robt., 378.
Bursted, Jeremy, 474, 478.
Burton, Wm., 429.
Busbo, Robt., 426.
Butcher, Francis, 316; John, 316; Katherine, 316, 448.
Butcher (tradesman), 292, 293.
Butler, Cecilius, 351; Margt., 399.
Butter, Alice, 399.

C

Cade, Robt., 349, 464.
Caine family, note, 437; Jas., Eleanor, 437, 451, 471, 476, 478; Jas., 71, 74.
Caldwell, 468; Jno., 254; Joshua, Presbyterian meeting place, 271.
Calloway family, note, 437; Anne, Eliz., Peter, Sarah, Wm., 437, 438; Peter, 280, 400.
Calvert, Gov. Chas., 5; protests against Scarburgh's invasion of Manokin-Annemessex, 45, et seq.; Philip, 13, 45, 48, 49, 51, 465.
Cammeday, Anne, 399, 401.
Campaison, Leonard, 397, 464.
Camplin, Thos., 464.
Canneday, Wm., 400, 464.
Cormon, Frances, 396; Ann, 440; Judith, 465; Stephen, 396, 464, 465.
Carey, Edwd., 397; Thos., 464.
Carlyle, Alex., 187.

Carne, Sarah, 399.
Carny (Carnee), Thos., 280, 471.
Carpe, Simon, 477.
Carpenter, Nicho., 281, 350, 464.
Carpenters (tradesmen), 293.
Carr family, note, 438; Ann, David, Eliz., Susanna, 438; Ann, 397, 401; Eliz., 397.
Carrell, Thos., 446, 464.
Carroll, Henry J., 433; Thos., 397; Thos. K., 433.
Carsley, Frances, 452.
Carter, Edwd., 464, 472; Geo., 397, 402, 453, 476, 478; Jane, 397, 401; Jno., 464; Philip, 154, 464.
Cary, Francis, 454; Thos., 181.
Cassaugh, Jno., 474, 492.
Cathell, Jas., 254.
Catherwood, Anne, 444; Robt., 425, 441, 444.
Cathol., Jas., 255.
Catlett, Jno., 37, 45, 49, 392.
Catlin (Cathing, Catling, Cattling, Catlyn) family, note, 438; Ann, Hannah, Jos., Robt., 438, 475; Ann, 400; Lynde, 432; Robt., 279, 397, 402.
Caulker, 303.
Cavalier expedition to Va. (1650), 454.
Carzara, Jno., 76, 492.
Cedar Neck, 183.
Chalkley, Thos. 90, 101, 108; excerpts from journal, 494-5.
Chambers, Richd., 153, 154, 192, 293, 350, 397, 401, 447, 464, 468.
"Chance" (tract), 192.
Chanceleer (Chancellor, Chancellour), Jno., 349, 402, 464.
Chapels of Ease in parishes in Somerset County, 186, et seq.; at Johnson's Mill, 208; near Stevens' Ferry, 201; at Stockton, 208.
Chares, Jno., 478.
Charles, Jno., 477.
Chappell Branch, St. Martin's River, 203.
Charleton, Stephen, 298.

CHASE, Jude Samuel, birthplace of, 514.
CHEESEMAN, Wm., 464.
CHELSE, Gideon, 476.
CHELTNAM, Jacob, 464.
CHENEY, Andrew F., 194.
CHERRY BRIDGE CREEK, 148.
CHESELDYNE, Kenelm, letter to Somerset Court, 343.
CHICKEN, Edwd., 464.
CHIEF JUDGE, 302.
CHISSAM, Jno., 397.
CHINCOTEAGUE PONIES, 362.
CHIPMAN'S MILL POND, 191.
CHIRURGEONS (surgeons), 281.
CHRISTOPHER, Jno., 350.
CHRIST CHURCH, Sussex Co., Del., 192.
CHURCH BRANCH, St. Martin's River, 203.
CHURCH OF ENGLAND FAMILIES, 468; Parish Churches in Somerset Co., 163, et seq.
CHURCHES; see Church of England, Presbyterian, Quaker, Baptist, Roman Catholic.
"CHURCHMANSHIP," liberal, 134.
CHURCHMEN, 348.
CHURCH OF ENGLAND, first clergyman in Somerset, 140; men in settlement, 131; organized in Somerset, 152, et seq.
CHURCH YARD AT ST. MARTIN'S, 202.
CHURCH, Ye, 422.
CLAGGETT, 442; Bishop, T. J., consecrates Coventry Parish Church, 177, 178.
CLAIBORNE, Wm., 8.
CLARK, Nath., 349.
CLARKE, Dorothy, 334, 399; Edwd., 334; Katherine, 400; Wm., 477.
CLARKSON, Phillis, 437.
CLAUSEN, 19; Jacob, 487.
CLAYLAND, Jno., 146, 360.
CLEMENT, Jno., 224, 226.
CLEMMY, Saml., 189.
CLERKS OF SOMERSET CO. (1666-1700), 393.

"CLIFTON," 181.
CLIFTON POINT, 422.
"CLOSURE," 433.
CLOYSE, Jacob, 477.
CLUGSTONE, Michael, 350.
COARD, Wm., 350.
COAST GUARD, beginnings, 363.
COCKEE, Wm., 400.
COGGIN, Geo., 477.
COLE, Peter, 475, 477; Richd., 350, 464; Robt., 264; Wm., 471, 475; Sarah, Susan, Jno., Eliz., 475.
COLEMAN, Ellis, 464.
COLEHOUNE, Jno., 397, 401.
COLLETT, Wm., 452, 478.
COLLIER, Jas., 436; Peter, 376; Robt., 153, 154, 397, 464.
COLLINGS, Thos., 262.
COLLINS, Edmund, 397; Saml., 378, 394, 397, 464.
COLMORE, Richd., 475.
COLSTON, Jno., 349.
COLVILLE, Thos., 372.
COMMISSIONERS, not to absent themselves during session of court, 73.
"CONCLUSION" (tract), 433.
CONNARD, Philip, 397, 401; Sarah, 398, 401.
CONNER, Ann, Philip, Sarah, 476.
CONNIEW (?), Jno., 397.
CONNOR, Jas., 349.
"CONTENTION" (tract), 333.
"CONVENIENCY" (tract), 257, 433.
COODE, John, letter to Somerset Court (1689), 342.
CONSTABLES, first Somerset, 71; in (1689), 71, 347.
COOKE, Mary, 398, 402; Thos., 478.
COOPER FAMILY, note, 438; Ann, Betty, Isaac, Jas., Phillis, Saml., Sarah, 437; Eliz., 400; Gabriel, 436, 440; Jane, 400; Jno., 280, 400, 436, 474, 475; Margt., 325, 438; Saml., 464; Susanna, 400.
COOPERS (tradesman), 292, 293.
COPLEY, Lionel, 356.
COPPINBALL (also COPPINHALL), Jane, 139, 400.

· 561 ·

CORD, Wm., 183.
"CORDICALL" (tract), 259, 331.
CORDRY, Danl., 464.
CORE, Toby, 477.
CORNEILLINSON, Harmon, 426.
CORNELIUS, Margrett, 398, 400.
CORNWELL, Nich, 349, 464.
CORNISH, Jno., 153, 419, 464.
COSTIN, Stephen, 445, 464.
COTTINGHAM FAMILY, note, 438; Chas., Esther, Jno., Mary, Sarah, Thos., 438; Mary, 433; Thos., 279, 306, 397, 433, 442, 454, 471.
COTTINGHAM'S BRANCH, 254; Ferry, 200.
COTTMAN, Ann., 437; Benj., 103, 131, 118, 120, 464, 468; Mary, 400.
COULBOURNE FAMILY, note, 438; Abigail, Frances, Katherine, Margt., 438-9; Anne, 323, 325, 438, 475; Benj., 199; Elijah, 198; Jno., 350; Mary, 325, 438, 474; Penelope, 325, 438; Robt., 325, 438, 445, 456; Solomon, 197, 325, 438; William, 58, 59, 74, 86-8, 92-6, 118-20, 138, 153-4, 197, 279, 309; sketch of, 322, *et seq.;* 340, 343, 349, 350, 393-7, 414, 438, 456, 463, 464, 468, 473; Wm. (currier), 397; Coulbournes of Somersetshire, Eng., 549.
"COULBOURNE" (tract), 300, 305.
COULBOURNE'S CREEK, 197, 300, 325, 422.
COUNCIL OF MD., protests against Scarburgh's demand on Annemessex-Manokin settlers, 36.
COURT HOUSES, 402-410.
COURT ORDERS TO BE SIGNED AT CONCLUSION OF SESSION OF COURT, 73.
COVAN, Jno., 397.
COVENTRY PARISH, Chapels of Ease, 197, *et seq.;* Parish Church, 163, 164, 174, *et seq.;* consecrated, 177; first vestry, 155.
COVINGTON (COVENTAN, COVENTON) FAMILY, note, 439; Abraham, Anne, Amy, Eliz., Isaac, Jacob, Jno., Jeremiah, Katherine, Levin, Mary,
Philip, Rachel, Rebecca, Sarah, Susanna, 439-440; Jeane, Jno., Katherine, Mary, Sarah, 474; Jane, 400, 463, 474; Margt., 396; Nehemiah, 72, 99, 100, 101, 280, 372, 397, 439, 443, 447, 463, 467, 470; Priscilla, 100, 367, 372 431, 439; Saml., 439, 442; Sarah, 398, 439; Thos., 118, 120, 190, 280, 400, 439-40, 439.
"COVINGTONS VINEYARD" (tract), 99.
COWDRY, Jno., 402.
Cox, Danl., 464.
COX'S BRANCH, 428.
"CRANBURN" (tract), 187.
CRAWFORD, Lawrence, 350, 461.
CRAWLEY, Jno., 350.
CREW FAMILY, note, 440; Ann, 396, 434; Eliz., 398, 440, 446, 449; Jno., 279, 440, 478.
CROCKET, Richd., 457.
CROFT, Herbert, 464.
CROPPER, 213, 223; Edmund, 260, 261; Eliz., 418; Jno., 418, 464, 468; Solomon, 203.
"CROPTON" (tract), 203.
CROSDALE, Henry, 197; Jno., 199.
CROUCH, Robt., 350, 464.
CROUTCH, Ambrose, 469.
CROUSH, Jno., 374.
CROW; see Crew.
CROWDER, Jos., 464.
CROWELEY, Jno., 477.
CULLEN, 458; Geo., 397; Jno., 397.
CULTLETT; see Catlett.
CURTIS FAMILY, note, 440; Chas., Catherine, Ellen, Esther, Mary, Rachel, 440; Danl., 72, 279, 397, 440, 478; Eliz., 397, 402, 438, 440, 478; Jas., 347, 397, 440, 445; Mary, 440, 478; Sarah, 457.
CURTIS, Martin, 271, 349.
CUSTIS, Edmund, 381.
CUTTYMOCKTICO CREEK, 332.
CUVINOE, Jno., 378.
CYPRUS BRIDGE, 190.

D

DAB, Thos., 477.

DALE, David, 465.
DANCE (?), Mary, 397.
DANFROY, Eliz., 459.
DANIEL, Rose, 401.
DANNELL, Mary, 397; Wm., 465.
"DANIEL'S FIRST CHOICE" (tract), 207.
DARLING, Abigail, Eliz., 474; Richd., 280, 474.
DASHIELL FAMILY, note, 440; Ann. 477; Benj. J., 149; C. M., 431; Eliz., 397, 477; Geo., 372, 440, 453; James, 72, 118, 120, 131, 135, 280, 338, 350, 358, 395, 396, 414, 440, 453, 468, 477; Jane, 330, 440; Katherine, 440; Robt., 440; Thos., 150, 181, 440.
DASHIELL'S CREEK, 123; mills, 429.
DAVEY, Edna, 186.
DAVIDSON, Wm., 465.
DAVIES, Jas., Jno., Jones, 476.
DAVIS FAMILY, note, 440; Abraham, 477; Ann, 399, 425; Edwd., 465; Eliz., 398, 440, 468; Humphrey, 465; Jas., 72, 280, 400; Jno., 350, 440, 471, 475, 479; Jonas, 465; Martha, 440, 445; Mary, 402; Richd., 118, 120, 280, 397, 401, 440, 436, 469, 478; Rosannah, 440; Sarah, 440, 478; Saml., 107, 128, 212, 215; sketch of, 222, *et seq.*; 242, 248, 350, 377, 381, 468, 538; Thos., 118, 120, 293, 321, 397, 401, 436, 440, 465, 469, 477, 479; Wm., 280, 350, 397, 400, 425, 440, 468, 472.
DAW, Jno., 477.
DAWES, Jno., 475.
DAY, Edwd., 187, 395, 397, 414, 465; Eliz., 441; Geo., 293, 397, 465.
DEALE, Jno., 349, 465.
DEANE, Anne, 398.
DEAS, Manniwell, 478.
DEATHS, register of; see "I. K. L."
DE BRULAGH, Jno., 465.
DEDECKER, Wm., 293.
DEEPE POINT, Town at (1668), 412, 421.
DEGAS, Devorax, 349.
DELAHIDE, Thos., 350.
DELAMUS, Jane, 478.

DELEGATES TO GENERAL ASSEMBLY, first from Somerset, 77.
DENBY, Eliza, 374.
DENNAHOE, Danl., 465.
DENNIS FAMILY, note, 441; Eleanor, Eliz., Henry H., Katherine, Margt., Theophilus, 441; Donnock, 131, 280, 441; Jno., 175, 198, 441; Littleton, 198, 267; Richd., 350; Wm., 377, 441.
"DENNIS PURCHASE" (tract), 200.
DENSON, Eliz., 443.
DENSTONES, Bridges, 428.
DENT, Margt., 397, 462; Peter, 127, 350, 362, 393, 396, 468; Wm., 378.
DENWOOD FAMILY, note, 443; Arthur, 100, 104, 416, 467, 443; Eliz., 397; Levin, 90, 98, 99, 100, 101, 104, 118, 120, 292, 298, 299, 303, 304, 414, 443, 464, 467, 475, 478; Mary, 98, 99, 464; Priscilla, 98, 99, 100, 443; Rebecca, 99, 100, 372, 439, 443; Sarah, 475, 478; Susanna, 99.
DERICKSON, Capt., 206; Wm., 442, 465.
DEVORAX, Jno., 465.
DIAS, Thos., 397.
DICKESON FAMILY, note, 443; Abraham, Chas., Eliz., Isaac, Jno., Peter, Teague, 443; Edwd., 279, 333, 443, 469, 470; Robt., 476.
DILLAMAS, Jane, 398, 452.
DISHAROONE, Michael, 465; mills, 429.
DITTY, Eleanor, 397.
DISSENTING MINISTERS, petition for their continuance in Somerset, 333.
DIVIDING CREEK, 200, 428; chapel (Coventry Parish), 200, *et seq.*
DIXE, Robt., 475.
DIXON FAMILY, note, 442; Adria, Abigail, Christiana, Diana, Robt., 442-3; Alice, 306, 442; Ambrose, 26, 40, 72, 86-94, 132, 279, 289, 299, 300-1; sketch of, 302, *et seq.*, 323; described by Scarburgh, 391, 397, 435, 438, 442, 453, 457, 467, 468, 470, 475, 479; Eliz., 306, 397, 475; Grace, 306, 401, 475, 479; Hannah, 306; Jno., 271;

· 563 ·

Mary, 302, 306, 333, 397, 402, 438, 442, 475, 479; Sarah, 306, 333, 435, 442, 457, 475, 479; Sturgis, 271; Thos., 153, 154, 175, 306, 350, 394-7, 442-3, 475, 479; Wm., 199.
DIXON FAMILY, graveyard, 305.
"DIXON'S CHOICE" (tract), 89, 304, 305, 322.
DOCTORS, first in Somerset, 285, *et seq.*
DONELSON, 418, 269.
DOONE, Geo., 477.
DORCHESTER Co., 63.
DORICKS, Margaret, 402.
DORMAN, Cattron, 264; Henry, 378; Jno., 118, 120, 293, 397, 465; Mary, 453; Matthew, 350, 397; Robt., 400, 475.
DORNEWELL, Robt., 475.
"DOUBLE PURCHASE," 27.
DOUGHERTY, Nathl., 465; Peter, 443; Rachel, 443.
DOUNIN, Wm., 465.
DOWNES FAMILY, note, 442; Anne, Betty, Bossman, Eliz., Esther, Isabel, Mary, Margt., Mitchell G., Priscilla, Robt., Sarah, 442; Geo., 131, 326, 402, 437, 442, 453, 468.
DOWTEY, Peter, 118, 120, 465.
DRAPER FAMILY, note, 443; Alex., 72, 75, 86-8, 118, 120, 279, 300, 301, 424, 426, 443, 469, 475; Katherine, 443, 469, 475.
DRIDEN (DREDON, DREADON), 465, 468.
DRESDON (DREADON, DRYDON?), David, 350.
DRIGGER, and others, free Negroes, 492.
DUETT, Mr., 199.
DUGGAR, Elias, Isaac, 474.
DUKES, Eliz., 90; Robt., 306, 397, 442, 465.
DULAP (DUNLAP), Ninian, 350.
DUNCAN, Jas., 350.
DUPARKE FAMILY, note, 443; Thos., 280, 443, 474; Eliz., 474.
DURHAM Co., 423.
DUSTE, Wm., 465.

E

EANES, Geo., 465.

"EASTERN SHORE (THE) BELOW CHOPTANK RIVER," commission for settling, 15; commissions of the peace (1662-1665/6), 19, 20, 22, 58, 59; encroachments by Virginians, 9; opened to settlement (Nov., 1661), 13; record, 61; record keeper, 61; first clerk, 62; presiding justice (1665), 61-2; nature of business transacted by court, 62; first settlement, 25, 386.
EDGAR, Jane, 397; Jno., 263, 370; Mary, 263; Mrs., 262.
EDMONSON, Jno., 359.
EDMUNDSON, Wm., 102.
EDWARDS, Thos., 350.
EDWYN (EDWIN), Marguerite, 476; Wm., 472, 476.
EDUCATION, early, 287, *et seq.*
EGIONS, Isabel, 477.
ELGATE, Hannah, 476; Jno., 476; Wm., 153, 472, 476.
ELEY, Bridgett, 399.
ELKSON (ELKISON, ELLISON?), Robt., 48, 49.
ELLIOTT, Henry, 469, 472; Stephen, 465, 471, 476.
ELLIS FAMILY, note, 443; Anne, Henry, Mary, Richd., Thos., 443-4; Eliz., 397, 398, 443; Jno., 280, 298, 350, 397; Warrick, 444; Thos., 350.
ELZEY FAMILY, note, 444; Alice, Eliz., Frances, Joan, 444; Arnold, 153, 181, 310, 312, 350, 395, 396, 421, 444; John 15, 16, 19, 20, 22, 27, 30, 31, 33, 41, 58, 131, 279, 308; sketch of, 310, *et seq.*, 312, 388, 386, 389, 435, 444, 448, 468, 470, 471, 472, 475; Major, 181, 444; Peter, 154, 280, 349, 444, 472; Sarah, 310, 312, 444.
ENGLISH IN SOMERSET SETTLEMENT, 282-3.
ENGLISH, Jas., 397.
ENNIS, Saml., 465; Wm., 395; see also Innis.
EMMETT, Jno., 465.
EMMIT, Jno., 350; Eliz., 458, 459.
EMPEROUR, Ellis, 465, 475.
EMPSON, Mary, 401.

ERSKINE, Archibald, 223, 292, 365, 465, 468; Margt., 365; Mary, 365.
ESKRIDGE, Wm., 439.
EVANS, Edwd., 349, 397; Elias, 262; John, 149, 457, 465, 468; Nicho., 149, 179, 396, 465; Rachel, 179; Thos., 293, 476; Walter, 206, 207.
EVERNDEN, Katherine, 467; Martha, 448; Nathl., 448; Thos., 90, 92, 93, 145, 319, 358, 394, 433, 448, 467.
"EVERNDEN'S LOT" (tract), 433.
EVERTON, Thos., 397.
EVITT, Arthur, 400, 465, 478.
EWELL, J. Paul, 267.
"EXCHANGE" (tract), 107.

F

FAREWELL, Richd., 350, 465.
FASSITT, 213, 223; Frances, 381; Jno., 465; Katherine, 332, 461; Wm., 259, 260-2, 350, 465, 468.
FENTON, Moses, 241, 350, 468.
FERREBY, Jas., 477.
FERRILL, Katherine, 397.
FIELD, Nehemiah, 457.
"FIRST CHOICE" (tract), 433.
FIRST SETTLERS, Somerset, from Accomack Co., Va., 280; Nansamond Co., Va., 281; Gloucester Co., Va., 281; Northumberland Co., Va., 281.
FISHER, Ann, 476, 477; Margt., 475; Philip, 451; Thos., 465; Wm., 474, 475.
FITCH, Adam, 350.
FLANNIKIN, Mary, 398, 449.
FLAXON, Thos., 475.
FLEMING, Patrick, 290.
FLINT, Jno., 255.
FLOYD, Thos., 475.
FLUTCHER, Wm., 397, 465.
FOSTER, Evis, 477.
FOUNDERS, sketches of, 295-334.
FOUNTAINE (FOUNTAIN, FONTAINE) FAMILY, note, 444; Baly, Bridget, Collier, Eliz., Grace, Hannah, Joanna, Mary, Priscilla Saml., Sarah, Stephen, Wm., Thos., 444; Dennis, 398, 402, 444, 449; John, 195, 444; Mercy (Macy), 397, 444; Neomy, 435; Nicholas, 131, 279, 468, 473, 474; Wm., 194.
FOWLER, Edwd., 465.
Fox, Geo., 60; visit to Somerset (1672), 95, et seq., 134, 328, 497-8; in Dorchester Co., 502; preaches in Dorchester, 502, 503; Mary, 402; Thos., 474.
FOXCROFT, Jos., 465.
FRAME, Arthur, 465.
FRANCIS, Arnold, 465.
FRANKLAND, Jno., 350.
FRANKLIN (also FRANKLYN, FRANCKLYN), 152, 154, 241, 395; Ebenezer, 460; John, 465, 468; Margt., 400, 461, 479; Wm., 261, 262.
FRANSELE, Jno., 520.
FREAKE, Mary, 478.
FREEMAN, Alicia, 334; Edmund, 334; Geo., Jos., 351; John, 397, 401, 465; Jos., 453, 465, 397.
FRENCH IN SETTLEMENT, 283.
FREE NEGRO, 280.
FREE-NEGROES; see Negroes, free, first in Somerset.
FRIENDS, early settlers of Somerset, 85.
FRIENDS' MEETINGS IN SOMERSET CO., Annemessex, 89, et seq.; Monie, 98, et seq.; Bogeternorton, 106, et seq. "Meeting-places": at Ambrose Dixon's, 88, 91; at Richd. Waters, 89, 92; at Levin Denwoods, 103; at George Trewett's (Truitt's), 108. "Meeting Houses": Annemessex, 89, 91; Monie, 104; Bogeternorton, 108. Burying Grounds: Annemessex, 89, 91; Monie, 105; Bogeternorton, 107, 108.
"FRIENDSHIP" (tract), 271.
FROWNIN (FROWIN), Ann, 379, 459.
FULLER, Humphrey, 474; Martha, 476; Servate, 477; Thos., 474.
FURLONG, Edwd., 465.
FURNIS (FURNISS, FURNESS, FURNISH) FAMILY, note, 445; Ann, Comfort, Eliz., Jas., Katherine, Priscilla, Ro-

zannah, 445; Mary, 402; Olive, 445, 474; Sarah, 396; Wm., 72, 74, 131, 280, 445, 471, 474.

G

GADDS, Jas., 465.
GAGER, Eliz., 401.
GAINES, Richd., 472.
GAMES, Richd., 476.
GALBRAITHS, 223; Jno., 465, 468.
GALE, Betty, 100, 102, 105, 467; George, 100, 102, 105, 372, 416, 443; Levin, 254, 372.
GALE'S CREEK, 26, 289.
GAMBRILL, Eliz., 446.
GATES, M. T., 431.
GEDDES, Robt., 194, 269.
GERMAN, Ann., 477.
GIBBS, Martha, 399.
GIDNEY, Diana, 475.
GILES, Clement, 349; Wm., 465.
GILL, Jas., 465.
GILLETT, German, 7, 465, 469, 470, 472; Henry, 476; Thos., 397.
GILLISS (GILLIS, GILLEY, GILLE) FAMILY, note, 445; Hannah, Jno., Mary, 445; Chas. J., Wm. W., 445; Mary, 476; Thos., 280, 451, 476.
GILLMAN, Philippa, 397.
GLADSTONE, Jno., 465.
GLANDENNING, Geo., 465.
"GLANDVILL'S LOT" (tract), 422, 423.
GLANDVILL, Wm., 416, 471.
GLASGOW, Patrick, 204.
GLOVER, Mary, 399.
GODDARD, Langdon, 465.
GODDARD'S CHAPEL, Stepney Parish, 186, et seq.
"GODDARD'S FOLLEY" (tract), 102.
GODDARD, Geo., 187, 397.
GODDIN, John, 90, 106, 107, 145, 316, 319, 358, 394, 395, 448, 467; Katherine 316, 319, 467; Mary, 316.
GOODIN, Judith, 397.
GODFREY, Judith, 397, 401.
GOLDSBOROUGH, Robt., 378.
GOLDSMITH (GOULDSMITH) FAMILY,

note, 445; Anthony, Hannah, Martha, Wm., 445; Jno., 280, 349, 445, 474; Mary, 445, 399.
"GOOD SUCCESS" (tract), 263, 265.
GOOSE CREEK, 27, 182, 421.
GORDAN, Thos., 350.
GOSLIN, Jno., 465.
GOSSE, Saml., 476.
GRADWELL, Isabell, 400.
GRAND JURY, first for Somerset, 72.
GRAY, Eliz., 399; Jno., 232, 350, 445; Jos., 241, 465; Mary, 400, 477; Miles, 154, 465; Sarah, 435; Wilis, 378.
GREARE, Wm., 271; Grizzle, 271.
GREENE, Edwd., 362; Eliz., 398, 401, 452, 440; Mary, 397; Wm., 397, 400, 452.
"GREENFIELD" (tract), 107.
"GREEN HILL CHURCH," 163-4; town, 179, 422.
GRIFFITH, Jno., 436, 465, 478; Margt., 399, 453.
GRIFIN, Sarah, 474.
GROVE, Mary, 477.
GROENENDYCK, Peter, 426.
GROTTIN, Avis, 397.
GULLET, Wm., 397, 465.
GULLICK, Wm., 465.
GUNBY, Francis, 402, 465; Jas., 198; Sarah, 398.
GUY, Sarah, 397.

H

HACK, Ann., 476.
HACALAND, Wm., 349.
"HACKLAND" (tract), 98.
HADSON, Wm., 474.
HADY, Eliz., 399.
HAGGAMORE, Jno., 474.
HALE, Henry, 350; Wm., 350; Oliver, 465.
HALL FAMILY, note, 445; Jno., Mary, Richd., 445; Alex., 416; Alice, 445, 458; Ellis (Alice?), 478; Chas., 132, 153, 279, 397, 398, 414, 445, 454, 468, 470, 473, 478; Henry, 153; Kath-

erine, 445, 454; Rachel, 445, 457; Robt., 350, 397; Sarah, 440, 445; Thos., 195; Wm., 378, 445, 465, 474.
HALL'S CREEK, 121.
HALSO, Wm., 476.
HAMBLIN, Geo., 401, 465.
HAMILL, Geo., 401.
HAMLIN, Francis, 332, 461.
HAMMOND, Edwd., 154, 396, 468.
"HAMPTON," 374.
HAMPTON, Frances, 370; John, 190, 219, 224, 245, 253, 262, 367, 369, 370; Marjory, 370; Mary, 190, 204; sketch of, 367, et seq.; Robt., 370.
HANCOCK, Stephen, 465.
HANDY, Arelia W., 431; Eliz., 247; Geo., 247; Jno., 254; Matilda, 431; Saml., 398; Jane, 438; Rachel, 438; Saml., 465, 468.
HANLEY, Arthur, 350.
HANNAH, Michael, 350, 465.
HARDIDGE, Jno., 477.
HARFORD TOWN, 418.
HARDY (HARDIE), Eliz., 457; Robt., 457, 471, 474; Margt., 400; Sarah, 396, 397, 435.
HARNEY, Timothy, 465.
HARPER, Edwd., 398; Henry, 447; Wm., 473.
HARRINGDON, Abigail, 402.
HARRIS, David, 465; Geo., 465; Eleanor, 402; Richd., 398; Wm., 398.
HARRISON, Jno., 397, 401, 465; Jos., 475; Miles, 350.
HART FAMILY, note, 445; Jone, 445; Robt., 71, 86-8, 118, 120, 279, 300, 445, 470, 475; Tomasen, 396.
HARVEY, Timothy, 398; Wm., 465.
HARWOOD, Thos., 472, 475.
HASFURT (HOSSFORD, etc.) FAMILY, note, 446; Geo., 75, 279, 286, 397, 446, 476.
HASSARD (HAZARD) FAMILY, note, 446; David, 438, 446; Edwd., 280, 397, 401, 438, 446, 478.
HASTE FAMILY, note, 446; Danl., 72, 102, 131, 153, 178, 280, 397, 446, 468, 471, 477; Eliz., 446; Sarah, 440, 446.

HASTE'S CREEK, 179, 422.
HASTINGS, Jno., 474.
HATTER (tradesman), 293.
HATTFIELD, Jno., 477.
HAWKINS, Philip, 474.
HAYMAN (HAMAN) FAMILY, note, 446; Anne, Chas., Jas., Wm., 446; Elinor, 446, 478; Henry, 280, 350, 398, 463, 471, 478.
HAYNES, Jno,. 465.
HAYWARD, Thos., 175, 194, 465.
HEADRIGHTS, list of, 473-479.
HEAP, Francis, 350.
HEARNE, Wm., 350, 465.
HEART, Jno., 215.
HEATCH, Adam, 253, 465.
HEATH, Abraham, 465; Jno., 237.
HEDGES, Thos., 478.
HELLAMY, Peter, 477.
HEMMING, Thos., 293.
HENDERSON, Jas., 350, 479; Jno., 350, 435, 465; Wm., 126, 378, 398.
HENRY, Hugh, 255, 261, 369; Helen, 369; Jannet, 369; John, 224, 367-70, 429; Robt. J., 175, 269, 368-70.
HEPWORTH, Jno., 465.
HERNE, Wm., 397, 401, 464.
HEYDEN, Saml., 398.
HICKS, Jno., 350; Thos., 443.
HIGGENBOTHAM, Richd., 293, 402; Robt., 465.
HIGGINS, Izabell, 400, 453.
HIGHWAY FOR SOMERSET ORDERED, 72; route designated, 73.
HIGNETT FAMILY, note, 446; Geo., Jno., Mary, Thos., Wm., 446; Eliz., 478; Jas., 478; Robt., 72, 280, 440, 446, 472, 478.
HILL, Francis, 472; Henry, 443; John, 397, 478; Matthew, 211; ordination of, 528-9; Richd., 349, 350; Robt., 332, 438, 461; Stephen, 475.
HILLIARD FAMILY, note, 446; Jane, Jno., Mary, Oliver, Thos., 446; Jno., 71, 450, 472, 476; Mary, 476; Isaac, 402.
HINDERSON, Jno., 398.
HOBBS FAMILY, note, 446; Eliz., Joy, Thos., 446; Jno., 190, 280, 446, 474.

HOBDAY, Mary, 397.
HODGKINS, Anthony, 52.
HODSON, Edwd., 475; Margt., 397.
HOGG, Jas., 203.
HOLBROOK, Matthias, 465; Thos., 154, 401, 465, 468.
HOLLAND, Geo., 293; Jno., 465; Michael, 198, 325; Richd., 153.
HOLLINSWORTH, 390.
HOLLYDAY, Jas., 439.
HOLSTON, Robt., 192, 479.
HOOKE, Jeremiah, 293, 465.
HOOPER, Anne, 397, 441; Eliz., 400; Henry, 7, 397, 443.
HOPE, Katherine, 461.
HOPKINS, Hannah, 381; Matthew, 269; Nathl., 260; Prudence, 477; Saml., 260, 340, 349, 350, 358, 394, 395, 429, 465, 468.
HORSEMAN, Wm., 293.
HORSEY FAMILY, note, 446; Anne, Eliz., Katherine, Randall, Smith, 446-7; Abigail, 300, 302, 398, 446, 474; Isaac, 398, 446, 477; John, 300, 302, 446, 470, 474; Mary, 300, 302, 446, 474; Nathl., 154, 309, 350, 446, 456, 477; Outerbridge, 198; Stephen, 6, 20-22, 26, 40, 58, 59, 61, 63, 67, 68, 74, 76, 78, 86-8, 92-3, 102, 198, 279; sketch of, 297, *et seq.*, 300, 304, 310; described by Scarburgh, 390, 393-5, 456, 458, 446, 468-71, 476; Saml., 300, 302, 446, 474; Sarah, 300, 302, 446, 474; Wm., 189, 446.
HORSMAN, Thos., 397, 465.
HORVISON, Wm., 293.
HOSTON, Ann., 399.
HOUFINGTON, Jonathan, 437.
HOUGH, Edmd., 381, 429.
HOULSTON, Robt., 118, 120, 465.
How, Jno., 457.
HOWARD, Edmund, 340, 350, 395, 397, 462, 465; Wm., 397, 465, 468, 476, 478; Wm. Stevens, 462.
HOWELL, Geo., 465.
HUDD, Eliz., 478.
HUDSON, Eliz., Nicho., Richd., Violetta, 446; Jno., 475, 478; Henry, 280,

472; Eliz., 397.
HUES, Jno., 465, Jos., 465.
HUETT, John, 128; sketch of, 140, *et seq.*, 154, 178, 233, 330, 358, 348, 349, 394, 453, 465; home place, 523-4; Ann, 453; Susanna, 453; note on family, 520-1.
HUGHES, Thos., 465.
HUGUENOT, 283.
HULL, Danl., 206.
HUMPHREYS, Thos., 253, 397, 449, 465.
HUNDREDS, bounds designated, 73.
HUNGARS PARISH, Northampton Co., Va., 87.
HUNT, Thos., 465, 476.
HUNTER, Henry, 267, 268.
"HUSK RIDGE," 104.
HUST, Jno., 465, 475.
HUTTSON FAMILY, note, 447; Henry, Lydia, Robt., 447; Lydia, 398.

I

"IKL," register of births, deaths and marriages in Somerset Co., note on, 515.
ILLEGITIMATE CHILD, 322.
ILLEGITIMACY (Boston-Best), 436; (Hassard-Carr), 438; (Brayfield-Cooper), 436.
INDEPENDENTS, congregation of, Canterbury, Eng., 316.
"INDIAN NECK," 7.
INDIANS, tribes in Somerset, 7; object to settlement, 16; threaten attack on Manokin - Annemessex settlement, 35; murder David Williams and family, 463.
INGLE, Wm., 465.
INGLISH, Jas., 465.
INGRAM FAMILY, note, 447; Anne, 397, 439, 447, 478; Jas., 398, 447, 478; Jno., 397, 447, 478; Robt., 280, 447, 478; Saml., 194.
INNIS, Saml., 465; see also Ennis.
IPSEWANSEY CREEK, 300.
IRVING, Jno., 436, 468.
IRVING, Jas., 269.
IVERY FAMILY, note, 447; Margt., 280,

399, 436, 447; Mary, 280, 397, 401, 436, 447, 474, 477; Nicho., 447.
IRISH IN SETTLEMENT, 282.
IRONSHIRE, 259.

J

JACKSON, Saml., 464, 474, 475.
JAMES, Gilbert, 465; Honor, 398; Richd., 398.
JARRETT, Graves, 445; Richd., 349.
JEFFERIES, Mary, 400, 401.
JEFFERSON, Richd., 465.
JEMISON (JEMMISON), Alex., 465; Eliz., 399; Jane, 398; Margt., 459.
JENINGS, Edmd., 372.
JENCKINS (JENKINS), Eliz., 475; Francis, 152, 154, 190, 339, 350, 358, 367, 368; sketch of, 373, et seq., 377, 393-5, 398, 414, 424, 426, 465; John, 293, 307; Rozanna, 374; Wm., 398.
JENNIFER, Danl., 476.
JOHNSON FAMILIES, notes, 447, 448, 507; Abraham, 449; Affradozi, 107, 507; Ann, 433; Anthony, 75, 131, 447, 474; Cornelius, 118, 120, 131, 280, 293, 447, 449, 463; Edwd., 317; Eliakim, 208; Eliz., 399, 400, 437, 477; George, 6, 26, 40, 59-63, 67-8, 71, 74, 86-8, 90, 93, 95, 106, 118, 119, 120, 279; sketch of, 316, et seq.; 330; described by Scarburgh, 390, 393, 394, 433, 449, 467, 469, 470, 471, 476, 478, 500; Gershom, 319, 448; James, 204, 206; John, 75, 280, 317, 350, 470, 474, 477, 459; Jone, 399; Jos., 149; Katherine, 90, 106, 316, 319, 448, 467, 476; Mary, 75, 131; Richd., 75; Robt., 349, 465; Susan, 280, 474; Wm., 293, 317, 475.
"JOHNSON's" (tract), 433.
JOHNSTON, Wm. W., 197.
JOICE, Francis, 350.
JOLY, Jas., 469, 472.
JONES FAMILIES, notes, 425, 449; Ann, 449; Andrew, 330, 398; Chas., 398, 436, 465; Danl., 104, 440, 448-9; Edwd., 288, 350, 362, 398, 435; Eliz., 449; Geo., 449; Howell, 330; Jane, 449; Jacob, 402, 475; James, 6, 59, 62, 67, 68, 94, 96, 101, 118, 119, 280; sketch of 329, et seq., 394, 425, 463, 467, 471, 477, 501, 552; John, 181, 182, 194, 349, 425, 449, 474; Johnson, 477; Katherine, 125, 398; Leonard, 465; Lucia, 396; Margt., 448-9, 477; Mary, 449; Matthew, 349; Morgan, 125, 126, 128, 516; Purnell, 475; Robt., 472; Saml., 280, 398, 402, 425, 449, 475; Sarah, 449, 477; Thos., 330, 340, 350, 358, 395, 414, 424, 425, 426, 441, 465; Wm., 52, 72, 131, 182, 247, 280, 395, 437, 440, 448, 473, 474, 477.
JONES' CREEK, 197, 325, 424.
"JONES' HOLE" (tract), 95, 329.
JORDAN (JORDEN), Sarah, 476; Thos., 312, 435, 444, 445.
JUDD, Michael, 187.
JUSTICES OF PEACE (1666-1700), 394-5.

K

KAREY (CAREY?), Richd., 465.
KEENE, Hannah, 396; Wm., 253, 396, 398, 435, 465.
KEITH, Robt., 165, 175, 237.
KELLY, Anne, 398.
KENNEDY, David, 375; Wm., 476.
KENNERLY, Hester, 448; Joshua, 448; Martha, 448; Wm., 433, 448.
KENNETT, Wm., 465.
KENT, Isle of, 8.
KER, Saml., 247.
KERNE (KEENE?), Clemence, 397, 446.
KEYES, Wm., 215.
KEYSER (KEYSAR, KEIZER), Benj., 349, 462, 465; Eliazer, 462; Geo., 462; Jno., 462; Sarah, 461.
KIBBLE, Abigail, 102, 103, 458; Jno., 102, 293, 398, 447, 465; Sarah, 447; Wm., 103, 447.
KILBY, Jno., 429.
KELLAM (KILLUM), Jno., 349; Wm., 378.
"KILLELEAH" (tract), 221.
KIMBLE (KIMBALL), Richd., 398, 465.
KINE, Jno., 350.
KING FAMILIES, notes, 365, 449; Anne M. (alias Aurelia), 431; Alex., 465; Capell, 416; Charlotte W., 430, 431;

Eleanor, 367, 435; Eliz., 398, 433, 450; family homes, 430; Jane, 476; Jeane, 449; Jesse, 194; John, 72, 181, 192, 280, 358, 395, 398, 414, 416, 435, 440 449, 465, 468, 469, 476; Laura, 431; Mary, 367, 372, 374, 397, 449, 476; Nehemiah, 372, 430-2; Robt. (I), 213, 319, 340, 350-1, 353, 358; sketch of, 365, *et seq.*, 374, 394-5, 414, 429, 430, 431, 439, 465; Robt. (II); sketch of, 371, *et seq.*, 430, 431; Robt. (III), 372; Robt. J. H., 430-3; Upshur, 192; Whittington, 193, 432; Thos. 319, 372, 433.
KINGS OF KINGSLAND, 100.
KING'S CREEK (KING'S BRANCH, TRADING BRANCH, MUDFORD), 192, 430, 404; note on, 432.
"KINGSLAND" (tract), 366, 430.
KING'S MILL, 192, 422.
KING'S MILL CHAPEL, Somerset Parish, 192, *et seq.*
"KINGSTON HALL," 319, 432.
KIRBY, Wm., 478.
KIRKE, Jno., 465; Sarah, 402.
KNIGHT, Eliz., 400.
KNOX, 468; Alex., 349; Jas., 349; Jno., 349; Malcolm, 349; Wm., 349.
KYLL (KYLE?), Alex., 350.

L

LAGGAN PRESBYTERY (Ireland), ministers of, 531-2.
LAKE, Henry, 398, 402, 466.
LAMAS, Jane, 400.
LAME'S FERRY, 190.
LAMPIN, Thos., 466.
LAND FOR COUNTY'S USE TO BE LAID OUT, 73.
"LAND DOWNE" (tract), 416.
LANE FAMILY, note, 449; Dennis, Eliz., Katherine, Mary, 449; Geo., 280, 350, 398, 436, 444, 449, 474, 477; Edwd., 475; Jasper, 465; Sarah, 475; Timothy, 398; Walter, 91, 394, 398, 465, 467; Wm., 175, 429.
LANGFORD, Jno., 466.
LANGLEY, Henry, 466.

LANGREENE, Jas., 350, 398, 466.
LANGREL, Jas., 347.
LANGWORTH, Mary, 474.
LANKFORD, Robt., 177.
LARRAMORE (LAREMORE), Thos., 398, 465.
LATHAM, Geo., 350.
LAURENCE, Jno., 472.
LAWE (LAW), Richd., 401; Wm., 347, 350.
LAWES FAMILY, note, 449; Jno., Mary, Robt., Wm., 437.
LAWRENCE, Barbara, 401; Henry, 203, 398, 401, 466; Mr., 392; Richd., 37, 45, 49; Sir Thos., 373; Wm., 350.
LAWS, Jno., 153, 280, 326, 378, 401; Robt., 182.
LAWYERS; see Attorneys.
LAXTONE, Wm., 477.
LAY, Henry C., 182.
LAYDEN, Thos., 476.
LAYFIELD, Eliz., 206, 376, 462; Geo., 154, 206, 329, 332, 350, 358; sketch of, 375, *et seq.*, 395, 461, 466; Mary, 376; Saml., 376; Thos., 376.
LAYTON, Wm., 350.
LEACH, Hanna, 477.
"LEADBURN," 433.
LEATHERBURY, Thos., 303, 323.
LEATON, Henry, 465.
LECKIE, Alex., 149.
LEE, Edwd., 475; Eliz., 398, 451; Henry, 436; Margt., 125, 399.
LEISTER (LISTER, LIDSTER), Thos., 398, 450, 465.
LESLIE, Thos., 465.
LESTER, Hannah, 474.
LEVERTON, Alce, 401.
LEWES, Thos., 398.
LEWIN, Robt., 399, 400, 466.
LEWIS, Henry, 290, 322, 402; Margt., 478; Wm., 466.
LIGHT, Jno., 398; Joshua, 350.
LINDOW, Jas., 468; Margt., 229.
LINDSAY, David, 398, 401.
LINNIS, Edwd., 465.
LISTON, Morris, 466, 470, 472, 477.
LITTLE, Christopher, 466.

LITTLETON, Esther, 381; Sarah, 441; Southy, 105, 381, 470.
LLOYD, Edwd., 100, 439; Richd., 473.
LLUELLEN, Saml., 398, 466.
LODGE, Walter, doctor, 543.
LOE, Robt., 465.
LONDON FAMILY, note, 449; Abigail, 398, 449, 450, 477; Ambrose, 92-3, 279, 395, 449, 477; Mary, 399, 400, 449; Ruth, 400, 449; Thos., 449-50.
LONDON, Bishop of, 189.
LONG FAMILY, note, 450; Ann, David, Jane, Jeffrey, Jno., Randolph, Wm., 450; Danl., 432, 450; Jno. D., 450; Eliz. 436, 450; Littleton, 177; Saml., 280, 398, 433, 450, 452, 476; Sarah, 433.
"LONG LOTT" (tract), 433.
LONGO, Mary, 445.
"LOTS PURCHASE" (tract), 433.
LONDRIDGE, Wm., 125, 398.
LOURY, Sarah, 402.
LOWE, Jane, 351.
LOWRY, Sarah, 399.
LUCAS, Jno., 350.
LUFFE (also LUFF, LUFE), Stephen, 312, 340, 350, 393-5, 435, 444, 466.
LUNN (LUN, LUNNE, LUM) FAMILY, note, 450; Edwd., 115, 116, 280, 450; Eliz., 116, 450.
"LYMSOME" (tract), 271.
LYNCH, Henry, 468.
"LYNNETH" (tract), 271.
LYTE, Jno., 465.

M

McCLAMME, 444.
McCLEMMY, Saml., 195.
McCLESTER, Jno., 396; Jos., 453; Neal, 180.
McGRAW, Jno., 194.
McKNITT, 213; Jno., 350, 399, 466.
McMASTER, Saml., 170; his note on Rehoboth Presbyterian Church, 535; S. S., 200.
MENEILL, Thos., 194.
McNISH, Geo., 219, 237, 245, 253, 262.
MACKBRIDE, Jno., 350.

MACKCULLAH, Alex., 350.
MACKETTRICK, Eliz., 397, 398; Jno., 400, 466.
MACKETT, Jno., 472.
MACKLURE, Richd., 349.
MACKMORIE, Margaret, 453.
MACRAH (MAGRAH, MAGRAW, MACCRAH, MACKRA, MAGRA, MACAH, MACKRUE, MACKARA) FAMILY, note, 450; David, Jno., Mary, Richd., Wm., 450, 451; Owen, 72, 247, 280, 350, 398, 471, 474, 476, 450-1.
MADDOX FAMILY, note, 451; Anne, Eliz., Mary, Nathl., Sarah., Wm. P., 451; Alex., 153, 280, 326, 350, 361, 394, 451; Danl., 444, 451; Eleanor (Maddox, Mattocks), 326, 437, 451; Lazarus, 280, 350, 394, 451, 476; Thos., 195, 451.
MADDOX (MATIX, MADOX, MADDOCKS, etc.), Robert, 115, 118; sketch of, 124, et seq., 131, 133, 247, 331; note, 514; his preaching stations designated and their locations, 512-514.
MAGISTRATES; see Justices of Peace.
MAHAUN, Jno., 466.
MAIDSTONE (Kent, Eng.), 316.
MAJOR, Alice, 460.
MAKEMIE, Anne, 367, 372; Francis, 128, 169, 170, 211, 215; sketch of, 216, et seq., 237, et seq., 269; Naomi, 218.
MALLIS (MALTIS), Katherine, 397, 401.
MANEUX, Margt., 399, 459.
MANINGETTOES CREEK, 148.
MANLOVE FAMILY, note, 451; Abia, 452; Ann, 435, 451-2, 475-6; Christopher, 452, 476; Eliz., 397, 400, 476; Geo., 452, 476; Hannah, 398, 400, 451-2, 476; John, 72, 398, 451, 476; Luke, 452; Mark, 280, 397-8, 401, 405, 451-2, 472, 476; Mary, 445, 451; Peerse (Percy), 400, 452, 476; Thos., 398, 400, 452, 476; Wm., 398, 401, 452, 476.
MANNING, Jno., 448; Sara, 448; Thos., 470.
MANNY; see Monie.

MANOKIN - ANNEMESSSEX, report of (1662), 18, 387-8; settlers' lands claimed by Scarburgh for Va., 30, *et seq.*
MANOKIN BRIDGE, 246; location of, 540.
MANOKIN HUNDRED, bounds designated, 73.
MANOKIN PRESBYTERIAN CHURCH, erection of, 244, *et se.;* records of, 529; location of, 539-40.
MANOKIN SETTLED, 16; area, 27; Quakers in, 27; settlers appeal to Accomack, Va., court for protection, 43; settlers submit to Scarburgh's demand for obedience to Va. government, 42.
MANYOTT, Jno., 475.
MARCHMENT, Saml., 398, 466.
MARCUM (MARCKUM, MARCAM, MARCOM) FAMILY, note, 452; Ann, 400; John, 87, 279, 452, 470, 474; Katherine, 476; Thos., 476.
MARINE, Harriet P., 467.
MARINERS IN SOMERSET CO., 292-3.
MARLETT, Jno., 400, 466.
MARRETT, Jno., 398, 452.
MARRIAGE BANNS, first in Somerset, 70.
MARRIAGES (Somerset Co.), 396-402.
MARSH, Geo., 398, 466; Paul, 394-5, 426, 466.
MARSHALL'S CREEK, 256.
MARSHALL, Geo., 433, 450; Isaac, 177, 199; Sarah, 177; Wm., 198.
MARTIN, 223, 442, 468; Edwd., 417; Eliz., 475; Francis, 399, 458, 466; John, 418; Mary, 417; Robt., 417, 418; Thos., 269.
MARYE, Wm. B., 256, 267.
MD.-VA., boundary line questioned by Edmund Scarburgh, 30; agreement (1668); boundary line, 53, *et seq.*
"MARY'S LOT" (tract), 369, 374.
MASON AND DIXON LINE, 429.
MASON, Geo., 351; John, 466; Michael, 476; Wm., 398.
MASSEY, Wm., 259, 332, 461.
MATHEWS, Wm., 466.
MATTAPANY HUNDRED, 74, 491.

MEAD, Wm., 350.
MEECH, Jno., 466.
MEETING HOUSE BRANCH, 256, 257, 258.
MEETING HOUSE LANDING (Pocomoke River), 266, 267.
MEETING HOUSE NEAR EDGARS, 262, *et seq.*
"MEETING HOUSES"; see under Friends and Quakers; Presbyterian Church buildings.
MELSON, Jno., 398, 401.
MELVELL, Wm., 349.
MELVIN, Wm., 198.
MENTIALE; see Minshall.
MERCHANTS IN SETTLEMENT, 291-2.
MEREDITH, Eliz., 477.
MESSEX (MESSICK, MEZICK), Julian, 439; Lawen (Julian), 398.
METHODIST CHURCH IN SOMERSET CO., 509.
MICHELL (MINSHALL?), Jane, 398; see also Minshall.
MICKLEY, Danl., 310.
"MIDDLE" (tract), 107.
MIDDLE BRANCH, St. Martin's River, 203.
MIDDLETON, Thos., 466.
MIDGLEY, Thos., 349.
MILBOURNE, Ralph, 349; Thos., 269.
MILES, Henry, 279, 400, 435, 457, 466; Wm., 193.
MILITARY FORCES, commander (1665), 60.
MILITARY OFFICERS, 395-6.
MILLARD, Symond, 477.
MILLER, Andrew, 350; John, 349, 429; Thos., 466, 474, 478.
MILLES, Jas., 466.
MILLIMAN, Thos., 466.
MILLNER, Rebecca, 322, 436; Robt., 466.
MILLS, Ann, 475; Henry, 350; John, 269; Moses, 269; Richd., 475; Susanna, 397.
MINARD, Sarah, 396.
MINISTERS OF THE GOSPEL: *Church of England:* see Adams, Alex.; Bell,

Hamilton; Huett, John; Keith, Robt.; Parkes, Henry; Teackle, Thos.; Trotter, Geo.; Robertson, Jas.; Wilkinson, Christopher. *Presbyterian:* see Davis, Saml.; Hill, Matthew; Glasgow, Patrick; Makemie, Francis; McNish, Geo.; Rogers, Jno.; Scougal, Jas.; Stewart, Wm.; Stevenson, Hugh; Tennent, Chas.; Traile, Wm.; Wilson, Thos.; Hampton, Jno. *Baptist:* see Palmer, Paul. *Church unidentified:* see Jones, Morgan; Maddox, Robt.; Moonerow, Geo.; Richardson, David and Robt.; Saulsbury, Benj.

MINSHALL FAMILY, note, 452; Anne, Alce, Eliz., Frances, Thos., 452, 478; Jane, 450, 452; Jeffery, 72, 87, 280, 452, 472, 478; Mary, 67, 399, 452, 460, 478; Randolph (Randall), 399, 452, 478.

MISKELL, Teague, 466.

MITCHELL FAMILY, note, 453; Anne, 399; Eliz., 440, 453; Geo., 131, 280, 400, 449, 453, 470, 474, 477; Humphrey, 475; Isabel, 440, 453; Margt., 280, 442, 453, 474; Mary, 67, 400; Priscilla, 440, 453; Rachel, 447; Robt., 263; Thos., 438; Wm., 299, 304.

MITCHELLER, Alex., 402, 459, 466, 471.
MITCHELLER'S BRANCH, 253.
MITFORD, Bulmer, 48.
MIVER (?), Ruth, 398.
MONCRIEF, Jean M., 221.
MONIE CHURCH (Church of England), 181; Friends Meeting, 98, *et seq.,* 467; Friends Meeting House location, 496, 505; Great and Little Monie Hundreds, bounds designated, 73; Indian Town, 485, 522.
MONKEY, Jno., 475.
MONMOUTHSHIRE, Wales, 94, 329.
MONOCAN (MANOKIN) TOWN, 181, 421, 422.
MOODEY, Rachel, 397, 401.
MOOLSON (MOLSON), Thos., 398, 466, 475.

MOONEROW (MONROE?), George, 116, 510.
MOORE (MOOR, MORE), Augustine, 320; Danl., 466, 479; Geo., 466; John, 349, 399, 466; Martin, 398, 400, 466, 477; Robt., 476; Saml., 476; Wm., 255.
"MORE AND CASE IT" (tract), 326.
MORGAN, Ann, 475; Henry, 416, 466; Margt., 397; Philip, 476; Thos., 350.
MORRIS, Cornelius, 466; Griffin, 399; Isaac, 381, 508; Jenkin, 466; Jeremiah, 441, 442; Manus, 398; Sarah, 455.
MORRISON, Francis, 454.
MORROE, Anguish, 401.
MOSELEY, Ann, 476.
MOULD, Mary, 462.
MOUNT, Richd., 478.
MOYER, Allen, 475.
MT. SCARBOROUGH, 424.
MUDFORD CREEK, 421, 432; see also Trading Branch and King's Creek.
MULBERRY GROVE QUAKER MEETING, 467.
"MULBERRY GROVE" (tract), 107.
MULLA, Cornelius, 466.
MULLEN, Chas., 350.
MUMFORD, James, 205, 206, 466; Sarah, 206; Thos., 206.
MURDAUGH, Robt., 466.
MURDRAKE, Robt., 477.
MURPHEE, Jno., 466.
MURPHY, Oliver H., 197.
MURRAH, Jas., 350.
MURRY, David, 429.

N

NANTICOKE HUNDRED, 74; river, 5, 429, 491.
NAPENIS, Jno., 477.
NASWORTHY, Geo., 469.
NAVAL OFFICER, 340.
NEARNE, Robt., 350.
NEGROES, free, first in Somerset, 75, *et seq.;* other free Negroes, 492.
NEHULIAN, Ellis, 441, 442.
NELSON (NELLSON) FAMILY, note, 453;

Bridget, 437; John, 131, 247, 280, 326, 349, 437, 468, 471, 476; Katherine, 401; Wm., 269, 350.
NESHAM, Benj., 347, 399, 466.
"NEWBERRY" (tract), 255.
NEWBOLD (also NEWBALL, NUBALL), Thos., 154, 340, 350, 395, 414, 460, 466, 468.
NEWGENT, Christopher, 466; Katherine, 399.
NEWMAN, Geo., 466.
NEWPORT CREEK, 204.
NEWTOWN (later Pocomoke City), 202, 267.
NICHOLSON (NICHOLLSON, NICOLLSON) FAMILY, note, 453; Chas., Eliz., Rachel, Richd., Roger, Saml., Sarah, 453; James, 280, 399, 453; Mary, 397, 401-2, 453.
NICOLS (NICHOLS, NICHOLLS), John, 401, 455-6, 474; Frances, 399.
NOBLE, Geo., 350, 362, 468; Isaac, 399, 401, 476, 478; John, 475; Wm., 153, 262, 264, 350, 466.
NODIN, Wm., 465.
NOLTON, Ann, 399, 400.
NON-CONFORMISTS, in settlement of Somerset, 85, *et seq.*
NORTHAMPTON-ACCOMACK, Va., men petition to settle in Maryland, 13.
NORTHAMPTON Co. (Va.), formation, 455, 493.
"NORTH PETHERTON" (tract), 183.
NORWOOD, Henry, 429, 454.
NOTTLE, Margt., 376.
NOUGHTON, Wm., 399.
NUTTALL (NUTHALL), John, 16, 298; note on, 486, 475.
NUTTER FAMILY, note, 453; Chas., Jno., Sarah, Thos., 453; Christopher, 280, 453, 472, 477; Mary, 453, 477; Matthew, 149.
"NUTTER'S PURCHASE" (tract), 247.
NUTTLEY, Mary, 402.

O

O'CANE, Roger, 441.
ODBER, Jno., 20, 21, 22, 58, 59, 279, 314, *et seq.*
OKE (OKEE) FAMILY, note, 453; Eliz., 453; John, 70, 280, 399, 400, 453, 477.
OLANDMAN, Donnan (Denham), 466, 476.
OLLIPHANTS, Presbyterian Meeting House at, 271.
OSBORNE, Atalanta, 381; John, 340, 381, 394, 414, 466.
OSWELL, Wm., 350.
OUTERBRIDGE, 447.
OWEN, Mary, 402; Thos., 399, 466; Wm., 349.
OXFORD, Thos., 350, 466.
OYSTER SHELL NECK, 420.

P

PAGE, I. Marshall, 262; Stephen, 350.
PAINTER (PANTER?), Eliz., 398, 401; John, 280, 474.
PAKE, Robt., 475.
PALMER, Paul, Baptist minister in Somerset (1739), 508.
PANTER, Jno., 74, 131, 154, 400, 466, 468.
"PAPISTS," 351.
PARAHAWKIN ROAD, 428.
PARIS, Geo., 254.
PARISH CHURCHES (Church of England); see Coventry, Somerset, Stepney, Snowhill Parishes.
PARISHES ORGANIZED, 153.
PARISH RECORDS LISTED, 519.
PARK, Geo,. 349.
PARKER, Geo., 52, 391; John, 466.
PARKES, Mr. [Henry], 138.
PARRAMORE, Jno., 208, 452, 466, 470.
PARSONS, Anne, 398; John, 349, 466; Peter, 466, 470.
PARTRIDGE, Richd., 399, 478; Robt., 125.
PASSERDYKE CREEK, 429.
PATE, Jno., 465.
PATERSON, Wm., 466.
PATENTS FOR LAND IN MD., granted by Va. government, 489.
PATRICK, Jno., 378; Rode, 466.
PATTERSON, Robt., 247.

PAYNE, John, 351; Thos., 474.
"PEACH BLOSSOM" (tract), 431.
PEACOCK, Richd., 475.
PEARLE, Jas., 399.
PEDDENTON (PEDDINGTON) FAMILY, note, 453; Henry, 279, 305, 399, 453; Margt., 453.
PEICKE, Jno., 466.
PELINGHAM, Jane, 397.
PENFAX POINT, location of, 542.
PENNINGTON, Henry, 475.
PENNY, Jone, 475.
PENY, Robt., 350.
PENT, Eliz., 477.
PEPPER, Margt., 401; Richd., 350, 466; Tobias, 350, 466.
PEPPER'S CREEK, 206.
PERCELL (also PERSILL), Sarah, 397, 401.
PERIMAN, Mary, 402.
PERKINS, Edwd., 478; John, 399, 458; Simon, 333.
PERRIE (also PIRRIE), Robt., 127, 362.
PERSONS, John, 382.
PETERFRANCK, Jno., 350.
PHESEY, Anne, 396.
PHILIPSON, Anne, 485.
PHILLIPS, Henry, 349; Roger, 350, 399; Thos., 476, 477.
PHILLPOT, Thos., 399.
PHOEBUS (PHEBUS), Geo., 293, 349, 399, 466, 476, 477.
PHYSICIANS, 281.
PIKE, Jno., 401.
PIPER, Tobias, 401; Wm., 153, 453.
PISHER (FISHER?), Ann, 400.
PITTS CREEK, 269.
PITTS CREEK (PRESBYTERIAN) CONGREGATION AND MEETING HOUSE, 267, *et seq.*
PITT, Robt., 472, 475, 479.
PLANNER FAMILY, note, 453; Rebecca, 453; William, 153-4, 279, 289, 315, 322, 350, 414, 445, 453, 470, 474-5, 478.
PLANTERS, 281.
PLATER, Geo., 378.
PLAYER, Jno., 316.

POCYTERNORTON; see Bogerternorton.
"POCOMOKE CHURCH" (1692), 161, *et seq.;* 169, *et seq.;* in use by Presbyterians and Church of England Congregations, 171.
POCOMOKE CITY (formerly Newtown), 267; chapel erected, now St. Mary's Church, 202.
POCOMOKE DISSENTING CONGREGATION, 267.
POCOMOKE FERRY (STEVEN'S FERRY), 264, 267; location of, 542.
POCOMOKE HUNDRED, bounds designated, 73.
POCOMOKE RIVER, 5, 429.
"POCOSAN ROAD," 245.
POINTER (also POYNTER), Thos., 154, 350, 466.
POLK, 468; Esther, W., 431; James, in Princess Anne, Presbyterian meeting place, 271; John, 232, 466; Robt., 350; Wm., 349.
POLLARD, Rebecca, 478.
POLLETT, Thos., 350.
"POMFRET" (tract), 198, 325.
POMFREY, Richd., 466.
PONIES; see Chincoteague ponies.
POOLE (POOL) FAMILY, note, 454; Andrew, Eliz., Grace., Jas., Jno., King, Rachel, 454; Thomas, 72, 131, 280, 290, 350, 454, 468, 474.
POPE, Jno., 350, 466.
POPLAR TOWN (IRONSHIRE), 261.
POPLEY, Martha, 401.
POPULATION, expansion of (1664-5), 60.
PORTER, Hugh, 441, 442; John, 350, 399, 466; Jos., 197; Patience, 476, 477.
PORTING, Emanuel, 474.
PORTLAND, Henry, 477.
POULSON, Wm., 476.
POTTER, ALICE, 399; Christiana, 306, 397, 442; Henry, 306, 442, 443; Thos., 289, 443.
POWELL, Catherine, 331, 461; Eliz., 399, 443; Jas., 292; Jno., 107; Walter, 107, 466-7, 506; Wm., 107, 467.

POYER, Robt., 399.
PRATE, Nicho., 475.
PREACHING STATIONS (Robt. Maddox, 1671/2), 121, *et seq.*; 512-14.
PRENTICE, Susanna, 317; Wm., 399, 466.
PRESBYTERIAN, 348; congregation southside Pocomoke, near the ferry, 266; origins in Somerset Co., 211, *et seq.*; early Presbyterians in Md., 528; remaining session records of Somerset churches, 529; ministers, fund raised toward support of, 532; families listed, 468.
PRESBYTERIAN CHURCH BUILDINGS IN SOMERSET; see Rehoboth, Manokin, Snow Hill, Sea Side Road, Buckingham, Pitts Creek, Pocomoke Church, Wicomico, Meeting House near Edgars, Broad Creek Bridge, Olliphants; Rider, Wilson; Polk, Jas.; Venables, Benj.
PRESBYTERY OF LAGGAN, petitioned for a minister for Somerset, 215.
PRESLEY, Peter, 381.
PRIESTLY, Henry, 472.
PRICE FAMILIES, notes, 454; Alex., 399; Edwd., 470; Jas., 72, 466, 470; Jean, 454; Jenkin, 71-2, 106, 280, 450, 454, 469, 472-4, 476, 478; John, 446, 454, 466, 474, 478; Katherine, 315, 472, 454, 478; Margt., 401, 454, 474, 478; Mary, 399, 453, 475; Martha, 454, 474, 478; Rachel, 454; Richd., 477; Sarah, 478; Thomas, 26, 40, 86-93, 106, 279, 301; sketch of, 315, *et seq.*, 316; described by Scarburgh, 390; 414, 453-4, 467, 470; William, 454, 472.
PRIDEAUX, Tangine, 402.
PRIM, Richd., 402, 466.
PRIMME (?), Alce, 398.
PRINCE GEORGE'S CHAPEL, Worcester Parish (Sussex Co., Del.), 206, *et seq.*
PRINCE, Sarah, 398.
PRINCESS ANNE TOWN, King's Mill Chapel removed to, 193.

PRISON, at Rehoboth, 419.
PRITCHETT, Wm., 475.
PROCTOR, Alex., 349.
PROTESTANTISM, in Somerset, 337.
PROUSE, Geo., 477.
PROUT (?), Jno., 399.
PUCKHAM, Jno., 143, 399.
PULBERRY, Sussex, Eng., 334.
PURNELL, Jno., 183; Thos., 153, 414, 466, 468.
PYLE, Thos., 466.

Q

QUAKERS, families listed, 467; burying ground near Snow Hill, Md., 507; at St. Dunstan's [Kent, Eng.?], 448-9; Va. law against Quakers, 121, *et seq.*; see also Friends.
QUEEN ANNE, 181.
QUEPONCOE, 257.
QUILLANE FAMILY, note, 454; Eliza, Judith, Lydia, Teague, Thomas, 454-5; Daniel, 280, 454, 455, 472.

R

RACIAL ELEMENTS IN EARLY POPULATION OF SOMERSET CO., 282-3.
"RACKLIFFE'S PURCHASES" (tract), 203.
RACKLIFFE, Sarah, 203.
RAMES, Francis, 478.
RATCLIFF (RATCLIFFE, RATCLIFE), Chas., 340, 349, 395, 400, 460, 466, 478, 479; Eliz., 460; Sarah, 478.
RAWLEY, Jas., 466; Jno., 349, 399.
RAYMOND, Jonathan, 382.
RAYNBOWE, Wm., 466.
READ, Amy, 475; Geo., 475; Humphrey, 350; Patrick, 350; Percifull, 466, 469; Walter, 350.
RED CAP CREEK, 6, 289.
REDELPHUS, Wm., 466.
REHOBOTH, Bay, 424; tract, 121, 328, 331, 374; home of Wm. Stevens, note, 551; church, 169; Presbyterian "meeting house," or church, erected, 237, *et seq.*; 170; town, 419; prison at, 419.
RELFE, Thos., 399, 436.
RELIGIOUS BODIES; see Quakers,

Friends, Church of England, Presbyterians, Baptists, Methodists, Roman Catholics.
RENNY, Jno., 466.
RENSHAW (RENSHA), John, 153, 349, 466, 468, 474, 475.
REVELL FAMILY, note, 455; Alice, 457; Anne, 138, 309, 325, 397, 438, 456; Ballard, 457; Chas., 440, 457; Frances, 456; Hannah, 307, 309, 446, 456, 474; John, 456; Katherine, 307, 309, 474, 456-7; Randall, 15, 18-21, 27-30-1, 34, 43-4, 76, 94, 131, 279; sketch of, 306, *et seq.*; 349, 386, 388, 391, 393, 435-6, 445, 455-7, 468-9, 474, 477; Rebecca, 325, 439, 453; Richard, 456; Sarah, 309, 446-7, 456-7; Wm., 457.
"REVELL'S NECK," 16, 27.
REVELL'S NECK ROAD, 422.
REVELL, Randall, town at, 413.
RHODES (RHOADES) FAMILY, note, 457; Comfort, Eliz., Patience, Robt., Werenia, Wm., 457; John, 44, 132, 279, 391, 457, 468, 478; Martha, 401, 457, 460.
RICE FAMILY, note, 457; Nicholas, 71, 280, 293, 395, 457, 471, 477.
RICHARDS FAMILY, note, 457; Grace, 457; John, 279, 306, 313, 401, 466, 457, 475, 477.
RICHARDSON, Daniel, 517; David, 126, *et seq.*; Robt., 126, 128, 206, 466; Susanna, 398.
RICKARDS, Jno., 401.
RICKETT'S ROAD, 190.
RIDER, Dorothy, 371; Wilson, 271.
RIGGIN, Teague, 399, 400, 450.
RIGHT, Robt., 474; Wm., 399.
RILEY, Lawrence, 332, 461.
RISBROOKE, Sevgan, 475.
RISDON, Blandina, 326, 437.
RIXON, Jno., 399.
ROACH FAMILY, note, 457; Arabella, Eliz., Hannah, Jos., Michael, Nathl., Rebecca, Saml., Wm., 458; Abigail, 396, 458; Chas., 457; John, 132, 279, 300, 350, 399, 445, 447, 457-8, 463, 470, 474; Mary, 399, 458; Sarah, 399, 457, 458; Wm., 457, 458.
ROAGUES, Ann, 478.
ROBBINS, Mary, 397, 401.
ROBERTS, Ann, 126, 396; Alce, 398, 402; Francis, 313, 466; Thos., 401; Wm., 441.
ROBERTSON, Jas., 175, 423.
ROBESON, Jno., 402; Mary, 401.
ROBINS, Alce, 398, 452; Esther, 443; Obedience, 297; Robt. P., 460; Thos., 466.
ROBINSON, Conway, 51; Frances, 400, 464; Jone, 478; James, 293; Martha, 478; Mary, 399, 478; Patrick, 466; Wm., 399, 466, 478.
ROCHE, Thos., 474.
"ROCHESTER" (tract), 90, 106.
RODE, Northamptonshire, Eng., 334.
RODGERS, Sarah, 446.
ROE, Thos., 118, 120, 139.
ROGERS, Jno., 271, 466; Mary, 399; Sarah, 397; Wm., 466.
ROGERSON, Eliz., 322, 396, 436.
ROLLENS, Margt., 401.
ROMAN CATHOLICS, 351; none discovered in Somerset Co. prior to 1700, **509.**
Ross, Allen, 350; John, 208.
ROUND, 213, 214, 223; James, 263, 340, 350, 358, 370, 394-5, 466, 461, 466; Wm. 152, 154, 350, 370, 466.
ROUSBY, Gertrude, 370.
Row, Thos., 466.
ROWASTICO BRANCH, 180.
ROWELL, Jno., 349, 399, 402.
RUSSELL, Geo., 347; Wm., 476.
RUST, Jno., 350.
RUSTALL, Jno., 183.

S

SADLER, Micayah, 349.
ST. ANDREW'S CHURCH, Princess Anne, 196.
ST. MARTIN'S CHAPEL AND CHURCH, 204, *et seq.*; church yard, 183, 202.
ST. MARY, the Virgin Church (Pocomoke City), 202.

St. Mary's (City), 8.
St. Peter's Church, Salisbury, 189.
St. Stephen's Church, Dividing Creek, removed to Upper Fairmount, 201.
Salisbury, Benj., 125, 128.
"Salisbury" (tract), 285.
Salisbury, Md., 429; Goddard's Chapel removed to, 189.
Sallaway, Ann, 475.
Sandy Hill, Worcester Co., 208; wharf, 416.
Sangster, Jas., 350, 362, 399, 460.
Sargent, Jno., 399.
Saucer (Sawser), Benj., 396, 466.
Saunders, Jno., 350.
Savage, Thos., 447.
Sawyer (tradesman), 293.
Sayer, Peter, 339.
Saywell, Thos., 475.
Scarborough, Jno., 429; Matthew, 154, 183, 394, 395, 466, 468.
Scarburgh, Edmund, 15, 21, 28, 29; demands submission of settlers, 30; letter to John Elzey, 37 et seq.; 307, 308, 313, 386; report proceedings Annemessex-Manokin (1663), 388-392; 479; Hannah, 218; Katherine, 437, 456.
Schoolfield, Benj., 466.
Schoolhouse (1696), 289.
School teachers, first in Somerset, 287-8.
"Sciper's [Skipper's] Plantation," 121.
Scotchmen in settlement, 282.
Scott, Jno., 197, 429; Wm., 466.
Scougal, Jas., 266.
Seaboard side, warrants for land, 473.
Seaman, Jno., 477; Wm., 477.
Searle, Susanna, 396.
Sea Side, road up, "Meeting House" on, 248, 256, et seq.
Seawell, Thos., 399, 466.
Selby, Danl., 466; Thos. 154, 466.
Sereeke, Paul, 477.
Serle, Susanna, 475.
Settlers, first families, 434-464.

Sewall, Henry, 351, 469; Nicholas, 351.
Seward, Josias, 288, 466.
Sewall, Jane, 396; Mary, 398.
Shankland, Wm., 350.
Shaw, Ann, 310; Cecill, 126, 399.
Shealy, Danl., 402.
Sheltenham, Jacob, 466.
Sheriffs (1666-1700), 393.
Sherman, Jno., 466, 478.
Shiall family, note, 458; Eliz., 458; John, 458; Thos., 131, 280, 458, 468.
Shild (Shiall?), Thos., 349.
Shiles, _____, 436.
Shiletto, Mary, 397, 444; Thos., 397, 399, 444, 466.
Shingle Landing Prong, St. Martin's River, 203.
Shipham, Edwd., 466.
Shipyard, 423.
Shipway, Jno., 466, 471, 475, 468.
Shipworth, Wm., 475.
Shoares, Wm., 475.
Shockley, Richd., 399.
Shoemaker (tradesman), 293.
Showell (also Shewell), Saml., 203, 350, 466.
"Showell's Addition" (tract), 203.
Shuttleworth, Vincent, 466.
Sidbury, Edwd., 466.
Sikes, Jno., 477.
Silvero, Nicholas, 401.
Simmons, Jno., 466.
Simson, Robt., 349.
Sinepuxent Bay, 429; neck, 260.
Skervin, Wm., 365, 381.
"Slater's Neck" (Del.), 315.
Small, Richd., 466.
Smart, Jno., 381; Tabitha, 381.
Smith family, note, 425; Archibald, 445; Anne, 401, 425; Baker, 474; Edwd., 394, 466; Geo., 399, 466; Henry, 118, 119, 126, 135, 338, 340, 350, 394, 414, 422, 424-6, 466, 473, 474, 479; James, 349; Joanna, 425; John, 374, 425; Robt., 459, 466; Saml., 137, 381, 471; Thos., 349, 472,

474; Tomasin, 425; Wm., 300, 349, 425, 472-3, 468.
"SMITH'S ADVENTURE" (tract), 137, 381.
"SMITH'S FOLLY" (tract), 200.
SMOCK, Eliz., 257; Henry, 256; John, 256, 349, 466; Saml., 257; Wm., 257.
SMYTON, Wm., 466.
SNOSSALL, Christopher, 466.
SNOW, Jno., 350, 446.
SOMERSET, Lady Mary, 5, 68, 485; Sir Jno., 485.
SOMERSET Co., erected and organized, first officials named, 5, 67-9; tithables ordered listed, 70; first court, 70; first marriage banns, 70; seaboard-side lands to be granted, 71; constables, 71-2; surveyors of highways, 72; highway ordered, 72; first grand jury, 72; courts held at Pooles, 72; highway route designated, 73; Hundreds laid out, 73, 490-1; first free Negroes, 75, et seq.; first representation in Assembly, 77, et seq.; evangelization proposed by grand jury (1671/2), 115, et seq.; representatives in Associators' Government, 353-4; arms kept in private homes, 355; representatives to Assembly, 1692, refused seats, and proceedings thereon, 359, et seq.; address to King William and Queen Mary, 349-50; social status of first settlers of Somerset Co., 281, et seq.; names of settlers (Aug., 1666-1700), 464-6; public roads (1696/7), 541-2; first volume of court records, 489.
SNOW HILL (or ALL HALLOWS) AND WORCESTER PARISHES, Chapels of Ease, 202, et seq.; Parish Church, 163, 164, 182, et seq.; first vestry, 154.
SNOW HILL PRESBYTERIAN CHURCH, erection of, 242, et seq.; location of, 538-9; session records, 529.
SNOW HILL TOWN, 416-418, 429; church in, 182, et seq.
SOMERSET PARISH, Church, 163, 164, 180, et seq.; 421; first vestry, 155; Chapels of Ease, 192, et seq.; communion silver, 444; glebe, 468.
SOMERSET TOWN, 181, 421, 422.
SOMMERTON, 181.
SOUTHERN FAMILY, note, 458; Cullett, 400; Edwd., 72, 280, 290, 458, 474; Mary, 474.
SOWELL, Thos., 477.
SPEER, Andrew, 399; Priscilla, 399.
SPENCE FAMILY, note, 458; Adam, 260, 269, 349; Alex., 458; Ann, 458; Bridget, 436; David, 75, 131, 280, 458, 468, 471, 477; Jas., 436, 458; John, 458.
SPRATT, Jno., 477.
SPRING HILL CHAPEL, Stepney Parish, 189, et seq.
SPRING HILL PARISH, 191.
STADLEY, Ann, 398.
STANBRIDGE, Thos., 466.
STANFORD, Augustine, 466.
STANDRIDGE, Matthewe, 398; Martha, 446; Thos., 398.
STANFORD, Rachel, 255; Thos., 255.
STANLEY, Hugh, 473.
STAPLEFORD, Raymond, 469.
STARRETT (STARRET), Jno., 153, 350, 466.
STATON (STAYTON), Jos., 466.
STEELE, Wm., 399.
STEELL, Jno., 350.
STEPNEY PARISH, Chapels of Ease, 186, et seq.; parish church, 163, 178, et seq.; first vestry, 155.
STERLING, Jno., 400, 466.
STEVENS, Ann, 459; Abigail, 459; Edwd., 263, 264, 265, 466; Elizabeth, 107, 264, 329, 375-6, 458, 461, 477; Frances, 458; Hannah, 459; Isaac, 459; Jno., 264-5, 326, 459; Philip, 454; Richard (of Wicomico), 101-2, 280, 447; note on family of, 458, 504; 467, 471, 477; Ruth, 263, 264; Saml. 264; Tabitha, 264; William (of Pocomoke), 264, 265; William (of "Rehoboth"), 6, 59, 60-3, 67-8, 77, 79, 118, 119, 131, 134 169, 206, 212, 214,

215, 259, 280, 302; sketch of, 326, *et seq.*; 338, 374-6, 394-5, 416, 447, 461, 472-3, 476; William (doctor), 543; William (of Dorchester), note on, 502.
"STEVENS' CONQUEST" (tract), 102.
STEVENS' FERRY (Pocomoke), 265.
STEVENSON, 223, 468; Christopher, 472; Hugh, 261, 262, 270; Jas., 271; Wm., 153, 350.
STEWARD, Jas., doctor, 543.
STEWART, Wm., 247, 270.
"STEWART'S NECK," 7.
STEWNES (STEVENS?), Wm., 399.
STIVENSON (STEVENSON?), Thos., 349.
STOCKDELL, Edwd., 399, 466.
STONE, Wm., 9.
STORY, Thos., 91, 101, 108; excerpts from his journal, 495-6; William, 449.
STOUGHTON, Wm., 444.
STRADLING, Margt., 475.
"STRAIGHTS" (tract), 318, 433.
STRATTON, Thos., 441.
STRAWBRIDGE, 213; John, 153, 350, 362, 445; Thos., 466, 468.
STREETE, Anne, 399.
STRETCHER, Henry, 457; Sarah, 457.
STRINGER, Col., 39.
STUART, Alex., 431.
STURGES, Geo., 399.
SUDNAM (SURNAM?), Ann, 474; Edwd., 474.
SUGAR, Jone, 476.
SUMMER FAMILY, note, 459; Benj., 279, 300, 400, 401, 459, 470, 474; Isabel, 459; Thos., 459; Wm., 399, 459.
SURNAM FAMILY, note, 459; Ann, 402, 459; Edwd., 280, 349, 399, 459; Peter, 459; Thos., 459.
SUTTON, Wm., 475.
SWAN, Peter, 316.
SWAINE, Jno., 350.
SWANNY CREEK, 121.

T

TAILORS (tradesmen), 293.
TARR, Jno., 350, 466; Michael, 208.

TAYLOR, Alce, 402; Ann, 398, 477; Anthony, 400, 466, 478; Eliz., 381, 475; Hope, 402; Jno., 325, 350, 439, 471; Joell, 477; Jos., 401, 466, 478; Sarah, 437; Walter, 466, 469.
TEACHERS, 287-8.
TEACKLE, Thos., 116, 132, 135, 299.
TEAGUE, Eliz., 399, 401.
TENNENT, Chas., 270.
THIRD HAVEN MEETING HOUSE (Friends), 467.
THOMAS, Alex., 126, 350, 399, 466; Henry, 477; Jno., 477; Marcum, 118, 120; Mary, 402; Philip, 372; Rebecca, 399; Roger, 182, 202; Wm., 471.
THOMPSON, Jno., 224, 466; Wm., 430.
THORNE, Wm., 6, 19, 20, 22, 27, 41, 58, 59, 60-3, 67-9, 74, 131, 213, 279, 311; sketch of, 312, *et seq.*; 363, 388, 389, 391, 394, 468, 471, 472, 475; Winifred, 213, 313, 475.
"THORNTON" (tract), 27, 313, 363.
THOROWGOOD, Francis, 259, 332, 461.
TILLMAN FAMILY, note, 459; Eleanor, Eliz., John, Moses, Solomon, 459; Gideon, 131, 280, 399, 459, 468; Isaiah, 194.
TILNEY, Jno., 391.
TILSLEY, Thos., 475.
TIMBELLS, Jno., 477.
TINGLE, Hugh, 349, 399, 466.
TITHABLES, Somerset, 1666, ordered listed, 70.
TIPQUIN, 418.
TIZARD, Jno., 293.
TOADVINE, Henry, 402, 442; Nicholas, 350, 399, 466.
TOFT, Anne, 27, 76, 307, 381, 474.
TOMPKINS, Wm., 262, 466.
TOMLINSON, Saml., 466.
TONIES' VINEYARD (home of free Negroes), location, 76, 492.
TORRENCE, Helen, 491.
TOWNS, first in Somerset Co., 410; on Elzey's land, 420; on south side Wicomico River, 414; on Smith and Glandvill's land in fork of Manokin River, 415.

TOWNSEND FAMILY, note, 459; Chas., Eliz., Jas., Jeremiah, Mary, Solomon, Wm., 459; Brickus, 204; John, 280, 459, 469.
TRADESMEN, 293; see also Carpenters, coopers, tailors, sawyer, blacksmith, shoemaker, boatright, butcher.
TRADERS, Indian, 290, 291.
TRADING BRANCH, or King's Creek, 192, 404, 421, 430, 485.
TRAHERNE (TREHERNE), GEO., 399, 401, 466; Sarah, 435.
TRAILE, Eleanor, 221; Jas., 222; Wm., 128, 212, 215; sketch of, 220, *et seq.;* 348, 350, 466; home of, 533.
TRANSQUAKING MEETING HOUSE (Friends), 449.
TREVETT, Eliz., 401.
TRICE, Alex., 399.
TROTTER, Geo., 147, 165.
TROUT, Paul, 212.
TRUITT (TREWETT, TRUET), 91, 103, 106, 107, 467; John, 103, 467.
TRUPSHAW, Jno., 350.
TUCKER, Florence, 264; Jno., 466.
TULL FAMILY, note, 460; Benj., Eliz., Geo., Jno., Mary, Rachel, Sarah, Wm., 460; Edwd., 186; Richd., 118, 120, 132, 279, 350, 400, 401, 457, 460, 468; Thos., 70, 132, 279, 350, 378, 399, 400, 452, 457, 460, 468.
TULL'S CREEK, 121.
TURNER, Mary, 399; Richd., 399, 401.
"TURNER'S PURCHASE" (tract), 229.
TURPIN, Eliz., 400; Jno., 400; Sarah, 435; Wm., 399, 447, 464.
TURVILE (TURVILL) PRESGRAVE, 203; Wm., 350, 460, 466.
TYFERD, Jno., 401, 466.
TYLER, Jno., 293, 399; Nicholas, 347.
TYRE, Thos., 466.
TYZARD, Jno., 466.

U

UPPER FERRY ROAD (Wicomico), 254.

V

VALENTINE, Luke, 437, 449.

VAUS, Sarah, 399.
VAUX, Henry, 99.
VAUGHAN, Wm., 466.
VANHACK, Jno., 470.
VENABLES, Benj., 253, 254, 255; Presbyterian meeting place at, 271; Joseph, 149, 178, 241, 253, 262, 333, 396, 466; Wm., 188, 189, 255; Presbyterian meeting place at saw-mill of, 271; 468.
VERRAZANO, Giovanni de, 429.
VESEY, Nathl., 350.
VESTRIES, order for election of, 154; first elected, 155.
"VERMIN DRANE" (tract), 205.
"VERNAM DEANE" (tract), 206.
VINCENT, Frances, 280, 400, 474; John, 280, 453; Mary, 67, 280, 399, 400, 474.
VIGOROUS, Jno., 543, 466.
VA. ASSEMBLY, Sept., 1663, Act relative to boundaries of colony on Eastern Shore, 37, *et seq.*
Voss (also VAUX), Henry, 303.

W

WAILES, Benj., 439, 446.
WALE (WALLE, later WHALEY) FAMILY, note, 460; Bridget, Chas., Eliz., Elias, John, Lewis, Nathl., Rachel, Sarah, Wm., 460; Edwd., 280, 400, 460; Geo., 460, 469, 472; Isabel, 400, 459, 477.
WALKER, Jane, 397; Jno., 401, 478; Susanna, 288; Thomas, 139, 148, 288, 292, 322, 393, 395, 400, 424, 426, 466, 468; William, 476.
WALL (WALLER?), Thos., 349.
WALLACE, 213; see also Wallis.
WALLAHANE, Philip, 466.
WALLER FAMILY, note, 460; Alice, 460; Jno., 72, 74, 131, 280, 460; Major, 444, 460; Wm., 193, 349, 460.
WALLEY FAMILY, note, 460; Eliz., 460, 477; Jno., 186, 460, 477; Margt., 460, 477; Rachel, 460, 477; Rebecca, 460; Thos., 186, 280, 460, 471, 477.
"WALLEY'S CHANCE" (tract), 186, 187.

WALLIS, 213; Jane, 399; Matthew, 153; Wm., 466, 468.
WALLOP, Jno., 479.
WALSTON, Thos., 450; Wm., 293, 400, 438.
WALTER, Wm., 466.
WALTHAM, Jno., 347, 382, 400, 452, 466.
WALTON (WALLTON), Jno., 378; Rebecca, 397; Richd., 289; Wm., 414.
WANCKLEN, Jno., 477.
WARD FAMILY, note, 460; Alice, Jno., Saml., Thos., Wm., 460-1; Cornelius, 132, 279, 400, 470, 479; Edwd., 476.
WARING, Jacob, 466.
WARNER, Geo., 360.
WARREN, Jno., 446; Richd., 349, 466.
WARWICK, 431; Wm., 466.
WATERS, Eliz., 92, 105; Geo., 176; Jno., 466; Mary, 440; Richd., 89, 93, 102, 105, 467; Wm., 470; Wm. A., 431.
WATKINS' POINT, 5, 428.
WATSON, Mary, 400, 401.
WATT, Jno., 350.
WATTS, Jno., 332, 376, 461.
WATTSON, Jno., 477.
WAUGHOP, Jno., 472.
WEATHERLY, Jas., 153, 154, 466.
WEBB, Ann, 401, 416; Nicholas, 476; Richd., 400, 401, 466.
WEEDON, Henry, 398; Jas., 374, 394, 465, 466; Lucy, 374, 465; widow, 398.
WELLS, Ellen, 475; John, 475.
WELLS, Somersetshire, Eng., 285.
WELSH IN SETTLEMENT, 282.
WEST, Jno., 241, 309, 332, 334, 347, 350, 362, 391, 393, 456, 466.
WESTLOCK FAMILY, note, 461; John, 7, 280, 461, 471, 474, 475; Magdalen, 461, 471, 475.
"WEYMOUTH" (tract), 127.
WHALEY; see Wale.
WHAPLES, Peter, 350.
WHARTON, Mary, 264, 398; Richd., 466.
"WHAT YOU PLEASE" (tract), 253.
WHEARLY (WHALEY?), Eliz., 459.

WHEATLEY, 447.
WHEELER, Edwd., 400, 466; Sarah, 264.
WHITE FAMILY, note, 461; Alex., 350; Ambrose, 466; Archibald, 221, 466; Edwd. J., 431; Eliz., 331, 461; Frances, 332; Francis, 461; Grace, 457; Henry, 303, 323; Jerome, 49; John, 6, 59, 67, 68, 153, 259, 280; sketch of, 331, et seq.; 349, 376, 393-5, 400, 461; Lewis, 451; Priscilla, 332, 376-7, 461-2; Phenix, 466; Phineas, 466, 472, 478; Sarah, 332, 376; 461; Stevens, 259, 332, 381, 461-2; Tabitha, 332, 461; Thos., 472; Wm., 259, 331, 461.
WHITEHALL, 420.
WHITEHAVEN, Md., 94.
WHITE HOUSE, 422.
WHITEMARSH, Richd., 470.
WHITFIELD (WHITTFEELD, WHITTFIELD), Thos., 300, 474; Wm., 466, 469.
WHITTAKER, Nath., 198.
WHITTINGHAM, Bishop W. R., 182, 200, 201; Heber, 447.
WHITTINGTON, Andrew, 342, 354, 466; Atalanta, 381, 461; Eliz., 381; Esther, 381; Hannah, 381; Smart, 381; Southy, 381; Tabitha, 381; William, 145, 298, 341, 344, 345, 352, 358; sketch of, 379, et seq.; 381, 393-6, 416, 466, 488.
WHITTY FAMILY, note, 462; Alce, 462; Dorothy, 462; Edwd., 474, 478; Eliz., 477; Richard, 153, 280, 424, 426, 471, 476.
WHOREKILL, 424, 426.
WICKHAMBRUX (Kent), 316.
WICOMICO, County, 428, 429; Hundred boundaries designated, 74; Presbyterian Congregation and Meeting Houses, 253, et seq., and Session records, 529.
WIFE-HIRING, case tried, 321.
WIGHCO RIVER, 5, 428.
WIGHCOCOMOCO RIVER, 5, 428.
WILDGOOSE, Richd., 350, 466.
WILKINSON, Christopher, 183; Mary,

399, 476; Wm., 470, 476.
WILLERS, Susan, 474.
WILLIAMS FAMILIES, notes, 462-4; Alex., 466; Ann, 400, 463, 476; Anthony, 475; Chas., 400, 401; David, 400, 439, 462, 463; Eliz., 398, 401, 463, 464; Evan., 402; Hannah, 464; Isaac, 175, 447; John, 118, 120, 350, 464, 476, 479; Mary, 400, 463, 464, 474, 475, 478; Michael, 279, 297, 300, 302, 400, 446, 458, 463, 464, 470, 474; Nathl., 463; Sarah, 279, 297, 300, 302, 399, 446, 458, 463, 464, 474; Thos., 175, 197, 199, 279, 300, 400, 414, 463, 464, 470, 474, 479; Walter, 463; William, 199, 433.
WILLIS, Jas., 400, 435, 466.
WILLS, Robt., 369.
WILMOT, Wm., 349.
WILSON FAMILY, note, 468; Alce, 402; David, 468; Eliz., 468; Ephraim, 349, 369, 393, 436, 468; Geo., 400, 466; Henry P. C., 247; Jane, 232, 399; John, 219; Margt., 228, 468; Mary, 402; Robt., 466; Sarah, 398; Thomas, 122, 128, 212, 215; sketch of, 226, *et seq.;* 245, 348-50, 364, 466, 468; William, 232, 349, 400.
"WILTSHIRE" (tract), 126.
WINDER FAMILY, note, 464; Bridget, 332, 477; Eliz., 330, 333, 398; John, 6, 59, 62-3, 67-8, 71, 102, 118, 119, 131, 280; sketch of, 332, *et seq.;* 340, 350, 358, 398, 396, 414, 424, 426, 464, 468, 471-2, 477-8; Miriam, 333; Susan, 332; Susanna, 477; R. H., 464; Thos., 254, 332, 395, 396; Wm., 255, 333.
"WINDER'S PURCHASE" (tract), 332.

"WINDSOR" (tract), 187.
WINGOD, Thos., 400, 466.
WINNIE, Anne, 396.
WINSAR, Jno., 401, 466.
WISE, Jno., 52, 218, 391; Mary, 218; 223.
WITHEROW, Prof., 228.
WOLSTON (WALSTON), Thos., 400.
WOOD, Ann, 397; Eliz., 474; Richd., 477.
WOODCOCK, Jno., 351.
WOODCRAFT, Richd., 350.
WOODGATE, Wm., 118, 120, 466.
WOOLDRIDGE, Agnes, 459; Deborah, 401.
WOOLFORD FAMILY, note, 464; Ann, Eliz., Jas., Rosanna, Sarah, 464; Jno., 365; Levin, 425, 464; Mary, 464, 475; Roger, 72, 98, 131, 135, 280, 292, 338, 340, 361, 394-5, 414, 443, 464, 468, 473-5, 478.
WOOTEN, Edwd., 400, 466.
WORCESTER Co., 423, 424, 428.
WORCESTER PARISH, 185.
WORTHINGTON, Saml., 104, 350, 362, 396, 444.
WOULDHAVE, Wm., 347, 350, 466.
WRIGHT, Abell, 400; Christopher, 400; Edwd., 439, 466; Francis, 17, 19, 487; Jno., 402; Wm., 400, 437, 466.
WYNE, Jno., 466.
WYNNE, Jas., 477; Lucy, 477.

Y

YALDING, Wm., 402.
YARRITT, Jas., 478.
YEO, Hugh, 307, 391.
YONSON, Francis, 477.
"YORKSHIRE" (tract), 257.

www.ingramcontent.com/pod-product-compliance
Lightning Source LLC
Chambersburg PA
CBHW071711300426
44115CB00010B/1389